13.95

ARCHITECTURE
residential drawing and design

by

CLOIS E. KICKLIGHTER
Associate Professor of Industrial Education
Eastern Michigan University
Ypsilanti, Michigan

RONALD J. BAIRD
Consulting Editor
Professor of Industrial Education
Eastern Michigan University
Ypsilanti, Michigan

South Holland, Illinois
THE GOODHEART-WILLCOX COMPANY, INC.
Publishers

Copyright 1979

by

THE GOODHEART-WILLCOX CO., INC.

Previous Editions Copyright 1973, 1976

No part of this book may be reproduced in any form
without violating the copyright law. Printed in U.S.A.
Library of Congress Catalog Card Number 79—14626.
International Standard Book Number 0—87006—277—8.

123456789—79—32109

Library of Congress Cataloging in Publication Data

Kicklighter, Clois E.
  Architecture: residential drawing and design.

  Includes index.
  1. Architecture, Domestic — Designs and plans.
I. Title.
NA7115.K46   1979   728.3   79—14626
ISBN 0—87006—277—8

INTRODUCTION

The purpose of this text is to provide basic instruction in preparing architectural working drawings and to serve as a reference for design and construction principles and methods. It is intended to help the student develop the necessary technical skills which will enable him to communicate and express his architectural ideas in an understandable, efficient and accurate manner.

ARCHITECTURE, Residential Drawing and Design is organized so that the content is presented in the logical order of use. The functional organization and layout of the text, the step-by-step procedures and the easy-to-understand language in which it is written appeals to students at all levels.

ARCHITECTURE, Residential Drawing and Design is profusely illustrated. Many of the drawings and photographs are enriched by use of full color. In addition to providing information on architectural drawing, design and construction, the text includes excellent coverage of industrialized housing, estimating, financing, workmanship specifications, standard architectural symbols, career opportunities and an extensive reference section.

This text is intended for architectural drawing students in high schools, vocational and technical schools, community colleges, universities and adult classes. It will also serve as a valuable reference for builders, carpentry classes, skilled tradesmen, and interior designers.

Sensitive skills of the architect are represented in this ultramodern residence. He has taken advantage of the lake and surrounding natural landscape to compliment the structural features of the house.

CONTENTS

Fig. 1-1. This picturesque brick home is a final reward for the experienced architect.
(Ideal Cement Co.)

Chapter 1
THE WORLD OF ARCHITECTURE

The fascinating study of architecture encompasses a sensitivity to design, skill in drawing techniques and a knowledge of the latest construction materials. It is the combination of these abilities that yields the outstanding architects of today's world. These architects design massive high-rise buildings, quaint lakeshore cottages, modern churches, and family homes as required to meet the needs of our society.

The world of architecture is all around us. It has been one of the major conquests of man to design structures to bring the thrill of lasting beauty to the eye of the beholder. Whether it is a symbolic monument, or a long awaited residence, Fig. 1-1, a rewarding experience belongs to the architect and years of pleasure to those who view the structure. Some structures are designed for commercial and industrial use, Fig. 1-2, while others are planned for organizations and private living. The emphasis of this book is on the design and architectural study of residential structures; however, the relationships of line, form, and material of almost any structure has an impact on home construction.

Fig. 1-2. Many commercial structures, such as this bank building, are the result of combined architectural design efforts.
(Libbey-Owens-Ford Co.)

Fig. 1-3. Refined version of the traditional Cape Cod as a two-story home. (Bird and Son, Inc.)

MAN AND HIS STRUCTURES

Over the years a number of architectural styles for house construction have been developed. Many of these structures were designed to meet climatic conditions and needs of families in various parts of the country. Others were planned especially for luxurious living. All of these factors provide a historical background that influences the design of today's homes. Some house styles became so popular that they took on names related to their shape, period of time, or area of the country in which they were built. The emphasis here is given to the design qualities that man has used over many years and now imitates or incorporates in modern homes.

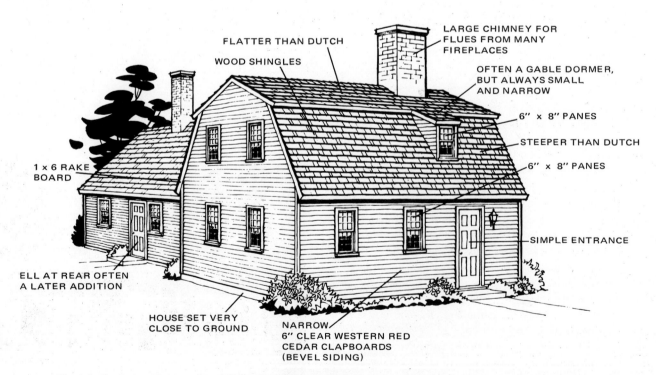

FLATTER THAN DUTCH

WOOD SHINGLES

LARGE CHIMNEY FOR FLUES FROM MANY FIREPLACES

OFTEN A GABLE DORMER, BUT ALWAYS SMALL AND NARROW

6" x 8" PANES

STEEPER THAN DUTCH

6" x 8" PANES

1 x 6 RAKE BOARD

SIMPLE ENTRANCE

ELL AT REAR OFTEN A LATER ADDITION

HOUSE SET VERY CLOSE TO GROUND

NARROW 6" CLEAR WESTERN RED CEDAR CLAPBOARDS (BEVEL SIDING)

Fig. 1-4. Rendering of the traditional Cape Ann. Many modern homes are distinguished by features taken from this early structure.   (Western Wood Products Assoc.)

THE CAPE COLONIAL

Two very popular home styles developed over 200 years ago are the Cape Cod and Cape Ann. These traditional homes have influenced structural design since they were first conceived. People have enjoyed them for their asthetic appeal. They provide a comfortable and livable atmosphere, and the rooms are large and functional.

Cape Cod are used in today's structures.

Another example of the Colonial style used in modern construction is the Cape Ann, Fig. 1-4. This differs from the Cape Cod in many respects. The chimney is centrally located and is usually larger. The tapering gambrel roof encloses an attic that is often converted into extra rooms. A growing family may take this into consideration when planning their first home. Modern use of the Cape Ann characteristics

Fig. 1-5. Contemporary styling of the typical New England Gambrel house.

The Cape Cod, Fig. 1-3, is one of the earliest and best known of the traditional Colonial styles. It originated as a fairly small house with a steep roof and little overhang. A central chimney accommodated the necessary room fireplaces. These homes were normally built as one or one-and-one-half story buildings, however, the same features have been incorporated in two-story styles. The eave line is always near the top of the windows, ending with a gable roof. Narrow trim lines of the siding, which appealed to New Englanders many years ago, are still used on these homes. Shutters are generally used on all windows, giving emphasis to the white or yellow painted siding which was preferred in earlier times. Many variations of the

provides a house with simple lines, sound construction, and a feel of colonial atmosphere. It makes a particularly attractive house along a tree shaded avenue or in a wooded development.

The New England Gambrel, as shown in Fig. 1-5, is a variation of other colonial styles. It features the gambrel roof where the pitch is abruptly changed between the ridge and eaves. Inherently American, the style is now used in most every section of the country. An advantage of the gambrel roof is the extra headroom and usable space available. The shorter rafter lengths required is an economic measure. Many adaptations of this architectural style provide pleasing and enduring homes for modern families.

Fig. 1-6. The Garrison home in a contemporary setting retains the original straight line features and overhanging second story.

THE GARRISON

An attractive house that includes a number of special features is a modern presentation of the traditional Garrison, Fig. 1-6. A distinguishing feature is the overhanging second story. This construction technique includes a number of advantages. (1) The separate corner posts on each floor make it possible to use shorter, stronger posts. (2) The short straight lines provide economy in framing materials. (3) Extra space is added at the second level by the overhang at very little extra cost. The steep pitch roof adds attic space. Narrow siding maintains the traditional styling. Fig. 1-7 shows the traditional Garrison from which modern design features have been developed.

8″ IN 12″ PITCH

NARROW 6″ CLEAR WESTERN
RED CEDAR CLAPBOARDS
(BEVEL SIDING) 4″ OR LESS
TO WEATHER, ALMOST
ALWAYS STAINED

5 1/2″ CORNER BOARD

NOT ALWAYS AN
OVERHANG AT SIDES

BLINDS WHEN NO
INTERIOR SHUTTERS
ARE USED

SIMPLE
ENTRANCE

CARVED DROP AT
CORNER POST

Fig. 1-7. The distinguishing characteristics of the traditional Garrison home.
(Western Wood Products Assoc.)

Fig. 1-8. A beautiful reproduction of the early New England Salt Box home.

THE SALT BOX

An interesting and easily recognizable Colonial is the Salt Box, Fig. 1-8. It is a direct offshoot of the basic colonial half house, resulting in a long roofline sloping gently from ridge to eaves. Many of today's beautiful homes have borrowed from this distinctive style, developed by master builders of early American times. The Salt Box house gets its name from the shape of coffee, tea, cracker, and salt boxes found in Colonial stores. The side elevations of these containers had the same general shape as this fascinating architectural style. Variations of this style are used to enhance many new homes.

The long low roofline at the rear of the house came about by the addition of "lean-to" structures being attached to add more living space. As further developments evolved, the low slanting roof was helpful in combatting the bitter winds common to New England winters. The basic style of the original Salt Box house is shown in Fig. 1-9.

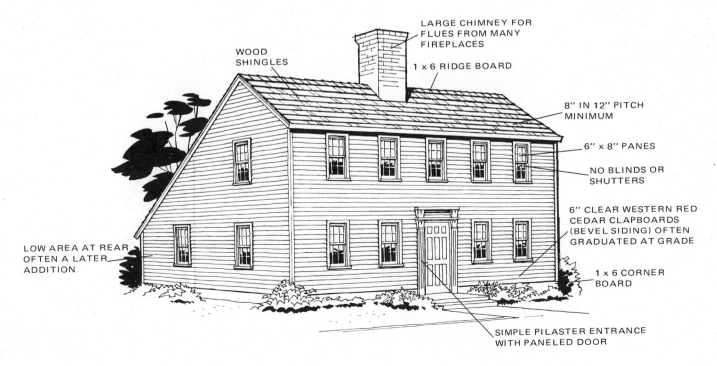

Fig. 1-9. Styling of the original Salt Box home with wood roof shingles, narrow wood siding, and no shutters.
(Western Wood Products Assoc.)

SOUTHERN COLONIAL

One of the most gracious of all the Colonials is the traditional Southern Colonial. The style, which reflects the warmth, quaintness, and hospitality of the old south, is shown in Fig. 1-10. This modern example borrows many of the fine details of the Southern Colonial to express a mood of elegance and traditional charm. The outstanding architectural features are the front colonnade and the giant portico. The extended portico sheltered the front entrance from the weather and kept direct sunlight from glaring into the first and second story rooms. These homes were usually massive, with upper and lower balconies, three story chimneys for bedroom fireplaces, ornate woodwork and iron trim, and a roof over the driveway to protect persons using the side entrance. Many of these features of the Southern Colonial may be adapted to the esthetic qualities of modern homes.

It is evident that the influences of the past, both in beauty and function, have had a profound effect on modern home designs. On the other hand, many new materials, appliances, and modes of living have caused the architect to "think out" ways to plan homes for all styles of modern living. The modern American home is a combination of many of these factors.

MODERN STRUCTURES

The style of houses, that is generally called modern, is the result of years of architectural planning, design and evolution. Many are well planned while others lack imagination or design balance. Some inexpensive homes are functionally satisfactory for a family, yet for economical measures, the exterior styling may have to be quite conservative in the use of a variety of

Fig. 1-11. A conservative modern home, using standard materials and a face of brick veneer. (Rodman Industries, Inc.)

Fig. 1-10. The most gracious of all the Colonial homes is this version of the Southern Colonial.

materials. See Fig. 1-11. The ability of the architect and the needs or finances of the family are two factors which generally dictate the modern styles being planned. Fig. 1-12 shows the use of various materials and expensive detailing in a modern home.

The term modern or contemporary does not denote any one particular architectural style. Most modern homes borrow some distinctive features from more traditional structures, Fig. 1-13. Others appear almost independent of past designs, Fig. 1-14. It makes little difference in our society just what constitutes modern styling. The most important job for the architect is to design a home that satisfies the customer, one that he may live in with pride and joy. In today's society, individual tastes vary to the extent that many people desire a house that is distinctly different from other houses. The owner

Fig. 1-12. Multimaterials and coordinated curves with straight lines give an architectural flair to this Spanish style home. (Brown and Kauffman, Inc.)

Fig. 1-13. A modern home with traditional characteristics including the overhanging gable, split shake roof, and grilled windows.

Fig. 1-15. Individuality is emphasized in this home, with heavy beams supporting the overhanging roof, horizontal plywood siding, and vertical glass panels surrounding the entrance.

Fig. 1-14. Unique styling is featured in this residence. Note the vertical plywood siding, flat roof, and heavy planked porch. (American Plywood Assoc.)

Fig. 1-16. The extensive use of wood for stained vertical siding and the split shake roof provide an attractive exterior for this home. (Marvin Windows)

may have a great satisfaction that his house represents his style of living and individuality, Fig. 1-15. He may enjoy the warmth of natural wood, Figs. 1-16 and 1-17, or solid structural design of a brick home as shown in Fig. 1-18.

Fig. 1-18. A brick home in a contemporary setting gives an unusual slant to architectural design. (Ideal Cement Co.)

The rapid development of new construction materials and methods of fabrication has made it possible to design homes that require a minimum of maintenance, Fig. 1-19, make extensive use of glass, Fig. 1-20, or place the emphasis on exposed structural members, Fig. 1-21.

Fig. 1-17. This attractive home makes use of heavy wood beams and wood siding combined with large areas of glass. (Georgia-Pacific Corp.)

Fig. 1-19. This home requires a minimum of maintenance through the use of solid vinyl siding, gutters, downspouts, ornamental shutters, fascia and soffits.

Fig. 1-20. Large exposed areas of glass are being used extensively in contemporary homes. (Red Cedar Shingle and Handsplit Shake Bureau)

Fig. 1-21. Visable roof support is illustrated by the structural columns at the entranceway. (Marvin Windows)

Fig. 1-22. A typical ranch design with modern materials and styling.

Fig. 1-23. Unusual and attractive architectural design for a ranch home. Note the variety of materials used.
(Western Wood Products Assoc.)

THE RANCH DESIGN

One prominent modern architectural home style is the ranch home, Fig. 1-22. This is basically a long, low, one story house that grew out of the "rancher's" homes of the southwestern part of the country. The plain ranch design generally has a low pitched roof with gables and overhanging eaves. It is normally built on a concrete slab with no basement. However, over the years ranch homes have taken on many newer features, Fig. 1-23. They usually have a one or two car attached garage. Basements are often added, and many have gone to an L shape to add interest and break up the straight line effect. Skylights and cathedral ceilings, provide variations.

New design concepts and additions to the basic ranch style have probably added more to the development of contemporary or futuristic homes than any other major factors, Fig. 1-24. The ranch has taken new twists, turns, angles and curves to the enchantment of the architect of today and tomorrow.

Fig. 1-24. A rectangular variation of a one story home with steel supports, flat roof, glass and metal panels.
(Bethlehem Steel Corp.)

TRENDS IN ARCHITECTURE

It is interesting to note that home styles for the near and distant future give the architect a freedom of design seldom known in the past. As indicated earlier, the multitude of individual preferences, materials, and structural techniques predicts a variety of unique expressions for architectural designing. Many of these homes are being designed for dramatic effects, as in Figs. 1-25 and 1-26, while others are styled for particular settings, Figs. 1-27 and 1-28, such as hillsides, seashores, and even cliffs.

The trends in architecture appear to lean toward the dramatic yet comfortable living styles. Homes designed to compliment the site, provide a feeling of openness, and still retain the required privacy are continually being developed. Fig. 1-29 gives an indication of spaciousness and sharp angular lines. Fig. 1-30 provides texture and curvature to exterior styling.

Fig. 1-25. A two-story twin cylindrical structure with graceful vertical lines. (Potlatch Forests, Inc.)

Fig. 1-26. Dramatic wood structure using roof shingles as the major area of exposure.

Fig. 1-27. Adaptation of an ultra-modern structure to a seashore setting. (American Plywood Assoc.)

17

Fig. 1-28. A combination of redwood siding and cedar shakes makes this home ideal for the rugged California coast. (California Redwood Assoc.)

A good idea of the new trends in architectural home designs may be obtained from Figs. 1-31 through 1-34. Each has its own unique styling, heavily emphasizing innovative construction techniques, and imaginative use of materials.

Another opportunity for the architect is in providing plans for the rebuilding of older homes, through the use of new materials. In redesigning older houses the cost factor is often a prime consideration.

Fig. 1-29. Angular lines and a sharp slanting roof give this home an expensive and attractive appearance. (Western Wood Products Assoc.)

Fig. 1-30. The curved concrete arches and roof beam extensions provide a classic expression to this contemporary home. (Ideal Cement Co.)

Fig. 1-31. An interesting use of tile, wood, concrete, and metal in a modern villa type structure reminiscent of old Mexico. (Brown and Kauffman, Inc.)

REVIEW QUESTIONS — CHAPTER 1

Write your answers on a separate sheet of paper. Do not write in this book.

1. Explain how soil and_____have contributed to the structural styles of homes.
2. List the three major factors that the fascinating study of architecture encompasses.
   a. _____.
   b. _____.
   c. _____.
3. Which of the following factors led to the name Salt Box for a particular style home?
   a.   Implement sheds.
   b.   Containers in village stores.
   c.   Early churches.
   d.   The shape of barn roofs.
4. What are the three main advantages of the architectural design of the Garrison style house?
   a. _____.
   b. _____.
   c. _____.

Fig. 1-32. Using modular units to bring together the total features of a modern home.

5. What are the outstanding architectural features of the Southern Colonial home?

a._____.

b._____.

6. What is different about the shape of the roof on a Gambrel style home?

7. Why do the terms contemporary or modern not describe a particular architectural style?

a._____.

b._____.

c._____.

8. The basic ranch home is a low, long one story house with a _____ roof and overhanging eaves.

9. Two factors that have probably contributed the most to the development of modern or futuristic homes are:

a._____.

b._____.

10. Factors that appear to be giving new trends in architectural design are:

a._____.

b._____.

c._____.

d._____.

SUGGESTED ACTIVITIES

1. Visit an architect and ask him the following questions: (a) What particular style home is most in demand today? (b) How did he become an architect and why? (c) In what ways does he communicate with his customers to provide the style home they desire. (d) How does he derive from a customer just what design features will be most appealing to his family. Write a brief report on the responses the architect has given you.

2. By using clippings from magazines and newspapers, make an architectural design folder indicating as many home styles as you can find. Indicate on each home any design feature that has been borrowed from the past or gives an

Fig. 1-33. A futuristic home design in raised modular units of rigid polyurethane foam. Ideal for a planned setting such as this. (Mobay Chemical Co.)

indication of a futuristic trend.

3. Visit a local contractor and ask him to specify new materials he is using for exterior structural features. Make a list of these materials and explain their use to your class.

4. Select a particular traditional style home and, using cardboard and glue, cut out and make a model of that design. Sketch in doors, windows, siding, etc. and put it on display in your classroom.

5. Make a collection of catalogs from lumber dealers and suppliers. From this material, prepare a list of new materials that are available to replace older exterior structural devices. An example might be the use of aluminum or plastic gutters that replace galvanized iron gutters. Present this as a discussion with your class.

Fig. 1-34. Imaginative use of textured concrete.
(Rohm and Haas Co.)

Excitement in house design. The architect has taken advantage of location for exterior view and compatibility of materials to present a beautiful home.

Fig. 2-1. One of many style variations for a typical one-story ranch house.   (Marvin Windows)

Chapter 2

BASIC HOUSE DESIGN

A residential home designer has basically four designs to choose from: the one-story or ranch, the one-and-one-half-story, the two-story, and the split-level. Each of these individual styles has strengths and weaknesses which should be considered before making a choice. Such factors as space available for the house, site contour, climate, convenience, cost, surroundings, and personal preference should all play a role in the final decision.

ONE-STORY RANCH DESIGNS

The one-story house has all the regular living space on one level, Fig. 2-1. It may have a basement depending on the section of the country in which it is built and preference of the prospective owner.

One of the chief advantages of the ranch is that it lends itself beautifully to indoor-outdoor living. Patios, porches and terraces may be added to virtually any room. With lots of glass, it is possible to bring the outdoor surroundings inside to make the house appear even larger than it is, Fig. 2-2.

Another advantage of this design is the absence of stairs . . . unless it has a basement. The ranch without a basement is popular with many older people.

The ranch usually has a low-pitched roof with wide overhangs since no headroom is necessary above the ceiling. The low-pitched roof and short walls make outside mainte-nance easy. Cleaning the gutters, removing the screens and

Fig. 2-2. An interior court within the living area of a ranch style house.
(Brown and Kauffman, Inc.)

Fig. 2-3. This ranch house minimizes the height problem in construction.
(Red Cedar Shingle and Handsplit Shake Bureau)

painting require no long ladders or other special equipment. Low height also simplifies construction. See Figs. 2-3 and 2-4.

The low and long appearance of the ranch is pleasing to most people, Fig. 2-5. The ranch may be built with a full basement, Fig. 2-6; crawl space, Fig. 2-7; or on a slab, Fig. 2-8. Great variation is possible. The ranch lends itself to expansion

Fig. 2-4. Standard, cut-to-length materials were an economical advantage in the construction of this ranch house.
(Wausau Homes)

Fig. 2-5. The attractiveness of this ranch is aided by the front gable, brick facing, and overhanging roof.
(Rodman Industries, Inc.)

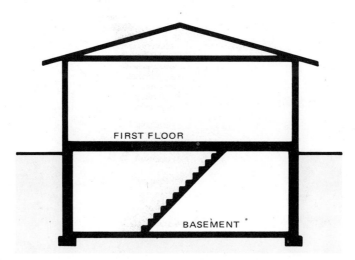

Fig. 2-6. Addition of a full basement provides valuable extra usuable space to a ranch house.

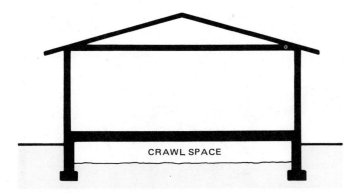

Fig. 2-7. A crawl space under the ranch house adds accessibility for service and maintenance.

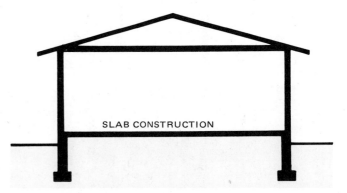

Fig. 2-8. The ranch on a concrete slab reduces cost and simplifies construction.

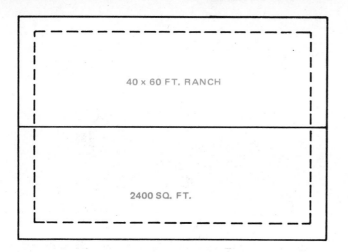

40 x 60 FT. RANCH

2400 SQ. FT.

FOUNDATION LENGTH = 200 FT.
ROOF AREA = 2500 SQ. FT.

30 x 40 FT. TWO-STORY

2400 SQ. FT.

FOUNDATION LENGTH = 140 FT.
ROOF AREA = 1300 SQ. FT.

Fig. 2-9. A comparison of the foundation length and roof area of a ranch and a two-story house having the same square footage of living area reveals the reason a ranch is usually more expensive to build.

Fig. 2-10. This spacious ranch house has extensive roof and wall areas and provides potential maintenance problems.

Fig. 2-11. Extreme hall space is required to make this ranch design serviceable. Better planning is desirable.

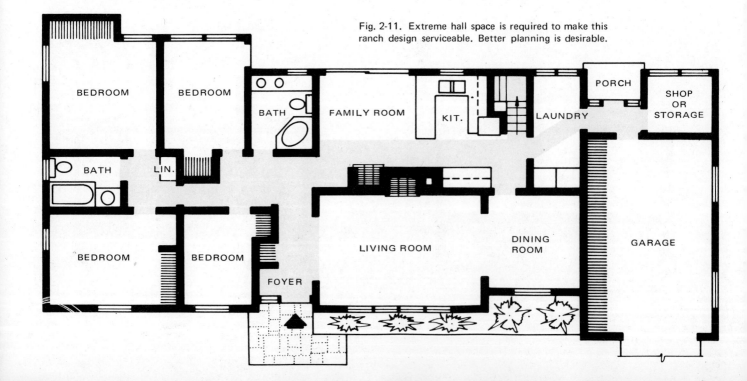

and modification with ease.

One disadvantage is that the one-story is usually more costly to build than other designs of the same square footage. This stems from the fact that the one-story requires more roof area and more foundation length, Fig. 2-9.

Another negative aspect of the ranch is that it requires a larger lot since it is spread out, rather than up. Furthermore, this increased area sometimes causes heating problems for certain areas of the house because of the distance from the furnace. There is generally no problem with electric heat.

Maintenance costs may be more on a ranch because of the larger roof and exterior wall surfaces, Fig. 2-10. Considerable hall space may be required in a large ranch style house to provide access to all rooms, Fig. 2-11. Careful planning should be done to keep hall space to a minimum.

ONE-AND-ONE-HALF-STORY DESIGNS

The one-and-one-half-story house (sometimes called a "Cape Cod") is essentially one-story with a steeper roof which allows for expansion of the attic, Fig. 2-12. Dormers are usually added to provide additional light and ventilation, Fig. 2-13. This has two distinct advantages; economy in cost per unit of habitable living space, and built-in expansibility.

Generally, bedrooms and a bath are provided in the attic space. Since any space with less than five feet headroom is considered unusable, the total square feet of space in the attic is about one-half that of the first floor.

Dormers, stairs and a slightly steeper roof are the principal additional costs required to build the one-and-one-half story.

The one-and-one-half-story is quite versatile. It can begin as a two-bedroom, one-bath house with the upper area left unfinished. This minimum house will meet the needs of a

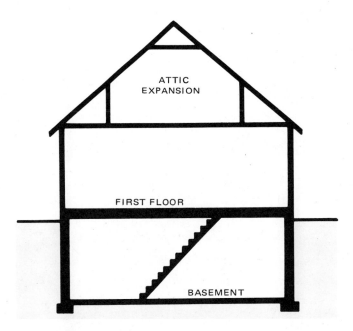

Fig. 2-12. Typical design section for a one-and-one-half-story house.

newly married couple or a retired couple. As the family of the younger people expands, the "expansion attic" can be finished to provide more livable room.

Heating costs are minimized due to the small outside wall area compared to the amount of interior space. Cooling may be accomplished through the use of louvered ventilators at each end of the structure and the generous use of insulation. Adequate ventilation and insulation is necessary since about one-third of the ceiling area is directly under the roof. This area tends to be quite warm in the summer.

Fig. 2-13. Dormers on this attractive one-and-one-half-story house provide natural light and ventilation to the upper living areas.   (Marvin Windows)

Architecture

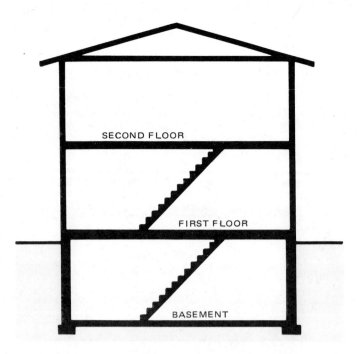

Fig. 2-14. A section of a "standard" two-story house.

Care must be taken in designing the one-and-one-half-story structure to best accommodate the number of persons it can ultimately house. The electrical and plumbing systems should be planned with expansion in mind. Failure to consider expansion at the outset will greatly reduce the efficiency of these vital systems. Other areas of the house, such as kitchen, dining, and living rooms should also be planned for the ultimate number of occupants.

TWO-STORY DESIGNS

Compared to ranch and one-and-one-half-story houses, the two-story house is more economical to build, Fig. 2-14. This may be built with or without a basement. It requires a smaller lot and has a small roof and foundation area compared to interior space of most other designs. Figs. 2-15 and 2-16 are typical examples.

Heating and cooling the two-story house is simple and comparatively economical. Heat from the first floor naturally rises to the second floor level. Even though the second floor is usually far from the furnace it is usually easy to heat. Cooling is facilitated due to the fact that the ceiling is not directly

Fig. 2-15. An attractively styled two-story house with attached garage.

Fig. 2-17. A contemporary adaptation of the two-story house. Roof design and windows tend to disguise the resemblance to older styles.

Fig. 2-16. Overhanging upper level and bay windows add charm to this modern two-story house.   (Bird and Son, Inc.)

Fig. 2-18. Typical example of the more traditional two-story house.

under the roof. Ventilation is easy and effective when ample windows are included in the design.

The two-story, however, in many localities is not as popular today as in former years. This is probably a result of the turn to more contemporary styles, Fig. 2-17. The two-story home is usually traditional in style, Fig. 2-18. The two-story home, unless located among other similar styles may appear to be out of place.

General exterior maintenance is usually more difficult and costly because of the height, Fig. 2-19. For some people the necessity of climbing stairs from level to level is considered a disadvantage. The two-story does not lend itself to variations in style as well as some other designs, but architects have added a contemporary flair, and as a result, have improved their overall appearance and saleability, Fig. 2-20.

As the cost and availability of land becomes more of a problem, the two-story house may gain in popularity.

Fig. 2-19. Construction variations and height make this older two-story house costly to maintain.

Fig. 2-20. The basic two-story house takes on a contemporary appearance with extended wings, overhanging porch roof, and post supports.

SPLIT-LEVEL DESIGNS

The split-level was conceived for the sloping or hilly lot. It takes advantage of what might otherwise prove to be a troublesome difference in elevation and uses it to advantage, Fig. 2-21. As a general rule, a split-level should not be built on a flat lot. Mounding up soil in front of the high section to give the appearance of a hill usually yields poor results, Fig. 2-22.

The split-level makes efficient use of space. The general arrangement of the split-level separates sleeping, living, and recreation on different levels, Fig. 2-23. Little or no hall space is required in a split-level house due to its basic design, a positive factor for consideration.

Fig. 2-22. Grading the ground level of a flat lot with an extreme slope, exposes the lower side of a split-level house and takes away from its attractive appearance.

Fig. 2-21. Contemporary split-level house well integrated with site atop a steep hill. (California Redwood Assoc.)

At the lowest level, there is a normal basement which houses the heating and cooling equipment, storage, and perhaps a shop or washroom, Fig. 2-24. This area is the usual depth of a basement. In some instances the basement may not be desired and a crawl space provided for maintenance and ventilation. The basement ordinarily equals about 40 to 60 percent of the space occupied by the house. This is usually enough for efficient use without wasted space.

The next level up from the basement, the intermediate level, generally houses the garage and recreation area, Fig. 2-24. This area is ground level and thus lends itself to these functions. Patios and terraces may be attached to the

Fig. 2-23. This rendering of a split-level house illustrates a standard arrangement of living quarters.

recreation area which further enhances its use. The intermediate level may also have a large foyer, mud room, or family room.

Slightly higher than the intermediate level is the living level, Fig. 2-24. Generally this area is located at grade also; the sloping grade makes this arrangement possible. The kitchen, dining room, living room and full or half bath normally are located on the living level. The foyer, mud room, and washroom may also be located at this level depending on the layout or preference. Again the use of patios and terraces adds to the usefulness and amplifies the attractiveness of the split-level.

cases, however, they are cheaper than a ranch. Heating may be a problem if not handled properly. The use of zoned heating (separate thermostats for the various areas of the house) will usually solve the heating problem.

VARIATIONS OF SPLIT-LEVEL DESIGN

There are basically three variations of the split-level design: the side-by-side, the front-to-back, and the back-to-front. Lots sloping from the left or right are suited for the side-by-side design. This design places the living area opposite the sleeping and intermediate areas, Fig. 2-25.

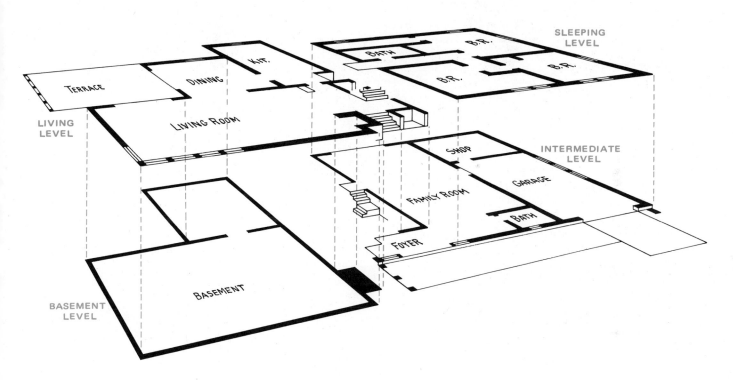

Fig. 2-24. This unusual perspective drawing provides a good insight into the arrangement of a four-level house.

At the highest elevation in the house is the sleeping area and bath, Fig. 2-24. The half-level difference between the living and sleeping levels affords greater privacy and quietness.

Split-level houses do have some negative aspects. They are generally more expensive to build than the two-story. In most

Variation number two, the front-to-back split-level, is suited for lots which are high in front and low in the back, Fig. 2-26. This house looks like a ranch from the front and a two-story from the back. The living area faces the street and the bedrooms are on the second level to the rear.

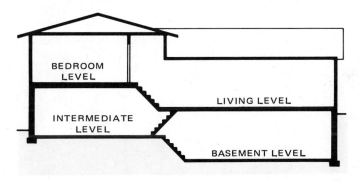

Fig. 2-25. A typical design of a side-by-side split-level house.

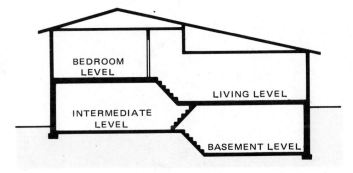

Fig. 2-26. Longitudinal section of a front-to-back split-level house.

The third variation, the back-to-front split-level, requires a lot that is low in front and high in back, Fig. 2-27. The intermediate level faces the street at grade. The bedrooms are above, also facing the street. The living level is at the rear. This model looks like a two-story in front and a ranch in the rear.

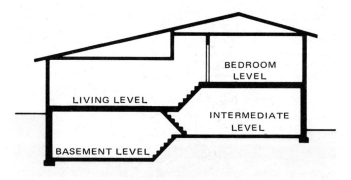

Fig. 2-27. The back-to-front split-level is adapted to a lot which slopes to the front.

Fig. 2-28 shows another style which some people call a traditional split-level. This is nothing more than a ranch with a raised basement which causes it to be taller than a ranch, yet not as high as a two-story. It also has a split entry (the foyer is half-way between levels) which is probably the reason for it being identified as a split-level.

TRAFFIC CIRCULATION

A primary consideration in designing a functional plan is traffic circulation. Traffic circulation involves those areas of the house which provide a means of moving from one area or room to another. Circulation must be planned for maximum efficiency. The pattern shown in Fig. 2-29 is an example of a well planned arrangement. The distance from the garage to the kitchen is short and direct. The foyer is centrally located and convenient to all parts of the house. All bedrooms are close to a bath. Few rooms have traffic planned through them. The family room and eating nook are exceptions. An analysis should be made of traffic circulation to determine if the plan is as functional as it could be. Frequently, a slight change in the floor plan can increase smooth flow of traffic to desirable locations.

REVIEW QUESTIONS — CHAPTER 2

1. The four basic residential home designs are:
   a._____.
   b._____.
   c. _____.
   d._____.

2. Identify five advantages of the ranch style house.
   a._____.
   b._____.
   c. _____.
   d._____.
   e._____.
   f. _____.

3. Five disadvantages of the ranch are:
   a._____.
   b._____.
   c. _____.

Fig. 2-28. An interesting split-level design which takes advantage of a raised basement to add height and better lighting.   (Wausau Homes)

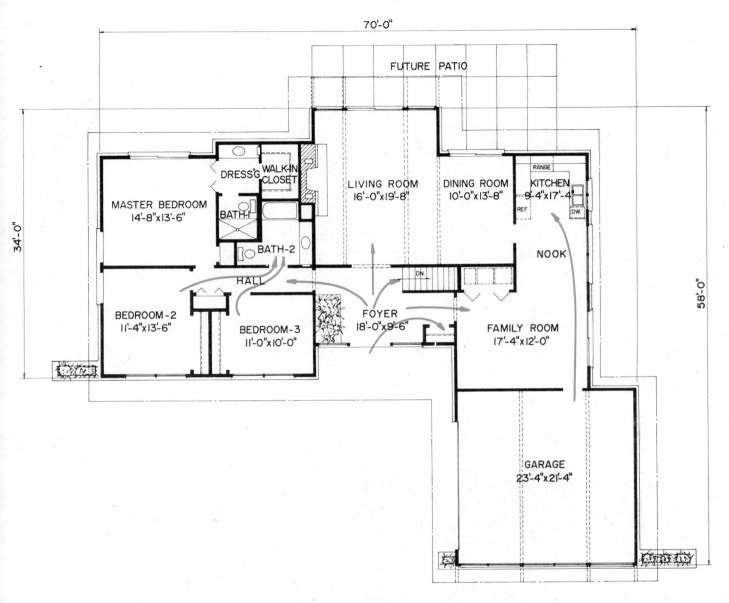

Fig. 2-29. A well planned arrangement for traffic circulation through the major living areas of a home.

d._____.

e._____.

4. A one-and-one-half-story house may be recognized by its _____ and _____.

5. The one-and-one-half-story house has two distinct advantages. They are _____ and _____.

6. One of the most economical houses to build is a _____design.

7. Four negative aspects of the two-story house are:

a._____.

b._____.

c._____.

d._____.

8. The_____design was conceived for the sloping or hilly lot.

9. The four levels of the split-level design are:

a._____.

b._____.

c._____.

d._____.

10. Three variations of the split-level are:

a._____.

b._____.

c._____.

11. What is one of the main advantages of the ranch type home?

12. Why are dormers usually added to the one-and-one-half story house?

13. In a split-level house, the basement usually equals what percentage of space occupied by the house?

a.   10 to 20 percent.

b.   20 to 40 percent.

c.   40 to 60 percent.

d.   60 to 80 percent.

14. What house design looks like a two-story from the front and a ranch from the rear?

SUGGESTED ACTIVITIES

1. Look through magazines and find an example (photo) of each of the basic house designs (one-story, one-and-one-half-story, two-story, and split-level). Mount the pictures on illustration board for display.

2. Identify houses in or near your community which are examples of the basic house designs. Describe materials used, colors and location of each house.

3. Obtain a floor plan of a house from a magazine, newspaper or other source. Determine the basic design and compile the following information about the house:

   a. How many square feet of living space is in the house?

   b. List the rooms identified in the house.

   c. How many sets of stairs are there in the house?

   d. Does the house have a basement?

4. Visit a contractor or architectural firm and ask for prints of basic house designs. Bring these to class and discuss the advantages and disadvantages of each in respect to the families of different members of the class.

5. Invite an architect to your class to discuss how basic house designs are chosen for various areas of your community.

6. Prepare a simple sketch of your own home showing the various levels for living and the contour of the property. Indicate what basic design your house resembles. If you live in an apartment, sketch the home of one of your friends.

7. Using your local newspaper for reference, read through the "houses for sale" section and make a list of the styles advertised. See if there seems to be a trend toward a particular basic design.

An important consideration when designing a home is to take advantage of the site. Surveyors provide land contour information which the architect should use as a guide.

Chapter 3
PRIMARY CONSIDERATIONS

Most everyone has a "dream home" in the back of his mind which he hopes to build some day. However, few people think beyond the house itself to the site location and characteristics, community attributes, zoning restrictions, family style of life, and quality of living. These considerations, in many instances, are just as important as the size and room arrangement of the house.

SITE CONSIDERATIONS

The site is more than just a plot of land--it is part of a larger community, Fig. 3-1. It is located in a certain school district and is either near or far from shopping areas. An airport or major traffic artery may be nearby. The site is in a growing community or a stagnant one. The topography is rolling or flat, high and dry or low and wet, big or small, wooded or treeless. It is located in a warm or cold climate. The site, next to the house itself, is probably the most expensive item of investment. It must be evaluated carefully to realize its potential as a vital part of the home and its setting.

The characteristics of a site frequently indicate the basic type of house which would be best suited for that site. For example, a flat topography lends itself to a ranch or two-story house. A hilly or sloping site is ideal for a split-level home. A site which has many trees may require a house with large windows and generous use of natural materials. Every effort should be made to take full advantage of site characteristics in planning the home. The structure should appear to be part of the site. It should blend in with the surroundings rather than stand apart from them.

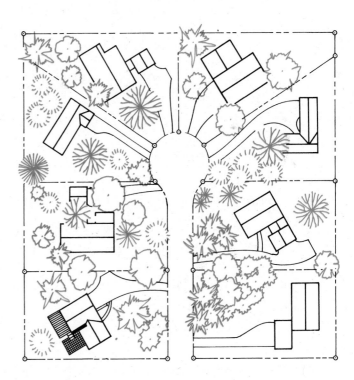

Fig. 3-2. A planned community neighborhood with no through traffic. A minimum of trees were removed to retain privacy and maintain a natural setting.

THE COMMUNITY

The neighborhood should be evaluated on the following points: (1) Is the community a "planned" community, Fig. 3-2, or one that has sprung up with no central theme of

Fig. 3-1. A homesite is always a part of a larger community--subdivision, city, or state. (Midwestern Consulting, Inc.)

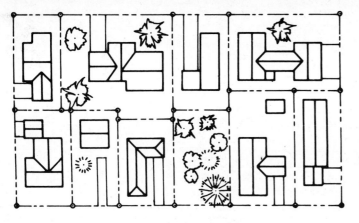

Fig. 3-3. This block of homes represents an example of little planning with no central theme.

forethought, Fig. 3-3? (2) Are the homes in this community in the price range of the proposed house? (3) Are the neighbors in about the same socioeconomic category as the prospective owner? (4) Is the community alive and growing or is it rundown and dying? (5) Does it have room for growth, or is it restricted? (6) Are the residents of the community people who take pride in their homes or seem indifferent toward them? (7) Does the community have modern churches, quality schools and shopping areas? (8) Are such facilities as fire protection, water, sewer, natural gas, and garbage collection available in this community? (9) Is the site near the prospective owner's work? (10) Is public transportation available in the com-

---

Lawyers Title Insurance Corporation

Form 561   5-71
WARRANTY DEED—Statutory Form
C.L. 1948, 565.151   M.S.A. 26.571

KNOW ALL MEN BY THESE PRESENTS: That William C. Brown and Arlene J. Brown, his wife

whose address is   813 Magnolia Lane, Saline, Michigan

Convey(s) and Warrant(s) to   Henry B. Jackson

whose address is   507 Highland Road, Jacksonville, Georgia

the following described premises situated in the   city   of   Melvinville
County of   Washington   and State of Michigan, to-wit:

Commence at the NE corner of the SW 1/4 of Sec. 13, T22S, R21E, run thence
N 89° 47' 38" W 1166.06 ft.; thence S 0° 12' 22" W 505 ft.; thence N 89° 47' 38" W
50 ft. to a POB; said point being on a curve concave to the SE/LY having a radius
of 50 ft.; thence from a T.B. of N 0° 12' 22" E run NE/LY along said curve 52.36 ft.
through an angle of 60°; thence N 0° 12' 22" E 36.70 ft.; thence N 89° 47' 38" W
145.79 ft.; thence S 0° 12' 32" E 80.0 ft.; thence S 89° 47' 38" E 120 ft. to the
P.O.B. together with ingress and egress rights.

Also known as Lot 13, Oak Hammock

for the full consideration of $10.00 and other valuable considerations
subject to   meeting sanitary sewer specifications

Dated this   fifth   day of   July   19

Witnesses: Signed and Sealed:

C. E. Howard   William C. Brown   (L.S.)

D. M. Foster   Arlene J. Brown   (L.S.)

_____   (L.S.)

STATE OF MICHIGAN
COUNTY OF   Washtenaw   }ss.

_____   (L.S.)

The foregoing instrument was acknowledged before me this
by

fifth   day of   July   19

My commission expires
   July 1, 19

Carol J. Bassett

Notary Public   Washtenaw   County, Michigan

Instrument
Drafted by   William C. Brown

Business
Address   813 Magnolia Lane, Saline, Mich.

County Treasurer's Certificate   City Treasurer's Certificate

Recording Fee_____

State Transfer Tax_____

When recorded return to_____

Send subsequent tax bills
to _____

Tax Parcel #_____

Fig. 3-4. A typical property deed containing a legal
description of the site.

BUILDING PERMIT

TOWNSHIP OF YPSILANTI

OFFICE OF THE BUILDING INSPECTOR

Owner_____ Date Filed_____19____

The undersigned hereby makes application for a Building Permit to (erect, move, alter, repair) a_____

Story_____on the_____side of_____street,

at House No._____between_____street and

_____street, on Lot No.____of_____Subdivision,

This building is to be____ft. wide by____ft. long, will be constructed of_____

In accordance with the accompanying plans and specifications, subject to Ordinances, Rules and Regulations governing the construction of all buildings within the limits of the Township of Ypsilanti, and laws of the State of Michigan, with which the undersigned agrees to comply.

APPROVED by Board of Appeals For_____

On_____

PLEASE NOTE: IF YOU INSTALL ANY ELECTRICAL, PLUMBING or HEATING, A SEPARATE PERMIT MUST BE OBTAINED FOR SAME.

SPECIFICATIONS

☐ BASEMENT   ☐ NO BASEMENT   CHIMNEY

Concrete Foundation_____

Wall_____Size_____

Columns_____Distance apart_____

Sills_____Joists {Floor_____ Ceiling_____} (Bolted to Foundation Wall)

Siding_____Finish_____

Side Yard, Minimum_____

Building Set-Back_____

Valuation $____Fee $____

Lined Masonry with Clean-out Door
Concrete Foundation with minimum projection of 6 inches beyond outside dimension of chimney x 12 inches deep.
Footings—Minimum area 4 square feet x 14 inches deep

Studding_____Rafters_____

Floor_____Plaster_____

_____
(Owner/Builder)

IMPORTANT: FIRST inspection shall be called for when foundation footings are in place and before proceeding with the basement walls. When earth trenches are used as the forming for foundation walls, the open trench must be inspected and approved before proceeding with walls.

SECOND inspection shall be called for when outside drain tiles are laid and outside of wall coated with foundation coating.

THIRD inspection shall be called for after the structural members are in place and before covering same with lath, plaster or other covering.

FINAL inspection shall be called for when structure is completed and BEFORE being occupied.

FAILURE TO NOTIFY the building official of the time for such inspection automatically cancels permit and a new one must be paid for before proceeding with structure.

BUILDING IS REQUIRED to be started three months from date of issuance.

PERMIT EXPIRES twelve (12) months from date of issuance.

BUILDING INSPECTION DEPARTMENT IS ENTITLED TO 24-HOURS' NOTICE ON ALL INSPECTIONS.

TREASURER'S COPY

_____
(Address)
City_____Phone_____
Approved_____19____
(Dept. of Building, Township of Ypsilanti)

PERMIT

№ 1685

____footing inspection
____backfill inspection
____open joist inspection
____framing inspection
____FINAL INSPECTION

HURON PRESS

Fig. 3-5. A building permit must be obtained before construction may begin.

munity? (11) Does the community have a high rate of turnover due to the resale of homes? These, and many other factors relate to the site selection and eventually to the happiness of the owner. These factors should be considered before selecting a site.

COST AND RESTRICTIONS

It is not possible to state exactly what percentage of the total cost of a home should be allowed for the site. This will depend on many considerations. The price, however, should be examined carefully to determine if it takes into consideration needed improvements such as grading, fill, tree removal, and drainage. The cost of the lot should also take into account the amount of frontage it has and whether or not it is a corner lot. Assessments are usually proportional to length of frontage, therefore, corner lots are more expensive.

A title search should be instituted before purchasing the lot to determine if there are any legal claims against the property. The deed, Fig. 3-4, will show any restrictions or easements attached to the property. Restrictions may specify the style of house that may be built on the lot, size of the house, type of landscaping, or even the overall cost of the house. Easements may allow utilities to cross the property or may prevent the filling of a low area which must remain for drainage purposes. The title and deed are very important documents and should be examined carefully by a competent attorney before the lot is purchased.

ZONING AND CODES

Investigate the zoning ordinances in the area where the site is located. It may be zoned commercial or for multiple-family dwellings. This could prohibit building a single family residential structure. Even if the selected site were zoned for single-family structures, you might find the large open area nearby which plays a large part in the selection of the site, is zoned for apartment buildings. Check the zoning!

Another area for consideration which many prospective buyers fail to explore is local building codes. It is possible that the codes (plumbing, electrical, and building codes) are so restrictive that the type of house that is being planned for the site cannot be built. The cost could also be much greater because of code requirements. On the other hand, the codes may be so lax that the quality of homes in the area is poor. Talk with the local building inspector to determine such things as cost of permits, inspections and regulations. Fig. 3-5 illustrates a typical building permit form.

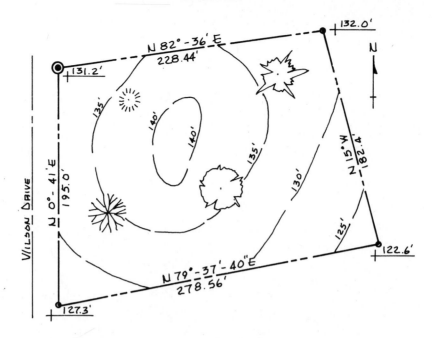

Fig. 3-6. A site plan which shows topographical features such as contour, elevations, trees and property lines.

TOPOGRAPHICAL FEATURES

The topography of the site is a primary concern. Study the topographical drawings of the site to determine its slope, contour, size, shape, elevation, trees, rocks, and soil conditions, Fig. 3-6. These factors may limit the type of structure that may be built on the site.

If the site is out of town and you must provide water and sewer, extra care must be taken in the selection of the proper

site. Very hard water, iron water, or the lack of water are problems to be aware of before the house is built. Equipment to handle these problems is expensive and requires constant maintenance. A site smaller than one acre may not meet the code requirements.

The shape of the site is important. Even though the site is large, it may be long and narrow or some odd shape which will limit construction possibilities, Fig. 3-7. Measure the site and have the measurements and lot lines checked by a surveyor to be sure the boundaries are located where you believe them to be.

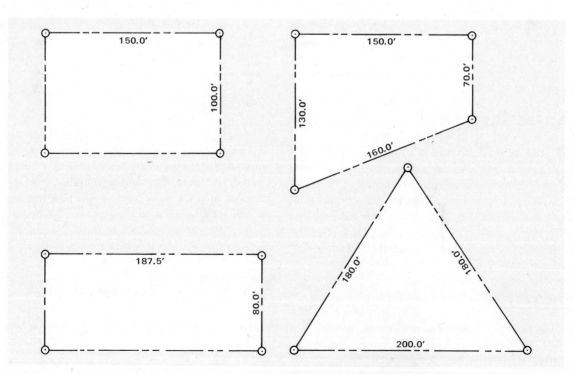

Fig. 3-7. Property shape is important in determining the size and style of the house to be designed. Note that each of these sites has 15,000 sq. ft. of area, yet the triangular plot appears the largest.

FAMILY NEEDS

A truly functional house will represent the style of life of those who occupy it. Rather than try to change a life style to fit the house, the structure should evolve from those who will use it.

Family size will be a major consideration in a house design. Ample space should be provided for each member of the family to perform his or her activities. Consideration should be given to providing space for these individual and family activities:

Preparing Food	Sleeping
Dining	Relaxing
Entertaining	Working
Family Recreation	Storage
Hobbies	Bathing
Laundering	Housekeeping
Studying	Accommodating Guests
Dressing	Planning

The above activities should not be thought of necessarily in relation to specific rooms. Some activities are performed throughout the house while others are restricted to certain areas. The important point is to provide for activities in which the family will be engaged. Let the structure take the shape and arrangement that best serves these needs.

OTHER CONSIDERATIONS

A residential structure should not be planned entirely from an "inside-out" approach. Consideration should be given to the exterior design, size and materials, Fig. 3-8. These additional factors add a unity to the structure and enhance its overall appearance. Consideration should be given too, to the saleability of the home.

MODULAR ASPECTS

Much is heard today about the advantages and disadvantages of modular construction (use of building materials based on 4 inch units of measurement, or modules). The fact remains that a house is a combination of many parts and these must fit together to form the whole. These parts are basic construction materials which are available across the country and are produced in standard sizes. If a home designer knows what these standard sizes are and actively plans his structure around them, a more economical building with less wasted material will result. For example, it would probably cost no more to build a house with overall dimensions of 40' x 60' than a house of 39' x 59'. The 40' x 60' house will provide considerable extra floor space.

A quick survey of representative construction material sizes

Fig. 3-8. Design is important. Note how the lines and use of materials
compliment each other in this ranch structure.
(Red Cedar Shingle and Handsplit Shake Bureau)

as shown below will provide some guidelines for the designer:

Plywood — 4' x 8'

Paneling — 4' x 8'

Construction Lumber — lengths of 8', 10', 12', 14', 16'

Concrete Blocks — modules of 4''

Typical guidelines:

1. Exterior walls should be modular lengths (multiples of 4').
2. Plan for the use of materials with as little waste as possible.
3. Plan interior rooms with an eye on standard sizes. (Example: carpet is produced in 12' and 15' widths.)
4. Walls should be modular heights (multiples of 4').

QUALITY OF LIVING

The location of the site, the characteristics of the site itself, Fig. 3-9, the size and layout of the house, and many other factors all add up to a certain quality of living. It is the designer's job to take advantage of as many aspects as possible to increase the quality of living in the structures being designed. The quality of living provided by the structure is a measure of the success of the designer in solving a problem.

Fig. 3-9. Imagine the site and design considerations necessary to construct this hillside house. (Potlatch Forests, Inc.)

DRAWINGS INCLUDED IN A SET OF PLANS

Most sets of plans for residential construction include these drawings:

Plot Plan	Electrical Plan
Foundation Plan	Construction Details
Floor Plan	Pictorial Presentations
Elevations	

A set of construction drawings is not complete without specification sheets. Specifications describe the quality of materials and workmanship. The drawings together with the specifications, form the basis for a legal contract between the owner and the builder.

BRIEF DESCRIPTION OF PLANS

The PLOT PLAN shows the location of the house on the site, Fig. 3-10. It usually shows also, utilities, topographical features, site dimensions, and any other buildings on the property.

A FOUNDATION PLAN illustrates the foundation size and material, Fig. 3-11. It may also be the basement plan as well if the house has a basement. The foundation plan gives information pertaining to excavation, waterproofing, and supporting structures.

The FLOOR PLAN shows all exterior and interior walls, doors, windows, patios, walks, decks, fireplaces, mechanical equipment, built-in cabinets and appliances, Fig. 3-12. A separate plan view is drawn for each floor of the house.

ELEVATIONS are drawn for each side of the structure, Figs. 3-13 and 3-14. These plans are typical orthographic projections showing the exterior features of the building. They show placement of windows and doors, type of exterior materials used, steps, chimney, roof lines and other exterior details.

THE ELECTRICAL PLAN is drawn from the floor plan, Fig. 3-15. It locates switches, convenience outlets, ceiling outlet fixtures, TV jacks, service entrance location, panel box and general information concerning circuits and special installations.

CONSTRUCTION DETAILS are usually drawn where more information is needed to fully describe how the construction is to be done. Typical drawings include details of kitchens, stairs, chimneys, fireplaces, windows and doors, foundation walls, and items of special construction, Figs. 3-16 and 3-17.

A PICTORIAL PRESENTATION is often included to show how the finished structure will look. The pictorial method commonly used is the two-point perspective. Sometimes a model is used instead, or in addition to the perspective, to show the total structure.

Other drawings which may be included in a set of residential construction drawings are:

Roof Plan	Plumbing Plan
Roof Framing Plan	Landscaping Plan
Floor Framing Plan	Furniture Plan
Heating and Cooling Plan	Expansion Plan

A ROOF PLAN should be included if the roof is complicated and not clearly shown by the other standard drawings.

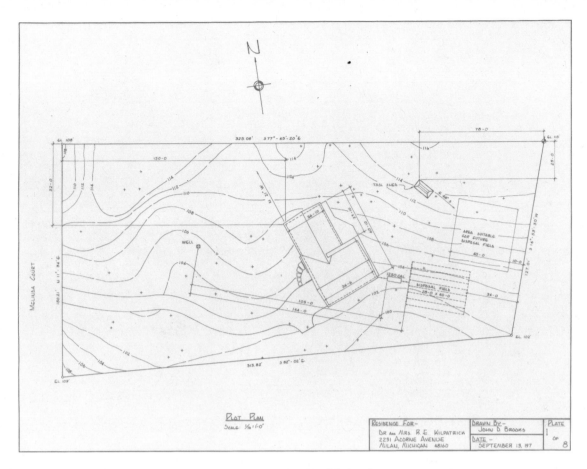

Fig. 3-10. A typical residential plot plan.

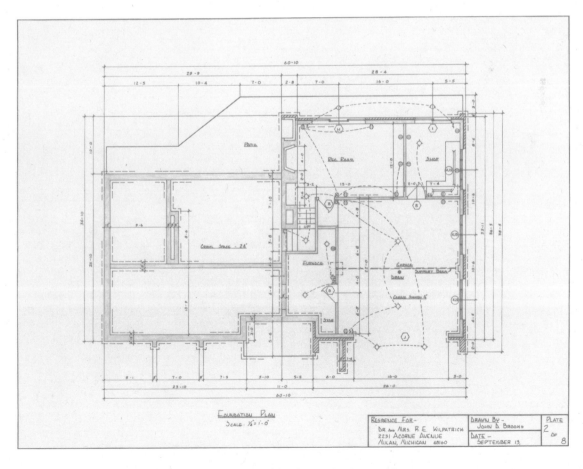

Fig. 3-11. A basement/foundation plan for a residence.

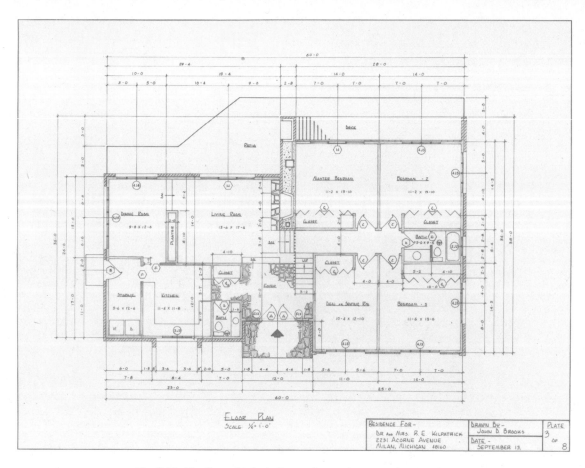

Fig. 3-12. The floor plan is the heart of a set of construction drawings.

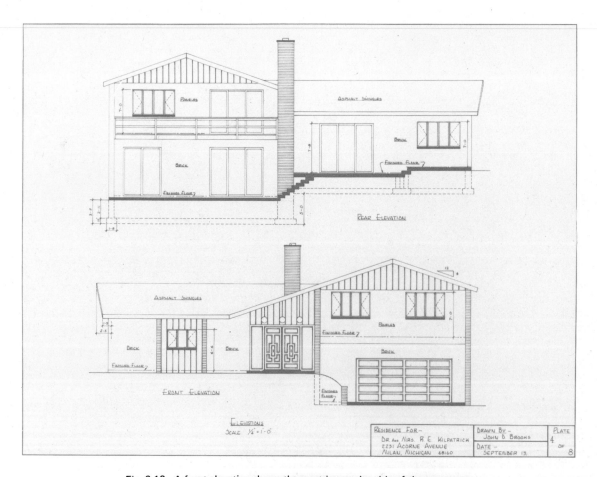

Fig. 3-13. A front elevation shows the most impressive side of the structure.

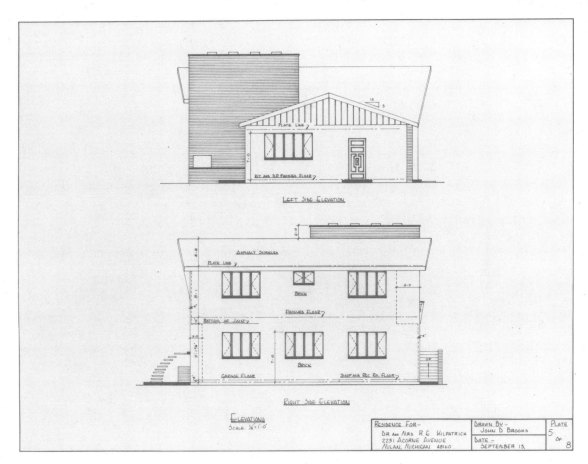

Fig. 3-14. Elevations are also drawn of the other sides of the house.

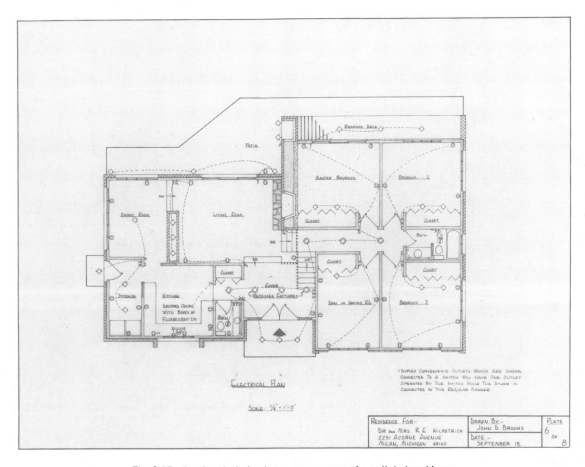

Fig. 3-15. An electrical plan is a necessary part of a well-designed home.

43

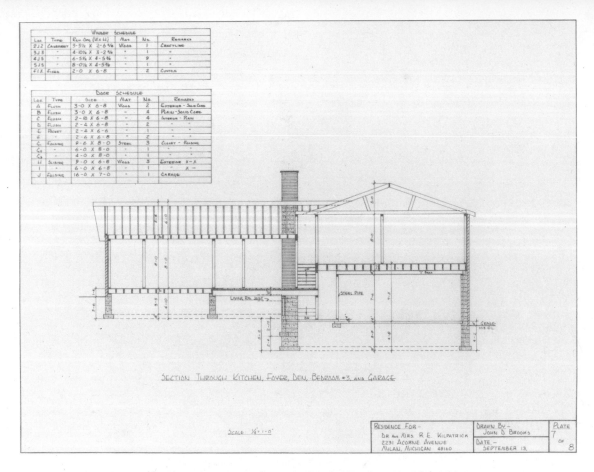

Fig. 3-16. A longitudinal section detail provides an excellent means of showing the various levels and vertical distances within a structure.

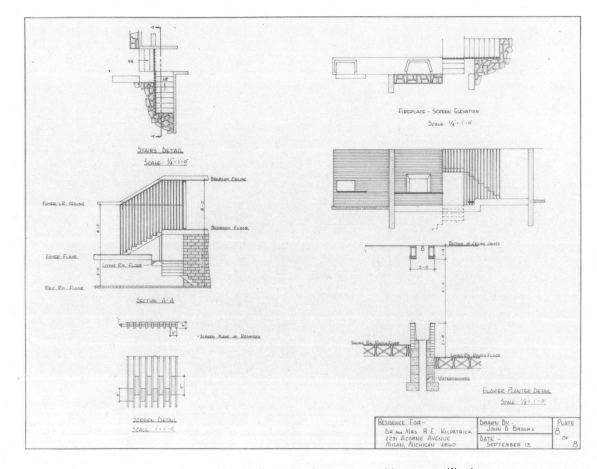

Fig. 3-17. Construction details provide the contractor with exact specifications.

The roof plan may be incorporated into the plot plan.

A ROOF FRAMING PLAN should be included in a set of residential plans in case of a complex roof or one that requires unique construction. A roof framing plan may be drawn to clarify construction aspects associated with the roof. The roof framing plan, normally shows the rafters, ceiling joists, and supporting members.

A FLOOR FRAMING PLAN shows direction of joists and major supporting members.

The HEATING AND COOLING PLAN illustrates components (furnace, air conditioner, heating and cooling ducts or hot water pipes of the climate control system of the house). The design of this system is usually performed by the contractor who installs the system.

A PLUMBING PLAN shows such features as the hot and cold water system, waste lines, vents, storage tank if needed, placement of plumbing fixtures and cleanouts.

The LANDSCAPING PLAN is sometimes combined with the plot plan. Its purpose is to locate and identify plants and other elements included in landscaping the site.

A FURNITURE PLAN identifies the furniture to be used and its placement in each area of the house. Even if no furniture plan is to be a part of the construction drawings, care should be taken in the design process to allow ample room for standard size furniture.

An EXPANSION PLAN shows how the structure has been designed to accommodate future expansion. Information on the expansion plan could be presented as part of the regular construction drawings.

REVIEW QUESTIONS – CHAPTER 3

1. List 12 factors which should be considered when planning a residential structure to the size of house and arrangement of rooms.
   a._____.
   b._____.
   c._____.
   d._____.
   e._____.
   f._____.
   g._____.
   h._____.
   i._____.
   j._____.
   k._____.
   l._____.
2. The document which lists any legal claims against the property is called a _____.
3. The document which shows any restrictions or easements attached to the property is the _____.
4. List four site features which are found on a topographical drawing of the site.
   a._____.
   b._____.
   c._____.
   d._____.
5. If a home is to have its own septic system and water supply, the lot should be at least_____in size. (The local code may require a larger site.)
6. What determines whether or not a house is functional?
7. List ten individual and family activities which should be provided for in a house.
   a._____.
   b._____.
   c._____.
   d._____.
   e._____.
   f._____.
   g._____.
   h._____.
   i._____.
   j._____.
8. Why should one plan a house using modular sizes?
9. Exterior walls should be lengths divisible by_____feet.
10. List the drawings which are ordinarily included in a set of residential house plans.
    a._____.
    b._____.
    c._____.
    d._____.
    e._____.
    f._____.
    g._____.
11. Why should a title search be made before purchasing a lot?
12. The measure of success of the architect in designing a house is:_____.
13. The cost of a site as a percentage of the total cost of a house will depend on _____.

SUGGESTED ACTIVITIES

1. Obtain a map of your city or community and identify the approximate location of your house on the map.
2. Using your house as an example, determine the following characteristics:
   a. How many square feet of living area does it have? (Do not include garage.)
   b. What are the dimensions of the lot on which your house sits?
   c. How far is it from your house to the closest grocery store?
   d. How far is it from your house to the school that you attend?
   e. Does your house have its own well and septic system?
   f. How many new homes are under construction within 1/2 mile radius of your home?
   g. How many older homes are for sale in the same 1/2 mile radius?
3. Visit your local building inspector and ask him to show you copies of the codes which are used in your community. Ask him how the cost of permits is calculated and what is required by his department before a permit may be obtained.
4. Look around your neighborhood for a vacant lot or piece

of property. Make a list of the "site considerations" that should be made if a house were to be constructed on this property. Include as many factors as necessary from this chapter that would apply to the property.

5. From your family needs, make a listing of the activity areas (space) that should be provided if you were planning a new home. Be sure to include all the needs of each member of your family and specific group activity areas.

6. Prepare a display for the bulletin board that illustrates the advantages of proper site consideration when planning a house. Use clippings from magazines and other publications to show how the architect made good use of all aspects of the property to enhance the beauty of the house.

Structural features of many parts of a house require exceptional skill in the use of instruments and drawing techniques. Note the roof framing members used in the room.

Chapter 4
DRAWING INSTRUMENTS AND TECHNIQUES

An understanding of basic drafting practices and the use of equipment is a necessary introduction to architectural drawing and style. Most of the equipment and many of the principles are similar to those used in a course in mechanical or technical drawing. A review of the basic drawing concepts will establish a foundation on which the techniques for architectural drawing may be developed.

ORTHOGRAPHIC PROJECTION

The use of orthographic projection is a means of representing an object from a point at infinity. For this reason, the projection lines are parallel to each other and no depth is represented in any of the primary views.

Orthographic projection is basic to any type of drawing. It

Fig. 4-1. This camp cottage shows the arrangement of a regular orthographic projection.

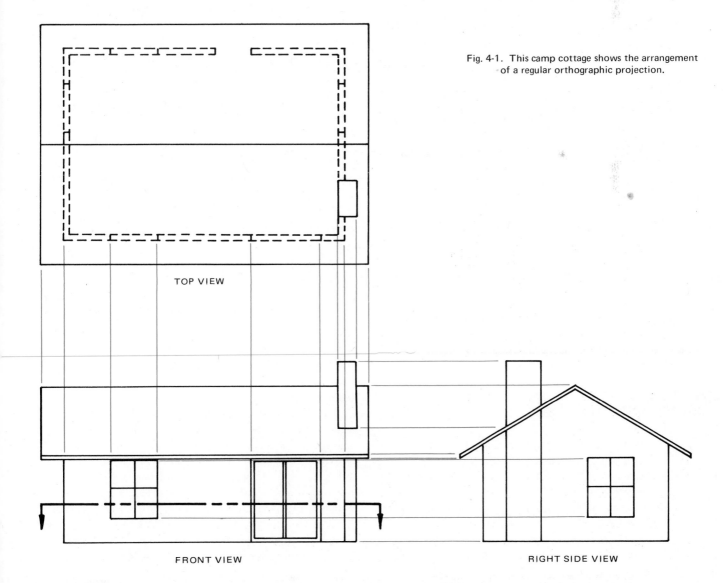

TOP VIEW

FRONT VIEW

RIGHT SIDE VIEW

47

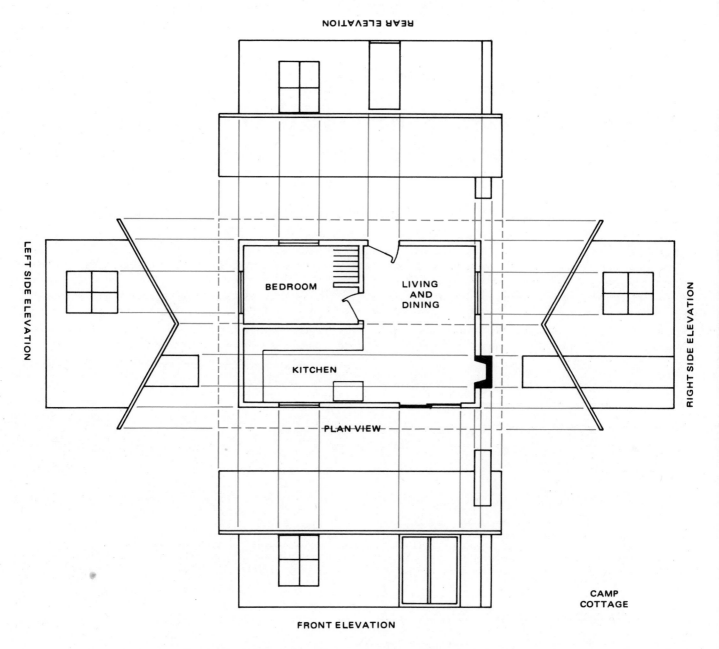

Fig. 4-2. How the four elevations of the camp cottage are projected from the plan view.

makes little difference whether you are drawing metal fasteners, electric motors or residences, the principles remain the same. Architectural drawing applies these principles with the primary difference being the objects drawn and symbols used to represent the various parts.

THREE PRINCIPAL VIEWS

The three principal views in orthographic projection are the top, front and right side views. In architectural drawing the names are changed slightly, but the views remain basically the same with minor exceptions.

The top view of an object in mechanical drawing is comparable to the roof plan of a house. The "plan view" or floor plan is the most important view and is actually a section view taken about halfway up the wall. The plan view is used as

the basis for most of the other views in a house plan and for most purposes will take the place of the top view. Fig. 4-1 shows a small cottage drawn in orthographic projection using the normal arrangement. A cutting plane line is shown in the front view to illustrate how the plan view is derived for use in architectural drawings.

The front view of an object in mechanical drawing is the same as the front elevation in architectural drawing. Note that the word "view" is changed to "elevation." Architectural draftsmen ordinarily draw an elevation of all sides of the structure rather than just the front and right side as is the practice in mechanical drawing. These elevations are called the FRONT ELEVATION, the RIGHT SIDE ELEVATION, the LEFT SIDE ELEVATION and the REAR ELEVATION. Some complex structures require more than four elevations to provide a complete description. Fig. 4-2 illustrates how the plan view is used to project the elevations. It should be noted that the elevations are NOT presented upside-down and on their side as shown in this illustration. In actual drawing, the plan view is revolved so that each elevation will be drawn in its natural position.

ARCHITECTURAL DRAFTING EQUIPMENT

An architectural draftsman uses equipment which is designed for specific purposes. Using the equipment requires skill and understanding. A brief description of the major items follows:

PENCILS

Pencils used in drafting are of two principal types--the common wood pencil and the mechanical pencil. Fig. 4-3 illustrates the two types of pencils most commonly used.

Wood pencils are still used by some draftsmen, but most are using the mechanical types. The mechanical pencil allows the draftsman to change the hardness of lead at will, but more important, the lead is easier to sharpen and may be used close to the end. Either type of pencil will give the desired results if kept sharp and used properly. (Be sure to sharpen the proper end of a wooden pencil so as not to remove the hardness identification.) The hardness number is printed on the side of the wooden pencil and along the lead used in mechanical pencils. Fig. 4-4 shows a variety of pencil sharpening devices which may be used to obtain a fine conical point.

ERASERS

Most draftsmen prefer to use an eraser not attached to the pencil. Several common drafting erasers are shown in Fig. 4-5. When selecting an eraser, care should be taken to choose one that will remove all traces of lead without destroying the surface of the paper or leaving colored marks. Some pink

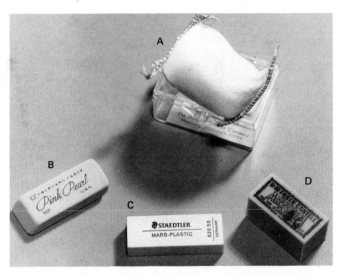

Fig. 4-5. An assortment of drafting erasers used by architects.

Fig. 4-3. Above. Both mechanical and wood pencils are used in architectural drawing. Fig. 4-4. Below. A pencil may be properly sharpened using a sandpaper board or a mechanical sharpener.

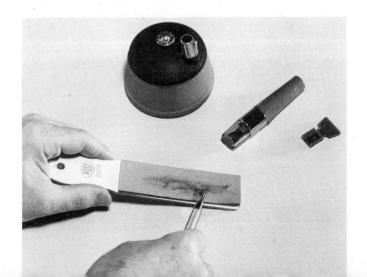

erasers will leave a pinkish color which distracts from the appearance of the finished drawing. Many of the newer plastic erasers are suitable for this type of work. Erasing with a large eraser can be difficult if an erasing shield is not used.

ERASING SHIELDS

Erasing shields, Fig. 4-6, are made of metal or plastic and are usually thin to provide for accurate erasing. The shield will allow lines to be removed without disturbing surrounding lines. Always use the erasing shield when there is a possibility of touching another line which you wish to save.

PAPER

Drafting paper may be purchased in standard size sheets or rolls. The sheets are easier to use but are usually more costly,

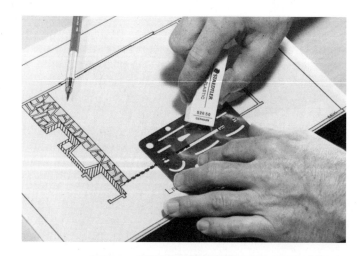

Fig. 4-6. The use of an erasing shield will improve the quality of a drawing.

Fig. 4-7. The chart below shows two systems of standard drawing sheet sizes.

Standard Drawing Sheet Sizes

Multiples of 8 1/2 x 11		Multiples of 9 x 12
Size	Letter Designation	Size
8 1/2 x 11	A	9 x 12
11 x 17	B	12 x 18
17 x 22	C	18 x 24
22 x 34	D	24 x 36
34 x 44	E	36 x 48

Both systems are approved by the American Standards Association and are commonly used. Most architectural drawings are executed on some type of vellum or tracing material which provides for ease of reproduction. Preliminary drawings are sometimes made on opaque drawing paper and then later traced for reproduction. Presentation plans are often executed on illustration board or some other special type medium designed for the particular artistic technique used in the presentation. As a general rule, the type of paper selected will depend on the intended use for which the drawing is being prepared and the presentation technique used.

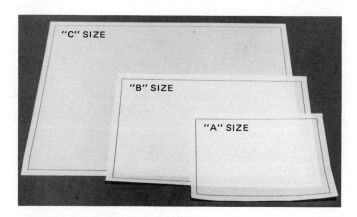

Fig. 4-7. Three standard sizes of tracing paper commonly used in archi-tectural drawing are: "A" size (9 x 12"), "B" size (12 x 18") and "C" size (18 x 24").

DRAWING BOARDS

Drawing boards are made in standard sizes of 12 x 18, 18 x 24, 24 x 36 and 30 x 42". Most boards have traditionally been white pine or basswood, but with the advent of vinyl covers, plywood and other species are now acceptable. The use of drawing boards seems to be giving way to drawing tables with tops which serve as boards. These tables are usually larger and have a drafting machine or straightedge permanently attached. Such an arrangement provides adequate working area with a straightedge as long as 96" and does away with the need for a T-square, Figs. 4-8 and 4-9.

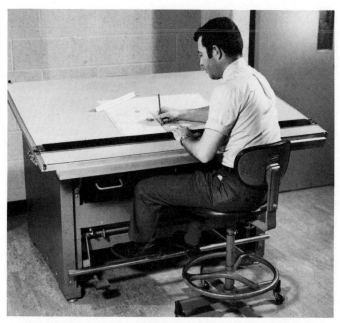

Fig. 4-8. A modern drawing table equipped with a straightedge.

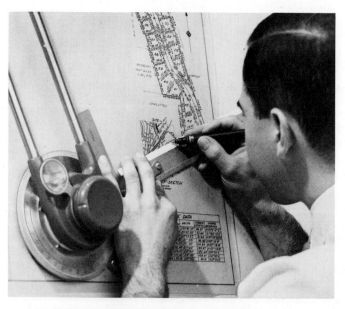

Fig. 4-9. A drafting machine enables the draftsman to draw lines and measure angles conveniently.

THE T-SQUARE

T-squares are manufactured from wood, metal, plastics and combinations of these materials. Fig. 4-10 shows one of the traditional models. The T-square is used to draw horizontal

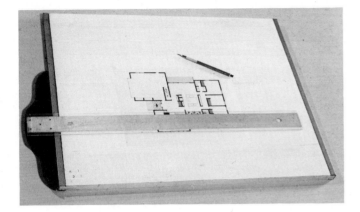

Fig. 4-10. The traditional T-square and drawing board are adequate for the beginning draftsman.

lines and provide an edge for guiding the triangles. The blade is held with the left hand and lines are drawn from left to right. (This is for a right-handed person. The process is reversed for a left-handed person.) The T-square should be used on only one side of the drawing board while making a drawing since the opposite edge may not be exactly parallel. Straightedges are used in much the same way as T-squares. Fig. 4-11 illustrates the use of a straightedge to draw a horizontal line.

Fig. 4-11. The procedure for drawing a horizontal line using a straightedge.

TRIANGLES

The 45° and 30°-60° triangles are the common triangles used in drafting work. They may be purchased in metal or plastic. Plastic is preferred because of its transparency. Fig. 4-12 shows the 30°-60°, 45° and adjustable triangles. Tri-

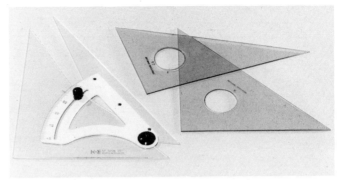

Fig. 4-12. A 30°-60°, 45°-45° and adjustable triangle.

angles are used for drawing lines which are not horizontal. Drawing vertical lines in an upward direction with the hand sliding along the triangle is shown in Fig. 4-13. Adjustable triangles are also available which take the place of the 30°-60° and 45° triangles. When using the adjustable type, care should be taken to adjust it accurately.

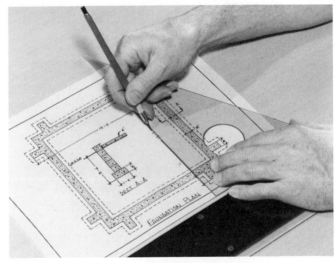

Fig. 4-13. A vertical line is drawn along the edge of a triangle from the bottom toward the top.

PROTRACTORS

Protractors are used for measuring angles. They are produced in semicircular and circular styles. The semicircular type is extensively used by most architectural draftsmen. Measurement finer than half a degree is not possible with most common protractors. However, metal protractors with a vernier scale may be purchased which will measure accurately to one minute. Fig. 4-14 illustrates the type of protractors commonly used by architectural draftsmen.

SCALES

Scales used in drawing are primarily of three types: the architect's scale, the engineer's scale and the combination

Fig. 4-14. Protractors are available in semicircular and full circle styles.

scale. Fig. 4-15 shows a typical architect's and engineer's scale. These are made of wood, plastics, metal or a combination of materials. The architect's scale is usually divided into 3/32, 3/16, 1/8, 1/4, 1/2, 1, 3/8, 3/4, 1 1/2 and 3'' to the foot and one edge divided into 16 parts to the inch. The engineer's scale is divided into 10, 20, 30, 40, 50 and 60 parts to the inch. The combination scale is just what the name implies--a combination of the architect's and engineer's scales. It is divided into 1/8, 1/4, 1/2, 1, 3/8 and 3/4'' to the foot and 50 and 16 parts to the inch. Decimal measurements may be made using the 50th scale.

The most significant difference in these scales is that the divisions of the architect's scale is based on twelve units to the foot while the engineer's scale is based on ten units to the inch. The combination scale is designed to bridge the gap and provide both features. An architectural draftsman usually needs both an architect's scale and an engineer's scale since certain drawings (topographical drawings and plot plans) require measurements in 10ths. The site plan and plot plan are good examples.

Scales are designed in various configurations which include two-bevel, four-bevel, opposite bevel and triangular shapes, Fig. 4-16.

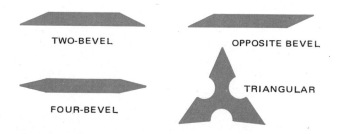

TWO-BEVEL

OPPOSITE BEVEL

FOUR-BEVEL

TRIANGULAR

Fig. 4-16. Four common scale designs.

HOW TO USE THE SCALE

The use of words SIZE and SCALE should be clarified. In drafting terminology, one may say the drawing is "half size." This means exactly what it says. The drawing is one half as large as the object in real life. When the notation at the bottom of the drawing indicates, Scale: 1/2'' = 1'-0'', then the drawing is 1/2 scale. One half scale means that 1/2'' on the drawing is equal to 1'-0'' on the object. If you were to draw a 40' x 60' house at a scale of 1/2'' = 1'' you would need a piece of paper a little over 20' x 30'. Most residential floor plans are drawn at 1/4 scale. (1/4'' on the drawing equals 1'-0'' on the house.)

Study the 1/4 scale shown in Fig. 4-17 and notice that the end 1/4'' is divided into twelve parts which represent the 12

Fig. 4-15. An architectural draftsman uses both an engineer's and architect's scale.

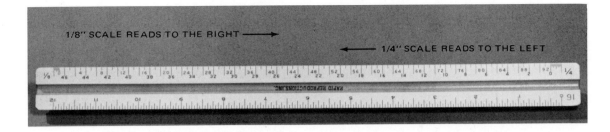

Fig. 4-17. The 1/8" = 1'-0" and 1/4" = 1'-0" are superimposed on the upper edge of this architect's scale. Note, however, that 1/4" = 1'-0" is standard in architectural work.

inches of one foot. Be careful not to confuse the 1/4 scale with the 1/8 scale which appear together on the same face. The 1/4 scale has longer lines denoting each foot.

Fig. 4-18 shows a measurement of 12'-0" being made on the 1/4 scale. The scale shown in Fig. 4-19 indicates a measurement of 16'-4" on the 1/4 scale. Always begin at zero on the scale and lay off the number of feet and then measure back from zero the number of inches. Use a sharp pencil and be very careful in pinpointing the exact length you wish to measure. ALWAYS DRAW AS ACCURATELY AS POSSIBLE. This is a good habit to form.

DIVIDERS

Architectural draftsmen use dividers in basically two sizes--large (about 6") and small (about 4"). The small dividers usually have an adjustment wheel in the center or on the side. The larger dividers often have a friction device of some type instead of the wheel. Both types are useful and are considered standard equipment, Fig. 4-20.

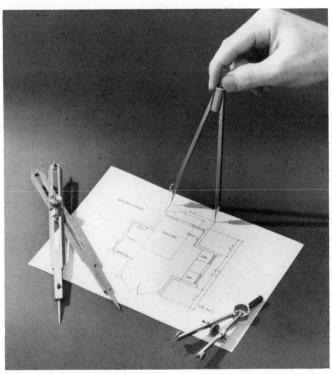

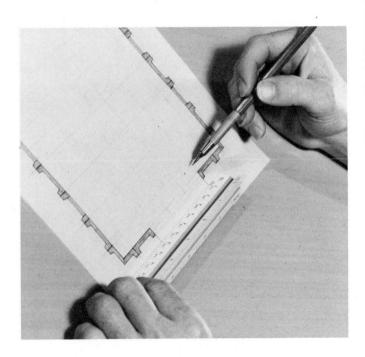

Fig. 4-18. Using the architect's scale to measure the width of an opening.

Fig. 4-20. Three types of dividers--a small center wheel divider, a large friction type divider and a proportional divider.

Fig. 4-19. The proper method of measuring 16'-4" using the 1/4" = 1'-0" scale.

The dividers are used to divide a line into proportional parts, provide a quick method of measuring a length which must be used a number of times, and other related uses.

Divider points are shaped like needles. They must be kept sharp to be useful.

THE COMPASS

The compass is produced in different styles and sizes to match the dividers. Some have center adjusting wheels and others have side adjusting wheels. The most common varieties used by architectrual draftsmen are the giant bow (about 6'' in length), medium size friction compass and the smaller center wheel compass as shown in Fig. 4-21.

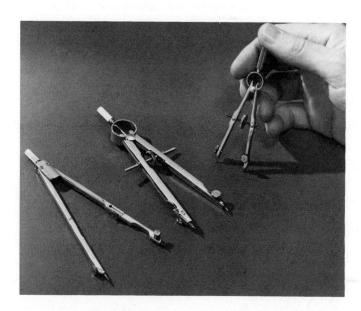

Fig. 4-21. Three common styles of compasses used in architectural drawing.

The compass is used to draw circles, arcs, or radii. Some practice is required to be able to draw sharp, smooth arcs. It is held between the thumb and forefinger and rotated in a clockwise manner while leaning it slightly forward. Large arcs may be drawn using a beam compass as illustrated in Fig. 4-22.

Lead in the compass should be adjusted to the proper length (slightly shorter than the center point) and sharpened to a fine point. Use an F or H lead.

The center point of a compass is different from points on the divider. The compass center point may be cup shaped or have a point with a shoulder. The shoulder prevents the point from going too deep.

LETTERING GUIDES

Lettering guides are used to draw guide lines which assist in producing neat letters. The Braddock-Rowe Lettering Triangle and the Ames Lettering Guide are shown in Fig. 4-23.

Fig. 4-23. Draw guidelines for lettering using either the Ames Lettering Guide or the Braddock-Rowe Lettering Triangle.

IRREGULAR CURVES

Irregular curves are used to draw curved lines which cannot be drawn with the compass. These lines usually have a series of centers and would be very difficult to construct with a compass. When using an irregular curve, line up at least four points and draw the line through three. Continue this process

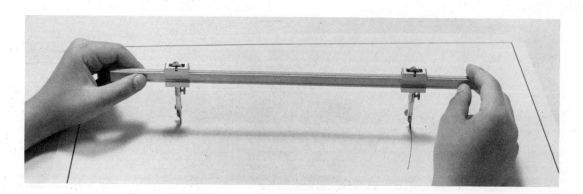

Fig. 4-22. A beam compass is used for drawing a large arc.

Fig. 4-24. Irregular curves are used to draw curved lines which are not arcs of a circle.

until the curve is completed. This procedure produces a smoother line. Fig. 4-24 shows how a flexible curve could be used to draw a long curved line.

CASE INSTRUMENTS

The case instruments may include dividers, compass, lining pens, pencil pointers, spare parts, small screwdriver, and various other instruments. Some students may wish to purchase a set of case instruments rather than individual parts. Fig. 4-25 shows a small set of case instruments.

LETTERING DEVICES

Lettering devices are used when uniformity of letters is essential. Many styles and sizes of letters are available. A popular type is the Leroy device shown in Fig. 4-26. Lettering in ink and pencil is possible with this set.

TECHNICAL FOUNTAIN PENS

Technical fountain pens are used by the draftsman to draw straight and curved lines in ink, Fig. 4-27. They have about replaced the old lining pen of years past. Pen points are interchangeable and range in size from 000 (very fine) to 8 (about 1/16 in. wide).

LINES USED IN ARCHITECTURAL DRAWING

Architectural draftsmen use a number of different line symbols which assist in clarifying the drawing to the reader. Drawings are usually made for a customer or as a presentation.

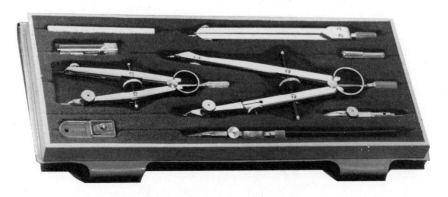

Fig. 4-25. A beginner's set of case instruments.

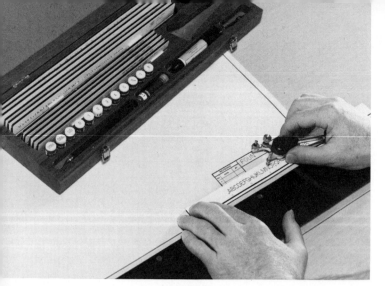

Fig. 4-26. A Leroy lettering device being used to letter a title block.

It is for the purpose of accurate communication that a specific line symbol is used in a given situation. Once the draftsman learns these lines and uses them properly, he will begin to communicate with others in a more precise manner. THE PURPOSE OF A DRAWING IS TO COMMUNICATE IDEAS ACCURATELY AND CLEARLY.

Fig. 4-27. A technical fountain pen used for inking lines and lettering.

Draftsmen refer to the line symbols used in drawing as the ALPHABET OF LINES. Many of the same symbols used in mechanical or technical drawing are also used in architectural drawing. However, one not familiar with architectural line symbols should study them carefully to be sure that their use is clearly understood. Some symbols may be slightly different in architectural work. Study Fig. 4-28 which illustrates the major lines used in architectural drawing.

BORDER LINES

Border lines are very heavy lines and are used to form a boundary for the drawing. They assure the reader that no part of the drawing has been removed and provide a "finished" look to the drawing.

OBJECT LINES

Object lines show the outline of the main features of the object. They are important lines and therefore should be easily seen. On an architectural drawing, such things as interior and exterior walls, steps, driveways, patios, fireplaces, doors and windows are represented by object lines.

BORDER LINE	────────────
OBJECT LINE	────────────
CUTTING PLANE LINE	←── ─ ─ ──→
SHORT BREAK LINE	∿∿∿∿∿
HIDDEN LINE	– – – – – –
CENTER LINE	── ─ ── ─ ──
SECTION LINE	──╱╱╱╱──
DIMENSION LINE	├─── 8'-9'' ───┤
LONG BREAK LINE	└──── ∿ ────┘
GUIDE LINES	ABCDEFGHIJKLMNO
CONSTRUCTION LINE	────────────
LEADERS	DRAIN TILE / 4'' CONCRETE

Fig. 4-28. General line symbols used in architectural drawing.

HIDDEN LINES

Hidden lines represent an edge which is not visible in a given view. Note that in a floor plan, hidden lines are also used to indicate features above the cutting plane, such as wall cabinets in a kitchen or an archway. Hidden lines are usually not as thick as object lines.

CENTER LINES

Center lines indicate the center of symmetrical objects such as windows and doors. Center lines simplify dimensioning, but should not be used as extension lines. Dimension to extension lines.

EXTENSION LINES

Extension lines are used to denote the termination point of a dimension line. They extend from a portion of the object to the dimension lines. Extension lines are thin lines, but are not construction lines, therefore, draw them sharp and clear to about 1/16″ past the dimension line.

DIMENSION LINES

Dimension lines are used to show size. They are usually placed outside the object, but it is sometimes proper to place them within the object if the area is large and not too cluttered with other lines. All dimension lines have a dimension figure halfway between the ends with some form of symbol at the two terminal ends. Fig. 4-29 shows accepted methods of terminating dimension lines and placing the dimension figures.

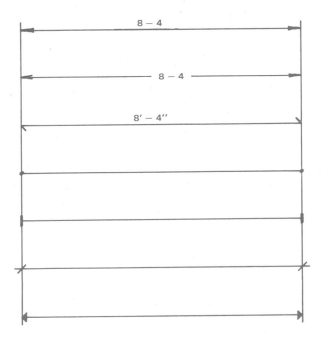

Fig. 4-29. Styles of dimension lines used in architecture.

LONG BREAK LINES

Long break lines are thin lines used to show that all of the part is not drawn. When the break line is two or three inches in length, then a long break line is usually used. An example of a long break line might be found across a paved driveway indicating that the drive was longer than shown on the plan.

SHORT BREAK LINES

Short break lines are used where part of the object is shown broken away to reveal an underlying feature or part of the object removed for some other reason. Short break lines are heavy lines drawn freehand.

CUTTING PLANE LINES

Cutting plane lines are heavy lines used to show where the object is to be sectioned. Ordinarily, cutting plane lines are labeled with a letter at each end so that the section detail will be easily identified.

SECTION LINES

Section lines or crosshatch lines are used to show that the feature has been sectioned. General section lines are usually drawn at a 45° angle, but specific symbols may represent various types of material.

GUIDELINES

Guidelines are used in lettering. They are drawn very light and are for the draftsman's use. Guidelines will help improve the quality of lettering and are, therefore, well worth the time and effort required to draw them.

CONSTRUCTION LINES

Construction lines are very light lines used in the process of constructing the drawing. Again, they are for the draftsman and should not reproduce when a print is made. Draw your construction lines sharp and light.

Fig. 4-30 shows most of the general line symbols applied in a floor plan. Other symbols will be found in areas pertaining to their specific use. A close examination of the lines shown in Fig. 4-30 shows that they vary in thickness (width) but not in shade. ALL LINES ARE BLACK AND VARY ONLY IN WIDTH. A thin line may look lighter than a thick line but in reality they are both black. Just remember that all lines (except construction lines and guidelines) must be dark so that reproduction of the drawing will be possible; light lines will not reproduce satisfactorily.

Certain types of lines lend themselves to hard or soft pencil leads. As a general rule, use 4H for dimension lines, extension lines, center lines, leader lines, long break lines, and section lines; 2H for object lines, hidden lines, cutting plane lines, short break lines and border lines; H for lettering; and 6H for construction and guidelines. These are not absolutes, but will vary with the type of paper being used and the pressure applied. The harder the lead, the more difficult it is to draw a dark line. The leads in the soft range (B-9B) are too soft to use in architectural drawing because they smear quite easily. Therefore, choose the lead which will allow you to draw a sharp dark line which will not smear. Note the following hardness range of pencil leads available to the architect to meet his many needs in line weight.

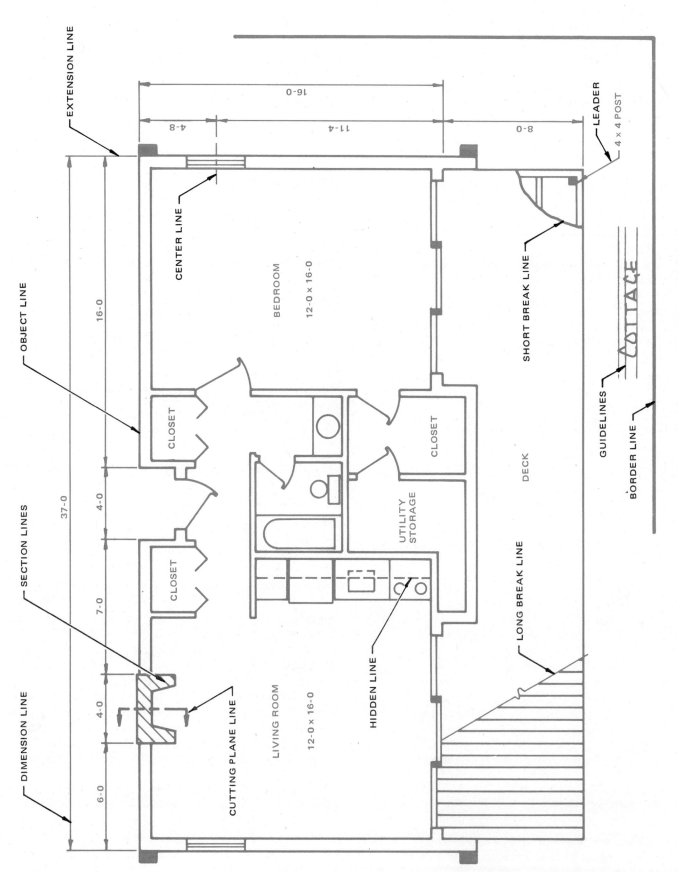

Fig. 4-30. A floor plan illustrating most of the line symbols used by the architectural draftsman.

9H 8H 7H 6H 5H 4H 3H 2H H F HB B 2B 3B 4B 5B 6B 7B 8B 9B
Very Hard   Medium   Very Soft

Always use the proper line symbol so that communication will be clear to the reader.

ARCHITECTURAL LETTERING

Architectural lettering is not the same as mechanical or technical lettering. The nature of an architectural drawing borders on art work and the "pure" letters used in mechanical drawing are not in keeping with architectural style.

There is no "one" correct architectural lettering style. Many acceptable styles present a certain artistic flair. Architects often like to develop their own personal style which is unique. Fig. 4-31 shows three individual styles developed by students of architecture. Each of the styles is different, but each is in keeping with the feeling of architecture.

ABCDEFGHIJKLM
NOPQRSTUVWXYZ
DAVID BROWNLEE

ABCDEFGHIJKLM
NOPQRSTUVWXYZ
E. FEGAN

ABCDEFGHIJKLM
NOPQRSTUVWXYZ
S REBLIN

Fig. 4-31. Each architectural student should develop his own personal lettering style.

SOME NOTES ON DEVELOPING A STYLE OF LETTERING

1. Draw guidelines and use them.
2. Experiment with variations of the capital letters of the alphabet to determine the ones you like best, Fig. 4-32.

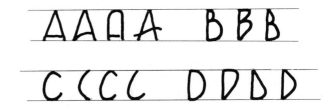

Fig. 4-32. Variations of standard letters may add interest to your style.

Lower case letters are seldom used in architectural lettering.
3. Select letter styles which are artistic but readily identifiable.
4. Apply a basic technique to all similar letters of the alphabet, Fig. 4-33.

AEFH BCDGOD
KR KR VM NX

Fig. 4-33. Treat similar letters the same way to increase unity of style.

5. Letter the entire alphabet large enough so that the proportion of the letters is distinct.
6. Make a mental picture of each letter so that you may reproduce it the same each time.
7. Practice "your" style until it becomes a part of you and flows easily.
8. Use your style.

Architectural lettering should be vertical. If you learn to letter that way, you should never have to worry whether your method will be acceptable. Slanted letters usually indicate that the word is in italics. This is only used for emphasis.

LETTER SPACING

The space between letters in a word is not a constant. The ability to judge the space between letters must be carefully learned. Only practice will perfect this ability. Fig. 4-34 shows

Fig. 4-34. Variable spacing of letters adds interest and is more pleasing to the eye.

an example of spacing as a constant, and then in a more pleasing arrangement with variable spacing. Constant practice in lettering words helps develop the ability to space letters in a pleasing manner.

WORD SPACING

The space between words is as important as the spacing between letters. Words must not appear to run together, nor should they be so far apart that valuable space is wasted. A good rule to follow in spacing words is to allow about the same distance between words as the letters are high.

LETTER SIZE

There are no absolute rules concerning lettering size. Generally, most information lettering on architectural drawings is 1/8" or 3/32" high. A technique which looks good and helps in the readability of lettering is to make the first letter of each word 1/8" high and the remainder of the word 3/32" high. This emphasizes the beginning of each word and tends to separate them, Fig. 4-35.

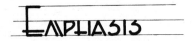

Fig. 4-35. Draw the first letter of each word larger than the succeeding letters for emphasis.

Titles and important words are usually lettered larger, with bold lines being used to direct attention to their importance. Underlining also helps to call attention to important information.

ARCHITECTURAL DRAWING TIME-SAVERS

In years past, architectural draftsmen drew all details with standard instruments. This was time consuming and hindered standardization of many common elements found on architectural drawings. Today we are fortunate in having at our fingertips many devices which speed up our work and add to the readability of our drawings. These devices are called architectural time-savers.

TEMPLATES

Templates serve as a guide in drawing special lines or symbols. Most templates used in drawing are made of plastic. Fig. 4-36 shows several plastic templates used in architectural drawing. These templates are similar in design and use. The cutouts represent standard symbols and may be traced to form the symbol on the drawing. Some of the features on the templates are general in nature and may be used to form symbols not represented on the template. Templates may be purchased in various scales to suit the requirements of most any drawing.

UNDERLAYS

Underlays are similar to templates. Symbols are printed or drawn on a sheet which is placed under the drawing and traced. Underlays are usually made for symbols which are used

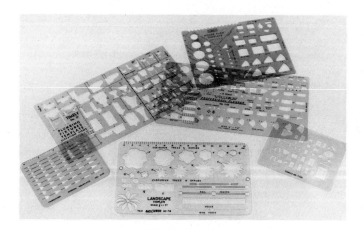

Fig. 4-36. An assortment of templates used in architectural drawing.

repeatedly. Symbols such as trees, bricks, stone, siding, and even doors and windows may be traced from underlays. Fig. 4-37 shows several underlays which are used by architectural draftsmen.

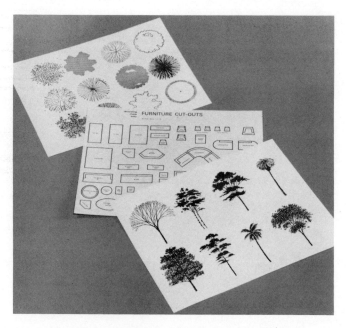

Fig. 4-37. Underlays are a useful aid to the draftsman in drawing difficult symbols.

OVERLAYS

Two types of overlays are commonly used in architectural drawing. The first type is printed on a transparent film and is attached directly to the original drawing by the use of an adhesive backing, Fig. 4-38. This overlay becomes a permanent part of the drawing and cannot be readily removed.

The second type of overlay is not permanently attached to the original drawing. The same materials may be used, but are attached to a transparent acetate sheet which is placed over the drawing, Fig. 4-39. This overlay may be used to emphasize specific features or provide alternate solutions. These overlays may be removed or used with a variety of other overlays.

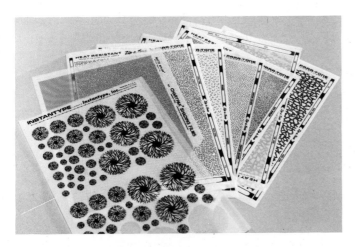

Fig. 4-38. A variety of permanent type overlays available to the draftsman.

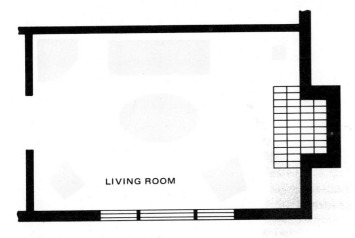

Fig. 4-39. Acetate overlays provide a technique for adding information to a drawing. Areas in color are on plastic overlay.

LIVING ROOM

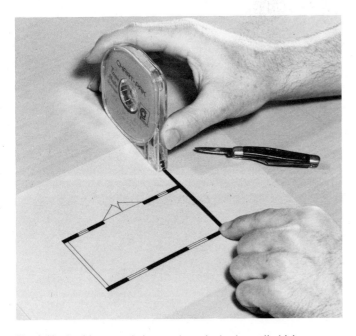

Fig. 4-40. Drafting tape being used to shade the wall thickness on a drawing of a storage house.

DRAFTING TAPES

Drafting tapes are manufactured in opaque and transparent color from 1/64'' to 2'' wide. They may be used on vellum, plastic overlays, or illustration board, Fig. 4-40. The transparent tapes are especially effective on overlays to represent areas of interest or to emphasize certain elements.

Pattern tapes are available which represent such standard symbols as hidden lines, arrowheads, north symbols, section lines, dot patterns, and many others, Fig. 4-41.

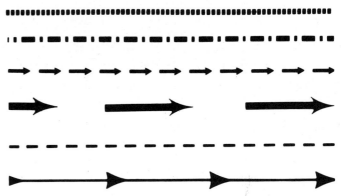

Fig. 4-41. Pattern tapes are available which represent many standard line symbols.

TRANSFER LETTERS AND SYMBOLS

Letters and symbols are easily applied to drawings using "transfer type." Large title letters and difficult symbols are available for use by architectural draftsmen. A smooth rounded object is used to burnish them on. These reproduce well. In some cases they may be removed if desired. Fig. 4-42 shows a sample of the transfer materials available to architectural drafting students.

Fig. 4-42. Transfer letters and symbols save time and add a professional touch to a drawing.

Fig. 4-43. A lettering stencil may be used for titles and for special effects as well as regular lettering.

STENCIL LETTERING GUIDES

Stencil lettering guides are available in plastic, metal and cardboard. Stencils are actually templates and are used in the same way, Fig. 4-43. There are a variety of styles on the market. Lettering guides probably should not be listed as time-savers. A draftsman who has developed a lettering style and practices it, will be able to letter faster freehand than when using a lettering stencil. A stencil also prevents the development of an individual style. In architectural drawing, the stencil should be reserved for special situations.

PHOTODRAWING

Photodrawing is a technique that can be a time-saver in a variety of situations. Photodrawing combines drafting and photography. Rather than redraw an entire plate when revisions are needed, you produce a paste-up, make a photograph, and in this way obtain a final drawing quicker. Old, dirty drawings can often be copied to obtain improved quality using photography. This technique can often be combined with other time-savers, Fig. 4-44.

GRIDS

Grids come in all sizes and forms and have many uses in architectural drawing, Fig. 4-45. Some grids are designed to be used under a sheet of tracing paper as an underlay, while others are designed to be drawn on directly. Square grids are useful in sketching idea plans and in modular construction

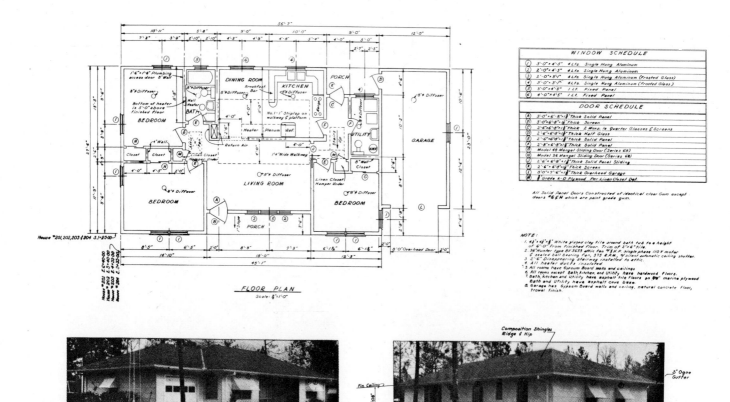

Fig. 4-44. An architectural photodrawing showing how additional information may be added to a drawing without redrawing the original. (Eastman Kodak Co.)

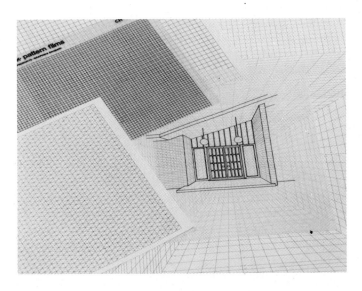

Fig. 4-45. A variety of useful grids.

drawings. These grids are produced in standard size sheets with 2, 4, 8, 16, and 32 squares per inch including reproducible and nonreproducible grid lines.

Another type of grid used in architectural drawing is the perspective grid. These grids are quite useful and usually serve as underlays. Vanishing points are pre-selected on perspective grids. Numerous variations are available.

RUBBER STAMPS

A relatively new timesaving technique in architectural drawing is the use of rubber stamps. Stamps are available of many standard architectural symbols. They are especially useful on plot plans and presentation plans. Fig. 4-46 shows a sample of tree stamps which range in size from less than one

Fig. 4-46. Tree stamps are a popular new addition to the architectural draftsman's equipment.

inch to over four. Trees require a certain amount of artistic ability to draw attractively. The tree stamp helps to solve the problem in a minimum of time.

BURNISH PLATES

Burnish plates are a special type underlay device. The plates, Fig. 4-47, are raised in the sections where lines are desired and recessed in all other areas. A pencil is used as a burnishing tool which results in a transfer of the symbol onto the surface of the tracing. The method is easy to use and accurate. It also reduces the time required to draw siding, bricks, trees, roofing, and many other symbols to a fraction of the time required by conventional methods.

Fig. 4-47. Burnishing plates enable the draftsman to add minute detail in a minimum of time.

REVIEW QUESTIONS — CHAPTER 4

1. The three principal views in orthographic projection are the _____ , _____ and _____ views.
2. The most important view or plan in a set of architectural drawings is the _____ .
3. The piece of drafting equipment used to erase accurately is the _____ _____ .
4. Drafting paper is produced in standard sizes. The dimensions of "B" size paper are _____ or _____ .
5. A newer piece of drafting equipment which replaces the T-square but not the triangles is the _____ .
6. The two triangles most commonly used in architectural drawing are the _____ and the _____ triangles.
7. The most accurate measurement possible with a common drafting protractor is _____ .
8. A scale that is only divided into 10, 20, 30, 40, 50, and 60 parts to the inch is an _____ scale.
9. If a drawing is half as large as the object then the scale is _____ .
10. If 1/4" on the drawing equals one foot on the object, then the scale is _____ .

11. The instrument, other than the scale, which is used to divide a length into proportional parts is the _____.

12. The instrument used to draw circles and arcs is the _____.

13. Guidlines may be drawn with a pencil using a _____.

14. The purpose of a drawing is the _____ _____.

15. The widest line on a drawing which provides a "finished" look is the _____ line.

16. Visible lines are also called _____ lines.

17. Lines which are not visible are _____ lines.

18. Lines which are used to indicate the length of a line or edge are called _____ lines.

19. A number H pencil is usually used for _____ on an architectural drawing.

20. Architectural lettering is different from mechanical lettering. It is more _____.

21. Space between letters in a word is _____.

22. The height of letters on an architectural drawing generally are _____ or _____ high.

23. Symbols on an architectural drawing may be traced using the following devices:
    a. _____.
    b. _____.
    c. _____.
    d. _____.

24. Symbols may be attached to the surface of a drawing using the following devices:
    a. _____.

b. _____.
c. _____.
d. _____.

SUGGESTED ACTIVITIES

1. Letter the alphabet using architectural style letters on a sheet of grid paper. Make the letters at least 1/4" high so the proportions will be distinct. Letter the numbers also.

2. Draw the "alphabet of lines" using proper line weights. Identify each line with its correct name. Design a title block which identifies the drawing. The following information should appear in this title block: your name, title of the drawing, the date, the class name, and the plate number.

3. Visit a drafting supply store and make a list with prices of the types of time-savers they carry in stock which are used in architectural drawing.

4. Obtain a sketch pad with square grid lines. Measure your drafting lab and sketch a plan view showing the walls, doors and windows. Dimension the plan as illustrated in this chapter. Use proper line symbols and line weights. Make the drawing at 1/4 scale.

5. Write letters to some of the major drafting equipment supply companies and ask for their specification literature. Prepare a bulletin board display by clipping and mounting illustrations of pieces of equipment and time-savers most used by the architectural draftsman.

Imaginative designing. This lakeshore home makes extensive use of wood shingles and glass for indoor and outdoor comfort.

Functional designing for recreational living. The straight line styling and use of natural materials keeps maintenance to a minimum.

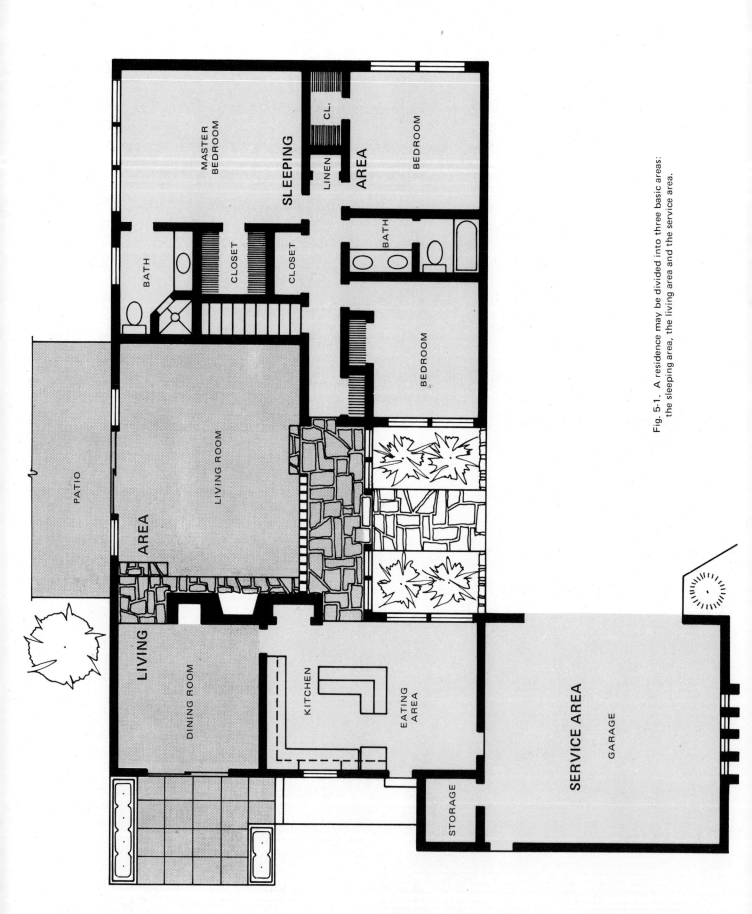

Fig. 5-1. A residence may be divided into three basic areas: the sleeping area, the living area and the service area.

Fig. 5-2. A boy's bedroom, designed for typical activities and interests. (Kirsch Co.)

Chapter 5
ROOM PLANNING, SLEEPING AREA

A residential structure may be divided into three basic areas, the Sleeping Area, the Living Area and the Service Area, Fig. 5-1. The Sleeping Area is where the family sleeps and rests. The Living Area is where the family relaxes, entertains guests, dines, and meets together. The Service Area is the part of the house where food is prepared, clothes are laundered, goods are stored, the car is parked and equipment for upkeep of the house is maintained.

These three basic areas are divided into rooms. Rooms provide privacy and help to separate and contain various activities. A house designer must understand the purpose for each room if he is to develop a functional plan.

SLEEPING AREA

Usually, about one third of the house is dedicated to the sleeping area which includes bedrooms, bath, dressing rooms, and nurseries.

Normally the sleeping area is in a quiet part of the house away from traffic and other noise. If possible, the sleeping area should have a south or southwest orientation so that it may take advantage of cool summer breezes which usually prevail from this direction.

BEDROOMS

Bedrooms are so important that houses are frequently categorized as "two-bedroom," "three-bedroom," or "four-bedroom." The size of the family usually determines the number of bedrooms needed. Ideally, each person would have his or her own bedroom, Fig. 5-2. In the case of a couple with no children, at least two bedrooms are desirable. The second bedroom could be used as a guest room and for other activities when there are no guests. A home with only one bedroom may be difficult to sell. In most localities three-bedroom homes have the greatest sales potential. A three-bedroom home

Fig. 5-3. An extra bedroom may be used as a den, for guests or the arrival of a new member of the family. (Celotex Corp.)

usually provides enough space for a family of four. It may be wise to include an extra bedroom in the plan which can be used for other purposes until needed, Fig. 5-3. It is usually more economical to add an extra room at the outset than to expand later.

Grouping bedrooms together in a separate wing or level of the house, Fig. 5-4, affords quietness and privacy. Each bedroom should have its own access to the hall. An attempt should be made to place each bedroom close to a bathroom. Some bedrooms may have their own private baths.

One of the first problems in designing a bedroom is determining its size. How large is a "big" bedroom, Fig. 5-5? How little is a "small" bedroom? The FHA (Federal Housing Administration) recommends 100 square feet as the minimum size. A small bedroom is shown in Fig. 5-6. It has 99 square feet and the bare essentials in furniture. An average size bedroom, Fig. 5-7, contains between 125 and 175 square feet. Such a room provides ample space for a double or twin beds, chest of drawers, dresser and other small pieces of furniture. A large bedroom has over 175 square feet of floor space, Fig. 5-8. A room of this size provides space for additional furniture. A desk, chair, or television set may be included as bedroom furniture, Fig. 5-9. The largest bedroom is usually considered to be the master bedroom. It may have its own private bath.

It is necessary for each bedroom to have a closet. The FHA recommends a minimum of four linear feet of closet rod space for a man and six feet for a woman. The minimum depth of a clothes closet is two feet. If space is available, a 30" depth is

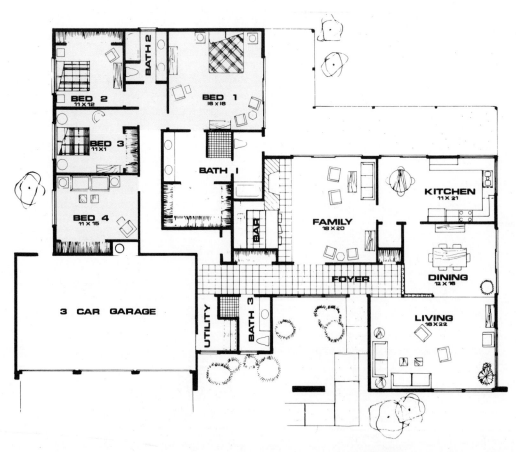

Fig. 5-4. Bedrooms should be clustered together in a wing or level of the house away from noise and other activities.

Fig. 5-5. A large bedroom allows for both study and recreational areas. (Azrock Floor Products)

desirable. When possible, closets should be located along interior walls rather than exterior walls. This provides noise insulation between rooms and does not reduce exterior wall space. A bedroom will normally have no more than two

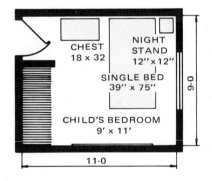

Fig. 5-6. A small bedroom with the minimum single bed, night stand and chest of drawers.

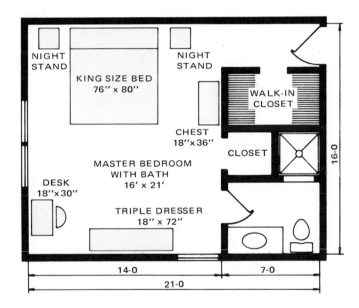

Fig. 5-8. An arrangement for a large master bedroom with private bath included. Note the area of floor space.

Fig. 5-9. This bedroom is large enough to include a comfortable relaxing or reading area. (American Plywood Assoc.)

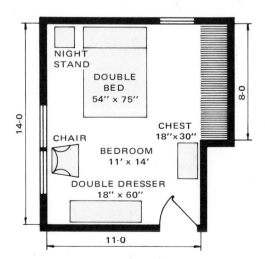

Fig. 5-7. The medium size bedroom contains room for a double bed, chest, chair, double dresser and night stand.

exterior walls, and the use of one for closets will reduce the chance of cross ventilation through windows.

Access to the closet should receive serious consideration. A variety of doors may be selected: sliding, bi-fold, accordion or flush. The usual height of a door is 6'-8", but bi-fold and accordion doors are also available in 8'-0" lengths. Using doors that provide easy accessibility and require but little space is desirable.

Good closet lighting is a necessity. Fixtures may be placed inside the closet.

Bedroom design is directly related to furniture size and arrangement. Determine common furniture sizes, Fig. 5-10, and design the bedroom with a specific arrangement in mind.

Fig. 5-11 shows the furniture cutout method of planning a definite arrangement. The steps are simple: (1) Determine the size of furniture to be used. (2) Draw the plan view of each item to the same scale as the floor plan. (3) Cut out each furniture representation. (4) Place the cutouts on the floor plan in the desired arrangement. (5) Trace around each one to "fix" the location. (6) Remove the cutouts and darken in the lines. Be sure to allow adequate clearance between the various room elements, as in Fig. 5-12.

Windows and doors are important bedroom features. An ideal bedroom will have windows on two walls. These should be located so that a draft will not blow across the bed. If the bedroom is on the first floor level, ribbon windows (wide,

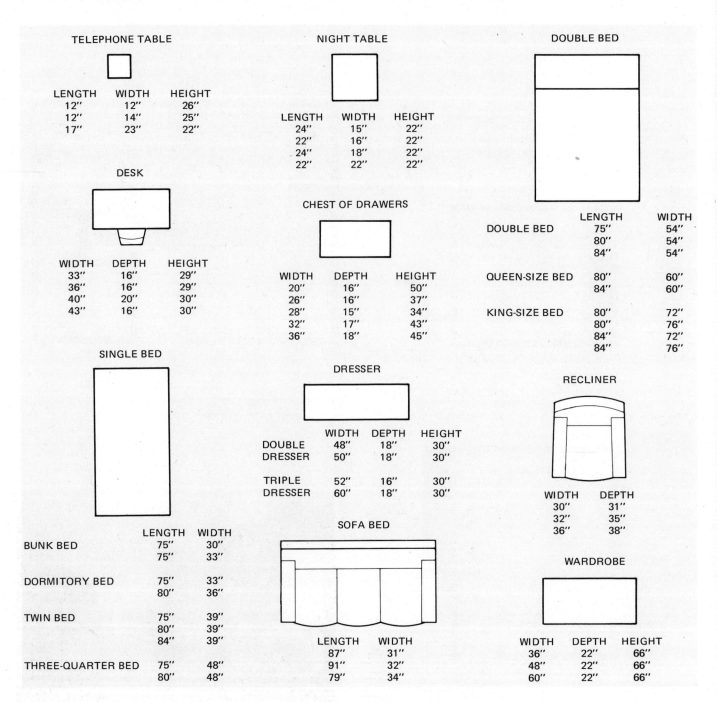

Fig. 5-10. Common sizes of standard bedroom furniture.

DOUBLE BED . . . . .54″ x 75″
TRIPLE DRESSER . . . . .18″ x 60″
NIGHT STAND . . . . . . .18″ x 24″
CHEST OF DRAWERS . . .18″ x 35″

STEP 1. DETERMINING FURNITURE SIZE.

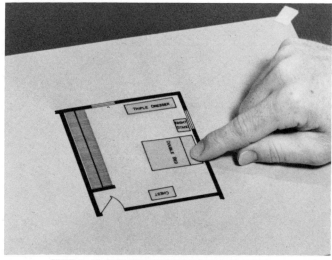

STEP 4. PLACE THE FURNITURE CUTOUTS
ON THE FLOOR PLAN.

STEP 2. DRAW THE PLAN VIEW OF EACH
PIECE OF FURNITURE.

STEP 5. TRACE AROUND EACH PIECE OF FURNITURE
TO LOCATE ITS POSITION.

STEP 3. CUT OUT EACH PIECE OF FURNITURE.

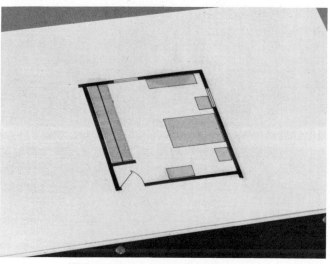

STEP 6. REMOVE THE CUTOUTS AND
DARKEN IN THE LINES.

Fig. 5-11. Using the furniture cutout method for planning a room arrangement.

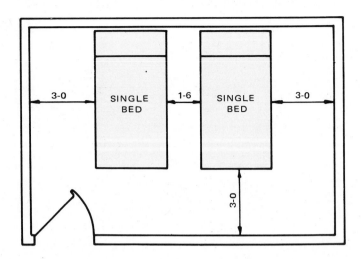

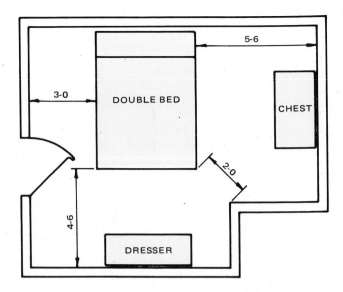

Fig. 5-12. Examples of minimum space clearances for bedroom furniture.

short windows) may be desired to provide added privacy. Window location and spacing is a definite consideration in all well-designed bedrooms.

Each bedroom will have at least one entry door. Interior doors are usually 1 3/8" thick and 6'-8" high. Standard widths range from 2'-0" to 3'-0" in increments of 2". The minimum recommended bedroom door width is 2'-6". A wider door, 2'-8" or 2'-10", provides for easier movement of furniture especially adjacent to a hall. The door should swing into the bedroom. Allow space along the wall for the door when it is open. Locating a door near a corner of the room usually results in less wasted space.

An average size bedroom is shown in Fig. 5-14. It could function as a master bedroom, guest room or regular bedroom. It provides adequate ventilation with large sliding windows. A private bath and large closet are assets. The lounge chair and small table provide a comfortable place to read or relax. Furniture is arranged in such a way that all pieces are easily accessible.

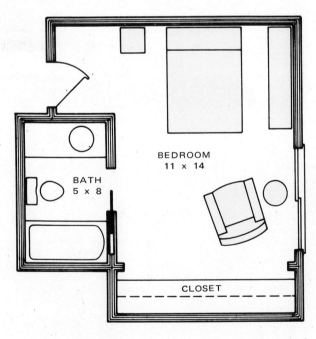

Fig. 5-14. An average size bedroom which is quite versatile.

Fig. 5-13. A well-designed and decorated bedroom is an area of lasting beauty and charm. (Georgia-Pacific Corp.)

A well-planned bedroom is a cheerful but restful place, Fig. 5-13. Carefully select colors which help to create a "quiet and peaceful," atmosphere.

Fig. 5-15 shows a bedroom with 156 sq. ft. plus closet and bath. It is a functional arrangement. Adequate space is provided for traffic by the furniture arrangement. Ventilation is sufficient, but could be improved if this were a corner room. The private bath is positioned in such a way that it could be shared with other rooms if desired.

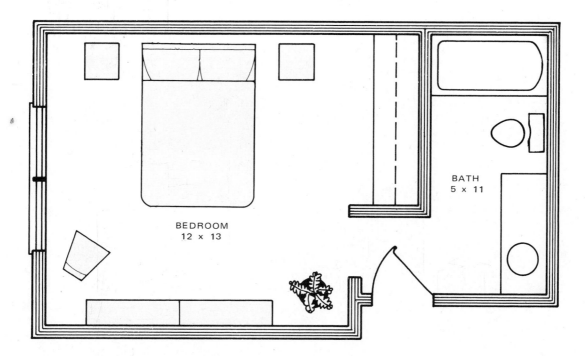

Fig. 5-15. A bedroom with one exterior wall provides for ease of furniture arrangement.

The architect has made use of multimaterials, texture and coordinated colors to enhance the environment of this residence.

Fig. 5-16. This large, attractively decorated bathroom illustrates the use of functional planning for convenience.. (Kohler Co.)

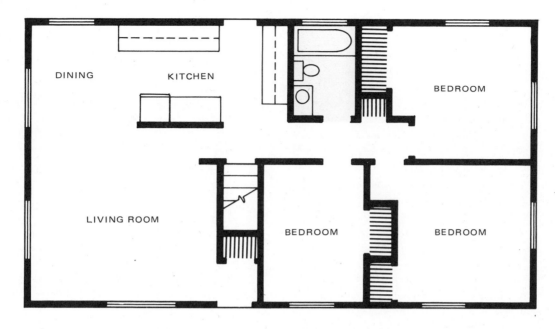

Fig. 5-17. A well-planned centrally located bath in a small house.

BATHROOMS

The small, drab bathroom of a few years ago is almost a thing of the past. Modern homes today have larger, brighter and more functional baths, Fig. 5-16. They also have more bathrooms than were used in the past. All homes require at least one bathroom, most modern homes have 1 1/2 or more. Ideally, every bedroom should have its own bath; however this is seldom possible.

Bathrooms should be located near the bedroom and living areas of the house. If the house is small, one bath may be sufficient. In this case, locate the bathroom in a place where it will be most convenient. See Fig. 5-17. Often the design of the house will indicate the minimum number of baths needed. A two-story design requires at least 1 1/2 baths - - a full bath on the second level near the bedrooms, and a half bath on the first floor near the living area. A half bath is one that does not have all three major fixtures. It usually has only a water closet and lavatory. A split-level house will also require at least 1 1/2 baths. Since the bedrooms are located on the upper level away

Fig. 5-19. This large functional bath provides room for dressing and grooming. Note the pleasing use of coordinated colors. (Kohler Co.)

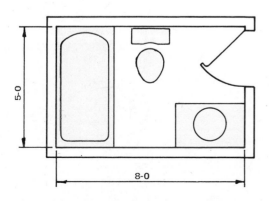

Fig. 5-18. Planned layout for a small size bathroom.

75

from the living area, the need for another bath on a lower level becomes evident. A large ranch house will require a minimum of 1 1/2 baths. The bedrooms are usually located in a wing of the house away from the living area and convenience dictates a second bath.

For years designers have emphasized the importance of locating baths close together and near the kitchen to reduce cost. Granted, the cost will be less if baths share a common wall or are placed above or below one another. However, this is a rather minor consideration compared to convenience and function. It is desirable to design a functional bath, and to place the bath in the most convenient location.

A minimum size bath is 5' x 8', Fig. 5-18. A large bath may be 10' x 10', 10' x 12' or larger. Most people prefer ample space for dressing, linen storage and for personal items, Fig. 5-19.

The three primary fixtures found in most bathrooms are the lavatory, the water closet, and the tub or shower. A fourth fixture, the bidet, Fig. 5-20, is gaining popularity in some of the more expensive homes. The arrangement of the fixtures will determine whether or not the bath is truly functional. Locating the lavatory or water closet under a window should be avoided. A mirror should be placed above the sink. Arrange the mirror so it will be well lighted and away from the tub to prevent fogging.

Provide ample space for each fixture in the room. Check the manufacturer's specifications and code requirements for placement of each of the fixtures. Most water closets require a space at least 30" wide for installation, Fig. 5-21.

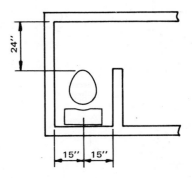

Fig. 5-21. Minimum clearance for a water closet installation.

Water closets should be placed so that they are not directly in line with the bathroom door.

Water closets are produced in a number of styles. The older style had a separate tank and stool. Most newer models are one-piece units, either floor or wall mounted, Fig. 5-22. Wall mounting makes cleaning easier.

Fig. 5-20. More and more bidets are being installed as people learn the advantages they offer to personal hygiene. (Eljer, Wallace-Murray Corp.)

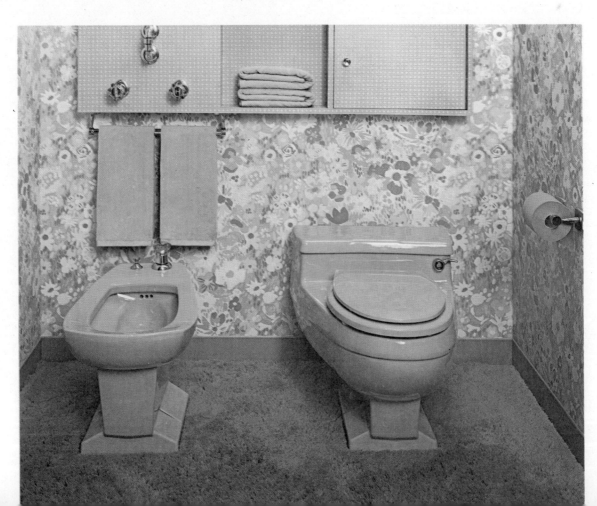

Bathroom fixtures vary in size as shown in Fig. 5-23. For example, regular bathtubs range in size from 54 to 72 inches long and 28 to 32 inches wide. The most common size is 30″ x 60″. It is accepted practice to install a shower above the tub. This provides the convenience of both and does not require two separate facilities.

Shower stalls are popular. Many homes have a tub and separate shower stall. Prefabricated showers are available in metal, fiber glass and plastics. Fig. 5-24 shows a prefabricated

Fig. 5-22. Contemporary styling of a one-piece water closet.

STANDARD TUB

WIDTH	LENGTH	HEIGHT
30 3/4″	54″	16″
30″	60″	14″
30″	60″	16 1/2″
31″	60″	15 1/2″
31 1/2″	60″	16″
31 1/2″	66″	18″
30 3/4″	72″	16″

SQUARE TUB

WIDTH	LENGTH	HEIGHT
37″	42″	12″
42″	48″	14″

WATER CLOSET

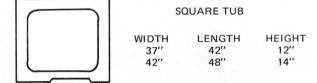

	WIDTH	DEPTH	HEIGHT
FLOOR MOUNTED TWO-PIECE	17″	25 1/2″	29 1/2″
	21″	26 3/4″	28″
	21″	28 3/4″	28″
FLOOR MOUNTED ONE-PIECE	20 3/8″	27 3/4″	20″
	20 3/8″	29 3/4″	20″
WALL HUNG TWO-PIECE	22 1/2″	26″	31″
WALL HUNG ONE-PIECE	14″	24 1/4″	15″

BIDET

WIDTH	DEPTH	HEIGHT
15″	22″	15″

WALL HUNG SINK

WIDTH	DEPTH
19″	17″
20″	18″
22″	19″
24″	20″

CIRCULAR LAVATORY

18″ DIAMETER

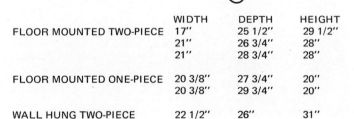

Fig. 5-23. Common sizes of bathroom fixtures.

Fig. 5-24. This one-piece, prefabricated shower is installed as a complete unit during construction. (Kohler Co.)

shower unit. More luxurious showers are usually made of ceramic tile, terrazzo, marble or similar materials, Fig. 5-25. Common shower sizes range from 30″ x 30″ to 36″ x 48″.

Sink cabinets or vanities, Figs. 5-26 and 5-27, are popular today and have just about replaced the old style wall hung lavatory. A variety of vanity base units is shown in Fig. 5-28. Lavatories are usually rectangular or circular. Today, the 18″ circular sink is very popular. All are available in cast iron and steel.

A bathroom must have ventilation. This may be provided by windows or an exhaust fan. If windows are used, care must

Fig. 5-25. This beautifully designed sunken shower makes use of durable ceramic tile. (American Olean Co.)

Fig. 5-26. This lavatory-vanity combination illustrates how beauty and function enhances a bathroom. (Eljer, Wallace-Murray Corp.)

Fig. 5-27. A simple, yet beautiful vanity which adds to the function of the modern bath. (H. J. Scheirich Co.)

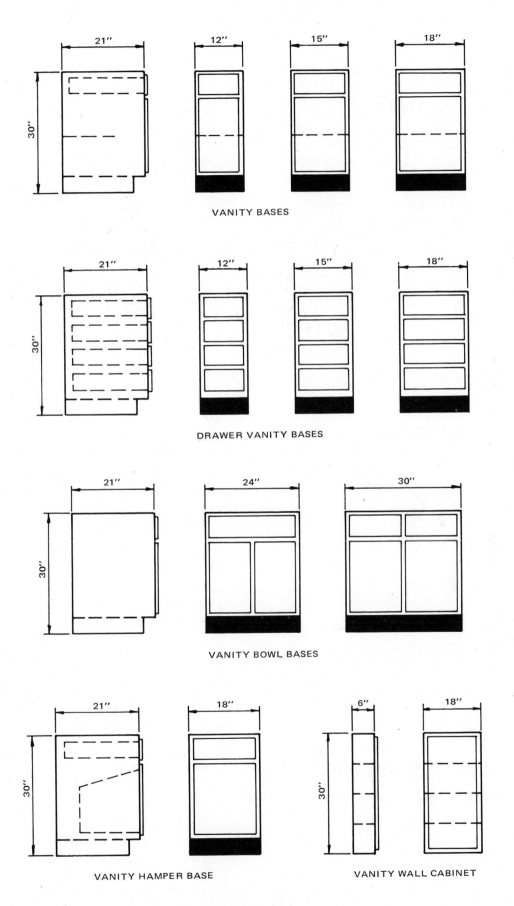

VANITY BASES

DRAWER VANITY BASES

VANITY BOWL BASES

VANITY HAMPER BASE   VANITY WALL CABINET

Fig. 5-28. Standard vanity sizes and designs.

be taken to locate them properly. Window placement should be such that a draft is not produced over the tub and maximum privacy is secured. If an exhaust fan is used, it should be located near the tub and water closet area. NO ELECTRICAL SWITCHES SHOULD BE PLACED SO THAT THEY CAN BE REACHED FROM THE TUB! Accessibility to the bathroom is important, Fig. 5-29. If there is only one bath

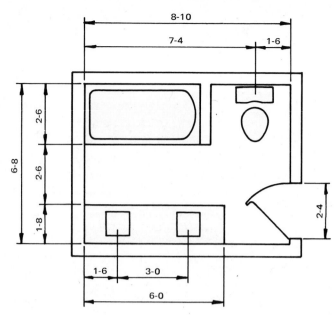

Fig. 5-31. A small bathroom containing only the necessary fixtures.

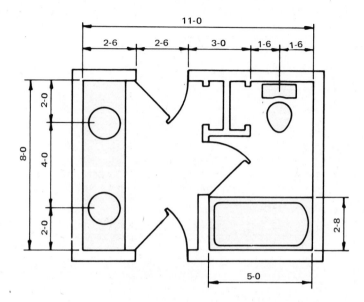

Fig. 5-29. A double-entry bath which provides maximum accessibility.

for all the bedrooms, locate the door in a hall common to all the bedrooms. One should not be required to go through another room to reach the bath. Bathroom doors are ordinarily not as wide as bedroom doors. A door that is 2'-6" or even 2'-4" is usually sufficient. In some instances pocket doors are used to subdivide the bath into two or more areas, Fig. 5-30, as in a two-compartment bath. Doors should swing into the bathroom and be designed so as not to interfere with the use of any fixture.

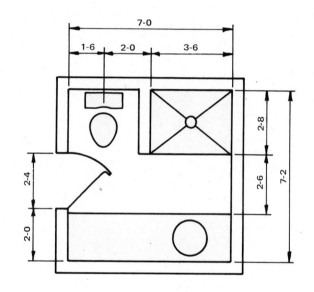

Fig. 5-32. A minimum size bath with shower.

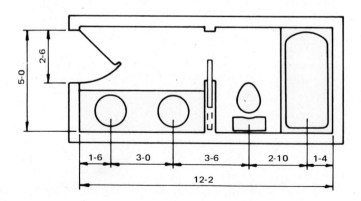

Fig. 5-30. Two compartment bath using a pocket door as a divider.

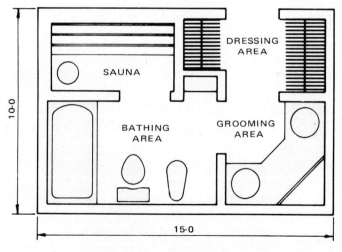

Fig. 5-33. An elaborate bath design which includes the bathing area, dressing area, grooming area and sauna.

Bathrooms may be simple with only the necessary fixtures, Figs. 5-31 and 5-32, or elaborate in design and function, Fig. 5-33. A dressing or exercise area may be incorporated in the

Fig. 5-34. Live plants, glassware and artwork provide a background of beauty for this bath.   (Kohler Co.)

bath. These activities require more space and added facilities. Plan the bath around the functions to be provided.

The decor of a well planned bath will provide for easy cleaning, resistance to moisture and a pleasing atmosphere. Select fixtures of a color appropriate for the desired color scheme of the room. Plants and art pieces may be added to enhance the beauty of the room, Fig. 5-34. The bathroom need not be a dull room void of design and beauty.

Fig. 5-35 shows a small bath which provides maximum convenience and practicality at a nominal cost. Economy is

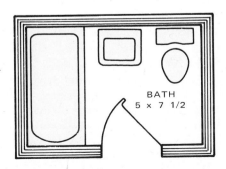

BATH
5 x 7 1/2

Fig. 5-35. An economical bath with the supply and drains on a single wall.

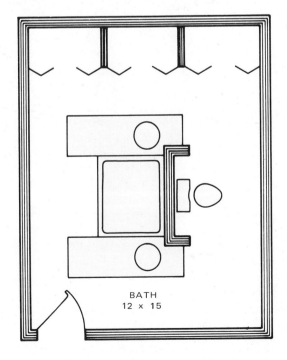

BATH
12 x 15

Fig. 5-36. A large island bath with plumbing fixtures in a center cluster.

partially obtained by the supply and drains being placed on a single wall. Also, there is no wasted space in this functional bath. Zones may be created through the use of open shelf cabinetry.

A large bath is shown in Fig. 5-36. This 12' x 15' bath groups all the plumbing fixtures into an island unit at the center of the room. The square tub and twin vanities create a unique design. The entrance and closets may be rearranged to suit the particular needs of a given plan. A vent fan, heater, lighting and shower curtain track are mounted in a cabinetized ceiling unit.

Fig. 5-37 represents a luxury bath. The 240 sq. ft. area provides separate, private dressing and grooming areas for the husband and wife. "Her area" may be decorated in a completely feminine decor while "his area" may be distinctly masculine. The sanitary area, tub and shower may be completely closed when desired. The shower and tub area are tiled and slightly sunken.

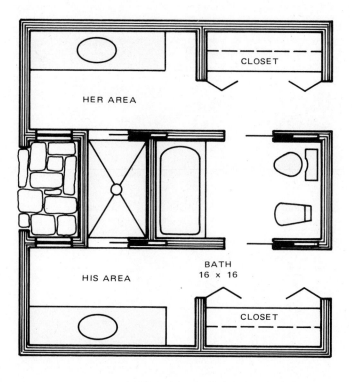

Fig. 5-37. This "his" and "her" bath represents a luxury dressing and grooming area.

REVIEW QUESTIONS — CHAPTER 5

1. In bathroom design, what electrical safety feature must always be followed?
2. The three basic areas into which a residential structure may be divided are:
   a. _____ .
   b. _____ .
   c. _____ .
3. In some design situations, _____ are used to subdivide the bath into two compartments.
4. The most expensive bathroom showers are usually made of:
   a. _____ .
   b. _____ .
   c. _____ .
5. Less space is wasted when the bedroom door is located near a _____ of the room.
6. FHA specifications recommend a minimum of_____ linear feet of closet rod space for a woman and _____ for a man.
7. The FHA recommends that the minimum bedroom size be no smaller than:
   a. 100 square feet.
   b. 150 square feet.
   c. 200 square feet.
   d. 250 square feet.
8. A minimum size bathroom is about_____ .
9. Bathtubs range in size from 28" x 54" to 32" x 72". The most common size is_____ .
10. Four types of doors generally selected for closets are:
    a. _____ .
    b. _____ .
    c. _____ .
    d. _____ .
11. Fixture arrangement will determine whether or not a bathroom is truly_____ .
12. The standard height of a bathroom vanity is_____ .

SUGGESTED ACTIVITIES

1. Select a floor plan of a house from a newspaper, magazine or other literature. Plan furniture arrangements for each of the bedrooms. Prepare a short writeup of each room describing the furniture and arrangement. Include sizes of all pieces of furniture.
2. Design a small bathroom (5' x 10'). Show the location and size of each fixture in a plan view.
3. Prepare a plan view for a clothes closet that is 3 feet deep and 8 feet in length. Show maximum door access, clothes rod and shelf storage area.
4. Design an average size bedroom according to FHA specifications. Make a plan view drawing of the room including bed, dresser, chest of drawers and other furniture to meet the needs of your own activities. You may want to include a study or reading area.
5. Look through a number of home design and planning magazines for closet arrangements. Prepare a display of clippings that illustrates maximum use of closet space for clothes, shoes and other wearing apparel.

Fig. 6-1. Note the "openness" of this gracious living and dining area. (Potlatch Forests, Inc.),

Chapter 6
ROOM PLANNING, LIVING AREA

The living area is the part of the house which most friends and guests see. This is the area that usually becomes the showplace. Comprising roughly one-third of the house, this area serves a variety of functions. It is the location for family get-togethers and dining. It is the area for recreation, entertaining and just relaxing. The living area is not restricted to the interior of the structure. It includes patios, decks and terraces. This area is designed for all activities not encompassed in the sleeping and service areas.

The living area is composed of a number of rooms. They include the living room, dining room, recreation or family room, den or study, special purpose rooms such as music or sewing rooms, foyer, outside patios, and guest bathroom. Some of the "rooms" may not be rooms in the true sense;

however they serve the same purpose. Modern trends are away from so many rooms or cubicles and toward a more open plan with fewer walls and doors. See Fig. 6-1.

LIVING ROOMS

The living room, for many families, is the center of activity. Depending on the specific occasion, it may be a play room for the children, a TV room or a conversation place. Its size and arrangement will depend on the life style of the members of the family who will ultimately use it. Figs. 6-2, 6-3, and 6-4 illustrate this point.

Living rooms are of all sizes and shapes. A small living room may have as few as 150 square feet; an average size, Fig. 6-5,

Fig. 6-2. The contemporary mood is expressed in the styling of this graceful living room. (Masonite Corp.)

around 250 square feet; while a large one may exceed 400, Fig. 6-6. The most important questions to ask regarding size and design of a living room are: (1) What furniture is planned for this particular room? See Fig. 6-7. (2) How often will the room be used? (3) How many people are expected to use the room at any one time? (4) How many functions are combined in this one room? (Is it a multipurpose room?) (5) Is the living room size in proportion to the remainder of the house? Answers to these questions should help establish the broad specifications of the room.

Specific furniture will reflect the use to which the room will be subjected, Fig. 6-8. For instance, if it is to be used primarily for viewing television, the arrangement should indicate that use. Conversely, if a separate room is provided for TV then this activity will probably not be a consideration. It's important to analyze the functions to be performed and provide for them.

The location of the living room should not be such that a natural traffic pattern will be established through it to other parts of the house, Fig. 6-9. Instead, try to locate the living room where members of the family will not feel the need to use it as a hall. Slightly raising or lowering the living room level helps to set it apart and discourage "thru traffic," Fig. 6-10. If

Fig. 6-3. Formality is emphasized in the design of this large living area. (Potlatch Forests, Inc.)

Fig. 6-4. Color, natural materials and warmth are found in this interesting living room design.   (Brown and Kauffman, Inc.)

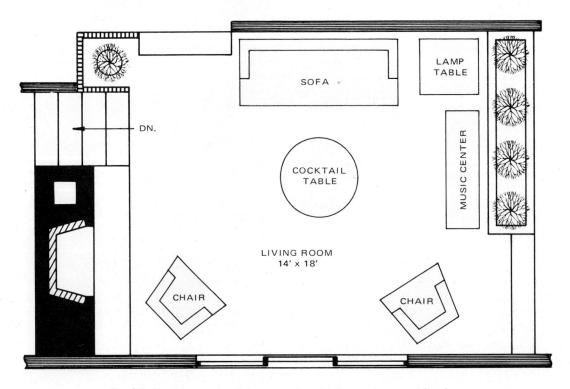

Fig. 6-5. A modern sunken living room plan with flower planter and fireplace.

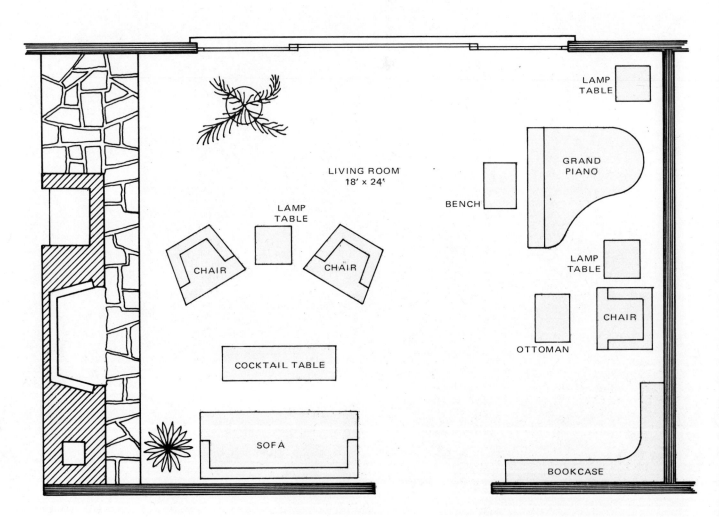

Fig. 6-6. A large living room, illustrated by the size and spacing of furniture requirements.

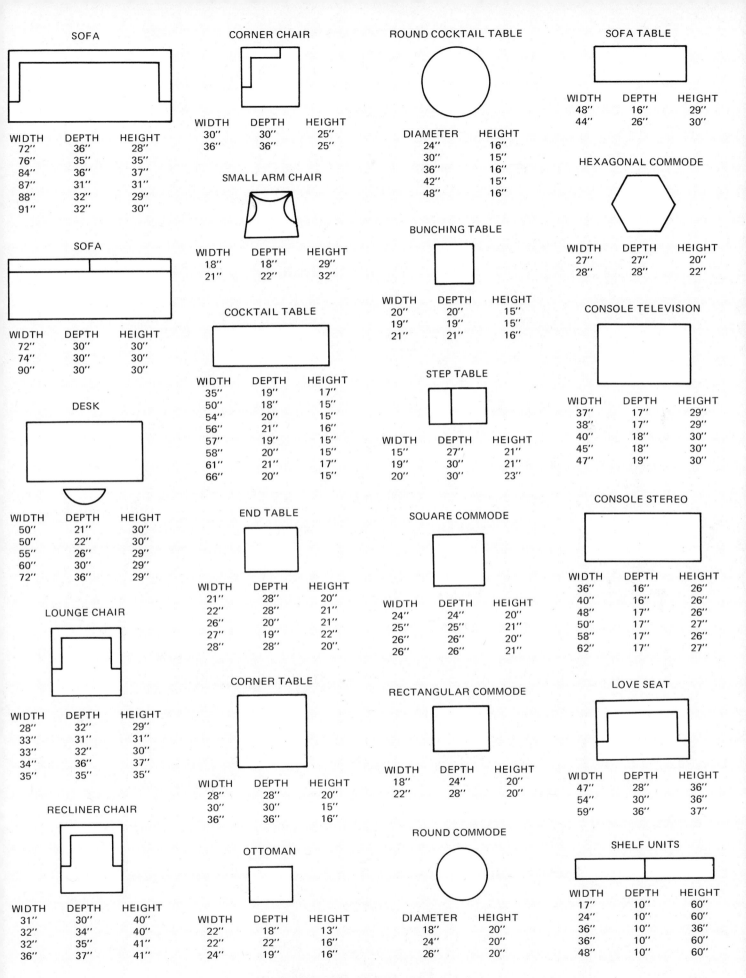

SOFA

WIDTH	DEPTH	HEIGHT
72″	36″	28″
76″	35″	35″
84″	36″	37″
87″	31″	31″
88″	32″	29″
91″	32″	30″

SOFA

WIDTH	DEPTH	HEIGHT
72″	30″	30″
74″	30″	30″
90″	30″	30″

DESK

WIDTH	DEPTH	HEIGHT
50″	21″	30″
50″	22″	30″
55″	26″	29″
60″	30″	29″
72″	36″	29″

LOUNGE CHAIR

WIDTH	DEPTH	HEIGHT
28″	32″	29″
33″	31″	31″
33″	32″	30″
34″	36″	37″
35″	35″	35″

RECLINER CHAIR

WIDTH	DEPTH	HEIGHT
31″	30″	40″
32″	34″	40″
32″	35″	41″
36″	37″	41″

CORNER CHAIR

WIDTH	DEPTH	HEIGHT
30″	30″	25″
36″	36″	25″

SMALL ARM CHAIR

WIDTH	DEPTH	HEIGHT
18″	18″	29″
21″	22″	32″

COCKTAIL TABLE

WIDTH	DEPTH	HEIGHT
35″	19″	17″
50″	18″	15″
54″	20″	15″
56″	21″	16″
57″	19″	15″
58″	20″	15″
61″	21″	17″
66″	20″	15″

END TABLE

WIDTH	DEPTH	HEIGHT
21″	28″	20″
22″	28″	21″
26″	20″	21″
27″	19″	22″
28″	28″	20″

CORNER TABLE

WIDTH	DEPTH	HEIGHT
28″	28″	20″
30″	30″	15″
36″	36″	16″

OTTOMAN

WIDTH	DEPTH	HEIGHT
22″	18″	13″
22″	22″	16″
24″	19″	16″

ROUND COCKTAIL TABLE

DIAMETER	HEIGHT
24″	16″
30″	15″
36″	16″
42″	15″
48″	16″

BUNCHING TABLE

WIDTH	DEPTH	HEIGHT
20″	20″	15″
19″	19″	15″
21″	21″	16″

STEP TABLE

WIDTH	DEPTH	HEIGHT
15″	27″	21″
19″	30″	21″
20″	30″	23″

SQUARE COMMODE

WIDTH	DEPTH	HEIGHT
24″	24″	20″
25″	25″	21″
26″	26″	20″
26″	26″	21″

RECTANGULAR COMMODE

WIDTH	DEPTH	HEIGHT
18″	24″	20″
22″	28″	20″

ROUND COMMODE

DIAMETER	HEIGHT
18″	20″
24″	20″
26″	20″

SOFA TABLE

WIDTH	DEPTH	HEIGHT
48″	16″	29″
44″	26″	30″

HEXAGONAL COMMODE

WIDTH	DEPTH	HEIGHT
27″	27″	20″
28″	28″	22″

CONSOLE TELEVISION

WIDTH	DEPTH	HEIGHT
37″	17″	29″
38″	17″	29″
40″	18″	30″
45″	18″	30″
47″	19″	30″

CONSOLE STEREO

WIDTH	DEPTH	HEIGHT
36″	16″	26″
40″	16″	26″
48″	17″	26″
50″	17″	27″
58″	17″	26″
62″	17″	27″

LOVE SEAT

WIDTH	DEPTH	HEIGHT
47″	28″	36″
54″	30″	36″
59″	36″	37″

SHELF UNITS

WIDTH	DEPTH	HEIGHT
17″	10″	60″
24″	10″	60″
36″	10″	36″
36″	10″	60″
48″	10″	60″

Fig. 6-7. Standard sizes of typical living room furniture.

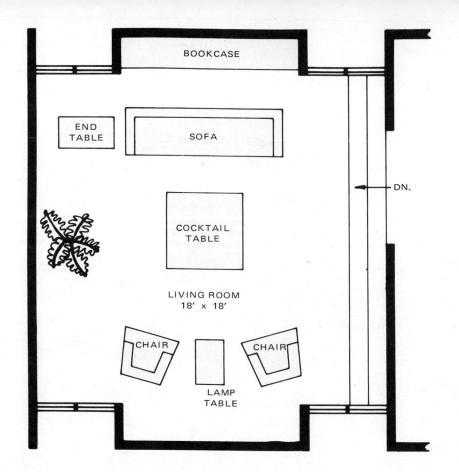

Fig. 6-8. Above. Designing a living room around "conversation" concept. Fig. 6-9. Below. Notice how this "poorly located" living room is in the traffic pattern from all of the surrounding rooms.

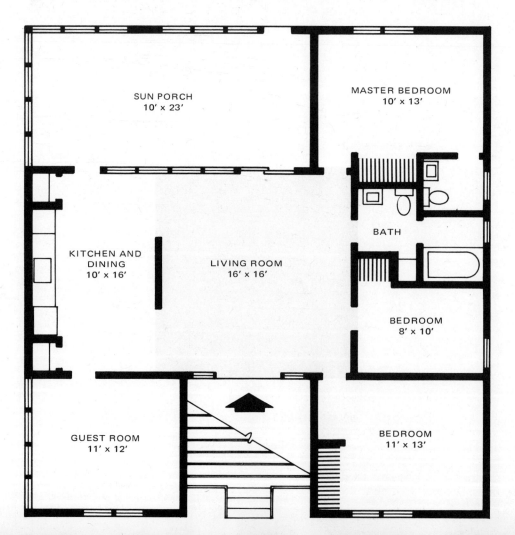

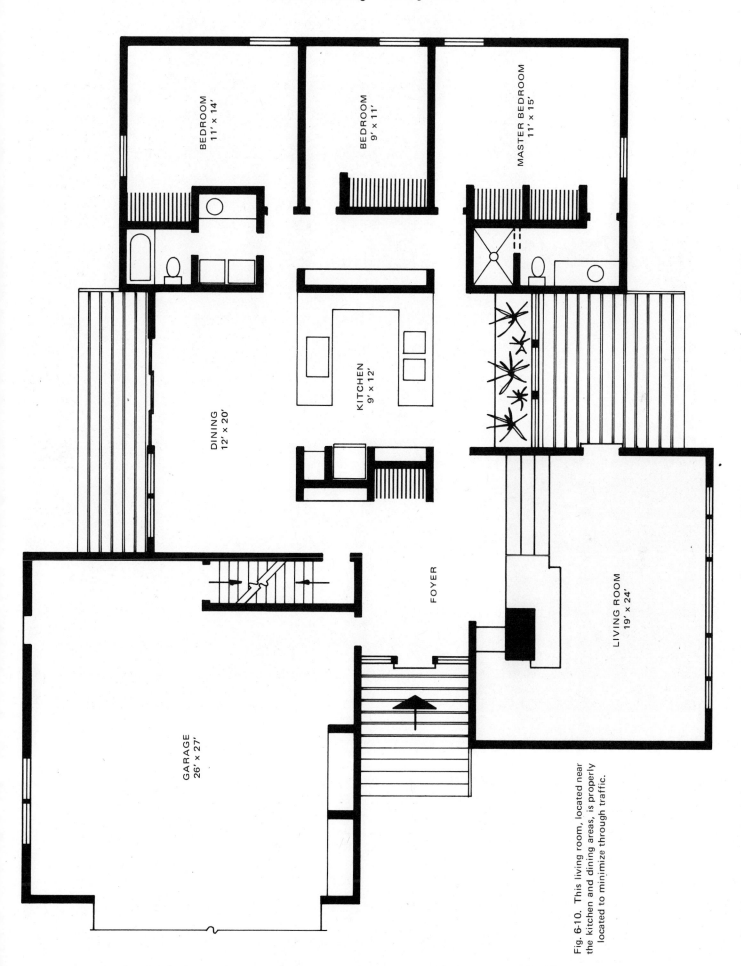

Fig. 6-10. This living room, located near the kitchen and dining areas, is properly located to minimize through traffic.

Fig. 6-11. Beauty and spaciousness are obtained in this living room by the use of large areas of glass.   (Andersen Corp.)

possible, the living room should be positioned at grade level. This allows for expanding activities to a patio or terrace. Such an arrangement enhances the use and often the beauty of the living room. The main outside entrance should not open directly into the living room, but through a hallway or foyer.

The use of large windows or sliding doors further encourages the feeling of "spaciousness" and increases the enjoyment of the living room, Fig. 6-11. Exterior wall areas should not be broken with too many small windows and doors and care should be taken to provide adequate wall space for required furniture.

The living room, like all other rooms in the house, should be used. It should not be planned just as a showplace. A properly designed living room can be a functional part of the house and at the same time a beautiful and charming area, Fig. 6-12.

Dining and entertaining are closely related; therefore, the living room should be located near the dining room. In some instances these areas may be combined to serve a dual purpose, as in Fig. 6-13. Usually some informal divider, short of a wall, is used to separate the two areas. A flower planter, furniture arrangement, screen or variation in level will effectively serve

Fig. 6-12. An attractive living room designed for entertaining and relaxing.   (Celotex Corp.)

Fig. 6-13. A well-designed living room dining combination.   (Azrock Floor Products)

Fig. 6-14. An inviting living room obtained by combining a variety of vivid colors with natural stone and wood.   (Potlatch Forests, Inc.)

this purpose. An open plan makes the house appear to be larger inside, while the closed plan tends to make the rooms look small.

Color, texture and design may be used to emphasize the good points and minimize weak aspects of the room, Fig. 6-17.

Fig. 6-15. Natural wood and marble are contrasted with warm colors.

Modern living rooms should be exciting, colorful and inviting. See Fig. 6-14. The selection of bright, vivid colors will compliment existing natural materials, Figs. 6-15 and 6-16.

Fig. 6-16. Warm color combinations put the finishing touch on this formal living room setting.   (Kirsch Co.)

Fig. 6-17. Striking color highlights the walls and gives emphasis to the cast iron fireplace and brick floor of this small living room. (Celotex Corp.)

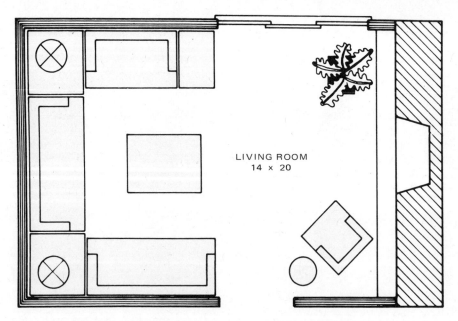

Fig. 6-18. An average size living room designed for conversation.

An average size living room designed for conversation is shown in Fig. 6-18. This layout lends itself to a corner location and restricts through traffic. Grade level placement permits access to a patio or porch. The fireplace is in an ideal spot for viewing from the conversation area.

Fig. 6-19 shows a well-planned living room adjacent to the dining area. An area rug unifies the furniture arrangement and adds interest. The screen defines the living room boundary and at the same time makes it appear larger. Large windows provide an excellent viewing area.

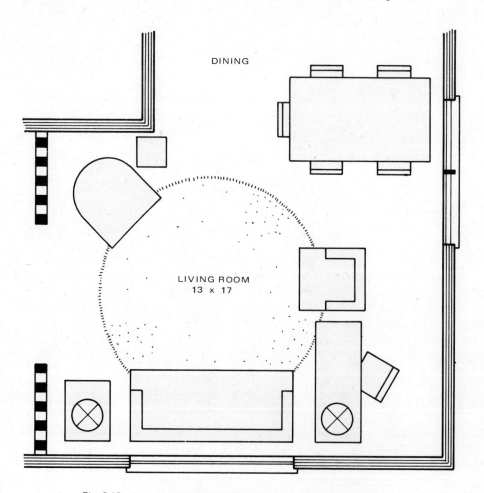

Fig. 6-19. An open style living room adjacent to the dining area.

DINING ROOMS

Most modern homes today have a dining room. Shortly after World War II fewer houses were being built with dining rooms, but in most localities that trend has been reversed and dining rooms have become popular again. However, in each individual case, the determining factor should be the life style of those who will live in the house rather than fad or fancy.

The main function of a dining room is to provide a special place for eating, Fig. 6-20. In some instances this activity is performed in the kitchen rather than in a separate room or area. At other times, eating is done in the kitchen as well as in some other location. Many modern homes provide eating facilities in the kitchen for informal meals and separate dining room for more formal gatherings.

Dining rooms vary greatly in size. A small room, capable of seating four people around a table and providing space for a buffet would require an area of approximately 120 square feet, Fig. 6-21. A medium size room, 12' x 15', would provide space for six to eight people with buffet and china

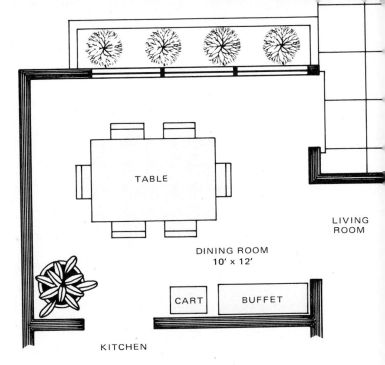

Fig. 6-21. Floor plan of a small dining room which seats four to six people.

Fig. 6-20. A typical small dining room arrangement with wood paneling and one central window. (Conwed Corp.)

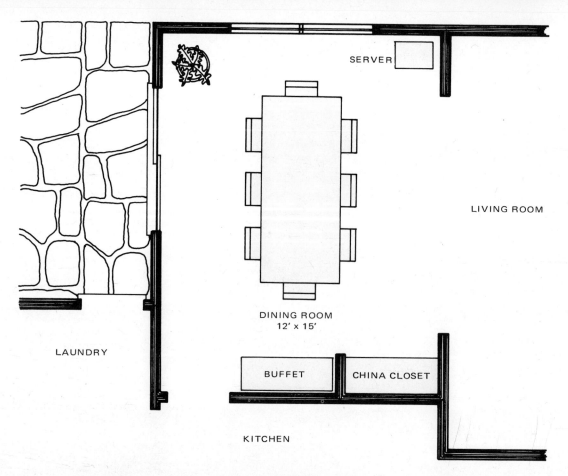

SERVER

LIVING ROOM

DINING ROOM
12' x 15'

LAUNDRY

BUFFET   CHINA CLOSET

KITCHEN

Fig. 6-22. Note planning for a medium size dining room arranged in respect to other living areas.

Fig. 6-23. A large dining room, seating eight or more people, designed for a large family or for those who entertain frequently.

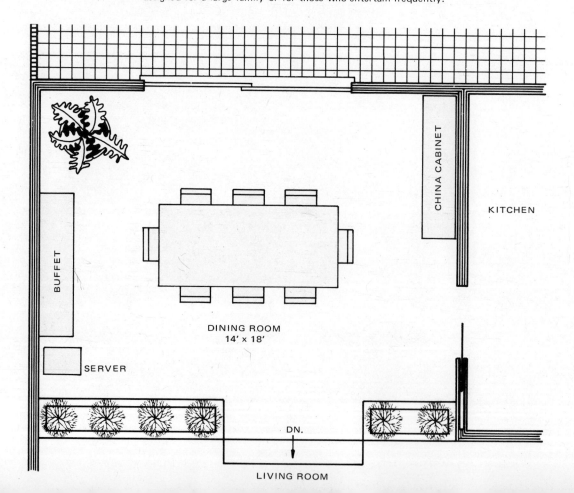

CHINA CABINET

KITCHEN

BUFFET

DINING ROOM
14' x 18'

SERVER

DN.

LIVING ROOM

closet, as shown in Fig. 6-22. Large dining rooms range in size from 14' x 18' or larger, Fig. 6-23. In most cases, the dining room size would depend on the number of people who will use the facility at a given time, the furniture to be included in the room and clearance allowed for traffic through the room.

Typical dining room furniture includes the table, chairs, buffet, china closet and server or cart, Fig. 6-24. Arrangement and spacing will depend on the layout of the room, a pleasant outdoor vantage point or orientation to other rooms, Fig. 6-25. At least 2'-3'' should be allowed from center line to center line of chairs around the table. Also, be sure to provide ample space for serving. Usually 2'-0'' is sufficent space between the back of the chairs and the wall.

RECTANGULAR DINING TABLE

LENGTH	WIDTH	HEIGHT
42''	30''	29''
48''	30''	29''
48''	42''	29''
60''	40''	28''
60''	42''	29''
72''	36''	28''

OVAL DINING TABLE

LENGTH	WIDTH	HEIGHT
54''	42''	28''
60''	42''	28''
72''	40''	28''
72''	48''	28''
84''	42''	28''

ROUND DINING TABLE

DIAMETER	HEIGHT
32''	28''
36''	28''
42''	28''
48''	28''

CHINA CABINET OR HUTCH

LENGTH	WIDTH	HEIGHT
48''	16''	65''
50''	20''	60''
62''	16''	66''

BUFFET

LENGTH	WIDTH	HEIGHT
36''	16''	31''
48''	16''	31''
52''	18''	31''

SERVER OR CART

LENGTH	WIDTH	HEIGHT
36''	16''	30''
52''	18''	33''
64''	16''	30''

CORNER CABINET

WIDTH	DEPTH	HEIGHT
36''	15''	80''
38''	16''	80''

DINING CHAIRS

WIDTH	DEPTH	HEIGHT
17''	19''	29''
20''	17''	36''
22''	19''	29''
24''	21''	31''

SEAT HEIGHT 16''

Fig. 6-24. Typical dining room symbols and dimensions.

Fig. 6-25. This dining room is styled to obtain a central location in relation to other living areas. (Rohm and Haas)

Fig. 6-26. The kitchen and living room surround two sides of this dining room. Note the planning for an outdoor view. (Potlatch Forests, Inc.)

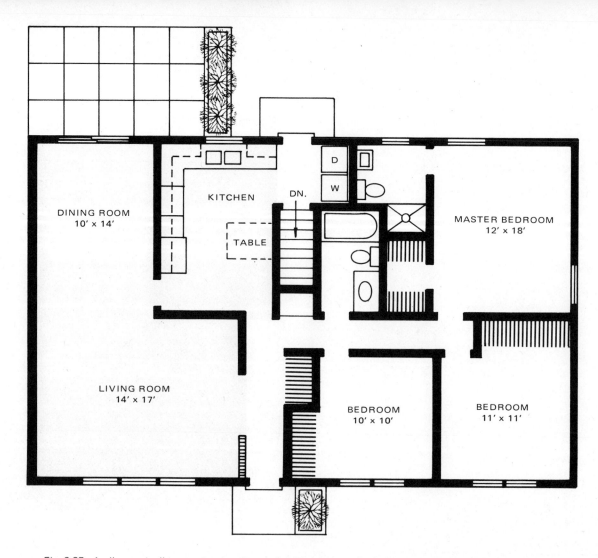

Fig. 6-27. An "open plan" layout showing the relationship between the dining room, kitchen and living room.

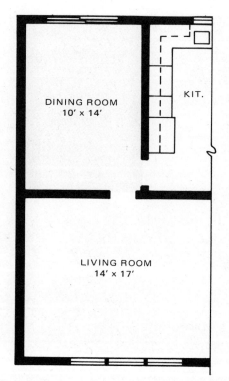

Fig. 6-28. Same basic plan as shown in Fig. 6-27 with a wall added to accomplish a "closed plan" dining room.

Fig. 6-29. A planter wall adds spaciousness to both the dining room and kitchen areas. (Rohm and Haas)

Fig. 6-30. A delightfully planned dining room with cheerful colors and extensive lighting. (American Plywood Assoc.)

Fig. 6-31. The graciousness of a dining room as viewed from the living area in an open plan. (Western Wood Products Assoc.)

Location of the dining room is important. For efficient use it should be adjacent to the kitchen and living room, as in Fig. 6-26. In some instances it may be desirable to locate it near the family room as well. An ideal arrangement is one that places the dining room between the living room and kitchen. This provides for natural movement of guests from living room to dining with minimum confusion. Furthermore, added space

is available in the living room if needed. This is especially true in an "open plan" layout as in Fig. 6-27.

When planning the dining room a decision should be made early as to whether an open or closed plan will be the most desirable. A closed plan places the dining room in a cubicle with little chance for overflow into other rooms, Fig. 6-28. The house appears smaller and less dramatic than in an open plan. Flower planters, screens, dividers and partial walls may be used effectively to divide the dining area from the living room or kitchen and at the same time make the rooms appear larger, Fig. 6-29. The function and efficiency of the rooms will be enhanced by using the open plan, Fig. 6-30. However, it is

Fig. 6-32. The glass patio wall admits outdoor light to the dining room. (Brown and Kauffman, Inc.)

Fig. 6-33. Planning is the keynote of this interesting dining room. The cathedral ceiling and sunken living room set off the dining area.

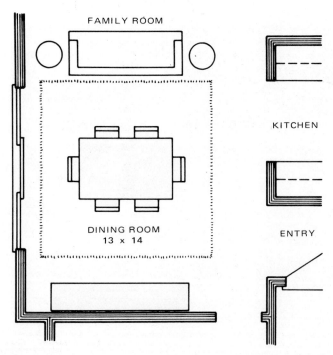

Fig. 6-34. An open plan dining room.

best if the dining room is separated from the kitchen in order to reduce the sight and smell of food preparation.

Dining is generally a happy conversation time, hence the decor and lighting are important factors, Fig. 6-31. Controlled lighting is desirable and makes possible a variety of moods, Fig. 6-32. The color scheme used in the dining room is often the same as the living room since it will most likely be an extension of that area. A bright, warm and cheerful atmosphere is the desired result, Fig. 6-33.

Fig. 6-34 shows a medium-size dining room. The relationship to the kitchen is ideal, but cannot function as an overflow area for the living room. Boundaries of the dining room are defined by the area rug and is a good example of an open plan. Traffic is confined to the space along the edge of the room and does not interfere with activities in the kitchen or dining room. The large sliding doors provide for a nice view of the patio or side yard.

The dining room in Fig. 6-35 is ideally located between the kitchen and living room. This semi-open plan is functional and creates a desirable atmosphere for dining. This arrangement is well suited for a site with a nice view to the rear. The room is large enough to allow for required traffic and to seat eight people.

100

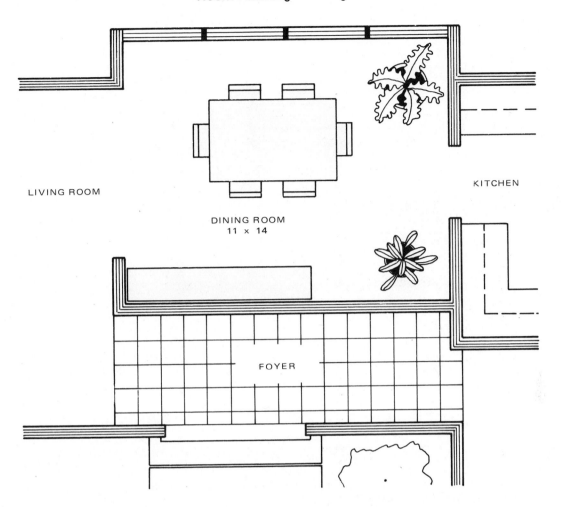

LIVING ROOM

DINING ROOM
11 x 14

KITCHEN

FOYER

Fig. 6-35. A dining room located in an ideal position between the kitchen and living room.

Making use of a natural setting, the architect has designed this home for privacy and outdoor enjoyment.
The extended porch can be used for dining and entertaining.

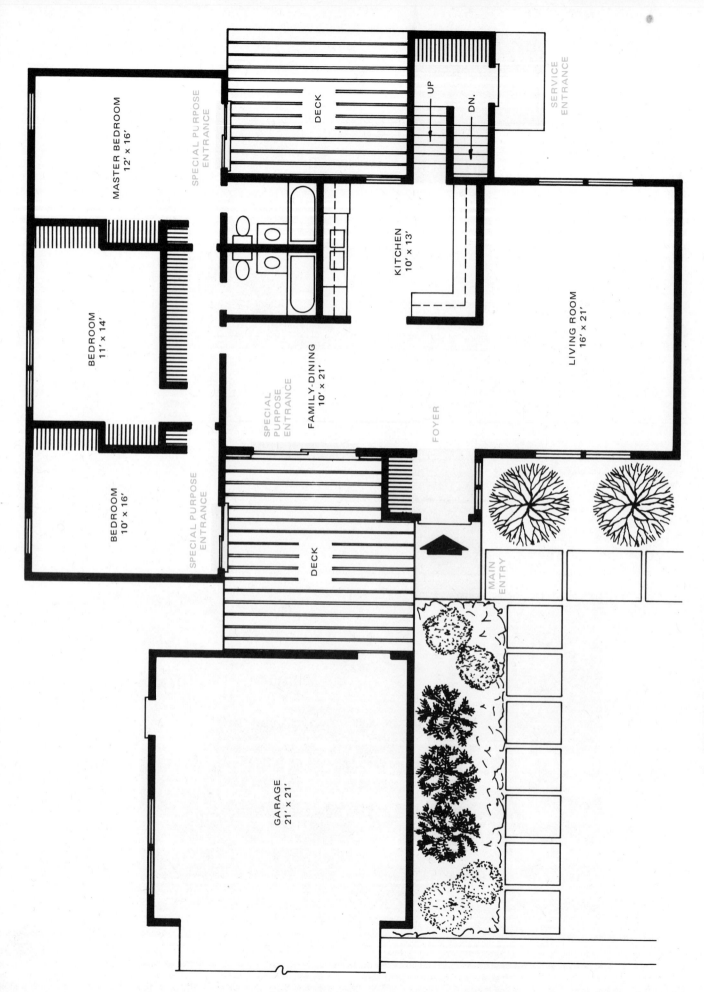

Fig. 6-36. This floor plan illustrates a variety of entryways used in a modern home. Note the main entry and foyer.

MASTER BEDROOM
12' x 16'

SPECIAL PURPOSE ENTRANCE

BEDROOM
11' x 14'

BEDROOM
10' x 16'

SPECIAL PURPOSE ENTRANCE

SPECIAL PURPOSE ENTRANCE

DECK

UP

DN.

SERVICE ENTRANCE

KITCHEN
10' x 13'

FAMILY-DINING
10' x 21'

LIVING ROOM
16' x 21'

FOYER

DECK

GARAGE
21' x 21'

MAIN ENTRY

ENTRYWAY AND FOYER

Every house has at least one entryway, but not all have a foyer. A well planned house will have both.

There are three basic types of entryways: main entry, service entry, and special purpose entry, Fig. 6-36. The main entry should be designed to be impressive because it is the first part of the house that guests see when they arrive. An entry need not be large to be attractive. Creative use of materials and a functional arrangement will enhance beauty and design.

The main entry should be centrally located to provide easy access to various parts of the house, Fig. 6-37. A main entry

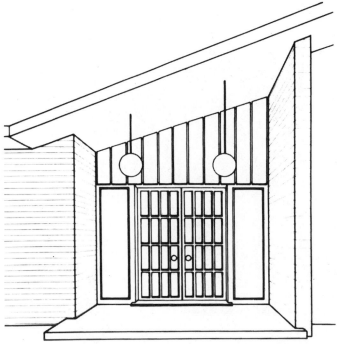

Fig. 6-38. Functionally designed, this entryway provides protection from the weather, electric and natural light to the foyer and visibility of callers.

Fig. 6-37. An outstanding example of a modern entryway capitalizing on the beauty of wood. (Evans Products Co.)

opening into a foyer is usually preferable to an entry leading directly into the living room. The entry should be designed in such a way that callers may be viewed without opening the door. Glass side panels provide visibility, natural light and add to the design, Fig. 6-38.

Protection from the weather is a major consideration in the design of an entryway. Either a large overhang may be provided or the entry may be recessed, Fig. 6-39. A recessed entry is impressive and helps to break up a long plain front

Fig. 6-39. This entryway is well protected from the weather by a wide overhanging roof section. (Kawneer Co., Inc.)

Fig. 6-40. A recessed entry, such as this, helps to break the straight line features of the front of the house. (Bird and Son, Inc.)

Fig. 6-42. These double doors add a spacious appearance to the entryway.

which might otherwise be uninteresting, Fig. 6-40. An extended overhang may also add design and interest to a plain roof. Regardless of the technique used, the lines of the entry should be compatible with the remainder of the house, Fig. 6-41. The use of totally different materials or a drastic change in proportion usually will not produce the desired results.

The size of the entry will depend somewhat on the size and

Fig. 6-41. Note how the entryway carries through the same theme of styling as the rest of the house. (Ideal Cement Co.)

Fig. 6-43. The service door to the rear of the house is designed to match the house style. (Ideal Cement Co.)

design of the house. However, sufficient space should be provided to accommodate several people at any given time.

Well-styled doors are a key element in any entry. Doors should be carefully selected to conform to the overall design of the house and add that special touch of creative design. Entry doors are normally 3'-0" wide and 1 3/4" thick. Standard door height is 6'-8". Added emphasis may be obtained by using two doors instead of one. This technique places more emphasis on the entry and also increases its function, Fig. 6-42.

intended to be as striking as the main entry, Fig. 6-43.

As stated earlier, a well-designed house should have a foyer. The foyer functions as a place to greet guests and (in colder climates) remove overcoats and overshoes. Consequently, the floor must be of a material which is not affected by water or dirt. Materials such as slate, terrazzo, ceramic or asphalt tile or linoleum are generally used for foyer floors. The foyer must have a coat closet. Minimum size required by FHA is 2' x 3' inside dimensions. A more desirable size would be 30" deep by 4'-0" wide. The closet floor covering material should also

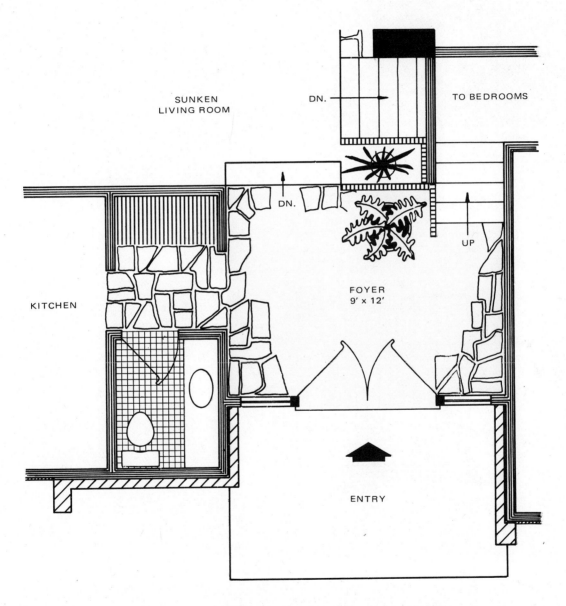

Fig. 6-44. Layout of a foyer designed as an extension of the entryway.

The service entrance is usually connected to the kitchen. The overall design may be improved by placing a mud room or utility room between the kitchen and service entrance.

Special purpose entries are those providing access to patios, decks and terraces. Sliding doors are often used for this type of entry. Service and special purpose entrances are not

withstand mud and water.

The foyer is an extension of the entry and, if possible, should capitalize on the design aspects of the entry, as shown in Fig. 6-44. For example, a two-story entryway may be extended to include the foyer as well, Fig. 6-45. This technique creates a unity between the inside and outside and

Fig. 6-45. This modern foyer includes the winding stairs to the upper living level. (Potlatch Forests, Inc.)

increases a pleasing effect. Planters or potted plants may be used in the same way. They may also serve as informal dividers between the foyer and other rooms. Lighting is an effective design tool that should not be overlooked. Plan the lighting for maximum effect both inside and outside the entry. Lighting outside walks and entries should be carefully considered.

The size of the foyer will depend on several factors: (1) The size of the house. (2) Cost of the house. (3) Location. (4) Personal preference. A minimum foyer is about 6' x 6'. An average size is 8' x 10'. Anything larger is considered a large foyer, Figs. 6-46 and 6-47.

Frequently the foyer provides access to other rooms of the house through halls. Hall space should be kept to a minimum, since any wasted area in halls reduces the space available for other rooms of the house. The FHA recommends a minimum hall width of 3'-0''. A width of 3'-6'' or 4'-0'' is more desirable.

Decor of the foyer will most likely reflect the color scheme and materials used in the living room or other adjacent rooms.

The foyer shown in Fig. 6-48 is well designed and functional. It is small to average in size, but well proportioned. The coat closet is easily accessible and the floor covering is

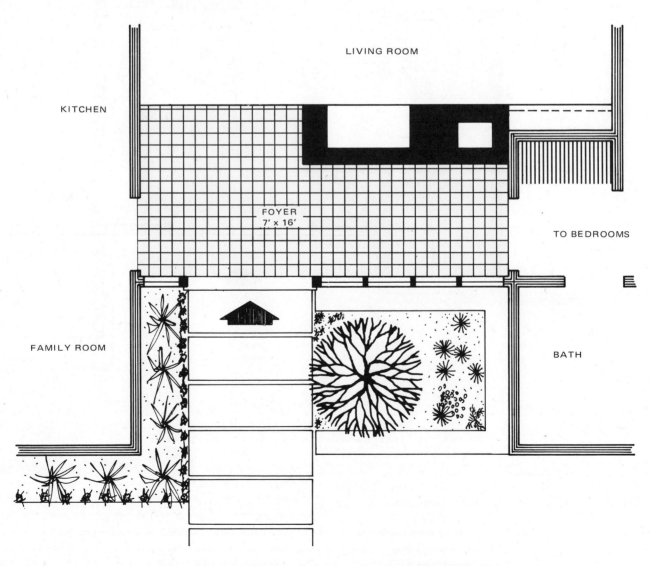

Fig. 6-46. Design of a large foyer leading to three living areas.

106

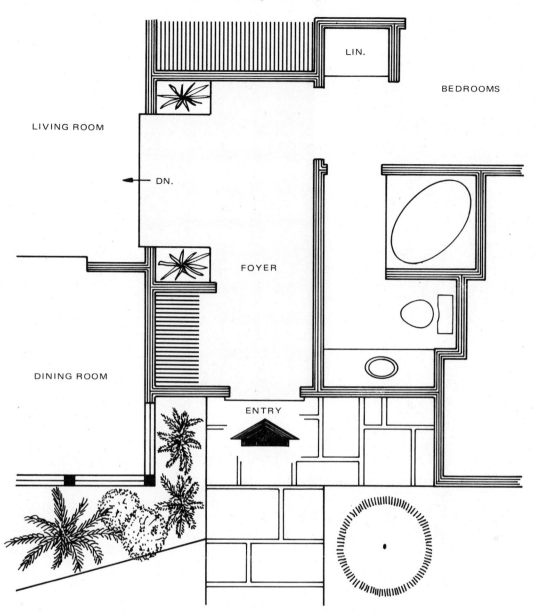

Fig. 6-47. An attractive entry and complimentary foyer design.

LIN.

BEDROOMS

LIVING ROOM

DN.

FOYER

DINING ROOM

ENTRY

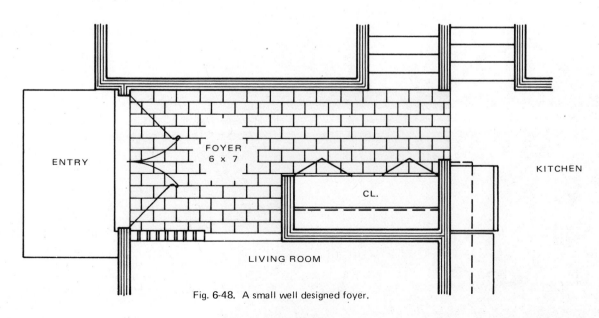

ENTRY

FOYER
6 x 7

CL.

KITCHEN

LIVING ROOM

Fig. 6-48. A small well designed foyer.

Architecture

durable. This is a functional design.

Fig. 6-49 shows a split-entry main and lower foyer. The main foyer is small, but adequate. The coat closet is convenient and the floor of both foyers is water and soil resistant. Even though the plan is complex with many walls and corners, this is a functional arrangement.

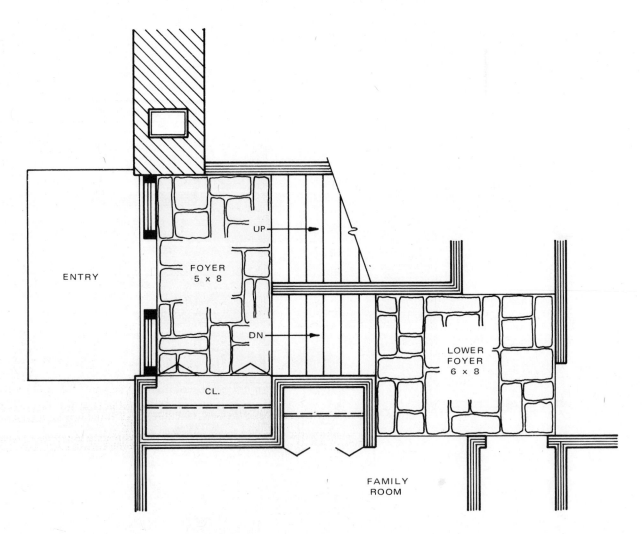

Fig. 6-49. This split-entry foyer is functional and convenient.

The architect has produced a dramatic effect upon the entryway of this home by the wise use of outdoor lighting for evenings.

FAMILY RECREATION ROOM

In modern homes there is a trend toward providing a specially designed room called a recreation room, family room, music room, hobby room or rumpus room. In some instances a

Fig. 6-51. The "entertainment wall" concept incorporates rear projection screen for home movies, music console and television. (Rohm and Haas)

Fig. 6-50. Using a game table and accessories as the central theme of a recreation room. (Conwed Corp.)

large house may have a number of these rooms each planned for specific activities, Figs. 6-50 and 6-51.

The basic purpose of a family recreation room is to provide a place where the family can play or pursue hobbies. Design this room so that it is functional and easily maintained, Fig. 6-52.

The family recreation room if located near the dining or living room will provide overflow space when needed. It may also be placed between the kitchen and garage, since this provides an ideal location of pursuing hobbies. In some cases, it may be wise to locate the family recreation room adjacent

Fig. 6-52. A well-designed recreation room for children and adults which provides extensive play area. (Azrock Floor Products)

Fig. 6-53. A triple combination design includes a game area, sewing center and open deck to swimming pool. (Brown and Kauffman, Inc.)

Fig. 6-54. Basement recreation room. Note the bi-fold door storage area.

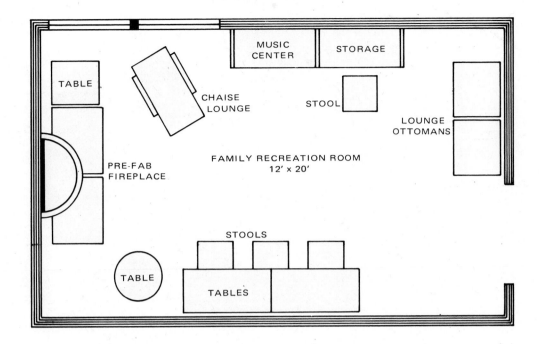

Fig. 6-55. A recreation room designed primarily for relaxation, writing and reading.
Note the furniture arrangement.

to a patio to take advantage of swimming pools, indoor-outdoor picnics or sunbathing, Fig. 6-53.

Some designers favor placing the recreation room in the basement, Fig. 6-54. This location takes advantage of a large area which separates noise from other living areas, contains the necessary structural details and is easy to decorate and keep clean. Wherever the room is located it should be convenient to those who use it.

Family recreation rooms range greatly in size. The number of people planning to use the room and the types of activities in which the family members are to be engaged are important considerations. A common size is 12' x 20', Figs. 6-55, 6-56 and 6-57. Of major importance is the furniture. Again, furniture selection will depend upon the activities anticipated, Figs. 6-58 and 6-59. Choose furniture which is serviceable and resistant to wear. This room will probably receive a great deal of use.

Decor of the family recreation room should feature floors

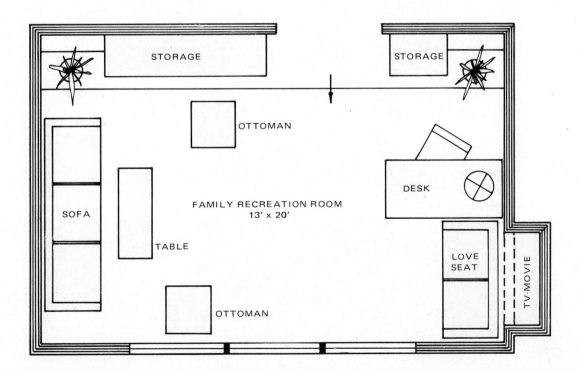

Fig. 6-56. This recreation room illustrates an arrangement for hobby work and a music center.

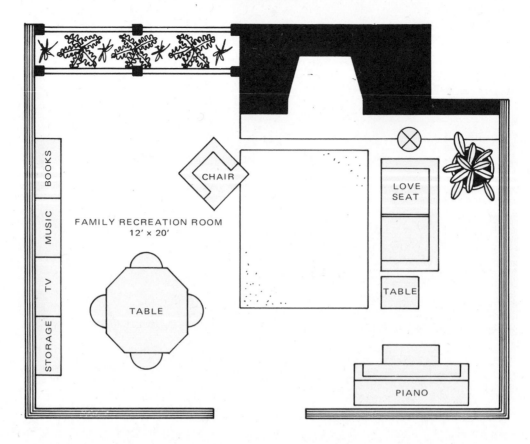

Fig. 6-57. Styled for board games, singing or a fireside chat, this illustration suggests further design ideas.

Fig. 6-58. Note the furniture selection which offers a warm surrounding for the pocket billiards table in this game room. (Masonite Corp.)

Fig. 6-59. Comfortable furniture emphasizes the theme of this general purpose recreation room.

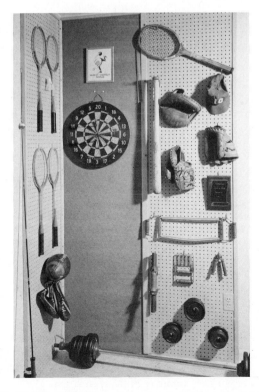

Fig. 6-60. Well-planned storage for recreational equipment keeps the room tidy and easy to clean.

Fig. 6-61. Architectural decorating makes the recreation room glow with excitement and warmth. (Masonite Corp.)

Fig. 6-62. A contemporary flair for color, texture and gracious living highlight this family recreation room. (Brown and Kauffman, Inc.)

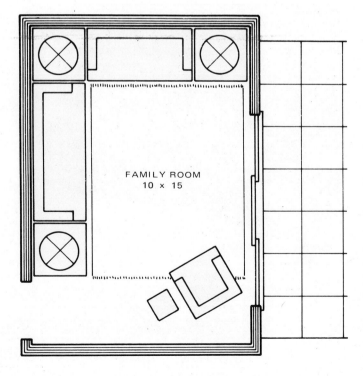

Fig. 6-63. A family room designed for reading, conversation, or relaxing.

FAMILY ROOM
10 x 15

which are easy to clean, suitable for a variety of activities, resistant to wear and not slippery. Linoleum and vinyl tile are commonly used. It is wise to select wall materials which are washable and mar resistant. Bright materials which are "alive with color" are desirable. Remember, this is a fun room!

This room should include storage space for games and hobbies, Fig. 6-60. Lighting must be good for those activities which require sensitive viewing, such as table tennis or exacting hobby work.

The family recreation room is a good place to try out decorating ideas. Emphasize your creative talents to develop individual and personal designs, Figs. 6-61 and 6-62.

Fig. 6-63 shows a compact family room designed for conversation, reading and relaxing. Large glass sliding doors opening onto the patio are an added attraction. This arrangement is quite functional for a "quiet" type family room. More vigorous activities may be performed on the patio, weather permitting.

The recreation room shown in Fig. 6-64 is truly an action room. This arrangement is designed especially for young people. The built-in conversation area is the focus point, but the raised dance area is a close second. This room would be popular in most any home with teenagers.

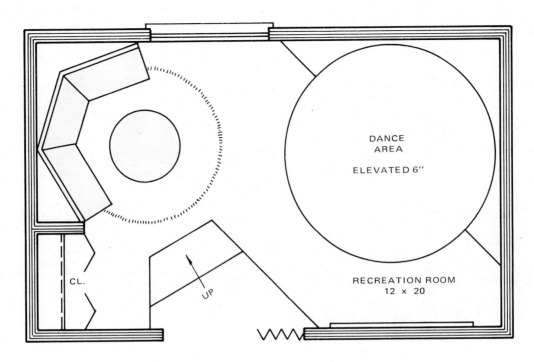

Fig. 6-64. This recreation room is truly an action room designed for young people.

Designing played on important part in the functional use of this study and recreation area of a remodeled attic.

Fig. 6-65. This enclosed court helps to provide the comfort of indoor-outdoor living.

PATIOS, PORCHES, AND COURTS

A well-designed house will extend its living facilities beyond its walls as shown in Fig. 6-65. The use of patios, porches and courts effectively enlarges the area and function of a house. In most localities outdoor living is popular and should be planned for, Fig. 6-66.

Patios are usually near the house but not structurally connected. These are ordinarily located at ground level and are constructed for durability. Concrete, brick, stone and redwood are commonly used materials.

Patios are used for relaxing, playing, entertaining and living, Fig. 6-67. Each function requires special consideration as to location, size and design. Try to locate patios designed for

Fig. 6-66. An attractive patio such as this complements the house and natural surroundings and provides extended outdoor living. (American Plywood Assoc.)

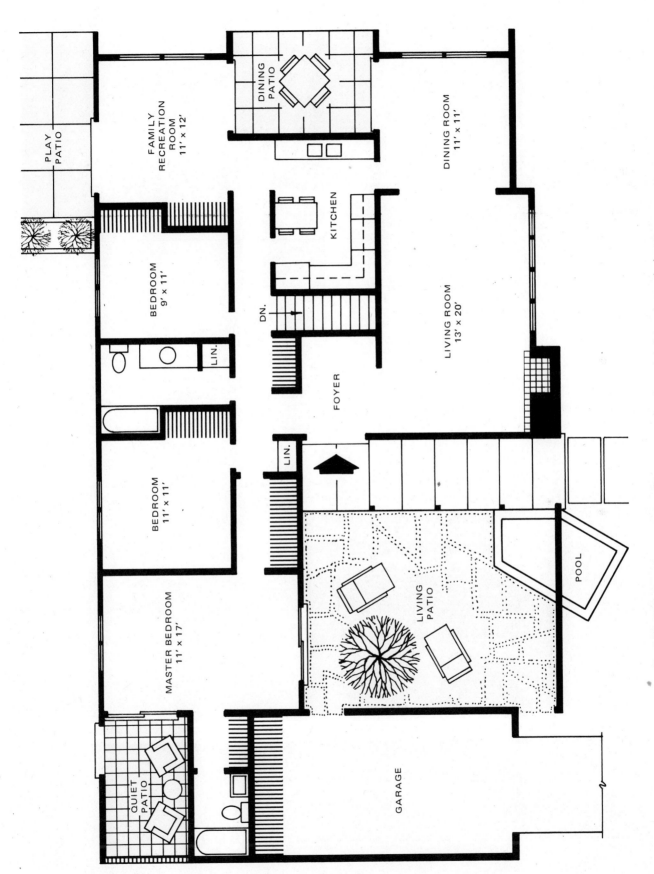

Fig. 6-67. This floor plan notes four different types of patios and their location to the house.

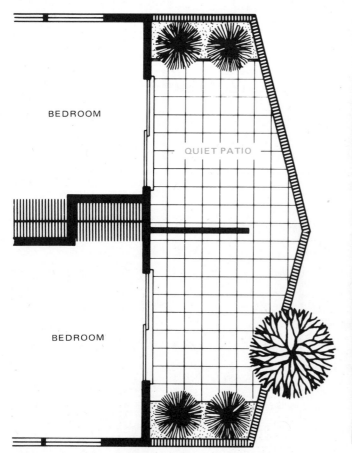

BEDROOM

QUIET PATIO

BEDROOM

Fig. 6-68. A quiet, secluded patio designed for privacy and comfort.

Fig. 6-69. The wood frame wall and planting provide privacy for this gateway patio.

Fig. 6-70. An extension of living off the recreation room, this large patio adds beauty and function of a barbecue pit.

relaxing, on a quiet side of the house near the bedrooms, where there is privacy, Fig. 6-68. Privacy may be achieved through the use of screens, walls or plants, Fig. 6-69.

A patio designed for living and entertaining will most likely be large and located off the living room, dining room or family recreation room. The redwood patio, Fig. 6-70, is an example of the contribution that an architecturally designed patio can make to the overall function of a house.

A 10' x 14' patio is considered small, while a 20' x 30' is considered large. Design the size of the patio proportional to the size of the house. The living or entertaining patio most likely will be located on the back side of the house where more space is available, Fig. 6-71. Again, privacy is a consideration that must be actively pursued in the planning, Fig. 6-72.

Consideration should be given to the orientation of sun,

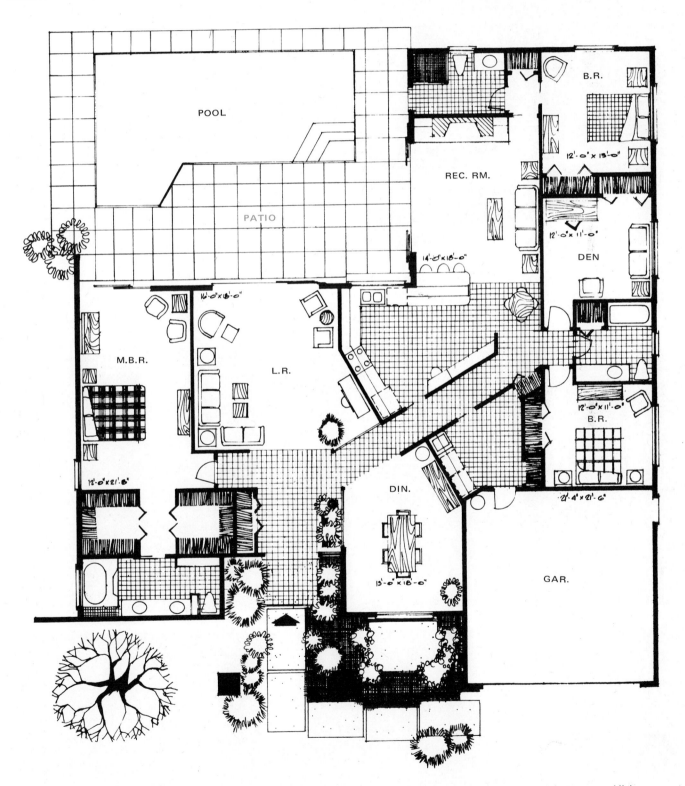

Fig. 6-71. A living-play patio with a swimming pool as the focal point. Access is from the master bedroom, recreation room and living room.

Fig. 6-72. Using an internal corner of the house and plantings to retain a degree of patio privacy. (ASG Industries, Inc.)

wind and view. In warm climates, shade may be a major factor; while in the far north, ample sun may be a prime objective. A well-designed patio is a pleasant place, so if the surrounding area lacks natural beauty, more emphasis should be placed on design and styling. The use of flowers, pools and screens helps to create a beautiful setting for dining, relaxing or entertaining.

If a swimming pool is planned, the encompassing area may well be designed as a patio. Fig. 6-73 is an example of a patio with a swimming pool as the main feature. This type of patio may be a living-entertaining type patio or a play patio. Play patios are usually less encumbered with furniture, planters and screens. The play patio is usually designed for use by children and adults for physical activities which require more open space. A patio of this nature is ordinarily located near or adjacent to the family recreation room or the service entrance. It sometimes doubles as a service entrance terrace, Fig. 6-74.

Porches differ from patios in at least two ways. First, they are structurally connected to the house and are raised above the grade level. Secondly, they are usually covered. Fig. 6-75 shows a porch which is an integral part of a modern frame cottage. Porches which are not under roof are usually called decks. Porches may function as outdoor dining areas, Fig. 6-76, and entryway extension. Balconies and verandas are types of porches which are generally higher than the standard porch.

Fig. 6-73. Making use of the swimming pool surroundings to form a beautiful and useful patio. (Ideal Cement Co.)

Porches need not appear to be "tacked-on." If the porch is planned as an integral part of the structure the result will be pleasing.

Usefulness of the porch (in northern states) may be increased by the addition of screens or glass, especially if the porch is to be used during the winter months.

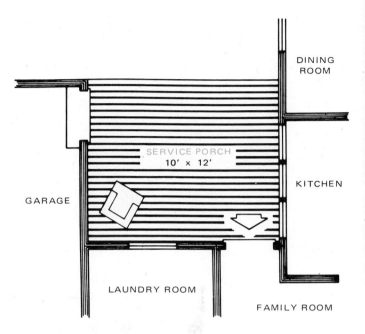

Fig. 6-74. Covered service porch located between the garage and family room may also serve as a play area.

Fig. 6-75. This serviceable cottage porch maintains the lines and details of the structure itself. (American Plywood Assoc.)

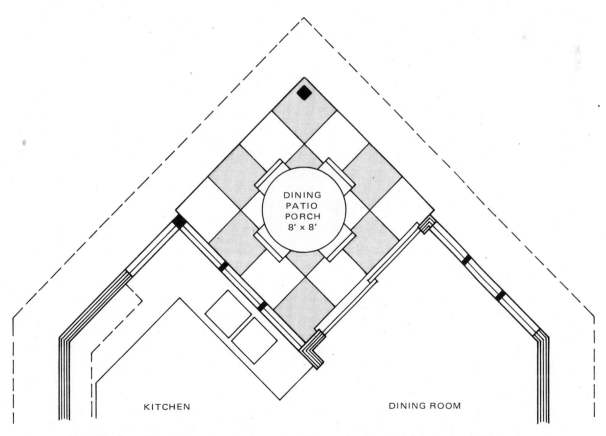

Fig. 6-76. A small roof covered dining patio-porch located adjacent to the dining room and kitchen.

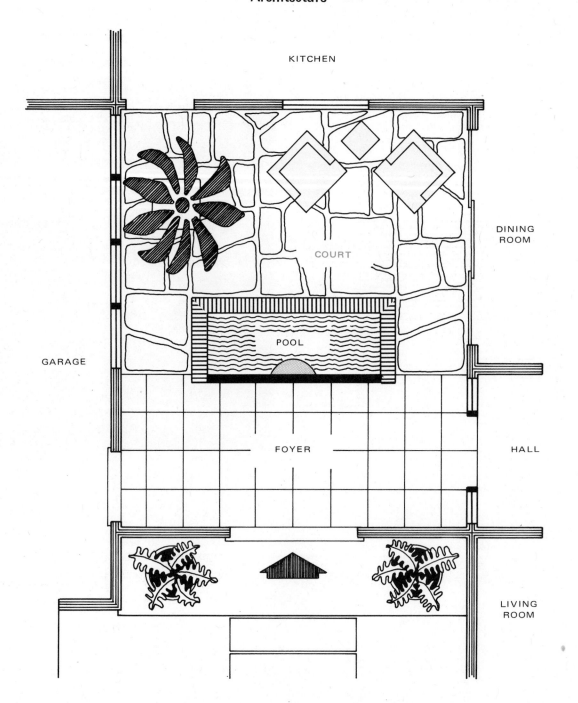

KITCHEN

DINING ROOM

COURT

POOL

GARAGE

FOYER

HALL

LIVING ROOM

Fig. 6-77. New approach to romantic old Spanish courtyard.

If possible, the porch should be large enough to act as a patio when needed. Porches are worthy of consideration in all modern plans.

Courts are similar to porches and patios and may have characteristics of both. They are totally or at least partially enclosed by walls or roof. Fig. 6-77 is a good example of an interior court. Courts may be used for dining, relaxing or entertaining, Fig. 6-78. They may also serve as interior gardens to add a touch of spring throughout the year. Courts are sometimes used to break up floor plans, add interest or serve the purpose of providing natural light to an interior part of the house which has no exterior wall space.

Lighting is an important feature of the patio, porch and court. Without proper lighting, use after dark may be limited, and much of the dramatic effect will be lost. Lighting should be used as a design tool to assist in accomplishing an atmosphere and extend the usefulness of the structure.

A large porch is shown in Fig. 6-79. This porch would be a welcome addition to most any home located in a warm climate. It could also be enclosed. It is convenient to the living and dining rooms as well as the bedroom area.

Fig. 6-80 shows an extensive porch and patio. The patio is enclosed with a fence to increase privacy and define the boundaries. The porch and patio extends the living area of the house to the outside and encourages outdoor living. The patio also provides a nice view from the living room.

Fig. 6-78. View of a beautiful court from the front entryway. Plantings provide a feeling of indoor-outdoor living.
(Brown and Kauffman, Inc.)

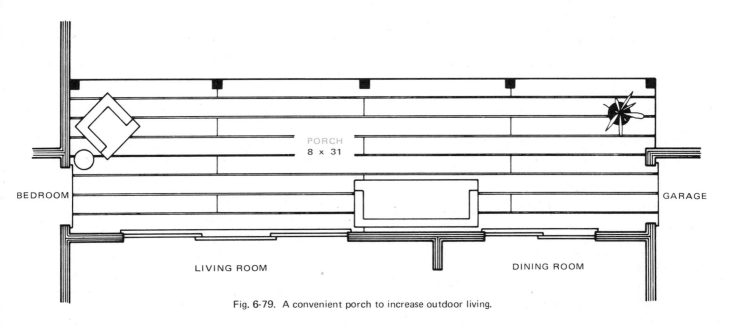

BEDROOM

PORCH
8 x 31

GARAGE

LIVING ROOM

DINING ROOM

Fig. 6-79. A convenient porch to increase outdoor living.

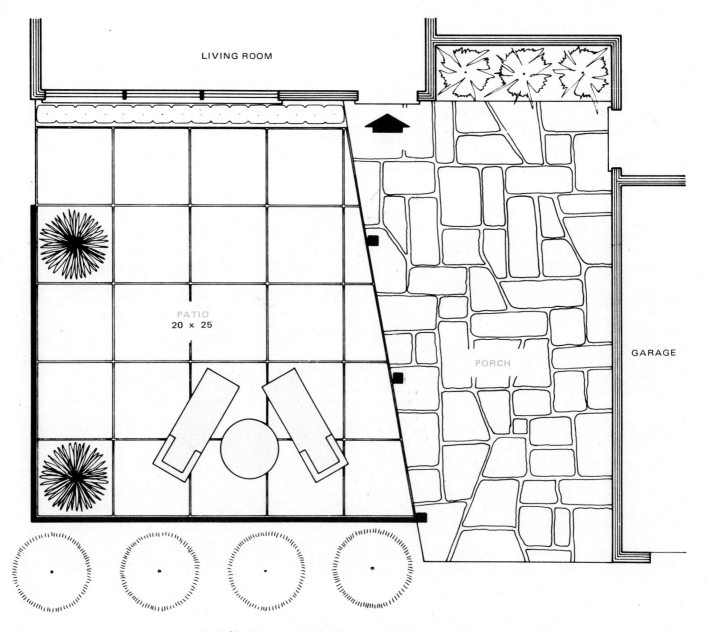

LIVING ROOM

PATIO
20 x 25

GARAGE

PORCH

Fig. 6-80. A large patio which increases the living area of the house.

REVIEW QUESTIONS — CHAPTER 6

1. The normal width of an entry door is _____.
2. What is the purpose of the foyer in a well designed house?
3. A dining room measuring 16 feet by 20 feet would be considered a _____ room.
4. Four ways in which the dining area may be separated from the living room without using a full wall are:
   a._____.
   b._____.
   c._____.
   d._____.
5. Other than the number of people expected to use the living room, four other factors to be considered are:
   a._____.
   b._____.

   c._____.
   d._____.
6. The living area of a residential structure comprises about _____ of the total area of a house.
7. There are many modern trends in planning the living area of a house. These include the following:
   a._____.
   b._____.
   c._____.
   d._____.
8. The three basic types of entryways are:
   a._____.
   b._____.
   c._____.
9. Standard interior and exterior door height is_____.
10. The usual parts of the typical house that most visitors or

friends see are the:

a. _____ .
b. _____ .
c. _____ .
d. _____ .

SUGGESTED ACTIVITIES

1. Plan a medium-size living room with furniture. Present your plan in color for a bulletin board display. Prepare a short description of the intended use.

2. Draw the plans for a modern dining room which is designed to accommodate six people.

3. Prepare a bulletin board display of entries from pictures cut out of magazines. Try to represent a broad range of designs.

4. Design a family recreation room for a specific hobby or activity. Describe the features of your design.

5. Select a house plan which has no patio and plan one. Draw the patio on tracing paper or acetate and present as an overlay on the house plan.

Split-level living areas. Skill in designing, material planning and construction techniques are all part of the architect's knowledge when planning rooms like these.

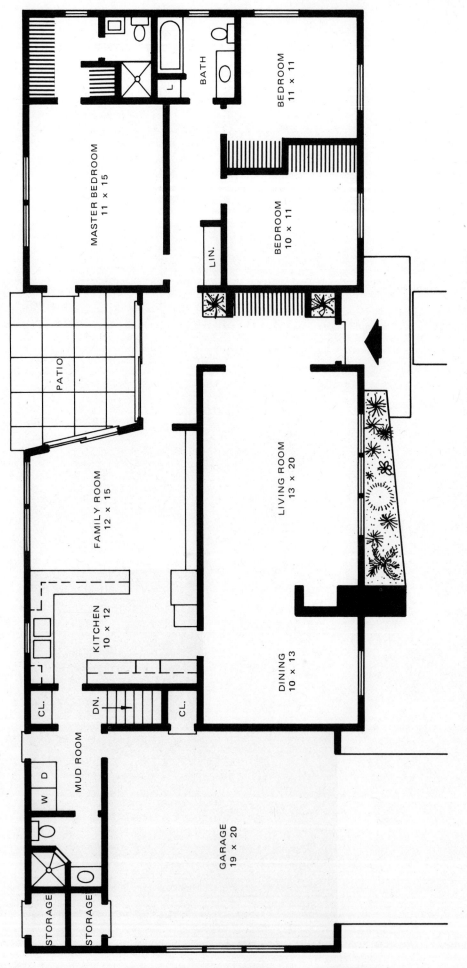

Fig. 7-1. The service area of this house includes the garage, kitchen, laundry, mud room, bath, and storage.

Chapter 7
ROOM PLANNING, SERVICE AREA

The Service Area supplements the Living and Sleeping Areas of the house. It supplies equipment and space for maintenance, storage and service. This includes the kitchen, laundry, work center, utility, garage and storage, Fig. 7-1. Due to its varied functions, the service area will require careful planning.

KITCHEN

A principal use for the kitchen is food preparation, Fig. 7-2. It may, however, be extended to include dining, laundry and storage. Kitchen design presents problems which are unique. Inefficiency and added cost will result if the problems are not

Fig. 7-2. A decorative and functional kitchen ideally designed for food preparation. (St. Charles Mfg. Co.)

Fig. 7-3. An example of creative design applied to the kitchen above to transform it into a lovely "new" kitchen, below.   (Wood-Mode)

Fig. 7-4. A compact kitchen which provides an exciting place to prepare food.

solved satisfactorily. From the standpoint of cost, the kitchen is usually the most expensive room in the house per square foot and receives the most active use of any room.

Efficient kitchen planning involves the placement of appliances, providing adequate storage cabinets and food preparation facilities. Fig. 7-3 shows a "before" and "after" kitchen. Note that in the "after" kitchen every inch of wall space is utilized. Angular shapes were replaced by bold, pleasing circular forms. There were no drastic structural changes. In designing kitchens, give considerable thought to the general location of each of the kitchen components. The arrangement should be logical and designed to minimize the amount of walking required by the homemaker, Fig. 7-4.

The work triangle is one measure of kitchen efficiency. It is determined by drawing a line from the front center of the range to the refrigerator to the sink and back to the range. The lengths of these three lines are added together to produce the length of the work triangle, Fig. 7-5. For practical kitchen design this distance should not exceed 21 feet.

Provision for food storage and cooking utensils should be located near the areas where they are to be used, Fig. 7-6. For example, the homemaker should not be required to walk across the kitchen to get pots and pans which are always used on the range. Store them near the cooking area.

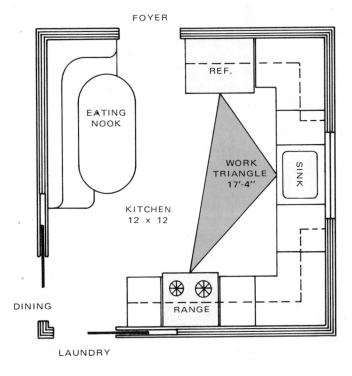

Fig. 7-5. The length of the work triangle is a good measure of the efficiency of a kitchen.

129

Fig. 7-6. Any homemaker would love the convenience these storage units provide. (St. Charles Mfg. Co.)

The kitchen designer has six basic styles to choose from:

Straight Line	"U" Shaped
"L" Shaped	Peninsula
Corridor	Island

THE STRAIGHT LINE KITCHEN. This design is frequently used in cottages and appartments. See Fig. 7-7. Little space is required and the design usually provides for an efficient arrangement of kitchen facilities. Two disadvantages are that it pro ides a limited amount of cabinet space and the result is usually not very interesting. The striaght line kitchen is seldom chosen for modern residences.

THE "L" SHAPED KITCHEN. The "L" shaped kitchen is located along two adjacent walls, Fig. 7-8. This design is efficient and an "L" shaped kitchen is usually more attractive than a straight line kitchen. Two work centers are generally located along one wall and the third on the adjoining wall. The

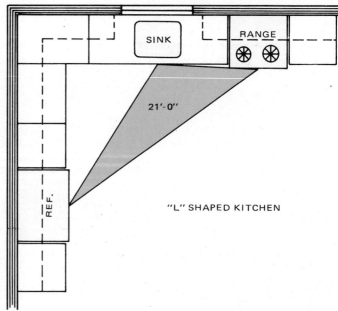

Fig. 7-8. The "L" shaped kitchen provides a traffic-free work triangle.

"L" shaped design is not intended for large kitchens because the effectiveness of the plan is lost if the walls are too long. Figs. 7-9 and 7-10 show modern "L" shaped kitchens.

Fig. 7-9. This "L" shaped kitchen combines the use of brick and wood to achieve a striking result. (Wood-Mode)

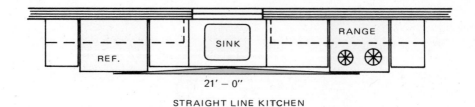

Fig. 7-7. An example of a straight line or one-wall kitchen.

Fig. 7-10. An "L" shaped kitchen which has a short work triangle to reduce steps. (Azrock Floor Products)

Fig. 7-12. A spectacular corridor which makes ample use of natural materials.

THE CORRIDOR KITCHEN. As implied by the name, the corridor kitchen is located on two walls opposite each other, Fig. 7-11. Corridor kitchens are usually small to medium in size and are ideal for a long, narrow room, Fig. 7-12. This design lends itself to an efficient arrangement, but is not recommended if traffic is to be heavy through the kitchen. Open space between the cabinets should be at least four feet.

efficiency and is one of the most attractive of the six designs, Fig. 7-13. There is no traffic through the kitchen to other areas of the house and the work triangle is compact and

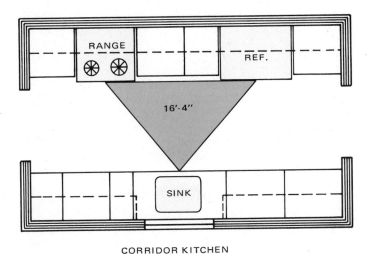

CORRIDOR KITCHEN

Fig. 7-11. Corridor kitchen design with plenty of cabinet space.

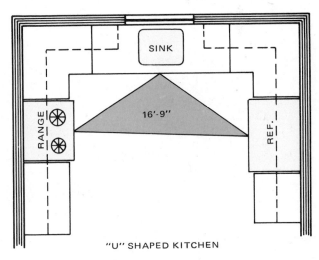

"U" SHAPED KITCHEN

Fig. 7-13. The "U" shaped kitchen is a popular design.

functional, Fig. 7-14. Most "U" shaped kitchens are medium in size with the open space between the legs of the U being 5 or 6 feet.

THE "U" SHAPED KITCHEN. Probably the most popular design, the "U" shaped kitchen retains a high level of

THE PENINSULA KITCHEN. The peninsula kitchen is popular because it provides plenty of work space, is attractive,

Fig. 7-14. Efficiency and beauty are the key elements of this unique "U" shape design. (St. Charles Mfg. Co.)

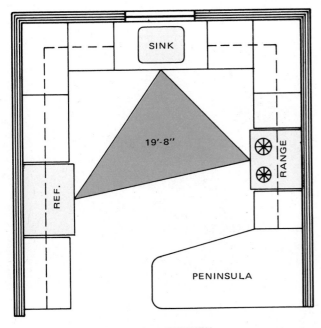

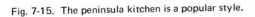

SINK

19'-8"

REF.

RANGE

PENINSULA

PENINSULA KITCHEN

Fig. 7-15. The peninsula kitchen is a popular style.

Fig. 7-16. The utilitarian exhaust hood which resembles a piece of modern wood sculpture becomes the focal point of this peninsula kitchen. (Wood-Mode)

and is easily joined to the dining room using the peninsula as a divider, Fig. 7-15. The peninsula may be used as the cooking center, Fig. 7-16; eating area, Fig. 7-17; or as a food preparation center, Fig. 7-18. As in the "U" shaped kitchen, traffic is reduced and the work triangle is compact.

Fig. 7-17. Here the peninsula is utilized as an eating area.

Fig. 7-18. The peninsula in this kitchen is used as a food preparation center. (H. J. Scheirich Co.)

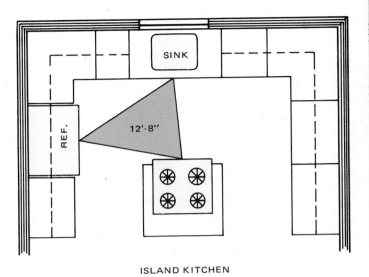

ISLAND KITCHEN

Fig. 7-19. An island kitchen design.

Fig. 7-21. An island kitchen tastefully decorated and designed to be functional. Note that the island serves as an eating area. (Wood-Mode)

THE ISLAND KITCHEN. The island kitchen may be a modification of the straight line, the "L" shaped or the "U" shaped design, Fig. 7-19. The island may house the sink, cooking center or food preparation area, and in some instances it may serve as a countertop or snack bar, Figs. 7-20, 7-21, and 7-22. The island should be accessible from all sides. At least four feet clearance should be allowed on all sides of the island for easy access.

Fig. 7-20. Kitchen with octagonal cooking island and oriental flair which should excite most any homemaker. (Wood-Mode)

Fig. 7-22. The function and efficiency of this island kitchen is difficult to overlook. (H. J. Scheirich Co.)

CABINETS AND APPLIANCES

Kitchen appliances are available in a variety of styles, colors and sizes. Symbols and standard sizes of kitchen appliances and sinks are shown in Fig. 7-23.

Kitchen cabinets provide the majority of storage space in most modern kitchens. They are produced in standard sizes, but may be custom made in other than standard sizes if required. Most standard base cabinets are 34 1/2" high, 24" deep, and width increments in 3 inch multiples. (15", 18", 21", etc.) Wall cabinets are either 12 or 13 inches deep (both are standard). Cabinets 12 to 30 inches high in increments of 3 inches and 12 to 36 inches wide in increments of 3 inches are also obtainable. A typical section through the base and wall cabinets is shown in Fig. 7-24. Fig. 7-25 illustrates the standard base and wall cabinets that most manufacturers produce as standard units. Be sure to check the specifications of the cabinets selected before drawing the kitchen plan.

REFRIGERATOR

CU. FT.	WIDTH	HEIGHT	DEPTH
9	24"	56"	29"
12	30"	68"	30"
14	31"	63"	24"
19	34"	70"	29"
21	36"	66"	29"

STANDARD FREE-STANDING RANGE

WIDTH	HEIGHT	DEPTH
20"	30"	24"
21"	36"	25"
30"	36"	26"
40"	36"	27"

DOUBLE OVEN RANGE

WIDTH	HEIGHT	DEPTH
30"	61"	26"
30"	64"	26"
30"	67"	27"
30"	71"	27"

DROP IN RANGE

WIDTH	HEIGHT	DEPTH
23"	23"	22"
24"	23"	22"
30"	24"	25"

BUILT-IN COOK TOP

WIDTH	HEIGHT	DEPTH
12"	2"	18"
24"	3"	22"
48"	3"	22"

RANGE HOOD

WIDTH	HEIGHT	DEPTH
24"	5"	12"
30"	6"	17"
66"	7"	26"
72"	8"	28"

SINGLE COMPARTMENT SINK

WIDTH	DEPTH
24"	21"
30"	20"

DOUBLE COMPARTMENT SINK

WIDTH	DEPTH
32"	21"
36"	20"
42"	21"

Fig. 7-23. Appliance symbols and sizes.

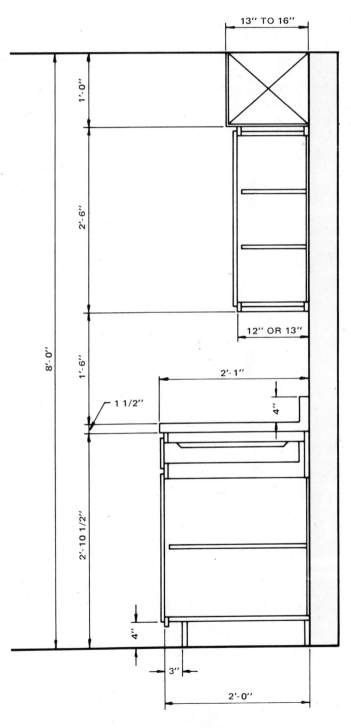

Fig. 7-24. A typical section through the base and wall cabinets.

WALL CABINETS

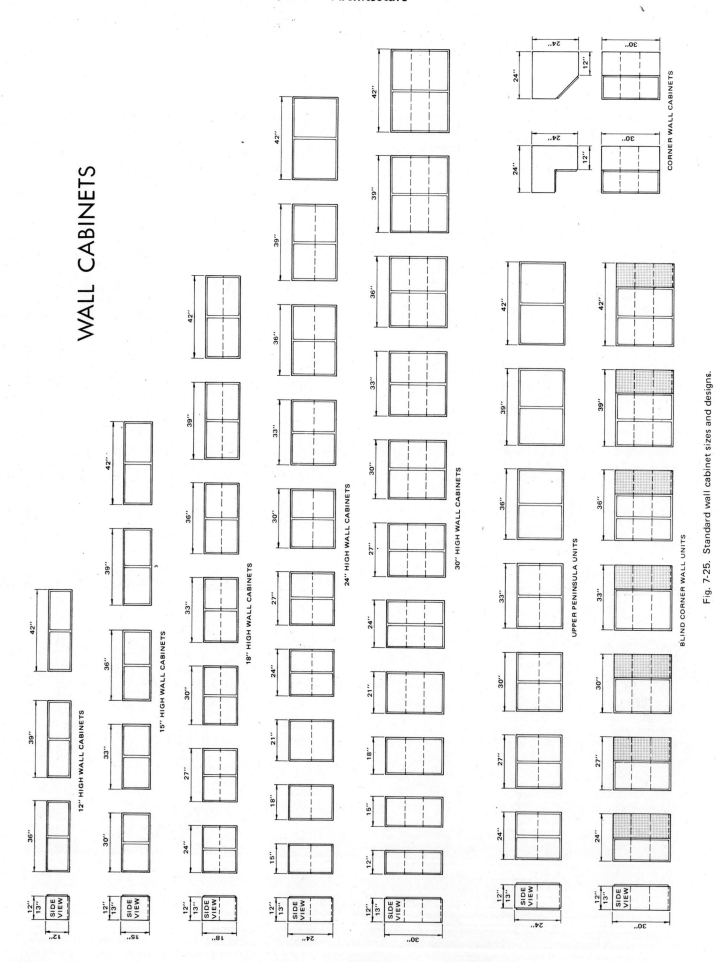

Fig. 7-25. Standard wall cabinet sizes and designs.

12" HIGH WALL CABINETS

15" HIGH WALL CABINETS

18" HIGH WALL CABINETS

24" HIGH WALL CABINETS

30" HIGH WALL CABINETS

UPPER PENINSULA UNITS

BLIND CORNER WALL UNITS

CORNER WALL CABINETS

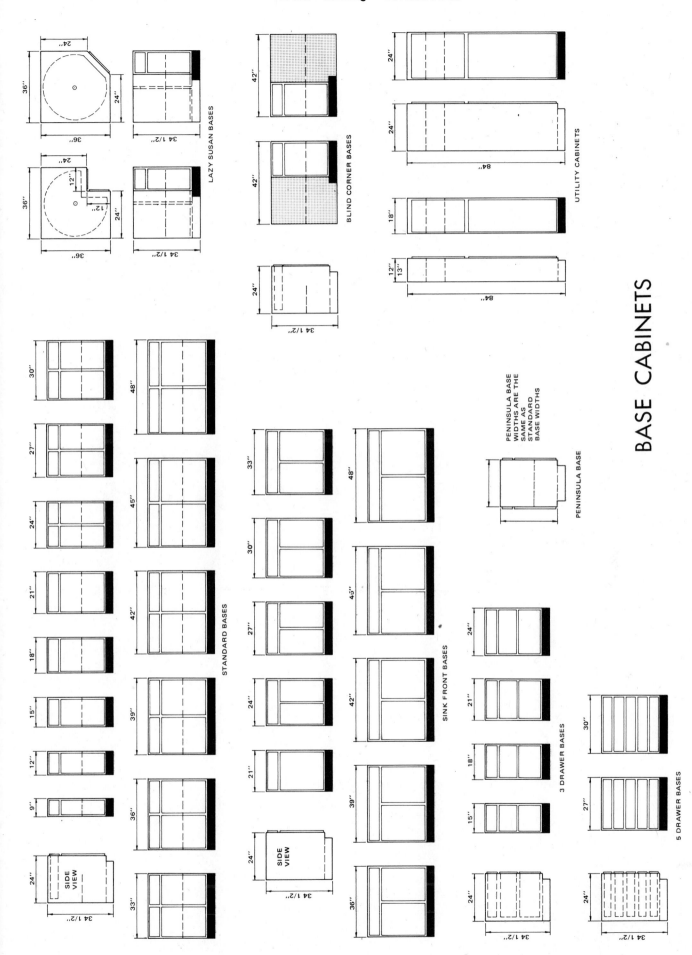

LAZY SUSAN BASES

BLIND CORNER BASES

UTILITY CABINETS

STANDARD BASES

SINK FRONT BASES

PENINSULA BASE WIDTHS ARE THE SAME AS STANDARD BASE WIDTHS

PENINSULA BASE

3 DRAWER BASES

5 DRAWER BASES

BASE CABINETS

Fig. 7-25. (Continued) Standard base cabinet sizes and designs.

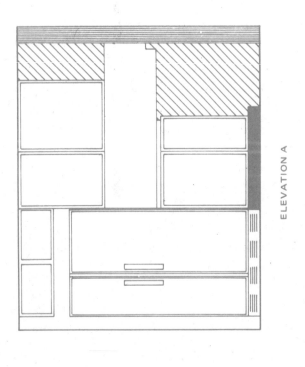

ELEVATION A

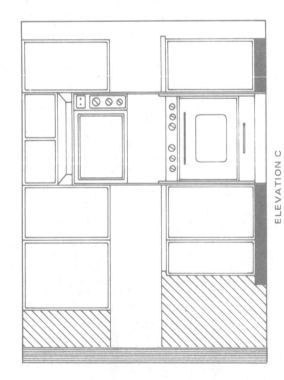

ELEVATION C

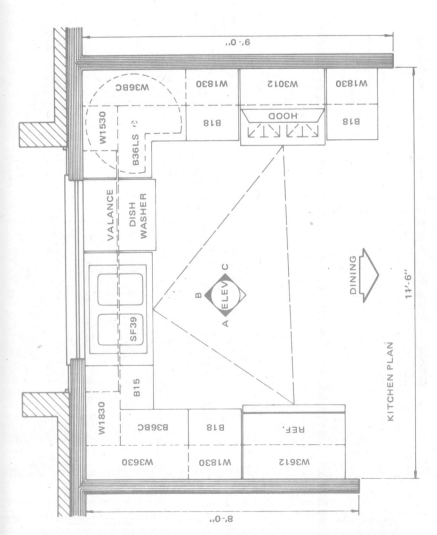

W3630 W1830 W3612

W1830

B15

B368C B18 REF.

SF39

VALANCE

DISH WASHER

W1830 W3012 W1830

B18 HOOD B18

W1530 B36LS (?) W36BC

9'-0"

8'-0"

11'-6"

DINING

A ELEV C
B

KITCHEN PLAN

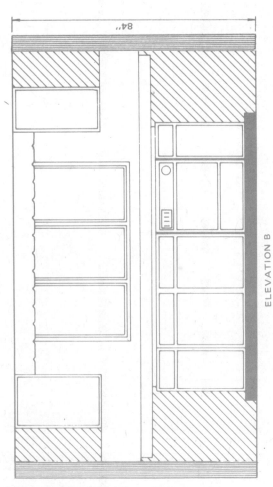

ELEVATION B

84"

Fig. 7-26. Construction drawings for a modern kitchen.

Fig. 7-26 shows the plan and elevation of a modern kitchen. Note how the wall and base cabinets are identified in the plan view. Numbers shown are manufacturers' stock numbers. The wall cabinets are illustrated with a hidden line symbol while the base units are shown as object lines. A kitchen plan should also show the work triangle and specify its length.

Proper location of the kitchen is important. It is the prime element of the service area and its relation to other areas of the house requires close examination. It is usually advisable to locate the kitchen near the service entrance and to provide easy access to outside trash containers. The kitchen should be located next to the dining room. Try to position windows in such a way that children in their play area may be observed from the kitchen. The laundry area and a bath should also be located in the general area of the kitchen.

Ventilation is a must in the modern kitchen. A wall fan is good, but a hood with a fan is better because it is more efficient in collecting fumes, Figs. 7-27 and 7-28. Provision for exhaust is necessary either through an outside wall or the roof. Exhaust from the kitchen fan should not be expelled into the attic.

Fig. 7-28. A modern range hood which requires no exhaust duct. It utilizes charcoal filters. (Nutone, Div. of Scovill)

Modern appliances are produced in many colors and styles. Select colors and styles which are consistent with the overall design of the kitchen. Choose materials which are easy to maintain and are durable, Fig. 7-29.

Fig. 7-27. This kitchen will remain free of excessive cooking odors because it has a large efficient hood over the range. (St. Charles Mfg. Co.)

Fig. 7-29. Modern kitchen sinks are designed to be functional. (Kohler)

Decor of the kitchen should be pleasant. The room should be well lighted. In addition to the main ceiling fixtures, lights over the sink, cooking center and food preparation areas are needed. A dropped ceiling with banks of fluorescent lights is a popular way to supply ample amounts of light and at the same time add to the appearance of the kitchen. A lowered ceiling makes the room look larger.

Fig. 7-30 shows a modified corridor kitchen. This efficient design provides a planning area, ample storage, and easy access to the work centers. The breakfast nook serves as a room divider and is convenient to the adjoining family room.

A "U" shaped kitchen with extras is presented in Fig. 7-31. This plan is designed for the woman who enjoys planning and preparing large meals. The design is efficient with lots of room provided for movement. The dining area is conveniently located next to the food preparation center. Another advantage of this plan is the service entrance, which facilitates garbage removal and restocking supplies.

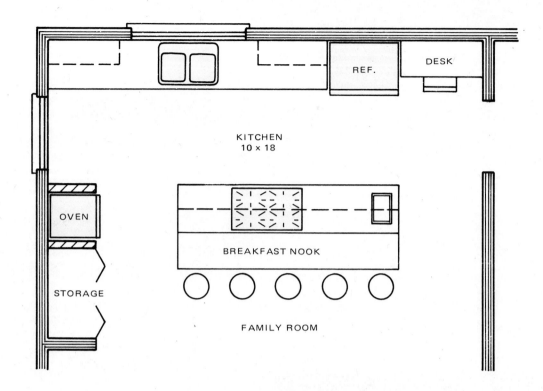

Fig. 7-30. A modified corridor kitchen with a breakfast nook.

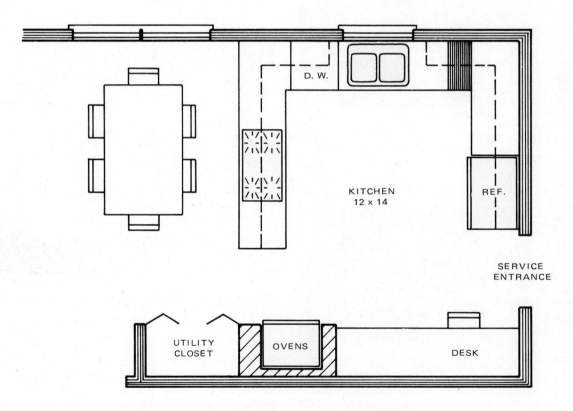

Fig. 7-31. A stylish "U" shaped kitchen designed for efficiency.

CLOTHES CARE CENTER

The clothes care center provides the location and facilities for washing, drying, pressing, folding, storing and mending clothes. It is intended to be more than a "utility" room. Many utility rooms are drab and are located away from other service areas of the house. The clothes care center is intended to be bright, cheerful and convenient, Fig. 7-32. It should be large enough to provide adequately for the activities to be performed there, Fig. 7-33.

It is desirable for the clothes care center to be ventilated and well lighted. The floor must be resistant to water and easily cleaned. Ceramic tile is preferred. Counter top space that is durable and soil resistant provides for a convenient work area, Fig. 7-34.

A well-designed clothes care center is illustrated in Fig. 7-35. Note that this room includes all the functions associated with clothes care. The built-in ironing board saves space and is functional. The laundry sink is near the washer for convenience. Cabinet storage space is provided above the washer and dryer.

If possible, locate the clothes care center near the kitchen. A homemaker spends a large amount of time in the kitchen and this location may save her many steps.

Fig. 7-32. This bright clothes care center provides ample workspace and convenient storage. (St. Charles Mfg. Co.)

Fig. 7-33. Storage space and convenience are the main features of this clothes care center. (Wood-Mode)

Fig. 7-34. This clothes care center provides ample counter space and utilizes a durable floor covering.

Fig. 7-36 shows the sizes and shapes of appliances and furnishings commonly used in a clothes care center. The clothes care center may be expanded into a full-fledged "homemakers center." Here is an all-purpose room where she can sew, arrange flowers, pursue hobbies and do many other things in addition to washing and ironing clothes. Fig. 7-37 shows such a room.

A compact clothes care center is presented in Fig. 7-38. This room is organized for efficiency. The ironing board swings up into the wall out of the way. Soiled clothes are collected in the bin below the clothes chute which is convenient for washday. A sewing and mending area is flanked by generous counter space. Storage is more than average in this well-planned center.

The clothes care center shown in Fig. 7-39 is designed especially for a basement location next to the family or recreation room. A series of storage shelves screens the area

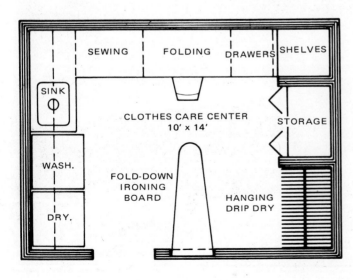

Fig. 7-35. A well-designed clothes care center with facilities for washing, drying, pressing, folding, storing and mending.

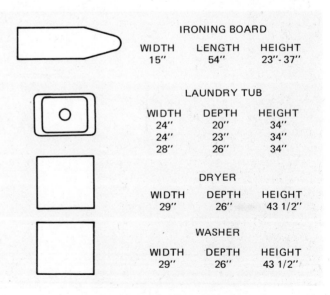

IRONING BOARD		
WIDTH	LENGTH	HEIGHT
15"	54"	23"-37"

LAUNDRY TUB		
WIDTH	DEPTH	HEIGHT
24"	20"	34"
24"	23"	34"
28"	26"	34"

DRYER		
WIDTH	DEPTH	HEIGHT
29"	26"	43 1/2"

WASHER		
WIDTH	DEPTH	HEIGHT
29"	26"	43 1/2"

Fig. 7-36. Furniture and appliance symbols used in a clothes care center.

Fig. 7-37. This homemaker center is an all-purpose room. Here she can sew, pursue creative activities and at the same time enjoy the fireplace. (Brown and Kauffmann, Inc.)

and adds many cubic feet of storage space. Wall cabinets line one wall and create a trim appearance as well as adding storage space. Counter area is sufficient for folding clothes or mending. Organization is the key in this plan.

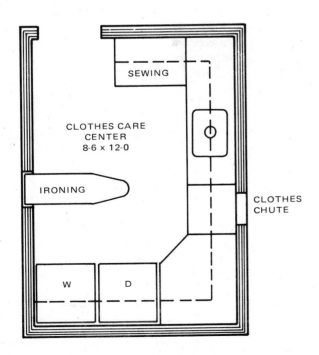

Fig. 7-38. A modern clothes care center which provides for washing, drying, sewing, storage and ironing.

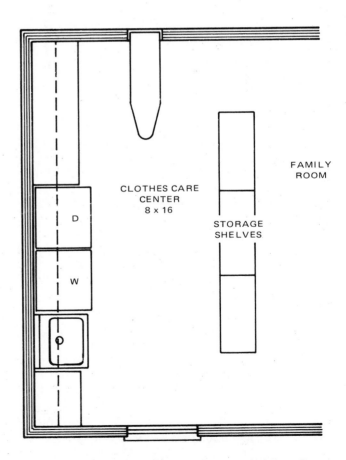

Fig. 7-39. A clothes care center designed for the basement.

GARAGE OR CARPORT

The primary purpose of a garage or carport is to provide shelter for the family automobile. It may be small and simple, large and complex, attached to the house, or free standing.

The size and location of the garage or carport will depend

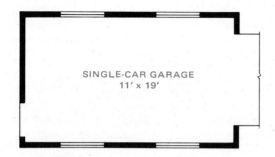

Fig. 7-40. A small garage with no storage facilities.

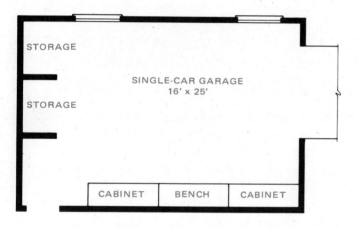

Fig. 7-41. Single-car garage with storage and work space.

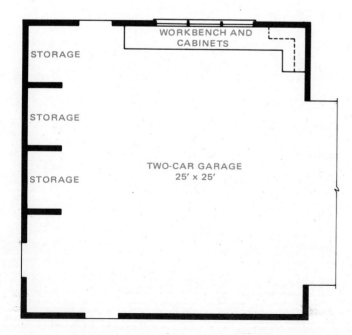

Fig. 7-42. Large two-car garage with workshop and storage.

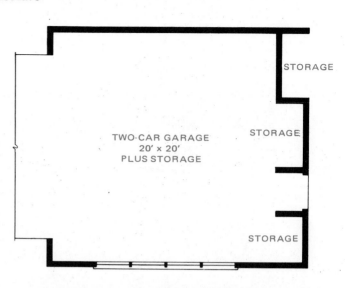

Fig. 7-43. A small two-car garage with a variety of storage space.

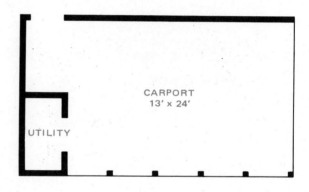

Fig. 7-44. Single stall carport open on two sides, with small utility area.

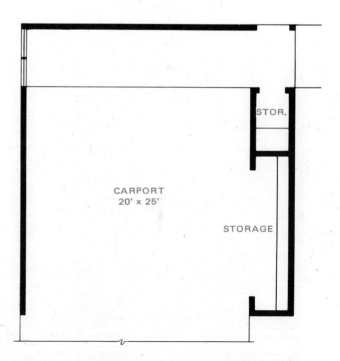

Fig. 7-45. A carport with space for two cars and lots of storage.

Fig. 7-46. A workshop adjacent to the garage is convenient and functional.   (Brown and Kauffmann, Inc.)

on the number of cars to be housed, the size and layout of the house and the space available. A single-car facility may range in size from 11' x 19' to 16' x 25', Figs. 7-40 and 7-41. A space designed for two cars may be as small as 20' x 20' or as large as 25' x 25', Figs. 7-42 and 7-43.

Several factors should be considered when deciding between a garage or a carport. A carport provides less protection for the car than a garage since it is open on one or more sides, Figs. 7-44 and 7-45. A garage supplies more security than a

carport. Certain house styles look better with one than the other. In cold climates, a garage may be more desirable. Carports are less expensive to build than garages and may be satisfactory for warm dry climates.

The overall space may be increased considerably if a work area or utility storage is planned into the facility, Fig. 7-46.

A garage or carport should be designed in such a way that it is an integral part of the total structure, Fig. 7-47. If care is not taken, a garage or carport could detract from the

Fig. 7-47. Garage is an integral part of the house.

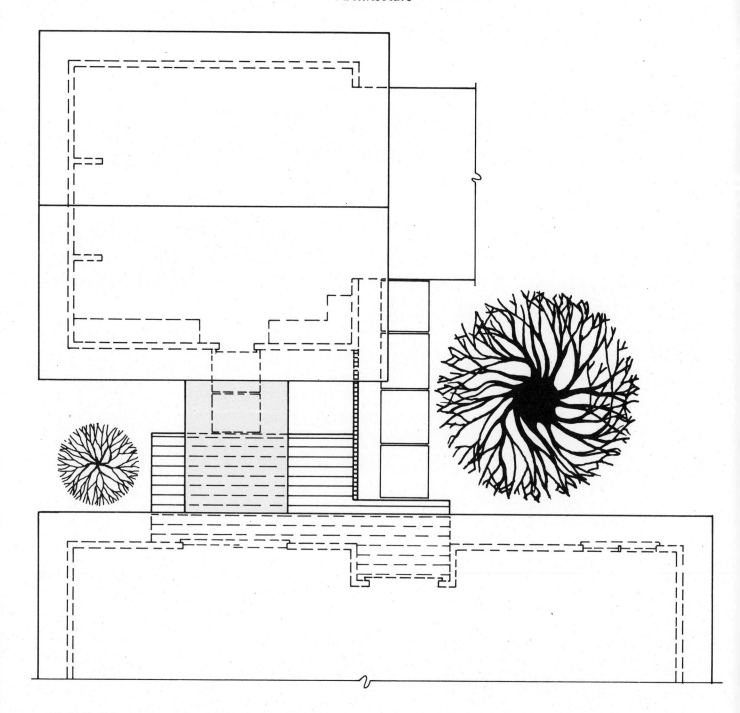

Fig. 7-48. This plan shows a free standing garage which becomes an integral part of the house by adding a covered walkway between the two.

appearance of the house.

If the garage is a free standing structure, providing a covered walkway to the house may be desirable, Fig. 7-48. The walkway should lead to the service entrance and provide easy access to the kitchen.

Plan the garage or carport with storage in mind, Fig. 7-49. Provide space for outdoor recreation equipment and gardening tools, if no other specific facility is provided for that purpose. Many homes have garages which are not used for storage of the car because they are full of tools and other equipment. This is often a result of poor planning.

A few design ideas may well be worth mentioning. The floor of the garage or carport should be at least 4" thick concrete reinforced with steel or wire mesh. Good floor drainage is important. Include ample windows and artificial lighting. If the garage is attached to the house, be sure to check the local building code for special requirements regarding fire protection.

Standard size garage doors are available in wood, fiber glass, plastics, aluminum and steel. Wood has been a traditional choice and is still preferred by many, but it requires frequent painting. Metal doors are popular and require little maintenance. Fiber glass is very durable and allows natural light to come through even with the door closed. A single-car garage door is usually 8 feet wide and 7 feet high. A two-car garage door is usually 16 feet wide and 7 feet high. Garage doors are also produced in widths of 18 feet. Fig. 7-50 shows four modern double garage door styles.

The driveway and turnaround should be planned concurrently with the garage. If space is available, a turnaround is often recommended. Backing directly onto the street should be avoided when possible. Fig. 7-51 shows two turnarounds with dimensions. Note that the minimum driveway width is 10 feet. Always plan garage facilities for a standard size automobile even though the prospective owner may have a compact car.

The garage shown in Fig. 7-52 is designed to utilize common building materials and techniques. A slab foundation and stud walls with bevel siding constitute the basic structure. Standard trusses are used to form the gable roof. The design is

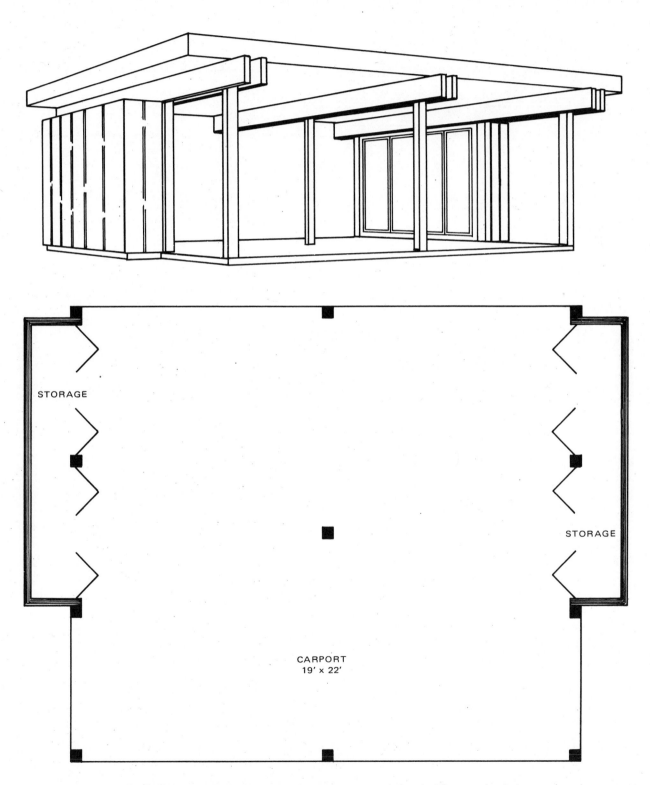

STORAGE

STORAGE

CARPORT
19' x 22'

Fig. 7-49. The plan and perspective of a modern carport designed with storage in mind.

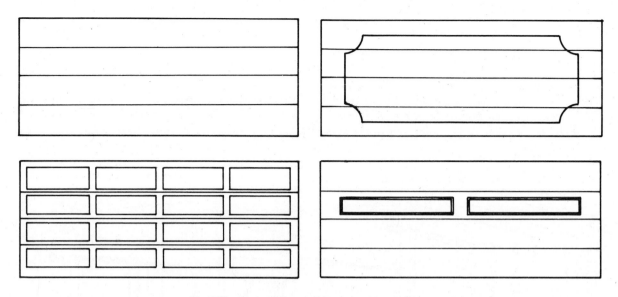

Fig. 7-50. Four modern double garage door designs.

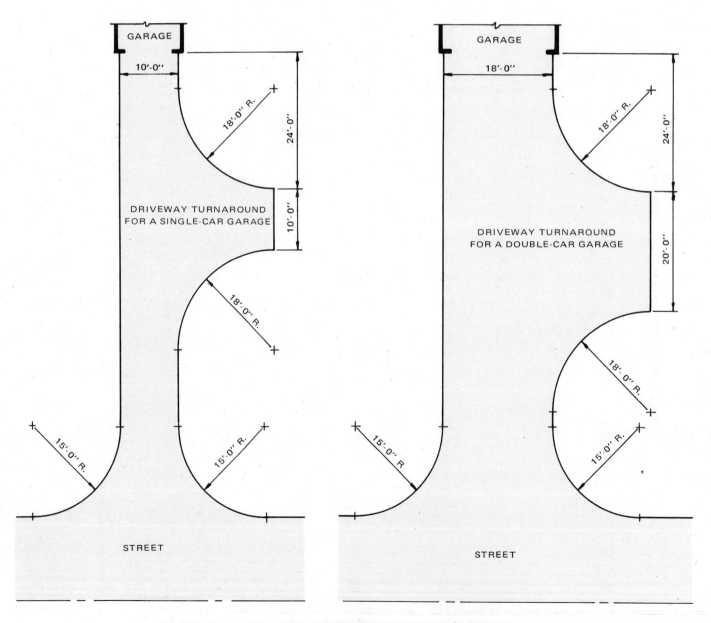

Fig. 7-51. Standard turnarounds with dimensions for single and double-car garages.

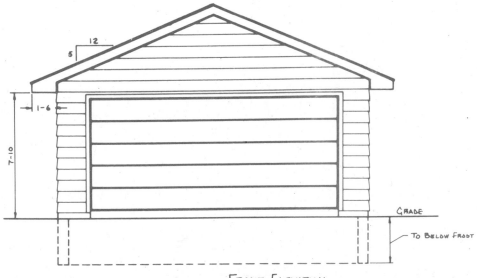

FRONT ELEVATION

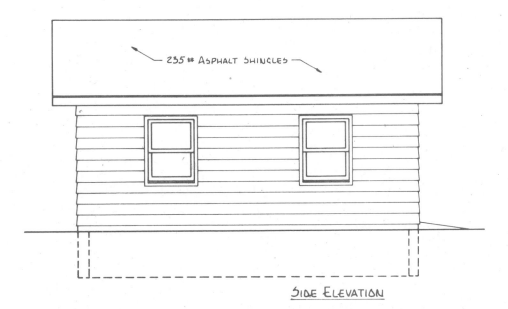

235 # ASPHALT SHINGLES

SIDE ELEVATION

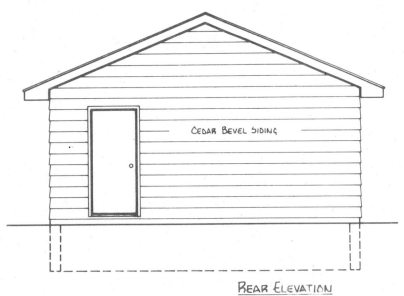

CEDAR BEVEL SIDING

REAR ELEVATION

Fig. 7-52. Plans for a conventional two-car garage.

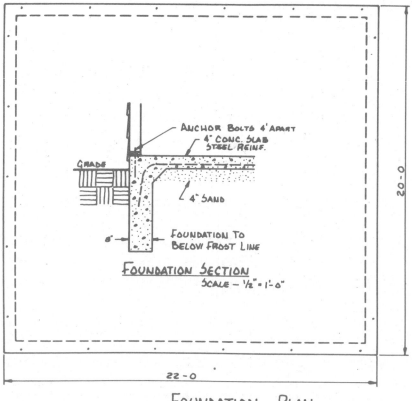

ANCHOR BOLTS 4' APART
4" CONC. SLAB
STEEL REINF.
GRADE
4" SAND
FOUNDATION TO
BELOW FROST LINE
8"

FOUNDATION SECTION
SCALE — 1/2" = 1'-0"

20-0
22-0

FOUNDATION PLAN
SCALE — 1/4" = 1'-0"

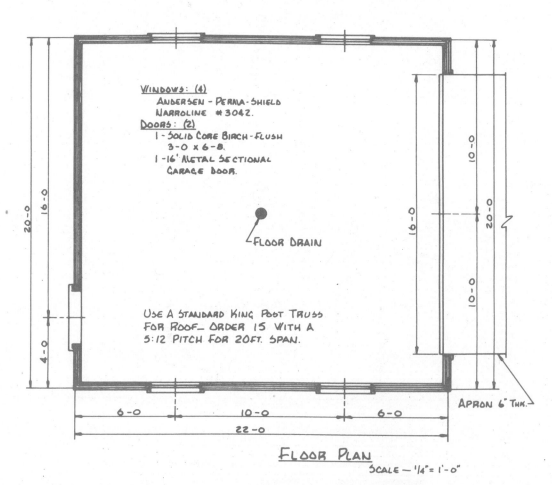

WINDOWS: (4)
ANDERSEN - PERMA-SHIELD
NARROLINE #3042.
DOORS: (2)
1 - SOLID CORE BIRCH - FLUSH
3-0 x 6-8.
1 -16' METAL SECTIONAL
GARAGE DOOR.

FLOOR DRAIN

USE A STANDARD KING POST TRUSS
FOR ROOF. ORDER 15 WITH A
5:12 PITCH FOR 20FT. SPAN.

20-0
16-0
4-0

10-0
20-0
16-0
10-0

6-0
10-0
6-0
22-0

APRON 6" THK.

FLOOR PLAN
SCALE — 1/4" = 1'-0"

Fig. 7-52. (Continued) Plans for a conventional two-car garage.

both economical and attractive.

Basic proportions of a garage are relatively fixed, but several ideas may be applied to improve the appearance. For example, an innovative roof may be used such as the Dutch hip, butterfly, or mansard. The roof style will change the overall appearance considerably. The use of modern siding materials may also improve an otherwise drab structure. Textured siding with rustic stain or weathered redwood boards add character and charm. Windows may be conventional types or fixed panels of colored glass or plastics. It is possible, with the application of a few innovative ideas, to transform a garage into an attractive and functional structure adding much to the total home environment.

REVIEW QUESTIONS — CHAPTER 7

1. Kitchen cabinets are produced in standard widths, heights and depths. The standard modular width increment is _____ inches.

2. The dimensions of a single-car garage are approximately _____.

3. The minimum width of a driveway is _____.

4. A clothes care center should provide for the following activities:

   a._____.
   b._____.
   c._____.
   d._____.
   e._____.
   f._____.

5. Identify the six basic kitchen designs.

   a._____.
   b._____.
   c._____.
   d._____.
   e._____.
   f._____.

6. The maximum acceptable length of the work triangle in a kitchen is _____ feet.

7. The service area of a home generally includes the following individual areas.

   a._____.
   b._____.
   c._____.
   d._____.
   e._____.
   f._____.

8. Kitchen base cabinets are normally _____ inches high.

9. Exhaust fumes from a kitchen hood fan should not be expelled into the _____.

10. Standard size garage doors are available in the following materials.

    a._____.
    b._____.
    c._____.
    d._____.

SUGGESTED ACTIVITIES

1. Visit an appliance store and obtain literature on the latest kitchen appliances. Prepare a bulletin board display using pictures from the literature.

2. Secure specifications and price lists of kitchen cabinets from a manufacturer. Calculate the total cost for the cabinets shown in Fig. 7-26.

3. Plan a modern kitchen which includes the major elements of the work triangle. Draw the plan view and elevations. Identify the cabinets using the manufacturer's numbers and dimension the drawings.

4. Obtain three floor plans from magazines or other sources and analyze the provisions for clothes care in each plan. Explain the strengths and weaknesses of each. Propose improvements.

5. Measure the length and width of a standard size automobile and design a single-car garage which provides adequate space for the car and extra storage.

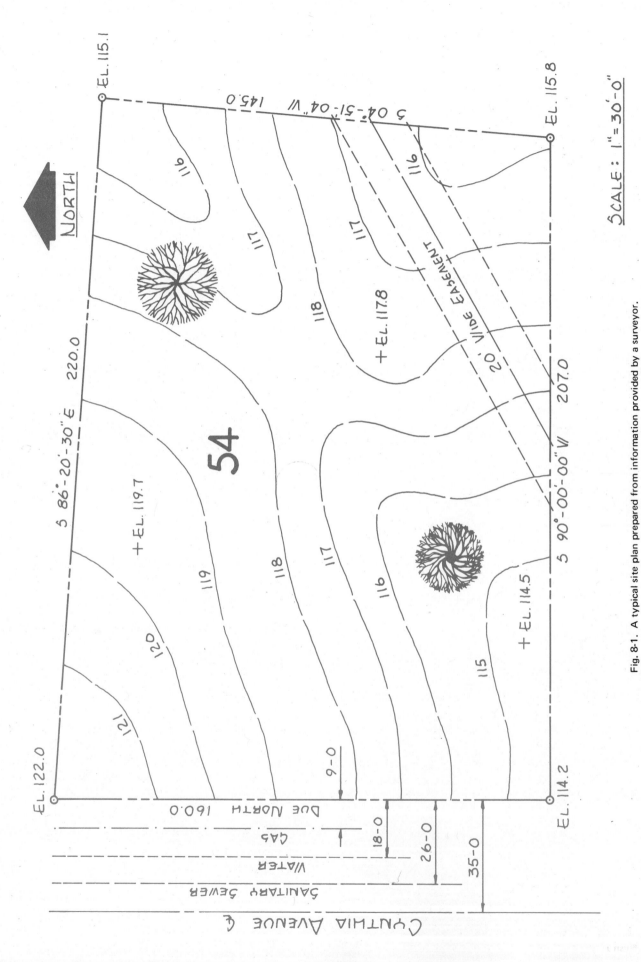

Fig. 8-1. A typical site plan prepared from information provided by a surveyor.

Chapter 8
PLOT PLANS

DEFINITION AND PURPOSE

A plot plan is a plan view drawing which shows the site and location of the buildings on the property. More specifically, a plot plan shows:

Length and bearing of each property line.
Location, outline and size of buildings on the site.
Contour of the land.
Elevation of property corners and contour lines.
Meridian arrow (north symbol).
Trees, shrubs, streams and gardens.
Streets, driveways, sidewalks and patios.
Location of utilities.
Easements for utilities and drainage (if any).
Well, septic tank and field.
Fences and retaining walls.
Lot number or address of the site.
Scale of the drawing.

The plot plan is drawn using information provided by a surveyor and recorded on a site plan, Fig. 8-1. Note that the site plan presents information only about the property and utilities. It does not show proposed construction. However, the plot plan shows both the property and proposed construction.

PROPERTY LINES

PROPERTY LINES DEFINE THE SITE BOUNDARIES. The length and bearing of each line must be identified on the plot plan. Property line lengths are measured with an engineer's scale to the nearest 1/100 foot. Fig. 8-2 illustrates a property line which is 175.25' long and has a bearing of N 89° E.

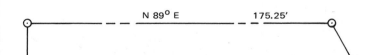

Fig. 8-2. This property line is 175.25' long and has a bearing of N 89° E.

Bearing angles are recorded in degrees and, if required, in minutes and seconds from either north or south. An example of a typical bearing might be, (S 63° W), while a more specific bearing would read, (S 63°-13'-05'' W). Fig. 8-3 shows a number of lines with bearings identified.

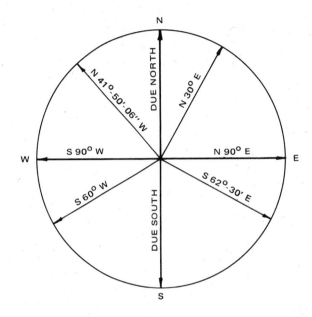

Fig. 8-3. Bearings are from North or South and may be as accurate as plus or minus one second.

If the property corner begins or ends on a bench mark it is usually identified with a special symbol. All other corners may be represented by drawing a small circle, the center of the circle being the property corner. See Fig. 8-4.

It is customary when drawing the property lines of a site to begin at a given corner and proceed in a clockwise manner

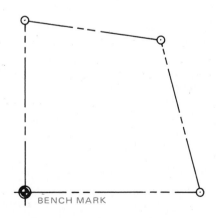

BENCH MARK

Fig. 8-4. Property corners which are located at a bench mark are identified with a bench mark symbol.

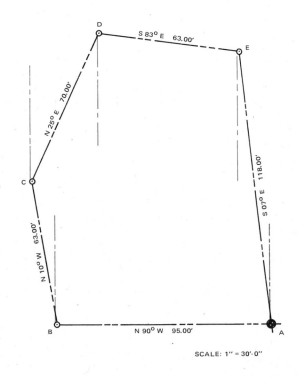

PROPERTY LINE DESCRIPTION

FROM POINT A   A LINE BEARS N 90° W   95.00' TO POINT B
FROM POINT B   A LINE BEARS N 10° W   63.00' TO POINT C
FROM POINT C   A LINE BEARS N 25° E   70.00' TO POINT D
FROM POINT D   A LINE BEARS S 83° E   63.00' TO POINT E
FROM POINT E   A LINE BEARS S 07° E   118.00' TO POINT A

SCALE: 1" = 30'-0"

Fig. 8-5. These property lines have been drawn to scale using the property line description provided.

until the beginning point is reached. Fig. 8-5 illustrates the procedure of drawing the property lines for a site.

CONTOUR LINES

A CONTOUR IS A LINE CONNECTING POINTS WHICH HAVE THE SAME ELEVATION. The shoreline of a lake is a good example of a contour. Contour lines help describe the topography of a site by depicting shape and elevation of the land. The accepted reference point for topographical surveys is mean sea level. Many times, however, it is not important to know how far a point is above or below sea level, but what the relative difference is between two or more points. In residential home construction, relative elevations are usually sufficient.

The examination of several characteristics of contours should help to clarify their use:

1. Contour interval is the vertical distance between two adjacent contours. This interval may be any distance which is functional for the specific drawing. Fig. 8-6 illustrates a contour interval of five feet. Be sure to identify the elevation of each contour line.

2. When contours are spaced closely together a steep slope is indicated, Fig. 8-7.

3. When contours are smooth and parallel, the ground surface is even. When contours are irregular the ground surface is rough and uneven, Fig. 8-8.

4. Summits and depressions are represented by closed lines as shown in Fig. 8-9.

5. Contours of different elevations do not cross. Only in the instance of a vertical slope would the contours appear to touch.

6. Contours cross watersheds and ridge lines at right angles with the concave side of the curve facing toward the higher elevation, Fig. 8-10.

Contour lines which are the result of a survey are usually represented by a series of long (one to two inch), thin freehand lines. Estimated contours are represented by a short dashed line similar to a hidden line, Fig. 8-11.

Fig. 8-12 shows the plotting of contours from a grid of elevations developed by a surveyor. Too few measurements

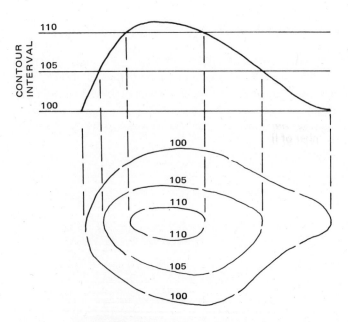

Fig. 8-6. The plan and elevation view of the contour using an interval of 5 feet.

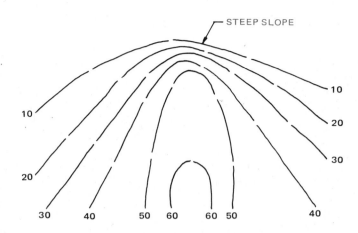

Fig. 8-7. The relative spacing of contour lines represents the slope angle.

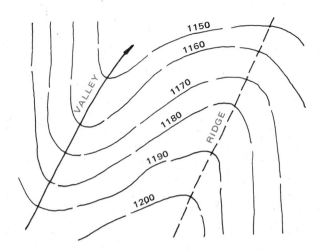

Fig. 8-10. Ridges and valleys should be identified using the proper symbols.

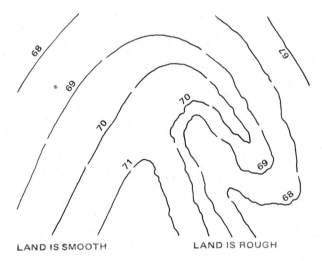

LAND IS SMOOTH   LAND IS ROUGH

Fig. 8-8. Contour lines show relative roughness of the land as well as elevation.

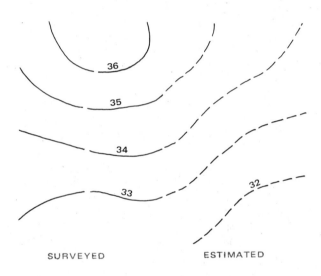

SURVEYED   ESTIMATED

Fig. 8-11. Estimated contours are shown with a dash line symbol. Surveyed contours are represented by solid or long dash lines.

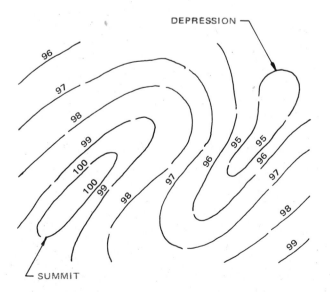

Fig. 8-9. Summits and depressions are represented by closed contour lines.

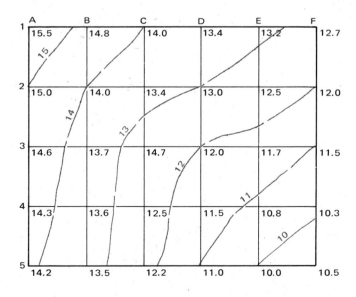

Fig. 8-12. Contour lines plotted from an elevation grid using data supplied by a surveyor.

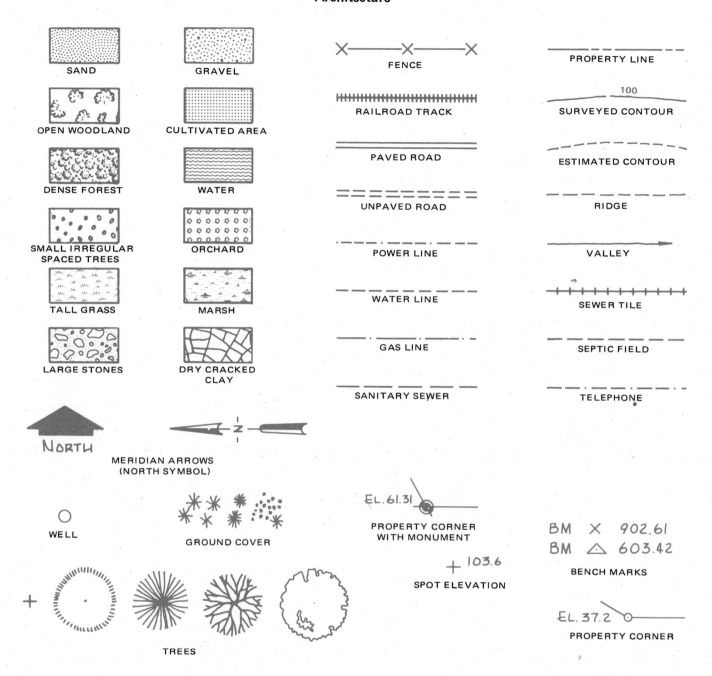

Fig. 8-13. Common topographical symbols used on plot plans.

taken for a given area will result in less accuracy of contour representations. When insufficient data is provided, the resulting contour will be only moderately accurate.

TOPOGRAPHICAL FEATURES

Topographical features are represented by symbols. Many symbols are standardized and readily recognizable. A few are not. When a symbol is designed for a specific purpose and is not standard it should appear in a legend on the drawing.

In some topographical drawings color plays an important role. When color is used the following guidelines should be applied: black is used for lettering and the works of man, such as roads, houses and other structures; brown represents all land forms such as contour lines; blue is used for water features such as streams, lakes, marsh and ponds; green for vegetation.

Fig. 8-13 illustrates some of the more common topographical symbols which might be used on a plot plan.

LOCATION OF STRUCTURE ON SITE

A complete analysis should be made of the site to determine the ideal location and placement of the structure on the site. The analysis should include such things as natural contour, trees, view, surrounding houses, code restrictions, style of house to be built, solar orientation, winds, placement of well and septic system, if needed, and size and shape of the site. Not all of these factors will apply in every situation, but they should be examined to determine their importance.

Once a specific location is decided on, the structure may be drawn on the plot plan. There are three commonly accepted methods of representing the house on the drawing. The first method is to lay out the outside of the exterior walls omitting all interior walls and roof. Shade or crosshatch the space covered by the house, Fig. 8-14. The second method of

overhang line to either of the other two methods. The distance from the roof overhang to the property may then be shown.

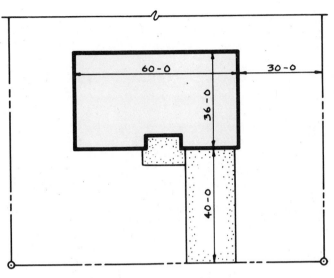

Fig. 8-16. Thickened exterior walls may show the location and size of a house on a site.

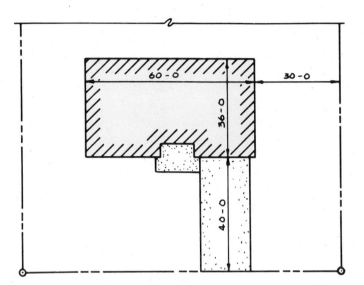

Fig. 8-14. A house may be represented on a plot plan by shading or crosshatching the area covered by the house. The roof is not included.

representing the house on the site is to draw the exterior walls as hidden lines with the roof shown as solid lines (typical roof plan), Fig. 8-15. The third method shows the exterior wall thickened with all interior walls, windows and doors omitted, Fig. 8-16.

When the distance between house and property line is critical it may be advisable to use the second method or add the

The location of the house on the site must be dimensioned. Standard procedure is to dimension the distance of one corner of the house from adjacent lot lines as shown in Figs. 8-14, 8-15, and 8-16. In some instances, this simple procedure will

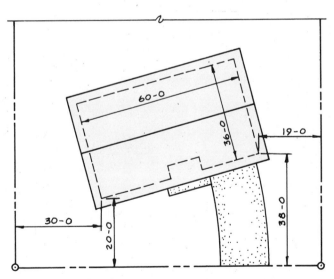

Fig. 8-17. A house which is not positioned parallel to the property lines may require more than two dimensions to properly locate it on the site. A bearing line could also be used to show the position of the house.

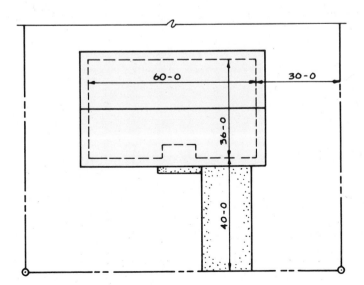

Fig. 8-15. A roof plan may be used to show the location and size of the house on a site. Exterior walls are represented as hidden lines.

not be sufficient to clearly locate the structure. Fig. 8-17 shows a more complex situation and its solution. In each instance, dimension the distance from the outside of the exterior wall to the property line and, if required, show the overhang distance.

PROCEDURE FOR DRAWING A PLOT PLAN

These steps are recommended for drawing a plot plan; omit items which do not apply:

1. Select a scale which will provide the largest drawing on the size paper that you have chosen. All of the sheets in set of drawings should be the same size for ease of handling. The property lines should be placed sufficiently inside the border to provide room for adding dimensions, notes and title block. Scales commonly used in drawing plot plans range from 1/8" = 1'-0" to 1" = 30'-0" and smaller.

2. Lay out the property lines using data supplied by the site plan or other source. Be extremely careful in this step to ensure an accurate drawing. Steps 2 through 4 are illustrated in Fig. 8-18.

3. Letter the bearing and length of each line and affix the scale near the bottom of the drawing.

4. Locate the meridian arrow (north symbol) in a place on the drawing where it will be easy to find.

5. Select a contour interval which is appropriate for your specific situation and plot the contour lines. Draw the lines lightly at this point. These are to be darkened in later. Steps 5 and 6 are illustrated in Fig. 8-18.

6. Letter the elevation of each contour line and property corner.

7. Locate the house on the site using one of the methods discussed earlier. Steps 7 through 9 are shown in Fig. 8-19.

8. Dimension the overall length and width of the house and the distance from the house to the two adjacent property lines. The elevation of a reference corner of the house is sometimes given.

9. Draw surrounding features such as driveway, sidewalks and patios. The size and elevation may be given for each if they are required.

10. Determine the center line of the street and location of utilities. Draw these features using proper symbols and dimension their location. If a well and septic system are required, draw them at this point. Steps 10 through 12 are illustrated in Fig. 8-20.

11. Draw other topographical features such as trees and shrubs. Now darken in all light contour lines.

12. Check your drawing to be sure you have included all necessary elements.

Fig. 8-21 shows a plot plan of a large home site and house which has its own septic system and well. This drawing is a typical plot plan.

LANDSCAPE PLOT PLANS

The landscape plan is designed to show the type and placement of trees, shrubs, flowers, gardens and pools on the

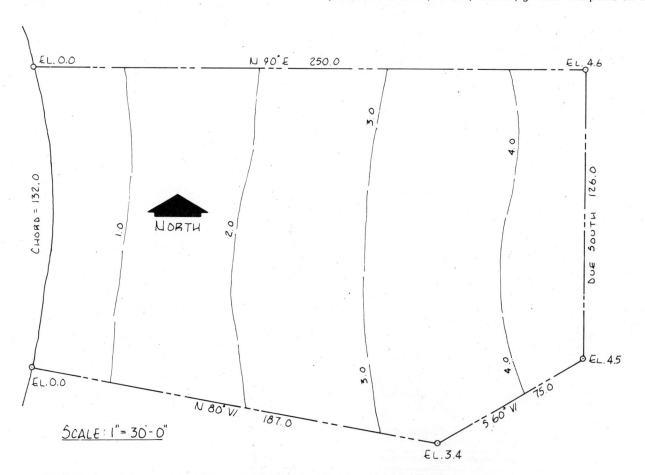

Fig. 8-18. A partially complete plot plan which has the property lines located and identified, meridian arrow positioned, the scale shown, and the contour lines and corner elevations added.

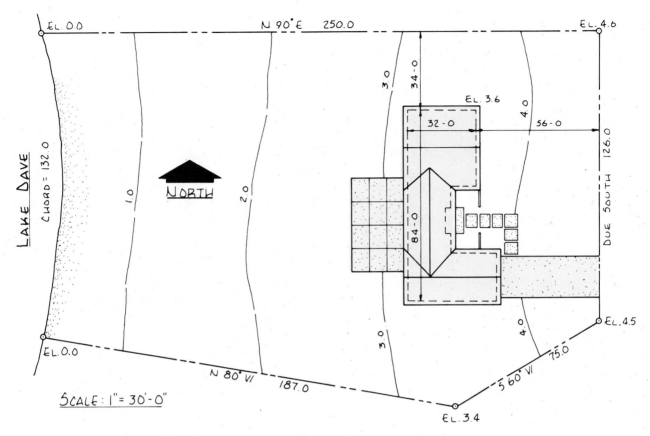

Fig. 8-19. The house, drive and patio are positioned on the site and dimensioned.

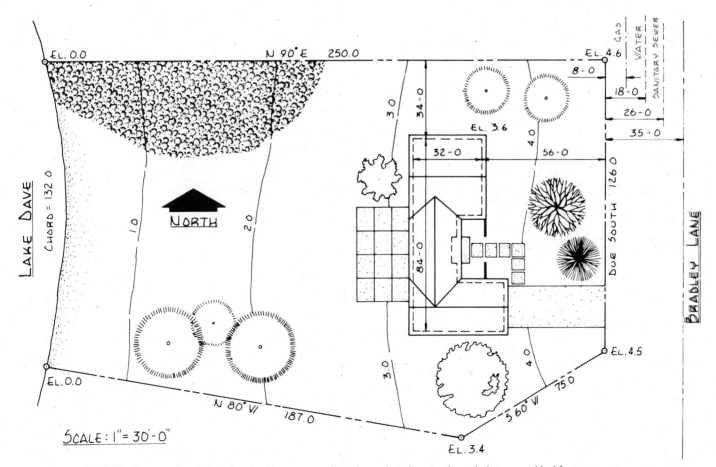

Fig. 8-20. The completed plot plan showing property lines, house location, north symbol, topographical features, center line of street and utilities.

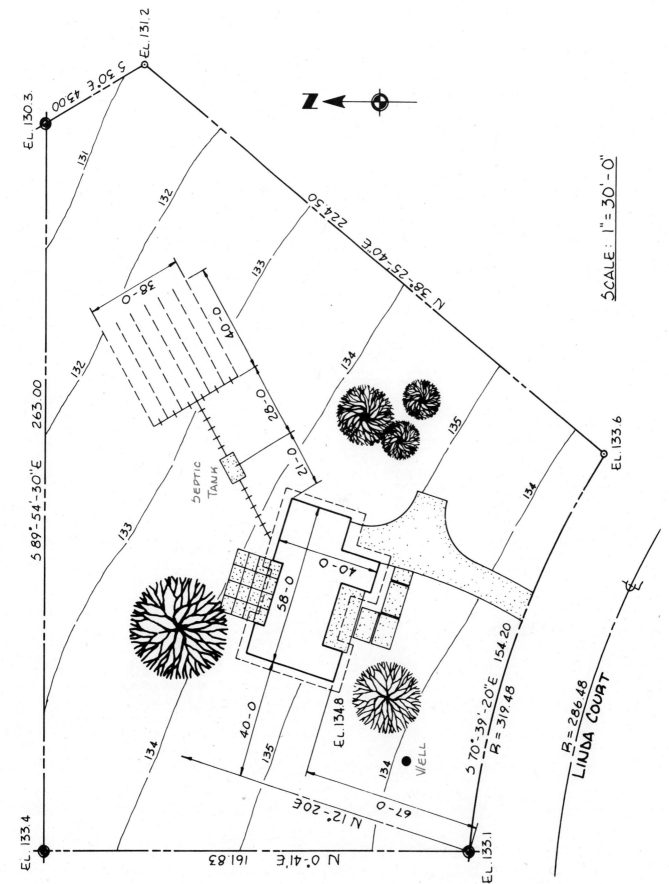

SCALE: 1" = 30'-0"

Fig. 8-21. A plot plan of a large site and house with its own septic system and well.

Plot Plans

site. A landscape plan (which is not always required) provides an excellent way to plan the total setting for the home.

Much of the information presented on the construction plot plan is required on the landscape plan. Boundary lines, meridian arrow, outline of the house, driveway, walks, patios and contour lines are needed to place the landscape elements into their proper perspective.

Symbols are used to represent various types of plants. These symbols should be keyed to a chart to avoid confusion. There are not sufficient symbols to allow each ornamental plant to have its own symbol.

Fig. 8-22 shows a typical landscape plot plan. When practical the plant symbols should be drawn to proper scale. This produces a realistic idea of the components on the plan.

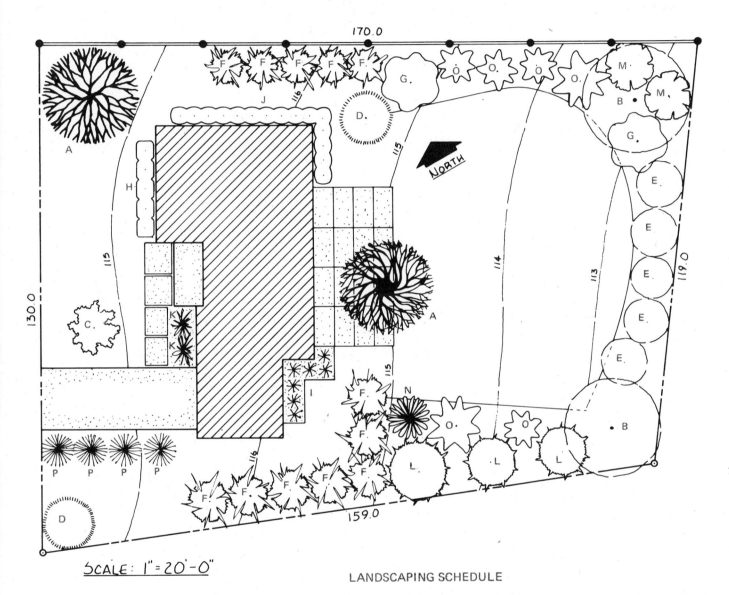

SCALE: 1" = 20'-0"

LANDSCAPING SCHEDULE

KEY	QUAN.	PLANT DESCRIPTION	KEY	QUAN.	PLANT DESCRIPTION
A	2	SHADE TREE	I	7	BUXUS
B	2	ORNAMENTAL TREE	J	15	PRIVET
C	1	FLOWERING CRAB	K	2	FLORIBUNDA ROSE
D	2	WILLOW TREE	L	3	PYRAMID YEW
E	5	RHODODENDRON	M	2	CAMELLIA
F	12	SPREADING JUNIPER	N	1	FRENCH HYBRID LILAC
G	2	FLOWERING SHRUB	O	6	VIBURNUM
H	5	TAXUS GLOBE	P	4	FORSYTHIA

Fig. 8-22. A typical landscape plot plan showing the type and location of trees and shrubs on the property.

163

REVIEW QUESTIONS — CHAPTER 8

1. A line connecting points which have the same elevation on a plot plan is:
   a. A bearing line.
   b. A property line.
   c. A contour line.
   d. None of the above.
2. The plot plan contains information collected by a _____ and recorded on a site plan.
3. Included in the analysis of a site for the ideal location and placement of a house are the following factors.
   a. _____ .
   b. _____ .
   c. _____ .
   d. _____ .
   e. _____ .
   f. _____ .
   g. _____ .
   h. _____ .
4. Symbols for plants should be drawn to the proper _____ whenever possible.
5. What is the purpose of the meridian arrow?
6. Estimated contours are represented on the plot plan by using _____ _____ lines.
7. List four topographical features represented on plot plans and indicate the color for the symbol if it were to be used.

Features

   a. _____ .
   b. _____ .
   c. _____ .
   d. _____ .

Color

   a. _____ .
   b. _____ .
   c. _____ .
   d. _____ .
8. Standard procedure for locating a house on a plot plan is to dimension the distance from one corner of the house to _____ lot lines.
9. Two types of information are needed about property lines, the length and _____ of each line.
10. The plan which shows the type and placement of trees, shrubs, flowers, gardens and pools is a _____ plan.

SUGGESTED ACTIVITIES

1. Select a vacant site in your community which is suitable for a home. Measure the site, determine north with a compass, and draw a site plan of the property to scale. Show any trees that may be on the site and indicate approximate contour lines.
2. Select a floor plan of a house from a newspaper, magazine or other source which is appropriate for the site you drew in No. 1 above. Locate the house on the site. Draw a plot plan showing the house and property.
3. Define these terms: property lines, meridian arrow, contour, site plan, plot plan, landscape plan, utilities, bearing, bench mark and depression.
4. Compile a list of fifteen ornamental trees and shrubs which grow in the area in which you live. Describe each one as to mature size and characteristics. Design a plan view symbol for each one.
5. Using the plot plan developed in No. 2 and the list of trees and shrubs hardy in your area, draw a landscape plan for the site.

Landscaping is a very important part of the total environment of a home. Care should be taken in choosing the plants so they will compliment the architectural style and climate.

Fig. 9-1. Slab foundations in various stages of completion.

Chapter 9
FOOTINGS, FOUNDATIONS, AND CONCRETE

In residential construction, providing a good foundation is very important. This requires careful planning and design on the part of the architect, if the foundation is to support the structure as required. See Figs. 9-1 and 9-2.

Fig. 9-2. This complex foundation is for a large split-level home.

STAKING OUT HOUSE LOCATION

The plot plan provides the necessary dimensions required for staking out the location of the house on the lot. The task is accomplished with a measuring tape, contractor's level and transit (if required). When angles other than 90° must be measured, the surveyor's transit is used.

The first step in staking out the house is to locate each corner by laying off the distances indicated on the plot plan. A stake is driven into the ground at the location of each corner of the foundation to identify its position. Square corners may be laid out using the 9-12-15 unit method, Fig. 9-3. These proportions define a right triangle and establish a 90° angle corner. The position of all corners should be checked for accuracy by diagonal measurement, Fig. 9-4.

Batter boards are used to retain the location of the foundation during excavation and construction. These are constructed of 2 x 4 stakes sharpened on one end and driven into the ground about 4 feet outside the footing line. A 1 x 6 board is nailed horizontally to the stakes so all are level and in the same horizontal plane. (They will have the same elevation.) A strong cord or string is stretched across the boards at opposite ends of the building and located directly above the corner stakes. A plumb bob is used for accurate placement of each stake. This is done for each side of the building. A saw kerf is usually made at the exact point on the horizontal batter board where the string is located. This prevents movement of the string along the board. After cuts are made in all eight batter boards, the lines of the house will be located, Fig. 9-5.

A control point is needed to determine the depth of excavation and foundation wall height. The corner with the highest elevation is usually selected for this purpose. The foundation should be higher than the the grade - - usually about 8 inches.

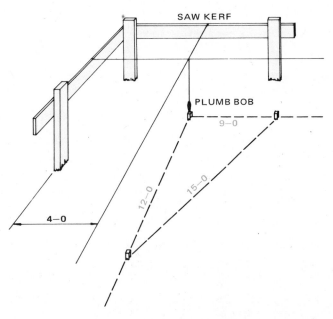

Fig. 9-3. Squaring a corner using the 9-12-15 unit method.

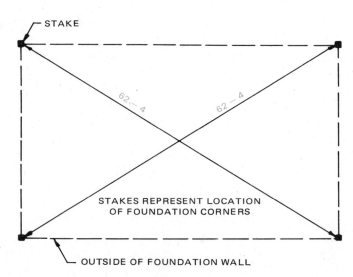

Fig. 9-4. The accuracy of layout may be checked by measuring the diagonals. They must be equal.

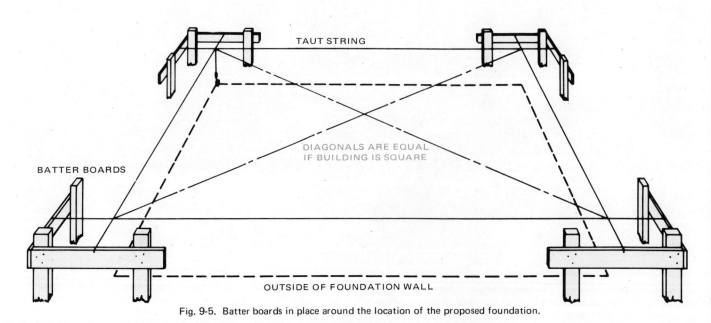

Fig. 9-5. Batter boards in place around the location of the proposed foundation.

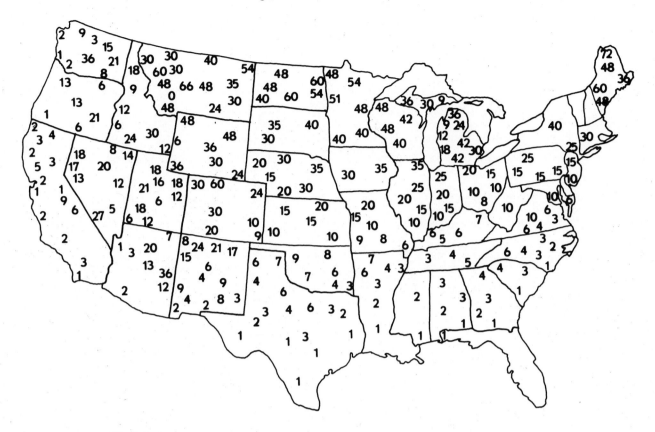

Fig. 9-6. Average depth of frost penetration in inches for locations throughout the United States. (U. S. Dept. of Commerce Weather Bureau)

EXCAVATION

In excavating for footings and foundation walls the top soil is usually removed using a bulldozer or tractor with a blade. This soil is saved for final grading. A trencher or backhoe may be used to excavate for foundations when either slab construction or crawl space is planned. In excavating for a basement, a backhoe or power shovel is generally used. Selection of excavating equipment is determined by the size of the excavation and type of soil.

Excavation for footings should extend down to a minimum of 6 in. into undisturbed earth. It must also be at least 6 in. below the average maximum frost penetration depth. See Fig. 9-6 for the frost depth in your area. Local codes usually specify the minimum footing depth for a given area.

No backfilling should be permitted under the proposed footings, because uneven settling of the house may occur. In instances where part of the footings bear on rock, about 6 in. of the rock should be removed under the proposed footing and replaced with compacted sand to equalize settling.

On sites which have recently been filled and regraded, it is recommended that the footings extend down to the original undisturbed earth. The exception is when soil tests prove that the earth is sufficiently compacted to properly support the structure.

Excavation must be large enough to allow space to work when constructing the foundation wall and laying drain tile. The steepness of the back slope will depend on the type of soil encountered. Sandy soil is likely to cave-in and therefore requires a gentle back slope, while excavating in clay may be nearly vertical.

FOOTING SHAPES AND SPECIFICATIONS

Footings increase the supporting capacity of the foundation wall by spreading the load over a larger area, Fig. 9-7. If a foundation was built on rock, a footing would not be necessary, however most houses are not built on such solid material and therefore need footings to support the heavy loads.

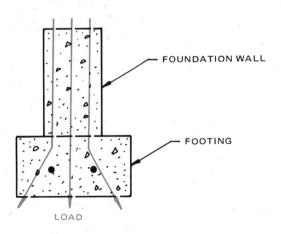

Fig. 9-7. The footing distributes the building weight over a broad area.

The size and type of footing should be suitable for the weight of the building and soil bearing capacity. Footings for most residential structures are made of poured concrete. The size of footing required is commonly determined by using the foundation wall thickness as a basis for its proportions. Fig. 9-8 illustrates the general proportions for a footing based on the foundation wall thickness. This size footing is designed for most normal soil conditions ranging from sand to clay.

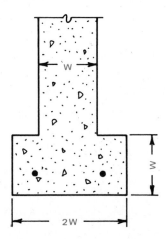

Fig. 9-8. General proportions of the footing as related to foundation wall thickness.

The footing thickness is equal to the foundation wall thickness and the footing width is twice the wall thickness. Foundation walls should be centered along the footing. Therefore, the footing will project beyond each side of the foundation wall a distance equal to one-half the thickness of the foundation wall. If the soil load bearing capacity is very poor, the size of footings should be increased and reinforced with steel.

During construction, the load increases on the footing which compresses the average subgrade soil. This compression causes a slight settlement of the structure. Whenever there are two or more different subsoils under various parts of the house, a variation in settlement may occur due to the unequal compressibility of the soil. Also, the weight of most homes is greater on two of the four walls which causes unequal loading. It is recommended that footings be large enough to minimize any of these differences in settlement to reduce cracking. Check your local code for recommended minimum footing size.

When footings must be located over soft or poorly drained soils, soils which are not uniform, or backfilled utility trenches, longitudinal reinforcement consisting of two No. 6 steel bars should be placed 2 in. from the bottom of the footing. The addition of continuous longitudinal reinforcing bars in the footings would be wise in most cases to provide further stability to the structure.

Footings for fireplaces and chimneys are more massive than regular house footings. They must support greater weight and are generally larger. A solid footing reinforced with steel is usually required. The footing should be 12 in. thick and extend 6 in. beyond the perimeter of the chimney on all sides.

The chimney footing should be cast integrally with the foundation wall footing if the chimney is located on an outside wall.

Stepped footings are frequently necessary when building on hilly terrain, Fig. 9-9. If stepped footings are required, the steps should be placed horizontally and the height of the vertical step should not be more than three-fourths of the distance between the steps. Step height and length should be multiples of 8 in. if the foundation is made of concrete block. Good building practice requires two 1/2 in. steel rods in the horizontal and vertical footing where steps are located. If steel rod is not used, the footing will very likely crack at these points.

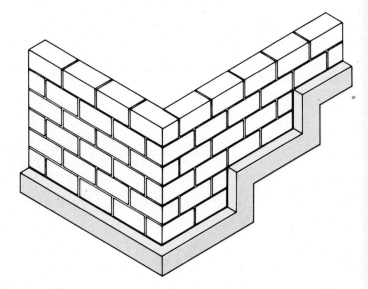

Fig. 9-9. A stepped footing and foundation wall for a sloping site.

FOUNDATION WALLS

Foundation walls are normally that part of the house which extends from the first floor to the footing. A foundation wall may also be a basement wall. Materials used to build foundation walls include cast (poured) concrete, brick, concrete block and stone in rare instances. Cast concrete and concrete block are widely used in residential structures. Brick is much more expensive than cast concrete or block and is seldom used. Stone was once used extensively, but is no longer of significance as a foundation material. Fig. 9-10 illustrates these common foundation materials in section.

Foundation walls are of three basic types: the T foundation, slab foundation and pier or post foundation, Fig. 9-11. The type chosen for a particular situation will depend upon the weight to be supported, load bearing capacity of the soil, location of the foundation in the building, climate and local codes. All should be considered when designing a foundation.

T FOUNDATIONS

The most common foundation type is the T foundation. The name is derived from the shape of the foundation and

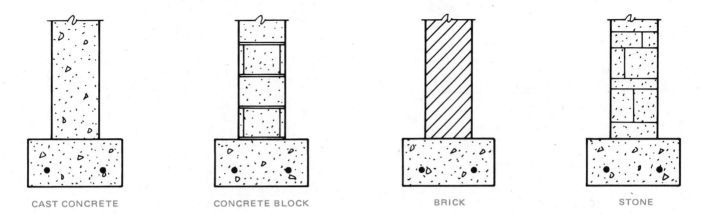

CAST CONCRETE   CONCRETE BLOCK   BRICK   STONE

Fig. 9-10. Materials commonly used for foundation walls.

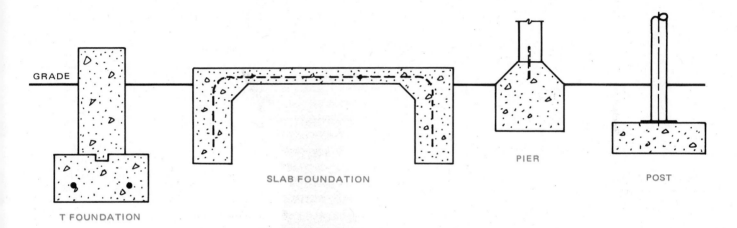

GRADE

T FOUNDATION   SLAB FOUNDATION   PIER   POST

Fig. 9-11. Common foundation types used in residential construction.

footing which looks like an inverted T. The foundation and footing are usually two separate parts but may be cast as a single unit.

Footings for the T foundation are usually poured in forms made from construction lumber, Fig. 9-12. The form boards are nailed to stakes once they are level. Stakes prevent movement while the concrete is being poured.

Fig. 9-13 shows several applications of the T foundation that are found in residential construction.

SLAB FOUNDATIONS

A slab foundation is an extension of a slab floor. It is poured at the same time the floor is poured and is not a separate unit. It is sometimes called a thickened edge slab. The foundation wall should extend down below the frost line, as in the case of the T foundation. Use of steel reinforcing rods or mesh is recommended for the slab foundation to prevent cracking due to settling.

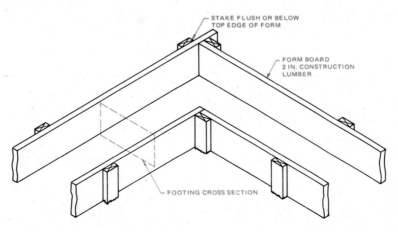

STAKE FLUSH OR BELOW
TOP EDGE OF FORM

FORM BOARD
2 IN. CONSTRUCTION
LUMBER

FOOTING CROSS SECTION

Fig. 9-12. Footings are usually poured using form boards made from construction lumber.

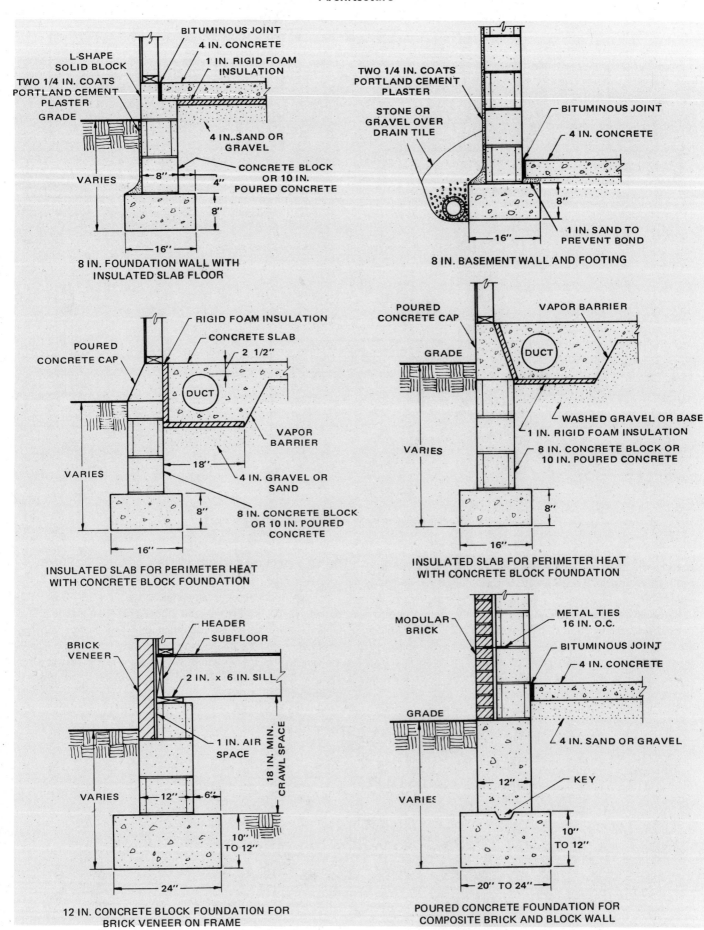

Fig. 9-14. Typical foundation details. (Continued)

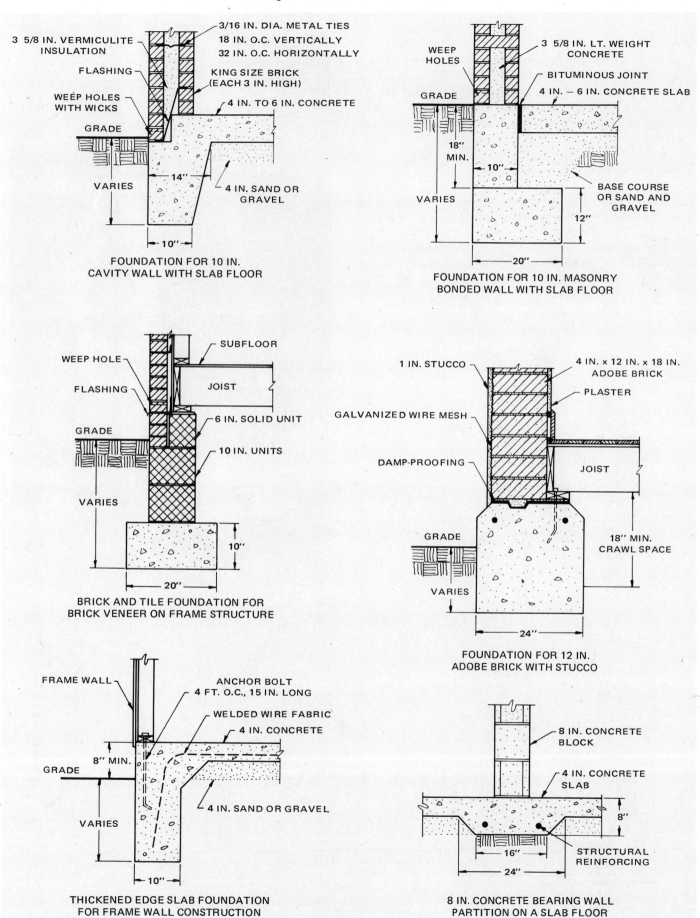

Foundation for 10 in. cavity wall with slab floor
3 5/8 IN. VERMICULITE INSULATION
FLASHING
WEEP HOLES WITH WICKS
GRADE
VARIES
3/16 IN. DIA. METAL TIES 18 IN. O.C. VERTICALLY 32 IN. O.C. HORIZONTALLY
KING SIZE BRICK (EACH 3 IN. HIGH)
4 IN. TO 6 IN. CONCRETE
14"
4 IN. SAND OR GRAVEL
10"
FOUNDATION FOR 10 IN. CAVITY WALL WITH SLAB FLOOR

Foundation for 10 in. masonry bonded wall
WEEP HOLES
GRADE
18" MIN.
VARIES
3 5/8 IN. LT. WEIGHT CONCRETE
BITUMINOUS JOINT
4 IN. – 6 IN. CONCRETE SLAB
10"
BASE COURSE OR SAND AND GRAVEL
12"
20"
FOUNDATION FOR 10 IN. MASONRY BONDED WALL WITH SLAB FLOOR

Brick and tile foundation
WEEP HOLE
FLASHING
GRADE
VARIES
SUBFLOOR
JOIST
6 IN. SOLID UNIT
10 IN. UNITS
10"
20"
BRICK AND TILE FOUNDATION FOR BRICK VENEER ON FRAME STRUCTURE

Foundation for 12 in. adobe brick
1 IN. STUCCO
GALVANIZED WIRE MESH
DAMP-PROOFING
GRADE
VARIES
4 IN. x 12 IN. x 18 IN. ADOBE BRICK
PLASTER
JOIST
18" MIN. CRAWL SPACE
24"
FOUNDATION FOR 12 IN. ADOBE BRICK WITH STUCCO

Thickened edge slab foundation
FRAME WALL
GRADE
8" MIN.
VARIES
ANCHOR BOLT 4 FT. O.C., 15 IN. LONG
WELDED WIRE FABRIC
4 IN. CONCRETE
4 IN. SAND OR GRAVEL
10"
THICKENED EDGE SLAB FOUNDATION FOR FRAME WALL CONSTRUCTION

8 in. concrete bearing wall
8 IN. CONCRETE BLOCK
4 IN. CONCRETE SLAB
8"
16"
24"
STRUCTURAL REINFORCING
8 IN. CONCRETE BEARING WALL PARTITION ON A SLAB FLOOR

Fig. 9-14. (Continued) Typical foundation details.

Some of the primary advantages of the slab foundation are that it requires less time, expense and labor to construct. Since no separate footing is required excavation is not as extensive as for the T foundation. Less time is required since the entire foundation and floor is cast in one operation. Examples and dimensions of the slab foundations are illustrated in Fig. 9-14. Note that this type foundation is also used for bearing wall partitions.

PIER AND POST FOUNDATIONS

Many situations in residential construction lend themselves to the use of piers, columns and posts. Frequently it is cheaper and just as satisfactory to use piers rather than the T foundation under parts of the building. For instance, when a crawl space is planned and the distance is too great for a single span, the pier foundation is a logical choice, Fig. 9-15.

Fig. 9-16. An aluminum lally column being put into place. Note the concrete footing for the column.

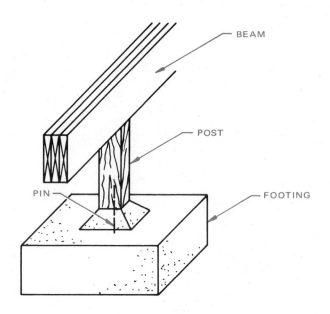

Fig. 9-15. Pier designed to support a heavy load.

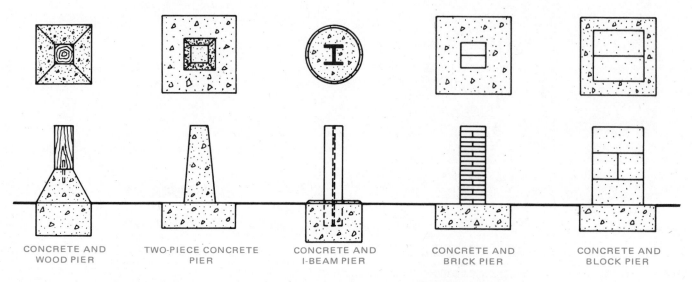

| CONCRETE AND WOOD PIER | TWO-PIECE CONCRETE PIER | CONCRETE AND I-BEAM PIER | CONCRETE AND BRICK PIER | CONCRETE AND BLOCK PIER |

Fig. 9-17. Piers may be constructed using a variety of techniques and materials.

Another common application which involves columns is in a basement or garage where the distance is too great to span with floor joists. Lally columns are used to support a beam which in turn supports the joists, rather than construct a bearing wall partition, Fig. 9-16.

The basic difference between a pier and column is the length. Piers are usually much shorter and ordinarily located under the house. Fig. 9-17 illustrates a few of the common types of piers used in residential construction.

The column is composed of two pieces; a footing and post, Fig. 9-18. The footing is usually square or rectangular with a minimum thickness of 8 in. for one-story construction and a minimum projection of 5 in. beyond the face of the column. Two-story homes require a minimum thickness of 12 in. and a minimum projection of 7 in. beyond the face of the column. The post may be masonry, steel or wood. If wood is used, it should be pressure treated to resist decay.

MINIMUM THICKNESS OF BASEMENT WALLS*			
Type of Unit	Minimum Wall Thickness, In. (Nominal)	Maximum Height of Unbalanced Fill, Ft.**	
		Frame Superstructure	Masonry and Masonry Veneer Superstructure
Hollow load-bearing	8†	5	5
	10	6	7
	12	7	7
Solid load-bearing	8†	5	7
	10	7	7
	12	7	7

*Basement walls should be at least as thick as the walls supported immediately above except as noted below.
**Heights shown may be increased to 7 ft. with approval of building official if justified by soil conditions and local experience.
†If the 8 in. basement wall supports an 8 in. wall, the combined height should not exceed 35 ft. If it supports brick veneer on wood frame or a 10 in. cavity wall, it may be corbeled out a maximum of 2 in. with solid units; but the total height of wall supported, including the gable, should not exceed 25 ft. Individual corbels should not project more than 1/3 the height of the unit. If a concrete first floor is used, it helps provide adequate bearing for these walls and corbeling can be omitted.
(Portland Cement Assoc.)

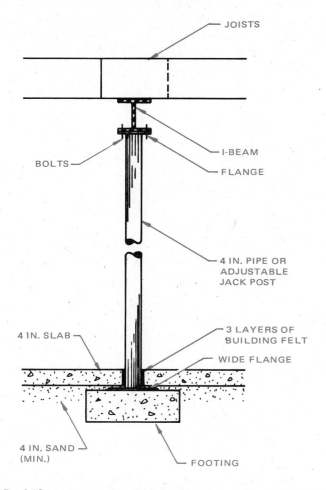

Fig. 9-18. A pipe or adjustable jack post is frequently used to support an I-beam.

JOISTS
BOLTS
I-BEAM
FLANGE
4 IN. PIPE OR ADJUSTABLE JACK POST
4 IN. SLAB
3 LAYERS OF BUILDING FELT
WIDE FLANGE
4 IN. SAND (MIN.)
FOOTING

BASEMENT WALLS

Concrete and masonry basement wall thickness depends on lateral earth pressure and vertical load to be supported. Recommended minimum thickness at various depths below grade are shown in the following chart.

These dimensions are based on conventional residential construction and average soils. The height of the unbalanced fill is measured from the finished grade (exterior) to the basement floor.

Several factors influence the strength and stability of a concrete or masonry basement wall to resist earth pressure. They include: height and thickness, the bond of the mortar, vertical loading, support from crosswalls, pilasters or wall stiffeners, and support provided by the first-floor framing. Lateral earth pressure may vary from almost zero to an amount equal to the hydrostatic pressure of a liquid with the density of mud.

When local conditions indicate strong earth pressures, pilasters, Fig. 9-19, can be used to strengthen the basement wall. Pilasters must be built at the same time the basement wall is laid. Pilaster block are frequently used for such construction. They should have a minimum width of 16 in. and project 8 in. inside an 8 in. thick basement wall. Ten inch basement walls will have a 6 in. inside projection. With 12 in. concrete masonry basement walls, pilasters or other wall stiffeners are not usually required. In 8 in. thick walls over 30 ft. long, the distance between pilasters should not be greater than 15 ft. In 10 in. thick walls over 36 ft. long, this distance should not be greater than 18 ft. Pilasters are also used for additional support for girders or beams.

Wall stiffeners provide another method of strengthing the walls. This is accomplished by placing a No. 4 bar in one core of the block from the top of the wall to the footing and filling the core with concrete.

A third procedure is to use continuous horizontal steel joint reinforcement at 16 in. intervals vertically. This method will provide additional lateral support to the basement wall and help prevent cracking.

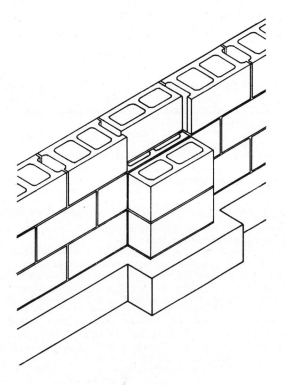

Fig. 9-19. Pilasters add strength to a basement wall and may be used to support a beam.

concrete walls may be dampproofed with a heavy coat of hot tar or two coats of cement based paints, commercially prepared specifically for dampproofing basements. This is applied from the grade line to the footing. Concrete block walls are dampproofed by applying two 1/4 in. thick coats of cement-mortar or plaster to the wall and then covered with hot tar, or a similar material when the cement is dry. This is called a parge coat (a thin coat of plaster over the foundation wall). In both instances, 4 in. drain tiles with open joints are used around the perimeter of the footing to remove excess ground water and reduce the chance of water problems, Fig. 9-21. The tile is covered with course stone or gravel to a depth of about 18 in. to allow water to seep into the tile. A piece of roofing shingle or tar impregnated felt is used to cover the joint between tiles. A newer plastic, continuous tile is also being used in some localities. It is easier and faster to install and appears to function as well as cement tiles.

In poorly drained and wet soils, added precautions may be advisable to insure against water damage. A sump pump may be installed in the basement to remove any water which seeps in. The floor slab may be reinforced to resist uplift by ground water pressure. A check valve in the floor drain will prevent water from flowing in through the drain.

Basement walls should extend at least 8 in. above the finished grade when using wood frame construction. Wood sills should be anchored to the basement walls with bolts 1/2 in. by 15 in. long and spaced approximately 8 ft. apart. Each sill piece should have at least two anchor bolts. Anchor bolts are placed in the cores of the top two courses of masonry and filled with mortar or concrete. Core filling may be supported by a piece of metal lath or similar material.

Basement walls may be slightly shorter than first and second floor walls. The distance from the top of the basement floor to the bottom of the floor joists above should be no less than 7 ft. A basement wall which is 11 courses above the footing with a 4 in. solid cap will provide a clear height of 7 ft. 5 in. from finished floor to the bottom of the floor joists, Fig. 9-20. This distance is more desirable since some space will generally be required for heating ducts, pipes and beams.

Load bearing crosswalls in the basement should not be tied to the exterior walls in a masonry bond. Instead, they should be anchored with metal tiebars. The tiebars are usually 1/4 in. thick, 1 1/4 in. wide, and 28 in. long. Each end has a 2 in. right-angle bend which is embedded in cores filled with mortar or concrete.

Floor loads are distributed more uniformly along the wall if the top course of block supporting the first floor is capped using: (1) 4 in. solid block, (2) solid top block, in which the hollow cores do not extend up into the top 4 in. of the block, (3) reinforced concrete masonry bond beam, or (4) cores in the top course filled with concrete or mortar. When the wood sill bears on both the inner and outer face shells of the block, capping may be omitted.

Basement walls require dampproofing on the outside to prevent ground water from seeping through the wall. Poured

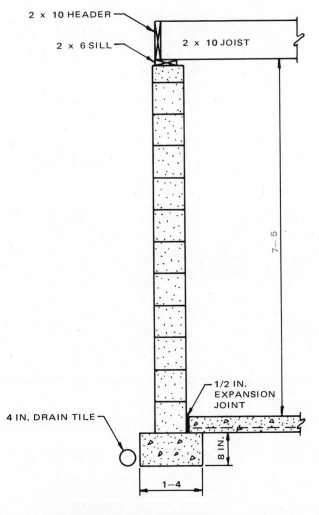

2 x 10 HEADER

2 x 6 SILL

2 x 10 JOIST

7—5

1/2 IN. EXPANSION JOINT

4 IN. DRAIN TILE

8 IN.

1—4

Fig. 9-20. A basement wall which provides a desirable floor to ceiling height.

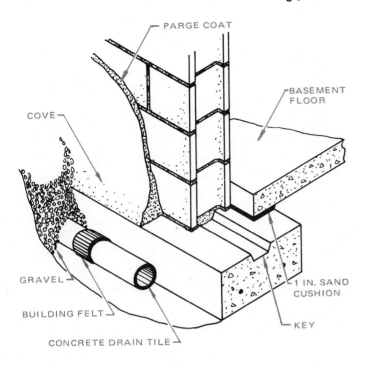

Fig. 9-21. A basement wall may be dampproofed by the application of a parge coat and drain tiles placed along the footing.

BEAMS AND GIRDERS

The size of most residences is such that the span is too great to use unsupported floor joists. Therefore, a beam or girder is required to support the joists and prevent excessive sagging. The beam is usually placed an equal distance from each outside wall or under a bearing wall. A bearing wall is designed to support part of the load of the structure.

Beams may be either wood or metal. Wood beams are of two types; built-up and solid. Built-up beams are used more frequently than solid ones because they are easier to handle, more readily available and do not check to the extent of solid beams. However, solid beams are generally stronger and more fire resistant.

Two types of steel beams are commonly used. These are: American Standard I-Beams and Wide Flange I-Beams, Fig. 9-22. The wide flange beam will support greater strength and is

AMERICAN
STANDARD
I-BEAM

WIDE FLANGE
I-BEAM

Fig. 9-22. Typical I-beams used in home construction.

more stable than the standard I-beam. For these reasons it is becoming more popular.

Calculation of the size beam needed is based on the weight of the structure, Fig. 9-23. Weights are designated either as live

loads or dead loads. Live loads are those fixed or moving weights, which are not a structural part of the house. Examples include furniture, occupants, snow on the roof, wind, etc. Dead loads are those static or fixed weights of the structure itself. Examples of dead loads are the weights of

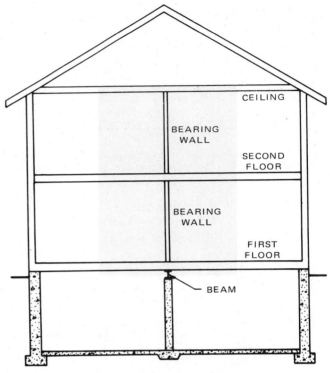

Fig. 9-23. Weight represented by the shaded area is supported by the I-beam.

roofing, foundation walls, siding, joists, etc. To simplify matters, it will be assumed that loads found in a typical residence are as follows.

FIRST FLOOR
Live load plus dead load = 50 pounds per square foot.

SECOND FLOOR
Live load plus dead load = 50 pounds per square foot.

CEILING
Live load plus dead load = 30 pounds per square foot.

WALLS
Dead load = 10 pounds per square foot.

ROOF
No load on the beam. Exterior walls generally support the roof.

Use these figures for load calculations.

WEIGHT CALCULATIONS
The example used is for a two-story frame structure which is 28'-0" x 40'-0". Fig. 9-24 shows the foundation walls and beam.

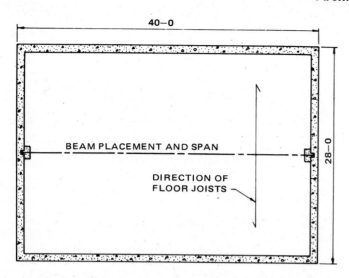

Fig. 9-24. A foundation wall with dimensions of 28'-0" x 40'-0" showing the direction of joists and placement of supporting beam.

Width x length = Area of the house.
28' x 40' = 1120 sq. ft. for each floor.
8' x 40' = 320 sq. ft. of wall area for each wall.

(This calculation assumes a bearing wall running the length of the house on both floors.)

Weight per sq. ft. x number of sq. ft. = total weight

Weight of first floor
(1120 sq. ft. x 50 lbs./sq. ft.) = 56,000 pounds
Weight of second floor
(1120 sq. ft. x 50 lbs./sq. ft.) = 56,000 pounds
Weight of ceiling
(1120 sq. ft. x 30 lbs./sq. ft.) = 33,600 pounds
Weight of roof on beam
(none in this example) = 0 pounds
Total = 145,600 pounds

One-half of the total weight bears on the center beam.
(1/2 x 145,600 pounds) = 72,800 pounds
Weight of first floor wall
(320 sq. ft. x 10 lbs./sq. ft.) = 3,200 pounds
Weight of second floor wall
(320 sq. ft. x 10 lbs./sq. ft.) = 3,200 pounds
Weight bearing on beam = 79,200 pounds

MAXIMUM ALLOWABLE UNIFORM LOADS FOR AMERICAN STANDARD I-BEAMS WITH LATERAL SUPPORT

SPAN IN FEET

SIZE OF BEAM	WEIGHT OF BEAM PER FT.	4	6	8	10	12	14	16	18	20	22	24	26	28	30	32	34	36	38	40
4 x 2 3/4	7.7	10	7	5																
	9.5	11	7	6																
5 x 3	10.0	16	11	8	6															
	11.3	20	13	10	8															
6 x 3 1/8	12.5	24	16	12	10	8														
	17.3	29	19	15	12	10														
7 x 3 3/4	15.3	35	23	17	14	12	10													
	20.0	40	27	20	16	15	13													
8 x 4	18.4	47	32	24	19	16	14	12												
	23.0	53	36	27	21	18	15	13												
10 x 4 3/4	25.4	80	54	41	33	27	23	20	18	16										
	35.0	97	65	49	39	32	28	24	22	20										
12 x 5	31.8	110	80	60	48	40	34	30	27	24	22	20								
	35.0	126	84	63	50	42	36	32	28	25	23	21								
12 x 5 1/4	40.8	144	100	75	60	50	43	37	33	30	27	25								
	50.0	168	112	84	67	56	48	42	37	34	31	28								
15 x 5 1/2	42.9	160	131	98	79	65	56	49	44	39	36	33	30	28	26	25				
	50.0	214	143	107	86	71	61	54	48	43	39	36	33	31	29	27				
18 x 6	54.7		196	147	118	98	84	74	66	59	54	49	45	42	39	37	35	33	31	
	70.0		226	170	136	113	97	85	76	68	62	57	52	49	45	43	40	38	36	
20 x 6 1/4	65.4		260	195	156	130	111	97	87	78	71	65	60	56	52	49	46	43	41	39
	75.0		281	211	169	140	120	105	94	84	77	70	65	60	56	53	50	47	44	42

LOADS ARE IN KIPS. 1 KIP = 1,000 POUNDS   (American Institute of Steel Construction)

Fig. 9-25. Span and load table for American Standard I-Beams.

SIZE OF BEAM	WEIGHT OF BEAM PER FT.	4	6	8	9	10	12	14	18	20	22	24	26	28	30	32	34	36	38	40
8 x 5 1/4	17	47	31	24	19	16	13	12												
8 x 6 1/2	24		46	35	28	23	20	17												
8 x 8	31		60	46	37	30	26	23	20	18	16									
10 x 5 1/4	21	62	48	36	29	24	21	18	16	14										
10 x 8	33		74	58	47	39	33	29	26	23										
10 x 10	49			88	73	61	52	46	40	36	33	30	28	26						
12 x 6 1/2	27		74	57	45	38	32	28	25	23	21	19								
12 x 8	40		87	69	58	49	43	38	35	32	29									
12 x 10	53			108	94	79	67	59	52	47	43	39								
12 x 12	65				117	98	84	73	65	59	53	49	45	42	39					
14 x 6 3/4	30		93	70	56	46	40	35	31	28	25	23	21	20	19					
14 x 8	43			105	84	70	60	52	46	42	38	35	32	30	28					
14 x 10	61				123	102	88	77	68	62	56	51	47	44	41					
14 x 12	78				156	135	115	101	90	81	73	67	62	58	54					
14 x 14 1/2	87						152	132	115	102	92	84	77	71	66	61	57	54	51	
16 x 7	36		124	94	75	63	54	47	42	38	34	31	29	27	25	24	22			
16 x 8 1/2	58			157	126	105	90	78	70	63	57	52	48	45	42	39	37			
16 x 11 1/2	88				202	168	144	126	112	101	92	84	78	72	67	63	59			
18 x 7 1/2	50			148	119	99	85	74	66	59	54	49	46	42	40	37	35	33	31	
18 x 8 3/4	64			188	156	130	111	98	87	78	71	65	60	56	52	49	46	43	41	
18 x 11 3/4	96				224	189	176	154	137	123	112	103	95	88	82	77	72	68	65	
21 x 8 1/4	62			211	169	141	120	105	94	84	77	70	65	60	56	53	50	47	44	42

MAXIMUM ALLOWABLE UNIFORM LOADS FOR WIDE FLANGE I-BEAMS WITH LATERAL SUPPORT
SPAN IN FEET

LOADS ARE IN KIPS. 1 KIP = 1,000 POUNDS   (American Institute of Steel Construction)

Fig. 9-26. Span and load table for Wide Flange I-Beams.

Tables giving the greatest safe loads which beams will support usually record the weight in kips. One kip equals 1,000 pounds. Fig. 9-25 presents span data for American Standard I-Beams. Fig. 9-26 presents span data for Wide Flange I-Beams. Loads shown are based on a fiber stress of 20,000 pounds, or pressure they will withstand per square inch. This stress is usually sufficient for common residential construction situations.

The length of beam needed in the example is 40 feet. If no posts were used, the span would be 40 feet. From previous calculations, the weight bearing on the beam was found to be 79,200 pounds. This weight is represented by the shaded area in Fig. 9-23. Convert 79,200 pounds into kips by dividing the weight by 1000. The weight then is 79.2 kips. Looking at the span data presented in Figs. 9-25 and 9-26, we find that an American Standard I-Beam would have to be 24" x 7 7/8" and weigh 120.0 pounds per foot to support 84 kips. A Wide Flange I-Beam would be 24" x 12" and weigh 100 pounds per foot to support 83 kips. One can see that such a huge beam is not feasible. The logical course of action would be to shorten the span by adding one or more post supports. Study the chart below and Figs. 9-27, 9-28 and 9-29, and note how the beam size and weight on the beam decreases with the addition of post supports.

COMPARISON DATA FOR EXAMPLE

	Span	Weight On Beam	Size of Beam and Weight	Kips Beam Will Support
No Post				
A. S. I-Beam	40'-0"	79.2 kips	24" x 7 7/8" x 120.0 lbs./ft.	84 kips
W. F. I-Beam	40'-0"	79.2 kips	24" x 12" x 100.0 lbs./ft.	83 kips
One Post (Fig. 9-27)				
A. S. I-Beam	20'-0"	39.6 kips	15" x 5 1/2" x 50.0 lbs./ft.	43 kips
W. F. I-Beam	20'-0"	39.6 kips	14" x 8" x 43.0 lbs./ft.	42 kips
Two Posts (Fig. 9-28)				
A. S. I-Beam	13'-4"	26.4 kips	10" x 4 3/4" x 35.0 lbs./ft.	28 kips
W. F. I-Beam	13'-4"	26.4 kips	8" x 8" x 31.0 lbs./ft.	26 kips
Three Posts (Fig. 9-29)				
A. S. I-Beam	10'-0"	19.8 kips	8" x 4" x 23.0 lbs./ft.	21 kips
W. F. I-Beam	10'-0"	19.8 kips	8" x 6 1/2" x 24.0 lbs./ft.	23 kips

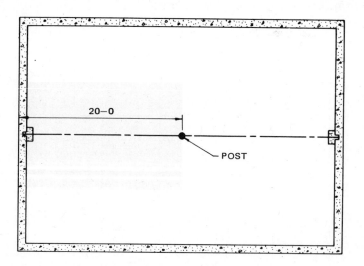

Fig. 9-27. The effective beam span with one post. The shaded area represents the weight supported by the 20'-0" beam section.

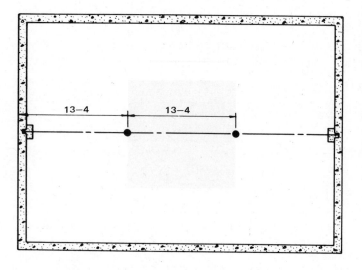

Fig. 9-28. The effective beam span with two posts. The span is 13'-4".

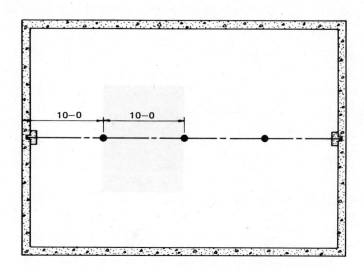

Fig. 9-29. Three supporting posts reduces the effective span to 10'-0".

Any one of the beams above would support the load of the structure. However, steel is sold by the pound, so it is desirable to choose the smallest beam which will adequately do the job with a reasonable span.

Once the size of beam and number of post supports have been determined, the size of each post must be calculated. This procedure is not as complex as the procedure for figuring beam sizes. In the previous calculation it was determined that if three posts were used, each beam segment or 10'-0" span would be required to support 19.8 kips or 19,800 pounds. This is the same weight that the center post must support since it must bear the weight on either side, half way to the next post. See Fig. 9-30 for a graphic representation of the load supported by the center post.

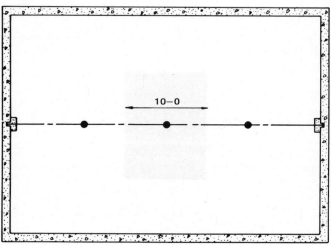

Fig. 9-30. Each post must support the weight represented by the shaded area.

Steel post design information is presented in Fig. 9-31. The size post needed is determined by finding the weight to be supported and length of the post needed on the chart. (Loads are recorded in kips.) In the example, the weight is 19,800 pounds or 19.8 kips and the unbraced length is 8 feet. The smallest column shown on the chart (nominal size of 3 in.) is more than adequate since it will support 34,000 pounds. Therefore, the support posts should be 3 inches in diameter and weigh 7.58 pounds per foot.

Steel posts must have a flange welded on both ends and provision for attachment to the beam. It may be bolted or attached with clips. The bottom flange (8" x 8") should be larger than the top flange to provide a larger bearing surface on the footing. Size of the top flange will be determined by the width of the beam to be supported.

LINTELS

A lintel is a horizontal structural member that supports the load over an opening such as a door or window. Lintels may be constructed of precast concrete, poured concrete, lintel blocks or angle steel, Fig. 9-32. When lintels are used in a masonry wall, the ends must extend at least 4 in. into the wall on either

NOMINAL SIZE IN INCHES	WEIGHT PER FT. IN POUNDS	UNBRACED LENGTH IN FEET									
		6	7	8	9	10	11	12	14	16	18
3	7.58	38	36	34	31	28	25	22	16	12	10
3 1/2	9.11	48	46	44	41	38	35	32	25	19	15
4	10.79	59	57	54	52	49	46	43	36	29	23
5	14.62	83	81	78	76	73	71	68	61	55	47
6	18.97	110	108	106	103	101	98	95	89	82	75

Table title: MAXIMUM ALLOWABLE CONCENTRIC LOADS FOR STANDARD STEEL PIPE COLUMNS

LOADS ARE IN KIPS. 1 KIP = 1,000 POUNDS
(American Institute of Steel Construction)

Fig. 9-31. Load table for standard steel pipe columns.

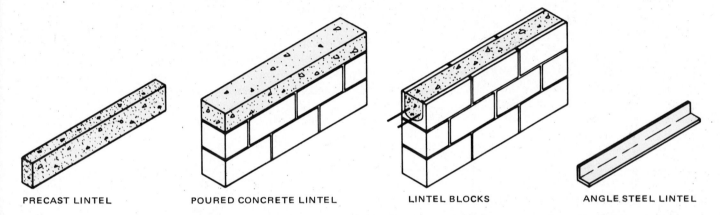

PRECAST LINTEL   POURED CONCRETE LINTEL   LINTEL BLOCKS   ANGLE STEEL LINTEL

Fig. 9-32. Four types of lintels frequently used in residential building construction.

side of the opening. Fig. 9-33 shows a precast lintel over a door in a concrete block wall. Common precast lintel sizes for residential construction are 4" x 8", 4" x 6" and 8" x 8". They are produced in a variety of lengths.

Lintels are also made of angle steel. They are available as equal angles (both legs the same size) or as unequal angles. The chart below identifies the size of angle required to support a 4 in. masonry wall above an opening.

**STEEL ANGLES TO SUPPORT
4 IN. MASONRY WALLS**

Span	Size of Angle
0'–5'	3" x 3" x 1/4"
5'–9'	3 1/2" x 3 1/2" x 5/16"
9'–10'	4" x 4" x 5/16"
10'–11'	4" x 4" x 3/8"
11'–15'	6" x 4" x 3/8"
15'–16'	6" x 4" x 1/2"

Fig. 9-34 shows a steel lintel supporting brick over a window opening.

CONCRETE AND MASONRY

The average modern home requires many yards of concrete. Fortunately, most contractors today are near a ready-mix

plant. Concrete is ordered by the cubic yard and the consistency is generally specified by how many bags of cement are contained in each yard of mix. A "five-bag mix" is considered minimum for most jobs while a "six-bag mix" will produce a stronger product and should be used when high strength or reinforcing is required.

Concrete is the result of combining cement, sand, aggregate (usually stone or gravel) and water. Cement is composed of a

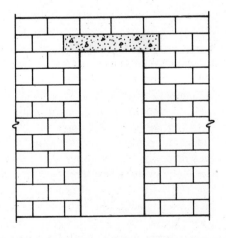

Fig. 9-33. A precast lintel in a masonry wall supporting the weight above a door opening.

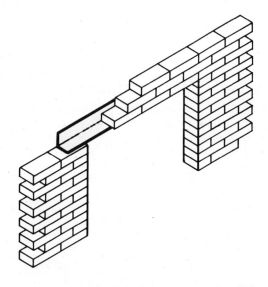

Fig. 9-34. A steel angle lintel in a brick wall.

mixture of lime, silica, alumina, iron components and gypsum. The proportions of the ingredients will vary with the requirements. However, sidewalks, driveways, footings and basement floors usually contain one part cement, three parts sand and five parts aggregate. Footings as well as concrete floors must have both a minimum compressive strength of 3,000 psi and a minimum cement content of 5 bags (470 lbs.) per cubic yard. The amount of water used will most likely be 6 or 7 gallons for each bag of cement (normally 94 pounds per bag).

Concrete cures over a long period of time and should be kept moist for several days after pouring. Failure to do this reduces strength and may harm the exposed surface. Temperature also affects the setup time of concrete. Cold weather slows down the process and concrete should not be allowed to freeze before it has set up.

When concrete is being poured, it commonly traps air pockets within the mixture. It is necessary to work these air pockets out by vibrating or tamping. This action helps to form a more dense material and removes weak spots due to air pockets.

After the concrete has been poured, a SCREED is used to smooth the surface. The screed is a long straightedge, usually a board, which is worked back and forth across the surface. This action brings excess water to the surface and settles the aggregate. Power screeds are also available for large jobs.

When screeding is finished, the surface is then worked over with a FLOAT. A float is a short board about a foot long with a handle attached to one of the flat sides. The purpose of floating is: (1) to embed the large aggregate just beneath the surface, (2) to remove any slight imperfections, humps, and voids to produce a flat surface, and (3) to consolidate mortar at the surface in preparation for final steel-troweling. As the mixture reaches the proper consistency, the troweling process is begun. The TROWEL is rectangular and is used in a circular motion. This troweling action further hardens the surface and develops a very smooth finish. If a slightly rough surface is desired, it may be swept with a broom to accomplish the desired texture.

As was indicated earlier, concrete is purchased by the cubic yard. A cubic yard is 27 cubic feet. When ordering concrete, one should figure only 25 cubic feet to the yard. Some of the material will remain in the mixer, some will be spilled and forms may sag. Experience has shown that it is better to have a little more concrete than you need than to have too little.

Large areas of concrete are likely to crack from expansion and contraction due to changes in temperature and moisture content. This cracking may be minimized or controlled by introducing contraction joints. Contraction joints should be placed in line with interior columns, at changes in the width of the slab, or at maximum spacing of about 20 ft. These joints may be formed by cutting grooves in the freshly poured concrete with a jointing tool. They may also be cut into the slab with a power saw after the concrete has hardened. The depth of joints or grooves should be one-fourth the thickness of the slab.

A concrete slab is usually placed directly on firmly compacted sand 4 to 6 inches thick. Dry sand should be dampened to prevent absorption of too much mixing water from the fresh concrete. The slab base (sand) should be thoroughly compacted to prevent settlement of the slab. It should also be sloped toward the floor drains to ensure a uniform slab thickness. Floor slabs usually have a minimum thickness of 4 inches.

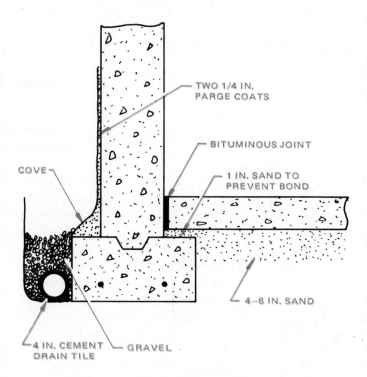

Fig. 9-35. Floor slabs should not be bonded to the footing or foundation wall.

Floor slabs should not be bonded to footings or interior columns. A sand cushion 1 in. thick may be used to separate the slab from the footing, Fig. 9-35. A sleeve of three thicknesses of building felt may be wrapped around columns to break the bond.

CONCRETE BLOCKS

Concrete blocks are used extensively in residential buildings. They are used to form exterior, and in some instances, interior walls. They may be purchased in a variety of sizes and shapes. In general terms, concrete blocks refer to hollow concrete masonry units, usually 8" x 8" x 16" in dimension. The actual size is 7 5/8" x 7 5/8" x 15 5/8". These dimensions allow for a 3/8 in. mortar joint. Therefore, the distance from the center line of one mortar joint to the center line of the next will be 8 or 16 inches. Fig. 9-36 shows a variety of concrete blocks that are frequently used in a residential structure.

A wide variety of decorative concrete blocks are available. They may be used to form a screen, fence or wall, Fig. 9-37. Use of decorative blocks should not be overlooked when searching for innovative materials. The application of concrete blocks is limited only to the designer's imagination.

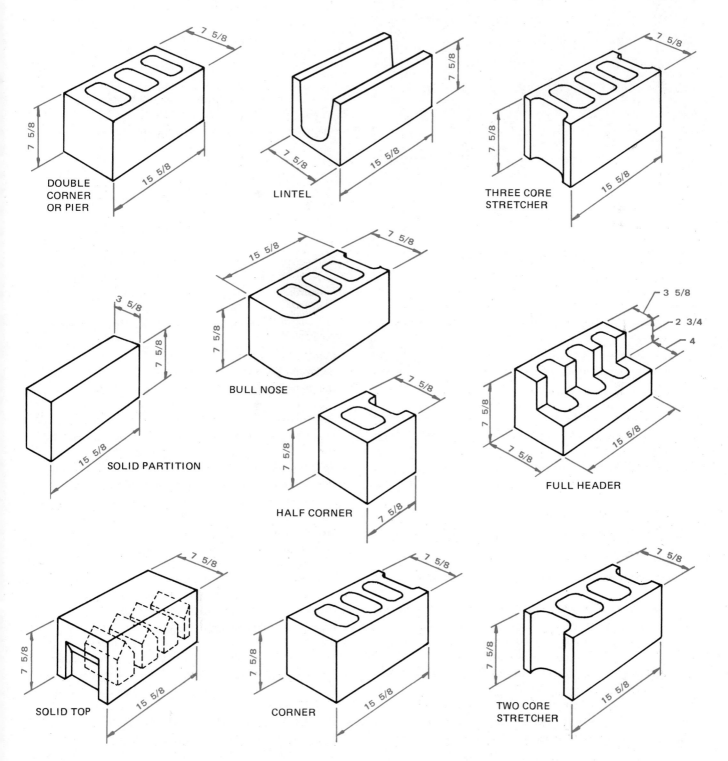

Fig. 9-36. Commonly used concrete blocks with actual sizes shown.

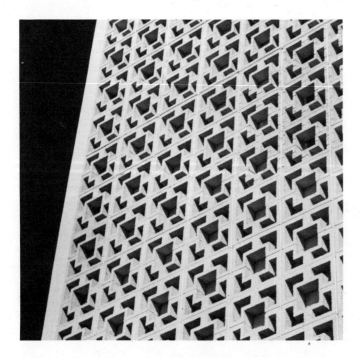

Fig. 9-37. Decorative concrete blocks may be used to add a new design dimension.

REVIEW QUESTIONS — CHAPTER 9

1. The necessary dimensions for staking out the house are found on the _____ plan.
2. What method may be used to check the accuracy of all corners of the house once it is staked out?
3. The purpose of batter boards is to _____.
4. The excavation must extend below the frost depth and down to _____.
5. The size and type of footing should be suitable for the weight of the building and _____.
6. The thickness of the footing is usually the same thickness as the _____.
7. Stepped footings are necessary when _____.
8. Cement may be reinforced using _____ inch steel rod.
9. The most common foundation type is the _____.
10. List two advantages of the slab foundation.
    a. _____.
    b. _____.
11. The basic difference between a pier and column is the _____.
12. The minimum clear height between a basement floor and ceiling should be _____.
13. Long basement walls may need added lateral support. A _____ is used to provide this support.
14. The materials commonly used to dampproof basement walls are _____ and _____.
15. When the span is too great to use unsupported floor joists, a _____ is used to provide this support.
16. Two types of I-beams used in residential construction are:
    a. _____.
    b. _____.

17. Weights are designated as live loads and dead loads. Snow on a roof is an example of a _____ load.
18. Safe loads which I-beams will support are usually given in _____.
19. A horizontal structural member which supports the load over an opening such as a door or window is known as a _____.
20. The ingredients in concrete are:
    a. _____.
    b. _____.
    c. _____.
    d. _____.
21. Temperature affects the curing time of concrete. Cold weather _____ the process.
22. A _____ is a long straightedge (board) which is worked back and forth to smooth concrete.
23. Large areas of concrete are likely to crack from expansion and contraction due to temperature change. This cracking may be minimized or controlled through the use of _____.
24. The nominal size of a concrete block is 8" x 8" x 16". The actual size of this block is _____.

SUGGESTED ACTIVITIES

1. Choose two or more friends and as a team stake out a one-car garage (12' x 20') using string, stakes and a 50' measuring tape. Use the 9-12-15 unit method of laying out a 90 deg. corner. (Refer to Fig. 9-3.) Check the accuracy of your work by measuring the diagonals. Record the diagonal measurement.
2. Using a carpenter's level on a stool or other fixed surface, determine the difference in elevation at the four corners of the garage which you staked out in number 1 above. Procedure: Have one member of the team hold a pole or strip of wood vertically, with bottom end resting on the ground, over one of the corner stakes. Sight down the level and have your partner make a mark on the pole even with your line of sight. Be sure the level is not tilted. Duplicate this procedure for each corner. Using the tape, measure the difference between the marks on the rod. These distances represent the variation in elevation. The same procedure can be done much more accurately with a contractor's level. Record your results.
3. Visit an excavation site for a residence in your community. Measure the depth and size of excavation. Determine the size of footings and thickness of foundation walls. Prepare a sketch of the foundation layout with dimensions. Note the type of soil supporting the footings.
4. Select a foundation plan of a small structure with a slab floor, such as a garage or storage building, and calculate the amount of concrete required to pour the footings, foundation wall and floor. Show your calculation and the foundation plan.
5. Calculate the size of I-beam and columns required to support a frame house with foundation dimensions of 34'-0" x 48'. The spacing of your columns should not exceed 12'-0" for this problem.

Chapter 10
THE FOUNDATION PLAN

DEFINITION AND PURPOSE

The foundation plan is a plan view drawing in section which shows the location and size of footings, piers, columns, foundation walls, and supporting beams. It is usually drawn after the floor plan and elevations have been roughed out. A foundation plan ordinarily includes the following:

Footings for foundation walls, piers and columns (hidden lines).

Foundation walls.

Piers and columns.

Dwarf walls (low walls built to retain an excavation or embankment).

Partition walls, doors and bath fixtures if the house has a basement.

Openings in foundation wall such as windows, doors and vents.

Beams and pilasters.

Direction, size and spacing of floor joists.

Drains, sump (if required).

Details of foundation and footing construction.

Complete dimensions and notes.

Scale of the drawing.

The foundation plan is prepared primarily for the excavator, masons and cement workers who build the foundation. Be sure to present the information they need to build the foundation. Symbols which are commonly used on a foundation plan are shown in Fig. 10-1.

PRELIMINARY STEPS TO DRAWING A FOUNDATION PLAN

The foundation is drawn from information presented on the floor plan, plot plan and elevations. It is important that dimensions on the foundation plan and floor plan are accurate and consistent. The preliminary floor plan may be used as an underlay for drawing the foundation plan. This procedure is common and usually reduces the time required to make the drawing. It also helps to keep errors to a minimum.

Before drawing the foundation plan, examine the floor plan to determine the type of exterior walls specified. This step is important because the dimensions of the foundation may not be the same for different types of exterior walls. For example, the foundation size will be larger for a brick veneer house than

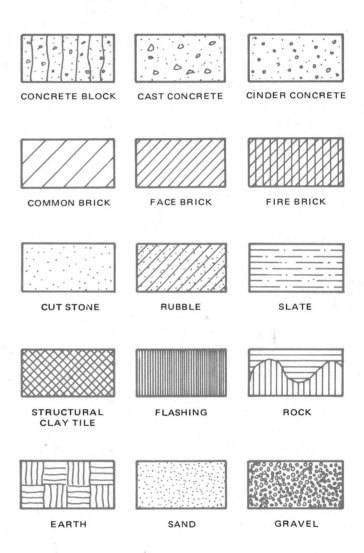

Fig. 10-1. Material symbols commonly used on a foundation plan.

a house with stud wall structure. The reason for the difference is that the basic house size is measured to the outside of the stud wall for both types of construction. A 4 in. brick ledge is required for the brick veneer house. This adds 8 in. to the length and width of the foundation. See Fig. 10-2.

The plot plan and elevation should also be examined to anticipate the need for stepped footings, retaining walls and problems related to the grade, Fig. 10-3.

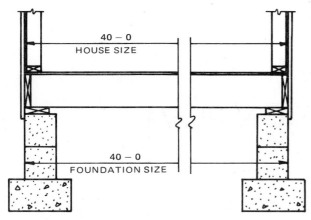

FRAME STRUCTURE

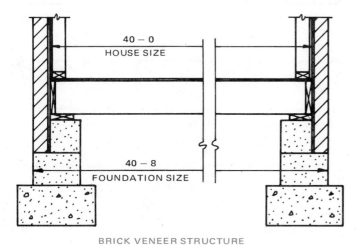

BRICK VENEER STRUCTURE

Fig. 10-2. A brick veneer house requires a foundation wall eight inches longer and wider than does a frame wall structure.

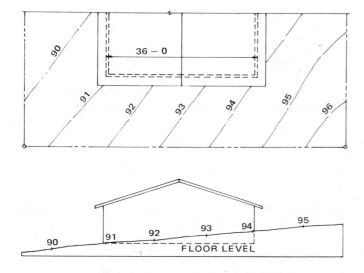

Fig. 10-3. No consideration for the existing grade has been made in this example. The finished floor level is below grade and most likely is in conflict with the building code.

Determine the size of footings and foundation walls required from information available. Check the frost penetration depth for the area where the house is to be built. Refer to the building code to be sure that all requirements are met, before proceeding. If the soil bearing capacity is questionable, have a soil bearing test made, Fig. 10-4.

Fig. 10-4. A soil test is being made to determine load bearing capacity.

DRAWING FOUNDATION PLAN

Drawing a foundation plan includes the following steps. Not all items will apply to every situation:

1. Select the scale to be used. Residential structures are usually drawn to 1/4" = 1' — 0" scale. Be sure to use the same size tracing sheets for all drawings in the set.
2. Locate the outline of the foundation walls on the paper allowing ample space for dimensions, notes and title block. Use the floor plan as an underlay or draw the foundation plan from dimensions obtained from the floor plan.
3. Draw the foundation walls, piers and columns and foundation for chimney (fireplace).
4. Indicate breaks in the foundation wall for windows, doors, access holes and vents. Steps 1 through 4 are shown in Fig. 10-5.
5. Lay out and draw the footings for the foundation walls. Use a hidden line symbol.
6. Draw the footings for the piers and columns.
7. Draw the footings for the fireplace and chimney.
8. Locate the supporting beam if one is required. Draw the beam using a thick center line symbol.
9. Show the size, spacing and direction of floor joists using

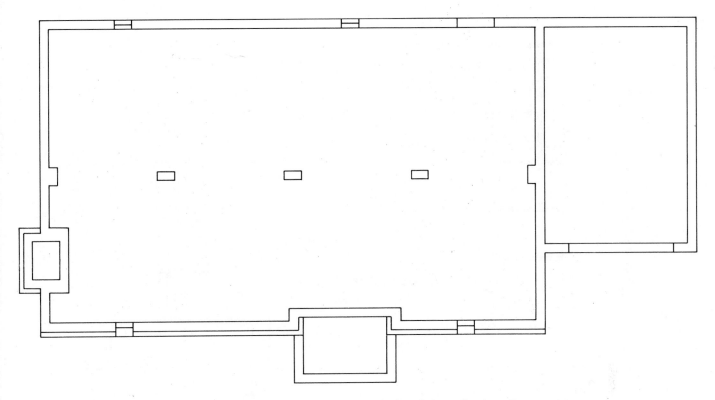

Fig. 10-5. A partially completed foundation plan which shows the foundation walls, piers, pilasters and vent openings.

the standard symbol.

10. Identify the location of sections needed to provide additional information. Steps 4 through 10 are shown in

Fig. 10-6 below.

11. Draw the necessary sections and dimension them as shown in Fig. 10-7.

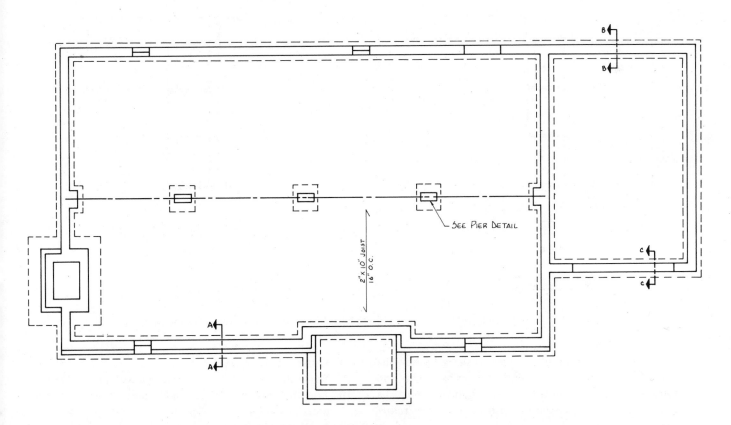

Fig. 10-6. Footings for the foundation walls and piers, supporting beam, section symbols and floor joist data have been added to the foundation plan.

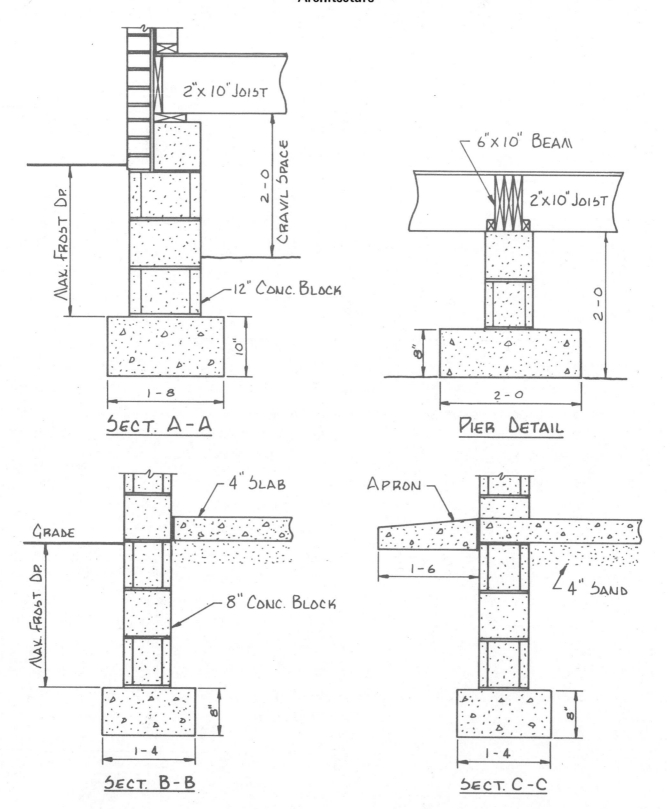

Fig. 10-7. Foundation details which are required to further describe the foundation construction.

12. Determine the location of dimensions needed to show the size of all aspects of the foundation. The length and thickness of all foundation wall segments must be dimensioned. Piers are dimensioned to the center rather than to the edge.

13. Draw the dimension lines and add dimensions.

14. Letter any necessary notes.

15. Shade the foundation wall drawings with proper symbols.

16. Add the title block, scale and name of drawing in the proper location.

17. Check drawing to be sure you have included all necessary information. Steps 12 through 17 are shown in Fig. 10-8.

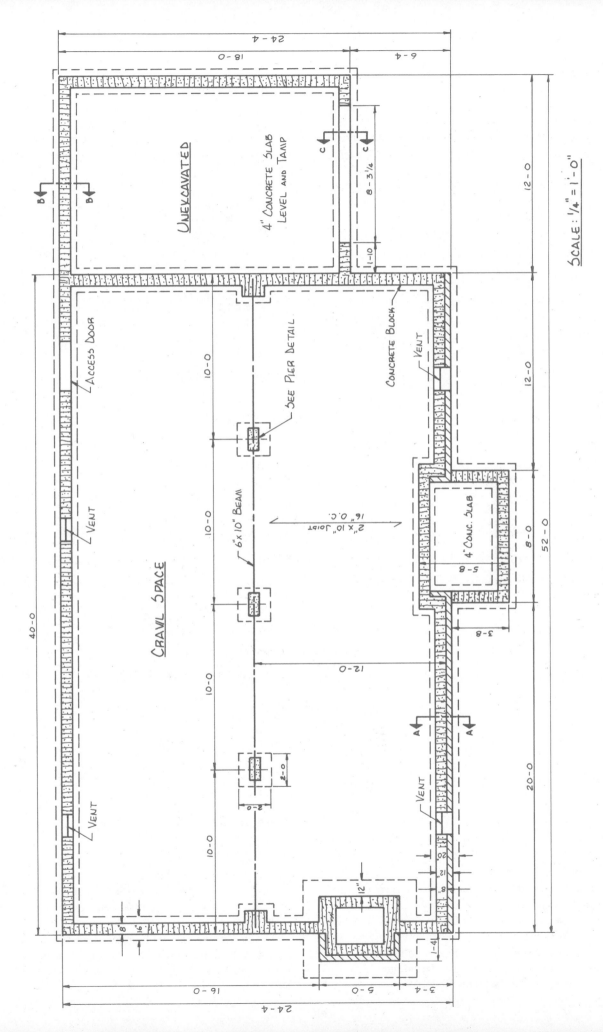

Fig. 10-8. The completed foundation plan showing dimensions, notes, foundation material symbol and scale. The house is frame with brick veneer along the front.

Architecture

THE BASEMENT/FOUNDATION PLAN

In cold climates where the frost penetration depth is several feet, basements are usually included in the plans. Since the footings must be below the frost depth, it is comparatively inexpensive to excavate the soil under the house and extend the foundation down a few more feet. This provides additional usable space at much less cost per square foot than the first floor level. Basements are also popular in areas where space is crowded and building sites are small.

PROCEDURE FOR DRAWING A BASEMENT PLAN

The procedure for drawing a basement plan is much the same as for a foundation plan except for the addition of several features. The following steps should help to clarify the procedure and insure the inclusion of all necessary information:

1. Select the proper scale to be used. Again, most residential plans are drawn 1/4'' = 1' − 0'' scale.

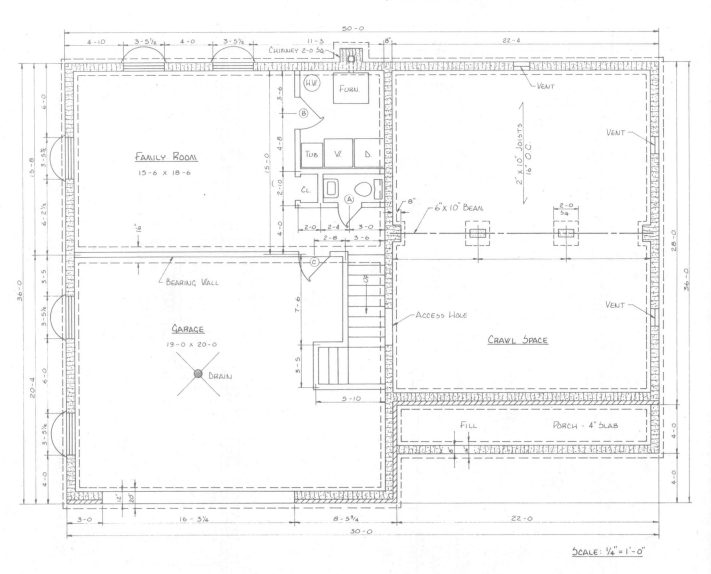

Fig. 10-9. A finished basement/foundation plan for a split-level house. The house is a frame structure with some brick veneer.

The basement plan is a combination foundation and floor plan. It includes the information commonly shown on the foundation plan and at the same time shows interior walls, stairs, windows and doors. The split-level house is a good example of a house which requires a foundation plan for one section of the house and a basement plan for the other. Fig. 10-9 illustrates the use of a basement and foundation plan to show construction for a split-level house foundation.

2. Draw the exterior foundation walls using the floor plan as an underlay or from information taken from the floor plan. Be sure the foundation walls are correctly positioned with respect to the first floor walls.

3. Draw the footings for the foundation walls, chimney, and columns. Steps 1 through 4 are shown in Fig. 10-10.

4. Locate and draw the beam and supports or bearing wall partition.

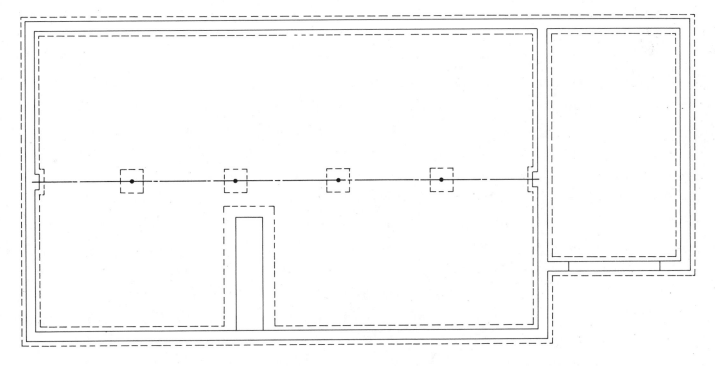

Fig. 10-10. A partially complete basement plan showing the foundation walls, footings, beam and columns.

5. Design the room layout in the basement area and darken in the lines.

6. Indicate breaks in the basement walls where windows and doors are to be located.

7. Locate and draw the stairs leading to the basement.

8. Show size, spacing and directions of floor joists using the standard symbol.

9. Identify the location of sections required to provide additional information about the basement construction. Steps 5 through 9 are shown in Fig. 10-11.

10. Draw the necessary sections and insert dimensions, Fig. 10-12.

11. Locate and draw permanent bath fixtures such as water closet, tub and lavatory. Also, locate the furnace, hot

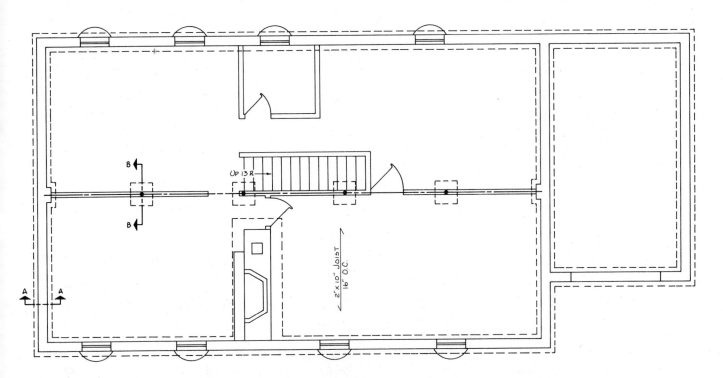

Fig. 10-11. Interior basement walls and doors, windows, joint information, stairs and section symbols have been added to the partially completed plan.

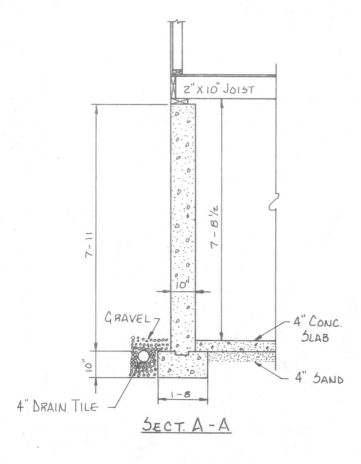

2" X 10" JOIST

7 - 11

7 - 8½

10"

GRAVEL

10"

4" DRAIN TILE

4" CONC. SLAB

4" SAND

1 - 8

SECT. A - A

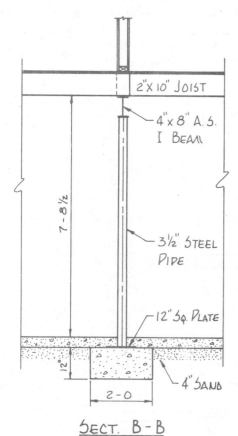

2" X 10" JOIST

4" x 8" A.S. I BEAM

7 - 8½

3½" STEEL PIPE

12" SQ. PLATE

12"

4" SAND

2 - 0

SECT. B - B

Fig. 10-12. Foundation details required for the basement plan shown in Figs. 10-11 and 10-13.

water heater, water storage tank, water softener, sump and floor drains. (All of these may not be necessary.)

12. Determine the location of dimensions needed to show all features. Dimension interior frame walls to the center of the wall. Do not dimension to the center of foundation walls.

13. Draw the dimension lines and add the dimensions.

14. Letter any necessary notes.

15. Show electrical switches, outlets and fixtures if no basement electrical plan is intended.

16. Shade the foundation walls with the proper symbol.

17. Add the title block, scale and name of drawing in the proper location.

18. Check the drawing to be sure you have included all necessary information. Steps 11 through 18 are shown in Fig. 10-13.

REVIEW QUESTIONS — CHAPTER 10

1. What is the definition and purpose of the foundation plan?

2. Residential foundation plans are usually drawn at _____ _____ scale.

3. List eight features which are usually shown on a foundation plan.

   a._____.
   b._____.
   c._____.
   d._____.
   e._____.
   f._____.
   g._____.
   h._____.

4. The foundation plan is prepared primarily for the _____ , _____ and _____ .

5. The foundation plan is drawn from information presented on the _____ plan, _____ plan and _____ .

6. A brick ledge is at least _____ inches wide.

7. The following considerations should be checked to help determine the height of foundation walls and size of footings:

   a. _____.
   b. _____.
   c. _____.

8. The symbol for a supporting beam is _____ .

9. The purpose of a section is _____ .

10. The foundation wall should be shaded to _____ .

11. How is a basement plan different from a foundation plan?

12. Why is a basement a logical choice for cold climates?

SUGGESTED ACTIVITIES

1. Select the floor plan for a garden or storage house and develop a foundation plan for the structure. Add necessary dimensions, symbols and notes. Provide sufficient information so that the foundation could be constructed from your drawings.

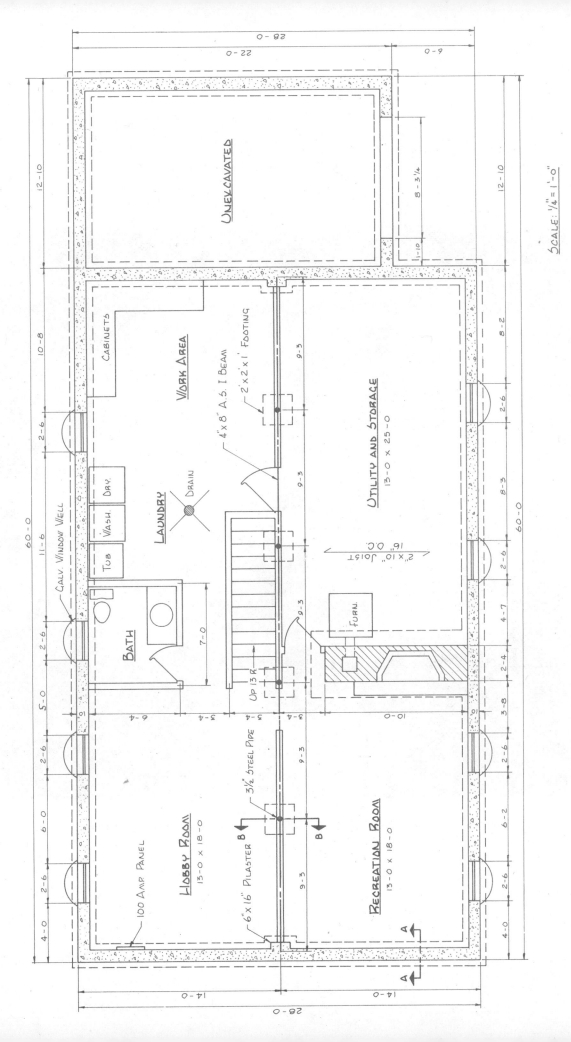

Fig. 10-13. A completed basement plan. The foundation walls are poured concrete and the structure is frame.

2. Using the floor plan for a cottage or vacation home, design and draw the foundation for this house. Completely dimension the drawing and indicate details needed to explain the construction. Draw the details.

3. Draw the foundation plan for a double-car garage which has a slab type foundation. Assume the garage is frame construction and is 20' − 0'' x 20' − 0''. Show anchor bolts every 4' − 0'' along the perimeter. Check the required footing depth for your area.

4. Select a floor plan from a magazine or other source and draw the foundation plan for the house. Calculate the size of beam required, number and size of piers or columns needed and the size and spacing of floor joists. Include dimensions and notes.

A bay window requires special framing in floor and sill construction to support the added weight.

Chapter 11
SILL AND FLOOR CONSTRUCTION

Methods of floor framing vary from one section of the country to another. Even builders in a given area may use different methods, based on personal preference and experience. The basic types of floor framing are PLATFORM and BALLOON framing. Of these two, platform framing is used more extensively. Plates, joists and studs are the structural members used in both types of framing.

PLATFORM FRAMING

Platform framing is popular for several reasons. It is satisfactory for both one and two-story structures and is easy and fast to construct. Shrinkage is uniform throughout the structure. A firestop is automatically provided. Construction is safe because the work is performed on solid surfaces.

In platform framing the SILL is the starting point in constructing a floor. A sill is the lowest member of the frame of a structure, resting on the foundation and supporting the floor joists or the uprights (studs) of the wall. The sill in most residential construction is a 2″ x 6″. (Actual dimensions 1 1/2″ x 5 1/2″.) Platform framing utilizes a method of sill construction known as BOX SILL construction, Fig. 11-1. The box sill consists of a 2″ x 6″ plate (also called a sill or mudsill) and a header which is the same size as the floor joists. Fig. 11-2 shows a detail of the first and second floor of a structure using platform framing and box sill construction.

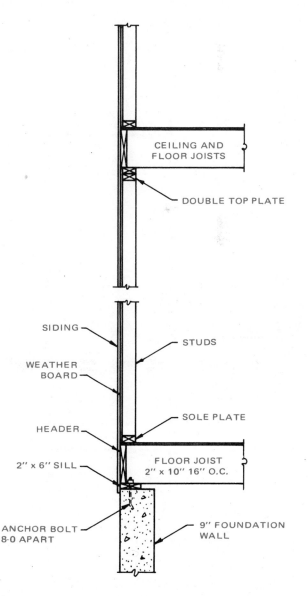

Fig. 11-2. Detail of first and second floors using platform framing and box sill construction.

Fig. 11-1. Box sill construction.

193

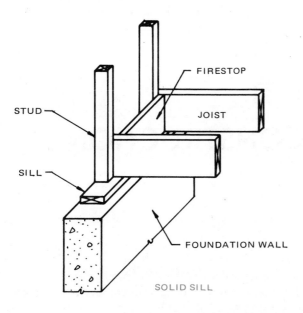

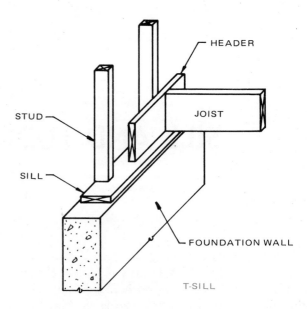

Fig. 11-3. Two types of sill construction used in balloon framing.

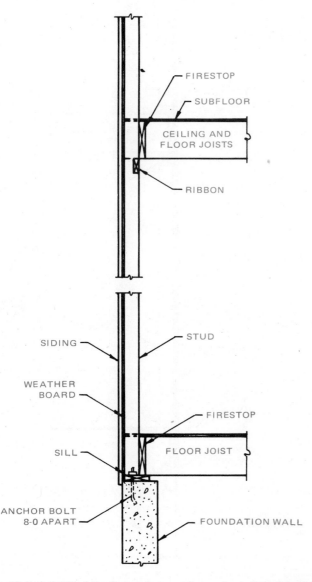

Fig. 11-4. A detail of the first and second floor using balloon framing and solid sill construction.

BALLOON FRAMING

Balloon framing was once used extensively, but in recent years has diminished in importance. Its distinguishing feature is that the wall studs rest directly on the sill plate. In balloon framing two types of sill construction are used, the solid or standard sill and the T-sill, Fig. 11-3.

The studs are nailed directly to the sill and joists in solid sill construction. No header is used. Joists are supported by a ribbon and nailed to the studs on the second floor level, Fig. 11-4. A firestop must be provided between the studs using pieces cut to the proper length.

In T-sill construction, a header is used which serves as a firestop. The studs rest on the sill plate and are nailed to the header as well as the sill plate. It should be noted that the sill plate in T-sill construction may be eight or ten inches wide to provide a broader supporting base upon which the joists may rest. Solid sill construction is used more extensively in two-story homes.

Two advantages of balloon framing are small potential shrinkage and vertical stability. Balloon framing is suitable for two-story structures with brick veneer or stucco exterior wall finishes. The vertical shrinkage in a two-story house using platform framing is sometimes great enough to cause cracking. This is usually not the case with balloon framing.

Disadvantages of balloon framing include a less than desirable surface to work on during construction and the need for firestop blocks.

JOISTS AND BEAMS

Joists provide support for the floor. They are usually made from a common soft wood such as southern yellow pine, fir, larch, hemlock or spruce. Joists are also available in aluminum, Fig. 11-5, and steel.

The size of floor joists ranges from a nominal size of 2″ x 6″ to 2″ x 12″.

Fig. 11-5. This house has aluminum joists.
(Aluminum Co. of America)

STANDARD LUMBER SIZES

DIMENSION LUMBER

PRODUCT CLASSIFICATION (NOMINAL SIZE)	ACTUAL SIZES	
	UNSEASONED*	DRY*
2 x 2	1 9/16 x 1 9/16	1 1/2 x 1 1/2
2 x 3	1 9/16 x 2 9/16	1 1/2 x 2 1/2
2 x 4	1 9/16 x 3 9/16	1 1/2 x 3 1/2
2 x 6	1 9/16 x 5 5/8	1 1/2 x 5 1/2
2 x 8	1 9/16 x 7 1/2	1 1/2 x 7 1/4
2 x 10	1 9/16 x 9 1/2	1 1/2 x 9 1/4
2 x 12	1 9/16 x 11 1/2	1 1/2 x 11 1/4

BOARD LUMBER

PRODUCT CLASSIFICATION (NOMINAL SIZE)	ACTUAL SIZES	
	UNSEASONED*	DRY*
1 x 2	25/32 x 1 9/16	3/4 x 1 1/2
1 x 3	25/32 x 2 9/16	3/4 x 2 1/2
1 x 4	25/32 x 3 9/16	3/4 x 3 1/2
1 x 6	25/32 x 5 5/8	3/4 x 5 1/2
1 x 8	25/32 x 7 1/2	3/4 x 7 1/4
1 x 10	25/32 x 9 1/2	3/4 x 9 1/4
1 x 12	25/32 x 11 1/2	3/4 x 11 1/4

*Dry lumber is defined as being 19% or less in moisture content. Unseasoned lumber is over 19% moisture content. The size of lumber changes approximately 1% for each 4% change in moisture content. Lumber stabilizes at approximately 15% moisture content under normal use conditions. (National Forest Products Assoc.)

The size joist required for a given situation will depend on the length of space, load to be supported, specie and grade of wood and distance the joists are spaced apart. Spacing of floor joists may be 12, 16 or 24" o. c. (on center). A spacing of 16" o. c. is most common. Span data for floor joists is presented in

Fig. 11-6. The span data presented assumes a maximum deflection of 1/360th of the span with a normal live load. This is the amount which most codes require. The normal live load is 40 pounds per square foot. The procedure for using the chart is as follows: (1) Determine the specie of wood to be used. The chart includes data for the three most common species. (2) Select the appropriate live load capacity required for the structure. (3) Determine the lumber grade to be used. Construction grade is the usual choice for fir and larch, while No. 1 dense is a comparable grade for southern yellow pine. (4) Scan the column under the lumber grade and note the maximum allowable spans for various joist spacing. (5) Select the joist size and spacing, ordinarily 16" o. c., which will adequately support the desired live weight. Example: The span is 14'-0" and No. 1 dense yellow pine is to be used for the joists. The live load is 30 pounds per square foot. The chart shows that the following choices would be within the limits chosen: 2" x 8" joists — 12" o. c. and 16" o. c.; 2" x 10" joists — 12" o. c., 16" o. c. and 24" o. c.; 2" x 12" joists — 12" o. c., 16" o. c. and 24" o. c. The most reasonable selection would be a 2" x 8" joist placed 16" o. c. Such a joist will span 14'-9" which exceeds the span by 9 inches.

The distance which joists must span is usually so great that a beam or load bearing wall is needed to reduce the span. The beam may be a solid timber, a built-up beam from dimension lumber or a metal I-beam. Load bearing walls may be concrete block, poured concrete or frame construction.

Several methods of supporting floor joists with a beam are commonly used. Fig. 11-7 shows some of these methods.

Partition walls which are supported by the floor joists require added support. It is good practice to double the joists under parallel partition walls. If space between the joists is

SOUTHERN YELLOW PINE – 30 LB. LIVE LOAD				
JOIST SIZE (NOMINAL)	SPACING OF JOISTS O. C. IN INCHES	LUMBER GRADES			
		NO. 1 DENSE KILN-DRIED 2″ DIM.	NO. 2 DENSE KILN-DRIED 2″ DIM.	NO. 1 DENSE 2″ DIM.	NO. 2 DENSE 2″ DIM.
2 x 6	12	12′- 5″	12′- 5″	12′- 5″	12′- 5″
	16	11′- 4″	11′- 4″	11′- 4″	11′- 4″
	24	10′- 2″	10′- 2″	10′- 0″	9′- 2″
2 x 8	12	16′- 1″	16′- 1″	16′- 1″	16′- 1″
	16	14′- 9″	14′- 9″	14′- 9″	14′- 9″
	24	13′- 1″	13′- 1″	13′- 1″	12′- 4″
2 x 10	12	19′- 11″	19′- 11″	19′- 11″	19′- 11″
	16	18′- 3″	18′- 3″	18′- 3″	18′- 3″
	24	16′- 2″	16′- 2″	16′- 2″	15′- 7″
2 x 12	12	23′- 9″	23′- 9″	23′- 9″	23′- 9″
	16	21′- 9″	21′- 9″	21′- 9″	21′- 9″
	24	19′- 2″	19′- 2″	19′- 2″	18′- 11″

SOUTHERN YELLOW PINE – 40 LB. LIVE LOAD				
JOIST SIZE (NOMINAL)	SPACING OF JOISTS O. C. IN INCHES	LUMBER GRADES			
		NO. 1 DENSE KILN-DRIED 2″ DIM.	NO. 2 DENSE KILN-DRIED 2″ DIM.	NO. 1 DENSE 2″ DIM.	NO. 2 DENSE 2″ DIM.
2 x 6	12	11′- 5″	11′- 5″	11′- 5″	11′- 5″
	16	10′- 5″	10′- 5″	10′- 5″	10′- 1″
	24	9′- 2″	9′- 2″	8′- 11″	8′- 3″
2 x 8	12	14′- 9″	14′- 9″	14′- 9″	14′- 9″
	16	13′- 6″	13′- 6″	13′- 6″	13′-6″
	24	12′- 0″	12′- 0″	11′- 11″	11′- 0″
2 x 10	12	18′- 3″	18′- 3″	18′- 3″	18′- 3″
	16	16′- 9″	16′- 9″	16′- 9″	16′- 9″
	24	14′- 10″	14′- 10″	14′- 10″	14′- 10″
2 x 12	12	21′- 9″	21′- 9″	21′- 9″	21′- 9″
	16	19′- 11″	19′- 11″	19′- 11″	19′- 11″
	24	17′- 7″	17′- 7″	17′- 7″	16′- 11″

LARCH AND DOUGLAS FIR – 30 LB. LIVE LOAD					
JOIST SIZE (NOMINAL)	SPACING OF JOISTS O. C. IN INCHES	LUMBER GRADES				
		SELECT STRUCTURAL	DENSE CONSTRUCTION	CONSTRUCTION	STANDARD	UTILITY
2 x 6	12	11′- 4″	11′-4″	11′- 4″	11′- 4″	8′- 4″
	16	10′- 4″	10′- 4″	10′- 4″	10′- 4″	7′- 2″
	24	9′- 0″	9′- 0″	9′- 0″	9′- 0″	5′- 10″
2 x 8	12	15′- 4″	15′- 4″	15′- 4″	15′- 4″	12′- 4″
	16	14′- 0″	14′- 0″	14′- 0″	14′- 0″	10′- 8″
	24	12′- 4″	12′- 4″	12′- 4″	12′- 4″	8′- 8″
2 x 10	12	18′- 4″	18′- 4″	18′- 4″	18′- 4″	16′- 10″
	16	17′- 0″	17′- 0″	17′- 0″	17′- 0″	14′- 8″
	24	15′- 6″	15′- 6″	15′- 6″	15′- 6″	12′- 0″
2 x 12	12	21′- 2″	21′- 2″	21′- 2″	21′- 2″	19′- 8″
	16	19′- 8″	19′- 8″	19′- 8″	19′- 8″	17′- 0″
	24	17′- 10″	17′- 10″	17′- 10″	17′- 10″	14′- 0″

LARCH AND DOUGLAS FIR – 40 LB. LIVE LOAD					
JOIST SIZE (NOMINAL)	SPACING OF JOISTS O. C. IN INCHES	LUMBER GRADES				
		SELECT STRUCTURAL	DENSE CONSTRUCTION	CONSTRUCTION	STANDARD	UTILITY
2 x 6	12	10′- 6″	10′- 6″	10′- 6″	10′- 6″	7′- 4″
	16	9′- 8″	9′- 8″	9′- 8″	9′- 8″	6′- 4″
	24	8′- 4″	8′- 4″	8′- 4″	8′- 2″	5′- 2″
2 x 8	12	14′- 4″	14′- 4″	14′- 4″	14′- 4″	10′- 0″
	16	13′- 0″	13′- 0″	13′- 0″	13′- 0″	9′- 6″
	24	11′- 6″	11′- 6″	11′- 6″	11′- 0″	7′- 10″
2 x 10	12	17′- 4″	17′- 4″	17′- 4″	17′- 4″	15′- 2″
	16	16′- 2″	16′- 2″	16′- 2″	16′- 2″	13′- 0″
	24	14′- 6″	14′- 6″	14′- 6″	14′- 0″	10′- 8″
2 x 12	12	20′- 0″	20′- 0″	20′- 0″	20′- 0″	17′- 8″
	16	18′- 8″	18′- 8″	18′- 8″	18′- 8″	15′- 4″
	24	16′- 10″	16′- 10″	16′- 10″	16′- 10″	12′- 6″

Fig. 11-6. Span data for floor joists of southern yellow pine, larch and Douglas fir. Maximum deflection is 1/360th of span with a normal live load. A normal live load is 40 pounds per square foot.   (National Forest Products Assoc.)

Sill and Floor Construction

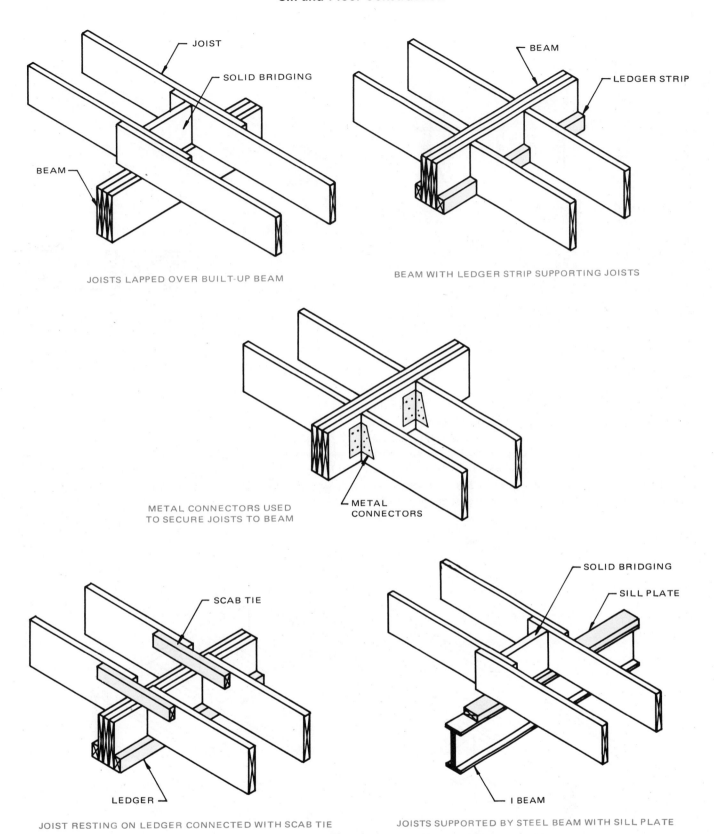

JOIST
SOLID BRIDGING
BEAM

JOISTS LAPPED OVER BUILT-UP BEAM

BEAM
LEDGER STRIP

BEAM WITH LEDGER STRIP SUPPORTING JOISTS

METAL CONNECTORS

METAL CONNECTORS USED TO SECURE JOISTS TO BEAM

SCAB TIE
LEDGER

JOIST RESTING ON LEDGER CONNECTED WITH SCAB TIE

SOLID BRIDGING
SILL PLATE
I BEAM

JOISTS SUPPORTED BY STEEL BEAM WITH SILL PLATE

Fig. 11-7. Common methods of supporting floor joists with beams.

used as a cold air duct, solid blocking is used between the joists, Fig. 11-8.

Openings in the floor for stairs and chimneys require double joist framing. Fig. 11-9 shows how such an opening is

framed and identifies the various parts.

Cross bridging is commonly used to stiffen the floor and spread the load over a broader area, Fig. 11-10. Bridging boards are ordinarily 1'' x 3'' in size with the ends cut at an

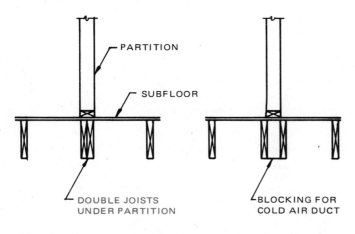

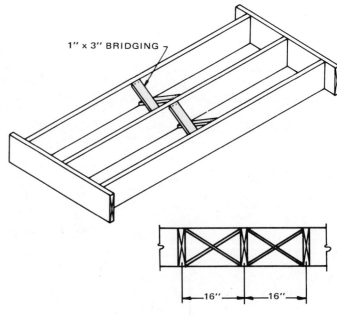

Fig. 11-8. Joists should be doubled under partition walls which run parallel to the joists.

angle so they fit snugly against the joist. They are nailed securely in place midway between the beam and wall. Metal bridging is also available, Fig. 11-11.

SUBFLOOR

Plywood, shiplap, and common boards are used for subfloors. The large size of plywood sheets (4' x 8'), and comparatively short time required to nail the sheets in place has drastically increased the use of plywood for subfloors. One-half inch thick plywood may be used when joists are spaced 16" o.c. but some builders prefer 5/8 in. stock. When plywood is used, it is important that the joist spacing is very

Fig. 11-10. Bridging is required by many codes.

accurate. All edges of the plywood must be supported, Fig. 11-12.

In some localities there is a trend to combine the subfloor and underlayment (ususally 5/8" particle board) into a single thickness which is usually 1 1/8" thick. The sheets have tongue-and-groove edges and require no blocking between the joists.

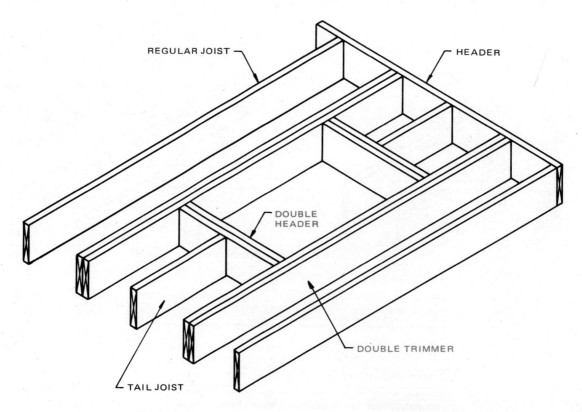

Fig. 11-9. Floor framing around openings such as fireplaces and stairs.

Fig. 11-11. Metal bridging may be quickly installed.

Plywood should be installed so that the grain direction of the outer plies are at right angles to the joists. It is stronger when positioned in this manner. Sheets of plywood should also be staggered so that end joints in adjacent panels break at different joists, Fig. 11-13. A slight space must be allowed between sheets for expansion.

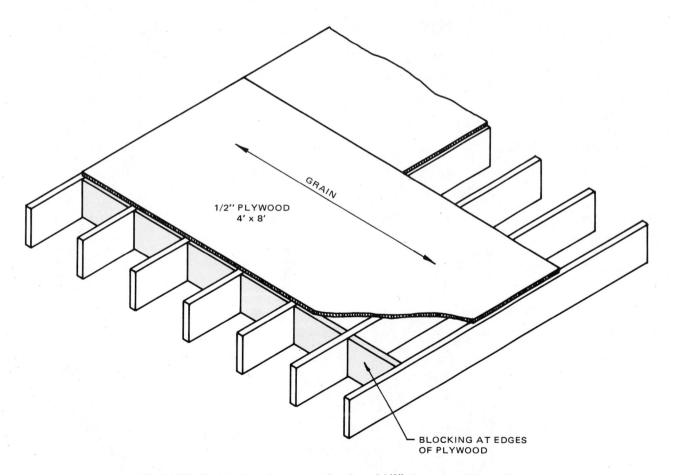

GRAIN

1/2" PLYWOOD
4' x 8'

BLOCKING AT EDGES
OF PLYWOOD

Fig. 11-12. Blocking is used to support the edges of 1/2" plywood used for subfloor.

Fig. 11-13. Grain direction of plywood should be perpendicular to the joists and the sheets staggered so that end joints in adjacent panels break at different joists. (American Plywood Assoc.)

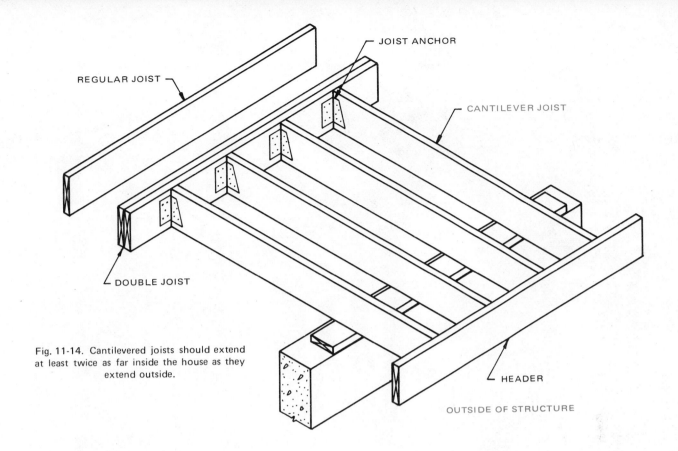

Fig. 11-14. Cantilevered joists should extend at least twice as far inside the house as they extend outside.

Labels in figure: REGULAR JOIST, JOIST ANCHOR, CANTILEVER JOIST, DOUBLE JOIST, HEADER, OUTSIDE OF STRUCTURE

CANTILEVERED JOISTS

Some home designs include a section of the floor which projects beyond a lower level. There is no particular problem when the floor joists run perpendicular to the cantilevered section, but when the joists are parallel to the overhanging area the situation requires cantilevered joists. Fig. 11-14 illustrates a typical framing technique for an overhanging section. A rule of thumb to follow in determining the necessary length of the cantilevered joists is to extend the joists inside at least twice the distance they overhang outside. If the inside distance is too short the result may be a sagging floor along the outside wall. If a ledger strip is used, it should be located along the top of the inside double header joist since the force will be up rather than down as in a normal situation.

FRAMING UNDER SLATE OR TILE

Certain areas of the home frequently have ceramic tile, slate or stone floors. These materials require a substantial base. If a

Fig. 11-15. A framing technique commonly used to support slate and ceramic tile areas . . . smaller size joists and placed closer together.

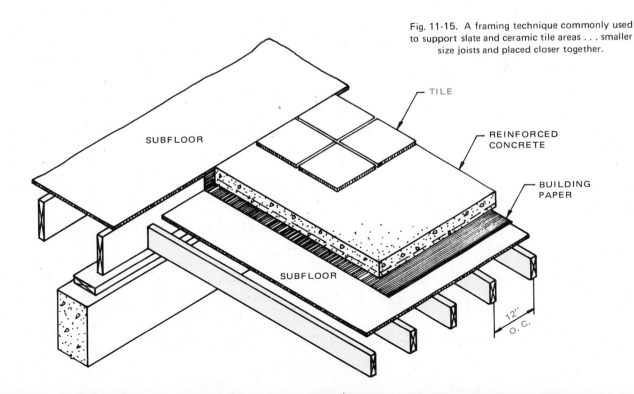

Labels in figure: SUBFLOOR, TILE, REINFORCED CONCRETE, BUILDING PAPER, SUBFLOOR, 12" O.C.

Fig. 11-16. An example of post and beam construction in a modern home.
(California Redwood Assoc.)

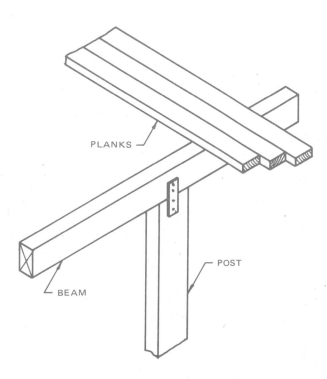

Fig. 11-17. The three components of post and beam construction.

concrete base is provided, the floor framing must be lowered to provide for the concrete. Several techniques are used to provide the needed support. A smaller size joist may be used and the space between joists reduced to provide adequate support, Fig. 11-15. This is a common solution to the problem. Another technique is to use one or more beams under the section to support the added weight. The dead weight may be as much as 40 or 50 pounds per square foot in a bathroom with a tile floor and heavy fixtures.

The concrete base for the tile or stone should be reinforced with wire mesh and poured on a plywood subfloor covered with building paper. A special type of concrete is generally used. It is a mixture of 1 part portland cement and 6 parts sand, known as a cement mortar mix.

POST AND BEAM CONSTRUCTION

In post and beam construction large framing members (posts, beams, planks) are spaced farther apart than conventional framing members, Figs. 11-16 and 11-17. Post and beam construction provides a greater freedom of design than conventional framing techniques. The system is basically simple, but presents problems related to larger structural sizes,

Fig. 11-18. Post and beam construction permits broad expanses of glass and provides the warm glow of natural wood. (Potlatch Forests, Inc.)

framing connectors and methods of joinery.

Most of the weight of a post and beam building is carried by the posts. The walls are called curtain walls. Curtain walls provide for wide expanses of glass without the need for headers, Fig. 11-18. Wide overhangs are also possible by extending the large beams to the desired length. Spacing of the posts is determined by the design of the building and the load to be supported.

The foundation for a post and beam structure may be a continuous wall or a series of piers where each post is to be located. Size of footings will be determined by the weight to be supported, soil bearing capacity and local building codes.

Check local codes.

The size of posts required will be at least 4" x 4". If the floor is also to be supported by the posts, they should be at least 6" x 6". Vertical height of the posts will be a factor in determining the size. Again check local codes.

Beams may be solid, laminated, reinforced with steel or plywood box beams. Fig. 11-19 shows a variety of beam types. Spacing and span of the beams will be determined by the size and kind of materials and load to be supported. In most normal situations a span of 7'-0" may be used when 2" thick tongue-and-groove subfloor or roof decking is applied to the beams. Thicker beams must be used if a greater span is

SOLID BEAM

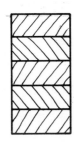

HORIZONTAL LAMINATED BEAM

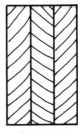

VERTICAL LAMINATED BEAM

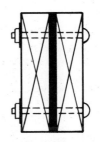

STEEL REINFORCED BEAM

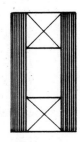

BOX BEAM

Fig. 11-19. A variety of beams used in post and beam construction.

Architecture

SPAN DATA FOR GLUED LAMINATED ROOF BEAMS*
MAXIMUM DEFLECTION 1/240TH OF THE SPAN

BEAM SIZE (ACTUAL)	WGT. OF BEAM PER LIN. FT. IN POUNDS	SPAN IN FEET											
		10	12	14	16	18	20	22	24	26	28	30	32
		POUNDS PER LIN. FT. LOAD BEARING CAPACITY											
3 x 5 1/4	3.7	151	85										
3 x 7 1/4	4.9	362	206	128	84								
3 x 9 1/4	6.7	566	448	300	199	137	99						
3 x 11 1/4	8.0	680	566	483	363	252	182	135	102				
4 1/2 x 9 1/4	9.8	850	673	451	299	207	148	109					
4 1/2 x 11 1/4	12.0	1,036	860	731	544	378	273	202	153				
3 1/4 x 13 1/2	10.4	1,100	916	784	685	479	347	258	197	152	120		
3 1/4 x 15	11.5	1,145	1,015	870	759	650	473	352	267	206	163	128	104
5 1/4 x 13 1/2	16.7	1,778	1,478	1,266	1,105	773	559	415	316	245	193	154	124
5 1/4 x 15	18.6	1,976	1,647	1,406	1,229	1,064	771	574	438	342	269	215	174
5 1/4 x 16 1/2	20.5	2,180	1,810	1,550	1,352	1,155	933	768	586	457	362	290	236
5 1/4 x 18	22.3	2,378	1,978	1,688	1,478	1,308	1,113	918	766	598	478	382	311

EXAMPLE: CLEAR SPAN   = 20'- 0"
BEAM SPACING = 10'- 0"
DEAD LOAD   = 8 LBS./SQ. FT. (ROOFING AND DECKING)
LIVE LOAD   = 20 LBS./SQ. FT. (SNOW)
TOTAL LOAD   = LIVE LOAD + DEAD LOAD x BEAM SPACING
= (20 + 8) x 10 = 280 LBS./LIN. FT.
THE BEAM SIZE REQUIRED IS 3 1/4" x 13 1/2" WHICH SUPPORT 347 LBS./LIN. FT. OVER A SPAN OF 20'- 0"

*BEAMS MAY BE DOUGLAS FIR, LARCH OR SOUTHERN YELLOW PINE.

SPAN DATA FOR GLUED LAMINATED FLOOR BEAMS*
MAXIMUM DEFLECTION 1/360TH OF THE SPAN

BEAM SIZE (ACTUAL)	WGT. OF BEAM PER LIN. FT. IN POUNDS	SPAN IN FEET											
		10	12	14	16	18	20	22	24	26	28	30	32
		POUNDS PER LIN. FT. LOAD BEARING CAPACITY											
3 x 5 1/4	3.7	114	64										
3 x 7 1/4	4.9	275	156	84	55								
3 x 9 1/4	6.7	492	319	198	130	89							
3 x 11 1/4	8.0	590	491	361	239	165	119						
4 1/2 x 9 1/4	9.8	738	479	298	196	134	96						
4 1/2 x 11 1/4	12.0	900	748	541	359	248	178	131	92				
3 1/4 x 13 1/2	10.4	956	795	683	454	316	228	169	128	98			
3 1/4 x 15	11.5	997	884	756	626	436	315	234	178	137	108		
5 1/4 x 13 1/2	16.7	1,541	1,283	1,095	732	509	367	271	205	158	123	96	
5 1/4 x 15	18.6	1,713	1,423	1,219	1,009	703	508	376	286	221	173	137	109
5 1/4 x 16 1/2	20.5	1,885	1,568	1,340	1,170	939	678	505	384	298	235	187	151
5 1/4 x 18	22.3	2,058	1,710	1,464	1,278	1,133	886	660	503	391	309	247	200

EXAMPLE: CLEAR SPAN   = 20'- 0"
BEAM SPACING = 10'- 0"
DEAD LOAD   = 7 LBS./SQ. FT. (DECKING AND CARPET)
LIVE LOAD   = 40 LBS./SQ. FT. (FURNITURE AND OCCUPANTS)
TOTAL LOAD   = LIVE LOAD + DEAD LOAD x BEAM SPACING
= (40 + 7) x 10 = 470 LBS./LIN. FT.
THE BEAM SIZE REQUIRED IS 5 1/4" x 15" WHICH WILL SUPPORT 508 LBS./LIN. FT. OVER A SPAN OF 20'- 0"

*BEAMS MAY BE DOUGLAS FIR, LARCH OR SOUTHERN YELLOW PINE.

Fig. 11-20. Span data for glued laminated floor and roof beams. Local building codes should be checked for specific requirements. (Potlatch Forests, Inc.)

Sill and Floor Construction

required. See the span tables, Fig. 11-20.

Two systems of beam placement are possible with post and beam construction. The first system is the longitudinal method. Here the beams are placed at right angles to the roof slope. Roof decking is laid, therefore, from the ridge pole to the eaves line. The second system is called the transverse method. The beams follow the roof slope and decking runs parallel to the roof ridge. See Fig. 11-21.

A post and beam structure has a limited number of joints. The conventional method of fastening small members by nailing does not provide a satisfactory connection. Therefore, metal plates or connectors are used. These are fastened with

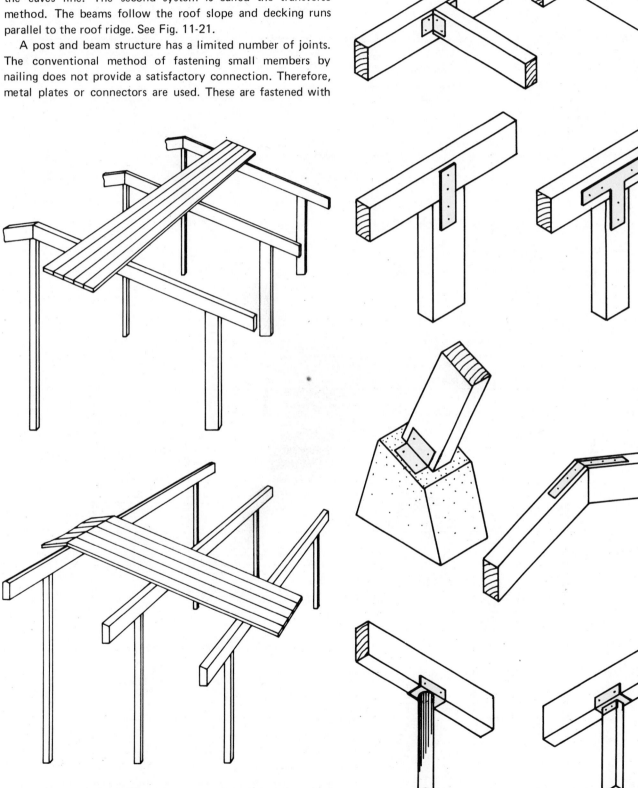

Fig. 11-21. Above. Roof beams follow the roof slope and decking runs parallel to the roof ridge in transverse post and beam construction. Below. The roof beams are perpendicular to the roof slope in longitudinal post and beam construction. Planks are parallel to the roof slope.

Fig. 11-22. Metal fasteners (typical) used to connect large beam segments.

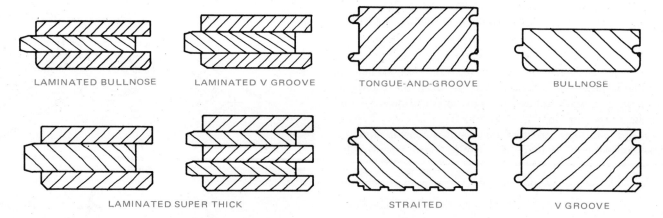

LAMINATED BULLNOSE LAMINATED V GROOVE TONGUE-AND-GROOVE BULLNOSE

LAMINATED SUPER THICK STRAITED V GROOVE

Fig. 11-23. Several plank designs produced commercially for use in post and beam construction.

SPAN DATA FOR ROOF DECKING
WITH A MAXIMUM DEFLECTION OF 1/240TH OF THE SPAN
LIVE LOAD = 20 LBS./SQ. FT.

THICKNESS IN INCHES (NOMINAL)	LUMBER GRADE	SIMPLE SPANS	
		DOUGLAS FIR, LARCH, SOUTHERN YELLOW PINE	WESTERN RED CEDAR
		SPAN	SPAN
2	CONSTRUCTION	9'- 5''	8'- 1''
2	STANDARD	9'- 5''	6'- 9''
3	SELECT DEX.	15'- 3''	13'- 0''
3	COMPL. DEX.	15'- 3''	13'- 0''
4	SELECT DEX.	20'- 3''	17'- 3''
4	COMPL. DEX.	20'- 3''	17'- 3''

THICKNESS IN INCHES (NOMINAL)	LUMBER GRADE	RANDOM LENGTHS	
		DOUGLAS FIR, LARCH, SOUTHERN YELLOW PINE	WESTERN RED CEDAR
		SPAN	SPAN
2	CONSTRUCTION	10'- 3''	8'- 10''
2	STANDARD	10'- 3''	6'- 9''
3	SELECT DEX.	16'- 9''	14'- 3''
3	COMPL. DEX.	16'- 9''	13'- 6''
4	SELECT DEX.	22'- 0''	19'- 0''
4	COMPL. DEX.	22'- 0''	18'- 0''

THICKNESS IN INCHES (NOMINAL)	LUMBER GRADE	COMB. SIMPLE AND TWO-SPAN CONTINUOUS	
		DOUGLAS FIR, LARCH, SOUTHERN YELLOW PINE	WESTERN RED CEDAR
		SPAN	SPAN
2	CONSTRUCTION	10'- 7''	8'- 9''
2	STANDARD	10'- 7''	6'- 9''
3	SELECT DEX.	17'- 3''	14'- 9''
3	COMPL. DEX.	17'- 3''	13'- 6''
4	SELECT DEX.	22'- 9''	19'- 6''
4	COMPL. DEX.	22'- 9''	18'- 0''

Fig. 11-24. Span data for Douglas fir, larch, southern yellow pine and western red cedar planking.

lag screws or bolts. Fig. 11-22 shows a number of metal fasteners used to connect various beam segments.

Decking planks for the roof and floor range in thickness from 2 to 4 inches. The planks are usually tongue-and-grooved along the edges and they may be tongue-and-grooved on the ends as well. Fig. 11-23 illustrates several plank designs which are available. It is customary to leave the underside of a planked roof exposed. If added insulation is required, it may be placed above the decking and under the roofing material. Rigid type insulation should be used. Roof decking span information is given in Fig. 11-24.

REVIEW QUESTIONS — CHAPTER 11

1. The two basic types of floor framing in use today are _____ and _____ framing.
2. The lowest member of the frame of a structure which rests on the foundation and supports the floor joists and wall studs is the_____.
3. The actual dimensions of a 2″ x 6″ are_____ .
4. Platform framing utilizes a method of sill construction known as_____ sill construction.
5. Two types of sill construction used with balloon framing are_____ and _____ sill construction.
6. Two advantages of balloon framing are:
   a._____ .
   b._____ .
7. The floor of a house is supported by_____ .
8. Name three soft woods which are commonly used for joists.
   a._____ .
   b._____ .
   c._____ .
9. Spacing of floor joists is usually_____ inches o. c.
10. Dry lumber is defined as wood which has less than _____percent moisture content.
11. What size floor joist should be used if the span is 14'-0″, No. 1 dense yellow pine is to be used, the live load is 30 pounds per square ft. and the joist spacing is 16″ o.c.? (Use the span data chart.)
12. The purpose of cross bridging is to stiffen the floor and _____ .
13. The thickness of plywood commonly used for subfloors is _____ .
14. When a part of the house extends out over a lower section, the term_____ is used to describe the structure.
15. The three elements of post and beam construction are:
   a._____ .

b._____ .
c._____ .
16. Identify four types of beams used in post and beam construction.
   a._____ .
   b._____ .
   c._____ .
   d._____ .
17. Two systems of beam placement are used in post and beam construction. They are the_____and the _____ method.
18. Roof decking is manufactured in various thicknesses and widths. The span chart for planking presents data for three thicknesses. They include:
   a._____ .
   b._____ .
   c._____ .
19. What type of insulation is used with a planked roof?

SUGGESTED ACTIVITIES

1. Obtain a set of house plans and identify the following:
   a. Size of floor joists required.
   b. Spacing of floor joists.
   c. Type of sill construction specified.
   d. Thickness and type of subfloor material to be used.
   e. Size of sill plate.
   f. Type and size of bridging.
   g. Specie and grade of lumber specified for joists.
   h. Method of framing used (balloon or platform).
   i. Type of construction details shown relating to sill and floor.
2. Define the following terms:
   a. span
   b. live load
   c. dead load
   d. cantileverage
   e. beam
   f. partition
   g. post
   h. reinforced concrete
   i. construction grade
   j. nominal dimension
   k. firestop
   l. dimension lumber
   m. header
   n. sill
   o. laminated
   p. slope
   q. tongue-and-groove
   r. straited
3. Select a floor plan of a house and prepare a list of materials for the first floor. (Sill, header, joists and subfloor.)
4. Design and draw the floor framing for a house of your design. Show the spacing, size, specie and grade of joists used. Draw the necessary construction details.

Fig. 12-1. All framing in this house is aluminum. The floor is 1/2" plywood and the walls are covered with weatherboard. (Aluminum Co. of America)

Chapter 12
WALL AND CEILING CONSTRUCTION

Residential wall construction is usually one of three types: frame, masonry, or combination frame and masonry. The wall panels may be constructed on site or prefabricated at another location and transported to the site for erection. The trend is toward more prefabrication and less on-site construction.

FRAME WALL CONSTRUCTION

Frame wall construction involves the proper arrangement of the wall-framing members which may be either aluminum, Fig. 12-1, or lumber, Fig. 12-2, used in conventional construction. This includes the sole plate, top plates, studs, headers and braces. Plates and studs are usually nominal 2 x 4 inch lumber. Headers or lintels are ordinarily constructed from larger stock. Bracing may be 1 x 4 or 2 x 4 stock. Fig. 12-2 shows a frame wall with the framing members identified.

Wall framing lumber must have good stiffness and nail-holding properties, be free from warp and easy to work. Species which meet these criteria include Douglas fir, southern yellow pine, hemlock, spruce and larch. The most common lumber grade used is construction grade or its equivalent. Moisture content should be between 15 and 19 percent.

Residential framing members are also available in aluminum, as shown in Fig. 12-1. The Aluminum Company of America has developed a system called the "Alumiframe" building system. This includes all of the structural framing members required to construct a house. Fig. 12-3 shows an Alumiframe exterior wall being put into place. The weather-

DOUBLE
TOP PLATE

1" x 4"
BRACING

STUD

SOLE PLATE

BLOCKING

Fig. 12-2. A frame wall corner showing the various framing members and their relationship to each other.

Fig. 12-3. Aluminum wall sections are much lighter than conventional stud walls.

board has already been attached. Aluminum framing members are not subject to warping, cracking, rotting or being destroyed by termites. Special self-drilling, self-tapping screws are used to fasten the various parts together. Fig. 12-4 shows a typical exterior wall corner and how it is designed. Aluminum framing may be prefabricated or assembled on the site.

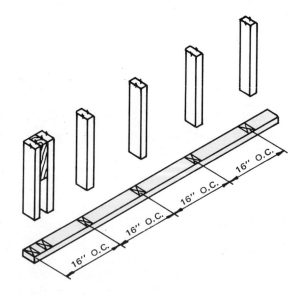

Fig. 12-5. A sole plate showing the location of studs.

Fig. 12-4. The aluminum corner post shown here is one piece designed especially for this purpose.

Frame wall construction usually begins with the sole plate. The spacing of the studs is marked off on the sole plate, Fig. 12-5. Construction of the wall is ordinarily performed on the subfloor. Exterior frame walls are flush with the outside of the foundation wall or moved 1/2'' inside to allow for the thickness of sheathing or weatherboard, Fig. 12-6. The sole plate acts as an anchor for the wall and a nailer for interior and exterior wall sheathing. A wall panel may extend along an entire side of the building if sufficient help is available to raise the wall. Otherwise, the wall may be built in smaller sections.

Wall studs are cut to length (usually 7'-9'' when 1 1/2'' material is used) and are nailed to the sole and top plates. A second plate is added after the wall is in place. The distance from the top of the subfloor to the bottom of the ceiling joists is usually 8'-1 1/2''. This distance provides a finished wall height of 8'-0''.

Openings for doors and windows are framed before the wall

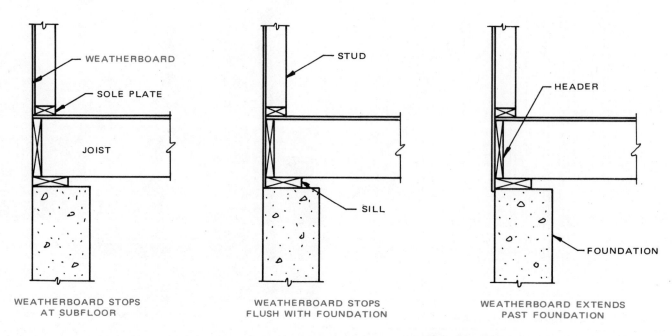

WEATHERBOARD STOPS AT SUBFLOOR

WEATHERBOARD STOPS FLUSH WITH FOUNDATION

WEATHERBOARD EXTENDS PAST FOUNDATION

Fig. 12-6. The weatherboard may terminate at the subfloor, the top of the foundation, or extend below the top of the foundation. The treatment used will most likely depend on the construction procedure.

is moved to the vertical position. Headers are cut to length and nailed into position with cripple studs and trimmers firmly nailed to the sole and top plates, Fig. 12-7. Cripples are studs which are not full length due to a wall opening. Trimmers are studs which support the header over an opening in the wall.

Corner bracing is required in many areas. Two methods of

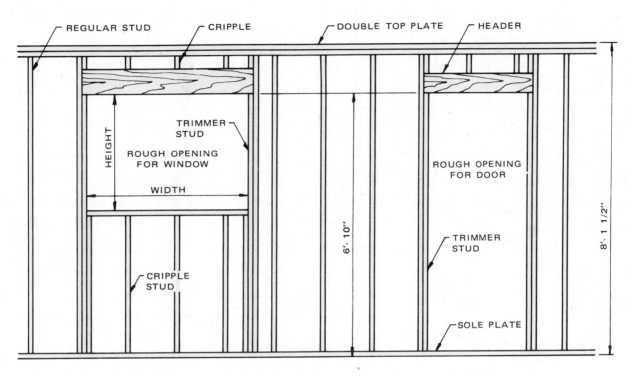

PLATFORM FRAMING 16" O.C.

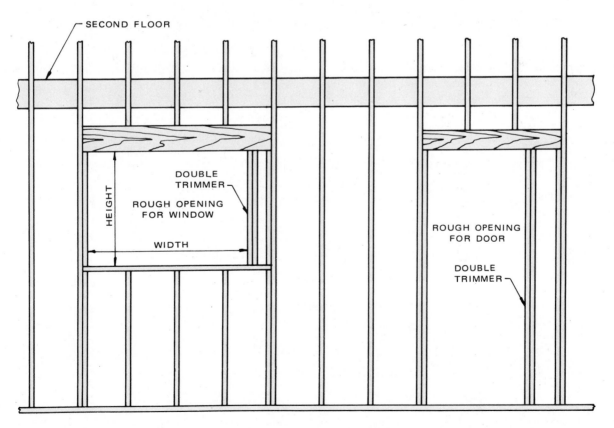

BALLOON FRAMING 16" O.C.

Fig. 12-7. Wall sections, platform and balloon framing.

shown in Fig. 12-2. The second method, which seems to be gaining in popularity, makes use of a sheet of 1/2" plywood nailed to the studs at each corner, Fig. 12-8.

Typical methods of framing used to form exterior wall corners are shown in Fig. 12-9. The corner must provide a nailing edge for the interior wall material and adequate support for the structure.

Interior frame walls are constructed the same way as exterior walls. They have sole plates and double top plates. Interior walls must be securely fastened to the exterior walls they intersect. Again, a nailing edge must be provided for the plaster base or drywall. This may be accomplished by using a 2 x 6 secured to cross blocking or by doubling the exterior wall studs at the intersection of the partition. Fig. 12-10 shows both methods. The same arrangement is used at the intersection of all interior walls.

Rough openings for windows and doors shown on the floor plan are dimensioned to the center of the opening. Specific dimensions are usually provided by the window and door schedule. The width is listed first and the height second. The rough opening height of most doors is 6'-10''. Tops of all windows will probably be the same distance above the floor. Each wall opening requires a header above the opening to support the weight above. Headers are formed by nailing two pieces of dimension lumber (2 x 6, 2 x 8, etc.) together with a 1/2'' plywood spacer between to equal the stud width. (If traditional 1 5/8'' x 3 5/8'' studs are used, the plywood will be 3/8'' thick.) The length of the header will be equal to the width of the rough opening plus the thickness of two trimmers, Fig. 12-11. Header sizes vary with the span and load requirements. The chart on page 213 shows sizes for various situations. Check the code to be sure these specifications are permitted in your area. Trussed headers are required for openings wider than 8'-0'' or in situations involving extremely heavy loads. Fig. 12-12 illustrates two types of trussed headers.

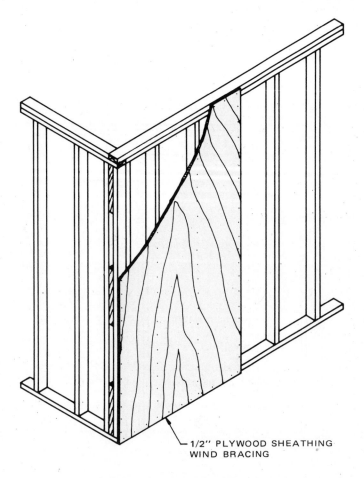

Fig. 12-8. One-half inch plywood sheathing may be used as bracing for the exterior wall corners.

1/2'' PLYWOOD SHEATHING WIND BRACING

bracing are commonly used to provide added support. Diagonal corner braces of 1x4 inch material is used from the top corner of the walls down to the sole plate. This method is

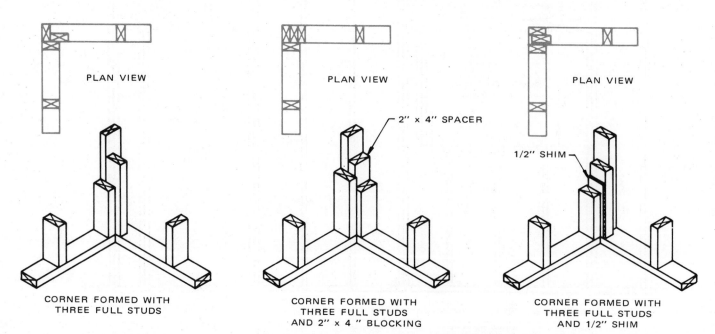

PLAN VIEW

PLAN VIEW

PLAN VIEW

2'' x 4'' SPACER

1/2'' SHIM

CORNER FORMED WITH
THREE FULL STUDS

CORNER FORMED WITH
THREE FULL STUDS
AND 2'' x 4 '' BLOCKING

CORNER FORMED WITH
THREE FULL STUDS
AND 1/2'' SHIM

Fig. 12-9. Corner posts are framed in a variety of ways. This illustration shows three accepted methods.

Wall and Ceiling Construction

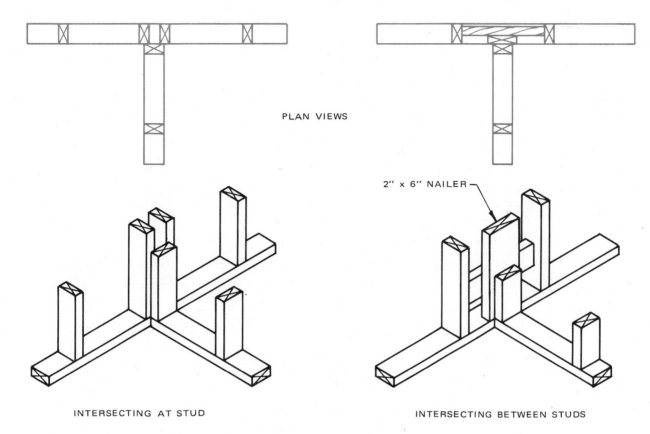

PLAN VIEWS

INTERSECTING AT STUD

INTERSECTING BETWEEN STUDS

2" x 6" NAILER

Fig. 12-10. The framing for the intersection of partitions and exterior walls is accomplished by using extra studs or blocking and a nailer.

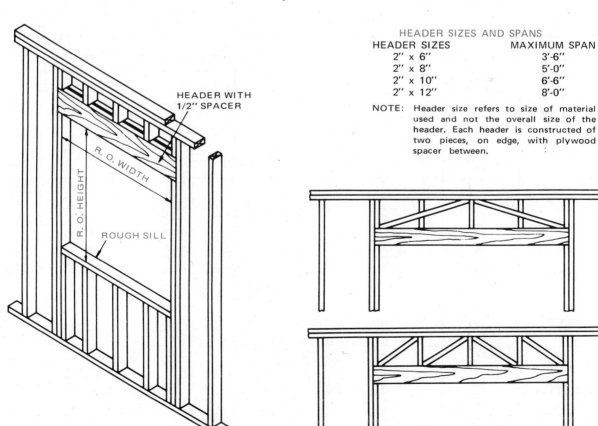

HEADER WITH 1/2" SPACER

R. O. WIDTH

R. O. HEIGHT

ROUGH SILL

Fig. 12-11. The rough opening for a window is the area between the trimmers and the rough sill and header.

HEADER SIZES AND SPANS

HEADER SIZES	MAXIMUM SPAN
2" x 6"	3'-6"
2" x 8"	5'-0"
2" x 10"	6'-6"
2" x 12"	8'-0"

NOTE: Header size refers to size of material used and not the overall size of the header. Each header is constructed of two pieces, on edge, with plywood spacer between.

Fig. 12-12. Trussed headers increase the supporting strength and increase the span.

SOUTHERN YELLOW PINE					
JOIST SIZE (NOMINAL)	SPACING OF JOISTS O. C. IN INCHES	LUMBER GRADES			
		NO. 1 KILN-DRIED 2″ DIM.	NO. 2 KILN-DRIED 2″ DIM.	NO. 1 2″ DIM.	NO. 2 2″ DIM.
LIMITED ATTIC STORAGE					
2 x 6	12	14'- 4″	14'- 4″	14'- 4″	14'- 4″
	16	13'- 0″	13'- 0″	13'- 0″	12'- 10″
	24	11'- 4″	11'- 4″	11'- 4″	10'- 6″
2 x 8	12	18'- 4″	18'- 4″	18'- 4″	18'- 4″
	16	17'- 0″	17'- 0″	17'- 0″	17'- 0″
	24	15'- 4″	15'- 4″	15'- 4″	14'- 4″
2 x 10	12	21'- 10″	21'- 10″	21'- 10″	21'- 10″
	16	20'- 4″	20'- 4″	20'- 4″	20'- 4″
	24	18'- 4″	18'- 4″	18'- 4″	18'- 4″
NO ATTIC STORAGE					
2 x 6	12	17'- 2″	17'- 2″	17'- 2″	17'- 2″
	16	16'- 0″	16'- 0″	16'- 0″	16'- 0″
	24	14'- 4″	14'- 4″	14'- 4″	14'- 4″
2 x 8	12	21'- 8″	21'- 8″	21'- 8″	21'- 8″
	16	20'- 2″	20'- 2″	20'- 2″	20'- 2″
	24	18'- 4″	18'- 4″	18'- 4″	18'- 4″
2 x 10	12	24'- 0″	24'- 0″	24'- 0″	24'- 0″
	16	24'- 0″	24'- 0″	24'- 0″	24'- 0″
	24	21'- 10″	21'- 10″	21'- 10″	21'- 10″

DOUGLAS FIR AND LARCH					
JOIST SIZE (NOMINAL)	SPACING OF JOISTS O. C. IN INCHES	LUMBER GRADES			
		SELECT STRUCTURAL	DENSE CONSTRUCTION	CONSTRUCTION	STANDARD	UTILITY
LIMITED ATTIC STORAGE					
2 x 6	12	14'- 4″	14'- 4″	14'- 4″	14'- 4″	9'- 6″
	16	13'- 0″	13'- 0″	13'- 0″	12'- 10″	8'- 4″
	24	11'- 4″	11'- 4″	11'- 4″	10'- 6″	6'- 8″
2 x 8	12	18'- 4″	18'- 4″	18'- 4″	18'- 4″	14'- 4″
	16	17'- 0″	17'- 0″	17'- 0″	17'- 0″	12'- 4″
	24	15'- 4″	15'- 4″	15'- 4″	14'- 4″	10'- 0″
2 x 10	12	21'- 10″	21'- 10″	21'- 10″	21'- 10″	19'- 6″
	16	20'- 4″	20'- 4″	20'- 4″	20'- 4″	16'- 10″
	24	18'- 4″	18'- 4″	18'- 4″	18'- 4″	13'- 10″
NO ATTIC STORAGE					
2 x 6	12	17'- 2″	17'- 2″	17'- 2″	17'- 2″	13'- 6″
	16	16'- 0″	16'- 0″	16'- 0″	16'- 0″	11'- 8″
	24	14'- 4″	14'- 4″	14'- 4″	14'- 4″	9'- 6″
2 x 8	12	21'- 8″	21'- 8″	21'- 8″	21'- 8″	20'- 2″
	16	20'- 2″	20'- 2″	20'- 2″	20'- 2″	17'- 6″
	24	18'- 4″	18'- 4″	18'- 4″	18'- 4″	14'- 4″
2 x 10	12	24'- 0″	24'- 0″	24'- 0″	24'- 0″	24'- 0″
	16	24'- 0″	24'- 0″	24'- 0″	24'- 0″	22'- 6″
	24	21'- 10″	21'- 10″	21'- 10″	21'- 10″	19'- 6″

Fig. 12-13. Ceiling joist span data for Southern Yellow Pine, Douglas Fir and Larch. To use the chart you must know the lumber grades and specie, the spacing of joists and whether or not attic storage is anticipated. (National Forest Products Assoc.)

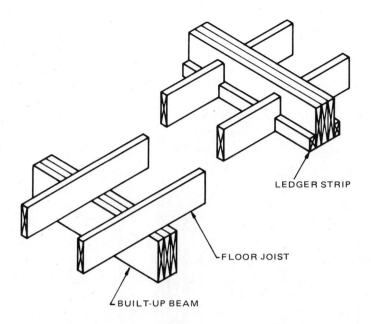

Fig. 12-14. Two methods of supporting ceiling joists with built-up beam.

CEILING CONSTRUCTION

After the exterior and interior walls are erected, plumbed, braced and top plates added, ceiling joists may be put in place. These are usually positioned across the width of the house and in the same direction as the rafters. The size of ceiling joists required will depend on the load to be supported, span distance, wood specie, spacing of joists and grade of lumber used. Span data for ceiling joists is presented for three common species of wood in Fig. 12-13. Examine the local code to be sure that your selection is acceptable.

Basic construction of the ceiling is similar to floor construction. The main differences are that a header is not required around the outside and smaller lumber is used. Long spans may require a bearing wall partition or beam. If a beam is used, it may be located below the joists or placed flush with them using ledger strips. Both methods are illustrated in Fig. 12-14.

The upper corner of the ceiling joists often interferes with the roof slope. To prevent this interference, the corner is usually cut to match the slope as shown in Fig. 12-15.

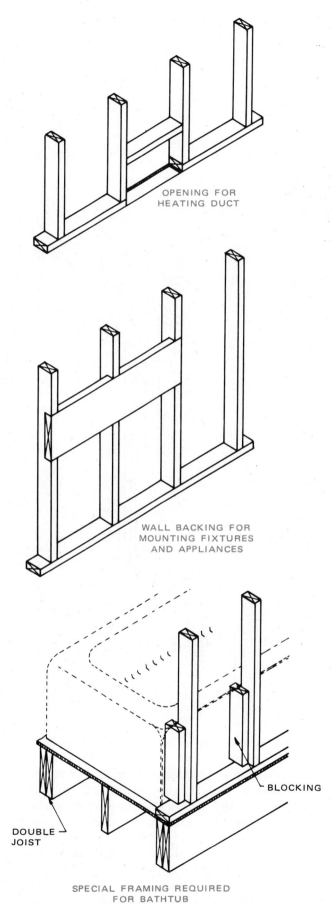

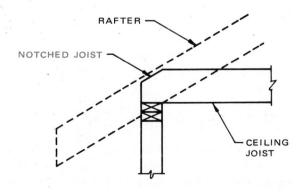

Fig. 12-15. Ceiling joists are usually notched to match the roof slope to prevent interference with the roof sheathing.

Fig. 12-16. Areas in the house which usually require special framing consideration.

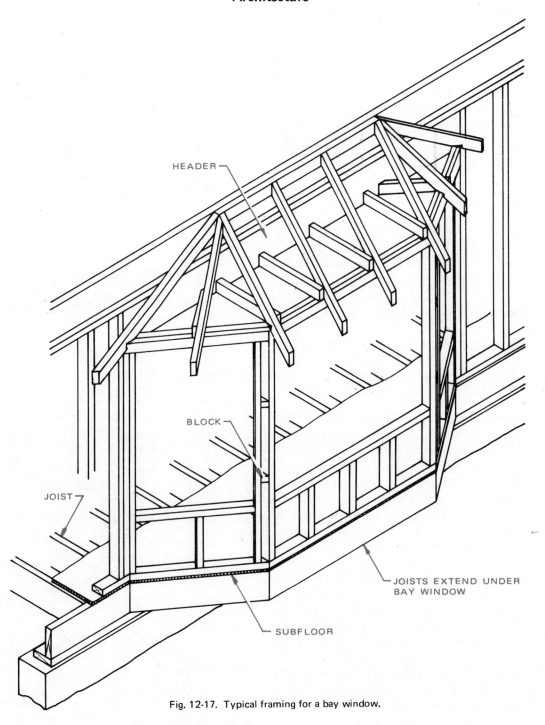

HEADER

BLOCK

JOIST

JOISTS EXTEND UNDER
BAY WINDOW

SUBFLOOR

Fig. 12-17. Typical framing for a bay window.

An access hole must be provided in the ceiling (usually in a closet) to afford entry to the attic. The size of this opening may be as small as 2 feet square. Framing around the opening is the same as for openings in the floor. Double headers are used for large holes (for example, when installing a disappearing stairway) but are usually not required for minimum size openings.

There are a number of areas in the house which require special framing. Openings for heating ducts, wall backing for various fixtures and extra support for the bathtub are examples of situations which require attention. Fig. 12-16 illustrates some of these special framing details.

Framing for a bay window presents special problems. Fig.

12-17 shows one accepted method for this type of framing. Note that the floor joists extend beyond the wall to provide support for the unit. If the unit is to be set at right angles to the joists, then cantilevered joists should be used. See previous illustration.

MASONRY WALL CONSTRUCTION

A masonry wall is constructed entirely of brick, concrete block, stone, clay tile, terra cotta or a combination of these materials. Walls which require more than one thickness of masonry must be bonded together. They may be bonded by using a header course every 16″ vertically, Fig. 12-18, or

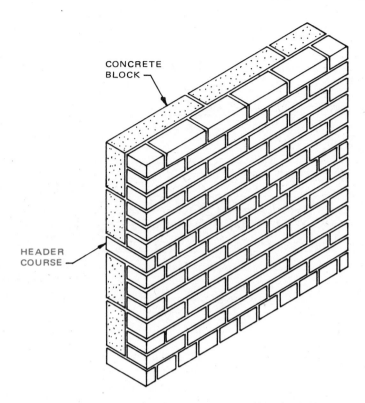

Fig. 12-18. A solid masonry wall using a header course to bond the two thicknesses together.

corrugated metal wall ties placed in the mortar joints, Fig. 12-19. Metal wall ties should be placed no more than 16″ apart vertically and 32″ horizontally.

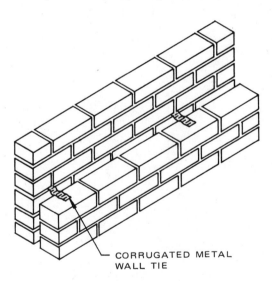

Fig. 12-19. Using corrugated metal wall ties.

Solid masonry walls for residential construction are usually 8″ thick. Concrete block walls (cavity walls) are popular in many sections of the country. Block walls are relatively inexpensive to construct and a variety of textures and designs are possible. One disadvantage of a solid masonry wall is that furring strips (usually 2″ x 2″ or 1″ x 3″) are required on the inside of the wall if dry wall, plaster or paneling is used, Fig.

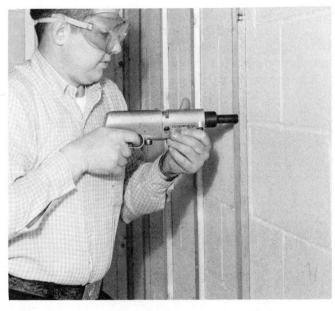

Fig. 12-20. Furring strips must be installed over masonry walls if paneling, dry wall or plastic is to be used. (Conwed Corp.)

12-20. Insulation may be added as shown in Fig. 12-21.

Solid brick and stone walls have been used extensively in years past, but because of the cost are diminishing in importance for residential purposes. The same exterior effect may be obtained with a brick or stone veneer on frame construction and the wall will be better insulated, less expensive to construct and present fewer construction problems.

Fig. 12-21. Insulation with a moisture barrier backing is commonly applied to reduce heat loss. (Conwed Corp.)

217

Floor joists are placed directly into openings in solid brick and stone walls. Each joist is cut at an angle on the end to prevent toppling the wall if the house should catch fire. The cut is known as a "firecut," Fig. 12-22.

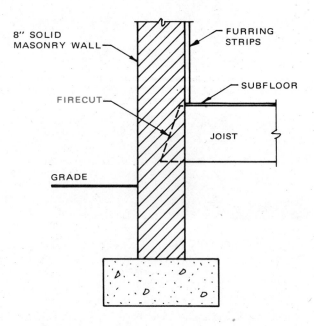

Fig. 12-22. Floor joists in a solid masonry wall require a firecut to prevent excessive wall damage in the event of a fire.

Stonework involves artistry on the part of the mason due to the varied size and texture of the material ordinarily used.

Stonework is commonly referred to as "ashlar" or "rubble." Ashlar stonework uses dressed, cut or squared stones. Each stone is a specific size and fits in an exact place in the pattern, Fig. 12-23. Rubble stonework is made up of irregular shaped stones. If the stones are basically flat the result may look like courses of stone, then the term "coursed rubble" is used. If no coursing effect is evident, the term "random rubble" is applied. Fig. 12-24 shows coursed and random rubble stonework.

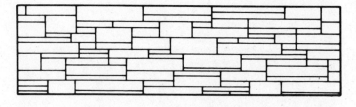

Fig. 12-23. An example of "ashlar" stonework.

Masonry veneer is usually placed one inch away from the frame wall to provide a dead air space for insulation and a means of escape for moisture which condenses on the inside of the masonry. The term veneer is commonly used to indicate that a less expensive or desirable material has been covered up with some type of facing material. The facing is usually 4" thick. The veneer does not help support the weight of the building. Fig. 12-25 shows a construction detail of brick

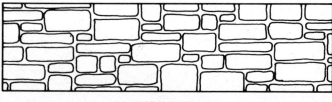

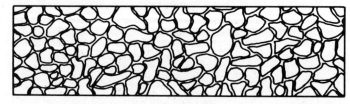

Fig. 12-24. Rubble stonework may be classified as random or coursed rubble.

veneer being used as a facing material over frame construction.

Flashing and termite shields should be used at the base of solid masonry or brick veneer walls. Flashing prevents the entrance of moisture. Termites are a threat in a large part of the country and do millions of dollars in damage to homes each year. Fig. 12-26 shows flashing and a termite shield in brick veneer and solid masonry walls.

If solid masonry wall is used, the top plate must be

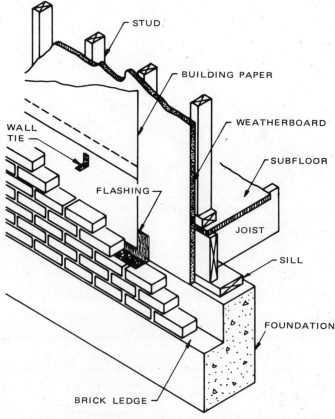

Fig. 12-25. Construction detail of a brick veneer wall section.

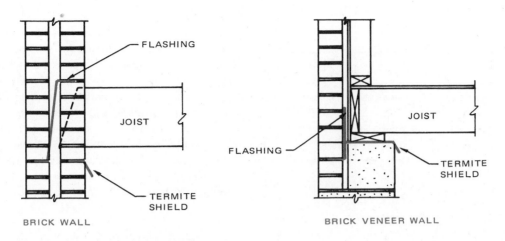

Fig. 12-26. Flashing is used to control moisture. Termite shields are required where termites are a threat.

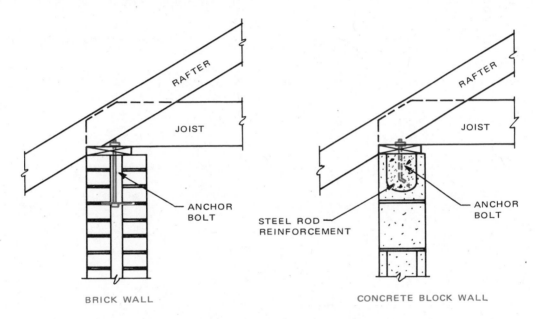

Fig. 12-27. The top plate is attached to masonry walls with anchor bolts embedded in the wall.

anchored securely to the wall, Fig. 12-27. The usual procedure in a brick wall is to place anchor bolts between the bricks and bolt the plate in place. A lintel block is used in concrete block

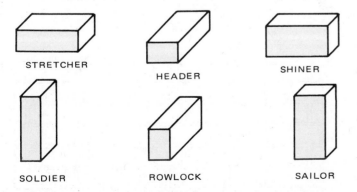

Fig. 12-28. Bricks are laid in six basic positions. Each position has a specific name.

construction and anchor bolts are cast in place. The plate is then secured by the use of bolts.

BRICK NAMES AND SIZES

Brick is a fired clay product. The color is ordinarily determined by the natural color of the clay, but sometimes earth colors are added to produce a wider variety. Brick may be purchased in single colors or in a mixture to produce a blend.

There are two basic types of brick used for wall construction, common brick and face brick. Face brick is usually uniform in size and has sharp corners and lines. Common brick is not as uniform in size and color and may have a lip on one or more edges. In recent years common brick has been used more widely as a facing material. They produce a character which is quite different from the face brick. They look rustic and the texture is much more distinct. They look especially

FLUSH CONCAVE RAKED FLUSH AND RODDED

STRUCK WEATHERED V-SHAPED BEADED

Fig. 12-29. Types of mortar joints.

Specific terms apply to the position or way the brick is laid. Fig. 12-28 illustrates accepted terminology. Note that the term "stretcher," "header," etc. applies to the position of the brick in the wall and not the type or size of the brick.

Numerous types of mortar joints are used in brickwork. Fig. 12-29 shows some joints used in residential construction. Masons have tools designed specifically for making the joints.

A discussion of brickwork would not be complete without mentioning some of the brick bonds which are recognized standards. Fig. 12-30 illustrates a few of the many bonds. The running bond is used extensively in brick veneer construction. The common bond is popular for solid masonry walls.

good with a deep rake joint which accents the individual character of each brick.

The names of brick shapes are well established, but sizes are not standardized. Sizes of brick frequently used in residential construction are shown in the following chart.

BRICK NAMES AND SIZES		
NAME	NOMINAL SIZE	ACTUAL SIZE
ROMAN	4 x 2 x 12"	1 5/8 x 3 5/8 x 11 5/8"
MODULAR	2 2/3 x 4 x 8"	2 1/4 x 3 5/8 x 7 5/8"
SRC BRICK	2 2/3 x 6 x 12"	2 1/8 x 5 1/2 x 11 1/2"
STANDARD	2 2/3 x 4 x 8"	2 1/4 x 3 3/4 x 8"
NORMAN	2 2/3 x 4 x 12"	2 1/4 x 3 5/8 x 11 5/8"
FIRE BRICK*	2 2/3 x 4 x 9"	2 1/2 x 3 5/8 x 9"

*Fire brick is not used for exterior wall construction but is included because it is used in fireplaces.

REVIEW QUESTIONS - UNIT 12

1. The size of ceiling joists depends on:
   a._____ .
   b._____ .
   c._____ .
   d._____ .
   e._____ .

2. The standard parts of a frame wall are:
   a._____ .
   b._____ .
   c._____ .
   d._____ .
   e._____ .

3. Wood framing lumber must have the following properties:
   a._____ .
   b._____ .

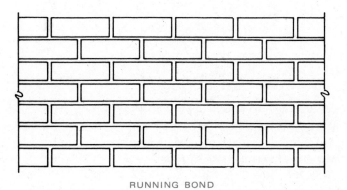

RUNNING BOND

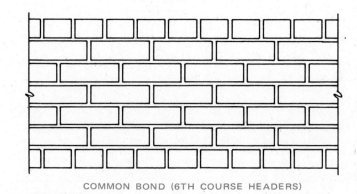

COMMON BOND (6TH COURSE HEADERS)

Fig. 12-30. Four of the most frequently used brick bonds.

STACK BOND

FLEMISH BOND

c. _____.

d. _____.

4. Name three soft woods commonly used as framing lumber.

   a. _____.

   b. _____.

   c. _____.

5. The acceptable range of moisture content for framing lumber is _____ percent.

6. Aluminum framing is also available. List some of its advantages.

   a. _____.

   b. _____.

   c. _____.

7. Finished wall height in most residential structures is _____.

8. The framing member used to span the distance over an opening in the wall such as a door or window is called a _____.

9. What are studs called which are not full length and are used above or below wall openings?

10. The rough opening height of most doors is _____.

11. If a window has a rough opening width of 5'-2", the Header Sizes and Span Chart indicates that the header size will be _____.

12. Name three areas in the house which require special framing consideration.

    a. _____.

    b. _____.

    c. _____.

13. The purpose of a header course of brick in a masonry wall is to _____.

14. The spacing of metal wall ties should be no greater than _____ apart vertically and _____ horizontally.

15. Solid masonry walls for residential construction are usually _____ inches thick.

16. Concrete block walls are sometimes called _____ walls.

17. An angle cut on the end of floor joists in a solid masonry wall is called a _____.

18. The two types of stonework are called _____ and _____.

19. In a brick veneer wall, the space between the brick veneer and stud wall is usually about _____.

20. The top plate is secured to a solid masonry wall by the use of _____.

21. Brick is made primarily of _____.

22. There are basically two types of bricks. They are _____ and _____.

23. The most popular brick mortar bond is called the _____ bond.

SUGGESTED ACTIVITIES

1. Build a scale model, 1" = 1'-0", of a wall section which has at least one door, one window and in intersecting partition. Identify the parts.

2. Select a simple floor plan for a frame house and lay out the wall framing indicating trimmers, cripples, spacing blocks and full studs.

3. Collect samples of building materials to be displayed in class. Identify each of the materials and explain where each might be used in the construction of a house.

4. Build scale models, 1/4 size, of framing for corners, wall intersections and openings for doors and windows. Prepare plan view drawings for display with the models.

5. Visit a building site where a house is being constructed using conventional methods and determine the specie and grade of the framing lumber and identify the type of framing used. (balloon or platform)

6. Photograph as many different brick bonds as you can find in the area surrounding your home. Identify the bonds and prepare them for display.

Note how the use of doors and windows provide for natural viewing from many locations.

Chapter 13
DOORS AND WINDOWS

Doors and windows perform several functions in a residential structure. They shield an opening from the elements, add decoration, emphasize the overall design, provide light and ventilation and expand visibility. Windows and doors are necessary features of all residential structures and should be planned carefully to insure maximum contribution to the overall design and function of the structure.

INTERIOR AND EXTERIOR DOORS

A number of classification systems may be used to identify the various styles and types of doors in residential construction. Two broad classes are interior and exterior doors. Doors may be grouped according to method of construction, uses, function or location.

INTERIOR DOORS

Interior door types include flush, panel, bi-fold, sliding, pocket, double-action, accordion, Dutch, French.

FLUSH DOORS. Flush doors are smooth on both sides and are usually made of wood, Fig. 13-1. Standard interior wood flush doors are 1 3/8'' thick and 6'-8'' high. They are hollow core doors which have a wood frame around the perimeter and wood or composition material placed in the cavity to support the faces of the door. Interior flush doors are produced in a wide range of widths from 2'-0'' to 3'-0''. The standard increment width is 2''. Both surfaces of the door are usually covered with 1/8'' mahogany or birch plywood.

PANEL DOORS. A panel door has a heavy frame around the outside and generally has cross members which form small panels. The vertical members are called STILES and the horizontal pieces are RAILS. Panels which are thinner than the frame are placed in grooves on the inside edges of the stiles and rails to enclose the space. The panels may be wood, glass, metal, or other material, Fig. 13-1. Panel doors are usually produced in white pine, but may be constructed of oak or other woods.

BI-FOLD DOORS. A bi-fold door is made of two parts which together form the door. They may be attached to the

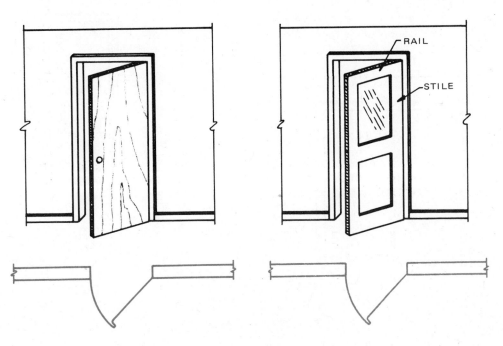

Fig. 13-1. Flush and panel doors with plan view symbol.

side jambs with conventional hinges or secured to the head jamb and floor using a pivot hinge, Fig. 13-2. Bi-fold doors may be flush, paneled or louvered. They are popular as closet doors, and are seldom used for other applications. Bi-fold doors are installed in pairs with each door being the same width. Usual widths are 1'-0" to 2'-0".

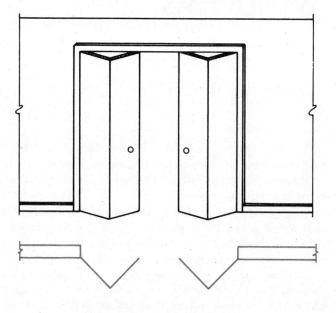

Fig. 13-2. Bi-fold doors with symbol.

Wood and metal bi-fold doors are produced in the standard 6'-8" height as well as 8'-0". The usual thickness is 1 1/8" for wood and 1" for metal.

SLIDING DOORS. Sliding or bi-pass doors are popular where there are large openings, Fig. 13-3. They are frequently used as closet doors. Any number of doors may be used. The width is not critical, because the doors are hung from a track mounted on the head jamb. Door pulls are recessed to allow the doors to pass without interference. Glides are installed on the floor to prevent swinging.

Sliding doors may be flush, paneled or louvered. They are usually construction from wood, but other materials may be used. The major problem with wood sliding doors is warping since they are not restrained by hinges.

POCKET DOORS. The pocket door ordinarily a flush door, is a variation of the sliding door. Ordinarily, only one door is used to close an opening. It is hung from a track mounted on the head jamb and rests in a wall pocket when open, Fig. 13-4.

Pocket doors are frequently used between rooms such as the kitchen and dining room. The chief advantage is that they require no space along the wall when open. However, they are

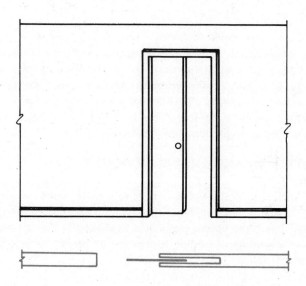

Fig. 13-4. Pocket door.

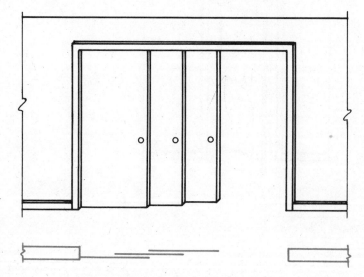

Fig. 13-3. Sliding doors and symbol.

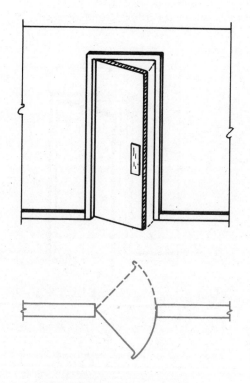

Fig. 13-5. Double-action door.

difficult to operate and present problems if outlets or cabinets are to be located on the wall space outside the pocket cavity. Pocket door frames of metal and wood are usually purchased already assembled.

DOUBLE-ACTION DOORS. Double-action doors are hinged in such a way that they may swing through an arc of 180°, Fig. 13-5. A special double-action, spring loaded hinge is used and is mounted in the center of the side jamb. This door is generally used between rooms which experience a great deal of traffic and require the door closed most of the time. Double-action doors may be single or double doors. A flush, panel or louvered door can be used.

ACCORDION DOORS. Accordion doors are frequently used to close large openings where bi-fold or sliding doors

would not be acceptable. They require little space and are produced in a large variety of materials and designs. They may be constructed from wood, plastics or fabric. Individual hinged panels are sometimes used as well as a large folded piece of fabric or other material. The door is supported on a track mounted on the head jamb, Fig. 13-6.

DUTCH DOORS. A Dutch door is composed of two parts-- an upper and lower half. The top section may be opened independently of the bottom to allow for light and ventilation, Fig. 13-7. This door may be used between the kitchen and dining room or as an exterior door.

FRENCH DOORS. French style doors are panel doors with the panels made from glass, Fig. 13-8. They are popular where the door leads to a patio or terrace. They may also be used between rooms.

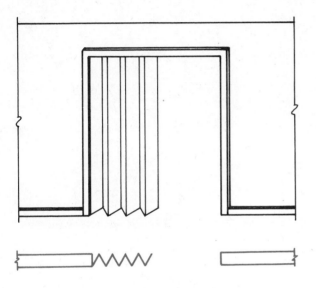

Fig. 13-6. Accordion door.

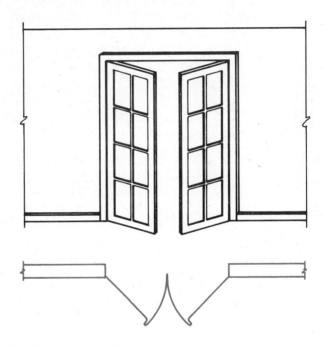

Fig. 13-8. French doors.

EXTERIOR DOORS

Exterior residential doors are similar to some of the interior types, but have decided differences. Exterior wood doors are usually not hollow core as are many interior doors. They are also thicker than interior doors and may have one or more glass panels to provide visibility. Doors commonly used include:

FLUSH DOORS. Standard exterior flush wood doors are usually 1 3/4" thick and 6'-8" high. Ordinarily, they are 3'-0" wide. The flush door is one of the most popular exterior doors, Fig. 13-9. These are produced from birch, mahogany, oak and several other woods. Moldings or other decorative mill work may be added to the flush door to enhance its appearance. Fig. 13-10 shows plan view symbols for various types of exterior doors.

PANEL DOORS. Exterior panel doors come in a great

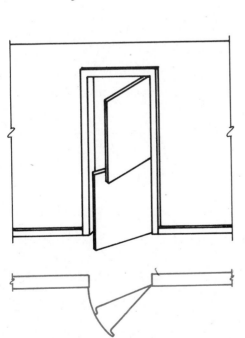

Fig. 13-7. Dutch door.

Fig. 13-9. Plain exterior flush door used in modern residence with lots of glass. (Andersen Corp.)

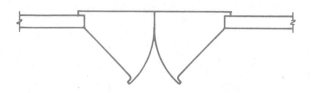

DOUBLE FLUSH OR PANEL DOORS IN FRAME WALL

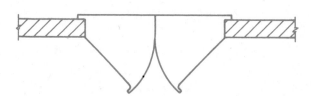

DOUBLE FLUSH OR PANEL DOORS IN MASONRY WALL

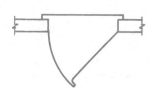

SINGLE FLUSH OR PANEL DOOR IN FRAME WALL

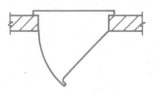

SINGLE FLUSH OR PANEL DOOR IN MASONRY WALL

SLIDING DOOR UNIT IN FRAME WALL

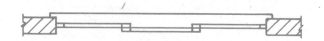

SLIDING DOOR UNIT IN MASONRY WALL

Fig. 13-10. These are standard plan view symbols of common exterior doors.

Doors and Windows

Fig. 13-11. Two vastly different styles of doors which accent the entry and communicate a definite architectural style.

Fig. 13-12. These glass "sliding" doors provide a panoramic view and easy access to the deck.   (Marvin Windows)

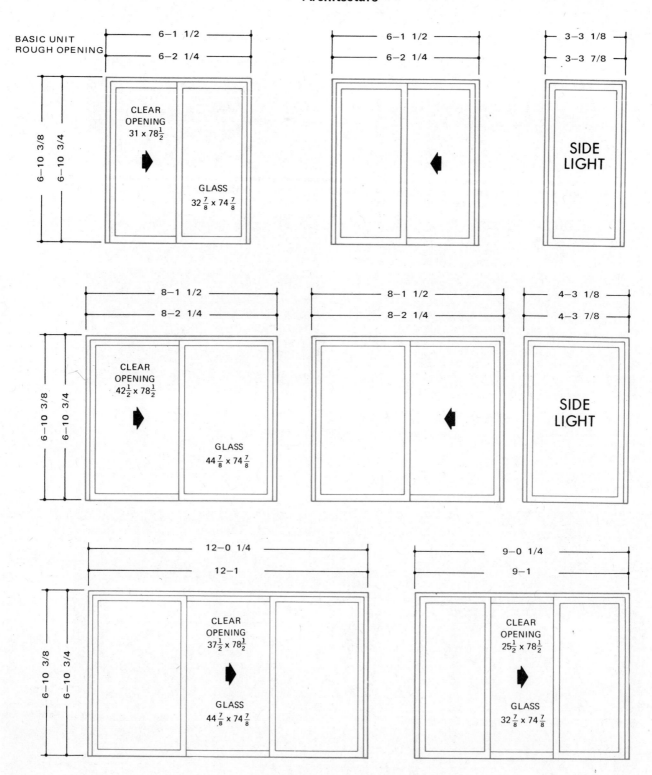

Fig. 13-13. Standard sizes of glass sliding doors.

variety of styles. They are constructed from white pine, oak, fir and various other woods. These doors are produced in the same sizes as flush doors. Fig. 13-11 shows two different styles of panel doors which are available.

SLIDING GLASS DOORS. In recent years sliding glass doors have increased in use and in popularity, Figs. 13-12 and 13-13. Sliding doors, Fig. 13-14 are produced in both wood and metal units. Fig. 13-13 shows some of the standard sizes

of exterior sliding glass doors which are available.

GARAGE DOORS. Two types of garage doors which account for most of the doors used are the overhead sectional and the one-piece overhead door, Fig. 13-15. Garage doors are available in wood, metal and plastics. Each material has its advantages and personal choice is usually the determining factor in selection. The following chart shows standard garage door sizes.

Fig. 13-14. Glass sliding door with vinyl coating which does away with painting. (Anderson Corp.)

Single Doors	Double Doors
Height x Width	Height x Width
6'-6'' x 8'-0''	6'-6'' x 15'-0''
*7'-0'' x 8'-0''	7'-0'' x 15'-0''
6'-6'' x 9'-0''	6'-6'' x 16'-0''
7'-0'' x 9'-0''	*7'-0'' x 16'-0''
	7'-0'' x 18'-0''

*These sizes are the most frequently used.

SPECIFYING DOORS

Each door identified on the foundation plan and floor plan should appear on a "door schedule." Information included on the door schedule should be obtained from manufacturers' literature. Specifications vary and it is important to have exact information for the schedule. A typical door schedule is shown in Fig. 13-16. The door schedule should be placed on the sheet with the floor plan or elevations if space permits.

DOOR DETAILS

An interior or exterior door is placed inside a door jamb. (A door jamb is the frame which fits inside the rough opening, Fig. 13-17.) Jambs may be constructed from wood or metal. Wood jambs are most common in residential construction. A jamb consists of three parts--two side jambs and a head jamb across the top. Jambs for exterior doors are ordinarily 1 1/8''

ONE-PIECE GARAGE DOOR

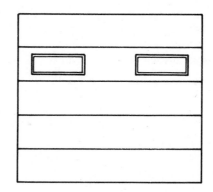

SECTIONAL GARAGE DOOR

Fig. 13-15. Two commonly used types of garage doors.

			DOOR SCHEDULE			
SYM.	QUAN.	TYPE	ROUGH OPENING	DOOR SIZE	MANUFACTURER'S NO.	REMARKS
A	2	FLUSH	3'-2 1/2'' x 6'-9 1/4''	3'-0'' x 6'-8''	EF 36 B	1 3/4'' SOLID CORE, BIRCH
B	6	FLUSH	2'-10 1/2'' x 6'-9 1/4''	2'-8'' x 6'-8''	IF 32 M	1 3/8'' HOLLOW CORE, MAHOGANY
C	2	FLUSH	2'-8 1/2'' x 6'-9 1/4''	2'-6'' x 6'-8''	IF 30 M	1 3/8'' HOLLOW CORE, MAHOGANY
D	8	BI-FOLD	SEE MANUFACTURER'S SPECS.	6'-0'' x 6'-8''	BF 36 AL	TWO UNITS EACH 36'' WIDE, ALUMINUM
E	2	SLIDING	4'-2 1/2'' x 6'-9 1/4''	4'-0'' x 6'-8''	IF 24 M	1 1/8'' HOLLOW CORE, MAHOGANY
F	1	GARAGE	SEE MANUFACTURER'S SPECS.	16'-0'' x 7'-0''	G 16 S	TWO-LITE OVERHEAD SECTIONAL, ALUM.

Fig. 13-16. A typical door schedule for a set of residential house plans.

Architecture

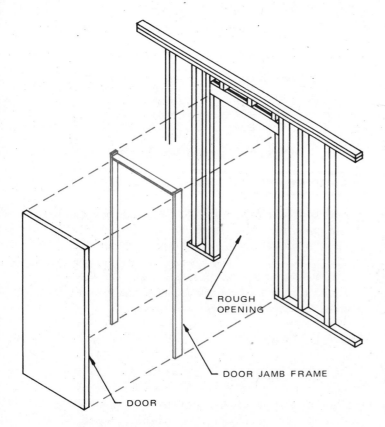

Fig. 13-17. The door jamb fits inside the rough opening and supports the door.

thick while interior jambs are 3/4". The door stop is rabbeted into the thicker exterior jambs, but is applied to the face of interior jambs, Fig. 13-18.

Jambs are available already assembled with the door hung and ready for installation. These are called pre-hung units. Pre-hung units are adjustable for slight variations in wall thickness.

Rough openings for interior doors are usually framed 3" more than the door height and 2 1/2" more than the door width. This provides ample space for the jambs and the necessary leveling and squaring. The space between the jamb and rough framing is covered with trim called "casing." Exterior casing is usually thicker. When installed in a masonry

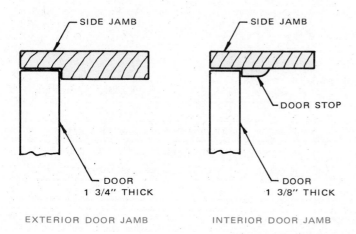

Fig. 13-18. Detail of interior and exterior wood door jambs.

wall it is called brick mold. A "drip cap" is used over the top piece of trim to shed water in frame construction. Such a strip is not necessary in masonry construction.

Exterior doors require a sill at the bottom of the door opening between the two side jambs. A sill is designed to drain water away from the door and provide support for the side jambs. Sills are constructed from wood, metal, concrete and stone. Fig. 13-19 shows a typical exterior flush door detail in frame and brick veneer construction. Door and window construction details are usually drawn in section through the head jamb (the jamb across the top of the opening), the side jamb and the sill. The drawings show head, jamb and sill details.

Construction details for exterior sliding door units are slightly more complicated than other doors, Fig. 13-20. Exterior sliding door jambs vary from one manufacturer to another. The number of door units may also affect the size and shape of the jambs. When specifying exterior sliding doors it is advisable to secure specifications from manufacturers to assure accuracy.

Ordinarily it is not necessary to draw detailed window and door section drawings in conventional construction. However, if special framing or uncommon construction is involved, then these drawings are a necessary part of a set of construction drawings.

WINDOWS

When selecting windows for a home it is important to remember the functions which windows perform. They admit light from the outside; provide fresh air and ventilation to the various rooms; help to create an atmosphere inside by framing an exterior view; and add detail, balance and design to the exterior of the house.

A uniform amount of light across a room is desirable. Proper design and placement of windows will help to eliminate dark corners and extremely bright areas. The following guidelines will help achieve a more evenly lighted room:

1. Glass area should be at least 20% of the floor area of the room. This amount of glass will provide an adequate amount of natural light even on cloudy days. When the light outside is very bright the intensity may be controlled with shades or drapes.

2. For increased light, face principal window areas toward the south. More light also means more heat, therefore, in warm climates a northerly orientation may be preferred.

3. One large window opening will produce less contrast in brightness than several smaller openings.

4. Better distribution of light will be accomplished if windows are placed on more than one wall.

5. Windows placed high on a wall will provide a greater degree of light penetration into the room than windows placed low.

6. Select the window shape which gives the type of light distribution desired in the room. Tall, narrow windows tend to give a thin and deep penetration while short, wide windows produce a shallow penetration over a broad area.

Natural ventilation in a home is necessary all year long, but

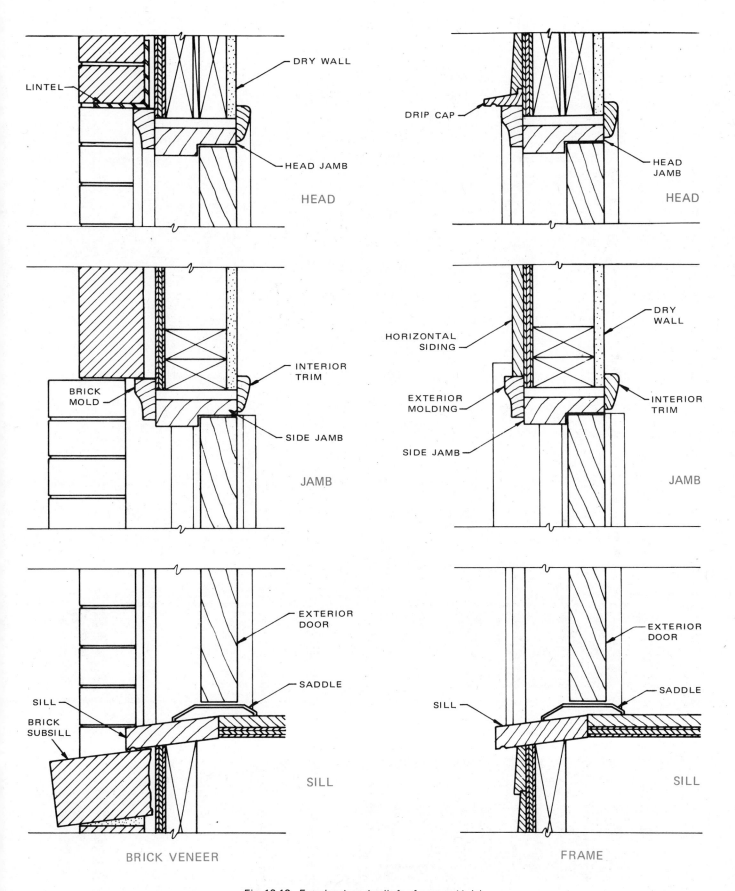

Fig. 13-19. Exterior door details for frame and brick veneer construction.

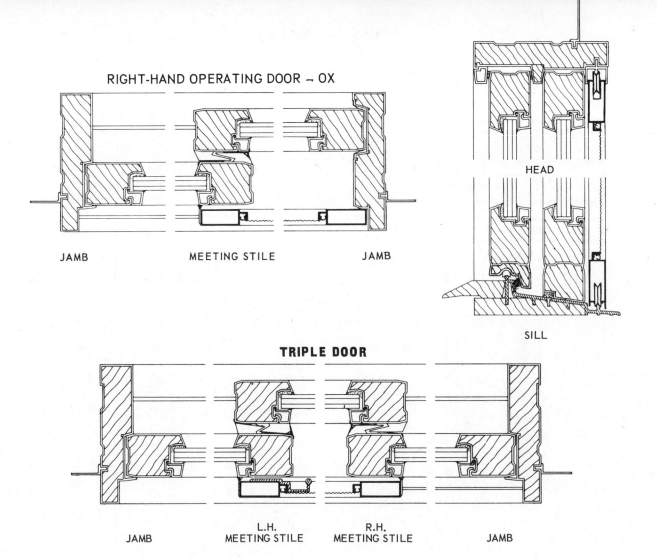

RIGHT-HAND OPERATING DOOR — OX

JAMB   MEETING STILE   JAMB

HEAD

SILL

TRIPLE DOOR

JAMB   L.H.   R.H.   JAMB
MEETING STILE   MEETING STILE

Fig. 13-20. Vinyl covered glass sliding door details.

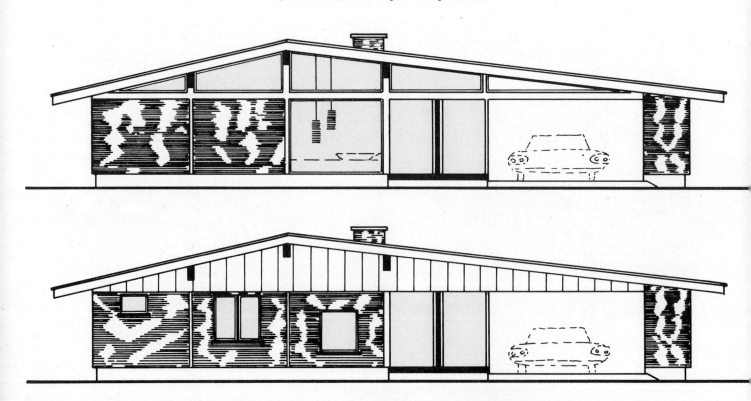

Fig. 13-21. A comparison of how the glass areas in two houses relate to the wall areas.

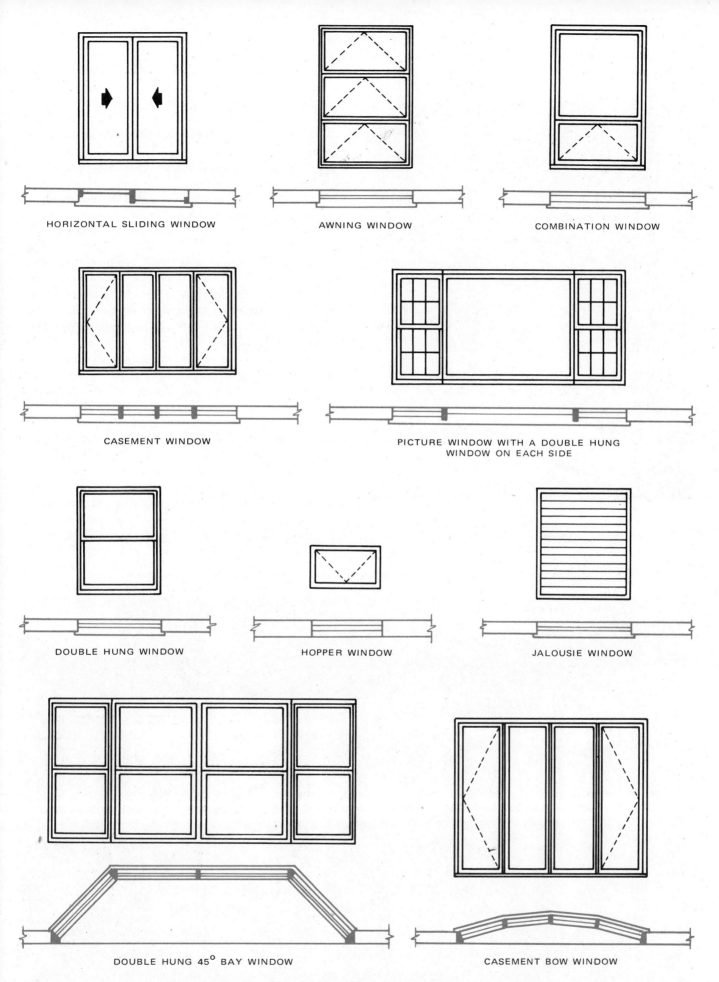

HORIZONTAL SLIDING WINDOW

AWNING WINDOW

COMBINATION WINDOW

CASEMENT WINDOW

PICTURE WINDOW WITH A DOUBLE HUNG
WINDOW ON EACH SIDE

DOUBLE HUNG WINDOW

HOPPER WINDOW

JALOUSIE WINDOW

DOUBLE HUNG 45° BAY WINDOW

CASEMENT BOW WINDOW

Fig. 13-22. Types of windows frequently used in residential construction.

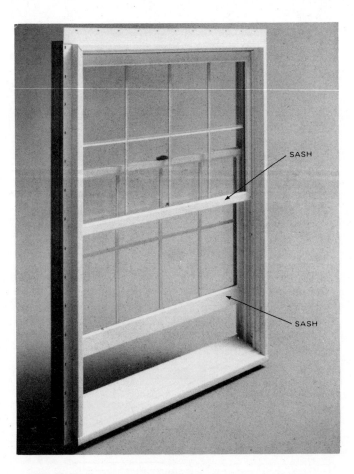

Fig. 13-23. A vinyl covered double hung window with muntins. (Andersen Corp.)

is especially important during the summer months. If windows are located with adequate ventilation in mind, comfort will be increased considerably. Apply these guidelines for efficient ventilation:

1. Openings for ventilation should be at least 10% of the floor area.

2. Placement of openings for ventilation should take advantage of prevailing breezes.

3. Locate windows in such a way that the best movement of air across the room will be achieved. Furniture should be planned so it will not interfere with the flow of air through the room.

Windows may often be used to enhance an existing view or provide a selective one. Large glass areas tend to make a room look larger. The size and shape of the windows will frame the view so it is important to select a window of the proper proportions ... one which does not have obstructions which interfere with the view.

The following points will aid the designer in specifying the proper window for a particular view:

1. A large area of fixed glass provides clear viewing without obstructions.

2. Horizontal and vertical divisions in the window or between windows should be thin to minimize obstruction.

3. Sill heights of windows should be determined on the basis of furniture, room arrangement and view.

Designing a home to be functional, efficient and pleasing to the eye on the outside is no small task. Some of the guidelines provided may conflict. A home which has been designed for light, view and ventilation may not have a pleasing exterior

Fig. 13-24. These double hung windows transmit the warmth of wood and solidarity. (Marvin Windows)

WINDOW UNIT SIZES

Fig. 13-25. Standard sizes of double hung windows.

235

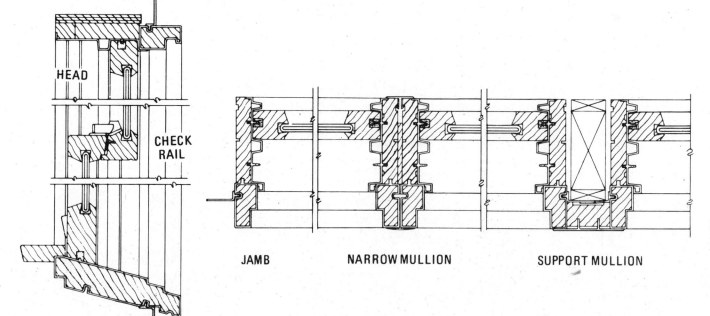

Fig. 13-26. Double hung window details.

appearance. The challenge is to meet all the requirement of good design in a creative way.

The placement and number of windows affect the overall design appearance of the home. Even though windows should be selected to fulfill interior needs, the size, placement and type may be varied slightly to improve the outside appearance of the home. Windows can add to the continuity of the design. They should relate to the solid wall areas rather than appear to be just a variety of openings in a wall, Fig. 13-21.

WINDOW TYPES

Many different types of windows are available. They are made of wood, aluminum and steel. Most types have their own proportions and are different in construction. To further complicate the matter, windows of the same general type, purchased from different manufacturers, will seldom be exactly the same. For these reasons, it is very important to

Fig. 13-27. Vinyl clad sliding window.

Fig. 13-28. Friction is reduced by installing a plastic or metal track rather than wood against wood.

SIZES AND LAYOUTS

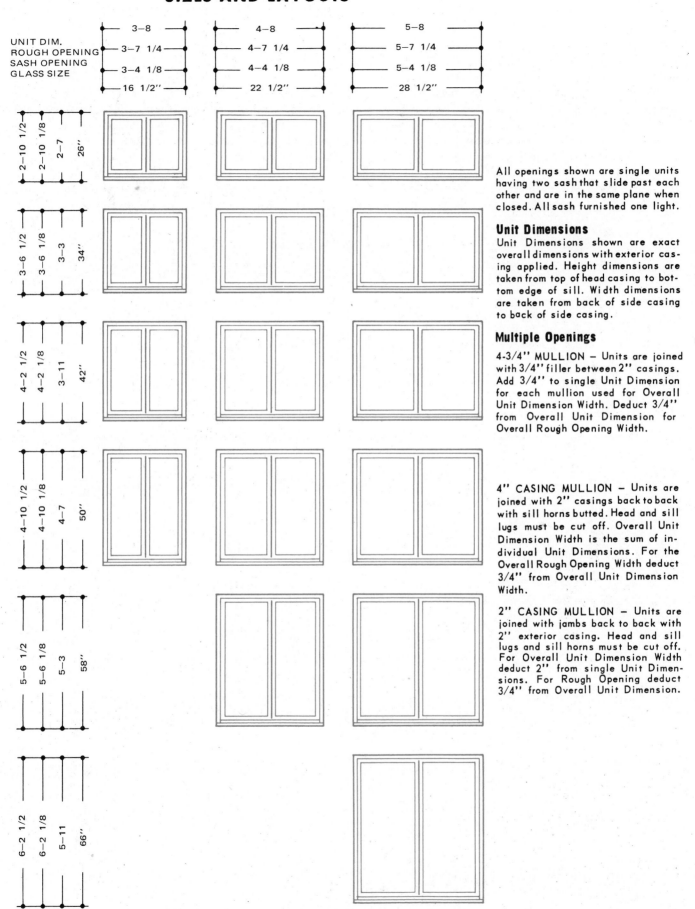

UNIT DIM.
ROUGH OPENING
SASH OPENING
GLASS SIZE

3—8	4—8	5—8
3—7 1/4	4—7 1/4	5—7 1/4
3—4 1/8	4—4 1/8	5—4 1/8
16 1/2"	22 1/2"	28 1/2"

2—10 1/2 / 2—10 1/8 / 2—7 / 26"

3—6 1/2 / 3—6 1/8 / 3—3 / 34"

4—2 1/2 / 4—2 1/8 / 3—11 / 42"

4—10 1/2 / 4—10 1/8 / 4—7 / 50"

5—6 1/2 / 5—6 1/8 / 5—3 / 58"

6—2 1/2 / 6—2 1/8 / 5—11 / 66"

All openings shown are single units having two sash that slide past each other and are in the same plane when closed. All sash furnished one light.

Unit Dimensions

Unit Dimensions shown are exact overall dimensions with exterior casing applied. Height dimensions are taken from top of head casing to bottom edge of sill. Width dimensions are taken from back of side casing to back of side casing.

Multiple Openings

4-3/4" MULLION — Units are joined with 3/4" filler between 2" casings. Add 3/4" to single Unit Dimension for each mullion used for Overall Unit Dimension Width. Deduct 3/4" from Overall Unit Dimension for Overall Rough Opening Width.

4" CASING MULLION — Units are joined with 2" casings back to back with sill horns butted. Head and sill lugs must be cut off. Overall Unit Dimension Width is the sum of individual Unit Dimensions. For the Overall Rough Opening Width deduct 3/4" from Overall Unit Dimension Width.

2" CASING MULLION — Units are joined with jambs back to back with 2" exterior casing. Head and sill lugs and sill horns must be cut off. For Overall Unit Dimension Width deduct 2" from single Unit Dimensions. For Rough Opening deduct 3/4" from Overall Unit Dimension.

Fig. 13-29. Sizes of horizontal sliding windows.

secure specifications for windows selected, from the producers.

Windows to be discussed in this Chapter include: double hung, horizontal sliding or glider, casement, awning, hopper, jalousie, bay or bow, picture and combination, Fig. 13-22.

DOUBLE HUNG WINDOWS. Double hung windows have two sashes, Figs. 13-23 and 13-24. The sashes slide up and down in grooves formed in the window frames. The weight of the sashes are usually counter balanced or have friction devices which hold the sash in the desired positions.

Muntins are small vertical and horizontal bars which separate the total glass area into smaller units. Mullions, not to be confused with muntins, are larger horizontal or vertical members which are placed between window units.

Fig. 13-25 gives the sizes of double hung windows produced by one manufacturer. Note that four different sizes are given for each window. The basic unit size represents the overall dimensions of the window unit. The rough opening size is the rough framed space in a wall required to install the window. Sash opening refers to the size of the opening inside the frame or outside dimensions of the sash. Glass size is the unobstructed glass size. This would be the same as the inside dimensions of the sash.

Double hung window details are presented in Fig. 13-26. Sections are traditionally drawn at the head jamb, side jamb and sill, just as in drawing doors. When a number of windows

CORNER WINDOW DETAIL

PLAN SECTION

HEAD

JAMB   MEETING STILE   JAMB

SILL   Fig. 13-30. Construction details of a horizontal sliding window.

238

Fig. 13-31. A modern casement window with grille.

are placed together to form a unit it is often necessary to draw a section of the support mullion also.

HORIZONTAL SLIDING OR GLIDER WINDOWS. Horizontal sliding windows ordinarily have two sashes, Fig. 13-27. In some models both sashes are movable; some models have one fixed sash. A track attached to the head jamb and sill provides for movement, Fig. 13-28. Rollers are usually not required for windows unless they are quite large. Fig. 13-29 gives the standard sizes of one brand of horizontal sliding windows. Construction details are presented in Fig. 13-30.

CASEMENT WINDOWS. A casement window has sashes hinged at the side which swing outward, Fig. 13-31. A single window unit may have several sashes separated by vertical mullions or a single sash, Fig. 13-32.

Fig. 13-32. Single sash wood casement window. (Andersen Corp.)

Fig. 13-33. Casement windows operated with hand crank. (Marvin Windows)

Architecture

A casement window may be opened or closed by using a crank, or push-bar on the frame, or a handle on the sash. See Fig. 13-33.

Casement windows are produced in a wide variety of sizes, see Fig. 13-34. Single units may be placed together to form a larger section. Fig. 13-35 shows the construction details for one type of casement window.

Hinge position on a hinged window may be shown in the elevation view of a plan by using a dashed line as shown in Fig. 13-36. It is usually advisable to indicate the direction of swing.

AWNING WINDOWS. An awning window may have several sashes or only a single sash. Each sash is hinged at the top and swings out at an angle like "awnings," Fig. 13-37.

Crank operated awning windows are manufactured in a

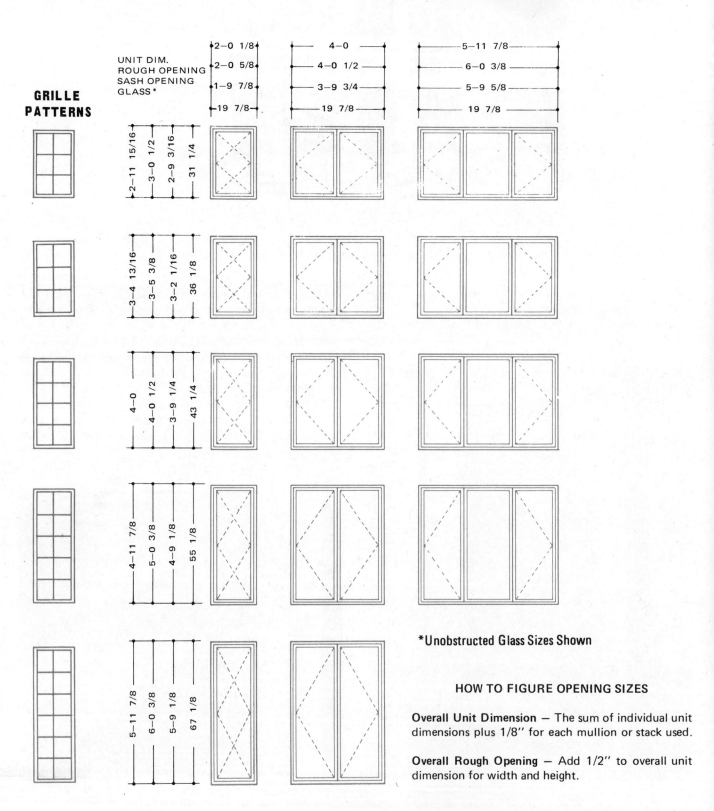

*Unobstructed Glass Sizes Shown

HOW TO FIGURE OPENING SIZES

Overall Unit Dimension — The sum of individual unit dimensions plus 1/8" for each mullion or stack used.

Overall Rough Opening — Add 1/2" to overall unit dimension for width and height.

Fig. 13-34. Standard casement window sizes.

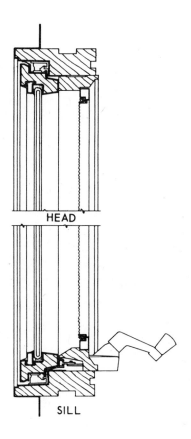

Fig. 13-37. A modern awning window with crank.
(Andersen Corp.)

HEAD

SILL

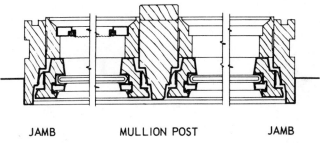

JAMB MULLION POST JAMB

Fig. 13-35. Casement window details.

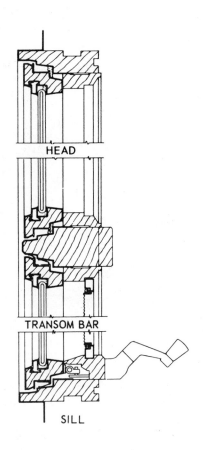

HEAD

TRANSOM BAR

SILL

wide variety of sizes. The head, jamb, sill and transom bar (horizontal divider) details are shown in Fig. 13-38 for the awning crank type window. Fig. 13-39 shows some of the standard sizes offered by one company.

HOPPER WINDOWS. The hopper window is usually an

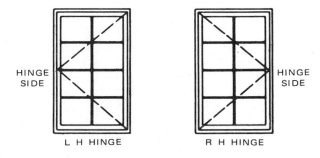

HINGE SIDE

HINGE SIDE

L H HINGE R H HINGE

Fig. 13-36. A dashed line symbol may be used to indicate hinged side of windows as shown above.

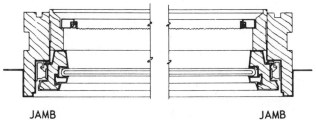

JAMB JAMB

Fig. 13-38. Awning window details.

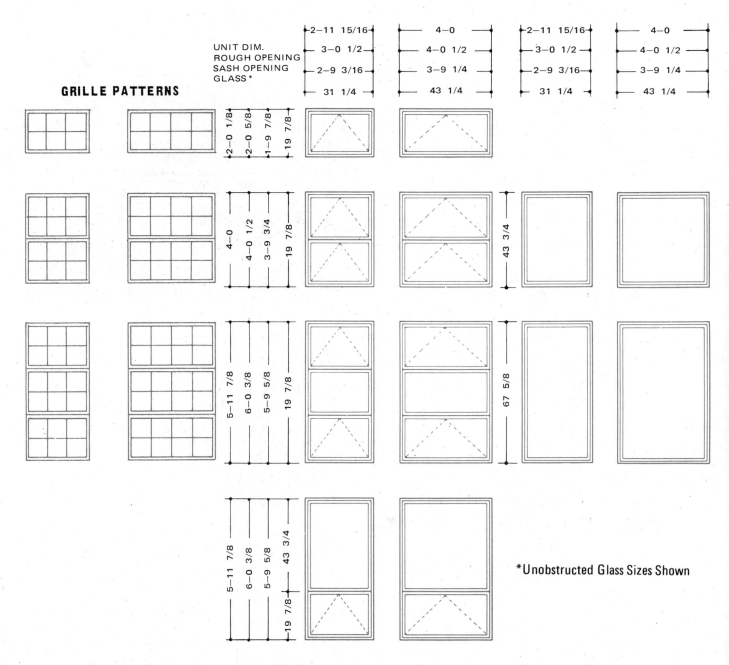

Fig. 13-39. Standard awning window sizes.

*Unobstructed Glass Sizes Shown

Fig. 13-40. Wood hopper window.

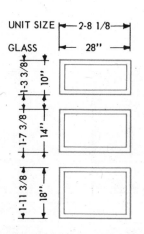

Fig. 13-41. Hopper window sizes.

inswinging window. It is hinged at the bottom and is opened by a lock-handle at the top of the sash. It is usually manufactured only as a single unit, Fig. 13-40. Hopper windows are popular for basement use.

Hopper windows direct air upward and should be placed low on the wall for best ventilation. They are easy to open and wash from the inside. The major disadvantage is that they swing inward. This interferes with the use of space in front of the window.

Hopper windows are produced in a relatively small number of sizes. Fig. 13-41 shows the sizes available from one company. Section details are shown in Fig. 13-42 for plaster and dry wall construction. Fig. 13-43 shows a section detail through a hopper window in a concrete block wall. This detail shows a typical basement installation.

JALOUSIE WINDOWS. A jalousie window has a series of narrow horizontal glass slats (usually 3″ wide in residential windows), which are held in metal clips and fastened to a frame. The slats operate in unison similar to venetian blinds.

Jalousie windows are produced in a variety of sizes (usually aluminum). Widths range from 18″ to 48″ in increments of 2 inches. Lengths are available from 17″ to 99 1/2″ in increments of 2 1/2 inches. Louver lengths are usually 2″ shorter than the window width (buck size). Head, jamb, sill and mullion details for an aluminum jalousie window are shown in Fig. 13-44.

PICTURE WINDOWS. The term "picture window" is used because the view is "framed" like a picture. Picture windows are fixed-glass units and are usually rather large. Fig. 13-45 shows the use of large fixed windows to provide an outdoor

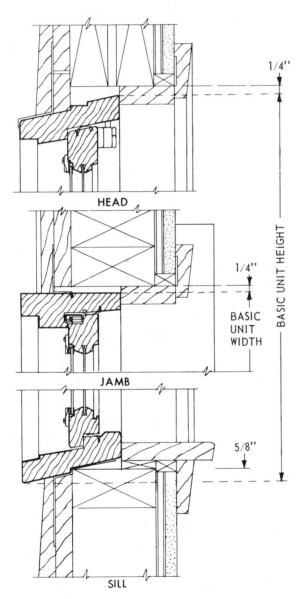

Shadow box installation with 3/4″ sheathing and lath and plaster on interior. Exterior casing and subsill omitted.

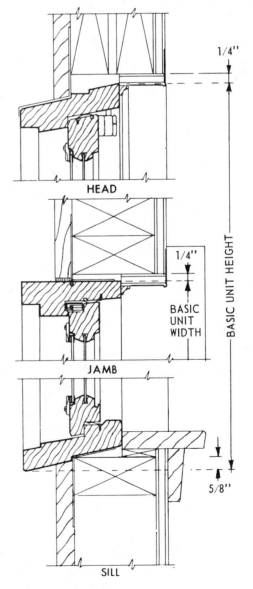

Single frame wall construction with dry wall interior returned into jambs. Note position of unit in wall.

Fig. 13-42. Details of hopper window used in plaster and dry wall construction.

mixture of two or more types of windows. Fig. 13-51 illustrates one type of combination window produced as a stock item. This particular window uses fixed and awning windows together to form the combination. Many variations are possible.

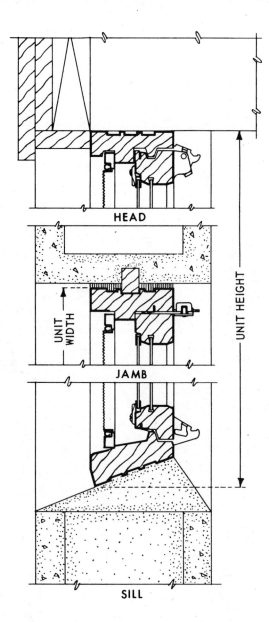

Fig. 13-43. A typical hopper window installation in a concrete block wall.

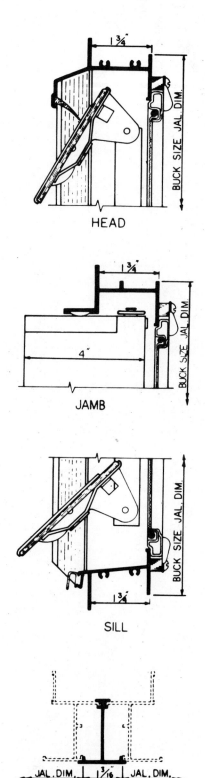

Fig. 13-44. Head, jamb, sill and mullion details of an aluminum jalousie window.

atmosphere to a modern post and beam structure. Picture windows are often the center unit of a group of regular windows. They do not function as ventilators, but they provide excellent views and admit large amounts of light.

Picture windows may be purchased in fixed sash or custom-made on the job. Fig. 13-46 gives the standard sizes of picture window units produced by one manufacturer. Fig. 13-47 illustrates the construction details of a manufactured picture window.

BAY OR BOW WINDOWS. Bay or bow windows may be constructed using most any kind of windows including double hung, casement, and fixed panels. Bay windows are frequently used in traditional styled homes, Fig. 13-48.

Fig. 13-49 shows a typical plan view layout for several bow windows using casement type windows. A typical 45° bay window detail is shown in Fig. 13-50.

COMBINATION WINDOWS. Combination windows are a

Fig. 13-45. This modern home provides an outdoor atmosphere through the use of large fixed glass panels.   (David Knox)

GLASS RABBET	EXACT GLASS SIZE FOR	
	1" INSULATING	1/4" PLATE
44 15/16 x 36 9/16	44 1/2 x 36	44 3/4 x 36 1/4
69 3/16 x 36 9/16	68 3/4 x 36	69 x 36 1/4
93 7/16 x 36 9/16	93 x 36	93 1/4 x 36 1/4
44 15/16 x 48 3/4	44 1/2 x 48 1/8	44 3/4 x 48 1/2
69 3/16 x 48 3/4	68 3/4 x 48 1/8	69 x 48 1/2
93 7/16 x 48 3/4	93 x 48 1/8	93 1/4 x 48 1/2
44 15/16 x 60 15/16	44 1/2 x 60 3/8	44 3/4 x 60 5/8
69 3/16 x 60 15/16	68 3/4 x 60 3/8	69 x 60 5/8
93 7/16 x 60 15/16	93 x 60 3/8	93 1/4 x 60 5/8
44 15/16 x 73 3/8	44 1/2 x 72 3/4	44 3/4 x 73
69 3/16 x 73 3/8	68 3/4 x 72 3/4	69 x 73
93 7/16 x 73 3/8	93 x 72 3/4	93 1/4 x 73

Fig. 13-46.. Standard picture window sizes in sash units.

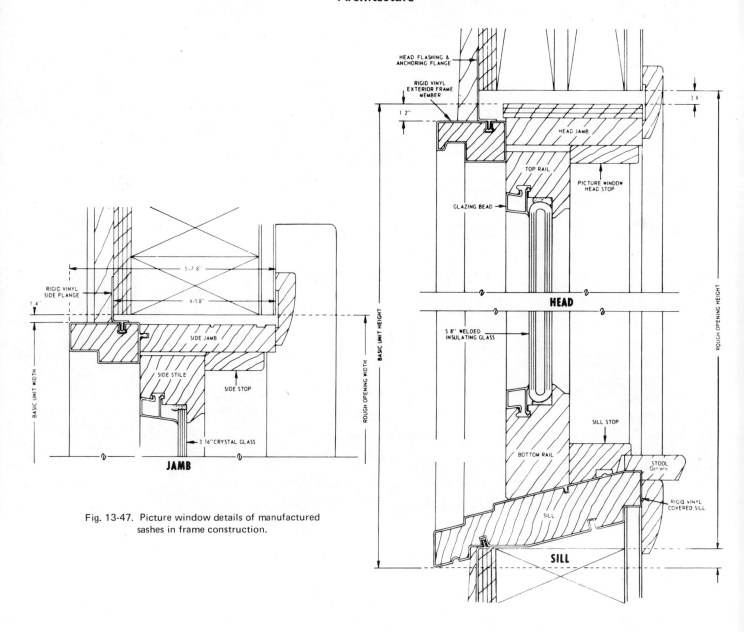

RIGID VINYL
SIDE FLANGE

1 4"

5-7 8"

4-5 8"

SIDE JAMB

SIDE STILE

SIDE STOP

3 16" CRYSTAL GLASS

JAMB

BASIC UNIT WIDTH

ROUGH OPENING WIDTH

HEAD FLASHING &
ANCHORING FLANGE

RIGID VINYL
EXTERIOR FRAME
MEMBER

1 2"

3 8"

HEAD JAMB

TOP RAIL

PICTURE WINDOW
HEAD STOP

GLAZING BEAD

HEAD

5 8" WELDED
INSULATING GLASS

SILL STOP

BOTTOM RAIL

STOOL
Optional

SILL

RIGID VINYL
COVERED SILL

SILL

BASIC UNIT HEIGHT

ROUGH OPENING HEIGHT

Fig. 13-47. Picture window details of manufactured
sashes in frame construction.

Fig. 13-48. This traditional style home is an ideal candidate for a bay
window.   (Marvin Windows)

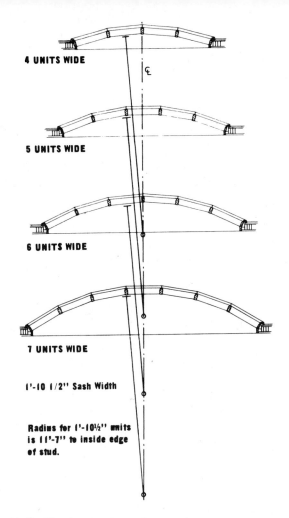

4 UNITS WIDE

5 UNITS WIDE

6 UNITS WIDE

7 UNITS WIDE

1'-10 1/2'' Sash Width

Radius for 1'-10½'' units
is 11'-7'' to inside edge
of stud.

Fig. 13-49. The plan view layout for several casement bow windows.

Fig. 13-51. A combination window which teams a picture window with an awning. (Andersen Corp.)

45° ANGLE BAY DETAILS

Metal or wood support brackets must be used below angle bay units.

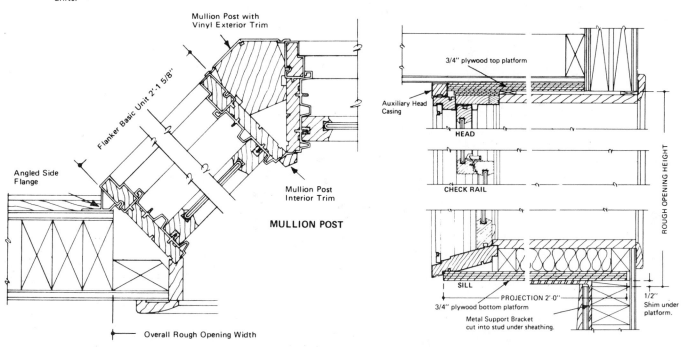

Mullion Post with
Vinyl Exterior Trim

Flanker Basic Unit 2'·1 5/8''

Angled Side
Flange

Mullion Post
Interior Trim

MULLION POST

Overall Rough Opening Width

SIDE JAMB

3/4'' plywood top platform

Auxiliary Head
Casing

HEAD

CHECK RAIL

ROUGH OPENING HEIGHT

SILL

PROJECTION 2'·0''

3/4'' plywood bottom platform

Metal Support Bracket
cut into stud under sheathing.

1/2''
Shim under
platform.

Fig. 13-50. Details of a typical 45° bay window.

247

WINDOW SCHEDULE						
SYM.	QUAN.	TYPE	ROUGH OPENING	SASH SIZE	MANUFACTURE NO.	REMARKS
A	6	CASEMENT	3'−6 1/8" x 5'−1"	3'−2 1/4" x 4'−9 1/4"	3N3	PRIMED, SCREENS, INSULATING GLASS
B	1	CASEMENT	3'−6 1/8" x 3'−3 1/4"	3'−2 1/4" x 3'−1 1/2"	2N3	PRIMED, SCREENS, INSULATING GLASS
C	1	CASEMENT	5'−6 1/2" x 8'−4 1/2"	5'−2 5/8" x 8'−1"	5N5	PRIMED, SCREENS, INSULATING GLASS
D	1	CASEMENT	2'−5 7/8" x 3'−5 1/4"	2'−2" x 3'−1 3/4"	2N2	PRIMED, SCREENS, INSULATING GLASS
E	5	HOPPER	1'−8" x 5'−5"	1'−4" x 5'−2"	314	EXTERIOR CASING OR SUBSILL NOT INCLUDED
F	2	FIXED	2'−4" x 6'−9 1/4"	SEE REMARKS	CUSTOM	GLASS SIZE − 2'−0" x 6'−8", INSUL.

Fig. 13-52. A typical window schedule layout which includes spaces for information required.

WINDOW SCHEDULES

A window schedule provides pertinent information about the windows in a structure; information such as type of window, size, identifying symbol, manufacturer's number, and installation.

The window schedule may be placed on the same sheet as the floor plan or elevation if space permits. Otherwise, it may be located on one of the other drawings.

Care must be taken to ensure that all windows are listed on the schedule and are properly identified. A sample window schedule is shown in Fig. 13-52.

REVIEW QUESTIONS – CHAPTER 13

1. List four functions of doors and windows.
   a._____ .
   b._____ .
   c._____ .
   d._____ .
2. Name eight types of interior doors.
   a._____ .
   b._____ .
   c._____ .
   d._____ .
   e._____ .
   f._____ .
   g._____ .
   h._____ .
3. Interior flush doors are usually_____ inches thick.
4. The horizontal members in panel doors are called _____ while the vertical members are _____ .
5. The main use of bi-fold doors in residential construction is _____ .
6. Standard height for most interior and exterior doors is _____ .
7. A door which is hung from a track mounted on the head jamb and is inside the wall when it is open is a _____ door.
8. A door which swings through a 180° arc is called a _____ door.
9. Name two ways in which exterior doors are different from interior doors.
   a._____ .
   b._____ .
10. Exterior doors are usually_____ wide.

11. What are the two types of garage doors most commonly used?
    a._____ .
    b._____ .
12. Door details are usually section-drawings cut through the _____ , _____ and _____ .
13. What is the function of a drip cap?
14. Glass area should be at least _____ percent of the floor area of any room.
15. Name one type of window which does not provide any ventilation.
16. Name eight different types of windows.
    a._____ .
    b._____ .
    c._____ .
    d._____ .
    e._____ .
    f._____ .
    g._____ .
    h._____ .
17. The small vertical and horizontal bars which separate the total glass area into smaller units are called _____ .
18. What does the "rough opening" size of a window represent?
19. What type of window is hinged at the side and swings out?
20. The name of the window which is commonly used in basements is the _____ window.
21. Information about windows used in a house is recorded on a _____ .

SUGGESTED ACTIVITIES

1. Make a list of the types and sizes of doors and windows in your home.
2. Build a scale model of an exterior or interior door, jambs, and rough framing. Present the model with plan, elevation, and section drawings.
3. Select a floor plan for a small to medium size house and plan the windows following the guidelines presented for ventilation, light, and view.
4. Visit a local lumber company and examine the cut-away models of the windows they handle. Measure the various parts of one model and prepare a sketch. Identify the type of window and the manufacturer. Collect any specification data about the windows that you can and bring it to class for reference purposes.

Chapter 14
STAIRS

A stairway is a series of steps with or without landings or platforms which is installed between two or more floors of a building. Stairs provide easy access to various levels of the home. All styles of homes, except the ranch with no basement, have stairs. Prime considerations in stair design should be easy ascent or descent and safety.

A house may have a main stairs (from the first floor to the second floor or from a split foyer to the first floor) and/or a service stairs. The main stairs are usually assembled with prefabricated parts and are of a much better quality than service stairs. They are generally made of hard woods such as oak, maple or birch. Service stairs are frequently constructed on location and are ordinarily made of Douglas fir or pine.

TYPES OF STAIRS

Six general types of stairs are commonly used in residential construction. They are the straight run stairs, L stairs, double L stairs, U stairs, winder stairs and spiral stairs.

THE STRAIGHT RUN STAIRS, Fig. 14-1, are the stairs used most in home construction. Straight stairs, as the name implies, have no turns. These stairs are not as expensive to construct as other types of stairs.

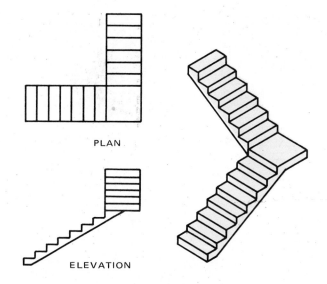

Fig. 14-2. L stairs.

difference. L stairs are used when the space required for a straight run stairs is not available.

DOUBLE L STAIRS, Fig. 14-3, require two 90 deg. turns along the flight. They may be used when space is not available for either the straight or L stairs. Double L stairs are not frequently used in residential construction.

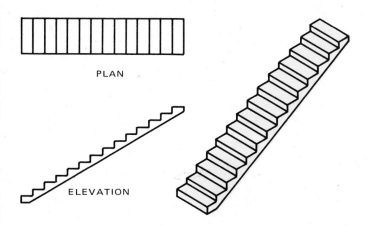

Fig. 14-1. Straight run stairs.

THE L STAIRS has one landing at some point along the flight of steps, Fig. 14-2. If the landing is near the top or bottom of the stairs, the term LONG L is used to describe the

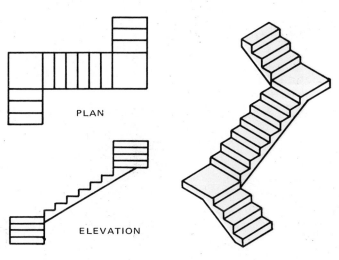

Fig. 14-3. Double L stairs.

U STAIRS may be constructed either as WIDE U or NARROW U stairs. Both have two flights of steps parallel to each other with a landing between, Fig. 14-4. The difference between wide and narrow U stairs is the space between the two flights. Narrow U stairs have little or no space between the flights while wide U stairs have a well hole between.

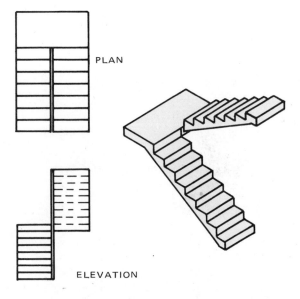

Fig. 14-4. U stairs.

WINDER STAIRS have "pie-shaped" steps which are substituted for a landing, Fig. 14-5. This type is used when the space is not sufficient for the L stairs. If winder stairs are used, the width of the triangular steps should be sufficient at midpoint to provide a tread width equal to the regular steps. For instance, if the regular tread width is 10 in., then the winder step should also be 10 in. at its midpoint. Winder stairs are not as safe as other types and should be avoided whenever possible.

SPIRAL OR CIRCULAR STAIRS are gaining in popularity and the components are now manufactured by several companies. They may be used where little space is available, Fig.

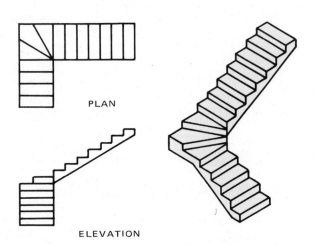

Fig. 14-5. Winder stairs.

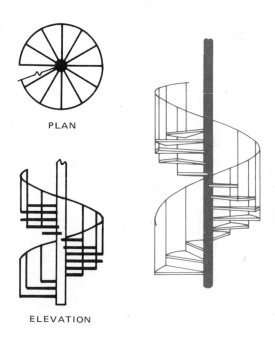

Fig. 14-6. Spiral or circular stairs.

14-6. Most spiral stairs are made from steel and welded together, however, it is possible to construct them from wood. Spiral stairs, as a rule, are not very safe since they generally have winder steps.

STAIR TERMINOLOGY

Several terms are associated with stairs which must be understood before considering design. The following list

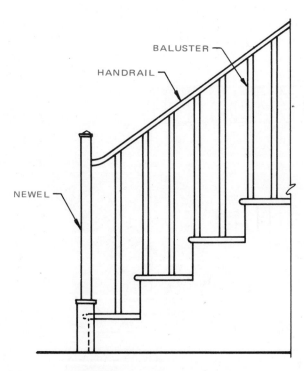

Fig. 14-7. A traditional type open stairs with newel, handrail and balusters identified.

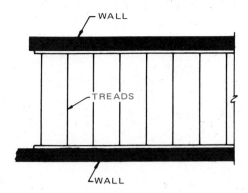

Fig. 14-8. A set of enclosed stairs which are built between two walls.

includes most of these terms:

BALUSTERS: vertical members which support the handrail on open stairs, Fig. 14-7.

ENCLOSED STAIRS: stairs which have a wall on both sides (also known as CLOSED, HOUSED, or BOX STAIRS), Fig. 14-8.

HEADROOM: the shortest clear vertical distance measured between the nosing of the treads and the ceiling, Fig. 14-9.

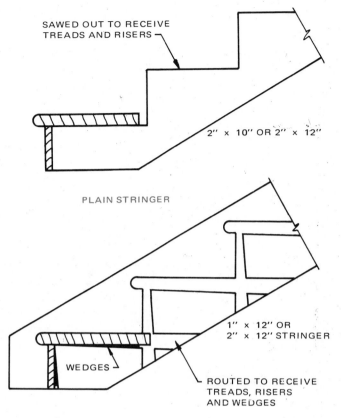

PLAIN STRINGER

HOUSED STRINGER

Fig. 14-10. The two most frequently used types of stringers are the plain and housed stringer.

HOUSED STRINGER: a stringer which has been routed or grooved to receive the treads and risers, Fig. 14-10.

LANDING: the floor area at either end of the stairs and possibly at some point between, as in the case of an L stairs.

NEWEL: the main posts of the handrail at the top, bottom or at points where the stairs change direction, Fig. 14-7.

NOSING: the rounded projection of the tread which extends past the face of the riser, Fig. 14-11.

OPEN STAIRS: stairs which have no wall on one or both sides, Fig. 14-7.

PLAIN STRINGER: a stringer which has been cut or

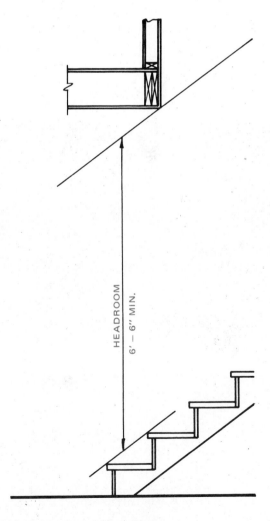

Fig. 14-9. Sufficient headroom is an important consideration in the design of stairs.

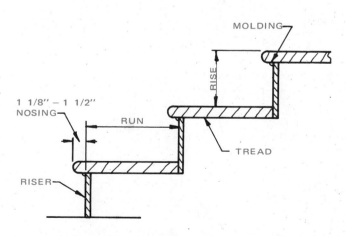

Fig. 14-11. Terms relating to treads and risers.

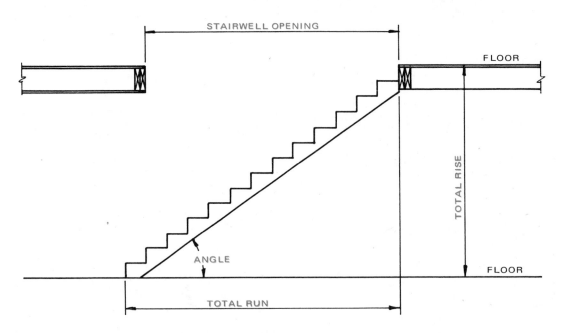

STAIRWELL OPENING

FLOOR

TOTAL RISE

ANGLE

FLOOR

TOTAL RUN

Fig. 14-12. Critical stair dimensions.

notched to fit the profile of the stairs, Fig. 14-10.

RISE: the distance from the top surface of one tread to the same spot on the next, Fig. 14-11.

RISER: the vertical face of a step, Fig. 14-11.

RUN: the distance from the face of one riser to the face of the next, Fig. 14-11.

STAIRWELL: the opening in which a set of stairs are constructed.

STRINGER: a structural member which supports the treads (also called the carriage), and risers.

TOTAL RISE: the total floor-to-floor vertical height of the

stairs, Fig. 14-12.

TOTAL RUN: the total horizontal length of the stairs, Fig. 14-12.

TREAD: the horizontal member of each step, Fig. 14-11.

Fig. 14-14. The simple techniques used in this modern stairs compliments the post and beam construction of the house.
(Potlatch Forests, Inc.)

Fig. 14-13. This well-designed contemporary U stairs is attractive and functional. (Brown and Kauffmann, Inc.)

STAIR DESIGN

A set of stairs which are properly designed and properly constructed will support the required weight, have width enough to provide ease of passage and movement of furniture, and slope between 30 and 35 deg., Fig. 14-13.

The main supporting members of the stairs are the stringers. Several types of stringers are used, but the plain stringer and housed stringer account for the majority. Fig. 14-10 shows these two types of stringers. Fig. 14-14 illustrates a type of stringer which is simple in design and appropriate for some types of construction. Usually two stringers are sufficient, however if the width of the stairs exceeds 3' – 0" a third stringer is required. (A main stairs should not be less than 3' – 0".) The extra stringer is placed in the middle of the treads and risers.

Plain stringers are generally cut from 2" x 12" straight-grain fir and the treads and risers are nailed directly to the stringers. This type of construction is used for service stairs and occasionally for main stairs if they are to be carpeted. Plain stringer stairs are sturdy, but they tend to squeak and do not have a finished appearance. The treads are usually 2 in. fir or other soft wood and the risers 1 in. white pine.

Housed stringers are made from finished lumber and are generally purchased precut. However, the stringers may be cut from 1" x 12" or 2" x 12" lumber. One-half inch deep grooves are usually routed in the stringers to hold the treads and risers. The bottom and back sides of the grooves are wider than the thickness of the treads and risers so that wedges may be driven in to hold them in place. Fig. 14-15 illustrates how the wedges are inserted in the grooves. The treads, risers and wedges are glued and nailed in place.

The two other primary parts of a set of stairs are the treads and risers. Standard treads are available in 1 1/4 in. oak in two widths - - 10 1/2 in. and 11 1/2 in. Both widths are 1 1/6 in. thick, actual size. The nose which is rounded is not included in calculations. A tread width of 10 1/2 in. is the most popular choice. Risers are 3/4 in. thick actual size and vary in width depending on the slope of the stairs. The ideal riser height is between 7 and 7 5/8 in. Clear white pine is the customary riser material.

Several rules have been devised for calculating the rise-run (riser-tread) ratio. Four of these rules are:

Rule No. 1. The slope of the stairs (rise-run ratio) should be between 30 and 35 deg.

Rule No. 2. The sum of two risers and one tread should equal 25 in.

Rule No. 3. The product of the riser height multiplied by the tread width should equal approximately 75 in.

Rule No. 4. The sum of one riser and one tread should equal 17 to 18 in.

The first rule generally will not be applied for service stairs since they are ordinarily steeper than main stairs. However, if the treads are 10 in. wide, the riser should be between 5 3/4 in. and 7 in. to produce a slope of 30 - 35 deg. A riser height of less than 7 in. is considered too short, therefore, a 7:10 ratio and 35 deg. slope is acceptable.

If a 10 in. tread is used for each of the rules, these riser heights will be required:

	Tread Width	Riser Height	Approx. Angle
Rule No. 1	10 in.	7 in.	35 deg.
Rule No. 2	10 in.	7 1/2 in.	37 deg.
Rule No. 3	10 in.	7 1/2 in.	37 deg.
Rule No. 4	10 in.	7 – 8 in.	35 – 38 deg.

A riser height of 7 in. is the only example used which falls within the proper slope angle. The angle can be reduced by increasing the tread width. For example, if the tread width is 10 1/2 in. then the riser height would be 7 1/4 in. using Rule No. 2. This combination would result in an angle slightly less than 35 deg. A ratio of 7 1/4 in. to 10 1/2 in. is considered ideal.

A stairway must provide a handrail for support while ascending or descending the stairs. Unless the stairs are very

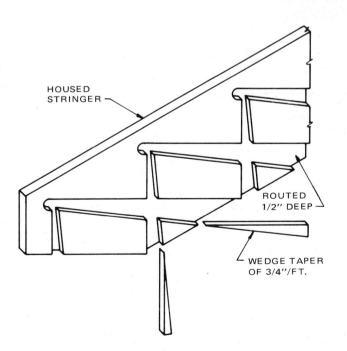

Fig. 14-15. A housed stringer showing how the wedges are positioned.

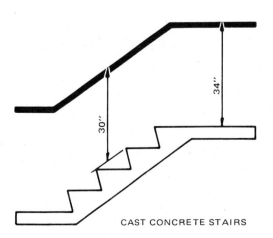

Fig. 14-16. Recommended handrail heights for all stairs.

wide, one rail is sufficient. Recommended height of the handrail is shown in Fig. 14-16. Note that the height is greater at a landing than along the incline.

STAIR CALCULATIONS AND DRAWING PROCEDURE

The following procedure may be used to determine the number and size of treads and risers for a set of stairs:

1. Determine the distance from finished floor to finished floor. This is the total rise of the stairs. The total rise is computed by adding the distance from finished lower floor to finished ceiling plus the thickness of the ceiling material plus the width of the floor joists plus the thickness of the subfloor and finished floor. See the following examples:

Finished lower floor to finished ceiling	8' − 0 in.
Thickness of ceiling material (dry wall)	0 − 1/2 in.
Width of the floor joists (2" x 10")	0 − 9 1/2 in.
Thickness of the subfloor (1/2" plywood)	0 − 1/2 in.
Thickness of the finished floor (particle board and asphalt tile)	0 − 3/4 in.
Total rise =	8' − 11 1/4 in.

Since the size of each step is computed in inches, the total rise is converted to inches. Total rise = 107 1/4 in. Fig. 14-17 shows the first step in drawing stairs.

STEP 1

FINISHED FLOOR

107 1/4" 8' − 11 1/4"

TOTAL RISE

FINISHED FLOOR

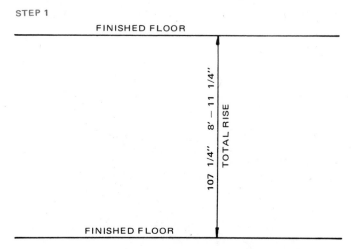

Fig. 14-17. Determine the total rise and lay out the finished floor lines.

2. Determine how many risers will be required by first dividing the total rise by 7. The reason 7 is used is because 7 in. is an ideal riser height and it is therefore a logical place to start. When 107 1/4 in. is divided by 7 the result is 15.32 risers. The number of risers must be an exact number, so either 15 or 16 risers will be required. When 107 1/4 in. is divided by 15 a riser height of 7.15 in. is produced. This figure seems to be acceptable so further calculations will be based on it. Fig. 14-18 shows how the total rise is divided into 15 equal

STEP 2

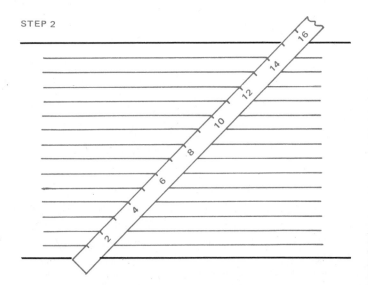

Fig. 14-18. Divide the total rise into the specified number of risers. The number of risers in this example is 15.

parts. EACH RISER MUST BE EXACTLY THE SAME HEIGHT.

3. Determine the tread size and total run which will yield a stair slope between 30 and 35 deg. It was determined earlier that a 10 1/2 in. tread was a commonly used width so it will be used for a trial calculation. THERE IS ALWAYS ONE LESS TREAD THAN THE NUMBER OF RISERS. This is because the floor serves as the top tread. Using Rule No. 2, the sum of two risers (7.15 in. + 7.15 in.) and one tread (10 1/2 in.) equals 24.80 in. This is very close to the required sum of 25 and indicates that this combination will be acceptable. For comparison Rules 3 and 4 will be applied. Rule No. 3 says that the product of the riser height and tread width should be approximately 75 in. Therefore if 7.15 is multiplied by 10.5 the product is 75.1. This is acceptable. Rule No. 4 indicates

STEP 3

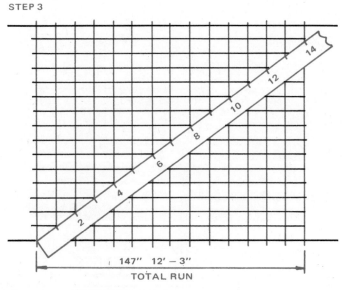

147" 12' − 3"
TOTAL RUN

Fig. 14-19. Lay out the total run and divide it into the number of tread widths required. In this case, 14.

that the sum of one riser and one tread should equal 17 to 18 in. If 7.15 is added to 10 1/2 the result is 17.65 in. This is within the required range. The tread width will be 10 1/2 in.

The total run is determined by multiplying the tread width (10 1/2 in.) by the number of treads (14). The product is 147 in. for the total run. Fig. 14-19 shows how the total run and tread widths are drawn.

4. Darken in the tread and riser lines, draw the bottom

edge of the stringer, and locate stairwell rough opening size. This dimension will be a function of the headroom dimension. Minimum headroom is 6' – 6". Step 4 is shown in Fig. 14-20.

5. Remove all construction lines and add dimensions and notes, Fig. 14-21.

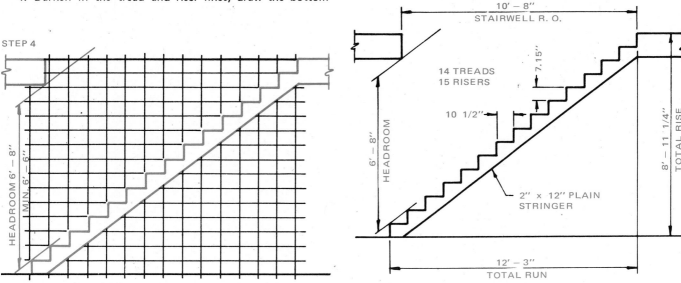

Fig. 14-20. Darken in the treads and risers and indicate the stairwell rough opening.

Fig. 14-21. Remove all construction lines and add dimensions and notes.

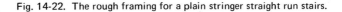

Fig. 14-22. The rough framing for a plain stringer straight run stairs.

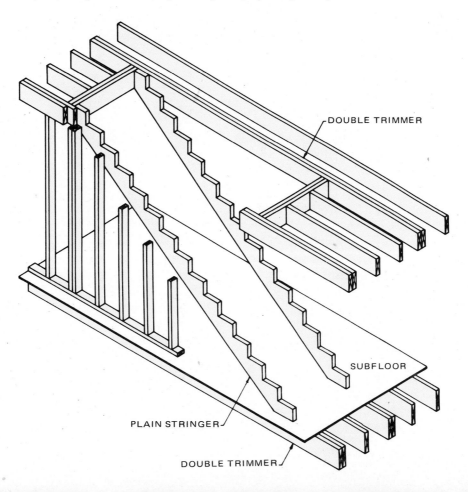

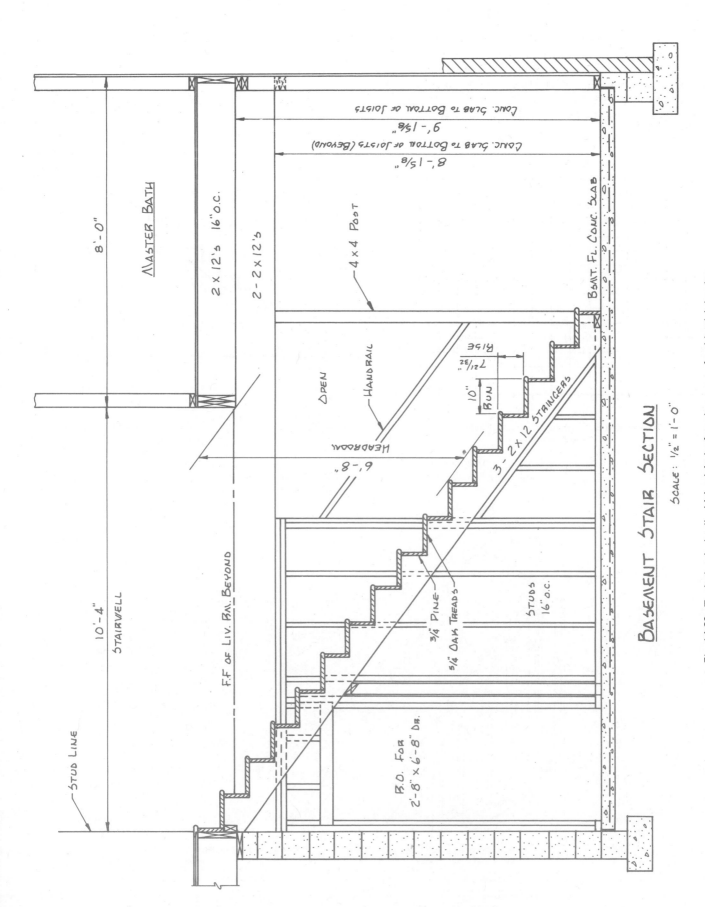

Fig. 14-23. Typical stair detail which might be found on a set of residential drawings.

STRUCTURAL DETAILS

Procedures for building stairs vary widely from one part of the country to another. Local codes often specify restrictions. Carpenters have their own preferences which add to the variations. Regardless of the procedure followed, the construction techniques must be sound. Fig. 14-22 shows the rough framing for a plain stringer, open straight run stairs. Ordinarily, this rough framing is not shown on a set of house plans, but a plan view and elevation with various section details are shown. Fig. 14-23 represents a typical stair detail drawing found in a set of residential plans.

REVIEW QUESTIONS — CHAPTER 14

1. Stairs which connect the first and second floor are known as _____ stairs.
2. Identify the six general types of stairs.
   a. _____ .
   b. _____ .
   c. _____ .
   d. _____ .
   e. _____ .
   f. _____ .
3. Which type of stairs always has two landings along the flight of steps?
4. The type of stairs which has two parallel flights of steps is the _____ stairs.
5. "Pie-shaped" steps are generally associated with two types of stairs. They are the _____ and the _____ .
6. Vertical members which support the handrail on open stairs are known as _____ .
7. Stairs which have a wall on both sides are known as _____ stairs.
8. Minimum headroom for stairs is _____ .
9. The two main types of stringers used in home stair construction are _____ and _____ stringers.
10. The rounded projection of the tread which extends past the face of the riser is the _____ .
11. A stair which has no wall on either side is a _____ stair.
12. A stringer which has been cut or notched to match the profile of the stairs is a _____ stringer.
13. Define rise. _____
14. Define run. _____
15. The total floor to floor vertical height of the stairs is known as the _____ .
16. The total horizontal length of the stairs is the _____ .
17. The proper slope angle for a set of main stairs should be between _____ and _____ deg.
18. The minimum recommended width for main stairs is _____ .
19. Treads on service stairs are frequently made from soft wood, but main stair treads are _____ .
20. The ideal tread to riser ratio is _____ to _____ .

SUGGESTED ACTIVITIES

1. Locate as many different stair designs as you can. Measure the width of tread and riser height. Draw a profile of the tread and riser and measure the angle with a protractor. Identify the materials used and rate the stairs as to ease of travel.
2. Locate a house in your community which is under construction and examine the stair framing. Measure the floor to floor distance and width of the stairs. If possible, interview the head carpenter and ask him to explain how he lays out a set of stairs. Report your findings to the class.
3. Design a housed stringer enclosed straight run stairs for a house which has a finished floor to finished floor distance of 9' — 1 1/4". Distance between the finished walls is 3' — 4". Provide the necessary drawings, dimension and add notes.
4. Visit a local lumber company which sells precut stairs. Collect information and literature about these stairs. Bring this literature to class to help build a file on stairs.
5. Select a basic type of stairs and build a scale model as accurately as possible. Display this model along with drawings of the construction.

Fig. 15-1. This contemporary fireplace is the focal point of the living room. Notice the raised hearth and log storage.   (Brown and Kauffman, Inc.)

Chapter 15

FIREPLACES AND CHIMNEYS

Most everyone enjoys the sound and warmth of a blazing fire. The fireplace is often a focal point in the living room or family room. In modern home planning it is an important design consideration, Fig. 15-1.

Many homes have fireplaces which are pleasing to the eye, but fail to operate properly. Care must be taken in the design and construction of a fireplace and chimney to make sure the fireplace will perform as desired.

FIREPLACE DESIGN CONSIDERATIONS

Several types of fireplaces are being constructed in modern residences. Some are traditional in design, Fig. 15-2, while others are contemporary. Increasingly, metal fireplaces are finding their way into the home. Some of these are wood burning, but many are gas fired, designed to look like a wood fire, Fig. 15-3. Often fireplaces draw on the building ma-

Fig. 15-2. A traditional fireplace with a flush hearth and marble front. (Vega Industries, Inc.)

Fig. 15-3. A wall hung fireplace which is prefabricated metal. This model is a gas fireplace. (Preway)

Fig. 15-4. This modern fireplace would be a welcome addition to most any room. (Vega Industries, Inc.)

terials for their charm, Fig. 15-4.

Generally, fireplaces may be identified as single face, two face opposite, two face adjacent, three face, or prefabricated metal fireplaces, Fig. 15-5. Each type has specific design requirements which must be met if the fireplace is to be safe and perform properly. (Design specifications are included later in this chapter.)

HEARTH AND FIRE CHAMBER

The function of the hearth is to protect the floor from sparks. It should extend at least 16 in. in front of the fireplace and be constructed from a noncombustible material. In conventional construction, the hearth extends beneath the fireplace to form an inner hearth, Fig. 15-6. It is usually covered with fire brick inside the fireplace, and stone, slate or ceramic tile in front of the fireplace. The hearth may be flush with the floor or raised to a desirable height.

The fire chamber is usually lined with fire bricks set in fireclay, (fire resistant mortar). Fireclay is a mortar-like refractory material used as a bonding agent between the fire

likely to smoke. Wall thickness should be a minimum of 8 in. on the back and sides of the fire chamber, Fig. 15-6.

When space is available below the fireplace and finished floor, an ash dump is desirable. A metal trap door is located in the middle of the fireplace floor and connected to the ash chamber below. A cleanout is provided in the ash chamber for

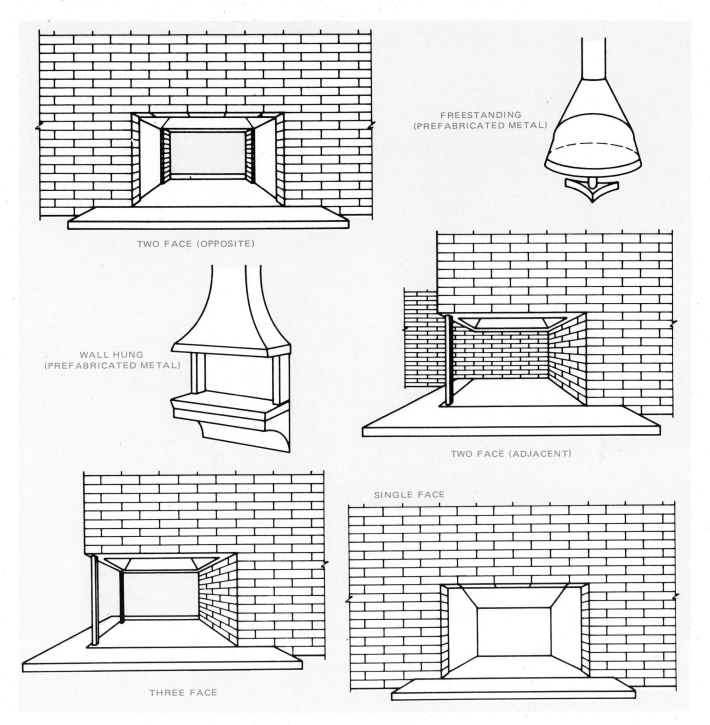

TWO FACE (OPPOSITE)

FREESTANDING
(PREFABRICATED METAL)

WALL HUNG
(PREFABRICATED METAL)

TWO FACE (ADJACENT)

SINGLE FACE

THREE FACE

Fig. 15-5. Types of fireplaces.

bricks. The shape of this area is critical and must be designed to lead hot gases and smoke into the throat for passage up the chimney. If the chamber is too deep, little heat will be reflected out into the room. If it is too shallow, the fireplace is

the removal of ashes.

In modern residential construction extensive use is made of prefabricated steel heat circulating fireplaces. The units include not only the firebox and heating chamber, but also the

261

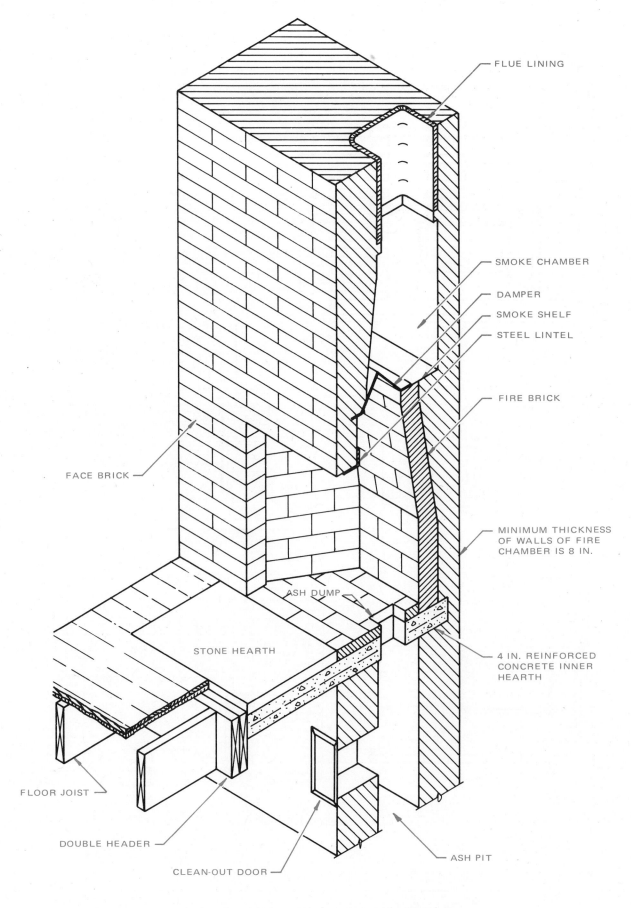

FLUE LINING

SMOKE CHAMBER

DAMPER

SMOKE SHELF

STEEL LINTEL

FIRE BRICK

MINIMUM THICKNESS
OF WALLS OF FIRE
CHAMBER IS 8 IN.

FACE BRICK

ASH DUMP

STONE HEARTH

4 IN. REINFORCED
CONCRETE INNER
HEARTH

FLOOR JOIST

DOUBLE HEADER

CLEAN-OUT DOOR

ASH PIT

Fig. 15-6. Single face fireplace with parts identified.

throat, damper, smoke shelf and smoke chamber, Fig. 15-7. Installation is generally easy. Fig. 15-8 shows the step-by-step procedure for installing a prefabricated stack heat circulating fireplace in frame construction. These units are very efficient because the sides and back consist of a double wall passageway where the air is heated. Cool air is drawn into the chamber, heated and returned to the room through registers located at a higher level.

DAMPER AND SMOKE SHELF

Every modern fireplace should have a damper to regulate the flow of air and stop down drafts of cold air when the fireplace is not in operation. The damper is located in the throat of the fireplace and opens toward the back of the throat. The damper opening should be larger than the area of the flue lining and as long as the width of the fireplace. Standard damper sizes are shown in Fig. 15-9. It should be placed 6 or 8 in. above the top of the fireplace opening. Dampers are produced in both steel and cast iron.

The smoke shelf height is determined by the location of the damper, Fig. 15-6. The smoke shelf causes cold air flowing

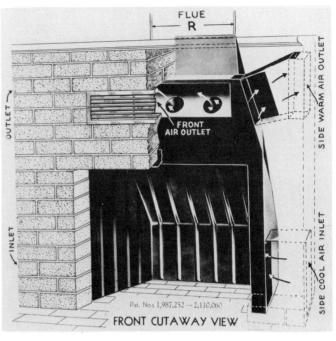

Fig. 15-7. A cutaway view showing the prefabricated steel heat-circulating fireplace. (Superior Fireplace Co.)

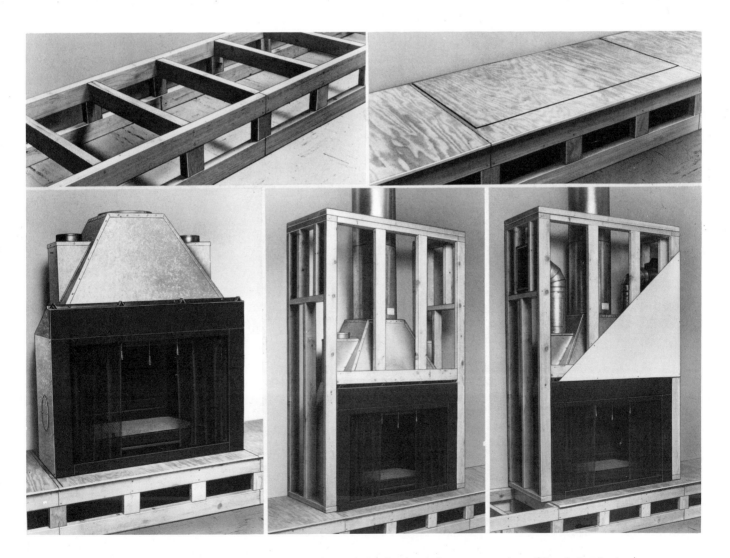

Fig. 15-8. Installation of a prefabricated steel heat circulating fireplace in frame construction. (Vega Industries, Inc.)

DAMPER SPECIFICATIONS

STEEL DAMPERS					
WIDTH OF FIREPLACE IN INCHES	DAMPER DIMENSIONS IN INCHES				
	A	B	C	D	E
24 TO 26	28 1/4	26 3/4	13	24	9 1/2
27 TO 30	32 1/4	30 3/4	13	28	9 1/2
31 TO 34	36 1/4	34 3/4	13	32	9 1/2
35 TO 38	40 1/4	38 3/4	13	36	9 1/2
39 TO 42	44 1/4	42 3/4	13	40	9 1/2
43 TO 46	48 1/4	46 3/4	13	44	9 1/2
47 TO 50	52 1/4	50 3/4	13	48	9 1/2
51 TO 54	56 1/4	54 3/4	13	52	9 1/2
57 TO 60	62 1/2	60 3/4	13	58	9 1/2
CAST IRON DAMPERS					
WIDTH OF FIREPLACE IN INCHES	DAMPER DIMENSIONS IN INCHES				
	A	B	C	D	E
24 TO 26	28	21	13 1/2	24	10
27 TO 31	34	26 3/4	13 1/2	30	10
31 TO 34	37	29 3/4	13 1/2	33	10
35 TO 38	40	32 3/4	13 1/2	36	10
39 TO 42	46	38 3/4	13 1/2	48	10
43 TO 46	52	44 3/4	13 1/2	48	10
47 TO 50	57 1/2	50 1/2	13 1/2	54	10
51 TO 54	64	56 1/2	14 1/2	60	11 1/2
57 TO 60	76	58	14 1/2	72	11 1/2

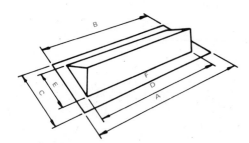

Fig. 15-9. Damper design specifications which are typical of products on the market.   (Donley Brothers Co.)

down the chimney to be deflected upward into the rising warm air. This action prevents downrushing cold air from forcing smoke into the room.

The smoke chamber is the area just above the smoke shelf and damper. This is basically pyramidal in shape with the back side usually being vertical. It is normally constructed from brick or other masonry.

CLAY FLUE LINER SIZES

NEW SIZES	ROUND (DIA.)	OLD SIZES
8 x 12	8	8 1/2 x 8 1/2
12 x 12	10	8 1/2 x 13
12 x 16	12	13 x 13
16 x 16	15	13 x 18
16 x 20	18	18 x 18
20 x 20	20	20 x 20
20 x 24	22	24 x 24

NEW FLUE SIZES CONFORM TO NEW MODULAR DIMENSIONAL SYSTEM. SIZES SHOWN ARE NOMINAL. ACTUAL SIZE 15 1/2" LESS EACH DIMENSION. ALL FLUE LININGS LISTED ABOVE ARE 2' – 0" LONG.

Fig. 15-10. Flue liners are available in round and rectangular shapes. Most are made of clay.

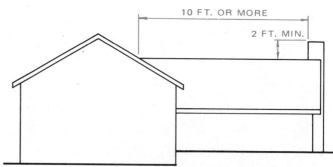

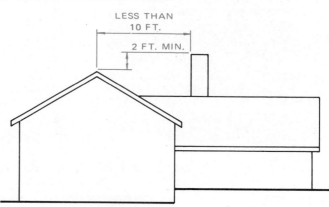

Fig. 15-11. Recommended above the roof chimney heights.

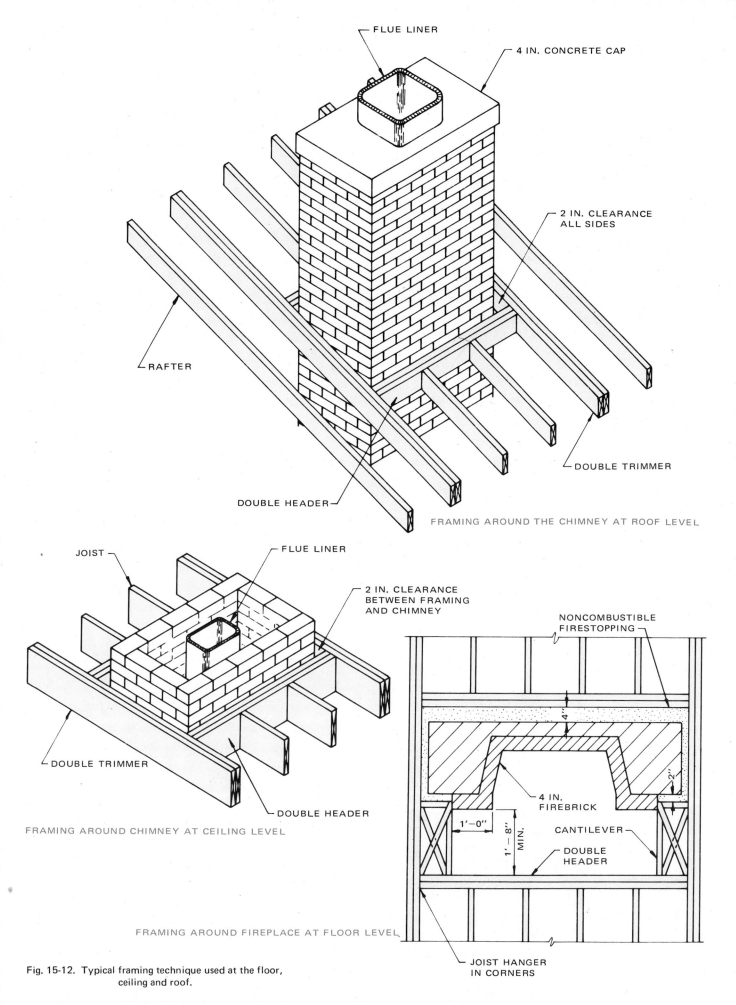

FLUE LINER

4 IN. CONCRETE CAP

2 IN. CLEARANCE
ALL SIDES

RAFTER

DOUBLE TRIMMER

DOUBLE HEADER

FRAMING AROUND THE CHIMNEY AT ROOF LEVEL

JOIST

FLUE LINER

2 IN. CLEARANCE
BETWEEN FRAMING
AND CHIMNEY

NONCOMBUSTIBLE
FIRESTOPPING

DOUBLE TRIMMER

DOUBLE HEADER

FRAMING AROUND CHIMNEY AT CEILING LEVEL

4 IN. FIREBRICK

CANTILEVER

DOUBLE
HEADER

1'—0"

1'—8" MIN.

4"

2"

FRAMING AROUND FIREPLACE AT FLOOR LEVEL

JOIST HANGER
IN CORNERS

Fig. 15-12. Typical framing technique used at the floor,
ceiling and roof.

FLUE

The flue usually has a clay lining which provides an avenue for smoke to pass up the chimney, Fig. 15-6. It begins at the top of the smoke chamber and extends to the top of the chimney. Each flue requires at least 4 in. of brick on all sides. If no liner is used the wall thickness must be a minimum of 8 in. EACH FIREPLACE MUST HAVE ITS OWN FLUE. Ideally, the flue will be centered directly above the fireplace and proceed upward in a straight line. A small amount of offset is permissible; however, efficiency is reduced when the flue is not straight.

The size of flue is important since it must be large enough to provide the necessary draft. A rule of thumb to follow in selecting the proper flue size is to choose a flue which has at least 1/10th the sectional area of the fireplace opening. For example, if the fireplace opening is 32" x 48" the area is 1536 sq. in. One tenth of 1536 sq. in. is 153.6 sq. in. A standard flue size which has at least this area is a 12" x 16" flue. It is better to have a flue which is too large than too small. Standard flue sizes are shown in Fig. 15-10.

Flue size is also related to several other factors. If the height of the flue is less than 14 ft., the size should be increased to provide the necessary draft. The draft is increased by making the flue higher. Prevailing winds and surrounding trees and buildings also affect the draft. If the flue is sheltered, the size should be increased. Most codes require that the flue extend at least 2 ft. above the highest point of the roof, Fig. 15-11. This is a safety factor, since sparks fly out the top and

may cause a roof fire.

A single chimney may have several flues. A flue is required for a gas furnace, a gas hot water heater, an incinerator and each fireplace. Efficiency of a chimney may be increased if it is placed within the house rather than on an outside wall. The warmer the chimney, the better the performance.

FRAMING AROUND FIREPLACE AND CHIMNEY

The chimney is a freestanding structure. It does not support any part of the house. In fact, fire codes prohibit direct contact of framing with surfaces of the fireplace or chimney. A minimum of 2 in. of clearance is required between the chimney and framing. This space should be filled with a noncombustible material. The opening through which the chimney passes through the floor, ceiling and roof requires double headers and trimmers to give the necessary support, Fig. 15-12.

If a chimney is located along the ridge line (the peak or highest point) of a roof, the chance of water problems is minimized. However, if the chimney must be located along a single slope of the roof, special precautions must be taken to prevent leaking. Water can back up along the chimney and roof intersections and seep under the shingles. To prevent this from happening, a saddle or cricket is built on the high side of the chimney to shed water. A saddle is especially necessary if the roof slope is low or the chimney is wide. Fig. 15-13 shows a saddle.

Masonry above a fireplace opening must be supported by a

Fig. 15-13. The framing for a saddle to shed water away from the chimney.

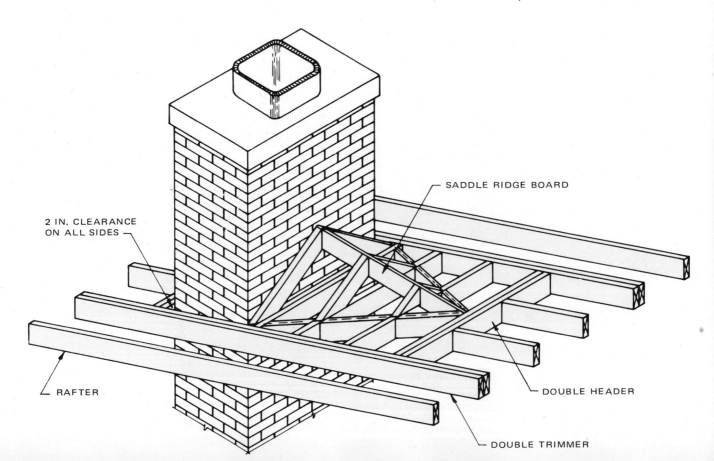

2 IN. CLEARANCE ON ALL SIDES

SADDLE RIDGE BOARD

RAFTER

DOUBLE HEADER

DOUBLE TRIMMER

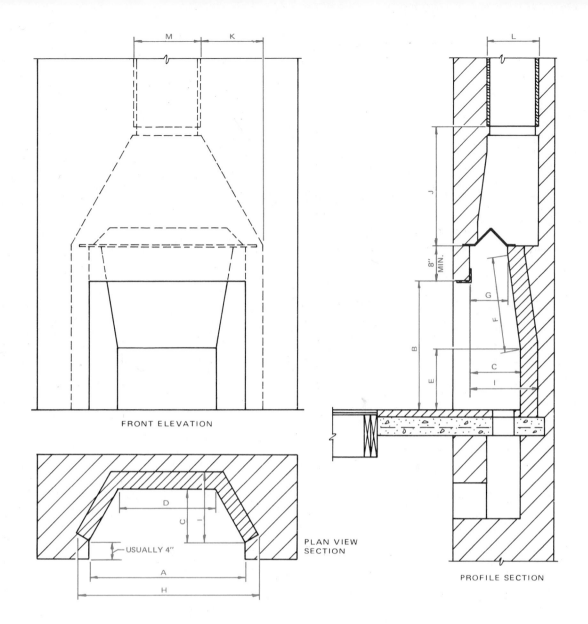

FRONT ELEVATION

PLAN VIEW SECTION

PROFILE SECTION

DESIGN DATA FOR SINGLE FACE FIREPLACES

WIDTH	HGT.	DEPTH	BACK	VERT. BACK	SLOPE BACK	THROAT	WIDTH	DEPTH	SMOKE CHAMB.	FLUE LINING SIZES				
										RECT.		RND.	MODULAR	
A	B	C	D	E	F	G	H	I	J	K	L x M		K	L x M
24	24	16	11	14	15	8 3/4	32	20	19	11 3/4	8 1/2 x 8 1/2	8	10	8 x 12
26	24	16	13	14	15	8 3/4	34	20	21	12 3/4	8 1/2 x 8 1/2	8	11	8 x 12
28	24	16	15	14	15	8 3/4	36	20	21	11 1/2	8 1/2 x 13	10	12	8 x 12
30	29	16	17	14	18	8 3/4	38	20	24	12 1/2	8 1/2 x 13	10	13	12 x 12
32	29	16	19	14	21	8 3/4	40	20	24	13 1/2	8 1/2 x 13	10	14	12 x 12
36	29	16	23	14	21	8 3/4	44	20	27	15 1/2	13 x 13	12	16	12 x 12
40	29	16	27	14	21	8 3/4	48	20	29	17 1/2	13 x 13	12	16	12 x 12
42	32	16	29	14	23	8 3/4	50	20	32	18 1/2	13 x 13	12	17	16 x 16
48	32	18	33	14	23	8 3/4	56	22	37	21 1/2	13 x 13	15	20	16 x 16
54	37	20	37	16	27	13	68	24	45	25	13 x 18	15	26	16 x 20
60	37	22	42	16	27	13	72	27	45	27	13 x 18	15	26	16 x 20
60	40	22	42	16	29	13	72	27	45	27	18 x 18	18	26	16 x 20
72	40	22	54	16	29	13	84	27	56	33	18 x 18	18	32	20 x 20
84	40	24	64	20	26	13	96	29	67	36	20 x 20	20	36	20 x 20
96	40	24	76	20	26	13	108	29	75	42	24 x 24	22	42	20 x 20

DIMENSIONS ARE IN INCHES.
FLUE SIZES FOR CHIMNEY HEIGHT OF AT LEAST 14′ − 0″.

Fig. 15-14. Design specifications for single face fireplaces.

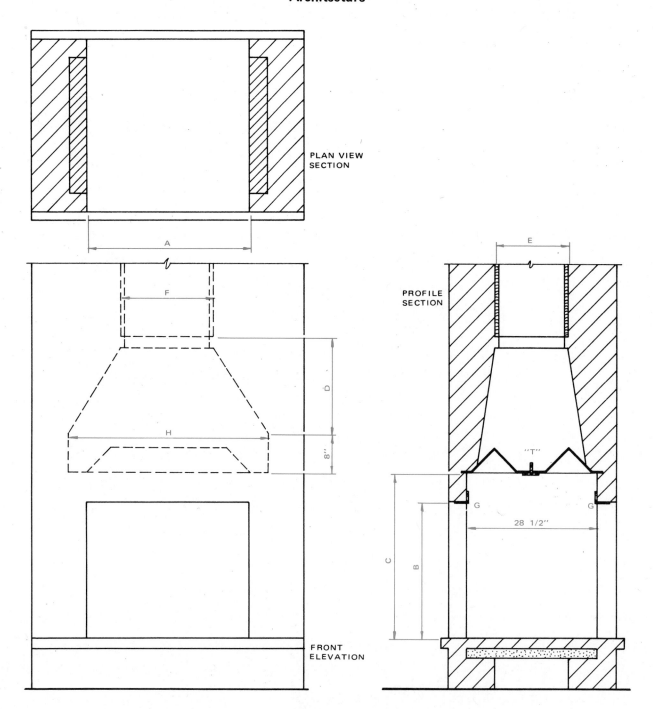

PLAN VIEW
SECTION

PROFILE
SECTION

FRONT
ELEVATION

DESIGN DATA FOR TWO FACE OPPOSITE FIREPLACES

A	B	C	D	OLD FLUE SIZE		RND.	NEW MOD. SIZE		ANGLE G	H	TEE
				E	F		E	F	2 REQ'D.		LENGTH
28	24	35	19	13	13	12	12	16	36	36	35
32	29	35	21	13	18	15	16	16	40	40	39
36	29	35	21	13	18	15	16	20	42	44	43
40	29	35	27	18	18	18	16	20	48	48	47
48	32	37	32	18	18	18	20	20	54	56	55

DIMENSIONS ARE IN INCHES.
FLUE SIZES FOR CHIMNEY HEIGHT OF AT LEAST 14' – 0''.
ANGLE G IS 3'' x 3'' x 1/4''

Fig. 15-15. Design specifications for two face opposite fireplaces.

Fireplaces and Chimneys

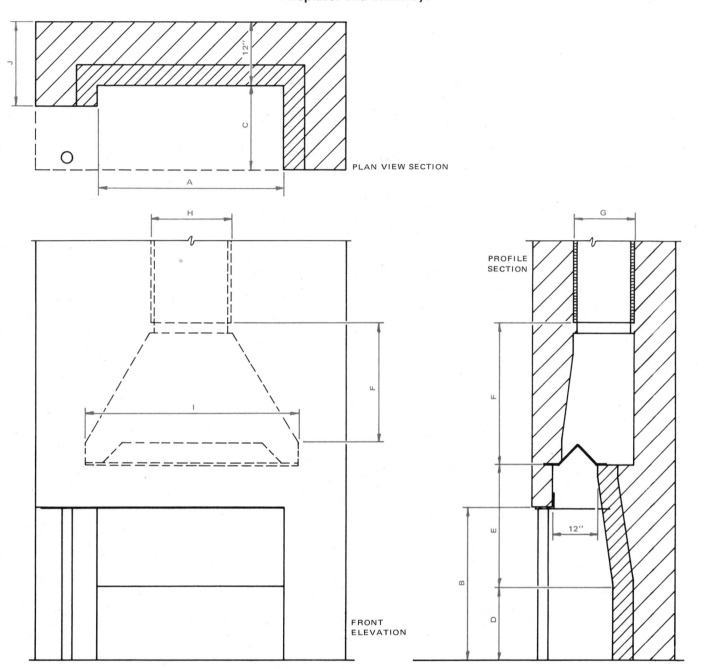

PLAN VIEW SECTION

PROFILE SECTION

FRONT ELEVATION

DESIGN DATA FOR TWO FACE ADJACENT FIREPLACES

| A | B | C | D | E | F | OLD FLUE | | RND. | MOD. FLUE | | I | J | CORNER POST |
						G	H		G	H			HEIGHT
28	26 1/2	16	14	20	29 1/4	13	13	12	12	12	36	16	26 1/2
32	26 1/2	16	14	20	32	13	13	12	12	16	40	16	26 1/2
36	26 1/2	16	14	20	35	13	13	12	12	16	44	16	26 1/2
40	29	16	14	20	35	13	18	15	16	16	48	16	29
48	29	20	14	24	43	13	18	15	16	16	56	20	29
54	29	20	14	23	45	13	18	15	16	16	62	20	29
60	29	20	14	23	51	13	18	15	16	20	68	20	29

DIMENSIONS ARE IN INCHES.
FLUE SIZES FOR CHIMNEY HEIGHT OF AT LEAST 14' – 0".

Fig. 15-16. Design specifications for two face adjacent fireplaces.

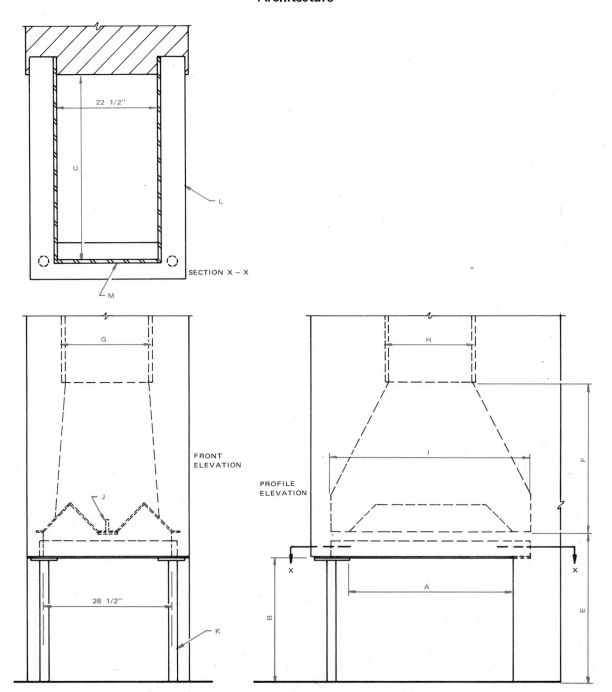

DESIGN DATA FOR THREE FACE FIREPLACES

A	B	C	E	F	OLD FLUE SIZE		RND.	NEW MODULAR FLUE SIZE		I	STEEL TEE	POST HEIGHT	ANGLE 2 REQ'D.	SPECIAL WELDED TEE
					G	H		G	H		J	K	L	M
28	26 1/2	32	32	24	18	18	18	16	20	36	35	26 1/2	36	34
32	26 1/2	36	32	27	18	18	18	20	20	40	39	26 1/2	40	34
36	26 1/2	40	32	32	18	18	18	20	20	44	43	26 1/2	44	34
40	26 1/2	44	32	35	18	18	18	20	20	48	47	26 1/2	48	34
48	26 1/2	52	32	35	20	20	20	20	24	56	55	26 1/2	56	34

DIMENSIONS ARE IN INCHES.
FLUE SIZES FOR CHIMNEY HEIGHT OF AT LEAST 14' – 0''.

Fig. 15-17. Design specifications for three face fireplaces.

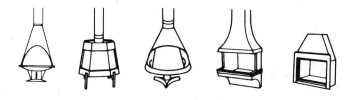

Fig. 15-18. Common wall hung and freestanding styles of prefabricated metal, wood and gas fireplaces.

lintel just the same as over a door or window. The common type of lintel used is angle steel. The size of angle required will vary with the length of opening. A 3″ x 3″ x 1/4″ angle will be sufficient for an opening of 60 in. wide.

FIREPLACE SPECIFICATIONS

The type of fireplace and size of opening is the beginning point in designing a fireplace. The following specifications are intended to facilitate the design process.

SINGLE FACE FIREPLACE

The single face fireplace is the most popular type. It is the least complicated to construct and usually functions better than the other types. Fig. 15-14 gives the specifications for several single face fireplaces. Damper size may be determined by studying the chart presented earlier.

TWO FACE (OPPOSITE) FIREPLACE

A two face (opposite) fireplace is open on both the front and back sides. Its primary advantage is that it opens into two rooms. Care must be taken to prevent a draft from one side to the other which may result in smoke. Fig. 15-15 presents specifications pertaining to this type fireplace.

TWO FACE (ADJACENT) FIREPLACE

A two face (adjacent) fireplace is open on the front and one side. It may be open on the right or left side. This type is also known as a projecting corner fireplace. Design specifications are shown in Fig. 15-16.

THREE FACE FIREPLACE

A three face fireplace is open on three sides. Ordinarily, two long sides and one short side are open. This is also known as a three-way fireplace. This type is somewhat of a novelty, however, it can add interest and design if the interior room

Fig. 15-19. Left. A modern gas fired fireplace. Fig. 15-20. Right. Freestanding metal fireplaces are popular for recreation rooms and cottages. (Preway)

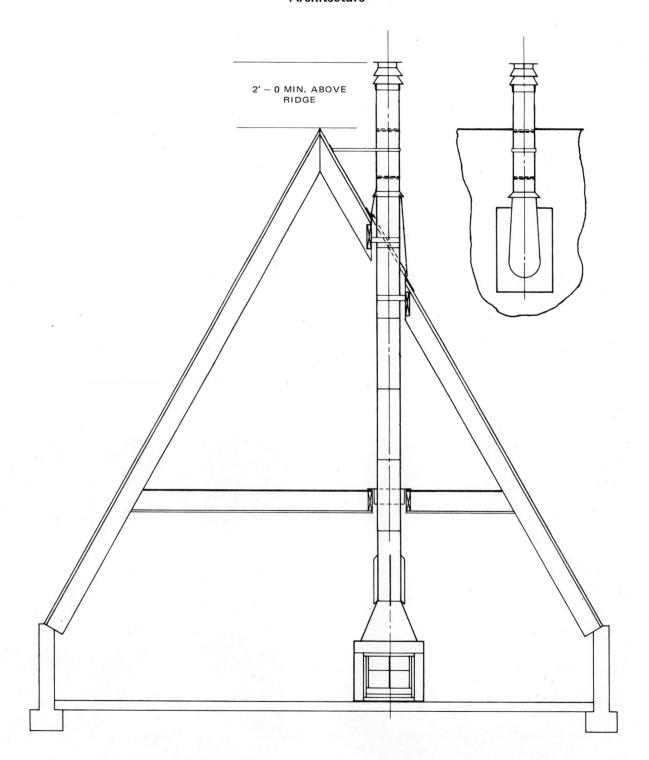

Fig. 15-21. A typical installation of a prefabricated metal fireplace in a cottage.

layout is properly arranged. Fig. 15-17 gives design specifications for the three face type.

PREFABRICATED METAL FIREPLACES

Prefabricated metal fireplaces are becoming more popular as a greater number of styles are produced, Fig. 15-18. Some are wall mounted, Fig. 15-19, and others are freestanding models, Fig. 15-20. These units may be purchased complete with all the necessary parts required to install them. No

masonry work is needed. Such fireplaces are ideal for cottages and basement installation. The local code should be consulted prior to installation. Fig. 15-21 shows installation details of a typical prefabricated metal fireplace.

Prefabricated steel heat-circulating fireplaces are manufactured in several designs, Fig. 15-22. These units require framing or masonry enclosures. Fig. 15-23 shows a heat-circulating fireplace. Vents are visible on the wall above the unit. Design specifications are shown in the chart on page 273.

Fig. 15-22. Three common designs of prefabricated steel heat circulating fireplaces; the single face, two face adjacent and two face opposite. (Superior Fireplace Co.)

PREFABRICATED STEEL HEAT-CIRCULATING FIREPLACE SIZES

Overall Dimensions			Finished Opening		Flue Size
Width	Height	Depth	Width	Height	(Approx.)
34 3/4	44	18	28	22	8 1/2 x 13
38 1/2	48	19	32	24	8 1/2 x 13
42 1/2	51	20	36	25	13 x 13
47 3/4	55	21	40	27	13 x 13
55	60	22	46	29	13 x 13
63	65	23	54	31	13 x 18

(The Majestic Co., Inc.)

REVIEW QUESTIONS — CHAPTER 15

1. Identify five different types of fireplaces which may be installed in the home.

   a. _____.

   b. _____.

   c. _____.

   d. _____.

   e. _____.

Fig. 15-23. This attractive fireplace is a prefabricated steel heat circulating model. (Vega Industries, Inc.)

2. The part of the fireplace designed to protect the floor from sparks is the _____ .
3. If the fire chamber is too shallow, a condition that may result is _____ .
4. One major advantage of a prefabricated metal firebox is _____ .
5. The function of the _____ is to deflect cold air flowing down the chimney into the rising warm air.
6. The area in the fireplace above the smoke shelf and damper and below the flue is called the _____ .
7. A rule of thumb to follow in selecting the proper flue size is to choose a flue which has at least _____ the sectional area of the fireplace opening.
8. Increasing the flue height will _____ the draft.
9. Most codes require that the flue extend at least _____ feet above the highest point of the roof.
10. Why will a chimney placed within the house function better than one on an outside wall?
11. A minimum clearance of _____ inches must be allowed between the chimney and framing.
12. The purpose of a saddle or cricket is to _____ _____ .
13. The type of lintel used above the openings of most fireplaces is _____ .
14. A fireplace which has but a single opening is known as a _____ .
15. A fireplace which is open on the front and one side is a _____ .
16. A type of fireplace that requires no masonry and is popular for cottages is _____ .

SUGGESTED ACTIVITIES

1. Select a residential plan which has a fireplace. Draw the fireplace details and dimension the drawings.
2. Build a scale model of a fireplace and describe the materials to be used in the actual fireplace. Draw the plan view and front elevation of the fireplace.
3. Collect literature and materials commonly used in modern fireplaces and bring to class. Display the literature and materials and describe them to the class.
4. Locate a residence under construction which has a fireplace. Measure the opening and depth. Sketch the fireplace and be prepared to discuss the construction techniques used.

The architect used an open plan with wall dividers to obtain a larger look for this living and dining area.

Fig. 16-1. Study this photo, then examine the floor plan, Fig. 16-2.

Chapter 16
THE FLOOR PLAN

DEFINITION AND PURPOSE

The floor plan is the heart of a set of construction drawings. It is the one plan to which all tradesmen refer. When designing a residence the floor plan is usually started first. It may be completed near the end of the designing, since modifications are frequently required during the development of the other plans in the set.

The floor plan is actually a section drawing. An imaginary cutting plane is passed through the structure about four feet above the floor and parallel to it. The plane may be higher or lower as necessary to "cut" through the required details. In some instances, the plane is offset (changes levels) as in the case of a split-level house.

The purpose of the floor plan is to show the location and dimensions of exterior and interior walls, windows, doors, major appliances, cabinets, fireplace and other fixed features of the house. See Figs. 16-1 and 16-2. Fig. 16-2 identifies many common features found on a floor plan. Sometimes when the structure is not complex, the floor plan may include information which would ordinarily be found on other drawings. For example, the electrical plan, heating/cooling plan or plumbing plan might be combined with the floor plan. Be careful not to include too much information on a single drawing or the drawing will become cluttered and confusing.

REQUIRED INFORMATION

Information about these features should be included on the floor plan: exterior and interior walls; size and location of windows and doors; built-in cabinets and appliances; permanent fixtures; stairs and fireplaces; walks, patios and decks; room names and material symbols; location and size dimensions; and scale. Frequently, related structures such as a freestanding garage or swimming pool are also shown on the floor plan.

275

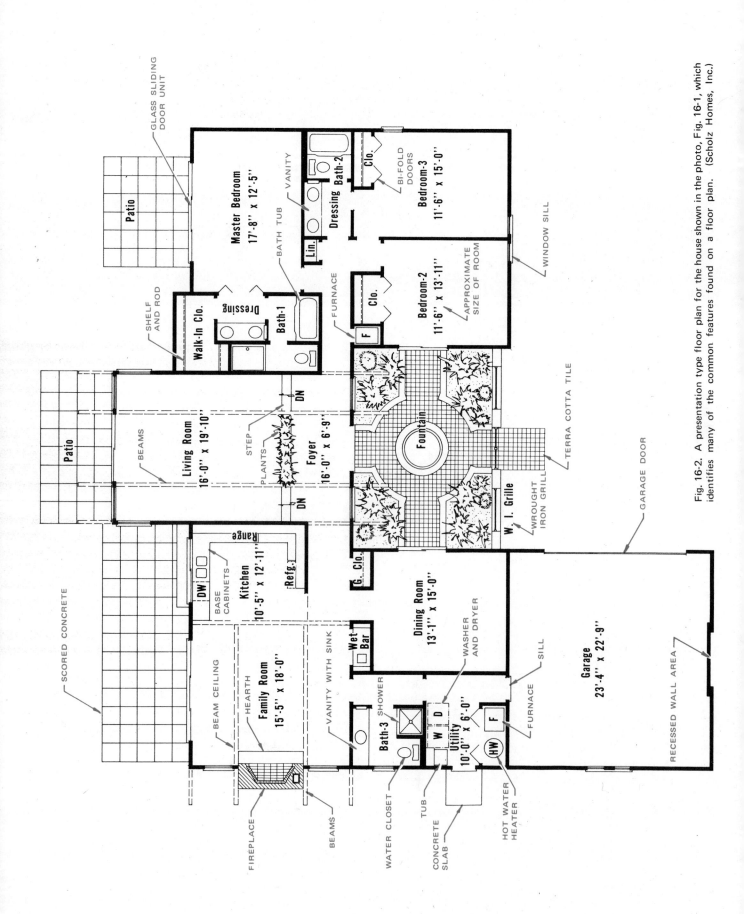

Fig. 16-2. A presentation type floor plan for the house shown in the photo, Fig. 16-1, which identifies many of the common features found on a floor plan. (Scholz Homes, Inc.)

276

LOCATION AND SIZE OF WALLS

Walls should be drawn accurately. You may use the following chart as a guide to wall thickness:

WALL THICKNESS CHART

Wood Frame Walls
Exterior walls (with sheating and siding)	6 in.
Interior walls (with dry wall both sides)	5 in.

Concrete Block Walls
Exterior walls	8, 10 or 12 in.
Interior walls	4 or 8 in.

Brick Veneer Exterior
Veneer on frame	10 in.
Veneer on concrete block	12 in.

Brick Exterior Walls
Two courses of brick	8 in.
Two courses with 2 in. air space	10 in.
Three courses of brick	12 in.

When drawing, a recommended technique for measuring wall thickness is to set your dividers to the proper dimension and use them rather than try to measure each time with your scale. Variations in wall thickness will be readily evident and will detract from the neatness of the drawing.

Since the floor plan is a section drawing, symbols should be used to indicate materials used. See Fig. 16-3.

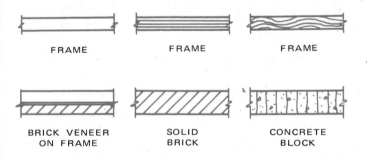

Fig. 16-3. Several methods of indicating interior and exterior walls on a floor plan.

LOCATION AND SIZE OF WINDOWS AND DOORS

When locating windows and doors on the drawing use a center line through the middle of the opening. The sash opening is shown for windows and the actual door width is used for doors. Sills are indicated for windows and exterior doors. Refer to Chapter 13 for appropriate window and door symbols. The door swing must be indicated on the floor plan. Fig. 16-4 shows how a window and door are represented on the floor plan.

Occasionally, a plain opening or archway may be desired rather than a door. In this case, hidden lines are used to show that the opening does not extend to the ceiling, Fig. 16-5. Hidden lines are used on the floor plan to indicate that a feature is above the cutting plane or hidden by some other detail.

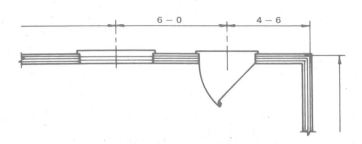

Fig. 16-4. Windows and doors should be located using a center line, type of window indicated and door swing shown.

CABINETS, APPLIANCES AND PERMANENT FIXTURES

The location and size of kitchen cabinets, bathroom vanities, fixtures and appliances must be indicated on the floor plan. These features are drawn using standard symbols which represent sizes. Never guess at the size of an appliance or fixture. Obtain information related to each item and record the necessary dimensions and specifications for inclusion in the plans.

Refer to symbols and location procedures presented in Chapters 5 and 7. Examine local codes relative to clearances and installation procedures acceptable in your area.

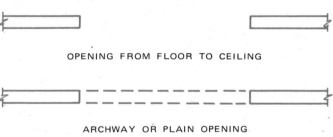

Fig. 16-5. Method of representing interior wall openings other than windows and doors.

STAIRS AND FIREPLACES

If stairs or fireplace is to be included, only basic size and location information needs to be recorded on the floor plan, because details will be included in the set of drawings for these two features.

Normally, the direction of flight and number of risers as

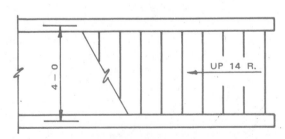

Fig. 16-6. Information about a set of stairs which is usually included on the floor plan.

well as the width of the stairs, is given on the floor plan. See Fig. 16-6. The basic width, length, location, and shape of opening of the fireplace is also shown on the floor plan. A simplified or more detailed symbol may be used to identify the fireplace, Fig. 16-7. Other flues which may be housed in the chimney are frequently added to the drawing.

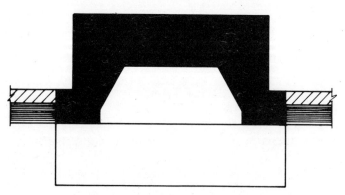

SIMPLIFIED FIREPLACE SYMBOL

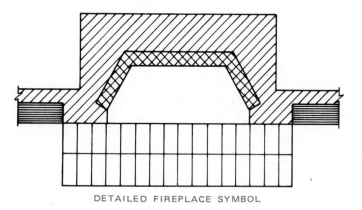

DETAILED FIREPLACE SYMBOL

Fig. 16-7. A fireplace may be represented using a simplified or detailed symbol. The detailed symbol is usually preferred.

WALKS, PATIOS AND DECKS

Several features which are outside the house are commonly included on the floor plan. Walks, patios and decks are examples. Sizes and materials to be used should be included on the plan. These features help to present the total plan and are important elements.

ROOM NAMES AND MATERIAL SYMBOLS

Room names add information which is important in communicating the plan to others. The room name should be lettered slightly larger (3/16 in.) than surrounding lettering. The ideal location for the room name is the center of the room. This may be shifted to one side or lowered if center space is unavailable. If desired, the approximate size of the room may be added immediately below the name. This is helpful to those not too familiar with construction drawings.

Material symbols are a type of shorthand for the draftsman. Symbols are used rather than try to describe each material

with words. Use a material symbol whenever the material should be identified. If the symbol is not a standard one, identify it. Several common building material symbols are shown in Fig. 16-8.

DIMENSIONING

Dimensions on a floor plan may show the size of a feature or its location. THE IMPORTANCE OF PROPER AND CAREFUL DIMENSIONING CANNOT BE OVEREMPHASIZED. Placement of dimensions requires good judgment. Locate dimensions where one would logically look for them. Dimension lines in architectural drawing are generally continuous lines with the dimension figure placed above the line. Dimensions are always parallel (never perpendicular) to the dimension line. Any of the termination symbols may be used as long as you are consistent. Review Chapter 4.

When drawings are so crowded with dimensions it is difficult to see the objects, move dimension lines out from the drawing far enough (at least 3/4 in.) so the dimension, as well as the object lines, may be clearly seen. Spacing between the dimension lines may be 1/4 in. or 3/8 in. as desired. Dimension lines may be located within the house area if that seems to be the logical place for them. Refrain from using long leaders. Maximum length of leaders should be two inches.

Dimensions in architectural drawing are recorded in feet and inches. When the dimension is less than one foot, one of two procedures may be used. Either place a zero in the foot location followed by the number of inches (0 – 6) or record the length as so many inches and show the inch mark (6″).

In drawing plans feet and inch marks may be omitted as a general rule. A dimension such as 12 – 6 could not mean anything other than 12 ft. 6 in.

Interior walls are commonly dimensioned to the center. A short line is drawn down the middle of the wall at the termination point of the dimension to show that the center is indicated, Fig. 16-9.

Exterior walls, if they are frame, are dimensioned to the outside of the stud wall. This usually includes the weatherboard or sheathing but not the siding, Fig. 16-9. Solid masonry walls are dimensioned to the outside of the wall, Fig. 16-10. Brick veneer walls are dimensioned to outside of the stud wall, Fig. 16-9.

Overall dimensions are necessary for the length and width of the structure. Always add all the dimensions which together equal the overall dimension. One of the most frequent errors in dimensioning is that partial dimensions do not add up to equal the total distance.

The overall length and width of major wall segments should be lengths which are multiples of 4 ft. Building material sizes are keyed to this dimension and much unnecessary waste will result if this rule is not applied.

Frequently, notes are required to present information which cannot be represented by a conventional dimension or symbol. These notes should be brief and located where they will be easy to see. Include only information which is required. Notes may be lettered 1/8 in. high or slightly smaller. They should be read from bottom of sheet - - not from edge.

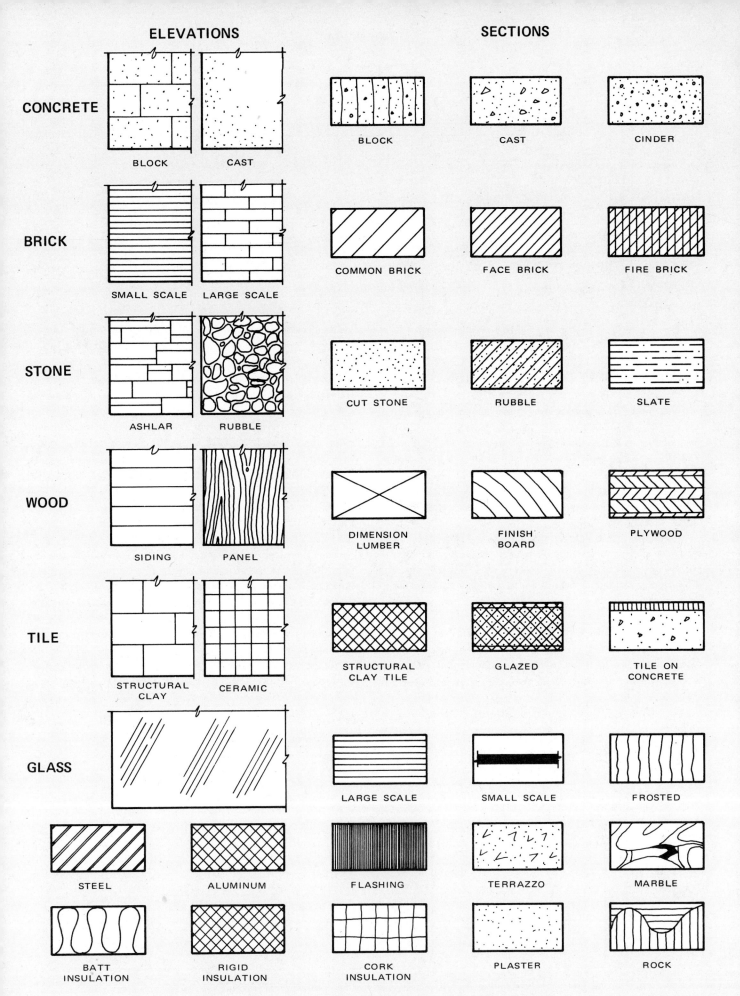

ELEVATIONS

SECTIONS

CONCRETE
- BLOCK
- CAST
- BLOCK
- CAST
- CINDER

BRICK
- SMALL SCALE
- LARGE SCALE
- COMMON BRICK
- FACE BRICK
- FIRE BRICK

STONE
- ASHLAR
- RUBBLE
- CUT STONE
- RUBBLE
- SLATE

WOOD
- SIDING
- PANEL
- DIMENSION LUMBER
- FINISH BOARD
- PLYWOOD

TILE
- STRUCTURAL CLAY
- CERAMIC
- STRUCTURAL CLAY TILE
- GLAZED
- TILE ON CONCRETE

GLASS
- LARGE SCALE
- SMALL SCALE
- FROSTED

- STEEL
- ALUMINUM
- FLASHING
- TERRAZZO
- MARBLE

- BATT INSULATION
- RIGID INSULATION
- CORK INSULATION
- PLASTER
- ROCK

Fig. 16-8. Several common building material symbols used on residential plans.

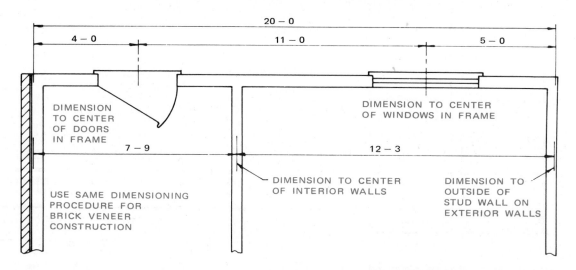

Fig. 16-9. Recommended method of dimensioning frame wall construction.

SCALE AND SHEET IDENTIFICATION

Residential floor plans are usually drawn to a scale of 1/4'' = 1' − 0''. A detail may be a larger scale and the plot plan smaller, but the other drawings should be 1/4'' = 1' − 0''. The size of paper selected for the plans will be determined by the size of the structure. A sheet of 18'' x 24'' paper is large enough for most plans. The scale must appear at the bottom of each drawing. An exception is the pictorial representation of the total house.

Numbering the sheets so the reader may determine if the set is complete is important. A method which works well is to number each sheet like this: Sheet 1 of 6, 2 of 6, etc. The sheet number should appear in the lower right hand corner of each sheet.

METRIC SYSTEM OF DIMENSIONING

Each year the metric system of measurement is used more world wide. It is anticipated that the United States will eventually convert to the metric system. Even though no standards have been agreed upon in the lumber and building industry, a simple floor plan has been presented, Fig. 16-11, to illustrate metric dimensioning. The basic unit of measure will most likely be the METER. However, before universal adoption of the system may be made by the building industry, new lumber sizes and standards must be decided upon and accepted.

PROCEDURE FOR DRAWING FLOOR PLAN

The first step in designing a house is to determine the requirements of the structure and record them as preliminary sketches. These rough sketches will provide direction for drawing the plan to scale. The following steps are presented as an aid to the student in drawing a floor plan once he has determined the basic requirements and developed some preliminary sketches.

1. LAY OUT THE EXTERIOR WALLS. Draw the walls as light construction lines. Be sure that the overall length and

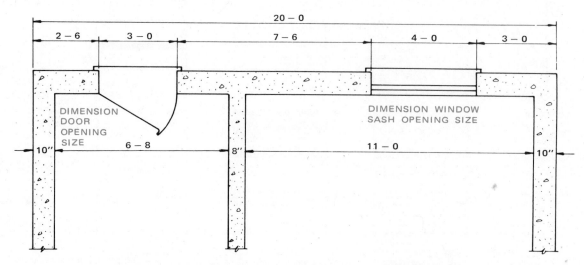

Fig. 16-10. Solid masonry walls (cast concrete, block, brick or stone) are usually dimensioned as shown.

Floor Plan

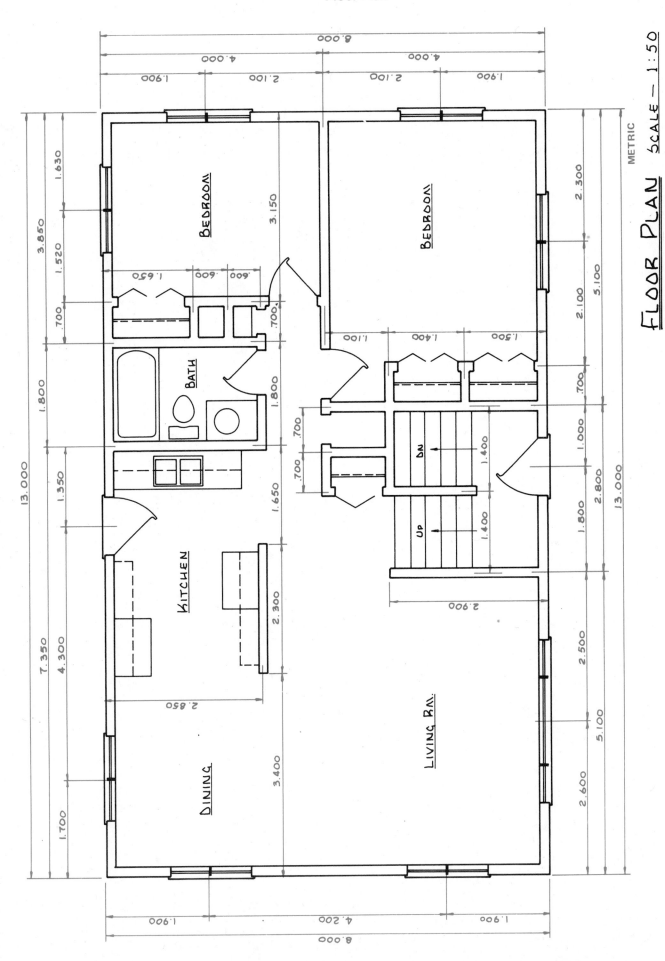

Fig. 16-11. Units for linear measurement in the construction industry should be restricted to the metre (m) and the millimetre (mm). Thus on drawings, whole number dimensions will always indicate millimetres, and decimalized numbers (to 3 places of decimals) will always indicate metres.

FLOOR PLAN SCALE — 1:50

METRIC

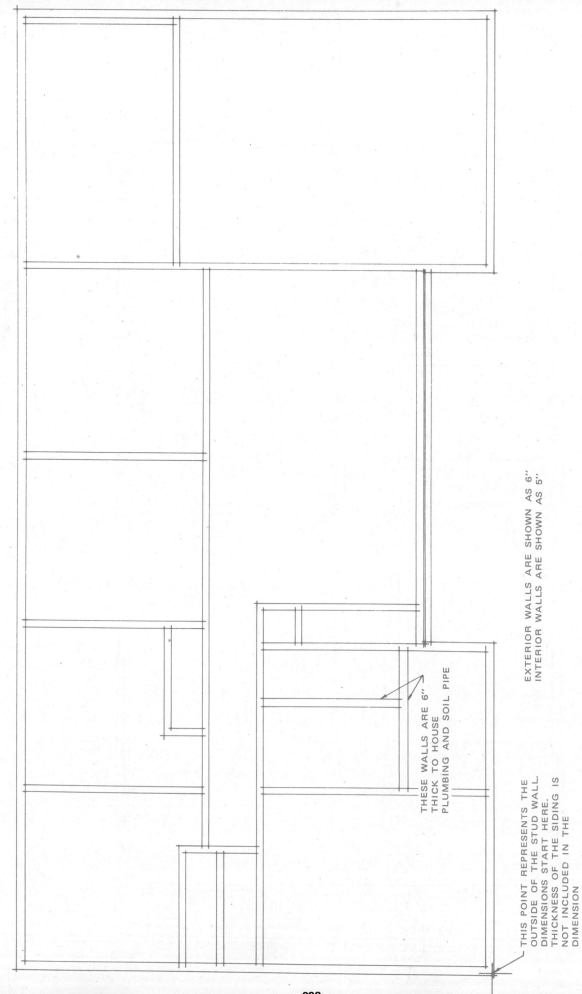

THIS POINT REPRESENTS THE
OUTSIDE OF THE STUD WALL.
DIMENSIONS START HERE.
THICKNESS OF THE SIDING IS
NOT INCLUDED IN THE
DIMENSION

THESE WALLS ARE 6"
THICK TO HOUSE
PLUMBING AND SOIL PIPE

EXTERIOR WALLS ARE SHOWN AS 6"
INTERIOR WALLS ARE SHOWN AS 5"

Fig. 16-12. A lay out of the interior and exterior wall locations using light construction lines for a small ranch type house with a basement.

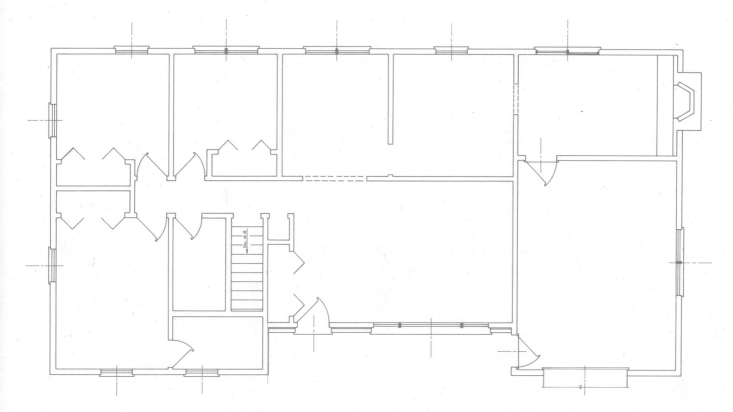

Fig. 16-13. Windows, doors, fireplace and stairs have been added to the layout. Lines showing walls and symbols have been darkened.

width of the house is measured to the proper place on the walls and that walls are the correct thickness.

2. LOCATE THE INTERIOR WALLS. Also draw these as light construction lines. Set your dividers to the desired wall thickness and use them to transfer the dimension. Use the center of the wall for locating its position. Steps 1 and 2 are shown in Fig. 16-12.

3. DETERMINE THE LOCATION OF THE WINDOWS AND DOORS. Both of these features will be dimensioned to the center line of the opening, so locate it first. Indicate the swing of doors and type of window used. Darken in lines used for windows and doors.

4. DRAW THE STAIRS. Measure the width of the stairs and lay out the treads. The finished floor to finished floor height must be determined and the tread and riser height calculated before this step may be completed accurately. See Chapter 14 for an explanation of stair design and construction. Draw equally spaced lines to represent the stair treads. Show direction of travel and number of risers. If the house has no stairs, then go to the next step.

5. LOCATE AND DRAW THE FIREPLACE. Review Chapter 15. If the house is to have a fireplace, draw the outline in lightly. Since the dimensions of a fireplace must be exact to ensure proper operation, some preliminary work must be done before it can be drawn on the floor plan. Identify the type and size of fireplace which is desired and record these dimensions for further use. Darken in the fireplace outline and fire chamber size. You may now darken in all exterior and interior walls. Steps 3, 4 and 5 are shown in Fig. 16-13.

6. LOCATE AND DRAW WALKS, PATIOS OR DECKS.

These elements of the plan should be well thought out and materials and designs selected which will complement the total structure. Lay out and draw these parts.

7. DRAW THE KITCHEN CABINETS, APPLIANCES AND BATHROOM FIXTURES. Kitchen base cabinets are usually 24 in. deep and wall cabinets 12 in. deep. The base units are shown as solid lines while the wall cabinets are indicated using a hidden line symbol. The refrigerator and range are usually deeper than 24 in. and should be represented as such. Bathroom vanities and fixtures should be located and drawn in the same way as kitchen cabinets and appliances. Be sure to check the code for clearances required for fixtures. Refer to Chapters 5 and 7 for information about bathrooms and kitchens.

8. ADD DIMENSIONS, NOTES AND ROOM NAMES. Keep in mind the guidelines for dimensioning that were presented earlier in this chapter. Make sure the dimensions are accurate and complete. Letter the room name in the center of each room and show the approximate room size below the name if desired. Look over the drawing and add any general or specific notes that seem warranted. Steps 6, 7 and 8 are shown in Fig. 16-14.

9. ADD MATERIAL AND IDENTIFICATION SYMBOLS. It is better to wait until the drawing is nearly finished to add material symbols so they do not interfere with dimensions or notes. Add the necessary symbols and darken in lines which are light. ALL OBJECT LINES, HIDDEN LINES, CENTER LINES, ETC. ON A DRAWING SHOULD BE BLACK AND ONLY VARY IN WIDTH. Exceptions are guidelines and construction lines. You may wish to remove the construction

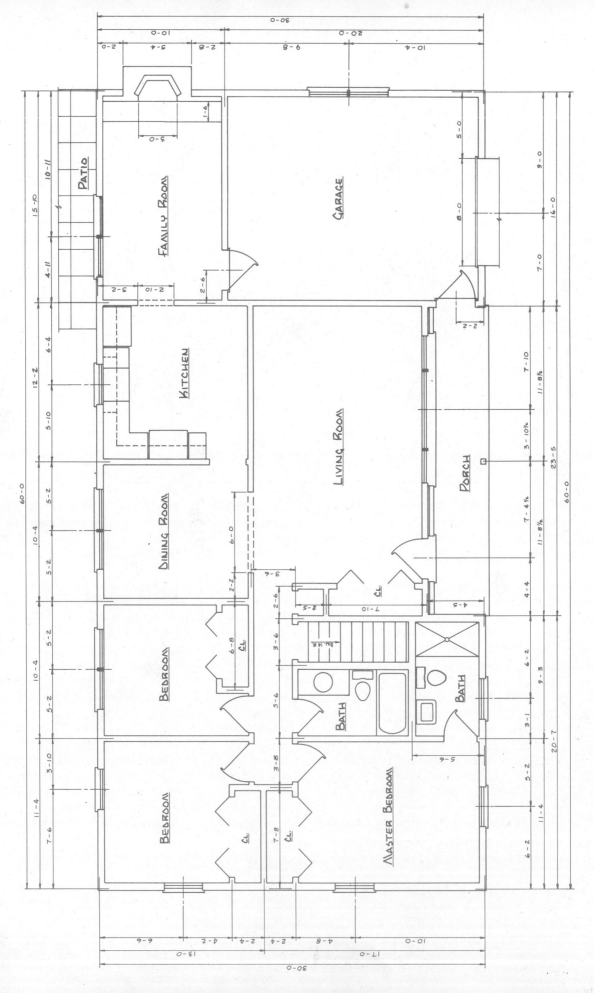

Fig. 16-14. A patio and porch, kitchen cabinets, bathroom fixtures, room names and dimensions have been added to the plan.

284

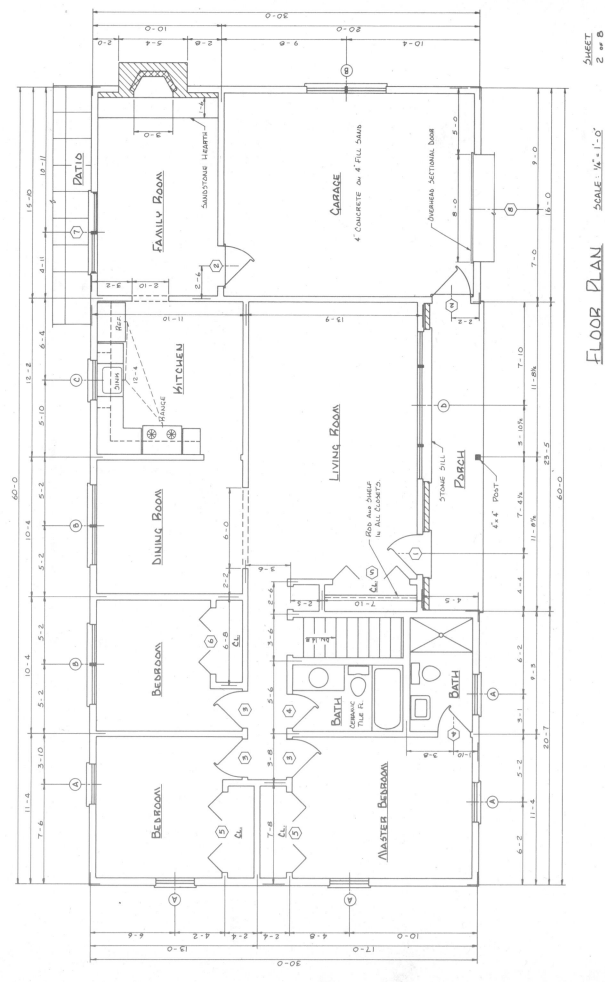

FLOOR PLAN   SCALE: 1/4" = 1'-0"

Fig. 16-15. The floor plan is completed by adding material and identification symbols, notes, scale and name of the drawing.

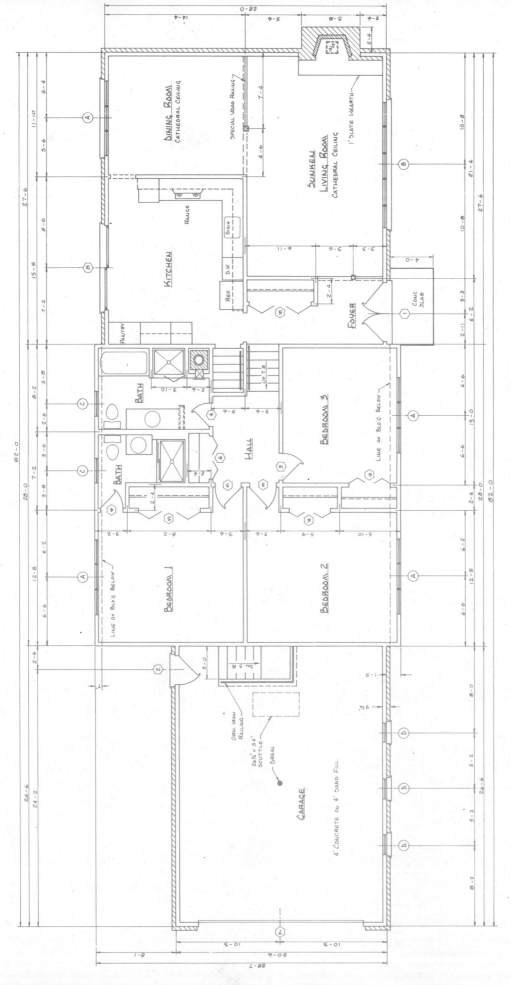

FLOOR PLAN
SCALE — 1/4" = 1'-0"

Fig. 16-16. Upper level floor plan for a split-level house. The basement/foundation plan of this house would present the lower level layout. (Donald F. Sowa, A.R.A.)

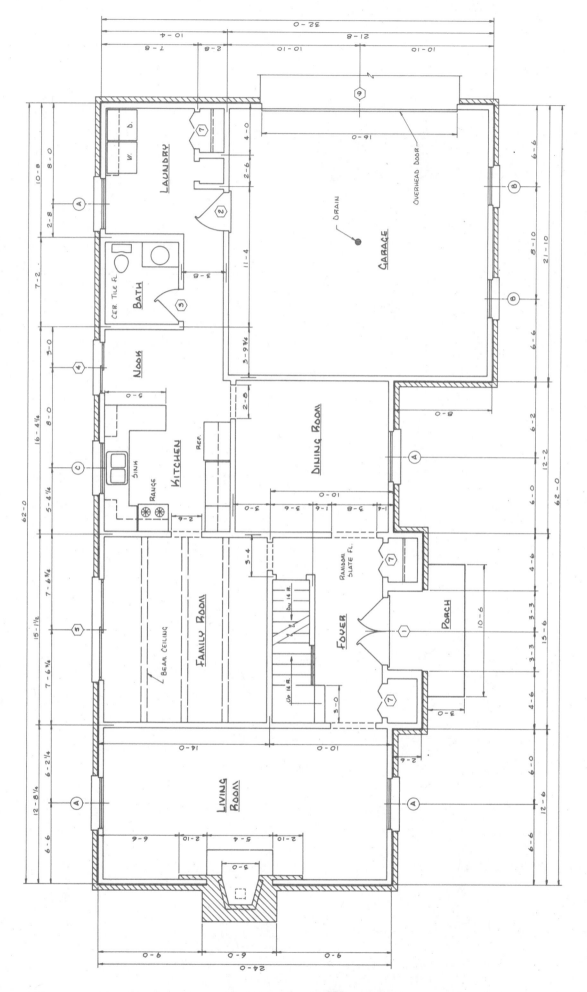

FIRST FLOOR PLAN
Scale — 1/4" = 1'-0"

Fig. 16-17. The first floor plan for a brick veneer, two-story house. Second floor plan is shown in Fig. 16-18.

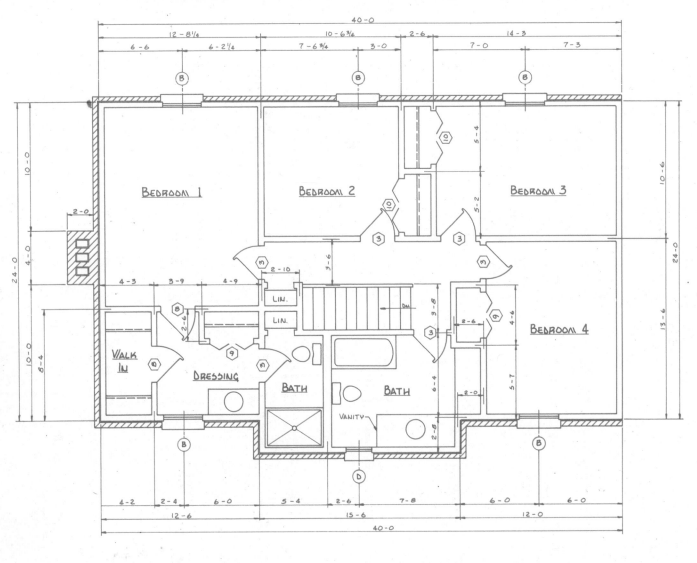

SECOND FLOOR PLAN
SCALE — 1/4" = 1'-0"

Fig. 16-18. The second floor plan for the two-story home shown in Fig. 16-17.

lines, but do not remove the guidelines.

10. DRAW THE TITLE BLOCK AND ADD THE SCALE. The scale is important and should be placed in a prominent location near the bottom of the drawing. It may be located in the title block if all drawings on the sheet are the same scale. The title block should include the following information: sheet number, name of drawing, scale, date, who the drawing is for, who made the drawing, and any other information which is deemed necessary. Steps 9 and 10 are shown in Fig. 16-15.

11. CHECK THE ENTIRE DRAWING. Examine all aspects of the drawing for accuracy and completeness.

The floor plan for a split-level house is presented in Fig. 16-16, to illustrate the typical way of drawing a split-level floor plan. First and second level floor plans of a common two-story house are shown in Figs. 16-17 and 16-18.

The plan shown in Fig. 16-19 is designed for expansion.

The basic house, 28 x 52 ft. contains the necessary space for a small family. As the family grows, the house may be enlarged to meet the needs. A bedroom and bath could be added first and the breezeway, bath and mud room later. Finally, the garage, storage and porch may be built to complete the expanded plan which is approximately 34 x 74 ft.

Expansion plans have much to offer. When additions are planned for in the initial design stage, the expanded house does not appear "added on to." Also, fewer basic changes are required when additions are ultimately made.

REVIEW QUESTIONS — CHAPTER 16

1. A floor plan is not a typical top view, but a_____ drawing.

2. The purpose of a floor plan is _____
_____

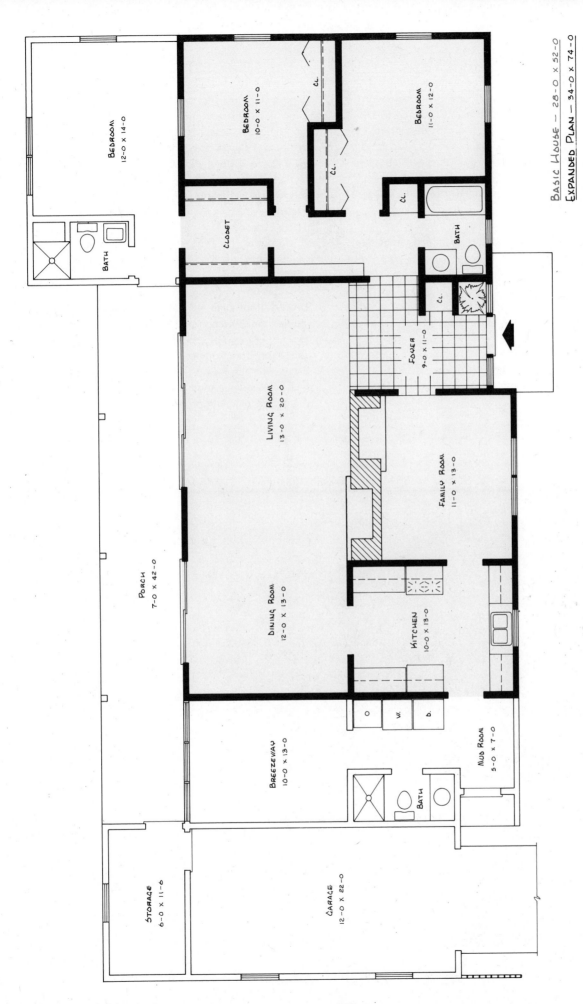

BASIC HOUSE — 28-0 × 52-0
EXPANDED PLAN — 34-0 × 74-0

Fig. 16-19. This basic house may be expanded from 1456 to 2516 sq. ft. The additions (which were preplanned) include a bedroom, two baths, a breezeway, mud room, storage, garage and porch.

Bedroom
12-0 × 14-0

Bath

Bedroom
10-0 × 11-0

cl.

cl.

cl.

Bedroom
11-0 × 12-0

Bath

Closet

cl.

Foyer
9-0 × 11-0

Living Room
13-0 × 20-0

Family Room
11-0 × 13-0

Porch
7-0 × 42-0

Dining Room
12-0 × 13-0

Kitchen
10-0 × 13-0

w.

Breezeway
10-0 × 13-0

Bath

Mud Room
5-0 × 7-0

Storage
6-0 × 11-6

Garage
12-0 × 22-0

289

3. The scale of most residential floor plans is _____.

4. The actual thickness of an exterior frame wall with 1/2" insulation board, 1/2" dry wall and 5/8" siding on a 1 1/2" x 3 1/2" framing member (stud) is 5 1/8", however an exterior frame wall is usually represented as _____ on the floor plan.

5. Windows and doors are dimensioned in frame construction as follows: _____.

6. Windows and doors are dimensioned in a solid masonry wall as follows: _____.

7. Indicate the symbol used to show an archway. _____.

8. Information generally given on the floor plan about a set of stairs is _____.

9. Indicate the section symbol for the following materials:
   a. Plaster
   b. Aluminum
   c. Rigid Insulation
   d. Dimension Lumber
   e. Common Brick
   f. Cast Concrete

10. Show the two ways of representing a dimension of 4 in. on a floor plan.

SUGGESTED ACTIVITIES

1. Find a floor plan for a small house or cottage in a magazine, newspaper or other source and draw it to 1/4" = 1' − 0" scale. Show all necessary dimensions, notes and symbols. Prepare a window and door schedule. Present your drawing along with the original.

2. Design a modern ranch type house which fulfills the following specifications:

Flat lot	Two-car garage
Three bedrooms	Slab floor construction
1 1/2 baths	No basement
Living room	Frame construction
Kitchen	Patio
Dining room	Fireplace

3. Draw a floor plan for a one-bedroom apartment with a living room, kitchen and dining area, a bath and storage area. Interior walls are frame and exterior walls are brick veneer on 8 in. concrete block. Calculate the living space.

4. Secure the floor plan for a house or apartment which you feel has a poor arrangement and utilization of space. Redesign this plan and present both for comparison.

Roof design and materials greatly influence the visual impact of a structure.

Chapter 17
ROOF DESIGNS

TYPES OF ROOFS

The overall appearance of a home is greatly affected by the roof lines and materials used for roof construction. The designer has many standard designs to choose from. He should be able to find one which will complement the basic design of the home being constructed. Fig. 17-1 shows traditional and modern roof types commonly used in residential construction.

GABLE. The gable roof is a very popular type of roof. It is easy to build, sheds water well, provides for ventilation, and is applicable to a variety of house shapes and designs.

HIP. The hip roof is slightly more difficult to build than a gable roof, but is still a popular choice. It does not provide for ventilation as well as some other designs and increases the chance for leakage due to the hips and valleys.

FLAT. A flat roof is the most economical roof to construct, but does not add much to the design of most houses. It requires a "built-up" roof covering rather than conventional shingles. A built-up roof consists of layers of roofing felt and tar topped with gravel. Actually, most so-called flat roofs are pitched at about 1/8 to 1/2 in. per foot to aid in drainage. The flat roof is popular in warmer areas of

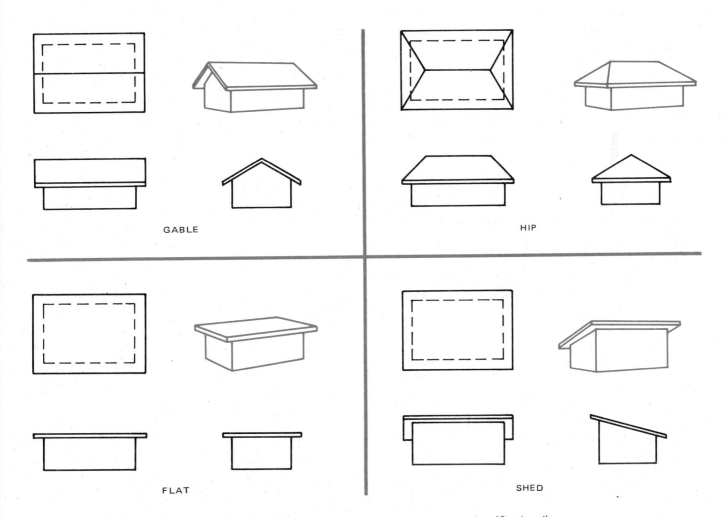

GABLE   HIP   FLAT   SHED

Fig. 17-1. Roof designs which may be used in residential construction. (Continued)

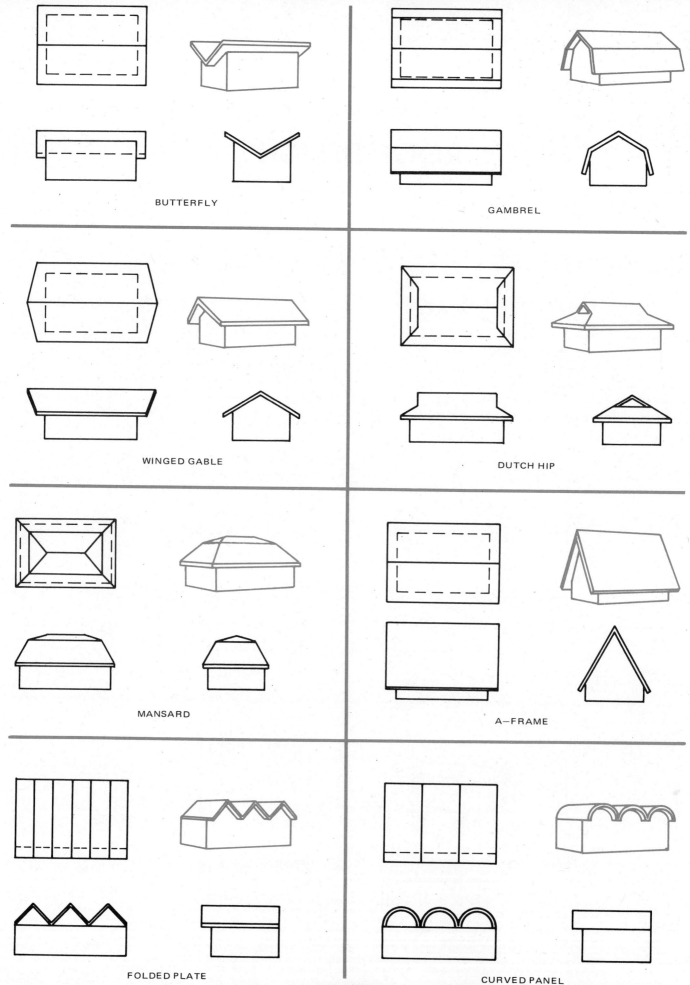

BUTTERFLY

GAMBREL

WINGED GABLE

DUTCH HIP

MANSARD

A—FRAME

FOLDED PLATE

CURVED PANEL

Fig. 17-1 Continued.

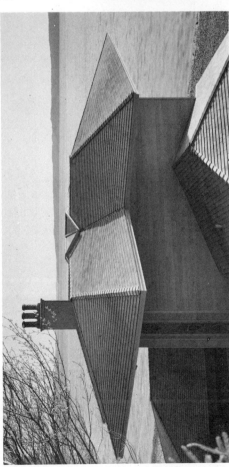

Fig. 17-2. The importance of a well-designed roof is illustrated by each of these contemporary homes. (Red Cedar Shingle and Handsplit Shake Bureau; Southern Forest Products Assoc.; American Plywood Assoc.)

the country where wide overhangs are desirable for shade and where little or no snow falls.

SHED. A shed roof is similar to a flat roof, but has more pitch. It is frequently used for additions to existing structures or in combination with other roof styles. A built-up roof is generally required unless the roof has a pitch of over 3:12. (Three feet rise for each 12 feet of run.)

MANSARD. The mansard roof is gaining in popularity after being used infrequently for several years. It is a French design and is more difficult to construct than the hip or gable.

GAMBREL. The gambrel roof is sometimes called a barn roof because it has been used extensively on barns. It provides the additional headroom needed for the Dutch colonial.

BUTTERFLY. The butterfly roof has not been used widely in the past, but seems to be gaining in acceptance. It has the advantage of providing plenty of light and ventilation, but drainage is a problem. Flashing should extend far up each slope along the valley to prevent leaking.

A-FRAME. The A-frame provides not only a roof but the walls as well. Originally, it was used for cottages, but in recent years it has been applied to homes, churches and other structures.

FOLDED PLATE. The folded plate roof is a contemporary design which is finding limited application in residential buildings. However, it is quite popular for motels and small commercial buildings. Modular, prefabricated roof units are being produced which will probably increase the popularity of this design.

CURVED PANEL. Curved panel roofs are similar to the folded plate in style and application. Thus far they have had only limited use in home construction. They too are being produced in prefabricated modules.

OTHER CONTEMPORARY ROOF TYPES. Several other modern roof types are being experimented with and should be identified. The PARASOL roof looks like an upturned parasol. It is usually constructed from concrete. WARPED roofs are

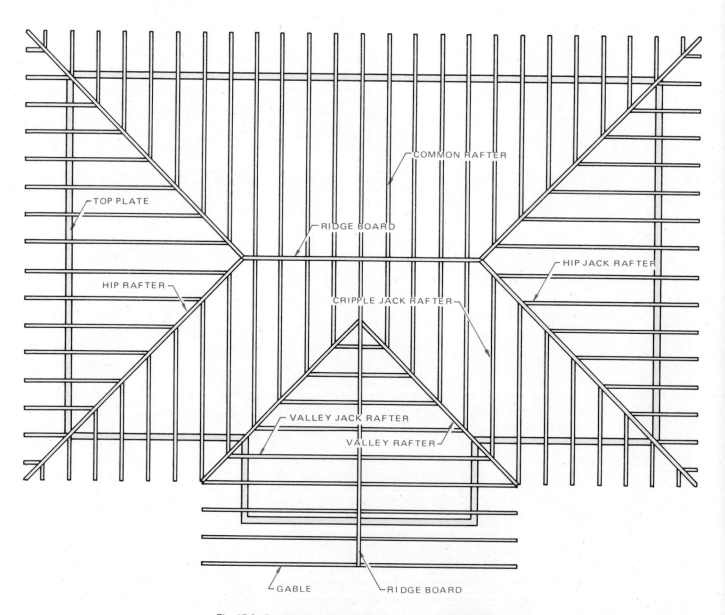

Fig. 17-3. Roof framing plan with structural members identified.

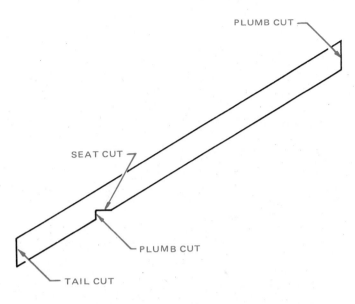

Fig. 17-4. A common rafter with the various cuts labeled.

limitless in design. They may be constructed from concrete, molded plywood or plastics. Complete freedom is possible with the FREE-FORM roof. Urethane foam is a popular choice of material for this roof. It is sprayed over a network of pipes and net material. It is strong and weather resistant. Fig. 17-2 shows several residential structures with modern roof styles.

FRAME ROOF CONSTRUCTION

RAFTERS. Roof covering material is supported by roof framing. The framing must be strong and rigid. Roof framing consists of several distinct structural elements. The first and most basic of these elements is the rafter. Common rafters are perpendicular to the top wall plate. They extend from the plate or beyond to the ridge of the roof. Fig. 17-3 shows a plan view of the roof framing for a simple structure. Note that several types of rafters other than common rafters are identified.

Rafters are cut to the proper dimensions by locating the ridge cut, the seat cut, the plumb cuts, and the tail cut, Fig. 17-4. The precise layout of these cuts is determined by the slope or PITCH of the roof and the width or SPAN of the building. Terms which must be understood before calculating rafter dimensions and roof pitch are: RISE, RUN and SPAN. The rise of a roof is the vertical distance measured from the top of the wall plate to the intersection of the center line of the rafters. The run of a roof is one-half of the span. Span is the horizontal distance from the outside of one stud wall to the outside of the opposite stud wall. Fig. 17-5 graphically illustrates these terms.

Roof slope may be given on a drawing by showing a slope ratio diagram or a fractional pitch indication. The slope diagram, Fig. 17-6, represents the ratio between the rise and run of the roof. The fractional pitch is calculated using the following formula:

$$\text{Pitch} = \frac{\text{Rise}}{\text{Span}}$$

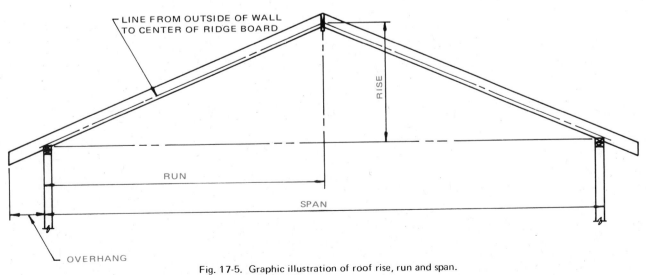

Fig. 17-5. Graphic illustration of roof rise, run and span.

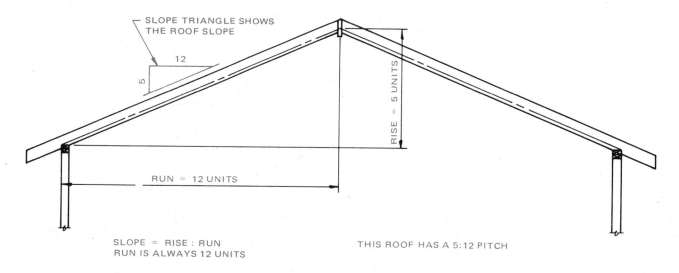

SLOPE TRIANGLE SHOWS
THE ROOF SLOPE

12

5

RISE = 5 UNITS

RUN = 12 UNITS

SLOPE = RISE : RUN
RUN IS ALWAYS 12 UNITS

THIS ROOF HAS A 5:12 PITCH

Fig. 17-6. The roof slope diagram represents the relationship of the rise
to the run.

Fig. 17-7 illustrates the fractional pitch for the same roof slope shown in Fig. 17-6.

Roof slope may also be shown using an angular dimension. However, this method is seldom used because it is difficult to measure as accurately as either of the other methods. A roof with a 45 deg. slope has a 12:12 or 1/2 pitch. Fig. 17-8 shows several common roof pitches used in residential construction. When designing a roof, try to use one of the standard roof pitches.

Rafter sizes will depend on the distance to be spanned, the spacing of the rafters and the weight to be supported. Rafter span data is presented in Fig. 17-9. Rafters for low slope roofs may also serve as a base for the finished ceiling. In this instance, they are acting as rafters and ceiling joists, Fig. 17-10. Normal rafters are listed in the table under roof slope of over 3:12 pitch. A light roofing is one which weighs less than four pounds per square foot. Anything more is con-

sidered heavy roofing.

CORNICE. The cornice is the overhang of the roof at the eaves line that forms a connection between the roof and sidewalls. In a gable roof it is formed on two sides of the building. The cornice continues around all four sides on a hip or flat roof.

The three types of cornices frequently used in residential buildings are the OPEN cornice, BOX cornice and CLOSE cornice. The open cornice, Fig. 17-11, may be used with exposed beam construction, contemporary or rustic designs. Rafter ends are exposed and are usually tapered to prevent a bulky appearance.

There are three basic types of box cornices: the NARROW BOX, WIDE BOX WITH LOOKOUTS and WIDE BOX WITHOUT LOOKOUTS. A narrow box cornice is usually between 6 and 12 in. wide. The soffit board is nailed directly to the bottom side of the rafter, Fig. 17-12. A wide box

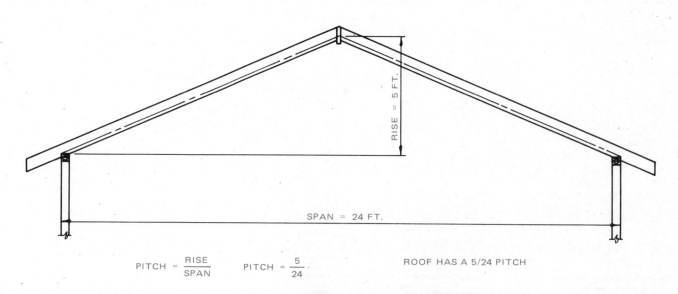

RISE = 5 FT.

SPAN = 24 FT.

$$PITCH = \frac{RISE}{SPAN} \qquad PITCH = \frac{5}{24}$$

ROOF HAS A 5/24 PITCH

Fig. 17-7. The roof slope shown as a fractional pitch denotes the relationship between the rise and span.

cornice with lookouts normally requires additional support members (lookouts) for fastening the soffit. Fig. 17-13 shows a wide box cornice with lookouts. A wide box cornice without lookouts has a sloped soffit. The soffit material is nailed to the underside of the rafters. This type of cornice is frequently used when the overhangs are very wide, Fig. 17-14.

A close cornice is one in which the rafter does not project beyond the wall. The roof is terminated by a frieze board and molding, Fig. 17-15.

RAKE OR GABLE END

The RAKE or gable end is the extension of a gable roof beyond the end wall of the house. The amount of overhang

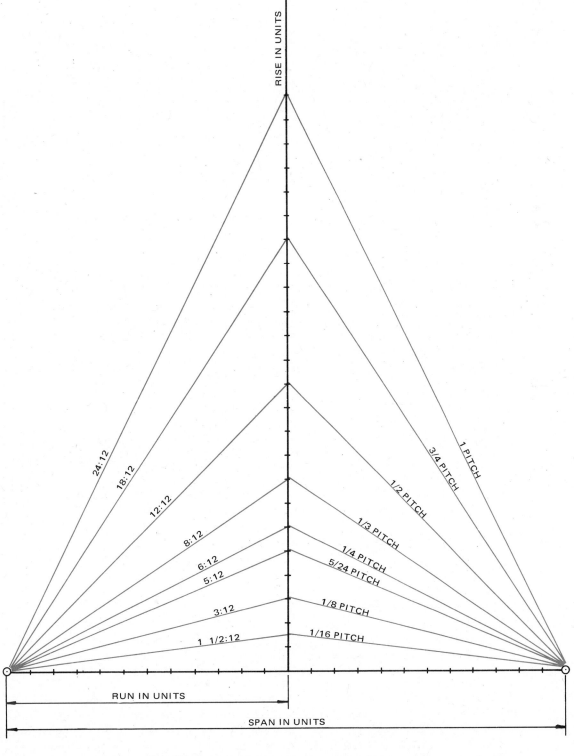

Fig. 17-8. Several roof pitches used in residential construction.

RAFTER SPAN DATA

NOMINAL SIZE IN INCHES	SPACING IN INCHES O.C.	NONSUPPORTING FINISHED CEILING					SUPPORTING FINISHED CEILING				
		DOUGLAS FIR AND LARCH									
		SELECT STRUCT.	DENSE CONSTR.	CONSTR.	STANDARD	UTILITY	SELECT STRUCT.	DENSE CONSTR.	CONSTR.	STANDARD	UTILITY
		SOUTHERN YELLOW PINE									
		NO. 1 K.D.	NO. 2 K.D.	NO. 1	NO. 2		NO. 1 K.D.	NO.2 K.D.	NO. 1	NO. 2	
2 x 6	12	14 4	14 4	14 4	14 4	9 6	13 8	13 8	13 8	13 8	8 10
	16	13 0	13 0	13 0	12 10	8 4	12 4	12 4	12 4	11 10	7 8
	24	11 4	11 4	11 4	10 6	6 8	10 10	10 10	10 8	9 8	6 2
2 x 8	12	18 4	18 4	18 4	18 4	14 4	17 8	17 8	17 8	17 8	13 2
	16	17 0	17 0	17 0	17 0	12 4	16 4	16 4	16 4	16 2	11 6
	24	15 4	15 4	15 4	15 4	10 0	14 8	14 8	14 6	13 2	9 4
2 x 10	12	21 10	21 10	21 10	21 0	19 6	21 0	21 0	21 0	21 0	18 0
	16	20 4	20 4	20 4	20 4	16 10	19 6	19 6	19 6	19 6	15 8
	24	18 4	18 4	18 4	18 4	13 10	17 8	17 8	17 8	16 8	12 10
2 x 12	12	24 0	24 0	24 0	24 0	22 8	24 0	24 0	24 0	24 0	21 0
	16	23 6	23 6	23 6	23 6	19 8	22 6	22 6	22 6	22 6	18 2
	24	21 2	21 2	21 2	21 2	16 2	20 4	20 4	20 4	20 2	14 10

SPANS ARE IN FT. AND INCHES.

(National Forest Products Assoc.)

*CALCULATIONS ARE BASED ON:

LIGHT ROOFING — LESS THAN 4 POUNDS PER SQ. FT.

A DEAD LOAD OF 15 POUNDS PER SQ. FT. AND A LIVE LOAD OF 20 POUNDS PER SQ. FT. FOR A FINISHED CEILING.

DEFLECTION NOT TO EXCEED 1/240TH OF THE CLEAR SPAN

NOMINAL SIZE IN INCHES	SPACING IN INCHES O.C.	ROOF SLOPE OVER 3:12*									
		LIGHT ROOFING					HEAVY ROOFING				
		DOUGLAS FIR AND LARCH									
		SELECT STRUCT.	DENSE CONSTR.	CONSTR.	STANDARD	UTILITY	SELECT STRUCT.	DENSE CONSTR.	CONSTR.	STANDARD	UTILITY
		SOUTHERN YELLOW PINE									
		NO. 1 K.D.	NO. 2 K.D.	NO. 1	NO. 2		NO. 1 K.D.	NO. 2 K.D.	NO. 1	NO. 2	
2 x 6	12	16 10	16 10	16 10	16 10	11 2	15 6	15 6	15 6	14 10	9 6
	16	15 8	15 8	15 8	15 0	9 8	14 4	14 4	14 0	12 10	8 4
	24	13 10	13 10	13 6	12 2	7 10	12 6	12 6	11 6	10 6	6 8
2 x 8	12	21 2	21 2	21 2	21 2	16 8	19 8	19 8	19 8	19 8	14 4
	16	19 10	19 10	19 10	19 10	14 4	18 4	18 4	18 4	17 6	12 4
	24	17 10	17 10	17 10	16 8	11 0	16 6	16 6	15 8	14 4	10 0
2 x 10	12	24 0	24 0	24 0	24 0	22 10	23 6	23 6	23 6	23 6	19 6
	16	23 8	23 8	23 8	23 8	19 8	21 10	21 10	21 10	21 10	16 10
	24	21 4	21 4	21 4	21 0	16 2	19 8	19 8	19 8	18 8	13 10

SPANS ARE IN FEET AND INCHES

(National Forest Products Assoc.)

*CALCULATIONS ARE BASED ON:

LIGHT ROOFING WHICH IS LESS THAN 4 POUNDS PER SQ. FT. OR HEAVY ROOFING — OVER 4 POUNDS PER SQ. FT.

A DEAD LOAD OF 15 POUNDS PER SQ. FT. AND A LIVE LOAD OF 15 POUNDS PER SQ. FT. FOR HEAVY ROOFING

DEFLECTION NOT TO EXCEED 1/240TH OF THE CLEAR SPAN

Fig. 17-9. The maximum allowable rafter span may be determined by referring to these charts. Rafter span is the horizontal distance between supports. This is not to be confused with rafter length, which must be calculated using the rise and run of the roof.

and treatment at the gable end should be about the same as the cornice. For example, if a close cornice is used, then a close rake should also be used. Fig. 17-16 shows the framing for a gable end with a wide overhang. A close rake is less expensive to build, but wider overhangs provide for sidewall protection and less frequent painting.

The style of house must be considered when designing the gable end. A narrow box cornice is normally used for Cape Cod or colonial homes. The same proportions should be extended to the gable end.

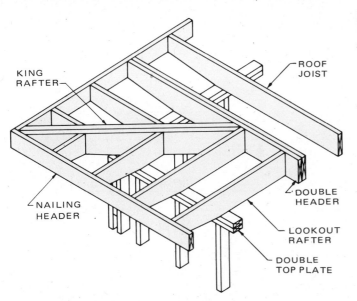

Fig. 17-10. Framing detail of the cornice for a flat or low pitched roof.

KING RAFTER

ROOF JOIST

NAILING HEADER

DOUBLE HEADER

LOOKOUT RAFTER

DOUBLE TOP PLATE

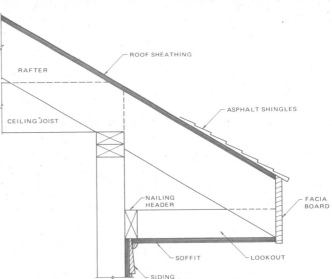

Fig. 17-13. A wide box cornice with lookouts.

RAFTER

ROOF SHEATHING

CEILING JOIST

ASPHALT SHINGLES

NAILING HEADER

FACIA BOARD

SOFFIT

LOOKOUT

SIDING

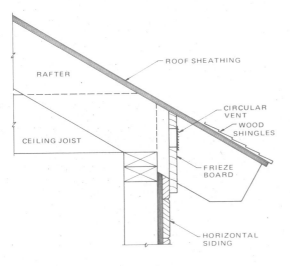

Fig. 17-11. Section through an open cornice.

RAFTER

ROOF SHEATHING

CEILING JOIST

CIRCULAR VENT

WOOD SHINGLES

FRIEZE BOARD

HORIZONTAL SIDING

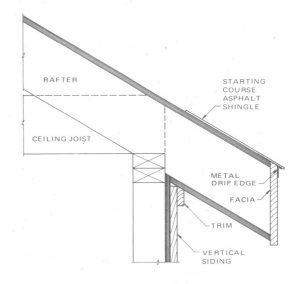

Fig. 17-14. A section of a wide box cornice without lookouts.

RAFTER

CEILING JOIST

STARTING COURSE ASPHALT SHINGLE

METAL DRIP EDGE

FACIA

TRIM

VERTICAL SIDING

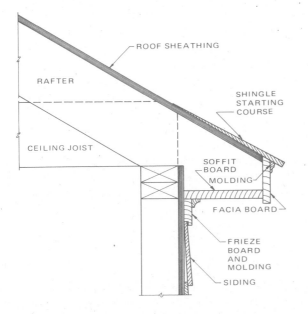

Fig. 17-12. Section through a narrow box cornice.

ROOF SHEATHING

RAFTER

CEILING JOIST

SHINGLE STARTING COURSE

SOFFIT BOARD

MOLDING

FACIA BOARD

FRIEZE BOARD AND MOLDING

SIDING

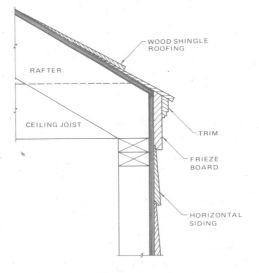

Fig. 17-15. A typical close cornice.

WOOD SHINGLE ROOFING

RAFTER

CEILING JOIST

TRIM

FRIEZE BOARD

HORIZONTAL SIDING

299

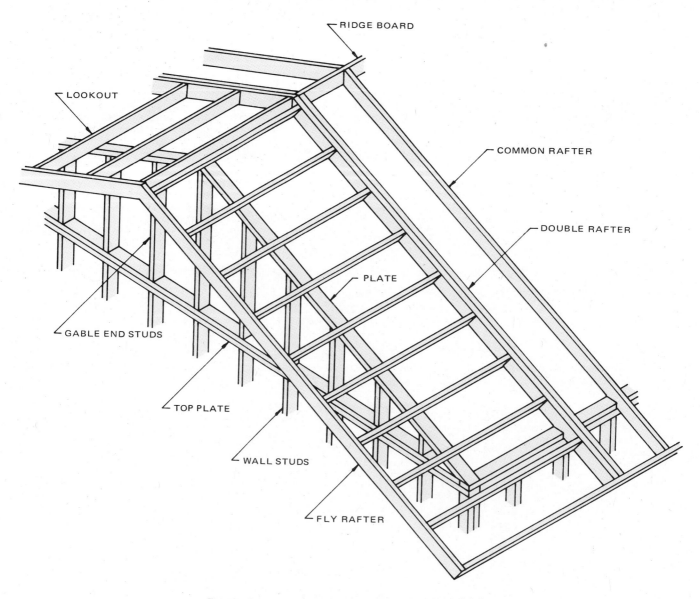

RIDGE BOARD

LOOKOUT

COMMON RAFTER

DOUBLE RAFTER

PLATE

GABLE END STUDS

TOP PLATE

WALL STUDS

FLY RAFTER

Fig. 17-16. Framing for a gable end with a wide overhang.

VENTILATION

Providing for adequate ventilation in the attic space is a necessity. If sufficient ventilation is not provided, moisture will probably form on the underside of the roof sheathing and in time damage will result. Also, a well-ventilated attic will help to cool the interior of the house during the summer.

Ventilation in the attic space is usually accomplished through the use of louvered openings in the gable ends and along the underside of the overhang. Ridge ventilators are also available which provide an efficient means of expelling hot air when coupled with soffit openings. The difference between the temperature of air in the attic and the outside causes air movement and thus reduces the temperature inside.

Experience has shown that the total area of ventilator openings should be at least 1/300th of the ceiling area. For example, if the ceiling area is 1200 sq. ft., then the ventilator area should be a minimum of 4 sq. ft. Fig. 17-17 shows several louvered gable type ventilator openings.

FLASHING

Flashing should be used where the roof comes in contact with a wood or masonry wall, chimney or roof valley. Wide strips of weather resistant metal such as aluminum, copper, and galvanized sheet steel are commonly used as flashing. This is worked beneath the surface materials a distance sufficient to prevent the penetration of water. Fig. 17-18 shows flashing around a chimney.

Roof valleys may be flashed with metal or two thicknesses of roll type roofing. The width of valley flashing should be no less than specified below:

Roof Slope	Flashing Width
less than 4:12	— 24 inches wide
4:12 to 7:12	— 18 inches wide
over 7:12	— 12 inches wide

Frequently a ribbon of asphalt-roofing mastic is used under the shingles adjacent to the valley flashing, to aid in waterproofing the roof. Fig. 17-19 shows valley flashing under

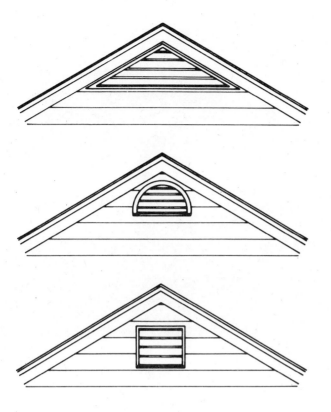

Fig. 17-17. Typical gable type louvered ventilators.

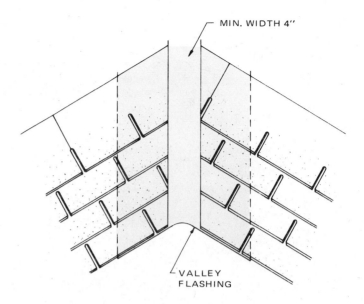

Fig. 17-19. The width of valley flashing is dependent upon the roof slope.

an asphalt shingle roof.

A small metal edging is normally used at the gable and eaves line to act as a drip edge. This flashing prevents water from entering behind the shingles and protects the facia and rake boards, Fig. 17-20.

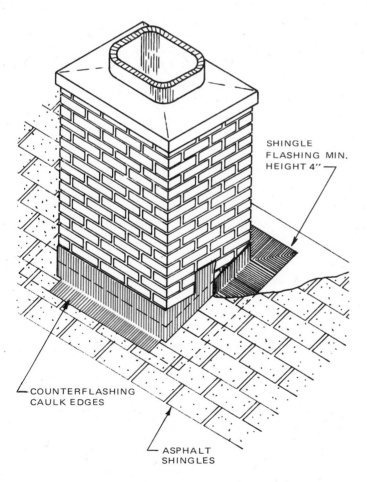

Fig. 17-18. Flashing around a chimney is composed of shingle flashing and counterflashing.

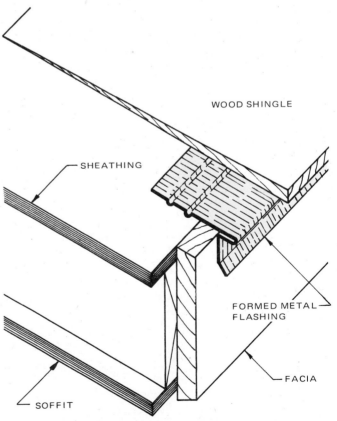

Fig. 17-20. Drip edge flashing prevents water from entering behind the shingles and protects the facia.

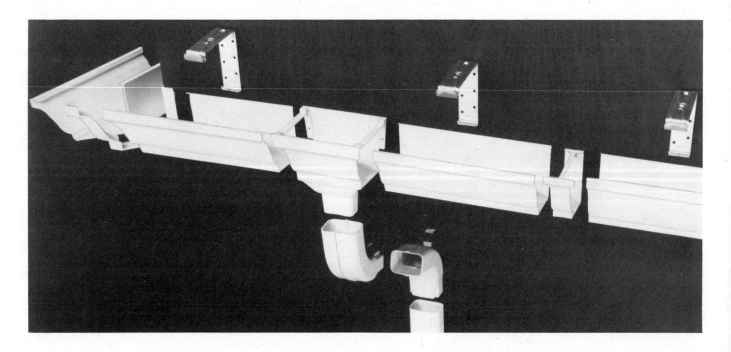

Fig. 17-21. Ogee style gutter made from vinyl plastic. (Bird and Son, Inc.)

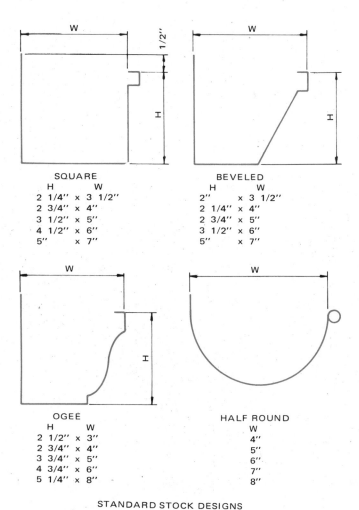

SQUARE	
H	W
2 1/4'' x	3 1/2''
2 3/4'' x	4''
3 1/2'' x	5''
4 1/2'' x	6''
5'' x	7''

BEVELED	
H	W
2'' x	3 1/2''
2 1/4'' x	4''
2 3/4'' x	5''
3 1/2'' x	6''
5'' x	7''

OGEE	
H	W
2 1/2'' x	3''
2 3/4'' x	4''
3 3/4'' x	5''
4 3/4'' x	6''
5 1/4'' x	8''

HALF ROUND
W
4''
5''
6''
7''
8''

STANDARD STOCK DESIGNS

Fig. 17-22. Typical gutter designs and sizes. Lengths are usually 10 feet.

GUTTERS AND DOWNSPOUTS

Gutters collect the water from the roof and direct it to an outlet. This prevents water from running directly off the eaves and splattering the house and running down the foundation wall. Gutters are usually pitched 1 to 1 1/2 in. in 20 ft. This slope permits even flow and prevents water from standing in the gutter.

Several styles of gutters and downspouts are available in copper, vinyl, aluminum and galvanized sheet metal. The ogee style gutter is a popular type, Fig. 17-21. Several common shapes and sizes of gutters are shown in Fig. 17-22. Wood gutters are attractive on some home styles, but they are diminishing in importance due to high original and maintenance costs.

ROOF SHEATHING AND ROOFING

Roof sheathing is placed over the rafters to support the roofing material. Sheathing may be planks as in post and beam construction, individual boards, or plywood, Fig. 17-23. Except in the case where wood shingles are used as the roofing material, plywood is a popular choice. Usually 1 x 3 in. strips, spaced several inches apart, are used for wood shingle roofs.

The thickness of sheathing will vary with the spacing of the rafters or supporting beams. However, in most situations (rafters spaced 16 or 24'' o.c.) 1/2 in. standard sheathing grade plywood is used. The plywood must be laid with the face grain perpendicular to the rafters as in floor sheathing. The sheets should be staggered so that two sheets side by side do not end on the same rafter.

When individual boards are used as sheathing, they are

usually no wider than 6 or 8 in. Minimum thickness is 3/4 in. for rafters 16 or 24'' o.c. Each board should be long enough to span a minimum of two rafters. Longer boards are desired for gable ends.

Roofing material used should be long-lived and provide a waterproof surface. Materials which have stood the test of time and have proven to be satisfactory include: asphalt shingles, asbestos shingles, wood shingles, tile, slate, roll roofing, copper, aluminum, galvanized steel, and layers of felt and tar. Factors which influence the selection are cost, local codes, roof pitch, design and individual preference.

More homes have asphalt shingle roofs than any other type. The usual recommended minimum weight of asphalt shingles is 235 pounds per square for square-butt strip shingles. A square of shingles will cover 100 sq. ft. The square-butt strip shingle is 12'' x 36'' and is laid on 5'' intervals. A layer of building paper (15 pound saturated felt) is ordinarily placed on the sheathing before laying the shingles. This acts as a moisture barrier.

The other roofing materials are less frequently used and are usually applied in special situations. Instructions for installation may be obtained from manufacturers.

Fig. 17-23. A shingled roof showing the exposed construction. (Southern Forest Products Assoc.)

ROOF TRUSSES

The roof truss is an assembly of members which form a rigid framework of triangular shapes. This arrangement permits

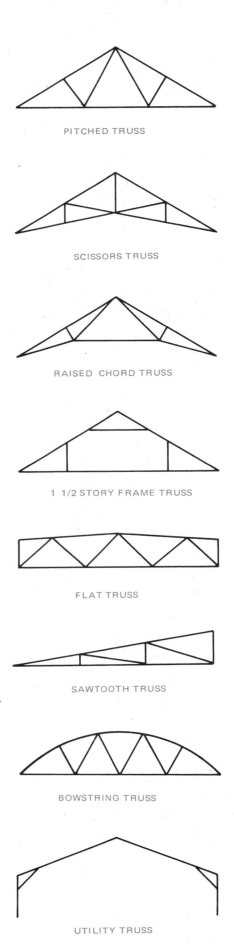

PITCHED TRUSS

SCISSORS TRUSS

RAISED CHORD TRUSS

1 1/2 STORY FRAME TRUSS

FLAT TRUSS

SAWTOOTH TRUSS

BOWSTRING TRUSS

UTILITY TRUSS

Fig. 17-24. Common roof truss designs used in residential construction.

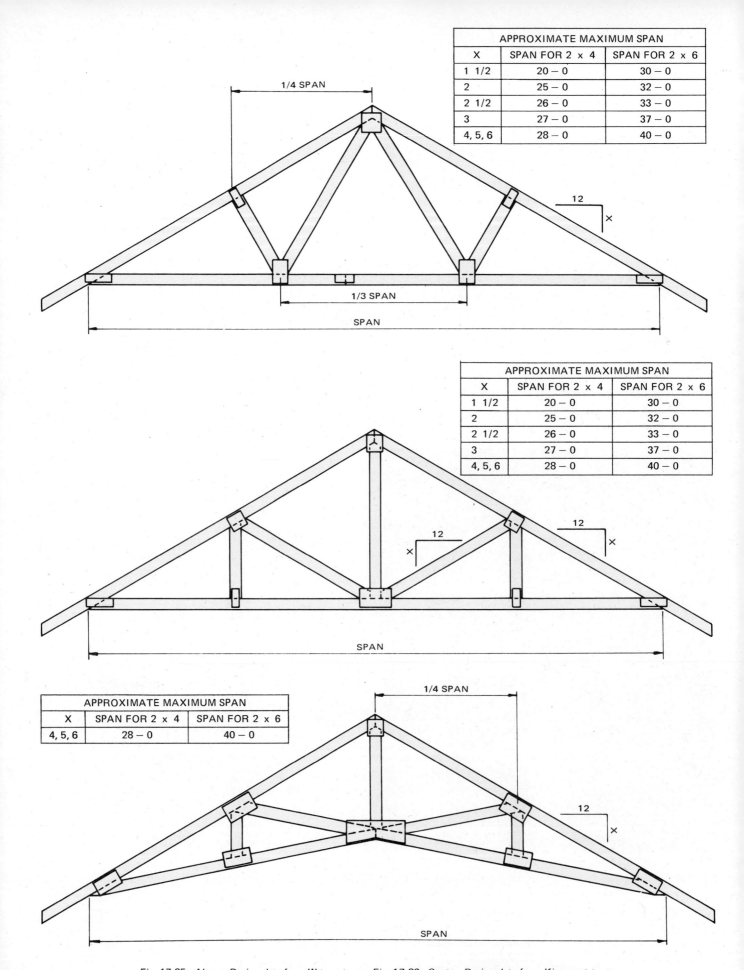

APPROXIMATE MAXIMUM SPAN		
X	SPAN FOR 2 x 4	SPAN FOR 2 x 6
1 1/2	20 — 0	30 — 0
2	25 — 0	32 — 0
2 1/2	26 — 0	33 — 0
3	27 — 0	37 — 0
4, 5, 6	28 — 0	40 — 0

APPROXIMATE MAXIMUM SPAN		
X	SPAN FOR 2 x 4	SPAN FOR 2 x 6
1 1/2	20 — 0	30 — 0
2	25 — 0	32 — 0
2 1/2	26 — 0	33 — 0
3	27 — 0	37 — 0
4, 5, 6	28 — 0	40 — 0

APPROXIMATE MAXIMUM SPAN		
X	SPAN FOR 2 x 4	SPAN FOR 2 x 6
4, 5, 6	28 — 0	40 — 0

Fig. 17-25. Above. Design data for a W-type truss. Fig. 17-26. Center. Design data for a King-post truss.
Fig. 17-27. Below. Design data for a Scissors truss.

wide unsupported spans with a minimum amount of material. Fig. 17-24 shows several roof truss designs.

Lightweight wood roof trusses are designed to span distances of 20 to 32 ft. and in some instances even more. Many times they are cheaper than conventional framing. Time and expense is saved in the erection. Prefabricated trusses are readily available for standard widths and pitches. Trusses for nonstandard dimensions may be built on the site or factory produced. Most lightweight trusses are made from 2 x 4 in. lumber.

Wood trusses which are commonly used in residential construction are the W-TYPE truss, Fig. 17-25; the KING-POST truss, Fig. 17-26; and the SCISSORS truss, Fig. 17-27. Most trusses are designed to be placed 24 in. apart. Ceiling materials are nailed directly to the bottom of the trusses.

Information needed to purchase the proper truss for a house includes the span, roof pitch, spacing of the trusses and the anticipated roof load. A roof load of 40 pounds per square foot is adequate for most applications.

Wood trusses are frequently fastened together with gussets, Fig. 17-28. These gussets are made from 3/8 or 1/2 in. plywood using exterior type glue, or from metal.

Aluminum trusses, Fig. 17-29, are comparable in strength to wood trusses. These are light in weight and easy to handle.

Fig. 17-28. Light wood trusses fastened together with plywood gussets form the roof framing for this house. (American Plywood Assoc.)

Fig. 17-29. The application of light aluminum trusses. (Aluminum Co. of America)

REVIEW QUESTIONS — CHAPTER 17

1. Identify, by name, ten distinct roof types.
   a. _____.
   b. _____.
   c. _____.
   d. _____.
   e. _____.
   f. _____.
   g. _____.
   h. _____.
   i. _____.
   j. _____.
2. The purpose of roof framing is _____.
3. The roof framing member which extends from the top plate to the ridge is called a _____.
4. If a roof has a pitch of 3:12 and the rise is 3 ft., the span is _____ ft.
5. The roof span is measured from _____.
6. The _____ of a roof is one-half the span.
7. The formula for calculating the fractional pitch of a roof is _____.
8. The pitch of a roof which has a slope of 45 deg. is _____.
9. Rafter size is dependent on three things:
   a. _____.
   b. _____.
   c. _____.
10. A lightweight roofing is one that weighs less than _____ pounds per square foot.
11. The _____ is the overhang of the roof at the eaves line that forms a connection between the roof and sidewalls.
12. Three types of cornices are frequently constructed on homes. They are:
    a. _____.
    b. _____.
    c. _____.
13. The purpose of attic ventilation is two-fold. Identify them:
    a. _____.
    b. _____.
14. The total area of ventilator openings should be a minimum of _____ of the ceiling area.
15. Two materials commonly used for roof flashing are:
    a. _____.
    b. _____.
16. Roof sheathing on most homes is _____ inch plywood.

17. Identify five roofing materials which are used on residential structures.
    a. _____.
    b. _____.
    c. _____.
    d. _____.
    e. _____.
18. The recommended minimum weight of asphalt shingles is _____ pounds per square.
19. Two advantages of the roof truss over conventional framing techniques are:
    a. _____.
    b. _____.
20. Identify three types of trusses which are commonly used in residential construction.
    a. _____.
    b. _____.
    c. _____.
21. Information required to purchase roof trusses for a home includes:
    a. _____.
    b. _____.
    c. _____.
    d. _____.
22. What is a gusset? _____.

SUGGESTED ACTIVITIES

1. Look through magazines to which you have access and cut out pictures of houses which represent various roof styles. Mount the pictures on illustration board for display.
2. Write to several manufacturers of roof covering materials and ask for specifications and descriptive literature about their products. Display the literature and then add it to the classroom collection.
3. Build a scale model of an open cornice, a box cornice or close cornice. Use a scale of 1'' = 1' − 0'' and label the various parts. Display your model along with a section drawing.
4. Design a contemporary roof for a 24' x 36' cottage or a small house of your choice. Try to be innovative in design. Draw a plan view, elevations and a section of the roof. Dimension the drawings and describe the materials used.
5. Design three different types of trusses. Compare their strength by building a scale model of each and applying weight until each breaks. Write a description of your testing procedure and report your results. Show the drawings and models.

Chapter 18
ELEVATIONS

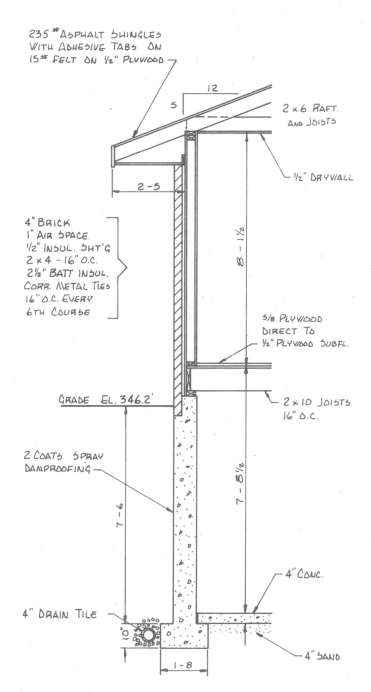

235 # Asphalt Shingles
With Adhesive Tabs On
15# Felt On ½" Plywood

12
5

2 x 6 Raft.
And Joists

2-5

½" Drywall

4" Brick
1" Air Space
½" Insul. Sht'g
2 x 4 - 16" O.C.
2½" Batt Insul.
Corr. Metal Ties
16" O.C. Every
6th Course

8 - 1½

5/8 Plywood
Direct To
½" Plywood Subfl.

Grade El. 346.2'

2 x 10 Joists
16" O.C.

2 Coats Spray
Dampproofing

7 - 6

7 - 8½

4" Conc.

4" Drain Tile

4" Sand

1 - 8

Fig. 18-1. Wall section for a typical brick veneer structure with a basement. This type of section would be included in a set of construction drawings.

DEFINITION AND PURPOSE

An elevation is an orthographic projection (drawing) which shows one side of the building. When the term "elevation" is used in connection with a set of construction drawings, it ordinarily refers to an exterior elevation. Various interior elevations may be drawn, but they are usually considered to be details.

The purpose of an elevation is to show the finished appearance of a given side of the building and furnish vertical height dimensions. Four elevations are customarily drawn - - one for each side of the house. In some instances, however, more than four elevations may be required to describe the structure.

Elevation drawings provide height information about basic features of the house which cannot be shown very well on other drawings. They also indicate exterior materials such as siding and roof covering.

REQUIRED INFORMATION

Several features should be included on elevation drawings: identification of the specific side of the house which the elevation represents, grade lines, finished floor and ceiling levels, location of exterior wall corners, windows and doors, roof features, vertical dimensions of important features, porches, decks and patios, and material symbols.

ELEVATION IDENTIFICATION

Each elevation must be identified as to the particular wall it represents. The two methods commonly used are front, rear, right side and left side or north south east and west identification. The first method of designation is preferred by most designers as there is a possibility of confusion when specifying directions. The right and left side elevations are determined by facing the front of the building. The right side elevation is then on the right side. Identify each elevation immediately below the drawing to avoid confusion.

GRADE LINE, FLOORS AND CEILINGS

The reference point for most elevations is the grade line. Study the plot or site plan to determine the existing grade along each exterior wall of the house. If the existing grade is not satisfactory, a final grade line should also be indicated on each elevation affected. It is frequently helpful to indicate the desired elevation height of the grade at each corner of the house. This information is recorded on the plot plan as well as the elevation drawing if the site is not relatively level.

All features which are below grade should be drawn in hidden lines. Examples are foundation walls, footings, and window wells (areaways).

Floor to ceiling height is an important feature of the elevation. Two methods of representing this height are commonly used. The first is to indicate the finished floor to finished ceiling distance. (The floor and ceiling are represented using a center line symbol.) The usual distance from the finished floor to finished ceiling is 8' – 0'' for the first floor and 7' – 6'' or 8' – 0'' for the second floor. The second method shows the construction dimension. This is measured from the top of the subfloor to the top of the wall plate. In this instance, the construction dimension for the first floor is 8' – 1 1/2'' and 7' – 7 1/2'' or 8' – 1 1/2'' for the second floor. Carpenters usually prefer the later method because it does not require them to do any calculation.

Minimum recommended height for garage ceilings is 8' – 0''. Basements must have a clear headroom space of at least 6' – 2'' with all beams and heating ducts above this height. A full height ceiling is more desirable and should be specified where practical.

Most codes require that the top of the foundation wall be at least 8'' above the grade. This is to protect the framing members from moisture. This requirement should be kept in mind when drawing elevations. The garage floor may be slightly higher than the grade, but should be at least 4'' lower than an interior floor when the garage is attached to the house.

WALLS, WINDOWS AND DOORS

All visible wall corners are shown on the elevation using object lines. In rare instances it may be desirable to show hidden walls. Exact wall height should be determined by drawing a section through the wall and locating the grade, sill, floor joists and top plate, Fig. 18-1. The section will be more helpful since the overhang will extend below the top of the wall in most instances. Determine the exact location.

Windows and doors which are located on an exterior wall must be included on the elevation. Placement along the wall may be projected from the floor plan, but the vertical height is shown only on the elevation drawing. It is customary to place tops of windows the same height as the tops of doors. The lower face of the head jamb is considered the height of the opening. This dimension is usually 6' – 10'' from the top of the subfloor.

Show sufficient detail on windows and doors to accurately indicate details. If windows are hinged, show the swing using the proper symbol. See Chapter 13. If the windows or doors have brick mold or other trim then show this on the elevation. The glass elevation symbol may be used if desired. Sometimes it is desirable to show the window and door identification symbols on the elevation as well as the floor plan.

ROOF FEATURES

Showing roof features on an elevation drawing is important. It is here that the roof style and pitch are shown as well as chimney height and size. The roof pitch may be indicated using the fractional pitch or slope triangle. The slope triangle is usually preferred.

Gable ends must be drawn first to determine roof height. If more than one roof height is anticipated, the highest section should be drawn first. When a roof is complex a single elevation may not be completed without constructing several details to determine various heights and termination points.

The procedure for drawing a gable end is as follows:

1. Locate the top of the upper wall plate and center line of the proposed ridge location (usually in the center between the walls).

2. Lay out the desired slope starting from the top outside corner of the wall plate. A line from this point to the ridge is known as the center line of the rafter.

3. Draw a line from the top inside corner of the wall plate parallel to the rafter center line to the ridge. This line represents the bottom edge of the rafter.

4. Measure the width of the rafter perpendicular to the bottom edge and draw the top edge parallel to the rafter center line and bottom edge.

5. Measure the amount of desired overhang. Do not forget to add the thickness of roof sheathing.

6. Repeat the procedure for the other side of the roof.

Chimneys which intersect the roof usually require more than one view to determine the points where they pass through the roof. Draw the view where the roof slope is shown first. This view will indicate where the chimney passes through the roof. These points may then be projected to other views.

The chimney height above the highest roof point must be dimensioned. A minimum height above the ridge is usually 2' – 0''.

Chimney flashing, roof covering material and gable ventilators are also shown on the elevation. Use proper symbols and adequate dimensions and notes on the drawings to describe these features. Other details such as roof ventilators, vent pipes and gutters may be shown if desired.

DIMENSIONS, NOTES AND SYMBOLS

Dimensions on the elevation drawing are mainly vertical height dimensions. Features which must be dimensioned include: thickness of the footing, distance from the footing to the grade, finished floor to finished ceiling distances, overhang width, height of the top of windows and doors, and height of chimney above the roof. Other dimensions may be required for details such as deck railing, retaining walls and planters.

Notes should be included where additional information is needed or would be helpful to the builder. Some of the typical notes found on an elevation drawing are: grade information, exterior wall material notation, roof covering material identification, facia material and flashing material. Other notes may be required for specific situations.

Several symbols are commonly used on elevations. The roof

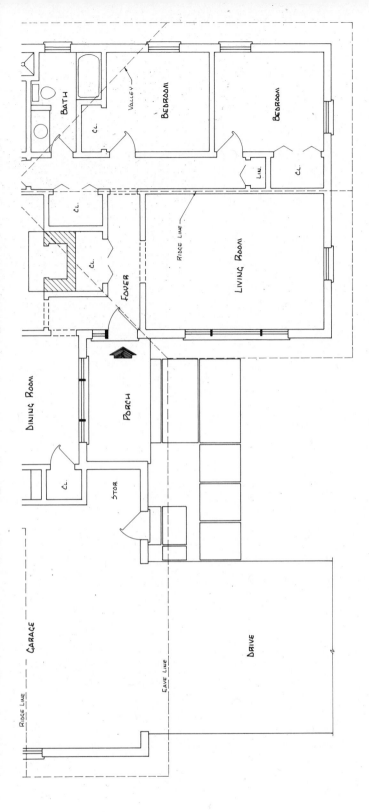

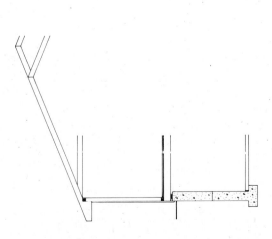

ELEVATION WILL BE DRAWN HERE

Fig. 18-2. The floor plan is placed above the space where the elevation is to be drawn and the section is to the left. This will provide a fast method of locating the various features on the elevation.

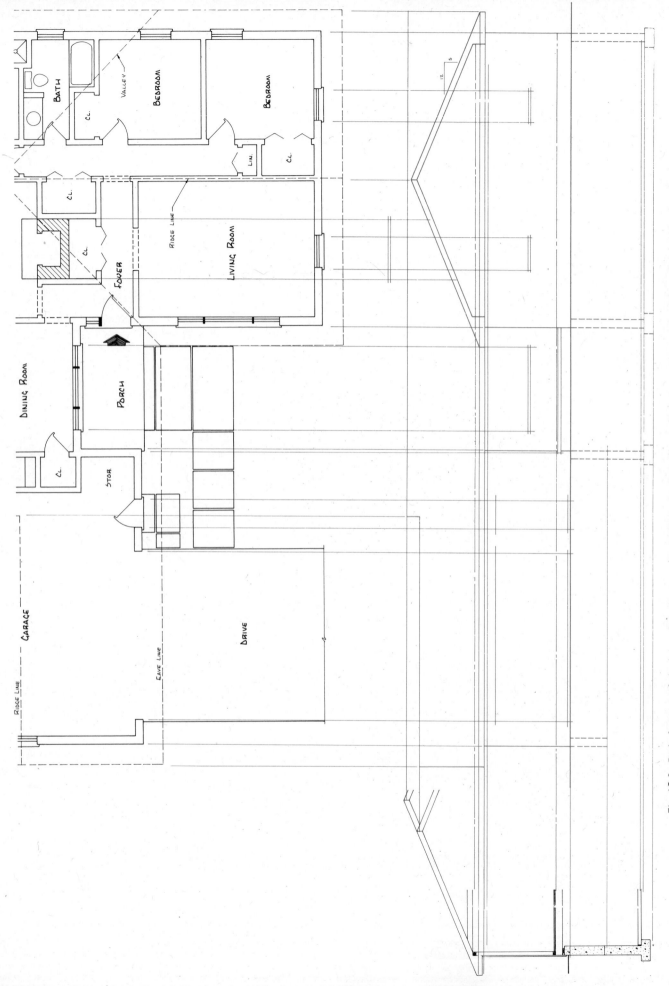

Fig. 18-3. Basic features of the house have been projected from the floor plan and section to the location where the elevation is to be drawn. Light construction lines are used.

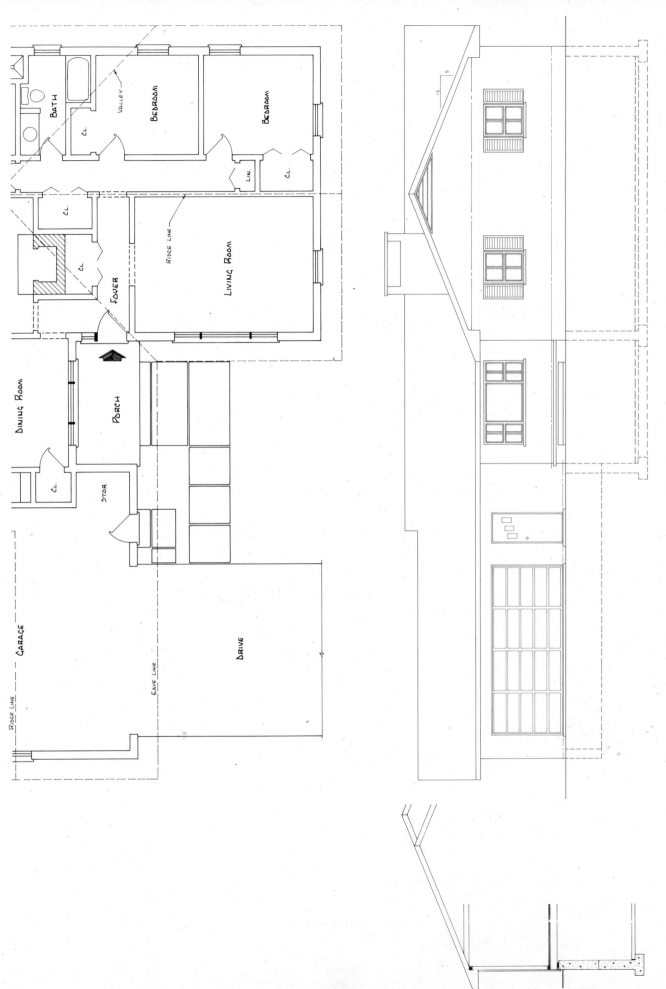

Fig. 18-4. Each feature has been darkened in and construction lines removed. Note that some dimensions were not provided by the floor plan or the section. These must be secured from other sources.

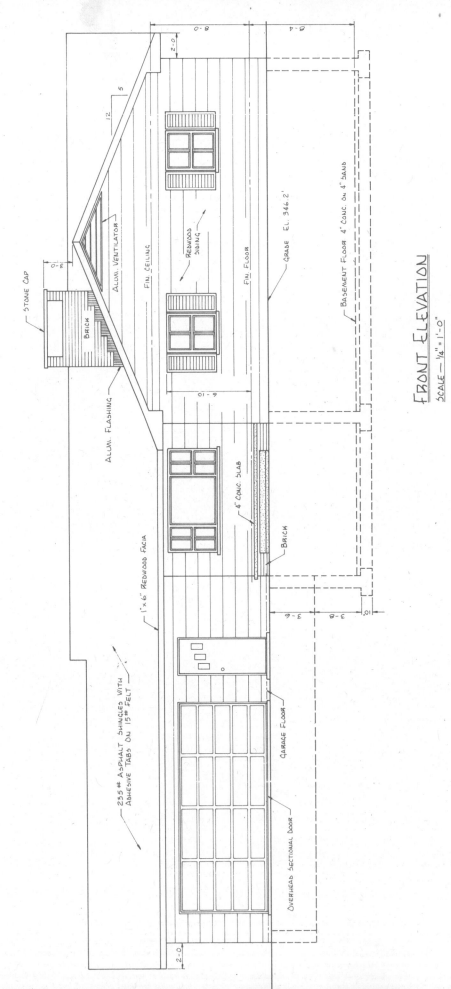

FRONT ELEVATION

SCALE — 1/4" = 1'-0"

Fig. 18-5. Dimensions, notes and symbols have been added to complete the elevation.

312

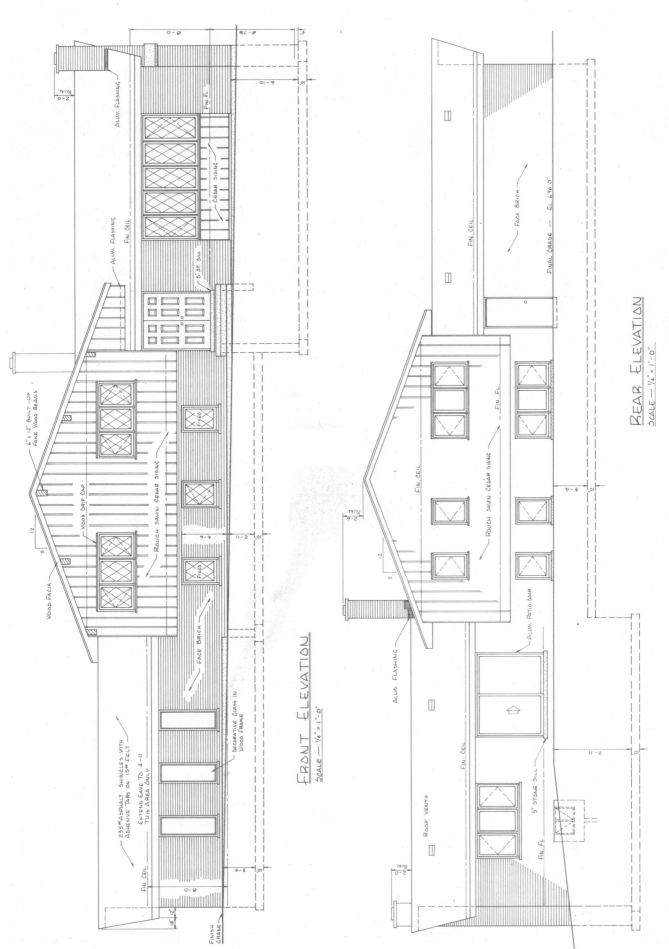

Fig. 18-6. Front and rear elevation of a modern split-level house.

Fig. 18-7. Photo above and floor plans below for the front elevation in Fig. 18-8.

FIRST FLOOR PLAN

SECOND FLOOR PLAN

pitch symbol is always shown and the exterior wall covering is usually symbolized. Many designers show material symbols extensively on the front elevation but sparingly on the remaining views. Window swing symbols which are cutting plane symbols are also drawn if needed.

PROCEDURE FOR DRAWING AN ELEVATION

There are numerous accepted procedures for drawing elevations. The procedure presented here is a logical approach

which yields fast and accurate results if followed carefully. The steps are:

1. Draw a section through the wall to be represented by the elevation. This section should be the same scale (1/4'' = 1' – 0'') as the floor plan and proposed elevation. The section drawing must be very accurate since it will be used to project the height of wall and roof elements to the elevation. If all the exterior walls of the house are the same type construction and height, then only one section will be required. However, if each wall is different, a section for each

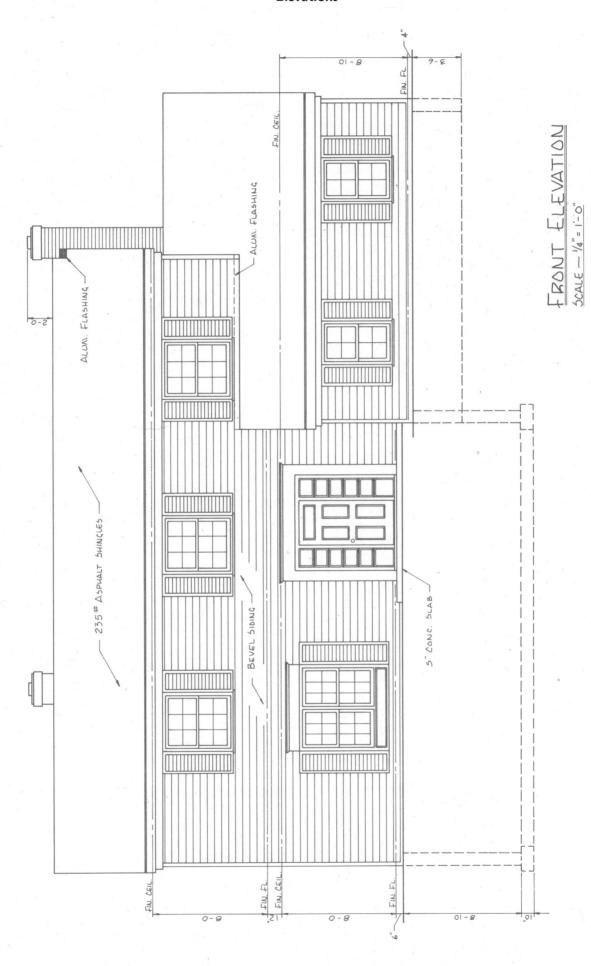

FRONT ELEVATION
SCALE — ¼" = 1'-0"

Fig. 18-8. The front elevation for the house shown in the photo and floor plans shown in Fig. 18-7.

wall will be needed. These section drawings may be discarded after the elevations are complete. Similar drawings will be made at a larger scale later.

2. Place the floor plan directly above the space where the elevation is to be drawn. The exterior walls to be represented by the elevation should be facing down toward the elevation. Some draftsmen prefer to draw the elevation on top of the floor plan rather than below it. Either method is acceptable. Steps 1 and 2 shown in Fig. 18-2.

3. Project the height of the grade line, depth and thickness of footings, window and door heights, eaves line and roof height across from the section to the space reserved for the elevation. These should be very light construction lines.

4. Project the horizontal length of exterior walls, windows, doors and other elements down from the floor plan. These may be drawn in dark since their proper length will already have been determined. Steps 3 and 4 are shown in Fig. 18-3.

5. Darken in each feature and remove the construction lines. At this point, the elevation is complete enough to determine if changes are desired in the overall design. Make any changes now.

6. Add details such as railings, window muntins, trim, window wells (areaways) and gable ventilators. Information on many of these features must be secured from reference sources such as Sweets Architectural File. Steps 5 and 6 are shown in Fig. 18-4.

7. Add dimensions, notes and symbols. It is good practice to draw material symbols last since they may interfere with other information if drawn earlier.

8. Check the drawing to be sure that all features are shown as desired. Add the title block and scale. See Fig. 18-5 which shows the finished elevation.

Repeat the eight steps for each elevation. It is customary to draw two elevations on a single sheet if space permits.

The front and rear elevations of a typical, modern split-level home are presented in Fig. 18-6. Note that material symbols are more brief on the rear elevation than appear on the front.

Fig. 18-7 shows the front elevation, floor plans and photo of a two-story house. The elevation, as illustrated by this example, provides a means of visualizing the overall appearance of the house.

REVIEW QUESTIONS – CHAPTER 18

1. What is the purpose of an elevation drawing?_____
_____.

2. How many exterior elevations are usually required for a home?_____Their names are_____
_____
_____.

3. The reference point for most elevations is the _____.

4. Features on the elevation which are below grade are represented with a _____ line.

5. On most houses, the distance from the finished floor to finished ceiling is _____.

6. Sometimes the second floor ceiling height is less than the first floor. The recommended dimension is _____.

7. The minimum recommended clear ceiling height of a basement is _____.

8. The foundation wall should be at least _____ inches above the grade.

9. A section through the wall is a helpful drawing for constructing the elevation because _____.

10. The lower face of the head jamb is considered to be the height of the opening for a window or door. The distance from the floor to this point is usually_____.

11. Where is the slope triangle located on an elevation drawing?_____.

12. The minimum height that a chimney must extend above the highest point of the roof is _____.

SUGGESTED ACTIVITIES

1. Select a floor plan of a house and draw a section through the front wall. Draw the section at a scale 1/2" = 1' – 0". Add dimensions and notes. Present the floor plan with the section.

2. Draw the four elevations for one of the floor plans that you drew for the Chapter on Floor Plans. Follow the procedure presented in this chapter. Add all dimensions, notes and submit the elevations with the floor plan.

3. Select a home from the newspaper or a magazine (photo and floor plan) and draw a front elevation of the home using a different style roof and exterior materials. Do not change the floor plan. Present your revision along with the original.

4. Select an older home in your community and sketch an elevation as it now appears. Measure the house to determine the required dimensions. Redesign the front using good design and unique application of materials. Draw an elevation of your new design.

Chapter 19
RESIDENTIAL ELECTRICAL

Planning for the electrical needs of a modern home requires a basic understanding of several factors. These factors include familiarization with related terms, electrical requirements for lighting and appliances, code restrictions and safety considerations.

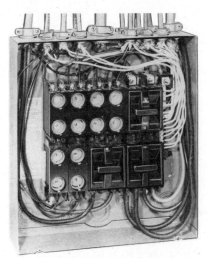

Fig. 19-1. Residential service entrance equipment may be: Above. Switch and fuse type. Below. Circuit breaker type. (Square D Co.)

ELECTRICAL TERMS

The following terms are identified to assist in familiarization and understanding of electrical terminology.

AMPERE: The unit of current used to measure the amount of electricity flowing through a conductor per unit of time.

CIRCUIT: A path through which electricity flows from a source to one or more outlets and then returns to the source.

CIRCUIT BREAKER: A device designed to open and close a circuit by nonautomatic means, and to open the circuit automatically on a predetermined overload of current.

CONDUCTOR: A material which permits the flow of electricity (usually refers to a wire).

CONVENIENCE OUTLET: A device attached to a circuit to allow electricity to be drawn off for appliances or lighting.

FUSE: A safety device which breaks the circuit when it is overloaded by melting a fusible link.

LIGHTING OUTLET: An outlet intended for the use of a lighting fixture.

RECEPTACLE: A contact device installed at an outlet for the connection of an attachment plug and flexible cord (same as a convenience outlet).

SERVICE DROP: The overhead service conductors between the last pole and the first point of attachment to the house.

SERVICE ENTRANCE: The fittings and conductors that bring electricity into the building.

SERVICE PANEL: The main distribution box that receives the electricity and distributes it to various points in the house through branch circuits. The service-panel contains the main disconnect switch, fuse or breaker which supplies the total electrical system of the house.

VOLTAGE: Pressure which forces current through a wire. One volt is the force that causes one ampere of current to flow through a wire with one ohm resistance. An ohm is the measure of electrical resistance in a circuit.

WATT: One ampere under one volt of pressure. Amps times volts equal watts. Most appliances are rated in watts.

SERVICE ENTRANCE AND DISTRIBUTION PANEL

The foundation for a residential electrical system is the service entrance and distribution panel. Residential service entrance equipment may be of the circuit breaker or switch and fuse type, Fig. 19-1. Either method provides overcurrent protection by opening the circuit if the current reaches too high a value.

A residence may have 120 or 240 volt service. Only two wires are required for 120 volt service, but three are necessary for 240 volt service. Fig. 19-2 illustrates how 120 volts is derived from 240 volt service. Even if no 240 volt appliances are to be installed when the home is built, 240 volt service entrance equipment is recommended. This is becoming standard procedure and it is less expensive to install initially than at a later date.

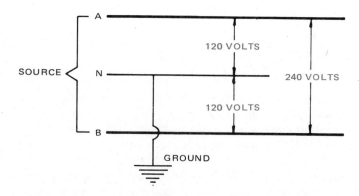

Fig. 19-2. Two voltages are available from this 240 volt, three-wire service drop. Half of the 120-volt circuits are connected to A and N and the other half to B and N. All 240-volt circuits are connected to A and B.

The most common arrangement of electrical service to a house is with the service conductors first terminating at the meter. The incoming service may be overhead or underground. Several service entrance designs are possible. Fig. 19-3 shows a common method of anchoring the service drop to the house. The use of a service head is a must if the service entrance is located along the eave line of a single story home. The service drop must be at least 10 feet above the ground at all points and 12 feet above driveways. No wires may be closer than 3 feet to windows, doors, porches or similar structures where they may be touched.

Electrical cable (copper or aluminum) is used to bring the current from the service head to the meter and on to the distribution panel. The size of this cable will depend on the size of service entrance equipment to be used in the home and the amount of amperage supplied by the electric company. The following table shows the size wire usually recommended for various amperage ratings.

SERVICE ENTRANCE CONDUCTOR SIZES
(WHEN DEMAND FACTOR IS 80 PERCENT OR LESS)

Number of Wires	Open Air Installation		Installed in Conduit	
	Size	Amperage	Size	Amperage
3	4	70	4	110
3	2	100	2	140
3	1/0	150	1/0	200
3	2/0	175	2/0	225
3	3/0	200	3/0	260

These sizes are for copper wire. If aluminum wire is used, at least two sizes larger will be required to handle the amperage indicated.

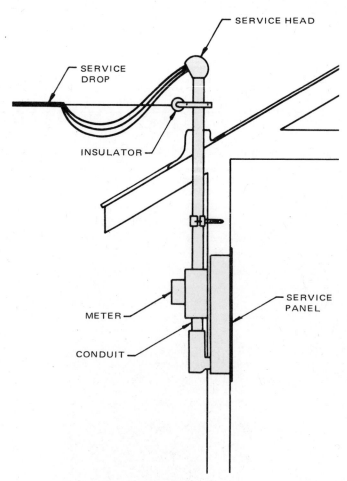

Fig. 19-3. The service head is commonly used for houses with low pitched roofs or when the service entrance equipment is located along the eaves line.

Fig. 19-4 shows how wire size is indicated. Number 12 is generally recommended for branch lighting circuits of modern residential installations. No. 14 is the smallest circuit conductor permitted by the National Code.

Fig. 19-4. Relative wire sizes and designations.

Wire size is important in a residential electrical system because current flowing through a wire produces heat. If the wire is too small for the amount of current it may cause a fire. Even if a fire does not result the heat increases resistance in the wire and electricity is wasted.

From the meter, the conductors are terminated at the distribution panel, Fig. 19-5. The main disconnect switch or breaker is usually located in the distribution panel. This switch disconnects all current to the house and should be located as close to the incoming service as possible.

Fig. 19-5. A typical distribution panel box with the cover removed to show service entrance conductors, main disconnect switch and wiring.

The capacity of the service entrance equipment should be sufficient to supply present and future demands. The National Electrical Code recommends that a minimum of 100 ampere service be provided for all residences. Many homes will require 150 or 200 ampere service.

Fig. 19-6. A compact type circuit breaker capable of providing over-current protection for two different branch circuits.
(Square D Co.)

The type of overcurrent protection devices most frequently used today is the circuit breaker. The heart of the system is the individual branch circuit breaker, Fig. 19-6. Breakers are safe, reliable and easy to use which accounts for their popularity. Fig. 19-7 shows a modern panel box designed for circuit breakers.

Fig. 19-7. Circuit breaker panel box with cover. Shown are the main breaker, two 240-volt circuits and eight 120-volt circuits.

BRANCH CIRCUITS

A modern residence has several branch circuits. Appliances and outlets are grouped together so that smaller breakers or fuses and smaller wire may be used. If a house had only one giant circuit which could supply 100 amperes of current, the wire would be very costly and impossible to handle. Switches and outlets are not designed for such large wire. Also if the fuse were to blow or breaker trip, the total structure would be without power. Just as important, it would not be possible to install the proper fuse protection for various appliances which require far smaller amounts of current. These reasons indicate the need for branch circuits.

The National Electrical Code specifies three types of branch circuits which should be used in a residential structure:

1. LIGHTING CIRCUITS: These are primarily for lighting

and serve permanently installed lighting fixtures, as well as receptacle outlets into which you plug lamps, radios, television, clocks, and similar 120 volt devices (but not kitchen appliances).

2. SPECIAL APPLIANCE CIRCUITS: Special appliance circuits are located in the kitchen, usually above the counter top. These are designed for electric fry pans, mixers, blenders, toasters and similar appliances which require large amounts of current.

3. INDIVIDUAL APPLIANCE CIRCUITS: These are circuits which serve permanently-installed appliances such as a range, water heater, washer, dryer, or water pump.

LIGHTING CIRCUITS: In modern systems lighting circuits are frequently wired with No. 12 copper wire with 20 amp. overcurrent protection. This combination will provide 2400 watts of lighting capacity (120 x 20 = 2400). The Code requires a minimum of 3 watts of lighting power for each square foot of floor space. One lighting circuit would be sufficient for 800 sq. ft. of floor space if this minimum were applied. Again, this is a minimum and probably not satisfactory to most homeowners. One lighting circuit for each 400 sq. ft. would be more advisable.

Calculation of the number of lighting circuits required is performed as follows:

1. Figure the total area included in the house.
   (48' x 60' = 2880 sq. ft.)
2. Divide the total area in the house by 400.
   (2880 ÷ 400 = 7.2 lighting circuits.)

The number of lighting circuits required for a house with 2880 sq. ft. is seven. The following table shows the number of lighting circuits recommended for various size houses:

RESIDENTIAL LIGHTING CIRCUITS

| No. of | Number of Lighting Circuits | |
Sq. Ft.	Code Minimum	Recommended
1000	2	3
1200	2	3
1600	3	4
2000	3	5
2400	4	6
2800	5	7

SPECIAL APPLIANCE CIRCUITS: Special appliance circuits require No. 12 copper wire with a 20 amp. circuit breaker or fuse. The National Electrical Code specifies a minimum of two special appliance circuits in the kitchen or similar type room. No lighting outlets may be operated from these circuits. Each of these circuits is capable of supplying 2400 watts (20 x 120 = 2400). This number of special appliance circuits may not be sufficient for a large modern kitchen.

Special appliance circuits may be appropriate in other areas of the house such as sewing room, garage and shop.

INDIVIDUAL APPLIANCE CIRCUITS: Some appliances require such a large amount of electricity that they must have their own circuit. Such circuits are called Individual Appliance Circuits. The following appliances are usually operated on

TYPICAL APPLIANCE REQUIREMENTS

Appliance or Equipment	Typical Watts	Usual Voltage	Wire Size	Recommended Fuse Size
Electric Range (with oven)	12,000	240	6	50–60 Amp.
Range Top (separate)	5,000	120/240	10	30 Amp.
Range Oven (separate)	5,000	120/240	10	30 Amp.
Refrigerator	300	120	12	20 Amp.
Home Freezer	350	120	12	20 Amp.
Automatic Washer	700	120	12	20 Amp.
Automatic Dryer (elec.)	5,000	120/240	10	30 Amp.
Dishwasher	1,200	120/240	12	20 Amp.
Garbage Disposer	300	120	12	20 Amp.
Roaster	1,400	120	12	20 Amp.
Rotisserie	1,400	120	12	20 Amp.
Furnace	800	120	12	20 Amp.
Dehumidifier	350	120	12	20 Amp.
Waffle Iron	1,000	120	12	20 Amp.
Band Saw	300	120	12	20 Amp.
Table Saw	1,000	120/240	12	20 Amp.
20,000 Btu Air Conditioner	1,200	120/240	12	20 Amp.
Bathroom Heater	2,000	120/240	12	20 Amp.
Ironer	1,500	120	12	20 Amp.
Water Heater	2,000–5,000	120	10	30 Amp.
Television	300	120	12	20 Amp.
Hand Iron	1,100	120	12	20 Amp.
Toaster	1,000	120	12	20 Amp.

Fig. 19-8. Chart showing the approximate requirements for several appliances.

individual appliance circuits:

Range	Clothes dryer
Counter Top Oven	Garbage Disposer
Water Heater	Air Conditioner
Water Pump	Furnace
Dishwasher	Clothes Washer
	Attic Fan

In addition to these, any 120 volt permanently connected appliance which is rated at over 1,440 watts or has an automatically-starting electric motor should have its own circuit.

Individual appliance circuits may be 120 or 240 volts depending on the requirements of the device it is to operate. Always check the rating of the appliance to determine these factors. The chart in Fig. 19-8 shows the approximate requirements of several appliances.

CIRCUIT REQUIREMENT CALCULATIONS

The size of service entrance equipment and number and type of branch circuits are dependent upon the size of the house, appliances and lighting to be installed and planning for the future. In an effort to show how circuit requirement calculations are performed the following example is included:

EXAMPLE OF A TYPICAL RESIDENCE — 1500 SQ. FT.

Lighting Circuits:
    1500 sq. ft. at 3 watts per sq. ft. = 4500 watts

Special Appliance Circuits:
    2 circuits for kitchen — 4800 watts
    (120 volts x 20 amps. x 2 = 4800 watts)

Individual Appliance Circuits:
    1 circuit (240 volts) for
        self-contained range   = 12,000 watts
    1 circuit (240 volts) for clothes dryer = 5,000 watts
    1 circuit for water heater   = 2,000 watts
    1 circuit for clothes washer   =   700 watts
    1 circuit for garbage disposer   =   300 watts
    1 circuit for dishwasher   = 1,200 watts
    1 circuit for furnace   =   800 watts
                            Total = 31,300 watts
    For 120/240-volt 3-wire system feeders,
    31,300 watts ÷ 240 = 130.4 amps.

This house will require 150 amp. service. Service breakers are produced in ratings of 30, 40, 50, 60, 70, 100, 125, 150, 175, and 200 amp. Since 130.4 is between 125 and 150, the logical choice is 150 amp. service. This would also provide a spare circuit for future use.

OUTLETS AND SWITCHES

All convenience outlets, switches and joints where wire is spliced must be housed in an electrical box. Also, all lighting fixtures must be mounted on a box. There are several types of

boxes for various uses. The three most common types of boxes are shown in Fig. 19-9. Most are made from metal with a galvanized coating, but some styles are made from Bakelite and other insulating materials.

Fig. 19-9. Typical electrical boxes used in residential construction.

Placement of convenience outlets, switches and lighting fixtures require some thought. Code requirements, furniture arrangements and personal preference all play a role in the location. The code states that in living areas no point along a wall should be more than 6 ft. from a convenience outlet and each room should have a minimum of three outlets, Fig. 19-10. Placement of outlets about 8 ft. apart is more satisfactory and recommended. The height of most convenience outlets is 12 or 18 inches above the floor. The kitchen is an exception where the special appliance outlets are usually placed above the countertop. It is common practice to switch one or more outlets in each room where lamps are to be located. This saves wear on the lamp and is more convenient.

Frequently home designers forget to include weatherproof outlets and ample exterior lighting. These outlets provide a source of power for outside work or play. Placing at least one outlet on each exterior wall is recommended. Exterior lighting enhances the appearance of the house and reduces the chances of vandalism. Lighting fixtures and convenience outlets should also be located in the attic and crawl space of the house.

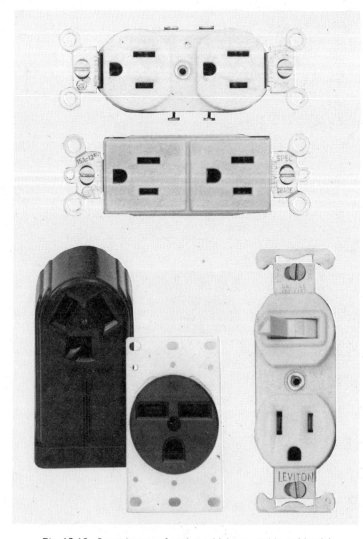

Fig. 19-10. Several types of outlets which are used in residential electrical systems. (Leviton)

Switches should be located in a logical place 48 in. above the floor. Care must be taken not to mount them behind doors or other hard-to-get-to places. Bathroom switches should not be located within reach of the bathtub or shower. This is an unsafe situation and must be avoided. Most switches in a house

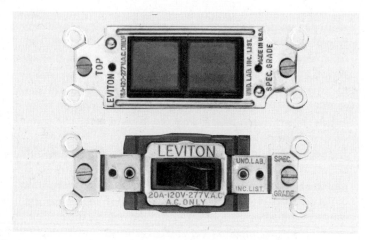

Fig. 19-11. Two styles of single-pole switches.

operate one fixture and are the single-pole type, Fig. 19-11. A single-pole switch simply opens and closes the circuit. In some instances three-way switches may be used for extra convenience. By using three-way switches a fixture may be switched from two locations, Fig. 19-12. Common locations

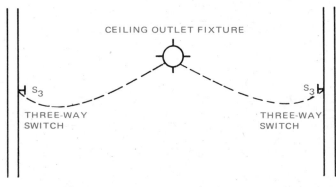

Fig. 19-12. A fixture or outlet may be switched from two locations using two 3-way switches.

for three-way switches are entrances, garages, stairs and rooms which have more than one entrance. Fixtures may also be switched from three locations using two three-way switches and one four-way switch, Fig. 19-13.

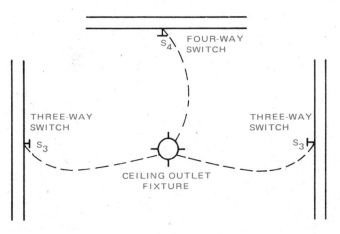

Fig. 19-13. One or more fixtures or outlets may be operated from three locations using two 3-way switches and one 4-way switch.

A special switch called a dimmer switch is commonly used for a main dining room ceiling fixture, Fig. 19-14. This allows the light to be adjusted to the desired brightness. The dimmer switch will fit into a regular electrical box.

There are several types of outlets which may be classified as "special outlets." These include telephone jacks, television antenna outlets, built-in hi-fi or stereo outlets for speakers, entrance signals (belts or chimes), burglar alarm systems and automatic fire-alarm systems. These are specialized installations. Information is usually supplied by the manufacturer or the systems are installed by them.

Fig. 19-14. A typical dimmer switch used to vary the intensity of an incandescent lighting fixture. (Emerson Electric Co.)

LOW VOLTAGE SWITCHING

In using low voltage switching convenience outlets are wired in the conventional way with No. 12 or 14 wire, and switches are wired to relays (electrically operated switches) using wire similar to that used for wiring door bells and chimes. These wires carry only 24 volts provided by a transformer which supplies current for the relays. The switches do not require boxes.

Low voltage switching, or remote control wiring as it is sometimes called, has possibilities for modern and unique installations. Remote control systems (low voltage switching) provide a simplified way of controlling lights in all parts of the home from one or more locations. For example, it is possible to operate fixtures located at various points in the house from the master bedroom. This is one of the advantages of the system. Fig. 19-15 shows a typical remote control wiring diagram.

REVIEW QUESTIONS – CHAPTER 19

1. The term that refers to the pressure which forces current through a wire is _____.
2. Two types of overcurrent protection devices are _____ and _____.
3. A material which permits the flow of electricity (a copper wire is an example) is called a _____.
4. Amps times volts equal _____.
5. How many service entrance conductors are required for 240 volt service? _____.
6. The service drop must be at least _____ feet above the ground at all points and _____ feet above driveways.
7. The material most wires are made from that are used in residential wiring is _____.
8. Which wire is larger in diameter: a No. 12 or No. 14 wire?
9. If the wire in a house is too small for the load, what is likely to happen? _____.
10. The smallest wire that may be used in a lighting circuit in a house is No. _____ wire.
11. The purpose of the main disconnect switch is _____.
12. The National Electrical Code recommends a minimum of _____ amp. service for all residences.
13. The type of overcurrent protection used in most homes today is the _____.
14. The three types of circuits used in a home are:
    a. _____.
    b. _____.
    c. _____.
15. The minimum number of special appliance circuits required for the kitchen is _____.
16. A lighting circuit has _____ amp. overcurrent protection if No. 14 wire is used.
17. The Code requires a minimum of _____ watts of lighting power for each square foot of floor space in the home.

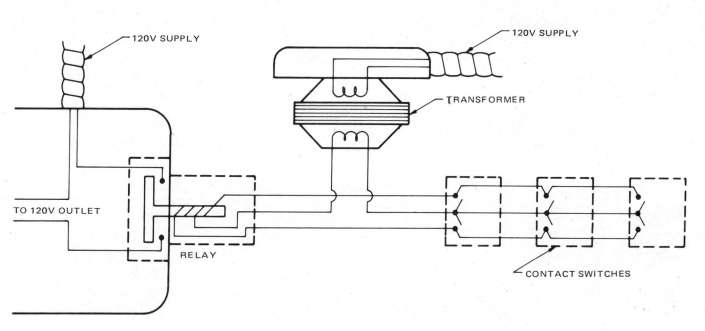

Fig. 19-15. Remote control electrical wiring diagram for a residential structure.

18. One lighting circuit should provide lighting for_____ sq. ft. if the Code were followed.

19. A 1500 sq. ft. house would require_____ lighting circuits.

20. A special appliance circuit is usually wired with No. _____ copper wire with a _____ amp. fuse.

21. If the voltage is 120 volts and the amperage is 20 amps., how many watts may be supplied? _____ .

22. Identify five appliances which would require an individual appliance circuit.

    a._____ .
    b._____ .
    c._____ .
    d._____ .
    e._____ .

23. Identify three factors which affect the size of service entrance equipment other than amperage serving the house, size of panel box and number of branch circuits.

    a._____ .
    b._____ .
    c._____ .

24. The minimum number of convenience outlets permitted in a single room is _____ .

25. No point along a wall should be more than_____ feet from a convenience outlet.

26. If you wanted to switch a lighting fixture from two locations, you would need a_____type of electrical switch.

27. Why would anyone use a low voltage switching system in a residence? _____ .

SUGGESTED ACTIVITIES

1. Determine the service entrance rating for your home or apartment. Count the number of 120 and 240 volt circuits. Calculate the amperage required for all the appliances, equipment and lighting. Determine if the incoming service is sufficient to operate all requirements. Show all your work.

2. Visit a home under construction which has the rough electrical wiring in place. Count the number of convenience outlets, switches and lighting fixtures in the house. Determine the number of circuits and size of main breaker. Organize your findings and report to the class. Is the house adequately wired?

3. Write to manufacturers that produce residential electrical supplies. Ask for literature and specifications for electrical boxes, wire, service entrance equipment switches and fixtures. Display the material and add it to the class collection for future use.

4. Prepare a bulletin board illustrating the circuits in a house and the equipment, appliances and lighting they serve.

Planned room lighting takes advantage of recessed spotlights along with the softer glow of diffused ceiling light.

Chapter 20
THE ELECTRICAL PLAN

DEFINITION AND PURPOSE

The electrical plan is a plan view drawing in section similar to the floor and foundation plans. It is usually traced from the floor plan. The electrical plan shows the meter, distribution panel box, electric outlets, switches and special electrical features. It identifies the number and types of circuits in the home. A schedule which specifies the lighting fixtures may be included.

The purpose of the electrical plan is to show the location and type of electrical equipment to be used. Convenience and trouble-free operation is dependent on a well-planned and properly installed electrical system.

REQUIRED INFORMATION

Information which should be on the electrical plan includes: service entrance capacity, meter and distribution panel

CEILING OUTLET FIXTURE	SINGLE RECEPTACLE OUTLET	SINGLE-POLE SWITCH
RECESSED OUTLET FIXTURE	DUPLEX RECEPTACLE OUTLET	DOUBLE-POLE SWITCH
DROP CORD FIXTURE	TRIPLEX RECEPTACLE OUTLET	THREE-WAY SWITCH
FAN HANGER OUTLET	QUADRUPLEX RECEPTACLE OUTLET	FOUR-WAY SWITCH
JUNCTION BOX	SPLIT-WIRED DUPLEX RECEPTACLE OUTLET	WEATHERPROOF SWITCH
FLUORESCENT FIXTURE	SPECIAL PURPOSE SINGLE RECEPTACLE OUTLET	LOW VOLTAGE SWITCH
TELEPHONE	230 VOLT OUTLET	PUSH BUTTON
INTERCOM	WEATHERPROOF DUPLEX OUTLET	CHIMES
CEILING FIXTURE WITH PULL SWITCH	DUPLEX RECEPTACLE WITH SWITCH	TELEVISION ANTENNA OUTLET
THERMOSTAT	FLUSH MOUNTED PANEL BOX	DIMMER SWITCH
SPECIAL FIXTURE OUTLET A,B,C ETC.	SPECIAL DUPLEX OUTLET A,B,C ETC.	SPECIAL SWITCH A,B,C ETC.

Fig. 20-1. Common electrical symbols.

location, placement and type of switches, location and type of lighting fixtures, special electrical equipment, number and types of circuits, electrical fixture schedule, symbols and legend, notes which help to describe the system.

SERVICE ENTRANCE

The Code requires that the service entrance equipment be located as close as practical to the point where the wires attach to the house. The service conductors should not run for 15 or 20 feet inside the house before they reach the main disconnect switch. The closer the main breaker is to the meter the better.

Another factor to be considered in locating the service entrance is where the largest amounts of electricity will be used. In most houses, this is the kitchen. Try to locate the meter and distribution panel close to the area of highest usage. It is less expensive and more efficient because larger loads require larger wire and the voltage drops over a long distance.

The meter may be located inside or outside the house, however, an outside location is usually preferred because it is easier to take readings. Electric meters are weatherproof and are designed for exterior installation.

Electrical symbols commonly used on an electrical plan are shown in Fig. 20-1. Amperage rating of the service required should be designated beside the symbol representing the distribution panel.

SWITCHES

The number and placement of switches throughout the house will be related to the number of lighting fixtures, switched convenience outlets and other equipment used. Try to select the logical location for each switch. Take into consideration the traffic patterns. The electrical plan must show whether the switches are single-pole, three-way, four-way, or another type. Use proper symbols to show types to be used.

The least expensive type of switch is a simple on-off TOGGLE SWITCH. A little more expensive, but preferred by many people, is the QUIET SWITCH, also the completely

silent MERCURY SWITCH. Other types include PUSH BUTTON, DIMMER and DELAYED ACTION switches. A modern home may require several types of switches.

On the electrical plan switches are shown connected to the fixtures, appliances, and outlets, which they operate. A thin hidden line symbol or center line symbol is generally used. These lines DO NOT represent the actual wiring, but merely indicate which switch operates a given outlet or fixture. Draw the lines using an irregular curve rather than a straightedge or freehand. Straight lines tend to become confused with other lines on the drawing and freehand lines are sloppy.

CONVENIENCE OUTLETS

Convenience outlets should be placed about 6 or 8 feet apart along the wall of all rooms. Most outlets are the 120 volt duplex type which have two receptacles. Special purpose outlets may have only one receptacle or several depending on their use. All convenience outlets should be grounded to prevent severe shock.

Convenience outlets may be switched or remain "hot" all the time. Most rooms will require at least one switched outlet for a lamp. It is wise to think about the furniture arrangement before drawing the electrical plan so that outlets and switches may be more accurately located.

Several kinds of special outlets may be desired. Each of these has a symbol to identify it. Use the proper symbol. If you are not sure the symbol is standard, identify it on the drawing.

LIGHTING

It is difficult to determine how many foot candles of light will be desirable for everyone. Some people prefer more light than others. Sufficient light should be provided for the activity to be pursued in a given area. Basically, two types of lighting fixtures are used in residences. They are the incandescent and the fluorescent types. All bulbs and tubes should be shielded in a way which will minimize glare. Exceptions are closets and storage areas. Diffusing bowls and shades are commonly used

LIGHTING FIXTURE SCHEDULE						
TYPE	MANUFACTURER	CATALOG NO.	NO. REQ'D.	MOUNTING HGT.	WATTS	REMARKS
A	SEARS	34K3546	2	7 – 0	100	BRUSHED ALUM.
B	LIGHTOLIER	4107	1	CEILING	150	
C	LIGHTOLIER	4233	2	CEILING	75	
D	SEARS	34K3113C	8	CEILING	80	RAPID START 48"
E	MOLDCAST	MP 232	4	GABLE PEAK	150	TWIN FLOODS
F	PROGRESS	P–180	7	CEILING	100	RECESSED 10" SQ.
G	SEARS	34K1899C	1	CEILING	240	POLISHED CHROME CHAND.
H	LIGHTOLIER	6349	2	6" ABOVE MIRROR	60	
I	ALKCO	330–RS	1	UNDER CABINET	40	
J	EMERSON	220	2	CEILING	60	FAN AND LIGHT COMBINATION
K	PROGRESS	P–318	2	18" BELOW CEILING	100	EXTERIOR – HANGING

Fig. 20-2. A typical lighting fixture schedule which includes the necessary information about each fixture.

LIGHTING FIXTURE SCHEDULE

TYPE	MANUF.	CAT. NO.	NO. REQ.	MOUNTING HGT.	WATTS	REMARKS
A	PROGRESS	P4014	1	CEILING	240	CHANDELIER
B	SEARS	34 K 5165	2	CEILING	100	CERAMIC HOLDERS
C	SEARS	34 K 3113	4	CEILING	80	SUSPENDED CEILING
D	PROGRESS	P7163	2	ABOVE MIRROR	80	RAPID START
E	SEARS	34 K 2734	2	CEILING	100	
F	PROGRESS	P6606	6	CEILING	100	RECESSED 10" SQ.
G	PROGRESS	P6676	7	CEILING	100	RECESSED 8" RND.
H	PROGRESS	P4449	2	12" BELOW CEIL.	100	EXT. HANGING
I	SEARS	34 K 3546	4	7'-0"	100	BRUSHED ALUM.
J	PROGRESS	P5228	3	1'-6"	60	
K	SEARS	34 K 3622	3	GABLE PEAK	150	TWIN FLOODS
L	PROGRESS	P7002	1	UNDER CAB.	40	

CIRCUIT DATA

LIGHTING CIRCUITS:
4 CIRCUITS PROVIDING 1800 WATTS EACH = 7200 WATTS
(1785 SQ. FT. X 3 WATTS/SQ. FT. = 5355 WATTS MIN.)

SPECIAL APPLIANCE CIRCUITS:
4 CIRCUITS PROVIDING 2400 WATTS EACH = 9600 WATTS
(2 CIRCUITS IN KITCHEN, 2 CIRCUITS IN SHOP)

INDIVIDUAL APPLIANCE CIRCUITS:
1 CIRCUIT FOR REFRIGERATOR = 2400 WATTS
1 CIRCUIT FOR GARBAGE DISPOSER = 2400 "
1 CIRCUIT FOR DISHWASHER = 2400 "
1 CIRCUIT FOR WASHER = 2400 "
1 CIRCUIT FOR GAS DRYER = 2400 "
1 CIRCUIT FOR GAS RANGE = 2400 "
1 CIRCUIT FOR GAS FURNACE = 2400 "
1 CIRCUIT FOR WATER PUMP (230 VOLTS) = 4800 "
1 CIRCUIT FOR TABLE SAW (230 VOLTS) = 4800 "
2 SPARE CIRCUITS   TOTAL = 43,200 WATTS

DISTRIBUTION PANEL:
150 AMP, 20 CIRCUIT, SQUARE D No. QOC - 20 M 200

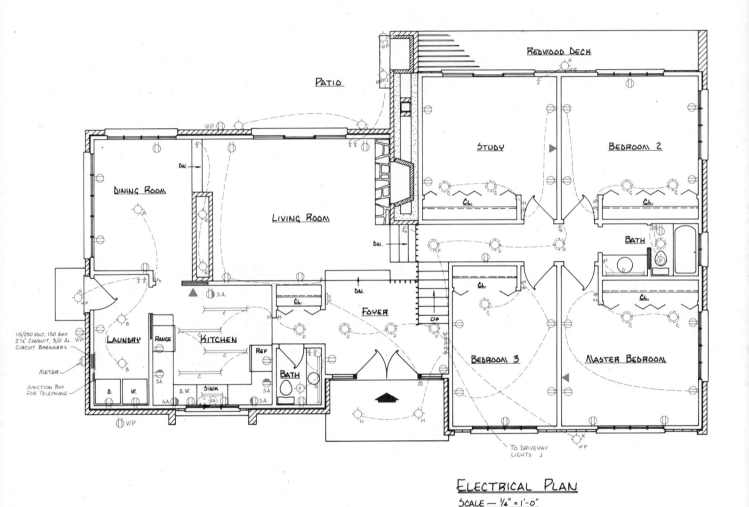

Fig. 20-3. A residential electrical plan showing the necessary electrical features for the first floor.

to reduce glare.

Lighting fixtures may be permanently mounted on the ceiling or wall, or they may be lamps which are plugged into convenience outlets. The trend seems to be toward more lamps and fewer ceiling mounted fixtures.

It is desirable to plan for a ceiling fixture in the dining room centered over the table. Another trend in lighting is to use fluorescent tubes above a suspended ceiling in the kitchen and bathrooms. This technique provides plenty of light and is also attractive.

Recessed lighting fixtures are suitable for certain areas of the home such as hallways, foyers and special emphasis areas.

Many varieties of recessed fixtures are available. Each should be evaluated carefully before making a selection.

Lighting fixtures which are to be located outside the house must be "exterior" fixtures. It is well to plan adequate lighting for walks, drives, porches, patios and other outside areas. Exterior lighting should be used to enhance the appearance of the home as well as make it more functional.

Each lighting fixture should be represented with the proper symbol placed in the location where the fixture is to be installed. If the placement must be exact, dimension the location.

Frequently, including a lighting fixture schedule is desirable. This schedule lists fixtures to be used, Fig. 20-2.

Several other electrical devices should be shown on the electrical plan. The permanent location of the telephone and all jacks should be indicated. Differentiate between the permanent unit and jacks (other telephone outlets). Items such as an intercom system, television antenna jack, door chimes and stereo or hi-fi outlets should also be included.

BRANCH CIRCUITS

A well-designed electrical plan will indicate the number and type of branch circuits required for the house. These are usually specified in note or diagram form on the same sheet as the electrical plan. It is not necessary to specify the exact circuit for each outlet, but the number of lighting, special appliance and individual appliance circuits, should be listed. This information must be determined before the size of the service equipment may be specified. Follow the guidelines discussed in the previous Chapter.

PROCEDURE FOR DRAWING AN ELECTRICAL PLAN

1. Trace the floor plan showing all exterior and interior walls and major appliances.

2. Locate the meter and distribution panel. Indicate the voltage and amperage rating. Check local code requirements.

3. Show all convenience outlets using the proper symbols. Be sure to indicate those which are 240 volts, split-wired (top half on different circuit from bottom or one half switched), weatherproof or other special purpose.

4. Locate all ceiling and wall lighting outlets. Carefully check the use of symbols.

5. Show all special outlets and fixtures such as telephone, chimes, intercom, etc.

6. Locate the switches and connect them to the outlets and lighting fixtures which they operate.

7. Add the lighting fixture schedule and symbol legend if necessary.

8. Note the number and type of circuits required.

9. Letter in all other notes, title, scale and sheet number.

10. Check the drawing carefully to be sure that all information is accurate and complete.

Fig. 20-3 shows an electrical plan for a split-level house in which the procedures just described have been followed.

REVIEW QUESTIONS — CHAPTER 20

1. An electrical plan may be defined as _____ _____.

2. A major factor which should be considered when locating the service entrance equipment is: _____.

3. The best location for the meter is _____ the house.

4. Identify the following electrical features with the proper symbol.
   a. Flush mounted distribution panel.
   b. Three-way switch.
   c. Push button.
   d. Telephone.
   e. Duplex convenience outlet.

5. Name three types of switches that may be used in the home.
   a._____.
   b._____.
   c._____.

6. Convenience outlets are grounded to prevent_____ _____.

7. The purpose of a lighting fixture schedule is _____.

8. A lighting fixture that is switched from two locations requires two _____ switches.

SUGGESTED ACTIVITIES

1. Select a floor plan of a small house or cottage and draw an electrical plan. Show all outlets, switches, distribution panel, meter and other required electrical features. Identify the number of lighting, special appliance, and individual appliance circuits. Follow the procedure presented in this chapter.

2. Using the same plan as in number 1 or some other plan, develop a pictorial schematic of the circuits in the house and the appliances, fixtures and outlets which each circuit serves. Indicate the size of wire and overcurrent protection required.

3. Visit your local utility company, building inspector and electrical materials distributor. Collect materials relative to house wiring, code requirements and materials used in residential electrical systems. Bring this information to class and share it with your classmates.

A combination of electrical and natural lighting is part of an architect's creative planning.

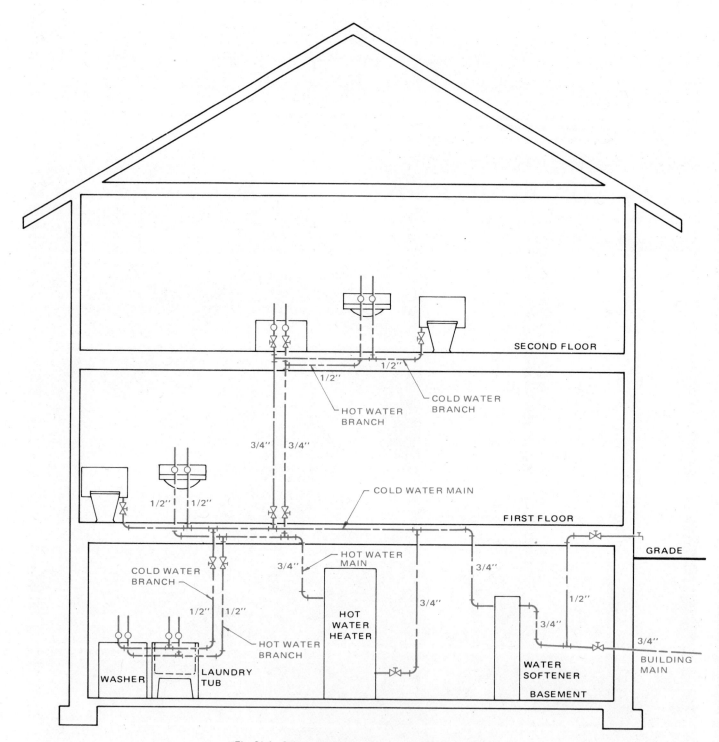

Fig. 21-1. Schematic of a residential water supply system.

Chapter 21
RESIDENTIAL PLUMBING

The residential plumbing system is taken for granted and is seldom a concern of homeowners. Yet, it is a very important part of the house. A well-designed and efficient system is necessary if it is to be functional and remain relatively trouble-free.

A residential plumbing system provides an adequate supply of water for household use in desired locations and removes the waste through a sanitary sewer or private septic system.

There are three principal parts to a residential plumbing installation: The water supply, water and waste removal and the fixtures which facilitate the use of water.

Fig. 21-2. A hot water heater installation using plastic pipe.
(B. F. Goodrich Chemical Co.)

WATER SUPPLY SYSTEM

A residential water supply system begins at the city water main or a private source such as a well, lake or stream. The pipe which enters the house is known as the BUILDING MAIN, Fig. 21-1. The building main branches into two lines - - the cold water and the hot water mains. It may be necessary to include in the system a water softener, filter or some other treatment device. It is customary to provide a branch line to hose bibs which do not require soft or filtered water.

The cold water main extends to various parts of the house to provide water to the fixtures. Since the water supply system is under pressure, pipes may follow any path which is convenient and practical from the view point of cost. Cold water branch lines are run from the cold water main to each of the fixtures. If a branch line is to supply more than one fixture, the diameter of the pipe must be increased to provide an ample amount of water. Branch lines are smaller than mains.

The hot water main emerges from the hot water heater, Fig. 21-2, and usually travels parallel to the cold water main where both hot and cold water are to be used. HOT WATER BRANCH lines run from the hot water main to each fixture.

Location of piping may depend on several factors. In cold climates, care should be taken to insulate pipes along exterior walls to keep them from freezing. Frost-free hose bibs are also available. Large, heavy pipes present a problem when they must pass through a joist. The customary solution is to place the pipe near the top of the joist and block the space above, Fig. 21-3.

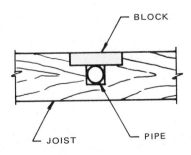

Fig. 21-3. When a large pipe such as a drain must pass through a joist, the joist should be blocked to prevent severe weakening of the member.

pipe. Some codes permit the use of plastic pipe for cold water or drain lines, Fig. 21-5. Check the local code requirements before planning the system.

Fig. 21-5. This plumbing installation utilizes copper pipe and fittings for the water supply system and plastic pipe for the drain system.

Fig. 21-4. Galvanized steel, copper and plastic pipe and fittings are used in residential plumbing systems.

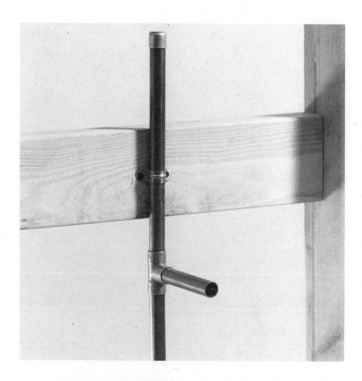

Fig. 21-6. A typical air chamber used at each faucet to reduce noise by cushioning the water flow.

Pipes used in the water supply system may be threaded galvanized steel pipe, plastic, or copper tubing with soldered joints when used inside the house, Fig. 21-4. Water supply pipes underground or in concrete are usually special heavy-duty copper tubing with soldered or flare-type joints or lead

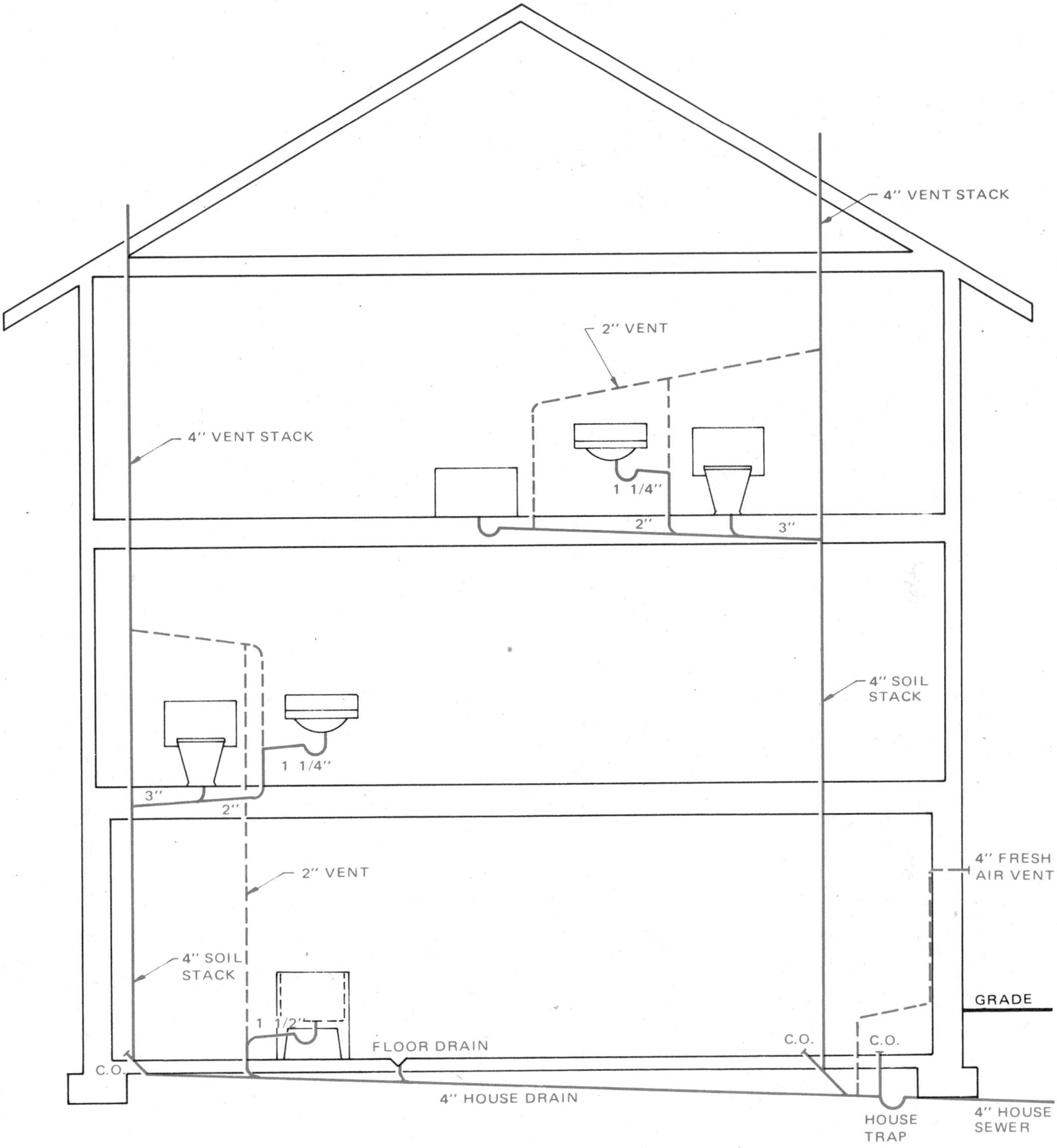

Fig. 21-7. Schematic of a residential water and waste removal system.

Today, copper tubing is used extensively for water supply systems. Rigid copper tubing (type L), copper fittings and copper valves are used for all inside installations. Copper pipe is available in 1/2, 3/4, 1 in. and larger diameters. Main lines are usually at least 3/4 in. in diameter and branch lines are a minimum of 1/2 in. in diameter.

Shutoff valves should be supplied for each main line, branch line and fixture. It should be possible to isolate a single fixture from the system without shutting off entire water supply.

Many codes require that an air compression chamber be located at each faucet. The chamber cushions the water flow and reduces pipe noise during use, Fig. 21-6. Most air chambers are simply short risers constructed from pipe with the end closed.

As stated earlier, cold and hot water branch lines usually run parallel to each other. Generally, they are placed about 6 in. apart. If they must be placed closer than this, some type of insulating material should be used to prevent the transfer of heat or cold from one pipe to the other. Efficiency may be improved in any system if the hot water lines are insulated.

WATER AND WASTE REMOVAL

Used water and other waste is carried to the sanitary sewer or septic tank through the waste removal or drainage system, Fig. 21-7. These pipes are isolated from the water supply system and require sufficient capacity, proper slope and venting and provision for cleanout.

Unlike the water supply system, the drainage system is not under pressure. It depends on gravity to carry the waste to the sewer. Waste creates gases with unpleasant odor which may be harmful. Disposing of these gases must also be provided for in the waste removal system.

All drain pipes must be pitched and large enough inside, usually 4 in. to prevent solids from accumulating at any point within the system. Drain pipes are generally smooth inside with minimum projections and sharp turns.

In planning a residential plumbing system careful consideration should be given to the drainage network. It is practical and economical to drain as many of the fixtures as possible into a single main drain.

A vertical drain pipe which collects waste from one or more fixtures is called a soil stack. Stacks which have water closets draining into them are called MAIN STACKS. Every house must have at least one main stack. There may be several if the house has more than one bath. Main stacks are generally about 3 in. in diameter if copper is used; 4 in. if cast iron. Stacks which do not drain water closets are called SECONDARY STACKS. These stacks may be smaller in diameter than main stacks, usually 1 1/2 in. Each fixture is connected to the stack using a BRANCH MAIN. These pipes must slope toward the stack at an angle to facilitate drainage. All stacks (main stacks and secondary stacks) extend down into or below the basement or crawl space and empty into the house drain. The house drain is basically horizontal with a slight slope and must be large enough to handle the anticipated load. All houses will have at least one house drain but may have several. Once the house drain passes to the outside of the house it is called a HOUSE SEWER. The house sewer finally empties into the city sanitary sewer or a private septic system.

As indicated earlier, sewer gases are a primary consideration in all waste systems. These are dissipated into the air through the soil stack which protrudes about 12 in. above the roof. Traps are installed below each fixture (except the water closet which has its trap built internally) to prevent gases from escaping through the fixture drain into the house. The trap remains filled with water and blocks the gases, Fig. 21-8.

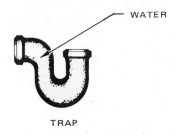

Fig. 21-8. A water trap blocks the escape of gases from the drain system.

Each stack requires a CLEANOUT located at the base of the stack. The cleanout permits the use of a cable to free waste from the house drain or sewer. A stack cleanout is shown in Fig. 21-9. Cleanouts should also be installed where the pipe makes a sharp bend.

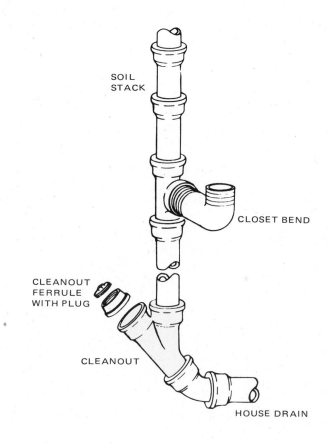

Fig. 21-9. Cleanouts are required by the National Code at the base of all stacks. This drawing illustrates a typical cleanout.

In addition to providing an escape for gases, the soil stack (technically a VENT STACK from the upper floor to the roof) provides an air inlet to the drainage system. Drains must have ventilation to operate properly.

Where 4 in. cast iron pipe is used for the soil and vent stack, a 2" x 4" stud wall will not provide sufficient space to house the pipe. In this case a 2" x 6" stud should be specified. This is commonly referred to as a STACK WALL.

Several types of pipe may be used for waste removal. Cast iron pipe is used extensively. Copper and brass alloy pipes which will not rust and are easy to install are also frequently used. Other materials used include fiber and plastic. Many local codes specify the type of pipe to use, so check the code.

House sewers are frequently not as deep as basement floors. Since a drain in the basement floor is desirable, and water will not flow up hill, a pump must be used. A concrete or tile pit or "sump" is located in an inconspicuous place in the basement and the floor is usually sloped toward a drain which flows into the sump, Fig. 21-10. A sump pump which will operate automatically is installed in the sump and connected to the house drain. When water reaches a predetermined level in the sump, the pump operates and removes the water.

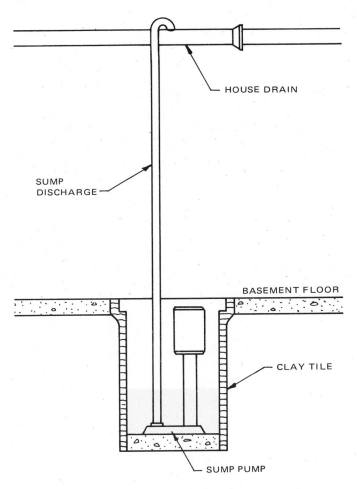

Fig. 21-10. A sump pump removes water from the basement and discharges it into the house drain or outside.

FIXTURES

The third part of the residential plumbing system is the fixtures. A fixture is any appliance such as a bathtub, shower, water closet, sink, dishwasher, etc. that requires water. Fixtures are the most obvious part of the plumbing system, because they are visible. The choice of fixtures is important. They are expensive to install and replace. Choose them wisely.

The National Code specifies minimum clearance and location dimensions which must be adhered to when installing various fixtures. Be sure ample space is allocated for the fixture specified.

PRIVATE SEWAGE DISPOSAL SYSTEM

Private sewage disposal systems (septic tank and disposal field) are used for rural and isolated homesites which cannot be connected to public sewers. Proper construction and maintenance of a private septic system are vitally important. The improper disposal of sewage may be a serious threat to the health and well being of those in the surrounding area. A large number of disease producing organisms thrive in sewage.

Usually before a building permit may be issued, the site is examined by a health department sanitarian to determine if the site is suitable for a private sewage disposal system. Suggested minimum dimensions for placement of well, septic tank and disposal field on a one acre site are shown in Fig. 21-11. A large land area and suitable soil conditions are necessary to isolate the disposal system from all water supply wells, lakes, and streams, to prevent contamination. Septic systems should also be isolated from property lines and

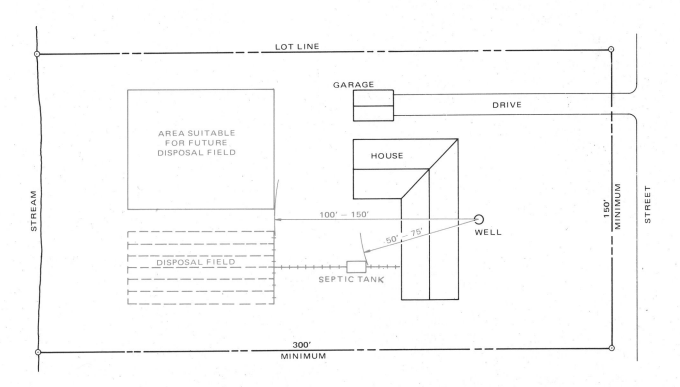

Fig. 21-11. Recommended minimum dimensions for placement of private septic system and water well with respect to the house and property lines. Minimum size site for this fixture is usually one acre.

buildings. Check with your local health department for minimum distances required.

SEPTIC TANK

Sewage from the house sewer first enters the septic tank. The septic tank performs two basic functions: (1) it removes about 75 percent of the solids from the sewage by bacterial action before discharging it into the disposal field; and (2) it provides storage space for the settled solids while they undergo digestive action.

A septic tank should be watertight. It is usually constructed of reinforced concrete or concrete blocks with mortared joints and interior surface coated with cement and sand plaster. Fig. 21-12 shows the construction of a typical septic tank.

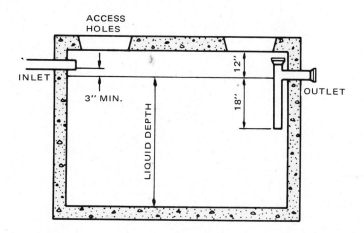

Fig. 21-12. Construction of a typical cast concrete septic tank.

The liquid capacity of the septic tank should be about 1 1/2 times the 24 hour sewage flow and in no case less than 750 gallons. Frequently the number of bedrooms in a home is used as an indication of the size septic tank required. The size should be increased particularly where automatic washers and garbage disposers are used. It is customary to double the liquid capacity when a garbage disposer is used.

DISPOSAL FIELD

The function of the disposal field is to receive sewage in liquid form from the septic tank and allow it to seep into the soil. Dry and porous soil containing sand or gravel is ideal for a disposal field.

The disposal or drain field may be constructed using clay tile, perforated fiber or plastic pipe. The drain field lines are laid nearly level (a slope of 1 in. in 50 ft. is the normal slope) about two feet below the surface of the ground. These are positioned in a bed of pebbles usually covered with straw. Fig. 21-13 shows some of the important construction features of a disposal field.

The field should be located in such a manner that surface water drainage is diverted away from it. If it becomes flooded, it will cease to be functional. The disposal field should also be

located downhill from any water supply well and never under a driveway, parking lot, paved area, or in a place where heavy vehicles may drive over it.

The suitability of the soil for a disposal field must be determined by soil tests. These tests are known as percolation tests. They determine how readily the soil will absorb water and provide a guide for design and size of the disposal field required. The percolation rate is determined by filling a test hole with water to completely saturate the immediate area. After complete saturation, water is added to provide 4 to 8 inches of water in the test hole. The drop in water level is measured at 30 minute intervals until the hole is dry. Drop that occurs during the final 30 minute period is used to calculate the percolation rate for that test hole. Standard percolation rate must be no greater than 45 minutes per inch. One test hole five feet or more deep is generally required to determine ground water level and consistency of subsoil. The following chart shows the recommended seepage area required for various percolation rates:

DISPOSAL FIELD DESIGN

Standard Percolation Rate Minutes Per Inch	Soil Drainage	Required Seepage Area Sq. Ft. Per Bedroom
15 or less	Good	275
16 — 30	Fair	375
31 — 45	Poor	500
Over 45	Not suitable	- - -

CALCULATION OF DISPOSAL FIELD SIZE

The following example is for a three bedroom home with a percolation rate of 25 minutes per inch:

1. If the tile is placed in individual trenches, the seepage area required would be 3 x 375 sq. ft. or 1125 sq. ft. (See chart above.) Using 2 ft. wide trenches, 562 lin. ft. of trench would be required. (1125 ÷ 2 sq. ft. per lin. ft. = 562 lin. ft.) Therefore, 8 trenches, each 70 ft. long would provide this.

2. If the tile is placed in a continuous bed, the seepage area required would be 3 x 375 sq. ft. or 1125 sq. ft. (See chart above.) A bed of 28' x 40' would provide this.

3. The minimum necessary gross area available to install the disposal field and provide space for future expansion and replacement would be:

2 1/2 x 1125 sq. ft. = 2812 sq. ft.

REVIEW QUESTIONS — CHAPTER 21

1. Identify the three parts of any residential plumbing system.
   a._____.
   b._____.
   c._____.
2. The pipe that enters the house from the city water main or private well is called the _____.
3. A faucet on the outside of the house is usually referred to as a_____.

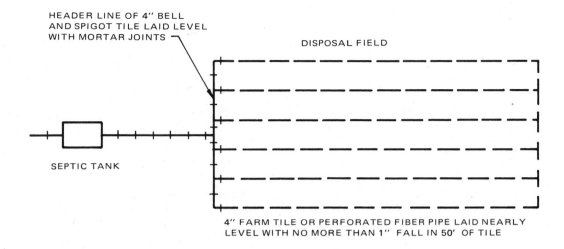

HEADER LINE OF 4″ BELL AND SPIGOT TILE LAID LEVEL WITH MORTAR JOINTS

DISPOSAL FIELD

SEPTIC TANK

4″ FARM TILE OR PERFORATED FIBER PIPE LAID NEARLY LEVEL WITH NO MORE THAN 1″ FALL IN 50′ OF TILE

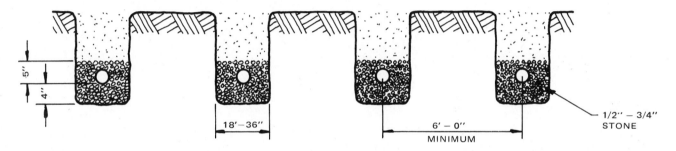

5″
4″
18′—36″
6′ — 0″
MINIMUM
1/2″ — 3/4″ STONE

TILE IN INDIVIDUAL TRENCHES

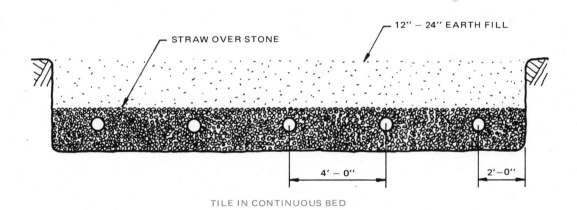

STRAW OVER STONE
12″ — 24″ EARTH FILL
4′ — 0″
2′ — 0″

TILE IN CONTINUOUS BED

Fig. 21-13. A disposal field may be constructed using either tile in individual trenches or in a continuous bed. A continuous bed requires less space than the individual trench bed.

4. The cold water line that connects to a fixture is known as a _____ _____ _____ line.
5. Two types of pipe commonly used in the water supply system.
   a._____.
   b._____.
6. Main water lines are usually at least _____ inch in diameter.
7. The purpose of an air chamber located at each faucet is _____.
8. List three places where a shutoff valve is required.
   a. _____.
   b. _____.
   c. _____.
9. The force that causes water to flow in the waste removal system is _____.
10. The usual size of most main drain pipes is _____ inches.

11. A vertical drain pipe which collects waste from one or more fixtures is called a _____.

12. Stacks which do not drain a water closet are known as _____ stacks.

13. All individual drains in the house empty into the _____ drain.

14. Gases are prevented from entering the house through fixture drains by_____.

15. Each stack requires a _____ at the base of the stack.

16. A wall that houses a soil and vent stack is called a _____ _____.

17. Water removal is provided for in a basement when the house drain is higher than the basement floor by a____ _____.

18. A _____ is any appliance which uses or helps you use water.

19. A private sewage disposal system is composed of two main parts.
    a. _____.
    b._____.

20. Identify two considerations that must be met before a private sewage disposal system may be installed.
    a._____.
    b._____.

21. The percentage of solids removed from sewage in the septic tank is _____.

22. The minimum size septic tank is _____ gallons.

23. The addition of one appliance may double the size of the septic tank. That appliance is _____.

24. The purpose of the disposal field is _____ _____.

25. The type of soil best suited for a disposal field is _____.

26. Recommended slope for drain lines in the septic field is _____.

27. Suitability of soil for a disposal field may be determined using a _____ test.

SUGGESTED ACTIVITIES

1. Visit a house under construction which has the rough plumbing installed. Trace the hot and cold water supply systems and the drainage system. Make notes as to the size and type of pipes used. Check to see where shutoff valves are located and determine if the house sewer is to be connected to a public sanitary sewer or private system.

2. Visit your local building or plumbing inspector. Ask for specifications and requirements for residential plumbing in your area. Invite him to speak to the class.

3. Write to several manufacturers of plumbing supplies and ask for catalogs showing their products. Examine the material and add it to the class collection.

4. Using a sand box, build a scale model of a private sewage disposal system for a three bedroom house with a soil percolation rate of 25 minutes per inch. Display the model.

5. Visit a local plumbing supply store and examine materials used in residential plumbing. Report your findings.

Chapter 22
THE PLUMBING PLAN

DEFINITION AND PURPOSE

The plumbing plan is a plan view drawing which shows the plumbing system. It is generally traced from the floor plan. The plan shows water supply lines, waste disposal lines and fixtures. It describes the sizes and types of all piping and fittings used in the system. Gas lines, also built in vacuum systems if required, are included on the plumbing plan.

The plumbing plan shows the location, size and type of plumbing equipment to be used. The plumbing system should be coordinated with the electrical and climate control systems. Convenience as well as health and safety depend to a considerable extent on a well planned plumbing system which operates efficiently.

REQUIRED INFORMATION

The plumbing plan should include: waste lines and vent stacks, water supply lines, drain and fixture locations, size and type of pipe to be used, plumbing fixture schedule, symbols and legend, and notes required to describe the system.

WASTE LINES AND VENT STACKS

Proper location and sufficient size are the major considerations in planning the waste lines. This network is usually designed first, because the whole system is ordinarily planned around it.

A main stack must be designated for each water closet and a sufficient number of secondary stacks included to properly vent other fixtures. The following chart indicates minimum sizes for residential waste and vent lines:

MINIMUM WASTE AND VENT PIPE SIZES

KIND OF FIXTURE	MIN. WASTE SIZE	MIN. VENT SIZE
Bathtub	1 1/2 in.	1 1/4 in.
Bidet	1 1/2 in.	1 1/2 in.
Water Closet	3 in.	2 in.
Lavatory	1 1/2 in.	1 1/4 in.
Service Sink	2 in.	1 1/4 in.
Shower	2 in.	1 1/4 in.
Laundry Tub	1 1/2 in.	1 1/4 in.
Floor Drain	2 in.	1 1/4 in.

As stated in the previous chapter, waste lines are not under pressure and depend on gravity to move the waste. The lines must be sloped slightly, usually 1/4 in. per foot, to facilitate even flow. The required slope should be shown on the plumbing plan, using either a general or specific note.

Waste lines and vent stacks are larger in size than water supply lines and are usually drawn using a wider line than used for supply lines, Fig. 22-1. Try to maintain a proper size relationship between all elements of the drawing.

Care should be taken in locating the house drain and sewer so they are the desired height to properly connect with the

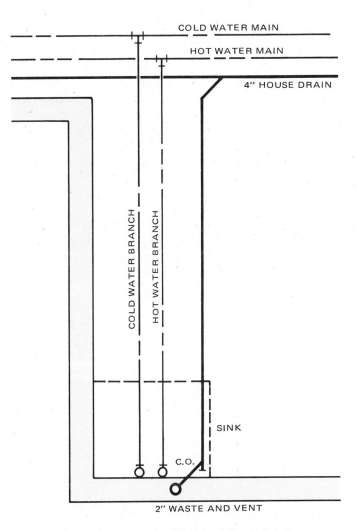

Fig. 22-1. Water supply and waste lines vary in width and are represented by different symbols.

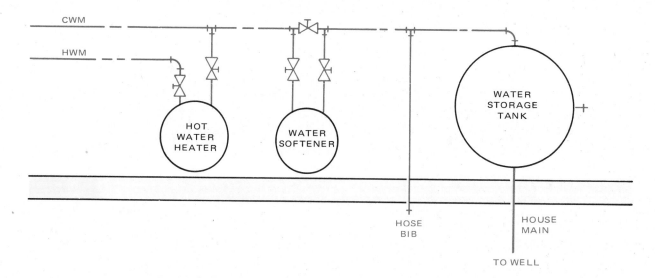

Fig. 22-2. Arrangement (typical) where a water storage tank, water softener and hot water heater are required.

public sewer or private septic system. The house drain should be no longer than necessary. Study all facets of the layout before deciding on the final location of the house drain and sewer.

WATER SUPPLY LINES

The water supply system begins at the city water main or private water source. Show the building main on the plumbing plan with proper shutoff valves, meter and size of pipe. Also show the water softener, filter, water storage tank or other treatment devices positioned along the building main, Fig. 22-2.

Hose bibs and other fixtures which do not require softened or filtered water should be connected to the building main before it reaches the softener. Shutoff valves must be provided for each fixture in the water supply system.

Study fixtures requiring a water supply and determine the size of pipe needed for each. Plan the size of each hot and cold water branch line so it will have the capacity to supply the amount of water needed. Show the location of the water heater and identify it.

Indicate the size of each line in the water supply system. Specify the type of pipe to be installed. Use the proper symbols.

Usually a single plumbing plan will be adequate for a ranch type house with or without a basement. A split-level or two-story house may require two or more plans. Piping which serves a given level of the house is shown on that plan view.

DRAIN AND FIXTURE LOCATIONS

Floor drains are usually located in basements and attached garages. They are usually connected to the storm sewer, or a dry well and not to the sanitary sewer system. Indicate drains with the proper symbol and show the location of the pipe leading to the storm sewer or dry well.

Draw the outline of all fixtures requiring plumbing. Check

the local code to determine clearance dimensions and minimum space requirements for fixtures. Locate plumbing for fixtures where access may be provided for servicing. This is a requirement of the National Plumbing Code.

SIZE AND TYPE OF PIPE

The proper size pipe required for a given installation will depend on the average amount of water used, peak loads, water pressure on the line, and length of the pipe run. (Friction reduces the flow of water and larger pipe should be used for long runs.) Rather than try to calculate the pipe size for each fixture and branch line in the house, it is suggested you refer to the minimum pipe sizes recommended by the Federal Housing Administration for most residences. These minimum sizes are shown in the following chart:

MINIMUM PIPE SIZES OF WATER SUPPLY LINES		
KIND OF FIXTURE	COLD WATER	HOT WATER
Bathtub	1/2 in.	1/2 in.
Bidet	1/2 in.	1/2 in.
Water Closet	3/8 in.	
Lavatory	3/8 in.	3/8 in.
Service Sink	1/2 in.	1/2 in.
Shower	1/2 in.	1/2 in.
Laundry Tub	1/2 in.	1/2 in.
Hose Bib	1/2 in.	
Building Main	3/4 in.	
Cold Water Main	3/4 in.	
Hot Water Main		3/4 in.
Cold Water Branch	1/2 in.	
Hot Water Branch		1/2 in.

The plumbing plan should specify the type of pipe to be used throughout the system. Several types are available. It is advisable to check the local code to be sure the type you wish to use is acceptable in your locality.

Copper pipe is a frequent choice for the water supply system. The nominal diameter refers to the approximate inside diameter of the pipe. For example, a 1 in. copper pipe, Type L, is 1.025 in. inside diameter and 1.125 in. outside diameter. This is a medium weight copper pipe with Type K being heavier and Type M lighter. Type L is usually used for inside installations for hot and cold water lines. Copper tubing with a designation of DWV is also available. It is thinner than Type M and is used in the sewage disposal system. (The DWV refers to drain, waste and vent.)

PLUMBING FIXTURE SCHEDULE

A plumbing fixture schedule is useful in planning the plumbing system, ordering the fixtures, and installing the system. Information which is customarily shown on a Plumbing Fixture Schedule includes: identifying symbol, name of the fixture, number of fixtures required, manufacturer and catalog number, pipe connection sizes, and a space for remarks. A typical residential Plumbing Fixture Schedule is shown in Fig. 22-3.

SYMBOLS AND LEGEND

Whenever possible, use standard symbols. Standard symbols are those that are recognized and accepted by draftsmen, designers, contractors and tradesmen. If there is a chance that the symbols used may not be standard or commonly used, then a legend is used to explain each symbol. The legend should appear on the plan where the symbols are used. Fig. 22-4 shows some of the commonly accepted plumbing symbols. It is important to note that symbols usually are not drawn to the exact size of the feature which they represent. For this reason, care must be taken in choosing the appropriate symbol size.

NOTES

Frequently, information other than that represented by symbols, dimensions and specifications is needed to describe the plumbing installation. This information is recorded in the form of general notes. The notes must appear on the drawing to which they refer. They are usually located above the title block or in some other prominent place.

Notes may refer to materials, installation procedures, or any facet of the plumbing system.

PROCEDURE FOR DRAWING PLUMBING PLAN

Several decisions and calculations must be made before the plumbing plan can be drawn. The exact fixtures to be used should be determined. Manufacturers' catalogs are good sources of this information. The exact placement of each fixture must be decided. The location of utilities such as sewer, water, storm drains and gas must be established. (The plot plan usually provides this information.)

After initial information has been gathered, the drawing may proceed. The following steps are suggested:

1. Trace the floor plan showing only the exterior and interior walls, doors and windows, and features which relate to the plumbing plan.

2. Draw the symbols for all fixtures which are to be connected to the house plumbing system. Fixtures may be outlined using a hidden line symbol to draw attention to them. Steps 1 and 2 are shown in Fig. 22-5.

PLUMBING FIXTURE SCHEDULE										
IDENT. SYMB.	TYPE OF FIXTURE	NO. REQ'D.	MANUFACTURER AND CATALOG NO.	C W	H W	S & W	VENT	TRAP	GAS	REMARKS
(WC)	WATER CLOSET	1	ELJER "SILETTE" NO. E 5000 ONE-PIECE	3/8"	—	3"	2"	—	—	VITREOUS CHINA TWILIGHT BLUE
(WC)	WATER CLOSET	1	ELJER "SILETTE" NO. E 5000 ONE-PIECE	3/8"	—	3"	2"	—	—	VITREOUS CHINA TUSCAN TAN
(T)	BATHTUB	1	ELJER "RIVIERA" NO. E 1120	1/2"	1/2"	2"	1 1/2"	2"	—	ENAMELED CAST IRON TUSCAN TAN
(L)	LAVATORY	2	ELJER "BRENDA" NO. E 3328	1/2"	1/2"	2"	1 1/2"	1 1/2"	—	VITREOUS CHINA TUSCAN TAN
(L)	LAVATORY	1	ELJER "BARROW" NO. E 3471	1/2"	1/2"	2"	1 1/2"	1 1/2"	—	VITREOUS CHINA TWILIGHT BLUE
(S)	SINK	1	ELJER "KENTON" NO. E 2325	1/2"	1/2"	2"	1 1/2"	1 1/2"	—	ENAMELED CAST IRON WHITE 32 x 20"
(WS)	WATER SOFTENER	1	SEARS "SERIES 60" NO. W 42 K 3482N	3/4"	—	—	—	—	—	17 1/2" DIA. x 42" HIGH DRAIN REQUIRED
(WH)	WATER HEATER	1	SEARS "MODEL 75" NO. 42 K 33741N	3/4"	3/4"	—	4"	—	1/2"	40 GAL. CAPACITY NATURAL GAS
(CW)	CLOTHES WASHER	1	WHIRLPOOL "SUPREME 80"	1/2"	1/2"	2"	1 1/2"	1 1/2"	—	AVOCADO GREEN
(DW)	DISH WASHER	1	WHIRLPOOL SSU 80	1/2"	1/2"	2"	1 1/2"	1 1/2"	—	AVOCADO GREEN
(HB)	HOSE BIB	3	CRANE B—106	3/4"	—	—	—	—	—	

Fig. 22-3. A typical Plumbing Fixture Schedule for a residence.

Architecture

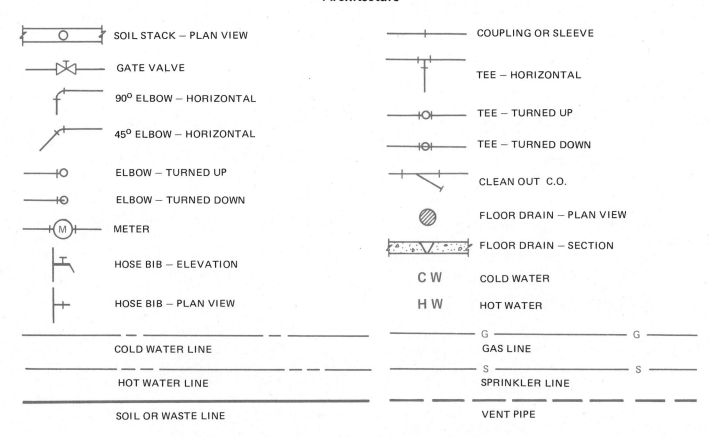

SOIL STACK – PLAN VIEW	COUPLING OR SLEEVE
GATE VALVE	TEE – HORIZONTAL
90° ELBOW – HORIZONTAL	TEE – TURNED UP
45° ELBOW – HORIZONTAL	TEE – TURNED DOWN
ELBOW – TURNED UP	CLEAN OUT C.O.
ELBOW – TURNED DOWN	FLOOR DRAIN – PLAN VIEW
METER	FLOOR DRAIN – SECTION
HOSE BIB – ELEVATION	C W COLD WATER
HOSE BIB – PLAN VIEW	H W HOT WATER
COLD WATER LINE	GAS LINE
HOT WATER LINE	SPRINKLER LINE
SOIL OR WASTE LINE	VENT PIPE

Fig. 22-4. Commonly accepted plumbing symbols used on a residential plumbing plan.

Fig. 22-5. A floor plan showing the location of all fixtures which are to be connected to the plumbing system.

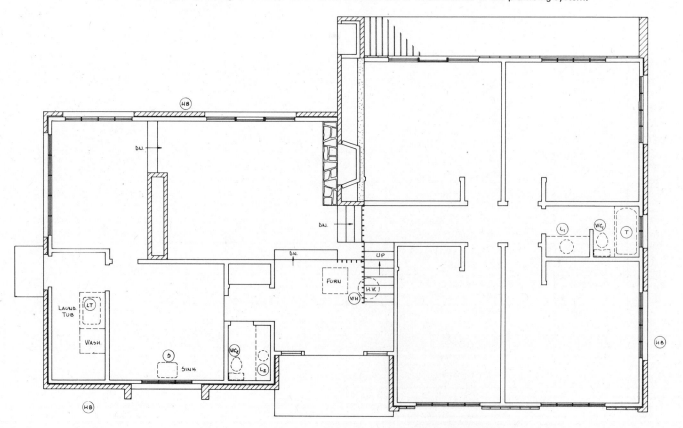

PLUMBING PLAN

SCALE – 1/4" = 1'-0"

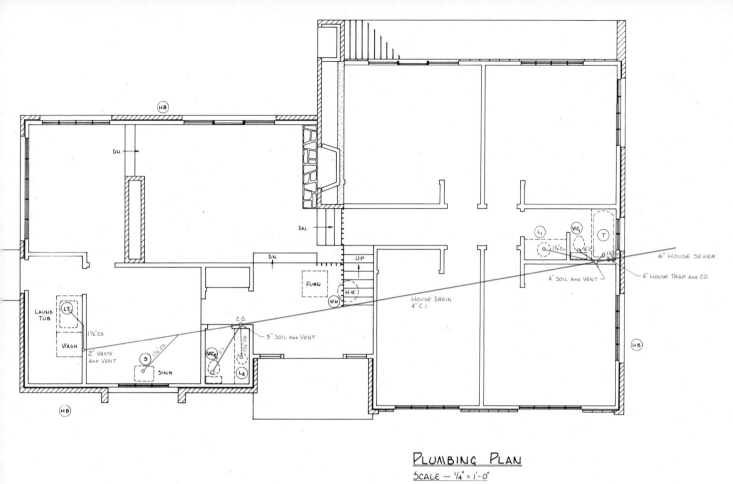

PLUMBING PLAN
SCALE — ¼" = 1'-0"

Fig. 22-6. Above. The plumbing system is planned around the water and waste system which includes drains, soil and vent stacks, and cleanouts.
Fig. 22-7. Below. Water supply system which traces the piping from the source to each fixture. Shutoff valves are included.

PLUMBING PLAN
SCALE — ¼" = 1'-0"

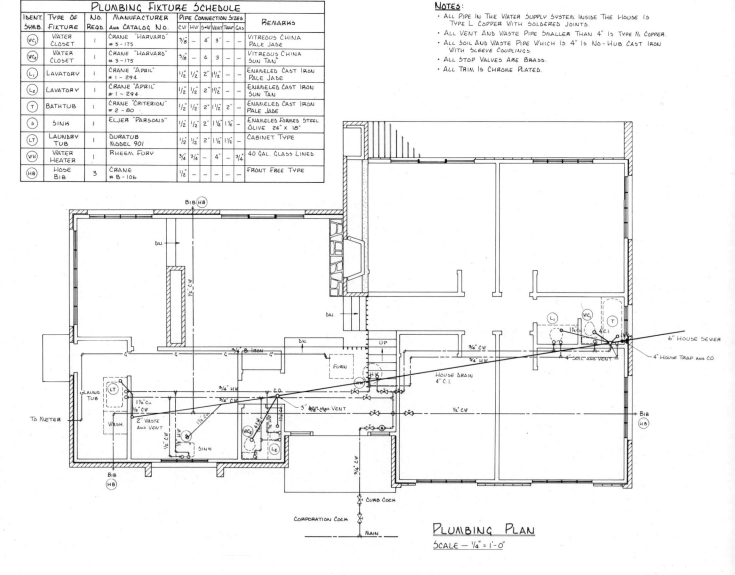

PLUMBING FIXTURE SCHEDULE

Ident. Symb.	Type of Fixture	No. Reqd.	Manufacturer and Catalog No.	CW	HW	S+W	Vent	Trap	Gas	Remarks
WC₁	Water Closet	1	Crane "Harvard" #3-175	3/8"	–	4"	3"	–	–	Vitreous China Pale Jade
WC₂	Water Closet	1	Crane "Harvard" #3-175	3/8"	–	4	3	–	–	Vitreous China Sun Tan
L₁	Lavatory	1	Crane "April" #1-294	1/2"	1/2"	2"	1½"	–	–	Enameled Cast Iron Pale Jade
L₂	Lavatory	1	Crane "April" #1-294	1/2"	1/2"	2"	1½"	–	–	Enameled Cast Iron Sun Tan
T	Bathtub	1	Crane "Criterion" #2-80	1/2"	1/2"	2"	1½"	2"	–	Enameled Cast Iron Pale Jade
S	Sink	1	Eljer "Parsons"	1/2"	1/2"	2"	1½	1½	–	Enameled Formed Steel Olive 24" x 18"
LT	Laundry Tub	1	Duratub Model 901	1/2"	1/2"	2"	1½	1½	–	Cabinet Type
WH	Water Heater	1	Rheem Furu	3/4"	3/4"	–	4"	–	3/4	40 Gal. Glass Lined
HB	Hose Bib	3	Crane #B-106	1/2"	–	–	–	–	–	Front Free Type

NOTES:
· All Pipe in The Water Supply System Inside The House is Type L Copper with Soldered Joints.
· All Vent and Waste Pipe Smaller Than 4" is Type M Copper.
· All Soil and Waste Pipe Which is 4" is No-Hub Cast Iron With Sleeve Couplings.
· All Stop Valves are Brass.
· All Trim is Chrome Plated.

PLUMBING PLAN
SCALE — 1/4" = 1'-0"

Fig. 22-8. A typical residential plumbing plan.

3. Locate and draw the house drain and soil and vent stacks. Be sure to include cleanouts.

4. Connect all fixtures and floor drains to the house drain showing fittings and secondary vents. Steps 3 and 4 are shown in Fig. 22-6.

5. Locate and draw the building main for the water supply system. Connect it to the hot water heater, water softener and hose bibs.

6. Draw cold and hot water mains. Include shutoff valves where required. Draw the cold and hot water lines paprallel where possible.

7. Locate and draw all cold water and hot water branch lines with shutoff valves. Use the proper symbols. Steps 5, 6, and 7 are shown in Fig. 22-7.

8. Identify each element of the plumbing system and show pipe sizes, Fig. 22-5.

9. Include a Plumbing Fixture Schedule, symbol legend, and general notes required, Fig. 22-5.

10. Add the scale and title block. Check the entire drawing for accuracy and omissions.

This procedure may be repeated for each floor level of the house which requires a plumbing plan.

REVIEW QUESTIONS — CHAPTER 22

1. The purpose of a plumbing plan is _____.
2. Name two major considerations in planning the waste lines.
   a. _____.
   b. _____.
3. The part of the plumbing system usually designed first is _____.
4. The fixture that requires a main stack is _____.
5. A water closet requires a waste line which is a minimum of _____ inches in diameter.
6. The force which carries waste and water down the waste lines is _____.
7. Once the house drain is outside the house it becomes the house _____.
8. Most house mains for the water supply system are

_____ inch in diameter.

9. Floor drains are usually connected to a dry well or _____.

10. Identify four factors which affect the size of pipe required for a given situation.

    a. _____ .

    b. _____ .

    c. _____ .

    d. _____ .

11. The nominal diameter of copper pipe refers to the _____ dimension.

12. The type of copper pipe usually used for drains, vents and waste lines is _____ .

13. The legend which shows the name of fixtures, manufacturer's catalog number, pipe connection sizes, remarks and identification symbols for fixtures is called _____ .

SUGGESTED ACTIVITIES

1. Select a simple floor plan and design the water and waste removal system. Determine the size pipe required for each drain and fixture. Specify the type of material to be used. Draw the plan to 1/4'' = 1' − 0'' scale. Add notes necessary.

2. Using the same floor plan as above, design the water supply system. Determine the pipe size for each branch and main line. Draw the plan using the proper symbols.

3. Sometimes a pictorial schematic is drawn of the entire plumbing system to further illustrate the layout. Using the drawings constructed in 1 and 2 above, make an isometric drawing of the total plumbing system. Omit the walls and floor of the house. Identify the important features of the system.

An island kitchen. Many variations incorporate the kitchen sink in the island while others use the island as a food preparation area as shown above. Plumbing considerations must be carefully planned when the island includes the kitchen sink.

Open space construction for air circulation is a climate control design problem for the architect.

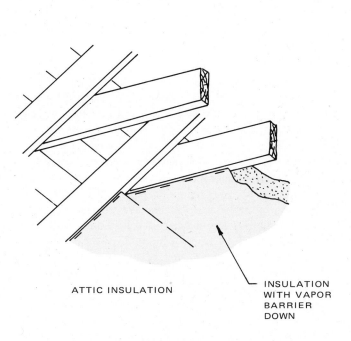

ATTIC INSULATION

INSULATION
WITH VAPOR
BARRIER
DOWN

Fig. 23-1. Adequate insulation which is properly installed will increase heating and cooling efficiency.

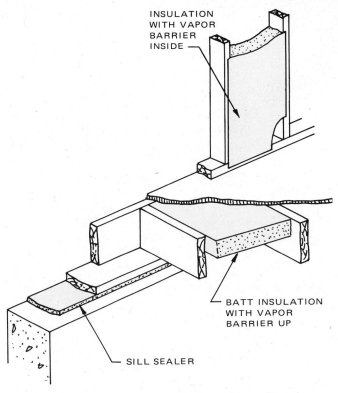

INSULATION
WITH VAPOR
BARRIER
INSIDE

BATT INSULATION
WITH VAPOR
BARRIER UP

SILL SEALER

FOUNDATION, FLOOR AND WALL INSULATION

Chapter 23
RESIDENTIAL CLIMATE CONTROL

Increasingly, modern homes are being built with complete climate control systems. A complete climate control system involves temperature control, humidity control, air circulation and air cleaning.

TEMPERATURE CONTROL

Temperature control includes both heating and cooling. The efficiency with which the control is accomplished is dependent on several conditions. Adequate insulation properly installed is of prime importance, Fig. 23-1. Insulation should be placed in the ceiling, in the exterior walls and under the floor when the house has a crawl space. Houses which are built on slab foundations should have rigid foam insulation along the inside of the foundation wall and horizontally along the perimeter of the floor, Fig. 23-2.

Insulation serves to prevent the transfer of heat or cold from one location to another. It helps to keep the house warm

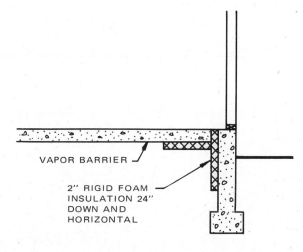

VAPOR BARRIER

2" RIGID FOAM
INSULATION 24"
DOWN AND
HORIZONTAL

Fig. 23-2. Rigid foam insulation is generally used to insulate a slab foundation. A vapor barrier prevents moisture from seeping through the slab.

347

in winter and cool in summer. Without insulation, efficiency in heating or cooling would require a much larger unit to maintain the desired temperature.

Ventilation is another important factor in an efficient temperature control system, Fig. 23-3. Ventilation reduces the temperature and moisture content in the house, crawl space, and attic. If the attic and crawl space do not have the proper amount of ventilation, moisture is likely to condense and cause damage. If the attic is hot and moist the house will be more difficult to cool.

A third factor which affects the effeciency of the heating or cooling system is the solar orientation of the house. The west walls of the house should be protected from the sun in the summer. In some cases this may be accomplished with trees or a garage which shades the side wall. In cold climates an attempt should be made to place all large areas of glass on the south side of the house away from the cold winter winds, and in position to take advantage of the winter sun.

Other factors such as weather stripping, color of roofing, length of overhang and landscape have a bearing on the efficiency of the temperature control system. Weather stripping seals small cracks around doors and windows to reduce heat loss. Light colored roofing materials absorb less heat from the sun than dark colored materials. If a house located in a warm climate does not have shade trees, then a light colored roof will most likely be preferred. Overhangs shade exterior walls and reduce the amount of heat entering the house. Landscaping not only serves to improve the appearance of a home, but may be used to block cold winds and provide shade. Insulated glass reduces heat loss and lowers the cost of heating and cooling.

HUMIDITY CONTROL

Air in our homes contains a certain amount of water (moisture). The amount of moisture in the air related to the temperature level is called humidity. More specifically, humidity is the ratio (percentage) of water vapor in the atmosphere to the amount required to saturate it at the same temperature. It is properly called RELATIVE HUMIDITY. The air will hold more water when the temperature is high than when it is low.

GABLE VENT

EAVE VENT

ROOF VENT

CUPOLA VENT

RIDGE VENT

FOUNDATION VENT

Fig. 23-3. The attic and crawl space should be ventilated for more efficient heating and cooling. Insufficient ventilation may cause damage to sheathing and other structural members due to excess moisture.

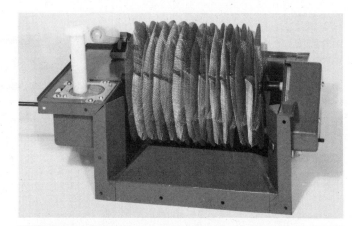

Fig. 23-4. Power humidifiers may be mounted on the plenum or supply duct of a forced warm air heating system. (Whirlpool Corp.)

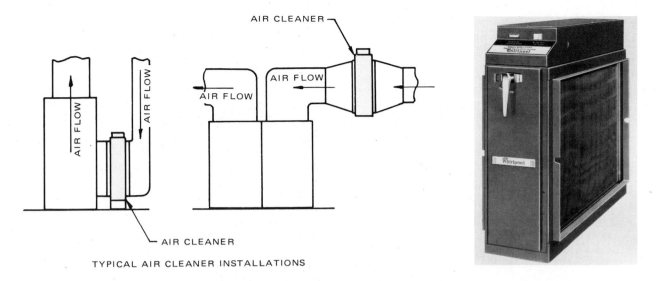

TYPICAL AIR CLEANER INSTALLATIONS

Fig. 23-5. Electronic air cleaners can be installed with most forced warm air heating, cooling or ventilating systems.   (Whirlpool Corp.)

A comfortable humidity level is around 50 percent when the temperature is about 75 deg. During the winter months, the amount of moisture in the air indoors drops to a low level because of expanding the air during heating and the low relative humidity outside the house. If water is not added to the air to increase the humidity, throat and skin irritations are likely. Also furniture may crack and separate at the glue joints. For these reasons, humidifiers are commonly used to increase the moisture level. Humidifiers may be attached directly to the plenum or heating ducts of a forced warm air system, Fig. 23-4, or a free standing model may be used.

In the summer the problem is too much moisture in the air. When the humidity is high, the air feels "sticky" and people are uncomfortable. Wood doors, windows and drawers swell and do not operate smoothly. When the moisture content is too high water is likely to condense on windows. This condition, if allowed to persist, may cause damage in the woodwork. A DEHUMIDIFIER may be installed to remove water from the air. This device condenses water on cold coils and thus removes it from the air and reduces the relative humidity. Humidity control is important for total comfort and should be considered when planning a climate control system.

AIR CIRCULATION AND CLEANING

If the same air in a house is used over and over without adding a fresh supply it will become stale and unhealthy. Therefore, some provision should be made to provide fresh air. Circulation helps to lessen the problems of dry air. High concentrations of moist air in the kitchen, laundry room and bath are distributed throughout the house when the air is circulated.

The air in most homes contains a sufficient amount of dust and other foreign particles so consideration should be given to adding some type of air cleaning device. Some furnaces have built-in filters, some have electronic air cleaning grids, Fig. 23-5. Electronic grids are effective and will remove up to about 95 percent of the dust particles as they pass through it.

A complete climate control system heats or cools the air, cleans, circulates, and controls moisture content in the house as required for comfort, Fig. 23-6. This provides a healthful atmosphere in which to live.

Fig. 23-6. This unit provides heating, cooling, humidification, dehumidification, and air cleaning.   (The Williamson Co.)

TYPES OF HEATING SYSTEMS

Modern heating systems are usually one of four basic types: FORCED WARM AIR, HYDRONIC SYSTEMS, ELECTRIC RADIANT SYSTEMS, and HEAT PUMPS.

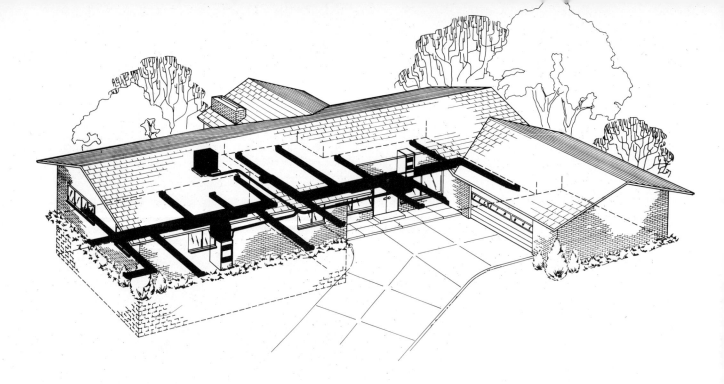

Fig. 23-7. Heating and cooling may use the same duct system or a combination of systems.

FORCED WARM AIR SYSTEMS

The forced warm air system heats air in a furnace and forces it through pipes or ducts to all parts of the house, Fig. 23-7. A fan or blower is used to push the warm air. Cool air is drawn through cold air return ducts to the furnace. Before it enters the heating chamber it passes through a filter which removes dust and other particles. Some forced warm air systems have built-in humidifiers, dehumidifiers, and air cleaners.

The forced warm air system is popular because it is relatively inexpensive to purchase and install, provides heat in adequate amounts quickly, the heating ducts may be used in a central air cooling system and humidification is simple.

Air conditioners can be installed in walls, Fig. 23-8, or as a part of the climate control system, Fig. 23-12.

Three basic kinds of forced air furnaces are available for residential installations: STANDARD UPFLOW FURNACE, COUNTERFLOW FURNACE and HORIZONTAL FURNACE. The upflow furnace, Fig. 23-9, is designed for

basement installation, because the plenum (chamber where warmed air is collected for distribution) is on top of the furnace. When the furnace is to be located on the main floor with ducts below the floor, a counterflow furnace is required,

Fig. 23-9. Left. Upflow furnaces are designed for basement installation because the plenum is located on top of the unit. Fig. 23-10. Right. Counterflow furnaces are specifically designed for closet, garage or utility room installation. The plenum is located on the bottom. (Whirlpool Corp.)

Fig. 23-8. Typical wall air conditioner.

Fig. 23-11. Horizontal furnaces are ideally suited for crawl space or attic installation. They require only minimum clearance and can be suspended from ceilings and floor joists or installed on a concrete slab.

Fig. 23-10. On this type of furnace the plenum is on the bottom and the warm air is forced downward. If the furnace is to be installed in the attic or crawl space, a horizontal furnace, Fig. 23-11, is a logical choice.

Modern forced warm air systems do have some disadvantages. Rapid movement of air is objectionable to some people because drafts are created. Noise is often transmitted through the ducts and the noise level is generally higher than with other systems due to the blower.

In modern furnace installations the ducts are designed to fit between the joists and wall studs, Fig. 23-12. Furnaces may be located in the attic, crawl space, or main level, Fig. 23-13. Furnace operation is controlled by the use of thermostats. A

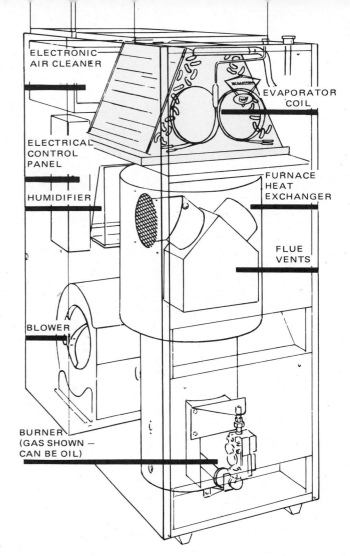

Fig. 23-12. Below. Forced warm air furnace installations in basement. (Lennox) Above. Using evaporator coil for summer cooling. (Williamson)

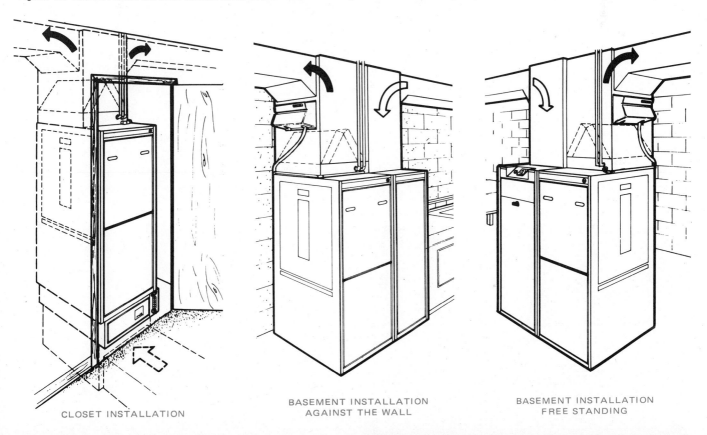

CLOSET INSTALLATION

BASEMENT INSTALLATION AGAINST THE WALL

BASEMENT INSTALLATION FREE STANDING

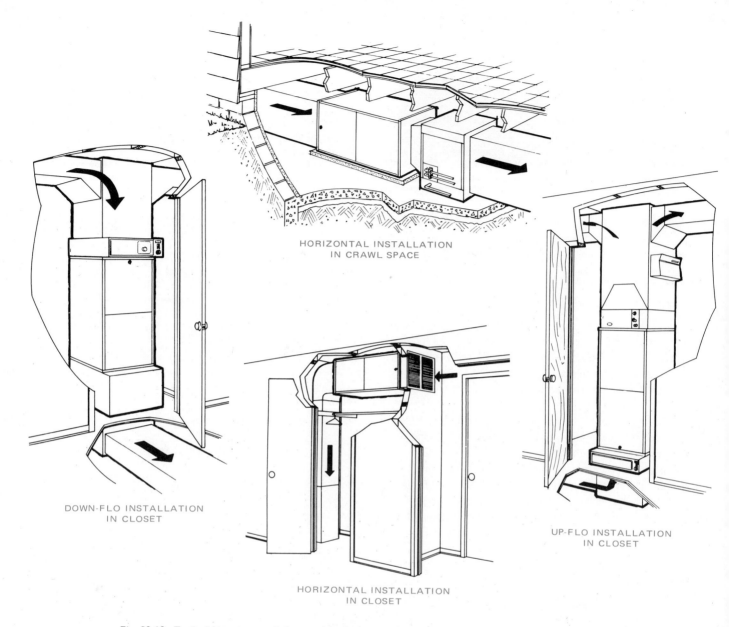

HORIZONTAL INSTALLATION
IN CRAWL SPACE

DOWN-FLO INSTALLATION
IN CLOSET

HORIZONTAL INSTALLATION
IN CLOSET

UP-FLO INSTALLATION
IN CLOSET

Fig. 23-13. Typical forced warm air furnace installations in the crawl space and closet on first floor.
(Lennox Industries, Inc.)

Fig. 23-14. Two common styles of thermostats used in residential heating and cooling systems. (Singer)

thermostat is an automatic sensing device that may be set to activate the furnace at predetermined temperatures, Fig. 23-14. The thermostat is usually located on an inside wall of the house. It should be located where it will be free from cold air drafts and heat from lamps. A typical forced warm air system for a small home uses one thermostat which controls the heat for the entire home. Large homes frequently require zoning into heating areas and utilize separate thermostats for each of the areas.

HYDRONIC SYSTEMS

A hydronic (hot water) system consists of a boiler to heat water (hot water), Fig. 23-15, water pipes and radiators or radiant panels. Hot water is pumped to the radiators which are located throughout the house. The cooled water is returned to

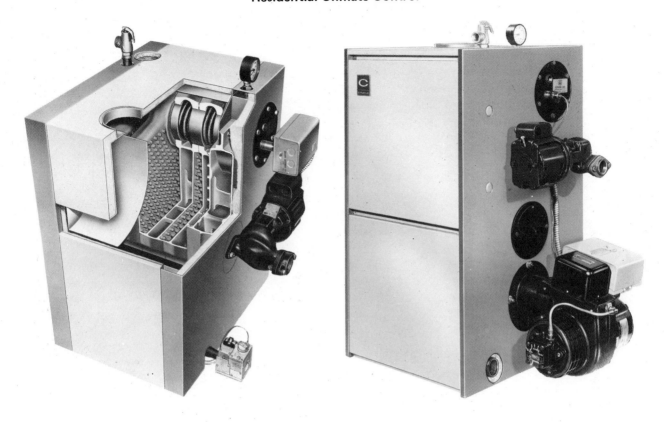

Fig. 23-15. Modern gas fired hydronic furnaces. (Crane Co.)

the boiler for reheating. The type of hydronic system used in most homes is known as the one-pipe system. The one-pipe system uses radiators or converters, as they are sometimes called, connected in series. Heated water carried in the main pipe is diverted to the radiators and is then returned to the furnace, Fig. 23-16. Special connectors allow small amounts of hot water to enter the radiators and equalize heat in radiators throughout the home.

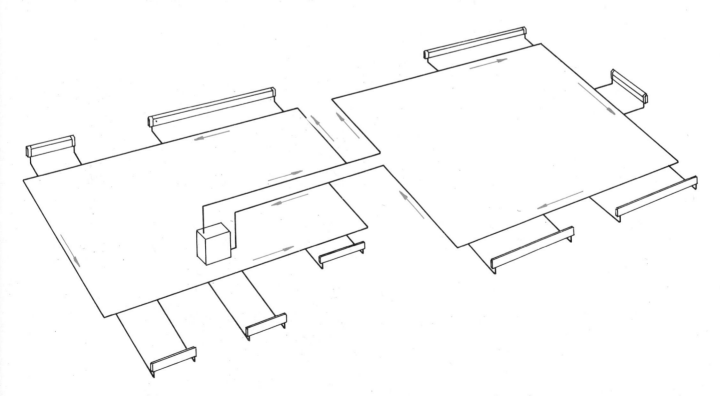

Fig. 23-16. A series loop type hydronic system with two zones of control.

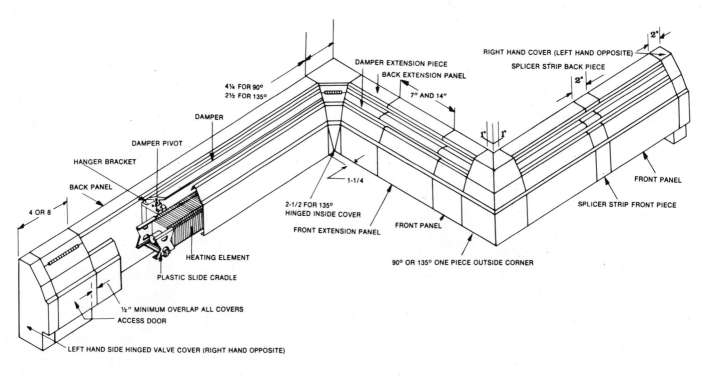

Fig. 23-17. A modern style baseboard convector for a hydronic system.   (Crane Co.)

Old style radiators are seldom used in new homes. Baseboard convectors, Fig. 23-17, are popular. These are produced in several styles. The convectors are efficient and readily transmit heat to the surrounding air.

Another type of hydronic heating system utilizes copper pipes embedded in a concrete floor or plastered ceiling. This system is often referred to as a RADIANT SYSTEM, Fig. 23-18. It is popular in mild climates and locations where the temperature is not likely to drop rapidly in a short period of time. A radiant heating system is silent and is completely hidden from sight.

One of the major advantages of a hydronic heating system is that each room may be controlled individually. Frequently the home is zoned into two or three areas which require about the same temperature and each zone is controlled by a separate thermostat. This adds to the heating comfort.

Other advantages include the absence of noise transmitted from room to room, no registers to occupy wall space, and no drafts. Hydronic heat is clean, quiet, and efficient. However, it has no provision for cooling, air filtration, or humidification. These may be considered serious deficiencies in some sections of the country.

ELECTRIC RADIANT SYSTEMS

Electric radiant systems use resistance wiring to produce heat in the wire. The wire is embedded in the ceiling, floor or baseboards, Fig. 23-19. This system is clean, quiet and produces a constant level of heat. The entire system is hidden if the wires are in the ceiling or floor. Heat control for each room or area is practical. No chimney is required as with gas or oil fired systems. The electric radiant system is dependable and free from maintenance problems.

Disadvantages of this system include no provision for

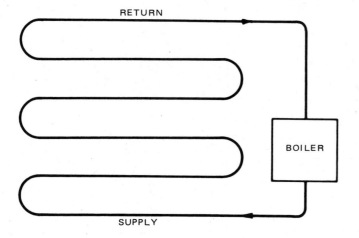

Fig. 23-18. Radiant hydronic system utilizing copper pipe embedded in concrete floor.

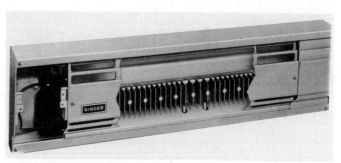

Fig. 23-19. Baseboard designed for an electric radiant heating system.

humidification, air filtration, cooling, and slow recovery if the temperature drops suddenly. In some areas of the country, electric radiant systems are expensive to operate due to the cost of electricity. Fig. 23-20 shows a typical installation.

HEAT PUMPS

Heat pumps, Fig. 23-21, serve the dual purpose of heating and cooling. They are essentially refrigeration units which

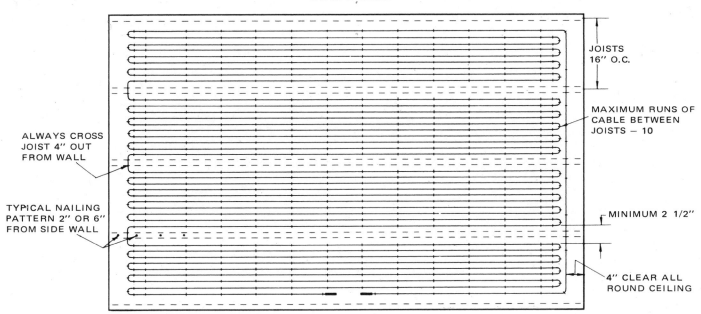

CABLE SPACING

JOISTS 16" O.C.

MAXIMUM RUNS OF CABLE BETWEEN JOISTS — 10

ALWAYS CROSS JOIST 4" OUT FROM WALL

TYPICAL NAILING PATTERN 2" OR 6" FROM SIDE WALL

MINIMUM 2 1/2"

4" CLEAR ALL ROUND CEILING

TYPICAL CEILING LAYOUT PATTERN

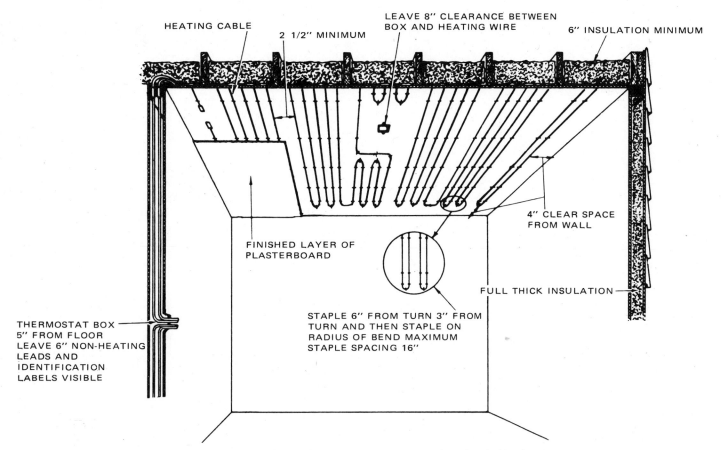

HEATING CABLE

2 1/2" MINIMUM

LEAVE 8" CLEARANCE BETWEEN BOX AND HEATING WIRE

6" INSULATION MINIMUM

FINISHED LAYER OF PLASTERBOARD

4" CLEAR SPACE FROM WALL

FULL THICK INSULATION

STAPLE 6" FROM TURN 3" FROM TURN AND THEN STAPLE ON RADIUS OF BEND MAXIMUM STAPLE SPACING 16"

THERMOSTAT BOX 5" FROM FLOOR LEAVE 6" NON-HEATING LEADS AND IDENTIFICATION LABELS VISIBLE

Fig. 23-20. Layout and spacing for resistance wiring used in radiant electrical heating systems. NOTE: 1 watt of electricity will provide 3.415 Btu's of heat.

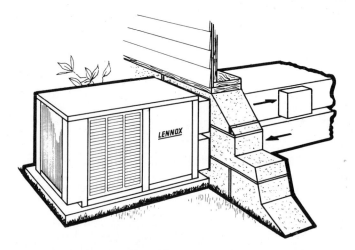

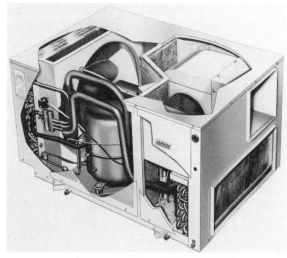

Fig. 23-21. A single package heat pump installed on a slab at grade level. The cutaway view shows the interior mechanism of the unit. (Lennox Industries, Inc.)

pump or transfer natural heat from air or water to heat or cool the house. Heat pumps operate on the principle that there is some heat in all air and water and this heat may be removed. Heat which has been removed is pumped into the house to heat it, and pumped from the house to cool it.

The heat pump requires electricity to operate a compressor. It is clean and needs no chimney. A disadvantage is that efficiency drops considerably when the temperature is below 30 deg. For this reason heat pumps are not practical for cold climates.

Choosing the "right" system for a particular home will depend on the availability of fuels, temperature variations, cost of installation and maintenance, type of house and personal preference of the owner.

HEAT LOSS CALCULATIONS

Before the proper size heating or cooling unit may be determined, heat loss calculations are required for exposed surfaces of the home.

Several terms with which you should become familiar are:

BRITISH THERMAL UNIT. A British Thermal Unit, or BTU as it is commonly called, is the quantity of heat required to increase the temperature of 1 pound of water 1 deg. Furnaces and air conditioners are rated in BTU's. Final heat loss calculation will be in BTU's.

HEAT LOSS. The amount of heat that passes through the exposed surfaces of the house for average temperatures.

INSIDE DESIGN TEMPERATURE. The desired room temperature level is called the inside design temperature. Seventy degrees is the usual level used for calculations.

OUTSIDE DESIGN TEMPERATURE. The outside design temperature is the average outdoor temperature for the winter months. An average of the coldest temperatures for the months of October through March is used to determine the outdoor design temperature.

DESIGN TEMPERATURE DIFFERENCE. The difference between the outside design temperature and the inside design temperature is the design temperature difference.

U FACTOR. The U factor, or U as it is commonly called, is the number of BTU's transmitted in 1 hour through 1 sq. ft. of a building material for each degree of temperature difference. U factors for common building materials may be determined by taking the reciprocal (dividing 1.00 by the resistance factor) of the resitivity of the material, see Fig. 23-22.

INFILTRATION. Heat lost through spaces around windows and doors is known as infiltration. For calculation purposes, it has been estimated that infiltration is equal to one air exchange per hour. For example, if a room is 10' x 18' and has an 8 ft. ceiling the total volume is 1440 cu. ft. This figure, 1440 cu. ft., is the amount of air infiltration.

RESISTIVITY. Ability to resist the transfer of heat or cold. Materials which transmit heat readily are known as conductors while those that do not are called insulators.

CALCULATION PROCEDURE

The procedure recommended for determining heat loss for walls, ceiling and floor of a room or the total house so the proper size heating or cooling unit may be established is:

WALLS

1. Find the total exterior wall area by multiplying the length by the height. This is the gross wall area.

2. Subtract the area filled by windows and doors in the exterior walls. The resulting area is called the net wall area.

3. Add the resistivity for each of the materials used in the construction of each wall. Take the reciprocal of the sum. This figure is the U factor for the net wall. (Each wall which is constructed differently must be calculated separately.)

4. Determine the U factor for each door and window in the exterior wall by taking the reciprocal of the resistivity.

5. Calculate the design temperature difference by subtracting the outside design temperature from the inside design temperature. Example: IDT = 70°, ODT = -10°, therefore 70° - (-10°) = 80°. The design temperature difference for this example is 80°.

6. Determine the BTU loss per hour (BTU/H) for the net wall area by multiplying the net wall area by the net wall U factor by the design temperature difference. Record this figure.

7. Determine the BTU/H for the windows by multiplying

the window area by the glass U factor by the design temperature difference. Record this figure.

8. Determine the BTU/H for the doors by multiplying the door area by the door U factor by the design temperature difference. Record this figure.

CEILING

1. Find the total ceiling area by multiplying the length by the width.

2. Determine the U factor for the ceiling by adding the resistivity for each material used and take the reciprocal.

3. Calculate the BTU/H by multiplying the ceiling area by the total ceiling U factor by the design temperature difference. Record this figure.

FLOOR

1. Find the total floor area (figure heat loss only for floors over non-heated areas such as crawl space or slab type floors) of the floor by multiplying the length by the width.

2. Determine the U factor for the floor by adding the resistivity for each material used and take the reciprocal.

3. Calculate the BTU/H by multiplying the floor area, by the total floor U factor, by the design temperature difference. Note that the design temperature difference may not be the same here as for walls and ceiling with heating ducts and hot water pipes which are not insulated. If the area is properly vented and pipes and ducts are insulated, then some design temperature difference may be used. Record this figure.

INFILTRATION

1. Determine the volume of air in the room or home under consideration by multiplying the length by the width by the height. This volume is equal to the air infiltration.

2. Calculate the air infiltration BTU/H heat loss by multi-

plying the volume of air infiltration by the U factor (.018) by the design temperature difference. Note that .018 BTU/H is required to warm 1 cu. ft. of air 1 deg. This is a constant and may be used in each calculation. Record this figure.

FINAL CALCULATIONS

1. List the BTU/H for the walls, windows, doors, ceiling, floor and air infiltration.

2. Add the results of each together to find the total heat loss in BTU's per hour. This figure represents the size of heating units required for the room or house being calculated.

Procedure for calculating the size of cooling unit is about the same except that the design temperature difference must reflect summer temperatures rather than winter and allowance should be made for very humid locations. A larger unit will be required.

EXAMPLE OF HEAT LOSS CALCULATION

The purpose of the following example is to apply the procedure just described to a room to show actual computation of heat loss. Fig. 23-23 shows the room used in the example. Details are also shown of the wall, ceiling and floor.

CALCULATION FOR WALLS

1. Total exterior area — 12' – 0" x 8' – 0" = 96 sq. ft.
   18' – 0" x 8' – 0" = 144 sq. ft.
   Gross wall Area = 240 sq. ft.

2. Window area — 6' – 0" x 5' – 0" = 30 sq. ft.
   6' – 0" x 5' – 0" = 30 sq. ft.
   Total window area = 60 sq. ft.

   Door area — 3' – 0" x 6' – 8" = 21 sq. ft.

RESISTIVITY TO HEAT LOSS OF COMMON BUILDING MATERIALS

	MATERIAL	RESISTIVITY		MATERIAL	RESISTIVITY
4"	CONCRETE OR STONE	.32	1/2"	PLYWOOD	.65
6"	CONCRETE OR STONE	.48	5/8"	PLYWOOD	.80
8"	CONCRETE OR STONE	.64	3/4"	PLYWOOD	.95
12"	CONCRETE OR STONE	.96	3/4"	SOFTWOOD SHEATING OR SIDING	.85
4"	CONCRETE BLOCK	.70		COMPOSITION FLOOR COVERING	.08
8"	CONCRETE BLOCK	1.10	1"	MINERAL BATT INSULATION	3.50
12"	CONCRETE BLOCK	1.25	2"	MINERAL BATT INSULATION	7.00
4"	COMMON BRICK	.82	4"	MINERAL BATT INSULATION	14.00
4"	FACE BRICK	.45	2"	GLASS FIBER INSULATION	7.00
4"	STRUCTURAL CLAY TILE	1.10	4"	GLASS FIBER INSULATION	14.00
8"	STRUCTURAL CLAY TILE	1.90	1"	LOOSE FILL INSULATION	3.00
12"	STRUCTURAL CLAY TILE	3.00		SINGLE THICKNESS GLASS	.88
1"	STUCCO	.20		GLASSWELD INSULATING GLASS	1.89
15 LB.	BUILDING PAPER	.06		SINGLE GLASS WITH STORM WINDOW	1.66
3/8"	SHEET ROCK OR PLASTERBOARD	.33		METAL EDGE INSULATING GLASS	1.85
1/2"	SAND PLASTER	.15	4"	GLASS BLOCK	2.13
1/2"	INSULATION PLASTER	.75	1 3/8"	WOOD DOOR	1.92
1/2"	FIBERBOARD CEILING TILE	1.20		SAME WITH STORM DOOR	3.12
1/2"	FIBERBOARD SHEATHING	1.45	1 3/4"	WOOD DOOR	1.82
3/4"	FIBERBOARD SHEATHING	2.18		SAME WITH STORM DOOR	2.94
	ROLL ROOFING	.15			
	ASPHALT SHINGLES	.16			
	WOOD SHINGLES	.86			
	TILE OR SLATE	.08			

Fig. 23-22. The resistivity of various common building materials has been determined by laboratory tests to be used in heat loss calculations.

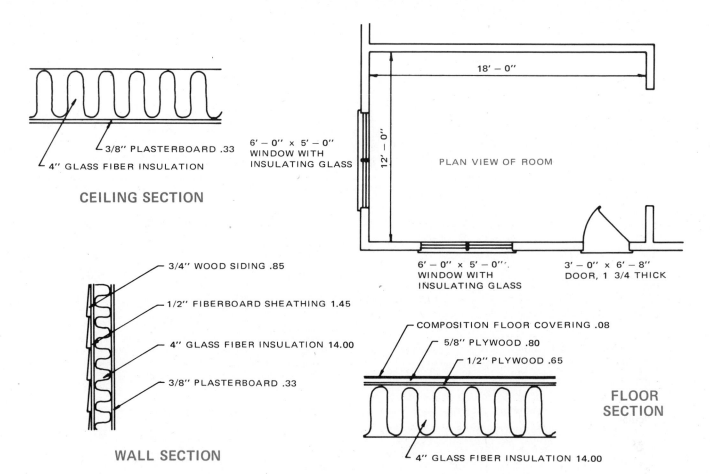

3/8" PLASTERBOARD .33

4" GLASS FIBER INSULATION

CEILING SECTION

6' – 0" x 5' – 0"
WINDOW WITH
INSULATING GLASS

12' – 0"

18' – 0"

PLAN VIEW OF ROOM

6' – 0" x 5' – 0".
WINDOW WITH
INSULATING GLASS

3' – 0" x 6' – 8"
DOOR, 1 3/4 THICK

3/4" WOOD SIDING .85

1/2" FIBERBOARD SHEATHING 1.45

4" GLASS FIBER INSULATION 14.00

3/8" PLASTERBOARD .33

WALL SECTION

COMPOSITION FLOOR COVERING .08
5/8" PLYWOOD .80
1/2" PLYWOOD .65

FLOOR SECTION

4" GLASS FIBER INSULATION 14.00

Fig. 23-23. Plan view and sections of a room with resistivity of materials shown.

Net wall area = Gross wall area-doors and window area
= 240 sq. ft. – 81 sq. ft.
Net wall area = 159 sq. ft.

3. Resistivity of wall materials
3/4" wood siding .85
1/2" fiberboard sheathing 1.45
4" glass fiber insulation 14.00
3/8" plasterboard .33
Total resistivity = 26.63

$1.00 \div 26.63 = .038$
U factor for net wall = .038

4. U factor for doors and windows
1 3/4" wood door .52
insulating glass window .53 for both

5. Design temperature difference
Inside design temperature = 70°
Outside design temperature = - 5°
Design temperature difference = 75°

6. BTU/H for net wall
Net wall area x U factor x temperature difference
159 sq. ft. x .038 x 75° = 453.150
BTU/H for the net walls = 453.15

7. BTU/H for the windows
Window area x U factor x temperature difference
60 sq. ft. x .53 x 75° = 2385.00
BTU/H for the windows = 2385.00

8. BTU/H for the door
Door area x U factor x temperature difference
21 sq. ft. x .52 x 75° = 819.00
BTU/H for the door = 819.00

CALCULATION FOR CEILING

1. Total ceiling area – 12' – 0" x 18' – 0" = 216 sq. ft.

2. U factor for ceiling
3/8" plasterboard = .33
4" glass fiber insulation = 14.00
Total resistivity = 14.33

$1.00 \div 14.33 = .069$
U factor for ceiling = .069

3. BTU/H for the ceiling
Ceiling area x U factor x temperature difference
216 sq. ft. x .069 x 75° = 1117.80
BTU/H for the ceiling = 1117.80

CALCULATION FOR FLOOR

1. Total floor area — 12' — 0'' x 18' — 0'' = 216 sq. ft.

2. U factor for floor

Composition floor covering	.08
5/8'' plywood	.80
1/2'' plywood	.65
4'' glass fiber insulation	14.00
Total resistivity =	15.53

1.00 ÷ 15.53 = .066
U factor for floor = .066

3. BTU/H for the floor
Floor area x U factor x temperature difference
216 sq. ft. x .066 x 75° = 1069.20
BTU/H for the floor = 1069.20

CALCULATION FOR AIR INFILTRATION

1. Volume of air
Length x width x hieght
18' — 0'' x 12' — 0'' x 8' — 0'' = 1728 cu. ft.
Volume of air = air infiltration

2. BTU/H for air infiltration
Volume of air x .018 x temperature difference
1728 cu. ft. x .018 x 75° = 2332.80
BTU/H for air infiltration = 2332.80

SUMMARY CALCULATIONS

BTU/H for net walls	453.15
BTU/H for the windows	2385.00
BTU/H for the door	819.00
BTU/H for the ceiling	1117.80
BTU/H for the floor	1069.20
BTU/H for air infiltration	2332.80
Total BTU/H =	8176.95

The total room heat loss is 8,177 BTU/H. A heating unit capable of producing this amount of heat is required for the room used in this example.

REVIEW QUESTIONS — CHAPTER 23

1. Identify the four features of a modern climate control system.
   a. _____.
   b. _____.
   c. _____.
   d. _____.
2. Name five conditions which help to increase temperature control efficiency.
   a. _____.
   b. _____.
   c. _____.
   d. _____.

e. _____.
3. The amount of water in the air as related to the temperature is called _____.
4. A comfortable humidity level is about _____.
5. Identify two possible outcomes from too little moisture in the air (low humidity).
   a. _____.
   b. _____.
6. Name two effects of too much moisture in the house.
   a. _____.
   b. _____.
7. The device which removes moisture from the air in a house is called _____.
8. List the four basic types of heating systems used in modern homes.
   a. _____.
   b. _____.
   c. _____.
   d. _____.
9. How does a forced warm air system operate? _____
   _____.
10. Identify three types of furnaces which are used in forced warm air systems.
    a. _____.
    b. _____.
    c. _____.
11. What is a thermostat? _____.
12. The three main parts in a hydronic system are:
    a. _____.
    b. _____.
    c. _____.
13. Name three advantages of the hydronic system.
    a. _____.
    b. _____.
    c. _____.
14. Heat is produced in the electric radiant system by _____.
15. A heat pump is essentially a _____ unit.

SUGGESTED ACTIVITIES

1. Select a plan of a medium size home and get an estimate from your local gas and electricity company as to the cost of heating this home. Also ask for their recommendations for installation and ventilation. Report your findings.
2. Using a plan supplied by your instructor, calculate the total heat loss and specify the size heating unit required. Show your calculations.
3. Contact people in your community who have forced warm air, hydronic and electric radiant heating systems and ask their opinion regarding dependability, advantages, disadvantages, economy and serviceability. Report their reactions.
4. Visit a local heating and air conditioning equipment supplier. Ask for catalogs and other literature showing heating and cooling equipment. Add this material to the classroom collection.

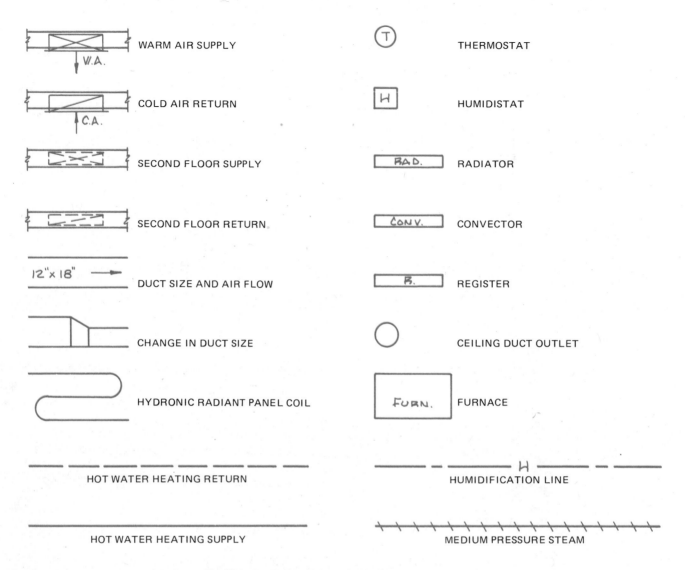

WARM AIR SUPPLY

W.A.

COLD AIR RETURN

C.A.

SECOND FLOOR SUPPLY

SECOND FLOOR RETURN

12"x 18"   DUCT SIZE AND AIR FLOW

CHANGE IN DUCT SIZE

HYDRONIC RADIANT PANEL COIL

HOT WATER HEATING RETURN

HOT WATER HEATING SUPPLY

T   THERMOSTAT

H   HUMIDISTAT

RAD.   RADIATOR

CONV.   CONVECTOR

R.   REGISTER

CEILING DUCT OUTLET

FURN.   FURNACE

H   HUMIDIFICATION LINE

MEDIUM PRESSURE STEAM

Fig. 24-1. Typical symbols used in a climate control system.

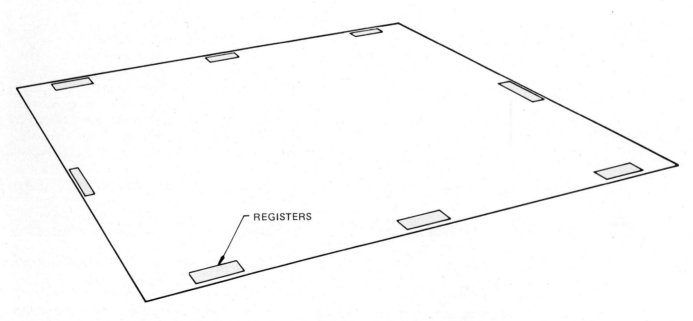

REGISTERS

Fig. 24-2. A perimeter system of outlets provides uniform heat or cooling.

Chapter 24
CLIMATE CONTROL PLAN

DEFINITION AND PURPOSE

A climate control plan is a plan view drawing in section of the home which shows the climate control system. It is traced from the floor plan. The plan shows piping or heating ducts, furnace and other climate control equipment.

A climate control plan shows the location, size and type of heating, cooling, ventilating, humidification and air cleaning equipment. This system should be closely coordinated with the structural, plumbing and electrical aspects of the home.

REQUIRED INFORMATION

The climate control plan should include information on size and location of distribution pipes or ducts, location of thermostats and registers or baseboard convectors, climate control equipment location and type, equipment schedule, heat loss calculations, and general or specific notes which help to describe the system.

DISTRIBUTION SYSTEM

The distribution system usually consists of ducts or pipes. Ducts (round or rectangular) are needed to move large quantities of air for heating or cooling. Pipes are used in hydronic systems to distribute hot water or steam from the boiler to radiators, baseboard units or radiant panels. The distribution systems to be used must be represented on the climate control plan using the proper symbols, Fig. 24-1. The ducts should be drawn as close to scale (1/4" = 1' – 0") as possible. Sizes should be shown on the plan. Pipes are indicated by single lines and are not drawn to scale.

PLANNING OUTLET AND INLET LOCATIONS. A perimeter system of outlets is generally specified. This provides uniform heat (or cooling) by concentrating heat where it is needed most - - along the outside walls, Fig. 24-2. There should be at least one outlet (register or baseboard unit) in each large area to be heated or cooled. This includes rooms, halls, stairwells, etc. which are to be conditioned. An average room has up to 180 sq. ft. of floor space. Usually larger areas should be counted as two or more rooms. If a room has more than 15 ft. of exterior wall, then two or more outlets should be used.

Inlets are required for forced warm air heating systems but are not needed for hydronic or electric radiant systems. If the house is a compact one-story house, one inlet (cold air return) will usually be sufficient. However, if the house is L-shaped, U-shaped or has several levels; then two or more inlets should be planned. Remember that closed doors and dead-end corridors block air circulation.

Registers or inlets are available in several sizes. The chart which follows shows some of the common sizes:

REGISTER SIZES

TYPE	SIZE	SUPPLY
Floor Diffuser	4" x 12"	6" Pipe
Floor Diffuser	6" x 12"	8" Pipe
Baseboard Diffuser	2 1/4" x 15"	6" Pipe
Baseboard Diffuser	2 1/4" x 24"	6" Pipe
Floor Diffuser	2 1/4" x 12"	6" Pipe

INLET SIZES

TYPE	SIZE	FURNACE SIZE
Baseboard Grille	6" x 14"	- - - - -
Baseboard Grille	6" x 30"	40,000 BTU
Ceiling or Wall Grille	16" x 20"	75,000 BTU
High Side Wall Grille	6" x 14"	- - - - -
Floor Grille	8" x 30"	60,000 BTU
Floor Grille	12" x 30"	80,000 BTU
Floor Grille	18" x 24"	90,000 BTU

PLANNING DUCTWORK. Two basic types of ductwork systems are the RADIAL SYSTEM and the EXTENDED PLENUM SYSTEM, Fig. 24-3. The extended plenum system is usually preferred because pipes (round) do not radiate out in all directions from the furnace as they do in the radial system. The extended plenum system uses rectangular ducts for the main supply and round pipes to connect to each register, Fig. 24-4.

Round pipe used to supply a register in the extended plenum system may be 6 or 8 in. in diameter. An 8 in. pipe is generally recommended when the duct system is to be used for cooling. The larger size is necessary when the same blower is used because cool air moves slower than warm air.

The ductwork size is based on the number and size of round pipes it serves. All rectangular ducts are 8 in. deep and vary in width from 10 to 28 inches. The sectional area of the supply duct must equal the total area of all the round register pipes. The extended plenum may remain the same size throughout its entire length or may be reduced in size as fewer registers remain to be supplied.

Duct size may be determined by using this procedure: For 6 in. pipes, multiply the number of pipes by 2 and add 2 to the product. The result is the width of the plenum duct

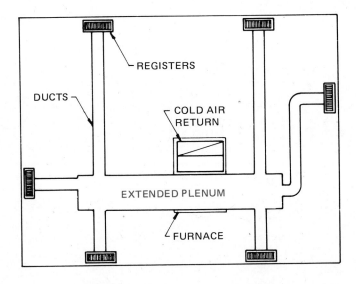

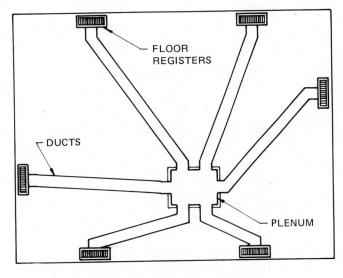

PERIMETER RADIAL SYSTEM

Fig. 24-3. Two ductwork systems are commonly used for residential climate control, radial and extended plenum systems.

required. Remember it is 8 in. deep. Example: A duct is to serve six 6 in. round pipes, therefore 6 x 2 = 12 + 2 = 14 in. The duct will be 8" x 14". For 8 in. pipes, multiply the number of pipes by 3 and add 2 to the product. If the round pipes in the previous example had been 8 in. pipes, then the duct size would have been 6 x 3 = 18 + 2 = 20 in. The duct size required is 8" x 20". A vertical duct designed to fit between the studs is called a wall stack and is usually 12" x 3 1/4".

PLANNING PIPING FOR HYDRONIC SYSTEM. The main hot water supply from the boiler must be large enough to provide for adequate heating. Copper pipe of these sizes is usually considered to be adequate for most installations:

    1 in. main for up to 71,000 BTU
    1 1/2 in. main for 72,000 — 160,000 BTU
    1 1/2 in. main for 161,000 — 240,000 BTU

The size baseboard unit or convector cabinet required will depend on the heat loss calculated for a given area. It is best to

calculate the heat loss for each room and then plan the number and size outlets to match this loss. The following chart shows the output rating for several common fin-tube baseboard units and common cabinets:

CONVECTOR CABINETS

LENGTH	THICKNESS	BTU/H OUTPUT
24 IN.	6 3/8 IN.	3,400
32 IN.	6 3/8 IN.	4,800
36 IN.	8 3/8 IN.	6,900
40 IN.	8 3/8 IN.	7,800
48 IN.	8 3/8 IN.	9,600
56 IN.	8 3/8 IN.	11,400
60 IN.	10 3/8 IN.	19,000

FIN-TUBE BASEBOARD UNITS

	BTU/H OUTPUT	
LENGTH	SINGLE	DOUBLE
2 FT.	- - - -	2,280
4 FT.	2,870	4,560
6 FT.	4,260	6,840
8 FT.	5,680	- - - -

Locate outlets below windows for most efficient heating. Any room which is over 15 ft. long should have at least two outlets.

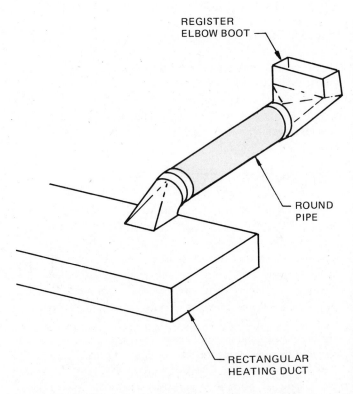

Fig. 24-4. Round pipe either 6 or 8 in. in diameter is frequently used to connect the register to the main supply duct.

THERMOSTATS AND CLIMATE CONTROL EQUIPMENT

Each automatic climate control system requires at least one thermostat. A forced warm air system will need only one thermostat if one furnace is used. Sometimes two furnaces are installed if the house is large, or if more than one zone is

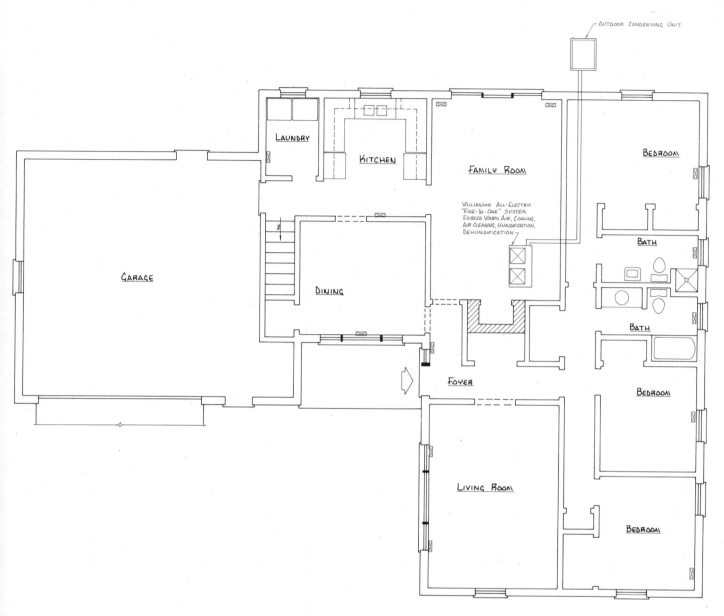

Fig. 24-5. Floor plan showing the location of the furnace, outdoor condensing unit, and registers. The furnace is in the basement below the main floor level.

required. As many zones as desired may be used with electric radiant or hydronic systems. Each zone needs a thermostat to provide accurate control.

Location of the thermostat is important because it measures the temperature and activates the furnace. If it is placed on a wall where the sun may shine on it, in a draft, or near a lamp the performance may not be satisfactory. Locate the thermostat on an inside partition in a place where the temperature will be representative of the room as a whole. Show the location on the climate control plan.

Other equipment should be indicated on the plan using symbols or notes.

SCHEDULES, CALCULATIONS AND NOTES

Various schedules may be useful on the climate control plan. An equipment schedule provides an orderly means of specifying equipment to be used in the system. Including a register schedule may be desirable because placing too much

information on the drawing will cause it to be crowded.

A complete climate control plan will show a summary of the heat loss calculations. These calculations form the basis for equipment selection and are important. If space permits, the summary should be located on the climate control plan.

Add any other information on the plan which you feel will be helpful or desirable to the builder or sub-contractors. Notes should be short and to the point.

PROCEDURE FOR DRAWING CLIMATE CONTROL PLAN

Just as in the plumbing and electrical plans, many decisions and calculations must be made before completing the climate control plan. The type of heating and cooling system or systems must be determined, and heat loss calculated for each room. Other drawings of the structure should be studied to determine the most practical layout before starting to draw.

After the preliminary details are disposed of, then you may

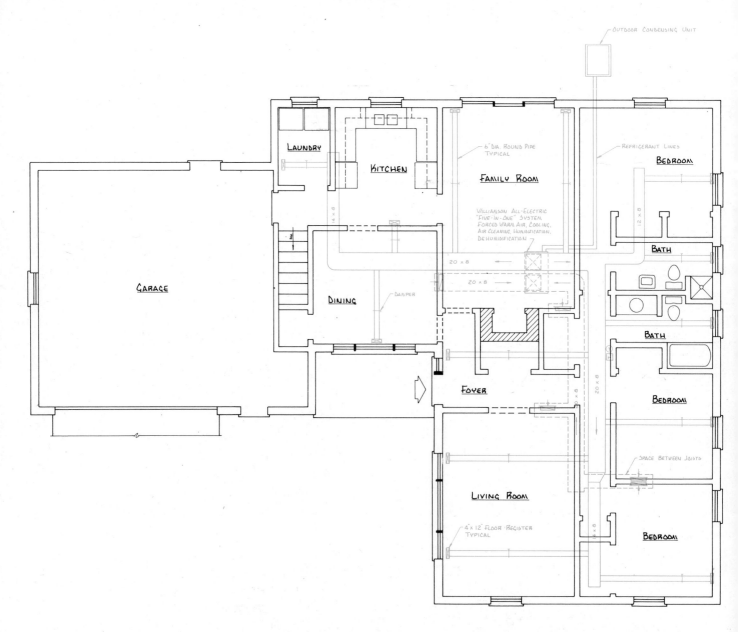

Fig. 24-6. A more complete climate control plan showing the location of supply and cold air return ducts and return registers.

proceed with the drawing of the plan. This procedure is suggested:

1. Trace the floor plan showing exterior and interior walls, doors and windows, and other features which relate to the climate control system.

2. Locate on the floor plan, equipment to be used for heating, cooling, humidification, and air cleaning.

3. Locate registers, coils, baseboard units or other means of heat exchange on the plan. Use the proper symbols. Steps 1, 2 and 3 are shown in Fig. 24-5.

4. Draw the air return ducts using a hidden line symbol. Also draw the cold air return grilles. (This step is for forced air systems and cooling only.)

5. Draw the supply duct or hot water main and connect it to registers, convectors, etc.

6. Locate thermostats and any other controls required.

7. Identify the size of ducts or pipe and other equipment.

Steps 4, 5, 6 and 7 are shown in Fig. 24-6.

8. Draw schedules required.

9. Add necessary notes, title block, scale and dimensions.

10. Check the drawing for accuracy and to be sure that is complete. Steps 8, 9 and 10 are shown in Fig. 24-7.

REVIEW QUESTIONS — CHAPTER 24

1. The purpose of the climate control plan is _____
_____.

2. Identify four features which should be included on a climate control plan.
   a. _____.
   b. _____.
   c. _____.
   d. _____.

3. The two most common devices used to distribute heat

Climate Control Plan

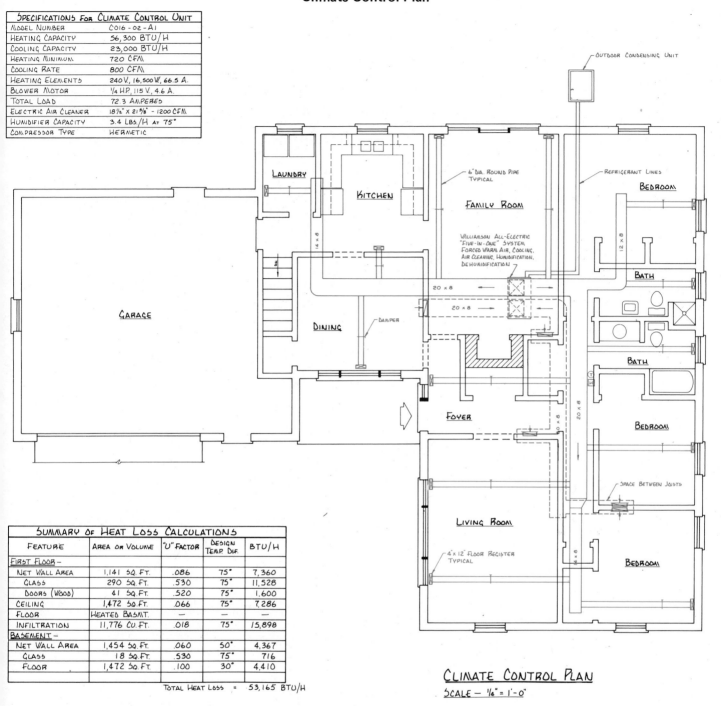

SPECIFICATIONS FOR CLIMATE CONTROL UNIT	
MODEL NUMBER	C016-02-A1
HEATING CAPACITY	56,300 BTU/H
COOLING CAPACITY	23,000 BTU/H
HEATING MINIMUM	720 CFM
COOLING RATE	800 CFM
HEATING ELEMENTS	240 V, 16,500 W, 66.5 A.
BLOWER MOTOR	1/4 H.P., 115 V, 4.6 A.
TOTAL LOAD	72.3 AMPERES
ELECTRIC AIR CLEANER	18½" x 21⅝" - 1200 CFM
HUMIDIFIER CAPACITY	3.4 LBS./H AT 75°
COMPRESSOR TYPE	HERMETIC

SUMMARY OF HEAT LOSS CALCULATIONS				
FEATURE	AREA OR VOLUME	"U" FACTOR	DESIGN TEMP. DIF.	BTU/H
FIRST FLOOR –				
NET WALL AREA	1,141 SQ. FT.	.086	75°	7,360
GLASS	290 SQ. FT.	.530	75°	11,528
DOORS (WOOD)	41 SQ. FT.	.520	75°	1,600
CEILING	1,472 SQ. FT.	.066	75°	7,286
FLOOR	HEATED BASM'T.	—	—	—
INFILTRATION	11,776 CU. FT.	.018	75°	15,898
BASEMENT –				
NET WALL AREA	1,454 SQ. FT.	.060	50°	4,367
GLASS	18 SQ. FT.	.530	75°	716
FLOOR	1,472 SQ. FT.	.100	30°	4,410

TOTAL HEAT LOSS = 53,165 BTU/H

CLIMATE CONTROL PLAN
SCALE – ¼" = 1'-0"

Fig. 24-7. A completed climate control plan with basement and first floor installations shown on the floor plan. The furnace and ductwork may be drawn on the foundation/basement plan and the registers shown on the floor plan if desired.

throughout a house are _____ and _____ .

4. The scale of a residential climate control plan will most likely be _____ .

5. A perimeter heat system is generally specified because _____ .

6. A room should have more than one register when _____ _____ .

7. The two basic types of ductwork systems are:
   a. _____ .

b. _____ .

8. The round pipes which are used to connect the registers to the main heating or cooling ducts are either _____ or _____ inches in diameter.

9. If four 6 in. pipes were to be supplied by a rectangular duct, the duct size should be _____ .

10. A vertical duct is generally called _____ .

11. If a house has three heating zones, it will normally require _____ thermostats.

12. Two types of schedules that may be useful on a climate control plan are:
    a._____.
    b._____.

SUGGESTED ACTIVITIES

1. Locate a house under construction which has the heating equipment in place. Examine the installation carefully and report on the following points:
   a. Type and size of house.
   b. Type of heating system and comfort provisions.

    c. Number of registers or convectors (if hydronic or forced air).
    d. Number of cold air returns.
    e. Size of heating and/or cooling unit.

2. Using a simple plan provided by your instructor or designed by yourself, plan an appropriate climate control system. The system should provide for heating, cooling, humidification, and air cleaning. If one (or more) of these is not necessary in your section of the country, omit it.

3. Draw a pictorial which represents the essential elements of a heating system. You may choose a forced warm air system, hydronic, electric radiant, or heat pump system. Label the parts and prepare the pictorial for display.

Fig. 25-1. This perspective rendering is a true representation of the actual home.   (The Aladdin Co.)

Chapter 25
PRESENTATION DRAWINGS

The purpose of a presentation drawing is to show the finished structure or to present various parts of the building in a form which is more meaningful than blueprints to those who are interested in the structure.

A type of presentation drawing commonly used is the PERSPECTIVE. This shows how the building will look when it is completed, Fig. 25-1. The result gives a three-dimension appearance by showing more than one side of the object. We

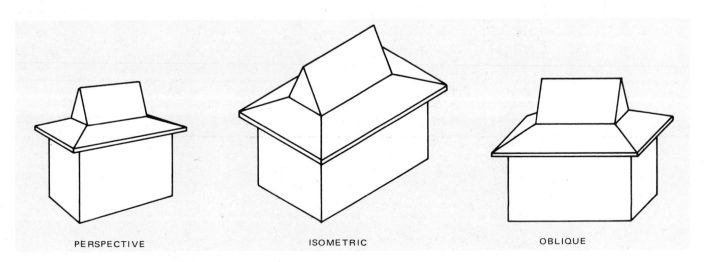

PERSPECTIVE

ISOMETRIC

OBLIQUE

Fig. 25-2. Any of these pictorial methods may be used for presentation drawings, however, the perspective produces a more realistic representation.

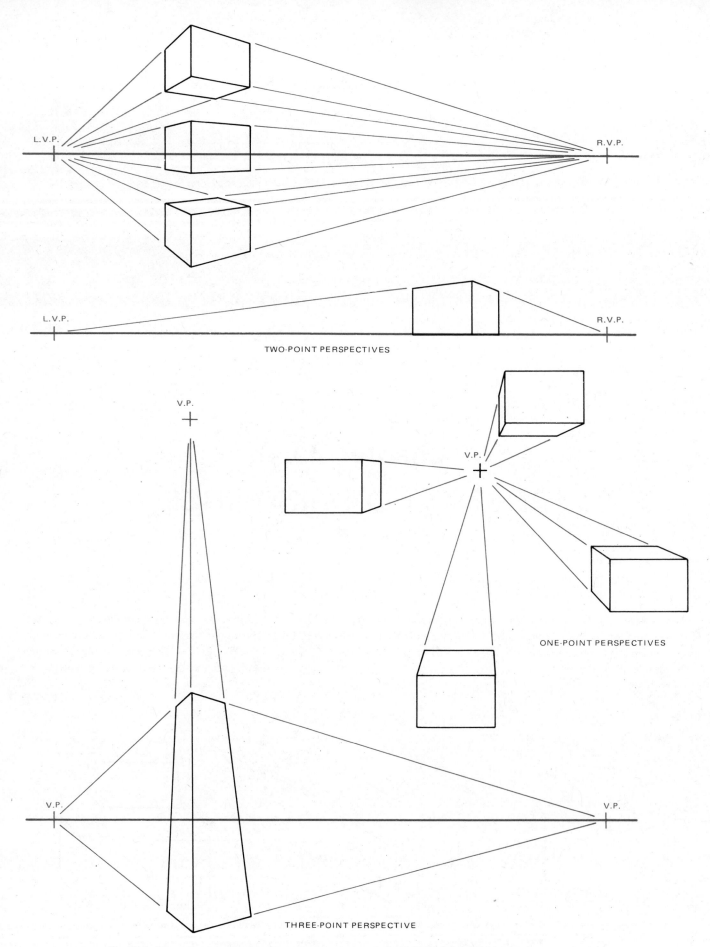

TWO-POINT PERSPECTIVES

L.V.P.

R.V.P.

V.P.

V.P.

ONE-POINT PERSPECTIVES

V.P.

V.P.

THREE-POINT PERSPECTIVE

Fig. 25-3. These three basic types of perspectives are so named for the number of vanishing points which they have. Notice how the object lines converge at the vanishing points.

know that things appear smaller when they are farther away. Perspective drawing applies this and other principles to achieve an accurate representation of the object.

Two other types of pictorial drawings are also used as presentation drawings, ISOMETRIC and OBLIQUE drawings. Fig. 25-2 shows an isometric, oblique and perspective of the same object to illustrate the difference between the three methods. Isometric and oblique drawings do not show a building as realistically as a perspective. However, both are useful for some types of presentations.

PERSPECTIVES

There are three basic types of perspectives: ONE-POINT or parallel perspective, TWO-POINT or angular perspective and THREE-POINT or oblique perspective, Fig. 25-3. One-and-two-point perspectives are commonly used for residential structures. Three-point perspectives are generally used for tall, commercial type buildings not covered by this text, and are therefore of little interest here.

A perspective drawing differs from an orthographic drawing in the position of the station point. THE STATION POINT IS THE LOCATION OF THE OBSERVER'S EYE. See Fig. 25-4. In orthographic projection, the station point is infinitely far away. Therefore, all visual rays or projection lines are parallel to one another. In perspective, the station point is a finite distance (measurable distance) away from the object or picture plane, Fig. 25-5. In all types of drawing the object is drawn as it would appear on an imaginary transparent picture plane. The picture plane could be in front of, behind or pass through the object.

Several terms should be clarified.

GROUND LINE (G. L.). The ground line represents a horizontal plane which is called the ground plane. In the least complex situation, the object to be drawn is positioned so that the foremost corner touches this plane. The ground line is drawn in the elevation part of the perspective layout. There are three parts to a perspective layout - - ELEVATION, PLAN, and PERSPECTIVE DRAWING. When the object touches the picture plane in the plan view, it must also touch the ground line in the perspective drawing. If the object is placed behind the picture plane, then the object will be above the ground line. Objects which pass through the picture plane will also extend below the ground line.

HORIZON LINE (H. L.). The horizon line represents the place where the ground and sky meet. It is therefore drawn in the elevation part of the layout. The distance between the ground line and horizon line represents the height of the observer's eye above the ground. This may be measured at the same scale as the plan view and elevation.

PICTURE PLANE (P. P.). The picture plane is a transparent plane on which the perspective is drawn. It is a vertical plane and therefore perpendicular to the ground plane. It is represented as a line (picture plane line) on the plan part of the layout and normally is located between the object and the station point or the observer's eye.

Any portion of the object which touches the picture plane will be true size in the perspective drawing. Any portion of the

object which is behind the picture plane will appear smaller than scale on the perspective drawing. Parts of the object which are in front of the picture plane (between the plane and the station point) will appear larger than scale in the perspective drawing.

STATION POINT (S.P.). The station point is the location of the observer's eye and therefore the beginning point of the visual rays or sight lines. The rays radiate out from the station point to the object which is represented in the plan view. They pass through the picture plane and locate the various points of the object on the picture plane.

In two-point perspective, the station point is located only in the plan view. In a one-point perspective it is located in the elevation view as well. In both instances, the distance that the station point is positioned from the picture plan may be measured using the same scale as the plan and elevation drawings.

TRUE LENGTH LINE (T.L.). A true length line or true height line as it is frequently called, is established where the object touches the picture plane. This true length line is used to project heights to the perspective drawing. It is always necessary to find at least one true length line in the perspective drawing so that height measurements may be made. If the object does not touch the picture plane then a side may be extended until it touches the picture plane thus establishing a true length corner.

VANISHING POINTS. One, two, and three-point perspectives are named for the number of vanishing points they include. Vanishing points are always located on the horizon line. The sides of the object recede toward the vanishing points and become smaller as they approach the point.

A two-point perspective has a right and left vanishing point (R.V.P. and L.V.P.). The procedure for locating these will be discussed later in this chapter. The one-point perspective has one vanishing point and it need not be formally identified, using popular construction techniques, unless desired.

TWO-POINT PERSPECTIVES

Two-point perspectives are especially appropriate for exterior views. They produce a photo-like result which is quite accurate in detail. An architectural draftsman should be able to draw objects similar to the way they would appear in real life, as this provides an effective way to communicate with prospective clients and other interested parties.

Before beginning to draw a perspective you should be aware that several relationships affect the final perspective drawing and these must be understood and controlled if the resulting drawing is to be satisfactory. These relationships include:

1. THE DISTANCE THE STATION POINT IS FROM THE PICTURE PLANE. Fig. 25-6 shows how the perspective grows larger as the station point is moved farther away from the picture plane. Proper location of the station point is critical to the final perspective. If it is too close, the drawing will be distorted and unrealistic. In most instances, a station point positioned so that it forms a cone of vision between 30 and 45 degrees is desirable. The procedure for determining this cone of vision is to draw a vertical line down from the corner of the

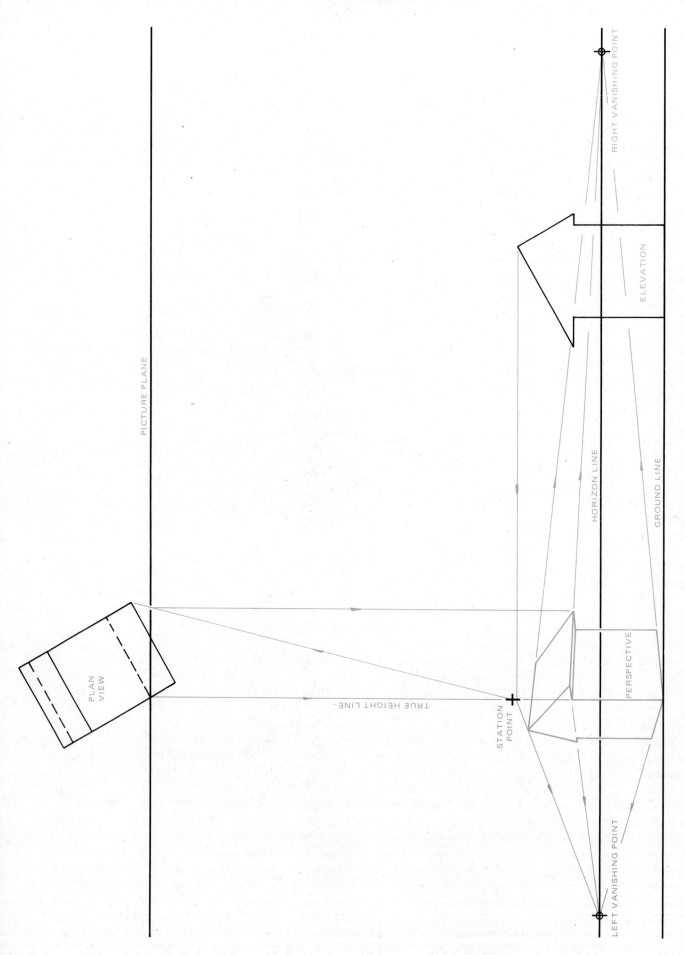

Fig. 25-4. A typical two-point perspective with the parts identified.

PICTURE PLANE

PLAN VIEW

TRUE HEIGHT LINE

STATION POINT

RIGHT VANISHING POINT

ELEVATION

HORIZON LINE

GROUND LINE

PERSPECTIVE

LEFT VANISHING POINT

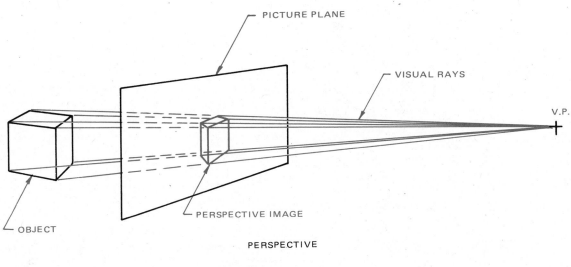

PICTURE PLANE

VISUAL RAYS

V.P.

OBJECT

PERSPECTIVE IMAGE

PERSPECTIVE

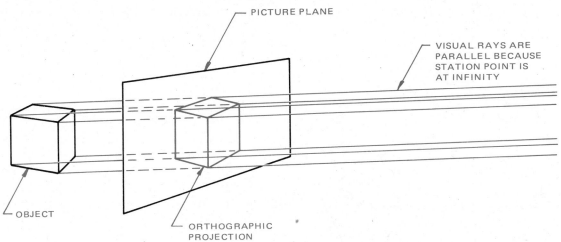

PICTURE PLANE

VISUAL RAYS ARE
PARALLEL BECAUSE
STATION POINT IS
AT INFINITY

OBJECT

ORTHOGRAPHIC
PROJECTION

ORTHOGRAPHIC PROJECTION

Fig. 25-5. In an orthographic projection drawing the station point is infinitely far away. However, it is a finite (measurable) distance in perspective. In both types of drawings the object is drawn as it would appear on an imaginary picture plane.

object which touches the picture plane and place a 30 or 45 degree triangle over the line so that 15° or $22 \ 1/2^O$, depending on the triangle used, fall on either side of the line. When the entire object is within the cone of vision represented by the triangle, the minimum distance has been established for the station point. Fig. 25-7 illustrates the procedure.

The station point may also be moved from side to side. This may improve the viewing position but should not be moved too far either way because distortion will result. The same effect may be accomplished by changing the angle of the plan view with respect to the picture plane, rather than move the station point.

2. THE POSITION OF THE OBJECT WITH RESPECT TO THE PICTURE PLANE. Two factors are at work. First, the angle that the object forms with the picture plane will affect the proportions of the finished drawing, Fig. 25-8. An angle of 30° on one side and 60° on the other is the most common position. This may be varied to suit the particular object.

The second factor relating to the position of the object with respect to the picture plane is whether the object is

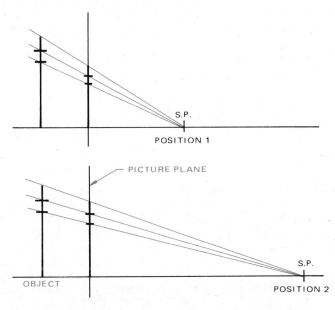

S.P.

POSITION 1

PICTURE PLANE

OBJECT

S.P.

POSITION 2

Fig. 25-6. The image on the picture plane is larger when the station point is moved from position 1 farther away to position 2.

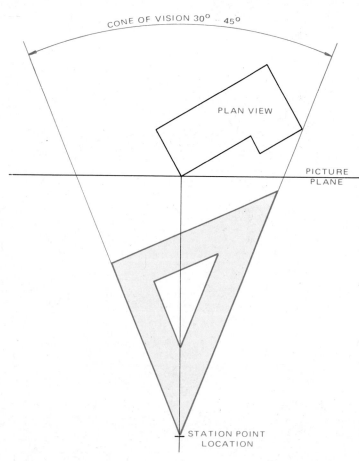

CONE OF VISION 30° 45°

PLAN VIEW

PICTURE
PLANE

STATION POINT
LOCATION

Fig. 25-7. The station point should be far enough away from the picture to include the entire object in the cone of vision.

behind, in front of, or passing through the picture plane, Fig. 25-9. When the object is behind the picture plane, it will appear smaller than one in front of the picture plane. Therefore, size will be dependent on this placement. Also, if the station point is not sufficiently far away when the object is in front of the picture plane distortion is greatly increased and will likely spoil the drawing.

3. THE VERTICAL HEIGHT OF THE STATION POINT OR HORIZON LINE. The finished result will vary greatly depending on the height of the station point. (Remember that this height is the distance from the ground line to the horizon line in a two-point perspective.) The horizon line may be located well above the ground line (20-30 ft.), a conventional height of 5 or 6 ft., on the ground line, or below the ground line, Fig. 25-10. Names have been attached to some of these relative positions such as "bird's eye view," "man's height" and "worm's eye view." The proper height will depend on the particular object and what features are to be emphasized.

These relationships must be kept in mind when laying out a perspective. In starting out only one factor should be varied at a time, to see the effect each has on the final outcome. If several things are changed at once, the effect of a single factor may never be known.

Several methods for drawing two-point perspectives are in use, but the method most frequently used is the COMMON or OFFICE METHOD. Procedure for drawing this type of two-point perspective is:

TWO-POINT PERSPECTIVE DRAWING SEQUENCE

1. Draw the plan view or roof plan of the object on a sheet

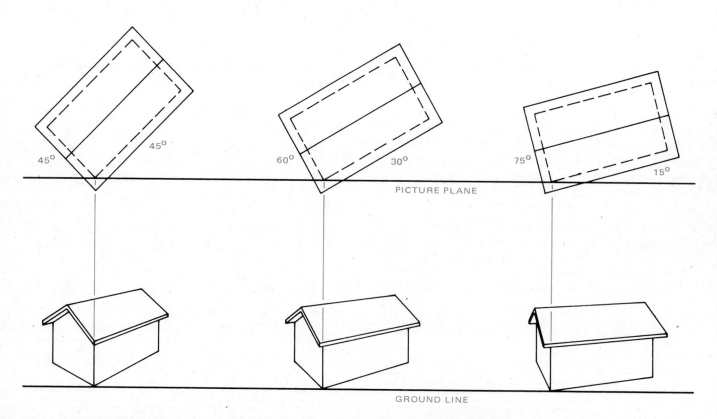

45° 45°

60° 30°

75° 15°

PICTURE PLANE

GROUND LINE

Fig. 25-8. The angle that the object makes with the picture plane may be varied to place emphasis on a certain part of the object.

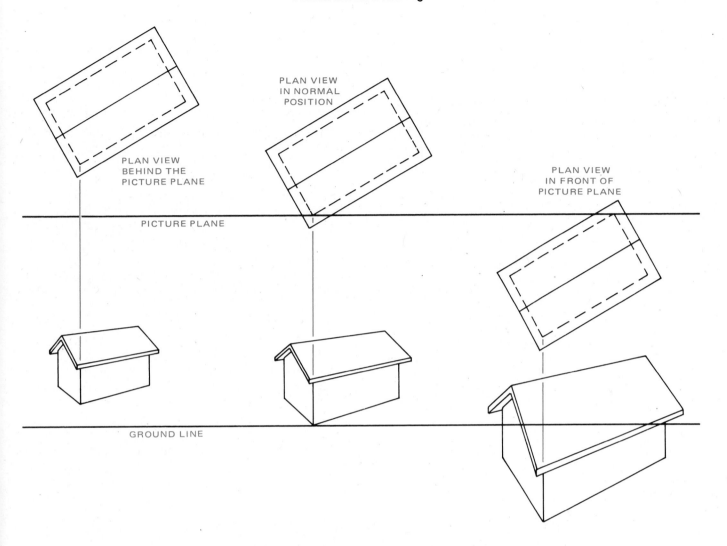

Fig. 25-9. As an object is moved from behind to in front of the picture plane, it increases in size.

of drawing paper. Draw an elevation view on a separate sheet of paper, Fig. 25-11.

2. Secure a large sheet of paper to the drawing table and draw the picture plane line near the top of the sheet, the ground line near the bottom of the sheet and the horizon line the desired distance above the ground line. These lines must be

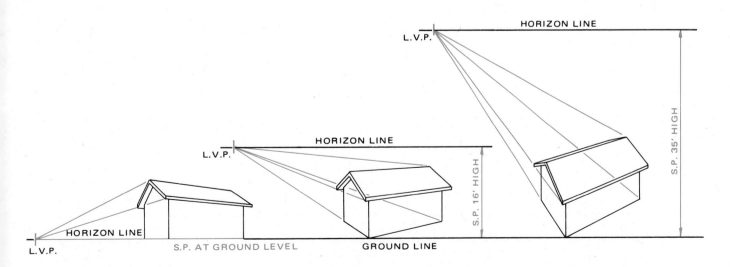

Fig. 25-10. The station point is commonly located either about 30 ft. high, a man's height, or at ground level in residential perspectives.

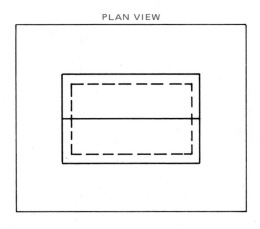

PLAN VIEW

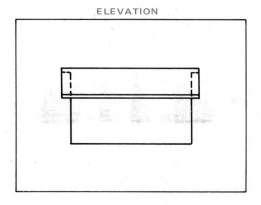

ELEVATION

Fig. 25-11. Procedure for drawing two-point perspective — Step 1.

parallel, Fig. 25-12.

3. Place the plan view or roof plan at a 30° angle with the picture plane so the forward corner touches the picture plane. Locate the elevation on the ground line to the extreme right or left hand side of the paper, Fig. 25-13.

4. Draw a vertical line down from the point where the object touches the picture plane and locate the station point using the 30 or 45 degree cone of vision procedure, Fig. 25-14.

5. Determine the location of the right and left vanishing points by drawing two construction lines from the station point, parallel to the sides of the object (in the plan view), to the picture plane line. Drop a vertical line from the point where each of these lines intersects the picture plane down to the horizon line. This is the location of the right and left vanishing points, Fig. 25-15.

6. Draw a true height line from the corner of the object which touches the picture plane down to the ground line. Project the object height of that corner to the T. L. line. The distance from the ground line to this point is the true height and location of the object corner in the perspective drawing, Fig. 25-16.

7. Determine the location of the other corners of the object by drawing sight lines from the station point to each corner in the plan view. The place where the sight line crosses the picture plane is projected down to the perspective. Each corner of the object will be on one of these lines, Fig. 25-17.

8. The length and vertical location of these corners may be found by projecting the vertical true length from the true

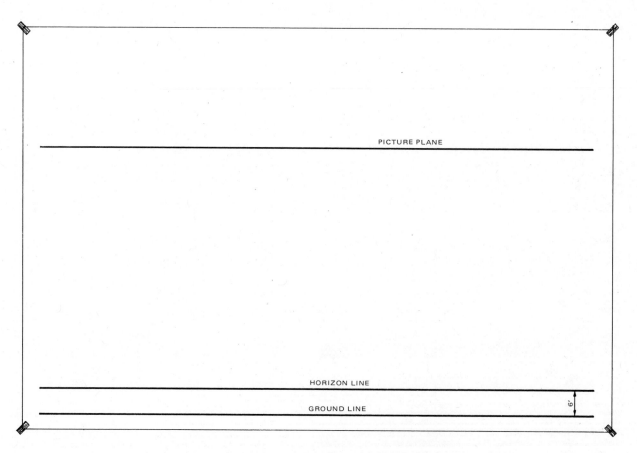

PICTURE PLANE

HORIZON LINE

GROUND LINE

Fig. 25-12. Procedure for drawing two-point perspective — Step 2.

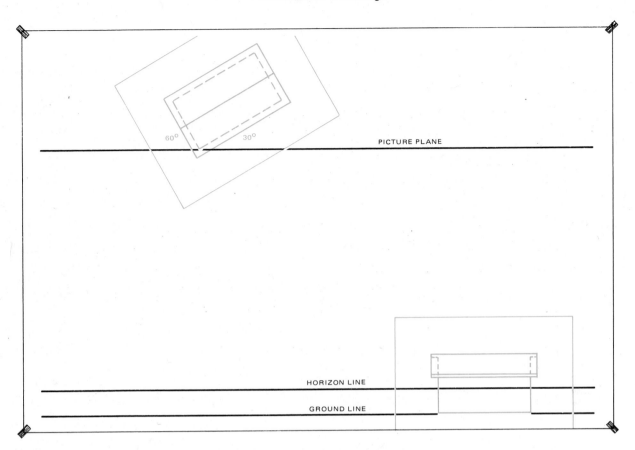

Fig. 25-13. Procedure for drawing two-point perspective — Step 3.

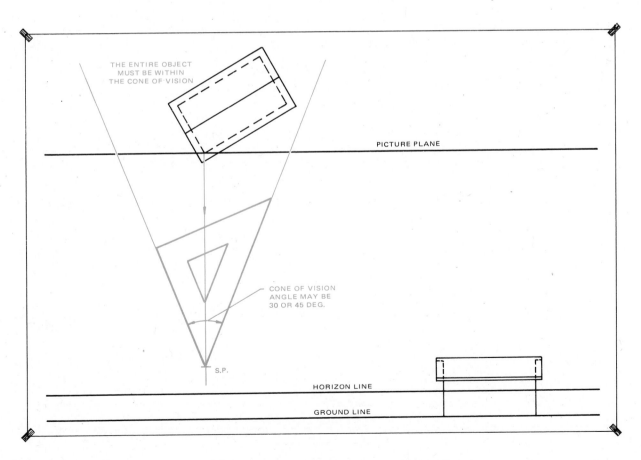

Fig. 25-14. Procedure for drawing two-point perspective — Step 4.

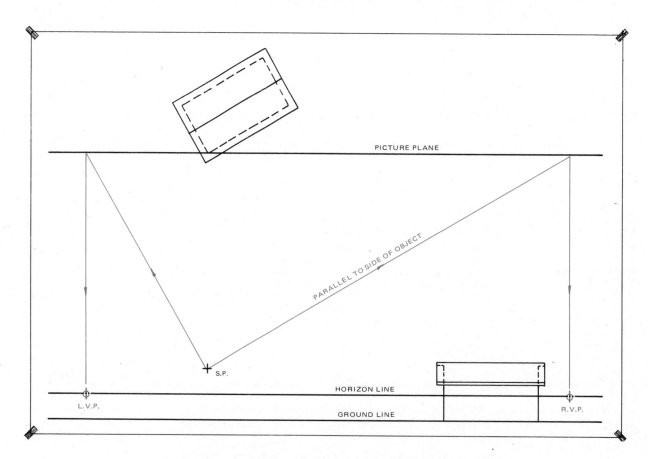

Fig. 25-15. Procedure for drawing two-point perspective — Step 5.

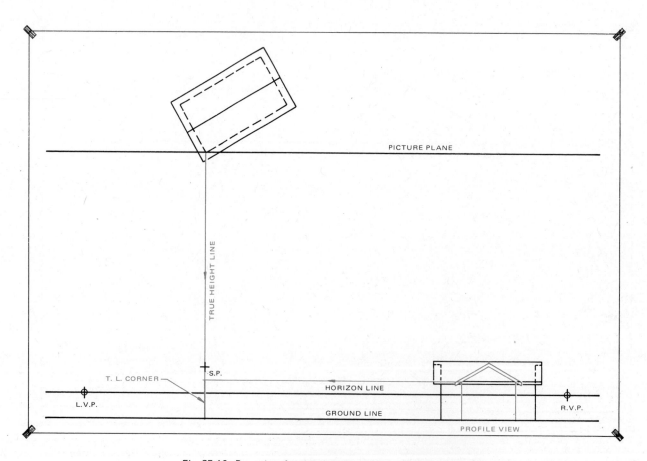

Fig. 25-16. Procedure for drawing two-point perspective — Step 6.

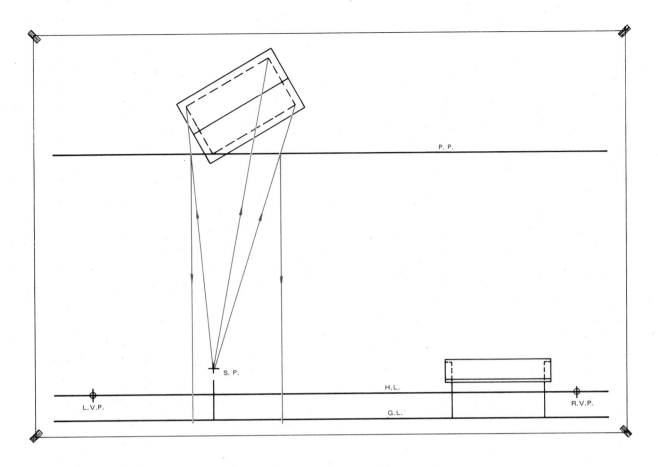

Fig. 25-17. Procedure for drawing two-point perspective — Step 7.

height corner to the vanishing points. Sides of the object which extend away to the right are projected to the right vanishing point and sides which extend to the left are projected to the left vanishing point. Inclined or oblique lines may not be projected to either vanishing point. Their end points must be located and simply connected, Fig. 25-18.

9. The back two sides of the object may be completed by projecting the corners to the vanishing points. Where the projection lines cross is the fourth corner. Check the accuracy of your work by drawing a vertical line down from the point where the sight line for the remaining corner crossed the picture plane. It should pass through the point where the two projection lines cross, Fig. 25-19. This corner will not be visible in the finished drawing.

10. The ridge of this object may be found by extending it until it touches the picture plane. This procedure establishes a new T. L. line. Project the height of the ridge over to the T. L. line and project this point to the right vanishing point. The right vanishing point is used because the ridge extends away to the right, Fig. 25-20.

11. Find the length of the ridge in the perspective by extending sight lines from the station point to the ends of the ridge on the plan view. The point where each sight line crosses the picture plane determines the length of the ridge, Fig. 25-21.

12. The roof overhang height may be determined by drawing a new T. L. line down from the point where the

overhang crosses the picture plane in the plan view. Project the fascia board width on the elevation over to this T. L. line. The top and bottom edge of the fascia passes through these two points. Project these points to the right vanishing point. The length of the fascia may be determined by extending sight lines from the station point to the corners on the plan view. The points where the sight lines cross the picture plane give the horizontal location for each corner, Fig. 25-22.

13. The perspective may be completed by locating the remaining roof corner and connecting the ridge to the three visible corners. The extreme left corner height is drawn by projecting the top and bottom of the fascia board at the front corner to the left vanishing point and dropping the sight line location from the plan view. Where they cross is the roof corner. Connect the roof corner to the roof ridge. Draw the gable trim boards as shown in Step 6 of the procedure. The peak point of the gable under the roof may be located by finding the point on the plan view and dropping a line down to the perspective. Connect the top of the left corner to this peak point, Fig. 25-23.

Establishing a new T. L. line is useful in rapidly determining the height of features which are not located on the principal sides of the object. Examples are roof ridges, overhangs, and chimneys.

A perspective of a more complex house is shown in Fig. 25-24. Note that the same procedures have been followed in drawing this perspective as the previous example.

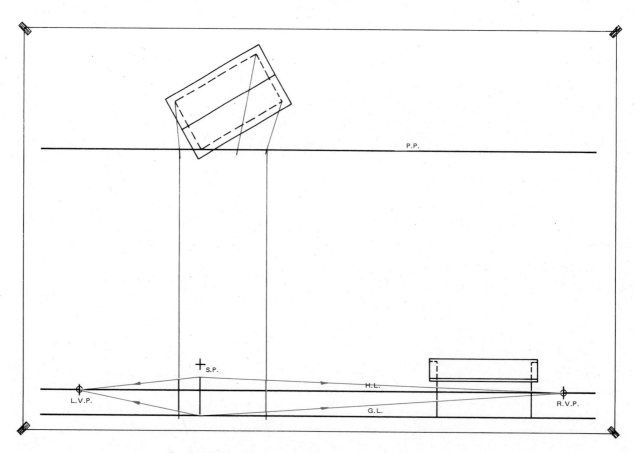

Fig. 25-18. Procedure for drawing two-point perspective — Step 8.

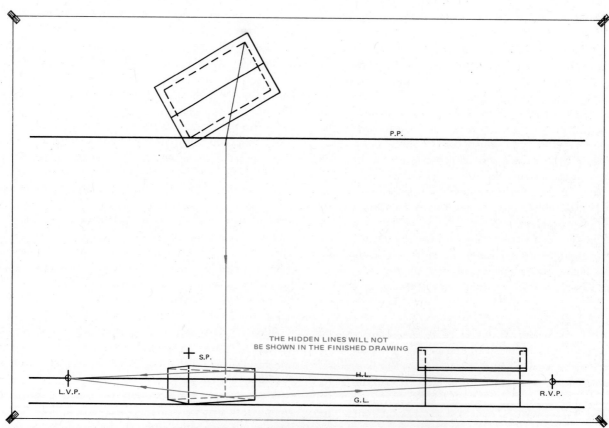

Fig. 25-19. Procedure for drawing two-point perspective — Step 9.

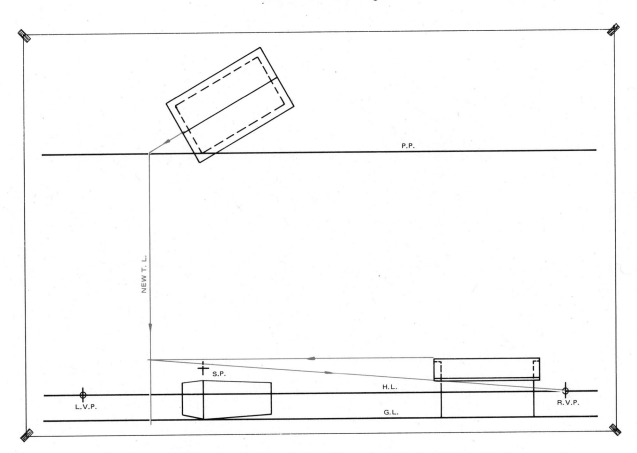

Fig. 25-20. Procedure for drawing two-point perspective — Step 10.

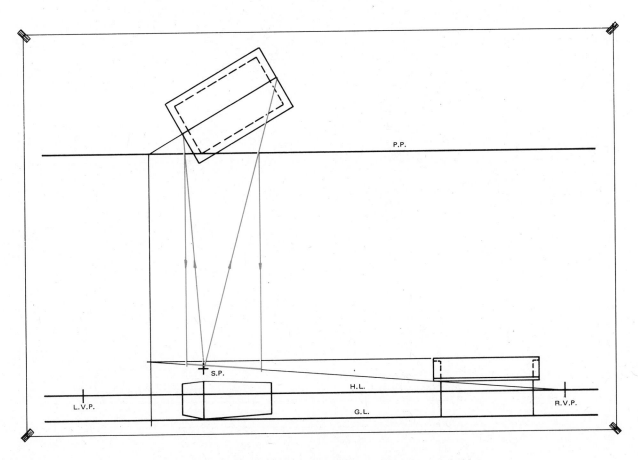

Fig. 25-21. Procedure for drawing two-point perspective — Step 11.

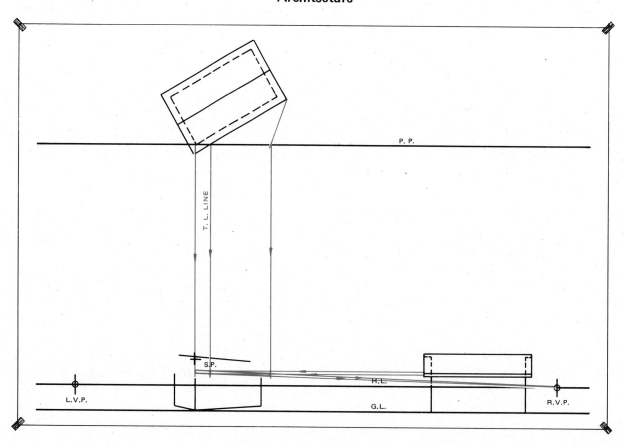

Fig. 25-22. Procedure for drawing two-point perspective — Step 12.

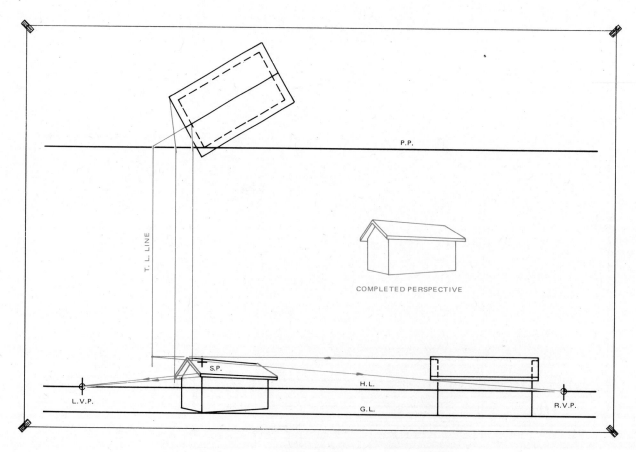

Fig. 25-23. Procedure for drawing two-point perspective — Step 13.

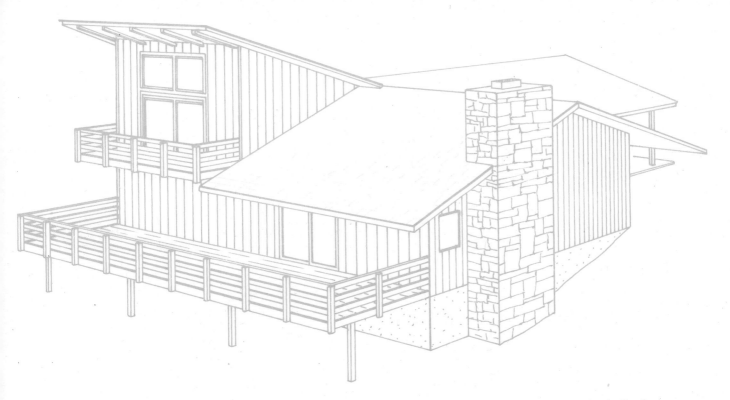

Fig. 25-24. A typical two-point perspective of a small residence. This drawing was made by following the steps previously described.

ONE-POINT PERSPECTIVES

One-point perspectives are not used as frequently as two-point perspectives, but they are well suited for interior drawings. Room and furniture layouts, kitchen cabinet pictorial details and interior space studies are all candidates for one-point perspective techniques, Fig. 25-25. One-point perspective may also be used for some exterior situations, Fig. 25-26. Entries, courts, porches and exterior architectural details may sometimes be shown best in one-point perspective, Fig. 25-27.

The procedure for drawing a one-point perspective using the COMMON or OFFICE METHOD is similar in some respects to the two-point perspective, but there are several

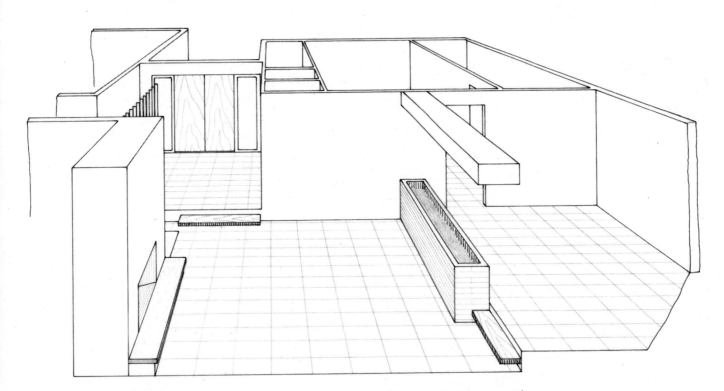

Fig. 25-25. A room layout and space study drawn in one-point perspective.

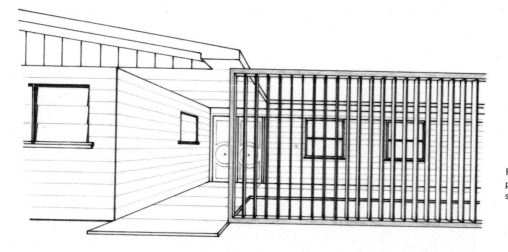

Fig. 25-26. This entrance detail in one-point perspective captures the major design elements as well or better than a two-point perspective could.

differences. One of the most important differences is the selection of an elevation to provide height measurements. Any elevation was acceptable for the two-point perspective, but a specific elevation is necessary for the one-point perspective. Another difference is that the vanishing point does not have to be located unless desired, in drawing the one-point perspective. The main difference is the most frequent position of the plan view which is placed parallel to the picture plane so that the horizontal and profile planes project to the vanishing point.

ONE-POINT PERSPECTIVE DRAWING SEQUENCE

These steps are presented to help clarify the procedure for drawing a common one-point perspective:

1. Select a sheet of drawing paper (about the size of a large drawing board) and draw the plan view near the top left side. With the paper in the same position, draw the right side elevation in the lower right corner. The picture plane should be drawn so that it touches the front of the plan view and the left side of the elevation. Draw the picture plane line in both

Fig. 25-27. An example of the type of exterior layout which lends itself to one-point perspective.

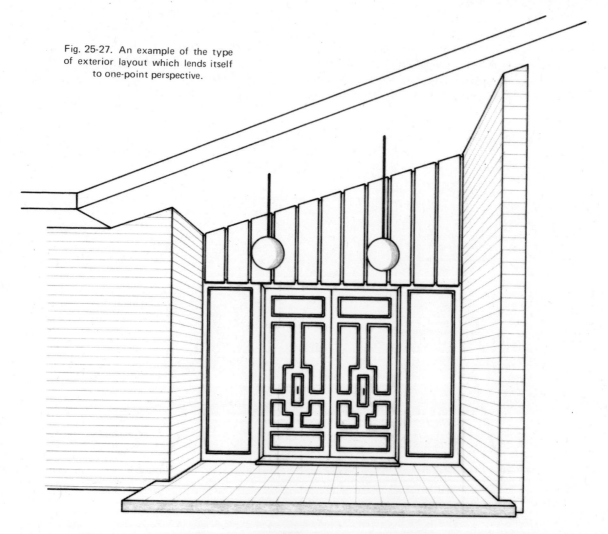

the plan and elevation views. Study Fig. 25-28 carefully to be sure that you understand which elevation is to be drawn. The space between these drawings (lower left corner) is where the perspective will be drawn.

2. Decide the location from where you wish to view the object. If one side should be emphasized more than the other then move the S. P. to the opposite side slightly. Locate the plan view of the S. P. first. Label it S. P.^{p}. This view of the station point indicates how far away and how much to the right or left you are viewing the object. Next, locate the

the points together in the perspective to outline each detail, Fig. 25-31.

5. The floor grid may be located by projecting the points which touch the picture plane in the plan view down to the floor line. The grid line ends which touch the back wall must be located by drawing a sight line from the station point to each end. The place where the sight line crosses the picture plane is the horizontal location of the point. The same procedure is followed in the elevation to determine the vertical location of each point. Connect the points, Fig. 25-32.

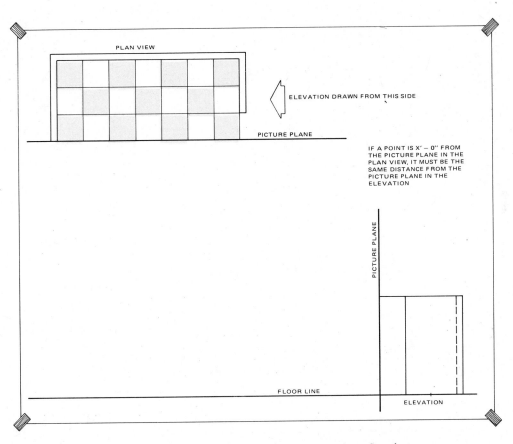

Fig. 25-28. Procedure for drawing one-point perspective – Step 1.

elevation view of the S. P. This view shows the height of the viewing position. The height is measured from the ground line or floor line vertically. Label this station point S. P.^{e} Fig. 25-29. BOTH VIEWS OF THE STATION POINT MUST BE THE SAME DISTANCE FROM THE PICTURE PLANE.

3. Any wall or other feature which touches the picture plane will be true size. You may project these points down from the plan view and across from the elevation. Where the lines cross is the location of each feature, Fig. 25-30.

4. Parts which are behind the picture plane will appear smaller than scale in the perspective. They may be drawn by projecting a sight line from the S. P.^{p} to each point of the detail in the plan view. Where the sight line crosses the picture plane is the horizontal location of the feature. The vertical location is determined by projecting sight lines from the S. P.^{e} to the elevation drawing. Where these lines cross the profile view of the picture plane is the height of each feature. Connect

6. Trace all object lines using the appropriate weight line for each feature. Fig. 25-33 shows the completed perspective.

Fig. 25-34 shows a typical one-point perspective of a kitchen. The procedures involved in this drawing were exactly the same as those shown in the step-by-step drawing sequence.

PERSPECTIVE GRIDS

One of the problems in constructing a two-point perspective is the large size layout. It is not uncommon for the vanishing points to be five feet or more apart for a residence. The use of a perspective grid, Fig. 25-35 will reduce the size work space needed and time required to draw a large perspective. The chief disadvantage is the limited freedom in choosing the position of the station point and placement of the picture plane. Many grid variations are available, but each is for a specific layout and several would be required if the

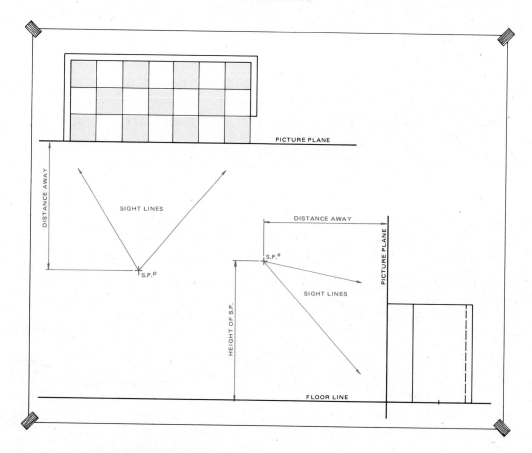

Fig. 25-29. Procedure for drawing one-point perspective — Step 2.

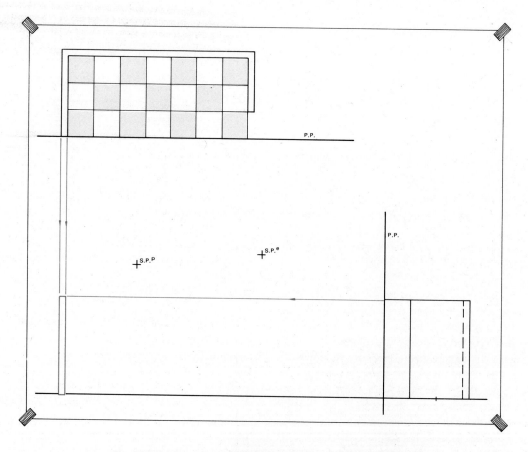

Fig. 25-30. Procedure for drawing one-point perspective — Step 3.

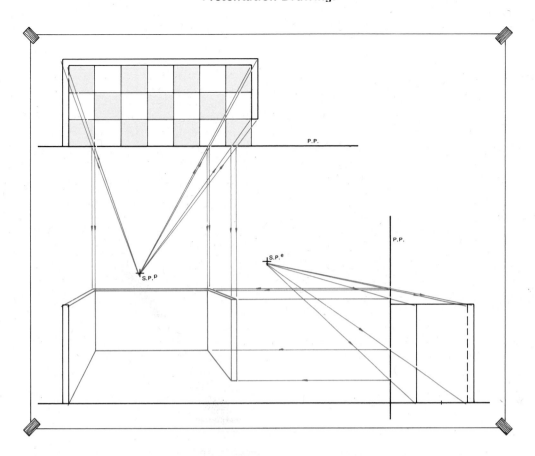

Fig. 25-31. Procedure for drawing one-point perspective — Step 4.

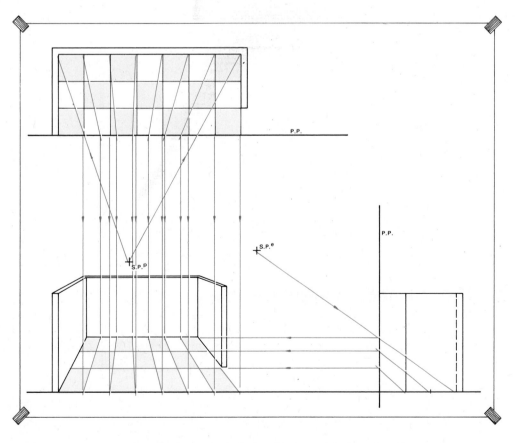

Fig. 25-32. Procedure for drawing one-point perspective — Step 5.

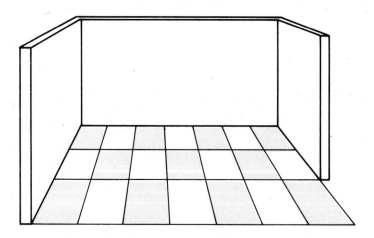

Fig. 25-33. Procedure for drawing one-point perspective — Step 6.

best position were to be achieved in each drawing.

A thorough understanding of perspectives is necessary before grids may be used effectively. A grid will not ensure a successful drawing if the person using it is not skillful in drawing perspectives beforehand.

PERSPECTIVES OF COMPLEX FEATURES

Frequently, objects to be drawn in perspective contain elements which are not parallel to any of the principal reference planes, or are circular, or curved. Such features may appear to be difficult to draw. Described in the following paragraphs are simple techniques which should be helpful:

Objects which are circular such as a round top table or oval area rug may be easily drawn if a series of points or a grid is superimposed over the surface to be drawn, Fig. 25-36. Several points on the curve may be located which define the details of the surface. Locate the points and draw the curve with a French or irregular curve.

Other objects which have a series of soft curves such as a sofa or chair may be drawn as though they had hard and sharp lines and then softened freehand, Fig. 25-37. Still other

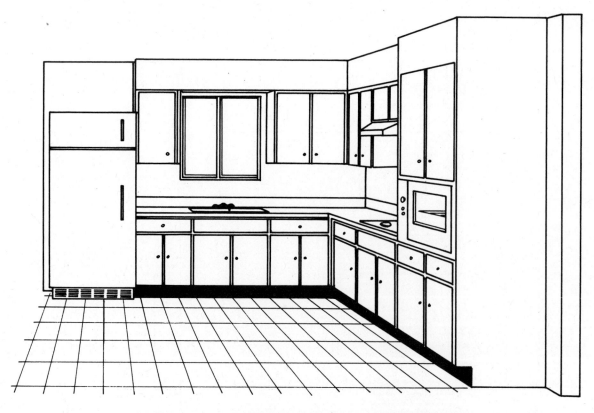

Fig. 25-34. A typical one-point perspective of a kitchen which was
drawn using the procedure presented in steps 1 through 6.
(David Brownlee)

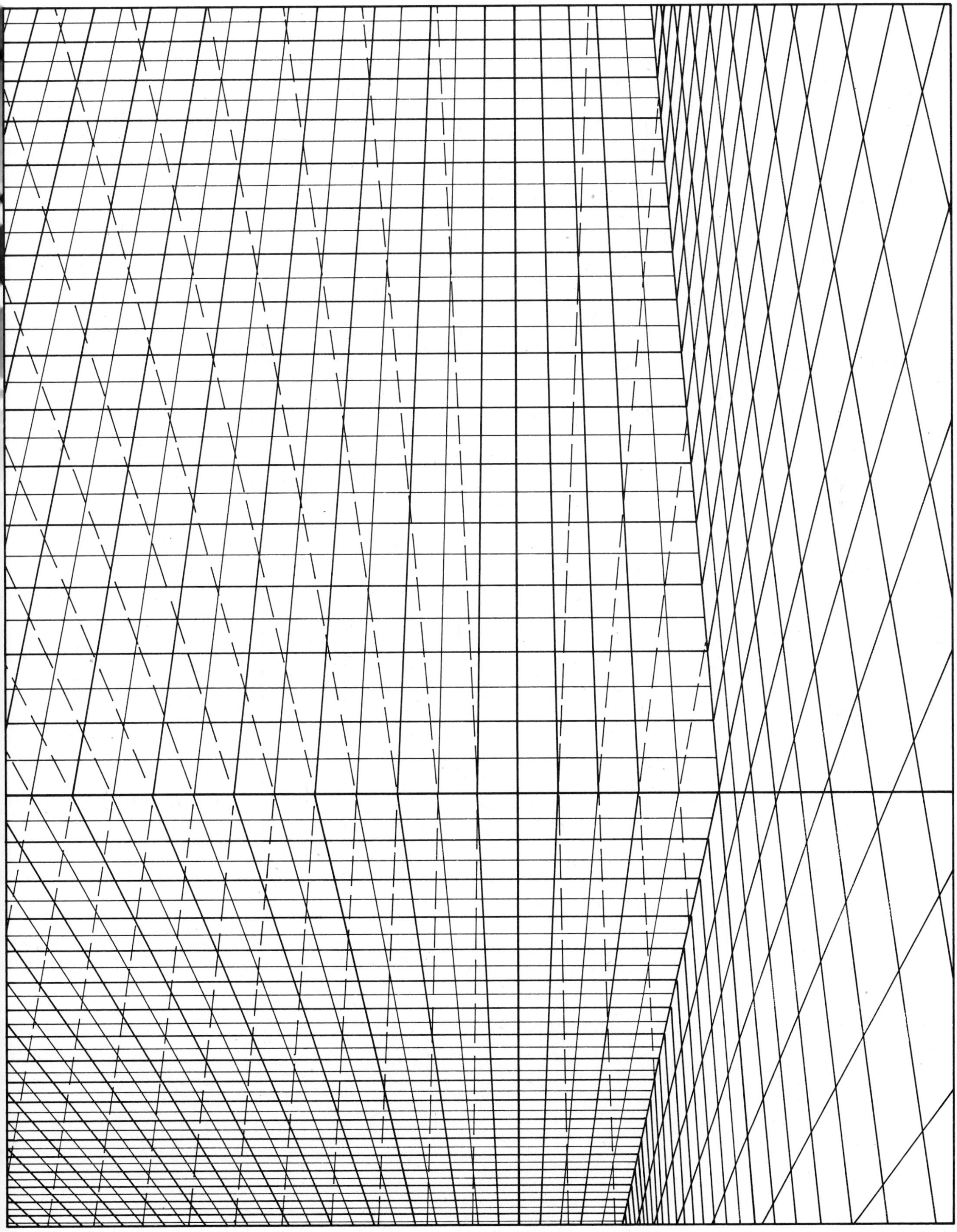

Fig. 25-35. A perspective grid used for drawing two-point perspectives.

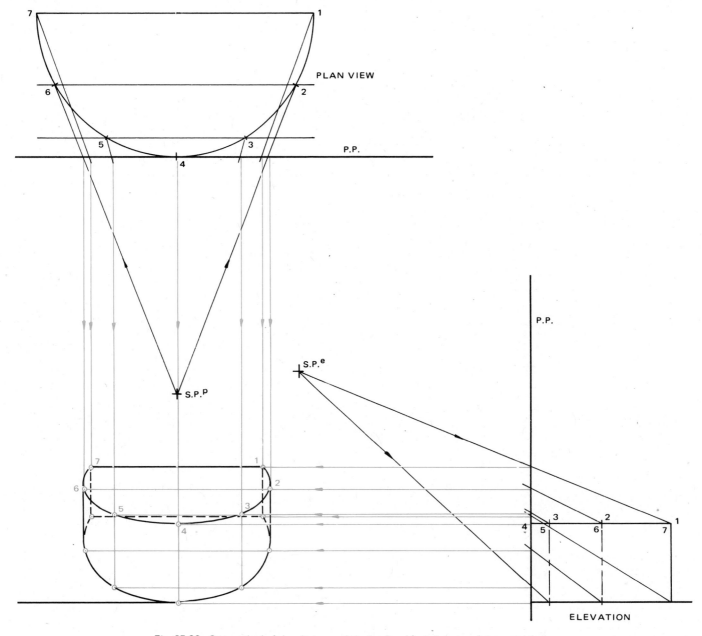

Fig. 25-36. One method of drawing curved or circular objects in one-point perspective.

objects which involve a great deal of free form must be boxed in and then drawn freehand within the space designated.

Remember that the drawing of any object is only a series of connected points. If a sufficient number of points are located and connected accurately, the result will be true to form. Reduce complex objects to simple parts and construct them one at a time rather than try to locate all points and then connect them. Once you understand the procedure used in drawing perspectives you will be able to draw complex objects by applying the procedure over and over again.

RENDERING

Presentation plans require a degree of realism which may be accomplished through rendering. Shades, shadows and textures provide much more realism than just clear sharp lines. For this

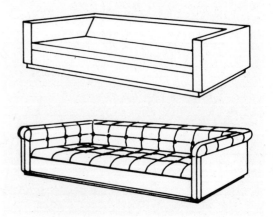

Fig. 25-37. An object with soft curves such as this sofa, may be "blocked in" first and then softened freehand.

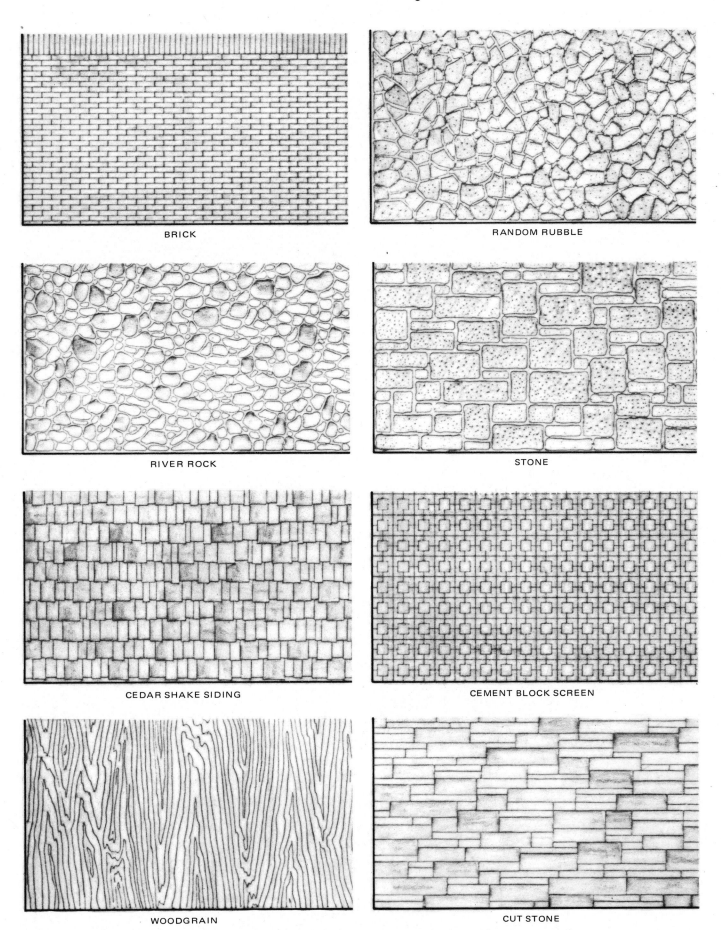

BRICK

RANDOM RUBBLE

RIVER ROCK

STONE

CEDAR SHAKE SIDING

CEMENT BLOCK SCREEN

WOODGRAIN

CUT STONE

Fig. 25-38. Common exterior materials rendered in pencil.

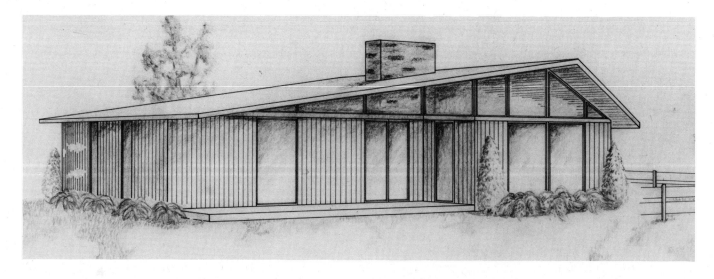

Fig. 25-39. An inked drawing rendered in pencil by a beginning student.

reason, presentation drawings are usually rendered using one or more of the common techniques.

Several methods of rendering are popular. They include:

Pencil	Water Color
Ink	Scratch Board
Tempera	Applique'
Colored Pencils	Air Brush
Magic Markers	Combination of Techniques

Each of these methods has advantages which should be considered before beginning the project.

PENCIL RENDERING

Pencil rendering is popular and probably the easiest. No special materials are needed and the product is highly acceptable if well done. Pencils softer than those generally used for construction type drawings are used. One of the problems encountered in pencil rendering is the difficulty in keeping the drawing clean. A good procedure is to cover the surrounding area to prevent smudges and smears.

Several common exterior materials are shown in Fig. 25-38 to illustrate the effect which may be achieved with pencil rendering. An ink drawing rendered in pencil by a student is shown in Fig. 25-39.

INK RENDERING

Renderings to be used for reproduction are best done in ink. Lines are sharper and fine detail is possible with ink, Fig. 25-40. Ink can be used to shade areas also. This may be

Fig. 25-40. A freehand pen and ink drawing.

Fig. 25-41. A pen and ink drawing with brushed ink and pencil shading.

accomplished with a series of parallel lines, dot pattern or solid shading. Drawing inks are produced in a broad spectrum of color which are also quite useful in rendering. Fig. 25-41 shows a pen and ink rendering with brushed and pencil shading. Various techniques and materials are often combined in a single rendering.

WATER COLOR RENDERING

Water color rendering is one of the most effective forms, Fig. 25-42. Vivid colors or broad expanses of light wash (very little paint with lots of water) are possible with water color. This type of rendering is one of the most difficult to execute.

Fig. 25-42. A faithful reproduction of a house in water colors. (Roy E. Zollinger)

Fig. 25-43. Water color rendering produces a very realistic effect.

Practice and patience are necessary to develop this technique. A water color rendering is shown in Fig. 25-43.

TEMPERA RENDERING

Tempera paint is also a type of water soluble paint. It differs from water color (transparent) in that it is opaque. Tempera is frequently used for monotone renderings as shown in Fig. 25-44. Advantages of this technique include a broad selection of colors which may be obtained by mixing and the ease of mending mistakes if the brush slips or the color is not satisfactory.

COLORED PENCIL RENDERING

Colored pencils may be used to obtain satisfactory renderings. Light shades or strong strokes are easily accomplished. Even the beginning student can achieve success with this technique, Fig. 25-45. Either regular colored pencils or water

color pencils may be used. Drawings rendered in water color pencil may be presented simply as a colored pencil rendering or transformed into a water color by adding water with a brush.

MAGIC MARKER RENDERING

Certain types of presentation drawings may be effectively rendered using magic markers or felt tip pens. Presentation plot plans are frequently rendered using these pens. The result is distinct and differs greatly from other techniques. Fine detail may be accomplished by mixing other techniques with the marker. Fig. 25-46 shows a perspective loosely rendered in felt tip pen.

SCRATCH BOARD RENDERING

Scratch board rendering produces a drawing with a great deal of character. Lines are scratched through a special black

Fig. 25-44. A monotone type rendering in tempera.   (The Aladdin Co.)

Fig. 25-45. The basic technique used in this rendering is colored pencil. It has been combined with ink and water colors.   (Ed Fegan)

Fig. 25-46. Felt tip pen has been used in this loose but effective rendering.

Fig. 25-47. Scratch board renderings.

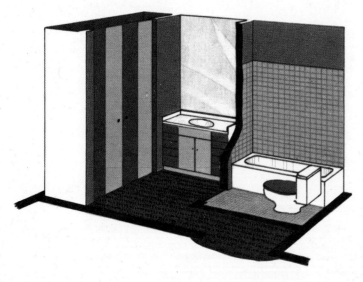

Fig. 25-48. A bathroom design rendered in applique' and ink.

coated illustration board type material. The result is a drawing of white lines on a black background. Such a rendering commands attention from the viewer. Fig. 25-47 shows two scratch board renderings.

APPLIQUE' RENDERING

Applique' rendering is accomplished by attaching a pressure sensitive transparent film over a drawing. The film may be a series of dots, lines, symbols or color. Several manufacturers are producing these films and it is possible to achieve striking results with them. Fig. 25-48 shows a drawing rendered using applique' and ink.

AIR BRUSH RENDERING

Air brush renderings are frequently produced by professional illustrators. Again, a great deal of practice is required to be able to produce a fine quality rendering using this technique.

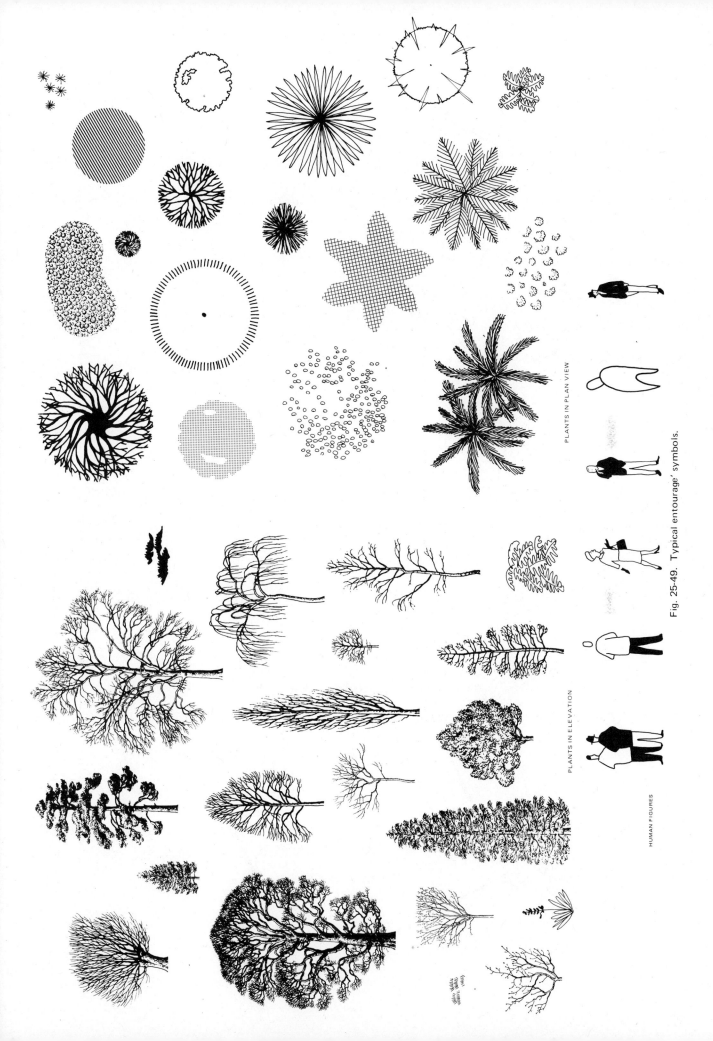

PLANTS IN PLAN VIEW

PLANTS IN ELEVATION

HUMAN FIGURES

Fig. 25-49. Typical entourage' symbols.

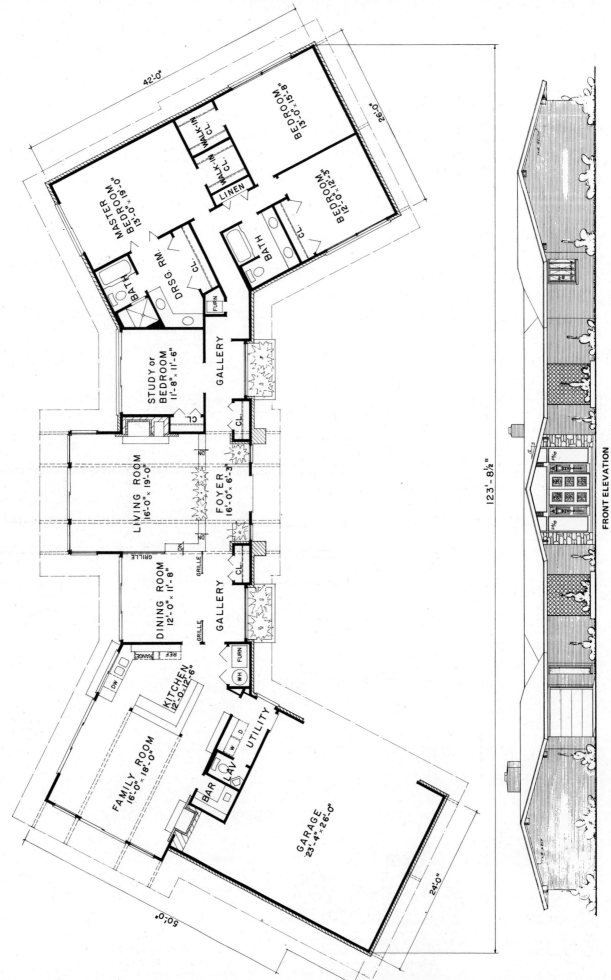

MASTER
BEDROOM
13'-0" × 19'-0"

WALK-IN CL.

WALK-IN CL.

LINEN

BEDROOM
13'-0" × 15'-8"

BEDROOM
12'-0" × 12'-3"

BATH

DRSG. RM.

CL.

CL.

FURN

BATH

CL.

STUDY or
BEDROOM
11'-8" × 11'-6"

GALLERY

CL.

CL.

42'-0"

26'-0"

LIVING ROOM
16'-0" × 19'-0"

FOYER
16'-0" × 6'-3"

DN

DN

GRILLE

DINING ROOM
12'-0" × 11'-8"

GALLERY

GRILLE

GRILLE

FURN

WH

CL.

123'-8½"

RANGE

REF

DW

KITCHEN
12'-0" × 12'-6"

FAMILY ROOM
16'-0" × 18'-0"

W   D

UTILITY

BAR

AV

GARAGE
23'-4" × 26'-0"

50'-0"

24'-0"

FRONT ELEVATION

Fig. 25-50. A presentation floor plan and elevation used to sell the house shown in the photo on the top of page 397.   (Scholz Homes, Inc.)

Fig. 25-50. (Continued) Home shown in the floor plan on page 396.

An air brush is simply an air nozzle which sprays paint. If examined closely, you will find the surface of the rendering is covered with many small dots of paint which form subtle shades and shadows. Areas not to be sprayed should be blocked out with paper or rubber cement since it is difficult to accurately control the spray.

Techniques described here represent the majority used for rendering presentation plans. Each requires a certain amount of artistic ability and skill to produce a satisfactory rendering. The ability to prepare renderings is well worth developing.

ENTOURAGE'

Entourage' (pronounced "n-tur-ahge") refers to surroundings such as trees, shrubs, cars, people, and terrain. These features add to the realism of a drawing and show an architectural structure in its proper setting. Entourage' is usually drawn to represent objects in simplified form rather than trying to make them look exactly as they would appear. Architects usually develop a personal style of drawing entou-

rage'. For those who feel inadequate in drawing these features; appliques, rub-on symbols, and rubber stamps are available which may be used to add a professional appearance to their drawings. Fig. 25-49 shows some entourage' symbols that are representatives of those commonly used by architects. Always draw surroundings to the proper scale. Information on appropriate sizes may be obtained from the Architectural Graphic Standards.

TYPES OF PRESENTATION PLANS

Several types of presentation drawings are used to represent a structure. Exterior and interior perspectives, rendered elevations, presentation plot plans, floor plans, and sections are commonly prepared to help "sell" the plan to a prospective client. These drawings are designed to present the structure to the layman who may not understand a set of construction drawings in an accurate and honest manner. They may also be used for advertising and other purposes, Fig. 25-50.

Fig. 25-51. A two-point perspective of an average home accurately represented. (Roy E. Zollinger)

Fig. 25-52. This rendering emphasizes the luxury of this modern home.   (Larry Campbell)

EXTERIOR PERSPECTIVES

The exterior perspective should present the structure as accurately as possible. Distortion, if permitted, could misrepresent the appearance and create a false impression. Fig. 25-51 shows an average home which is faithfully represented. Fig. 25-52 shows an elaborate home rendered in such a manner that the exquisite design is emphasized. Both examples are accurate representations of the actual homes.

RENDERED ELEVATIONS

An elevation is an orthographic type drawing which shows no depth. The addition of material symbols, trees and other surrounding features can transform an elevation into an effective presentation drawing, Fig. 25-53. Even though no depth is shown in the structure, the feeling of depth is accomplished through shades, shadows, textures and surroundings. Presentation elevations are frequently used instead of exterior perspectives because they are faster to draw and if presented well, are usually quite satisfactory, Fig. 25-54.

PRESENTATION PLOT PLANS

Presentation plot plans are used to show the site and structure relationship. This is essentially a plan view of the site showing important topographical features, house location, and property boundaries. The presentation plot plan gives a "bird's

Presentation Drawings

Fig. 25-53. Presentation elevations are sometimes used to represent a residential structure rather than a perspective, as this example of the home in Fig. 25-52 shows.

Fig. 25-54. A presentation elevation rendered in colored pencil by a student. (A. Sewell)

Fig. 25-55. A mixed media rendering of a plot plan. (Midwestern Consulting, Inc.)

Fig. 25-56. Presentation plot plan of residence in Fig. 25-52 drawn over elevation of the plot.

Lower floor plan

Upper floor plan

Fig. 25-57. A presentation floor plan with emphasis on space and furniture. (Fruehauf Corp.)

eye" view of the layout and provides an opportunity to show off the type of living afforded by the surroundings.

Several styles of presentation plot plans are possible. Figs. 25-55 and 25-56 show two different treatments.

PRESENTATION FLOOR PLANS

Presentation floor plans may be used to emphasize features such as furniture arrangement, area utilization and conve-

Fig. 25-58. This presentation floor plan of the home in Fig. 25-52 is rendered in ink and colored chalk. (Larry Campbell)

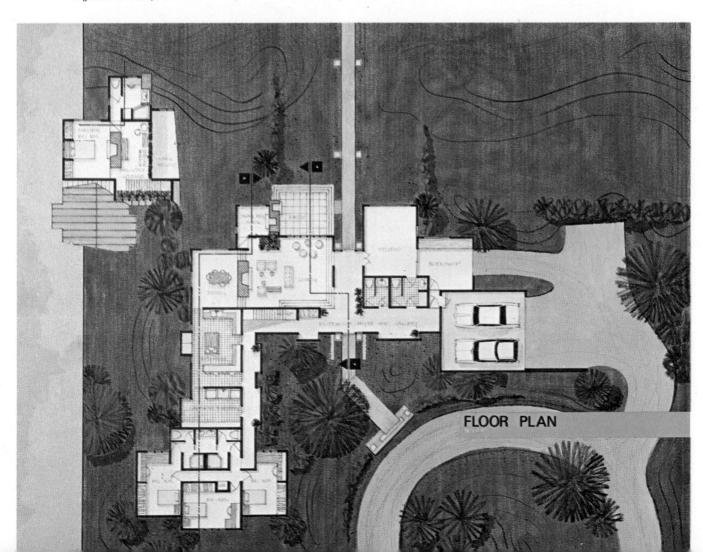

FLOOR PLAN

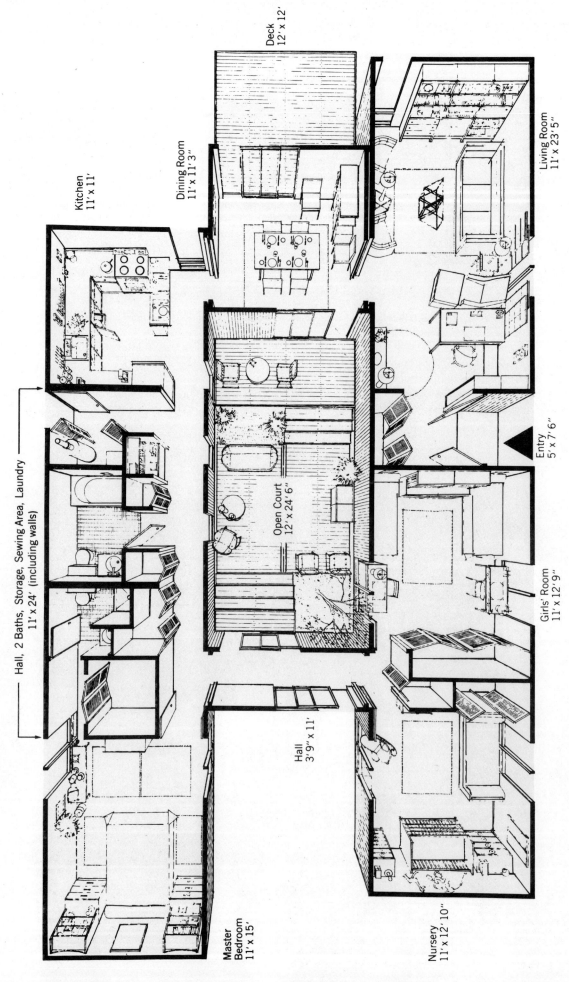

Kitchen
11' x 11'

Dining Room
11' x 11' 3"

Deck
12' x 12'

Living Room
11' x 23' 5"

Hall, 2 Baths, Storage, Sewing Area, Laundry
11' x 24' (including walls)

Open Court
12' x 24' 6"

Entry
5' x 7' 6"

Master
Bedroom
11' x 15'

Hall
3' 9" x 11'

Girls' Room
11' x 12' 9"

Nursery
11' x 12' 10"

Fig. 25-59. A pictorial type floor plan is frequently used to accomplish a more realistic presentation of the layout. (American Plywood Assoc.)

Fig. 25-60. Rendered sections of residence shown in Fig. 25-52 provide an effective means of illustrating complex structures. (Larry Campbell)

niences, Fig. 25-57. Color may be utilized to call attention to similar features or to separate areas. The color should be functional if possible rather than used just to "color" the drawings. The specific use intended for the drawing should be evident by the presentation technique utilized. Figs. 25-58 and 25-59 show contrasting styles of presentation floor plans.

RENDERED SECTIONS

Frequently, a complex structure requires a longitudinal section to emphasize the various levels. Such a plan is effective in communicating the internal layout of the house. Fig. 25-60 is an example of such a drawing. The realistic way in which information is presented helps to clarify the plan.

Presentation plans are being used more and more to communicate ideas. People understand architectural ideas better if they are presented in a manner in which they are accustomed. Presentation plans do just that and are therefore very useful, Fig. 25-61. They do require talents and skills which technical drawings do not, but they are definitely an integral part of architectural drawing and should be mastered by the architect.

Fig. 25-61. Two fine examples of presentation elevations rendered in ink. Note the attention given to fine details.

REVIEW QUESTIONS — CHAPTER 25

1. Name three types of pictorial drawings that are used as presentation drawings.
   a. _____ .
   b. _____ .
   c. _____ .
2. Identify the three basic types of perspectives.
   a. _____ .
   b. _____ .
   c. _____ . .
3. The type of perspective commonly used for exterior views is _____ .
4. The ground line is drawn in the _____ part of the perspective layout.
5. The distance between the ground line and the horizon line represents _____ .
6. An edge in the perspective is true height when _____ _____ .
7. Parts of the object which are in front of the picture plane appear _____ than scale.
8. The position of the observer's eye is called the _____ _____ .
9. How is the distance that an observer is standing away from the picture plane shown in a perspective layout? _____ .
10. All heights on a perspective must be measured on the _____ line.
11. Vanishing points are always located on the _____ line.
12. A two-point perspective has _____ vanishing points.
13. If a station point were moved from 20 ft. to 30 ft. away from the picture plane, the perspective would _____ _____ in size.
14. The standard angle which objects are usually placed with respect to the picture plane is _____ .
15. One may determine the closest place to stand to draw a perspective by _____ .
16. If the station point is too close to the picture plane the perspective may be spoiled because of _____ _____ .
17. Identify three common heights used in drawing two-point perspectives.
   a. _____ .
   b. _____ .
   c. _____ .
18. If the station point is moved closer to the picture plane, how will this affect the distance the vanishing points are apart in a two-point perspective? _____ .
19. One-point perspectives are well suited for _____ type views.
20. Heights are determined in one-point perspective by _____ .
21. The chief disadvantage of using a perspective grid is _____ .
22. The construction technique that may be used to draw a circular object in perspective is _____ .

23. The purpose of rendering is _____ .
24. Identify six common methods of rendering.
   a. _____ .
   b. _____ .
   c. _____ .
   d. _____ .
   e. _____ .
   f. _____ .
25. The most popular rendering technique is _____ _____ .
26. Renderings to be used for reproduction are best done in _____ .
27. A rendering which uses a pressure sensitive transparent film over the drawing is called _____ _____ rendering.
28. Professional illustrators frequently use _____ _____ rendering for their work.
29. What is entourage'? _____ .
30. Identify five types of presentation plans which may be used to "sell" a residential structure.
   a. _____ .
   b. _____ .
   c. _____ .
   d. _____ .
   e. _____ .

SUGGESTED ACTIVITIES

1. Using a simple straight-line object supplied by your instructor, draw several two-point perspectives from different distances and positions. Identify how far away and how high the station point was in each drawing.
2. Draw a two-point perspective of a small residence. Trace the finished drawing on vellum in ink. Do not render this drawing.
3. Look through old issues of Better Homes and Gardens, House and Home, House Beautiful, Home Modernizing Guide, or similar magazines and cut out perspective drawings of homes. Mount these pictures for display.
4. Select a large photograph (not a drawing) of a home or building from a magazine and mount it on a piece of illustration board or stiff paper. Locate the horizon line and vanishing points. Label.
5. Place a piece of tracing paper over the photograph used in No. 4 above and make a rendering in pencil. Do the drawing freehand. Compare your drawing with the photograph.
6. Collect renderings of architectural structures from magazines. Display these for style and inspiration in the drawing room.
7. Select a simple construction type floor plan and develop a presentation floor plan which emphasizes the furniture layout.
8. Render the two-point perspective that you drew in No. 2 above. Use a technique specified by your instructor or one of your choice.
9. Draw a one-point perspective of one of the rooms in the

house used for the presentation floor plan or one of your own design. Illustrate the furniture in your perspective.

10. Render the interior perspective above in color. Mount it on illustration board if drawn on paper. Display your drawing on the bulletin board.

11. Develop a presentation plot plan showing property boundaries, house location, drive, walks and topographical features. Present the plan in color and display.

Architectural models are used for both residential and community planning.

Chapter 26
ARCHITECTURAL MODELS

An architectural model provides the ultimate means of showing how the finished home will look in all three dimensions. The model may be viewed from any position and greatly increases the amount of information communicated. Models are useful in checking the finished appearance of an architectural design and "selling" a design to a client.

TYPES OF MODELS

Several types of models are used to represent architectural structures. One type is the SMALL SCALE SOLID MODEL, Fig. 26-1. This is frequently used to show how a building will relate to surrounding buildings. Scales used range from $1/32'' = 1' - 0''$ to $1/8'' = 1' - 0''$. Very little detail is shown on solid models.

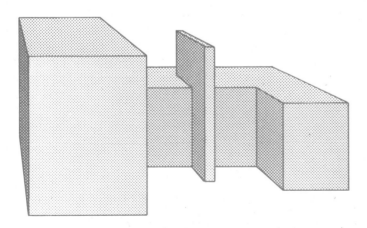

Fig. 26-1. A small scale solid model is frequently used to study the mass of a building or show its relation to surrounding buildings.

STRUCTURAL MODELS are frequently used to show features of a residence. All structural materials used should be cut to scale and proper building methods represented, Fig. 26-2. Structural models are usually $1/2'' = 1' - 0''$ or $1'' = 1' - 0''$ scale. If the scale is too small, the materials will be difficult to work with. Since the purpose of a structural model is to show the basic construction, most of the siding and roofing materials are left off to expose the structural aspects, Fig. 26-3. This type of model is useful when unique construction procedures are to be used, Fig. 26-4.

Fig. 26-2. A structural model under construction using materials cut to the proper scale. (Harry Smith)

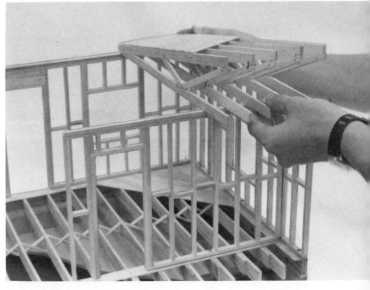

Fig. 26-3. Structural models show the framing of a building.

Fig. 26-4. This A-frame cottage has unique construction. Students are working as a group on this model. (Harry Smith)

Most residential models are PRESENTATION MODELS. The purpose of a presentation model is to show appearance of the finished building as realistically as possible, Fig. 26-5. A primary concern is to select materials that will closely resemble materials used in actual construction. Presentation models are usually 1/4'' = 1' – 0'' scale. They may be larger or smaller depending on the amount of detail desired, size of the structure, and funds available for model construction.

MATERIALS USED IN MODEL CONSTRUCTION

There are several basic materials which are commonly used for architectural model construction. Some model builders prefer Styrofoam sheets. This material is easy to cut and may be made to resemble various exterior building materials. Styrofoam is easy to glue and may be painted with various kinds of paint. However, it is soft and may be scratched or easily broken.

Another popular material for architectural models is cardboard or illustration board. This material is easy to obtain, glues well and may be painted with almost any type of paint. Two disadvantages are: Cardboard warps easily and it must be cut with a knife or razor type blade rather than by sawing. Pin holes are also more visible than with other materials.

A popular material for building models of homes is balsa wood. Balsa is available in a wide variety of sizes and is easy to cut with a sharp knife. It receives a finish well, and may be sawed or sanded and scored to represent exterior materials. A balsa model does not warp as much as cardboard and is stronger.

PROCEDURE FOR CONSTRUCTING BALSA MODEL

The following procedure (typical) is presented as an aid to building a presentation type balsa model with a removable roof:

1. Obtain a set of plans for the home which is to be built. If the plans are not 1/4'' = 1' – 0'' then they should be drawn to that scale. (In some instances it may be desirable to build a model to some other scale, but the majority of residential models are 1/4'' = 1' – 0'' scale.) In most instances only the floor plan, Fig. 26-6, and elevations, Fig. 26-7, will be needed to build the model. However, if the building site is not flat a plot plan should be drawn using the same scale as the other plans. It is usually not necessary to draw the entire site at 1/4'' = 1' – 0'' scale, but only the portion represented by the model. If the roof is complex, it may be desirable to develop a roof plan, Fig. 26-8, to aid in building the roof.

Fig. 26-5. Interior arrangement is frequently as important as exterior appearance in a residential model.

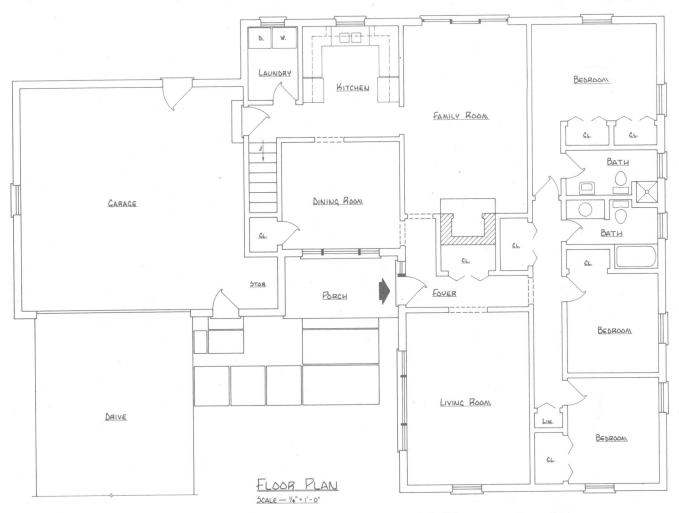

FLOOR PLAN
SCALE — 1/4" = 1'-0"

Fig. 26-6. A floor plan drawn at 1/2'' = 1' — 0'' scale to be used in building a presentation model.

Fig. 26-7. A front and left side elevation of the house shown in the floor plan.

LEFT SIDE ELEVATION
SCALE — 1/4" = 1'-0"

FRONT ELEVATION
SCALE — 1/4" = 1'-0"

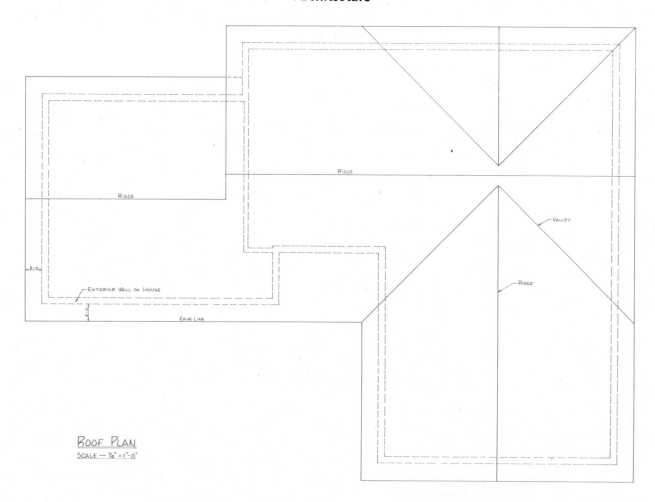

RIDGE

RIDGE

VALLEY

RIDGE

8-0"

EXTERIOR WALL OF HOUSE

EAVE LINE

ROOF PLAN
SCALE — ¼" = 1'-0"

Fig. 26-8. Roof plan of the same house to be used in constructing the model roof.

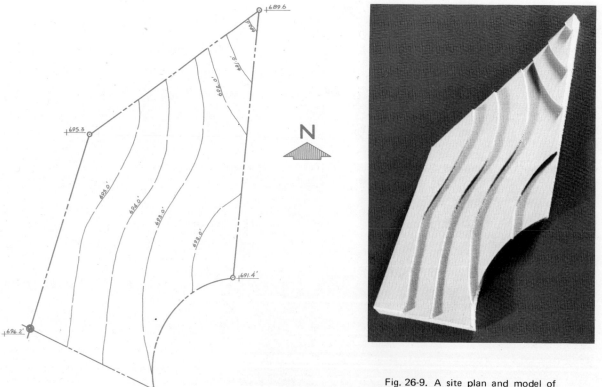

Fig. 26-9. A site plan and model of the site made from illustration board.

2. A decision must be made concerning the size of the base for the model. A prime consideration to be remembered is storage and handling. If the base is large it may be hard to store and transport. A good size base for an average residence is 30" x 30" or 30" x 36". The base should be 3/4 in. plywood if the site is relatively smooth. If the site is rolling, then a lighter base should be used to reduce weight. A rolling site must be accurately represented by building up the high spots with plaster of Paris, Styrofoam or cardboard, Fig. 26-9. It should be noted that if the site is flat the model may be completed on a workbench and placed on the base. If the site is rolling, Fig. 26-10, it may be easier to build the model on the base. (The procedure presented here relates to a house on a flat site.)

3. After studying the floor plan and elevations, select a piece of balsa which is about the thickness for the exterior walls of the model. Usually 3/16 or 1/4 in. thick material is used. Lay out the length of one exterior wall and openings in the wall such as windows and doors. Cut this piece accurately paying close attention to details. The corners may be mitered or butt jointed. A mitered corner is usually neater.

Proceed with the next exterior wall by cutting it to length and locating the windows and doors. Construct all the exterior walls in the same manner. The walls may then be glued together. Place them on the floor plan to insure accuracy, Fig. 26-11.

4. Lay out each section of interior wall on a piece of balsa

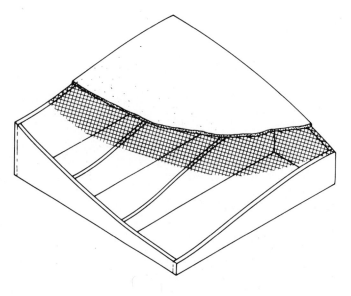

Fig. 26-10. A rolling site may be modeled by building a frame support, cut to the proper contour, and covered with screen and plaster of Paris.

1/8 in. thick. This thickness closely approximates the thickness of an interior wall drawn to scale. Cut out each interior wall segment and glue the pieces together in their proper locations on the plan.

5. Apply the trim around windows and doors and insert exterior doors (usually 1/8 in. thick). The window glass may

Fig. 26-11. Two exterior walls have been completed. Tools used included X-Acto knife, scale, square, and metal straightedge.

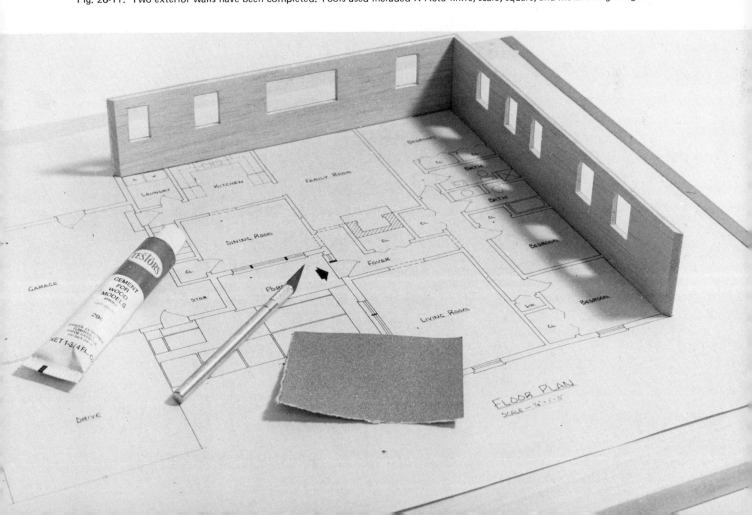

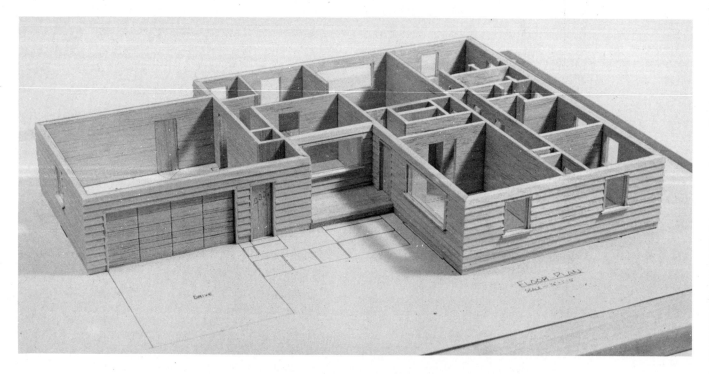

Fig. 26-12. Model with interior and exterior walls and siding in place. The siding was made from individual strips of balsa 1/4 in. wide by 1/32 in. thick and overlapped.

also be installed now or after the interior is painted. For best results, 1/16 in. thick Plexiglas may be used for windows. Exterior siding, brick or other material may be applied to the walls.

You may wish to make your own siding or represent other materials by scoring the board or gluing on thin strips. If you cut your own strips of siding be sure to make them to scale. Commercial materials are available at hobby and model train shops. Again, choose materials which are to scale. If materials in sheet form are to be used, rubber cement will work fine for

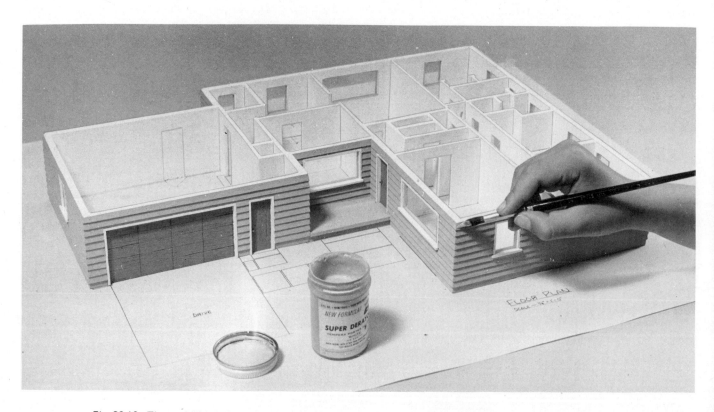

Fig. 26-13. The model has been painted both inside and out using tempera colors. Painting must be carefully done.

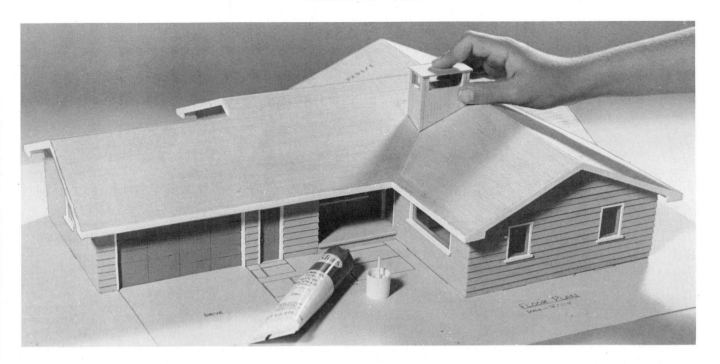

Fig. 26-14. The roof has been completed and placed on the model. The chimney is being held in place for glue to dry. Small blocks have been attached to the underside of the roof to insure proper placement of the roof on the house.

applying them to the walls. If individual strips are to be used, model cement or other fast drying cement is recommended. Fig. 26-12 shows the model after step 5 has been completed.

6. Paint the interior walls with tempera paint. The walls may be painted in soft pastels or white. Dark colors usually do not look realistic and should be avoided. Any wood siding or three-dimensional brick, stone or shingles used, should also be painted or stained. Exterior materials are available on plastic sheets which are embossed to provide a three-dimension effect. These should be finished with enamel. The mortar joints should be painted with a water base paint and wiped. This technique produces a realistic appearance. Fig. 26-13 shows the walls after painting.

7. Roof construction comes next. The roof may be assembled on the roof plan or on the model. Experience has shown that the most satisfactory results are usually obtained by assembling the roof on the roof plan. Since the roof framing will not be seen in a presentation model it is not necessary to cut each rafter and ceiling joist. Lay out the gables on 1/4 in. balsa and cut them out. Cut ridge boards from similar stock and glue in place at the peaks of the gables. Use straight pins to hold the pieces in place. The roof sheathing may be 1/4 in. balsa glued to the gables and ridge board. This thickness will approximate the thickness of the rafters and sheathing on the house. Use a strip of balsa 1/16 in. thick to represent a fascia board. If the home has a chimney,

Fig. 26-15. The completed model with landscape, drive and walk. The model was mounted on a piece of 3/4 in. plywood 24″ x 30″. The tree and plants were made from lichen purchased from the local hobby store. The grass is bright green flock made especially for models.

build a chimney to scale and accurately locate it on the roof, Fig. 26-14. Finish the roof by gluing strips of sandpaper or fine gravel to the sheathing. Be sure to represent the flashing. This may be aluminum foil or dark colored sandpaper.

8. After the floor area has been pained, or covered with an appropriate material, locate the model on the base and glue it in place. Next, paint the area surrounding the house bright green. For best results apply two coats and sprinkle grass flock before the second coat dries. Add trees, shrubs, drive and walk. The plants may be bought commercially or fabricated from a sponge and/or twigs. Use your imagination to develop a landscape that looks realistic. Do not add so many plants that the landscape appears to be cluttered. The walk and drive may be painted balsa or sandpaper glued in place.

9. Check the model to be sure all details are complete. Fig. 26-15 shows the completed model.

Furniture and major fixtures can be carved out of soap or wood and glued into place for added attraction. Again, the main consideration is scale. There is no limit to the amount of realism that may be incorporated in a model. Use your imagination. Be creative and develop a truly realistic presentation model.

REVIEW QUESTIONS — CHAPTER 26

1. Name three types of architectural models that may be used for homes.
   a._____.
   b._____.
   c._____.
2. The scale of most residential models is _____.
3. Identify three types of materials that are commonly used in model house construction.
   a. _____.
   b. _____.
   c. _____.
4. The first step in getting ready to build a model is_____

5. A plot plan would be a necessity for building a model when _____.
6. The size of base for an average size residence usually is about_____.
7. The base must be strong, so_____in. plywood is commonly used.
8. Exterior walls are usually thicker than interior walls. What is the thickness of most exterior walls on house models which are constructed at 1/4″ = 1′ − 0″ scale?_____.
9. Interior walls are usually_____in. thick on a 1/4″ = 1′ − 0″ scale model.
10. The type of paint frequently used for house models is _____.
11. Soap is used for _____ in a house model.

SUGGESTED ACTIVITIES

1. Visit a hobby shop and examine materials available for model home construction. Make a list of the materials and record prices. Also write down the address of the shop. Compare your findings with other members of the class.
2. Secure the plan of a modern freestanding garage and construct a balsa model to scale. A scale of 1/4″ = 1′ − 0″ is suggested. Mount the model on a base 12 in. square. Record the time required to build the model and total cost.
3. Obtain the plans for an attractive one-story type home. Build a presentation model of the home. Mount it on a suitable base and landscape the site. Display the model along with the plans.
4. Carve a permanent fixture such as a bathtub or water closet from soap. Check dimensions of the carving for accuracy.
5. Build a structural model of a modern storage or garden house of your design. Present your design and model for analysis.

Chapter 27
MATERIAL AND WORKMANSHIP SPECIFICATIONS

The architect is generally responsible for the preparation of material and workmanship specifications for residential structures. The specifications provide written information on details and products which supplement the drawings and become part of the complete set of building plans. When the house is to be constructed for sale, the architect supplies the specifications needed. When the home is being designed and constructed for a particular client, the architect and customer usually develop a "specification outline" together, Fig. 27-1.

Fig. 27-1. The architect, left, goes over details of the working drawings for a new residence with a client.

PURPOSE. Both working drawings and specification sheets (specs) become part of the total contract between the builder and owner and are legal and binding on both parties. This illustrates the necessity of carefully preparing specifications for materials, fixtures and workmanship that leaves little or no chance for misunderstandings between the contractor and owner.

The owner should carefully discuss the details of construction with the architect and, in most cases, rely upon the architect's judgment and suggestions for structural materials. On the other hand, the architect should accept the client's desires in such details as floor coverings, paint colors, type and style of hardware, plumbing fixtures, wallpaper and other items involving individual taste. Various forms for developing specifications are available. Some of these are short while others are long and highly detailed. In some instances the architect simply prepares specifications to the agreement of both parties.

While material specifications are quite factual, the question of workmanship and quality of construction is more difficult to define. What may appear to be a craftsman-like job of cabinet construction to one person may appear sloppy to another. It is the purpose of the specifications to include what both the contractor and owner agree on as an acceptable degree of workmanship quality. The contractor should employ or subcontract only to qualified skilled tradesmen.

SPECIFICATION FORMATS

There are many types and styles of standard long and short form specification formats. Specification guides or outlines may be purchased locally or supplied by the architect. Standard forms are also available from such organizations as the American Institute of Architects and the Veterans Administration. The V. A. form has become one of the leading guides for writing specifications.

Information provided by specification forms should include:

1. A description of the materials to be used. This includes sizes, quality, brand names, style and specification numbers.

2. List of required building operations. These are usually described under major headings such as excavation, masonry, carpentry, millwork, plumbing, electrical, insulation, etc.

3. Notes relative to cash allowances for such items as lighting fixtures and hardware which are to be selected by the owner. Expenditures over the cash allowance must be paid by the owner.

4. An indication that all specifications refer to the detailed plans of the working drawings.

5. A statement or agreement on quality of workmanship. This is often drawn up as a separate part of the contract.

6. Liability covered by the contractor during construction.

EXAMPLES OF SPECIFICATIONS

Fig. 27-2 shows a typical contract specification sheet prepared by an architect. The architect and owner went over the working drawings together and came to an agreement on details of construction, design and appliances.

A standard form as shown in Fig. 27-3 provides the necessary major headings for specifications. Each section may be filled in or left blank as agreed to by the architect and client. Each topic on this standard specification form should be carefully discussed with the architect, and in some cases the builder, so that all understand and agree to its content.

CONTRACT SPECIFICATIONS

Mr. Taylor D. Trask Residence
2402 Boyd Avenue
Avondale, Ohio

DATE_____

EXCAVATION: House to be excavated to depths shown on drawings, backfilled and graded with existing dirt. Excavation overcut in garage and lower level to be filled with sand. Twelve inches of sand to be furnished under garage floor. Tree removal is included only within building or drive area.

CONCRETE: All concrete to be 5 bag mix. Included is all foundation work, front sidewalk, garage floor, lower level floor, basement floor, and front stoop. Garage floor to have 6/6 wire mesh. All tie rods in lower level and basement are to be broken off on the inside and outside of foundation and inside of walls to have brushed cement finished coat. Furnish and install Kewanee basement windows complete with area wells and grates.

WATERPROOFING: Exterior of lower level and basement to receive two coats of sprayed tar.

STEEL: All steel beams, angles, plates, columns and lintels are a part of this contract.

LUMBER: All floor joists are to be 2 x 10 kiln-dried Southern Yellow Pine. All studs to be 2 x 4 white fir precuts. Ceiling joists and roof rafters to be 2 x 6 white fir. Roof sheathing and subfloor to be 4 x 8 x 1/2 C. D. plywood. Exterior siding to be channel type prestained rough sawn cedar. Fascia and soffit to be 1 x 8 prestained rough sawn cedar. Basement and lower level stairs to have 2 x 10 oak treads, pine risers and stringers. Two rows of 1 x 3 cross bridging to be installed.

MASONRY: Residence to have face brick four sides with an allowance of $80/1000. Fireplace to be face brick at $80/1000 allowance with slate hearth, colonial damper, cast iron ash drop and cleanout, 13/13 tile flue. Color mortar or raked joints will be extra.

CARPENTRY: All carpentry labor is included for all rough and trim work, including installation of all cabinets, tops, appliances, and hardware. Front door, garage service door, and door from garage to lower level to be weatherstripped, and to have aluminum thresholds.

STAIRWAY: Stairway from first to second floor to be mill made with oak treads and pine or white wood risers and stringers. Furnish railings for foyer and dining room.

MILLWORK: All trim to be Colonial white pine; all interior doors to be Colonial pine panel (first and second floor) 1 3/8 in. flush white birch on lower level; front and garage service doors to be 1 3/4 in. pine panel; door from garage to lower level to be 1 3/4 in. solid core birch. All windows to be Caradco Biltwell casements in insulating glass with screens on operating windows and muntin bars where indicated on drawings. All windows to have birch stools.

CABINETS: All kitchen and vanity cabinets to be birch or oak, prefinished, with ranch or provincial grooves and lap type doors with flush surface. Purchaser to select from standard finishes.

COUNTERTOPS: Kitchen and vanity countertops to be post formed one piece Formica or Textolite and scribed to the wall. Maple cutting block to be included over dishwasher.

FLOORING: Floors for living room, dining room, upper hall and bedrooms to be 5/8 in. plywood. Floors under ceramic tile in second floor baths and foyer to be 1/2 in. plywood. Floors in kitchen to be 5/8 in. underlayment plywood screwed in place. All floors to be laid directly on top of subfloors.

CERAMIC TILE: Foyer, lower hall and closet to have ceramic floor with an allowance of $3.20 per sq. ft. in place. Baths No. 1 and No. 2 to have ceramic floors and base with an allowance of $3.20 per sq. ft. in place. Ceramic tile walls and ceiling of 2 showers and walls only at 1 tub with an in place allowance of $3.40 per sq. ft. All ceramic to be laid in mastic.

RESILIENT FLOORS: Kitchen floor to be vinyl inlaid with an installed allowance of $12.00 per sq. yd. Stairway from kitchen to lower hall, lower hall, laundry room, and future powder room to have vinyl asbestos tile floor with an allowance of $.60 per sq. ft. installed. Rubber base to be installed in workshop, lower hall, laundry room, future powder room, and den. Five chrome fixtures to be supplied and installed in second floor hall bath, 4 chrome fixtures in master bath, and 2 chrome fixtures in lower powder room.

DRY WALL: All dry wall to be 1/2 in. adhesive applied before nailing (3 coat finish) garage ceiling and firewall to be 5/8 in. fire code with three exterior walls to be 1/2 in. regular dry wall.

INSULATION: Ceiling of house to have 4 in. blown fiber glass insulation except cathedral ceiling in living and dining room to have 4 in. fiber glass batt insulation. Walls of house to have 2 1/2 in. fiber glass batts. Garage ceiling and garage exterior walls are not insulated.

GLAZING: Obscure D. S. glass to be installed in basement sash. A 54" x 48" plate glass mirror to be installed in upper hall bath. Decorative glass panels to be installed in garage.

SHINGLES: All shingles to be 235 lb. asphalt with adhesive tabs laid over 15 lb. roofing felt.

HEATING AND SHEET METAL: A Carrier or Bryant gas forced air furnace and electric air conditioner to be installed with deluxe high wall returns on the second floor. A power humidifier, 26 gage galvanized iron gutters and downspouts and flashing, exhaust ducts for fans are a part of this contract.

WROUGHT IRON: A wrought iron railing is to be supplied and installed at stairway in garage.

PLUMBING: All plumbing fixtures to be American Standard in white, except green in bath No. 2. Two water closets to be "Cadet" model. Two lavatories to be "Cirocylyn" one tub to be "Bildor", two prefab

Fig. 27-2. A set of contract specifications for a home designed specifically for the owner. Details of the specifications are planned by hours of discussions between the architect and client. (Continued)

shower bases, one 32″ x 21″ stainless steel kitchen sink, one single compartment standard laundry tub. Water heater to be Rheam Fury 40 gal. glass lined. All faucets to be Moen mixing valve type. Shutoff valves are included at all sinks, lavatories and water closets. Three hose bibbs to be installed (front free type). Floor drain to be installed in basement, laundry room and garage. Drain tile to be installed around lower level and deep basement leading into a submersible sump pump for grade discharge. Gas lines to be run to furnace and water heater. Install dishwasher and disposal. All water lines to be copper and all sewer lines to be P.V.C. Install bypass for future softener by owner. Rough in only for powder room lavatory and water closet.

ELECTRICAL: 150 amp. underground electrical service with circuit breakers, one recessed chime with front and rear button. Install 220 volt outlet for range and oven. Provide electrical installation of furnace, power humidifier, dishwasher and disposal. Light fixture allowance is $500.00

HARDWARE: Interior and exterior door locks to be Schlage A Series. Kitchen cabinet and vanity hardware to be Amerock. Allowance for all finish hardware is $400.00 which includes closet rods, hinges, locks, latches, pulls, door bumpers, etc.

PAINTING: First floor and lower level trim to be stained, sealed and varnished. Walls and ceiling of house to receive a prime and finish coat. Exterior trim on windows and doors to receive two coats. Walltex is included at $7.00 per roll for baths No. 1 and No. 2. Second floor trim and doors to be painted (bedroom level).

APPLIANCES: Roper dishwasher No. 8581, Roper Disposal No. 8789,

Roper Range No. 2199 with Grille, Roper Double Oven No. 2069. All are part of contract.

DRIVEWAY: A blacktop drive is to be installed over blacktop base.

MEDICINE CABINETS: None in contract.

GARAGE DOOR: A 16′ − 0″ x 7′ − 0″ x 1 3/8 in. flush Masonite overhead garage door to be installed as manufactured by the Overhead Door Co.

SHOWER DOORS: Two shower doors are to be provided.

PATIO DOOR: An Arcadia aluminum framed patio door 8′ − 0″ wide with insulating glass and screen to be installed in kitchen.

GAS LIGHT: A standard gas post light is to be installed at front of driveway.

PERMIT: All permits and inspection fees are included in this contract.

SURVEY: Topography, survey, and building site are a part of this contract.

INSURANCE: Contractor to carry builders risk, covering fire, theft, liability and property damage. Purchaser to insure building upon final closing.

WORKMANSHIP: Contractor to provide all material necessary to build upon the real estate in a good, substantial and workmanlike manner.

Fig. 27-2. (Continued) Contract specification sheet prepared by an architect.

FHA Form 2005
VA Form 26-1852
Rev. 3/68

For accurate register of carbon copies, form may be separated along above fold. Staple completed sheets together in original order.

Form approved.
Budget Bureau No. 63-R055.11.

☐ Proposed Construction

☐ Under Construction

DESCRIPTION OF MATERIALS   No. _____

(To be inserted by FHA or VA)

Property address _____ City _____ State _____

Mortgagor or Sponsor _____ _____
                              (Name)   (Address)

Contractor or Builder _____ _____
                              (Name)   (Address)

INSTRUCTIONS

1. For additional information on how this form is to be submitted, number of copies, etc., see the instructions applicable to the FHA Application for Mortgage Insurance or VA Request for Determination of Reasonable Value, as the case may be.
2. Describe all materials and equipment to be used, whether or not shown on the drawings, by marking an X in each appropriate check-box and entering the information called for in each space. If space is inadequate, enter "See misc." and describe under item 27 or on an attached sheet.
3. Work not specifically described or shown will not be considered unless

required, then the minimum acceptable will be assumed. Work exceeding minimum requirements cannot be considered unless specifically described.
4. Include no alternates, "or equal" phrases, or contradictory items. (Consideration of a request for acceptance of substitute materials or equipment is not thereby precluded.)
5. Include signatures required at the end of this form.
6. The construction shall be completed in compliance with the related drawings and specifications, as amended during processing. The specifications include this Description of Materials and the applicable Minimum Construction Requirements.

1. EXCAVATION:
Bearing soil, type _____

2. FOUNDATIONS:
Footings: concrete mix _____; strength psi _____ Reinforcing _____
Foundation wall: material _____ Reinforcing _____
Interior foundation wall: material _____ Party foundation wall _____
Columns: material and sizes _____ Piers: material and reinforcing _____
Girders: material and sizes _____ Sills: material _____

Fig. 27-3. This standard Veterans Administration and Federal Housing Administration form lends itself well to all types of specifications for residential construction. (Continued)

Basement entrance areaway _____ Window areaways _____

Waterproofing _____ Footing drains _____

Termite protection _____

Basementless space: ground cover _____ ; insulation _____ ; foundation vents _____

Special foundations _____

Additional information: _____

_____

3. CHIMNEYS:

Material _____ Prefabricated *(make and size)* _____

Flue lining: material _____ Heater flue size _____ Fireplace flue size _____

Vents *(material and size)*: gas or oil heater _____ ; water heater _____

Additional information: _____

4. FIREPLACES:

Type: ☐ solid fuel; ☐ gas-burning; ☐ circulator *(make and size)* _____ Ash dump and clean-out _____

Fireplace: facing _____ ; lining _____ ; hearth _____ ; mantel _____

Additional information: _____

5. EXTERIOR WALLS:

Wood frame: wood grade, and species _____ ☐ Corner bracing. Building paper or felt _____

    Sheathing _____ ; thickness _____ ; width _____ ; ☐ solid; ☐ spaced _____ " o. c.; ☐ diagonal; _____

    Siding _____ ; grade _____ ; type _____ ; size _____ ; exposure _____ "; fastening _____

    Shingles _____ ; grade _____ ; type _____ ; size _____ ; exposure _____ "; fastening _____

    Stucco _____ ; thickness _____ "; Lath _____ ; weight _____ lb.

    Masonry veneer _____ Sills _____ Lintels _____ Base flashing _____

Masonry: ☐ solid ☐ faced ☐ stuccoed; total wall thickness _____ "; facing thickness _____ "; facing material _____

           Backup material _____ ; thickness _____ "; bonding _____

    Door sills _____ Window sills _____ Lintels _____ Base flashing _____

    Interior surfaces: dampproofing, _____ coats of _____ ; furring _____

Additional information: _____

Exterior painting: material _____ ; number of coats _____

Gable wall construction: ☐ same as main walls; ☐ other construction _____

6. FLOOR FRAMING:

Joists: wood, grade, and species _____ ; other _____ ; bridging _____ ; anchors _____

Concrete slab: ☐ basement floor; ☐ first floor; ☐ ground supported; ☐ self-supporting; mix _____ ; thickness _____ ";

    reinforcing _____ ; insulation _____ ; membrane _____

Fill under slab: material _____ ; thickness _____ ". Additional information: _____

7. SUBFLOORING: *(Describe underflooring for special floors under item 21.)*

Material: grade and species _____ ; size _____ ; type _____

Laid: ☐ first floor; ☐ second floor; ☐ attic _____ sq. ft.; ☐ diagonal; ☐ right angles. Additional information: _____

_____

8. FINISH FLOORING: *(Wood only. Describe other finish flooring under item 21.)*

Location	Rooms	Grade	Species	Thickness	Width	Bldg. Paper	Finish
First floor ___							
Second floor ___							
Attic floor ___	___ sq. ft.						

Additional information: _____

FHA Form 2005
VA Form 26-1852

1

DESCRIPTION OF MATERIALS

DESCRIPTION OF MATERIALS

9. PARTITION FRAMING:

Studs: wood, grade, and species _____ size and spacing _____ Other _____

Additional information: _____

10. CEILING FRAMING:

Joists: wood, grade, and species _____ Other _____ Bridging _____

Additional information: _____

11. ROOF FRAMING:

Rafters: wood, grade, and species _____ Roof trusses (see detail): grade and species _____

Additional information: _____

Fig. 27-3. (Continued) Standard V A and FHA specification form.

12. ROOFING:

Sheathing: wood, grade, and species _____; ☐ solid; ☐ spaced _____" o.c.

Roofing _____; grade _____; size _____; type _____

Underlay _____; weight or thickness _____; size _____; fastening _____

Built-up roofing _____; number of plies _____; surfacing material _____

Flashing: material _____; gage or weight _____; ☐ gravel stops; ☐ snow guards

Additional information: _____

13. GUTTERS AND DOWNSPOUTS:

Gutters: material _____; gage or weight _____; size _____; shape _____

Downspouts: material _____; gage or weight _____; size _____; shape _____; number _____

Downspouts connected to: ☐ Storm sewer; ☐ sanitary sewer; ☐ dry-well. ☐ Splash blocks: material and size _____

Additional information: _____

14. LATH AND PLASTER

Lath ☐ walls, ☐ ceilings: material _____; weight or thickness _____ Plaster: coats _____; finish _____

Dry-wall ☐ walls, ☐ ceilings: material _____; thickness _____; finish _____;

Joint treatment _____

15. DECORATING: *(Paint, wallpaper, etc.)*

ROOMS	WALL FINISH MATERIAL AND APPLICATION	CEILING FINISH MATERIAL AND APPLICATION
Kitchen _____		
Bath _____		
Other _____		

Additional information: _____

16. INTERIOR DOORS AND TRIM:

Doors: type _____; material _____; thickness _____

Door trim: type _____; material _____ Base: type _____; material _____; size _____

Finish: doors _____; trim _____

Other trim *(item, type and location)* _____

Additional information: _____

17. WINDOWS:

Windows: type _____; make _____; material _____; sash thickness _____

Glass: grade _____; ☐ sash weights; ☐ balances, type _____; head flashing _____

Trim: type _____; material _____ Paint _____; number coats _____

Weatherstripping: type _____; material _____ Storm sash, number _____

Screens: ☐ full; ☐ half; type _____; number _____; screen-cloth material _____

Basement windows: type _____; material _____; screens, number _____; Storm sash, number _____

Special windows _____

Additional information: _____

18. ENTRANCES AND EXTERIOR DETAIL:

Main entrance door: material _____; width _____; thickness _____". Frame: material _____; thickness _____"

Other entrance doors: material _____; width _____; thickness _____". Frame: material _____; thickness _____"

Head flashing _____ Weatherstripping: type _____; saddles _____

Screen doors: thickness _____"; number _____; screen cloth material _____ Storm doors: thickness _____"; number _____

Combination storm and screen doors: thickness _____"; number _____; screen cloth material _____

Shutters: ☐ hinged; ☐ fixed. Railings _____, Attic louvers _____

Exterior millwork: grade and species _____ Paint _____; number coats _____

Additional information: _____

19. CABINETS AND INTERIOR DETAIL:

Kitchen cabinets, wall units: material _____; lineal feet of shelves _____; shelf width _____

Base units: material _____; counter top _____; edging _____

Back and end splash _____ Finish of cabinets _____; number coats _____

Medicine cabinets: make _____; model _____

Other cabinets and built-in furniture _____

Additional information: _____

20. STAIRS:

STAIR	TREADS		RISERS		STRINGS		HANDRAIL		BALUSTERS	
	Material	Thickness	Material	Thickness	Material	Size	Material	Size	Material	Size
Basement ____										
Main ____										
Attic ____										

Disappearing: make and model number _____

Additional information: _____

2

Fig. 27-3. (Continued) Standard VA and FHA specification form.

21. SPECIAL FLOORS AND WAINSCOT:

	LOCATION	MATERIAL, COLOR, BORDER, SIZES, GAGE, ETC.	THRESHOLD MATERIAL	WALL BASE MATERIAL	UNDERFLOOR MATERIAL
FLOORS	Kitchen ___				
	Bath ___				

	LOCATION	MATERIAL, COLOR, BORDER, CAP. SIZES, GAGE, ETC.	HEIGHT	HEIGHT OVER TUB	HEIGHT IN SHOWERS (FROM FLOOR)
WAINSCOT	Bath ___				

Bathroom accessories: ☐ Recessed; material _____; number _____; ☐ Attached; material _____; number _____

Additional information: _____

22. PLUMBING:

FIXTURE	NUMBER	LOCATION	MAKE	MFR'S FIXTURE IDENTIFICATION NO.	SIZE	COLOR
Sink ___						
Lavatory ___						
Water closet ___						
Bathtub ___						
Shower over tub △ ___						
Stall shower △ ___						
Laundry trays ___						

△☐ Curtain rod   △☐ Door   ☐ Shower pan: material _____

Water supply: ☐ public; ☐ community system; ☐ individual (private) system.★

Sewage disposal: ☐ public; ☐ community system; ☐ individual (private) system.★

★Show and describe individual system in complete detail in separate drawings and specifications according to requirements.

House drain (inside): ☐ cast iron; ☐ tile; ☐ other _____   House sewer (outside): ☐ cast iron; ☐ tile; ☐ other _____

Water piping: ☐ galvanized steel; ☐ copper tubing; ☐ other _____   Sill cocks, number _____

Domestic water heater: type _____; make and model _____; heating capacity _____

_____ gph. 100° rise. Storage tank: material _____; capacity _____ gallons.

Gas service: ☐ utility company; ☐ liq. pet. gas; ☐ other _____   Gas piping: ☐ cooking; ☐ house heating.

Footing drains connected to: ☐ storm sewer; ☐ sanitary sewer; ☐ dry well. Sump pump; make and model _____

_____; capacity _____; discharges into _____

23. HEATING:

☐ Hot water. ☐ Steam. ☐ Vapor. ☐ One-pipe system. ☐ Two-pipe system.

☐ Radiators. ☐ Convectors. ☐ Baseboard radiation. Make and model _____

Radiant panel: ☐ floor; ☐ wall; ☐ ceiling. Panel coil: material _____

☐ Circulator. ☐ Return pump. Make and model _____; capacity _____ gpm.

Boiler: make and model _____   Output _____ Btuh.; net rating _____ Btuh.

Additional information: _____

Warm air: ☐ Gravity. ☐ Forced. Type of system _____

Duct material: supply _____; return _____   Insulation _____, thickness _____   ☐ Outside air intake.

Furnace: make and model _____   Input _____ Btuh.; output _____ Btuh.

Additional information: _____

☐ Space heater; ☐ floor furnace; ☐ wall heater. Input _____ Btuh.; output _____ Btuh.; number units _____

Make, model _____   Additional information: _____

Controls: make and types _____

Additional information: _____

Fuel: ☐ Coal; ☐ oil; ☐ gas; ☐ liq. pet. gas; ☐ electric; ☐ other _____; storage capacity _____

Additional information: _____

Firing equipment furnished separately: ☐ Gas burner, conversion type. ☐ Stoker: hopper feed ☐; bin feed ☐

Oil burner: ☐ pressure atomizing; ☐ vaporizing _____

Make and model _____   Control _____

Additional information: _____

Electric heating system: type _____   Input _____ watts; @ _____ volts; output _____ Btuh.

Additional information: _____

Ventilating equipment: attic fan, make and model _____; capacity _____ cfm.

kitchen exhaust fan, make and model _____

Fig. 27-3. (Continued) Standard VA and FHA specification form.

Other heating, ventilating. or cooling equipment _____

24. ELECTRIC WIRING:

Service: ☐ overhead; ☐ underground. Panel: ☐ fuse box; ☐ circuit-breaker; make_____ AMP's _____ No. circuits _____

Wiring: ☐ conduit; ☐ armored cable; ☐ nonmetallic cable; ☐ knob and tube; ☐ other _____

Special outlets: ☐ range; ☐ water heater; ☐ other _____

☐ Doorbell. ☐ Chimes. Push-button locations _____ Additional information: _____

25. LIGHTING FIXTURES:

Total number of fixtures_____ Total allowance for fixtures, typical installation, $_____

Nontypical installation _____

Additional information: _____

3   DESCRIPTION OF MATERIALS

DESCRIPTION OF MATERIALS

26. INSULATION:

LOCATION	THICKNESS	MATERIAL, TYPE, AND METHOD OF INSTALLATION	VAPOR BARRIER
Roof ___			
Ceiling ___			
Wall ___			
Floor ___			

HARDWARE: (make, material, and finish.) _____

_____

SPECIAL EQUIPMENT: (State material or make, model and quantity. Include only equipment and appliances which are acceptable by local law, custom and applicable FHA standards. Do not include items which, by established custom, are supplied by occupant and removed when he vacates premises or chattles prohibited by law from becoming realty.)_____

_____

_____

_____

_____

_____

27. MISCELLANEOUS: (Describe any main dwelling materials, equipment, or construction items not shown elsewhere; or use to provide additional information where the space provided was inadequate. Always reference by item number to correspond to numbering used on this form.) _____

_____

_____

_____

_____

_____

_____

_____

_____

PORCHES:

_____

_____

TERRACES:

_____

_____

GARAGES:

_____

_____

Fig. 27-3. (Continued) Standard VA and FHA specification form.

WALKS AND DRIVEWAYS:

Driveway: width _____ ; base material _____ ; thickness _____ "; surfacing material _____ ; thickness _____ "

Front walk: width _____ ; material _____ ; thickness _____ ". Service walk: width _____ ; material _____ ; thickness _____ "

Steps: material _____ ; treads _____"; risers _____". Cheek walls _____

OTHER ONSITE IMPROVEMENTS:

(Specify all exterior onsite improvements not described elsewhere, including items such as unusual grading, drainage structures, retaining walls, fence, railings, and accessory structures.)

_____

_____

_____

LANDSCAPING, PLANTING, AND FINISH GRADING:

Topsoil _____" thick: ☐ front yard; ☐ side yards; ☐ rear yard to _____ feet behind main building.

Lawns *(seeded, sodded, or sprigged)*: ☐ front yard _____ ; ☐ side yards _____ ; ☐ rear yard_____

Planting: ☐ as specified and shown on drawings; ☐ as follows:

_____ Shade trees, deciduous, _____" caliper.	_____ Evergreen trees. _____' to _____', B & B.
_____ Low flowering trees, deciduous, _____' to _____'	_____ Evergreen shrubs, _____' to _____', B & B.
_____ High-growing shrubs, deciduous, _____' to _____'	_____ Vines, 2-year _____
_____ Medium-growing shrubs, deciduous, _____' to _____'	_____
_____ Low-growing shrubs, deciduous, _____' to _____'	_____

IDENTIFICATION.—This exhibit shall be identified by the signature of the builder, or sponsor, and/or the proposed mortgagor if the latter is known at the time of application.

Date_____

Signature _____

Signature _____

FHA Form 2005
VA Form 26-1852

4

GPO 1968 c48—16—80081-1 296-152

Fig. 27-3. (Continued) Standard VA and FHA specification form.

REVIEW QUESTIONS – CHAPTER 27

1. Briefly list the six major types of information that should be included in any set of specifications for a residential structure.

    a._____ .

    b._____ .

    c._____ .

    d._____ .

    e._____ .

    f._____ .

2. It is important that the architect listen carefully to the desires of the client when writing specifications because:

    _____ .

3. The architect often writes the complete specifications for a house when _____ .

4. Specification sheets and working drawings become part of the_____between the builder and the owner.

5. A cash allowance is often provided for such items as:

    a._____ .

    b._____ .

    c._____ .

    d._____ .

6. An agreement on quality of workmanship is an important item on a specification sheet because: _____ .

7. Explain why many of the details of the actual building construction do not show up on the specification sheets.

_____

SUGGESTED ACTIVITIES

1. Prepare a specification sheet, as illustrated in Fig. 27-2, for one of the homes you have designed during the course or from a set of working drawings supplied by your instructor. For this porblem, have another person act as the client and use his suggestions for appliances, floor coverings, hardware and other items of personal choice.

2. Write to manufacturers of appliances, such as plumbing ware and residential cabinets, and plan a bulletin board display of all the latest fixtures a client has to select from when planning a new home.

3. Visit a brick supplier to gain information as to types of face bricks available for residential construction and present prices. Write a short report on how you would present the selection of face bricks and cost allowance to a client when planning specifications.

4. Using the Veterans Administration "Description of Materials" form as a format, secure a set of working drawings for a residence from your instructor, or other source, and fill in all necessary information. Plan the specifications as if you were to be the owner and make selections as listed in current catalogs and manufacturers' literature.

Fig. 28-1. The beautiful factory-built home is a prime example of good quality and design which applies the principles of modular construction. (Scholz Homes, Inc.)

Chapter 28
MODULAR APPLICATIONS

Traditionally, residential structures have been built by fastening together on the site, thousands of small pieces (boards, bricks, etc.). This requires a great deal of time and labor and is costly. In recent years much experimentation has been underway in an effort to speed up the process of building a house and reduce the cost. Experiments have involved precut lumber, factory wall assemblies, modular components and industrialized housing. Each of these has helped to further the technology of modern home construction, but the big pay off is still to be realized. Industries are just beginning to be truly successful in applying mass production techniques to house construction and home designers are using modular sizes in their plans. About 15,000 modular houses were built in 1969.

30,000 in 1970 and by 1980 it is estimated by the Department of Housing and Urban Development that two thirds of all new U. S. dwellings will be factory-built.

In the past, people associated factory-built houses with cheap, poorly constructed and designed boxes, but today this is no longer true. The modular concept can be applied to any style or house design, Figs. 28-1 and 28-2.

STANDARDIZATION

Application of the modular concept to on site construction or factory-built homes necessarily involves standardization. Manufacturers are moving toward standard size building

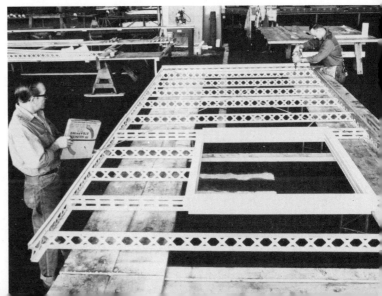

Fig. 28-2. The modular home, above, was constructed using aluminum structural members in factory-built wall panels and trusses shown to the right. (Aluminum Co. of America)

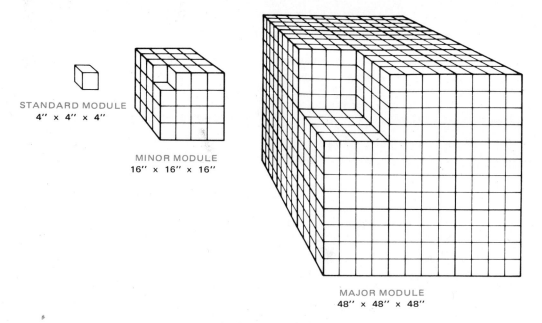

Fig. 28-3. All modules are multiples of 4 in. and each is a cube.

materials which lend themselves to modular construction. Some of the common size materials which are modular include:

4" x 8"	16" x 32"	48" x 48"
4" x 12"	16" x 48"	48" x 96"
8" x 16"	16" x 96"	48" x 120"
16" x 16"	48" x 32"	48" x 144"

Plywood sheets, interior paneling, floor tiles, etc. are all designed to be integrated into modular systems. Other materials will most likely join the ranks in the future.

The modular plan includes length, width and height using the STANDARD MODULE, a 4 in. cube. The 4 in. cubes are combined to produce larger units. For example, the MAJOR MODULE is 4' — 0" or 12 standard modules. Cubes which are

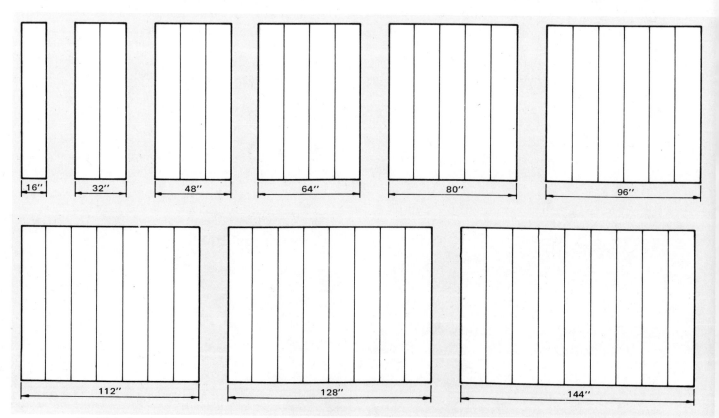

Fig. 28-4. Standard factory-built panels are produced in 16 in. increments. Windows are located in the panels with the top at a constant height.

16 and 24 in. are MINOR MODULES, Fig. 28-3. It is evident then, that a modular length must be a multiple of 4 inches. Minor modules of 16 and 24 in. are important because studs and joists are spaced those distances.

Modular panel components are usually produced in widths ranging from 16 to 196 in. in multiples of 16 inches, Fig. 28-4. These panels are then fastened together to form a wall. Exterior walls are generally multiples of 4' − 0" if feasible, in the modular system. This saves materials and reduces cutting time.

A structure which incorporates modular principles must be designed with definite modules in mind. Lengths, widths and heights must be planned to coincide with modular size materials and specifications given for materials to be used. The draftsman should use a modular grid as a guide in designing and dimensioning the structure. A typical modular grid is shown in Fig. 28-5.

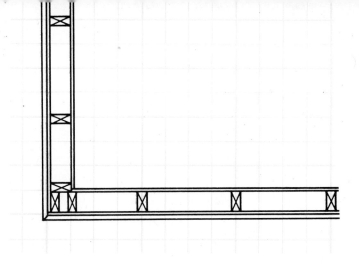

Fig. 28-6. House corners and other details should coordinate with the grid lines. Grid lines are shown on the plan.

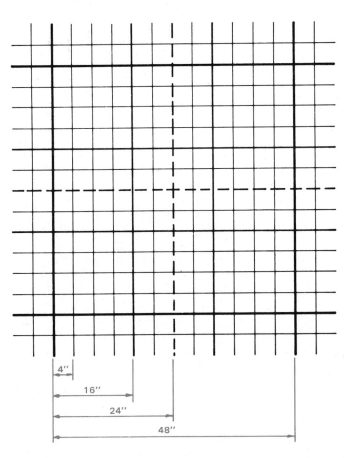

Fig. 28-5. A typical modular grid with three different weight lines to represent 4, 16 and 48 inches.

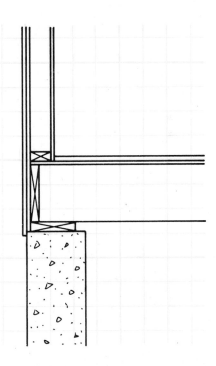

Fig. 28-7. Vertical location of grid lines with respect to frame floor above, and slab floor below.

A few simple rules have been devised for modular planning and dimensioning:

1. Lengths must be multiples of 4 inches.

2. Details of the structure should begin and terminate on a grid line, Fig. 28-6.

3. Grid dimensions are shown on the plan.

4. Floor levels are located on grid lines. The top of the subfloor and top of a finished concrete slab are located on the grid line, Fig. 28-7.

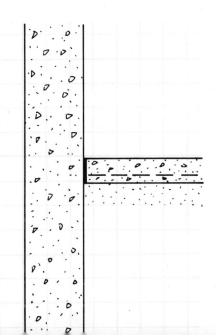

5. Dimensions terminating on a grid line are shown with an arrow. Dimensions terminating off the grid line are shown with a dot, Fig. 28-8.

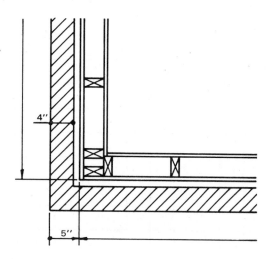

Fig. 28-8. In modular dimensioning, a dimension which terminates on a grid line is shown with an arrow. Dimensions which terminate off a grid line are shown with a dot.

6. Partitions are usually centered on grid lines, Fig. 28-9, but modular length interior walls are not nearly as important as outside walls.

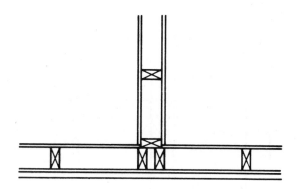

Fig. 28-9. Partitions are usually centered on a grid line.

MODULAR COMPONENTS

Modular components are building parts which have been preassembled either in a plant or on site. They are parts such as floor panels, roof panels, wall sections or roof trusses, Figs. 28-10 and 28-11. They may be constructed from wood, concrete, plywood, plastics, asbestos-cement, fiber glass, steel, aluminum, paper or most any other building material. Panels may also be made from layers of different materials.

Some of the advantages of prefabricated panels are: design freedom and esthetic appeal, high strength-to-weight ratios,

Fig. 28-10. The roof of this factory-built home is composed of preassembled roof panels which are complete with sheathing and insulation.
(Wausau Homes)

Fig. 28-11. A prefabricated wall panel is lifted into place. Notice that the electrical outlets, heating units, trim and wall finish have already been applied.

uniform quality, more efficient use of materials, lower cost and reduced time required for installation. Several companies are producing modular components in this growing field.

INDUSTRIALIZED HOUSING

The term industrialized housing refers to houses built in a factory. Many types of houses are being built in plants today,

all composed of modules, Fig. 28-12. Modules range in size from 12' x 20' to 12' x 40' and larger. A width of 12 ft. seems to be ideal because it is large enough for a fair size room and 12 ft. is the maximum width that most states will allow on the highway, Fig. 28-13. The larger modules are usually built on a production line much the same as an automobile, Fig. 28-14. Some facilities are so advanced that computer directed systems are being used. The computer calculates placement of

Fig. 28-12. A factory-built ranch style house which was erected on a regular type foundation. (Wausau Homes)

Fig. 28-13. A 12 ft. wide factory-built module being transported to the site. (American Plywood Assoc.)

studs for each wall panel and automatic nailers fasten the materials together. The trend toward more automatic equipment will continue as factory-built houses receive public acceptance and production increases. Fig. 28-15 shows some of the operations involved in producing a factory-built home.

The quality of many factory-built homes is better than traditional construction. Jigs and fixtures are used to cut and fit parts together and accuracy is improved. Better quality lumber is usually used because a warped board will not fit the jig properly.

These large modules are usually more than just a shell, Fig. 28-16. Most have the plumbing, wiring, finished floors and doors installed. They may be shipped to the site and lifted into place by a large crane one day, and be ready to move into in the next few days. Most are set on a regular foundation and ready to be connected to the water, sewer, gas and electricity as soon as they are located.

Fig. 28-14. Wall panels under construction on a production line.

Fig. 28-15. Some of the operations involved in producing a factory-built home. Upper left. Each module is built on a heavy steel frame on wheels. Upper right. Module walls have been erected, wiring completed, and interior is prepared for sprayed-on stucco surface. Lower left. Exterior wall panels are installed to complete the module. Lower right. Finished module, with wheels removed, is lowered onto concrete foundation. (American Plywood Assoc.)

Fig. 28-16. A modular house constructed from modular components. Most of the interior trim and mechanical equipment is already installed. (Wausau Homes)

Fig. 28-17. These kitchen modules are reaching completion on the production line. They will be complete with plumbing, wiring, cabinets and appliances.

Fig. 28-18. A bathroom module on the production line about to receive its drain and vent system. (Wausau Homes)

The versatility of these modules is evidenced by the fact that they may be set side by side, end to end, directly on top of each other or cantilevered to form interesting and functional shapes.

Modules within modules are also popular, Fig. 28-17. For example, a kitchen module which is complete with cabinets, range, refrigerator and floor covering may be plugged into a larger half-house size module. Bathroom modules are also being produced in the same manner, Fig. 28-18. As selection becomes greater, one will be able to select the kitchen, bath, and living room modules that he wishes to make up the total house, Fig. 28-19. A house may then be ordered just as a new car is now.

Factory-built houses of the future will not necessarily look like they do today. As new materials (new to the housing industry) are used for various house components and new processes are developed, complex shapes and rounded corners will be commonplace. The house of tomorrow should be more functional and afford a wider variety of configurations to choose from. If predictions are realized, the relative cost of housing will decline as factories move into full swing of home production.

Fig. 28-19. This kitchen module is being lifted into place. Other walls of the house will be located around it. Note the dishwasher, sink and lighting fixtures have been installed.

REVIEW QUESTIONS – CHAPTER 28

1. Some of the techniques that have been tried in an effort to reduce the cost and time required to build a residential structure are:_____.
2. The Department of Housing and Urban Development estimates that by the year 1980_____percent of the dwellings in the U. S. will be factory-built.
3. Building parts that have been preassembled in a plant are called _____ .
4. Identify four of the advantages of using prefabricated panels.
   a. _____ .
   b. _____ .
   c. _____ .
   d. _____ .
5. Identify the size of the following modules:
   a.   Standard module_____ .
   b.   Major module _____ .
   c.   Minor module _____and _____ .
6. All modules should be a multiple of_____inches.
7. Modular panels are usually produced in multiples of _____ inches.
8. When drawing a modular plan, dimensions terminating on a grid line are represented with a (an)_____ while dimensions terminating off a grid line terminate with a (an) _____ .
9. With respect to a frame floor the grid line is _____ _____ .
10. The term industrialized housing refers to _____ .

11. List two reasons why a 12' – 0" width appears ideal for industrialized housing modules.
    a. _____ .
    b. _____ .
12. Why is the quality of a factory-built home likely to be better than a "stick-built" home? Name two reasons.
    a. _____ .
    b. _____ .

SUGGESTED ACTIVITIES

1. Choose a non-modular floor plan and redesign it following the principles of modular construction. Dimension the plan and present both drawings for a comparison.
2. Invite a local builder to class to discuss methods which may be used in the design process that will conserve materials when building a house.
3. Design a residence which follows the principles of modular construction and makes use of standard roof and wall panels. Information about these panels may be secured from the American Plywood Association, The National Lumber Manufacturing Association, the Weyerhaeuser Company and others.
4. Design a modern two-car garage that makes use of formed roof modules. The modules may be plywood curved or flat stressed skin panels or precast concrete modules. Use your imagination and try for a unique but functional design.
5. Design a modular unit boat dock which may be expanded by simply adding more modules. Choose your own materials.

Construction costs are largely dependent upon the design features planned by the architect. Nonstandard sizes and unique styles will increase expenses considerably.

Chapter 29
ESTIMATING
BUILDING COST

After the house has been designed, construction drawings completed and material and workmanship specifications prepared, an estimate of cost should be made.

Estimating refers to an organized effort to determine the cost of materials and labor and other services required to build a house.

PRELIMINARY ESTIMATES

Two methods of estimating the cost of building a home are the SQUARE FOOT METHOD and the CUBIC FOOT METHOD. A rough estimate of the cost may be determined by using either method. In using the square foot method the first step is to compute the number of square feet in the house, then multiply this product by a constant which is determined by local conditions. The number of square feet is determined by multiplying the length of the house by the width. (All wall thicknesses are included in the total.) Garages, porches and basements are figured separately since they are not as expensive to construct as the living part of the house. (These are usually figured one half the cost per square foot of the living area.) For example, if a house is 24' x 60' and has a 20' x 20' garage, the area of living space would be 1,440 sq. ft. plus the garage area of 400 sq. ft. If the cost per square foot is $40 in a given area, then the living area would be 1,440 x $40 or $57,600. The cost of the garage would be 400 x $20 or $8,000. The estimated cost of the complete home then is $65,600. This price does not include the land. The constant of $40/sq. ft. (used for comparative purposes) is reasonable for some areas, but may vary several dollars in different localities and for different styles of homes and materials specified. For example, a ranch style home is more expensive to build than a two-story home which provides the same area of living space. Most builders use a different constant for each style house and add various amounts for special features such as an extra bath or fireplace. Before trying to calculate the cost of a home check with local builders to determine the constant for your area.

In estimating by the cubic foot method volume is used rather than area. The volume of a house is determined by finding the area and then multiplying this by the height. The height is figured from the basement floor to the ceiling. The attic volume is also included. It is calculated by finding the area (length by the width) and multiplying this figure by 1/2 the rise. The rise of the roof is the distance from the ceiling to the ridge. This procedure takes into account the volume lost due to the sloping roof.

If the 24' x 60' house is again used for the cubic foot method, the area is 1,440 sq. ft. and the height is 8 ft. Therefore, 1,440 x 8 = 11,520 cu. ft. for the living space, not including the attic. The area of the attic is 1,440 sq. ft. and the rise is 4 ft. Therefore, 1,440 x 2 = 2,880 cu. ft. for the attic. The total cu. ft. for the house then is 11,520 + 2,880 or 14,440 cu. ft. If the cost for a cubic foot is $4, then the estimated cost for the house would be 14,440 x 4 or $57,600.

The volume of the garage must also be computed and added to this figure. The volume is 400 x 8 or 3,200 cu. ft. The attic is 400 x 1 1/2 (the rise was 3 ft.) or 600 cu. ft. The total volume of the garage is 3,200 plus 600 or 3,800 cu. ft. The estimated cost of the garage is 3,800 x 2 or $7,600. The cost per cu. ft. of garage space is figured at one half the cost per cu. ft. of living space.

Total estimated cost of the house using the cubic foot method is $57,600 + $7,600 or $65,200. The difference in estimated cost between the two methods in this case is $400. Remember that you must use an accurate constant.

ESTIMATES WHICH ARE MORE ACCURATE

There are so many variables involved in the cost of a home that cost estimates obtained by the square foot or cubic foot method may vary considerably. A cost estimate which is more accurate may be obtained by determining the quantity, quality and cost of materials to be used, and cost of labor required for installation. You must include also an allowance for material waste, and for supervision and overhead.

The first step in compiling an accurate estimate is to study the construction drawings very carefully to become fully acquainted with the various elements of the structure. The specifications must also be examined carefully to determine the quality of materials and workmanship specified. Both of these factors will affect the final cost.

After one is intimately familiar with the plans, a list of materials may be compiled which will be required to construct the house. Most estimates follow the headings as listed on a good set of specifications. The order of the headings usually coincides with the construction sequence. When all the materials have been listed and priced, a total cost for materials may be identified. Prices should be secured from sources where the materials will be purchased to get an accurate price. A typical materials list is shown on the following pages.

Material List

Article And Description	Price	Amount	Article And Description	Price	Amount
General Information			Carpenter's Lumber List (Cont'd.)		
			Lintels		
Area of Basement, 1240 Sq. Ft. _____			2 Pcs., 2x12x15'0" (Flitch beams) _____		
Area of First Floor, 2250 Sq. Ft. _____			8 Pcs., 2x12x18'0" (Flitch beams) _____		
Height of Basement Floor to First Floor, 9'1-5/8" and 10'1-5/8" _____			6 Pcs., 2x12x3'4" _____		
First Floor Ceiling Height 8'0", 7'0" and Slopes _____			2 Pcs., 2x12x3'8" _____		
Ceiling to Roof, 4'6" and 3'1" _____			2 Pcs., 2x12x5'0" _____		
Size of Garage and/or Carport, 24'1"x22'10" _____			2 Pcs., 2x12x7'0" _____		
			8 Pcs., 2x12x9'0" _____		
			2 Pcs., 2x12x10'0" _____		
Excavating and Grading (will vary with local site conditions)			Stair Stringers		
			3 Pcs., 2x12x16'0" _____		
Rough Excavating, depends on site _____			Exterior Wall Plates, 2x4, 1260 Ft. _____		
Trench Excavating (wall footings), 19 Cu. Yds. _____			Exterior Wall Plates, 2x6x150 Ft. _____		
Backfill, depends on site and soil _____			Exterior Studs		
Finished Grading, depends on site _____			180 Pcs., 2x4x8'0" _____		
Hand Excavating (column footings), 1/2 Cu. Yd. _____			93 Pcs., 2x4x9'0" _____		
			7 Pcs., 2x4x10'0" _____		
Material Sub Total _____			9 Pcs., 2x4x11'0" _____		
Labor Sub Total _____			6 Pcs., 2x4x12'0" _____		
			Interior Plates		
			2x4, 800 Ft. _____		
Masonry			2x6, 30 Ft. _____		
			2x8, 105 Ft. _____		
Concrete Footings, 19.5 Cu. Yds. _____			Interior Studs		
Concrete Walls			55 Pcs., 2x4x9'0" _____		
4" Block, 40 Sq. Ft. _____			7 Pcs., 2x6x9'0" _____		
8" Block, 1600 Sq. Ft. _____			10 Pcs., 2x8x9'0" _____		
10" Block, 40 Sq. Ft. _____			210 Pcs., 2x4x8'0" _____		
12" Block, 420 Sq. Ft. _____			11 Pcs., 2x6x8'0" _____		
Exposed Concrete above Grade (block), 60 Sq. Ft. _____			25 Pcs., 2x8x8'0" _____		
Reinforcing Rods			Headers		
2-#4x4'0" _____			2 Pcs., 2x12x4'0" _____		
18-#3x30'0" _____			18 Pcs., 2x4x3'0" _____		
Wire Mesh Reinforcing, 2100 Sq. Ft. _____			16 Pcs., 2x4x2'8" _____		
Concrete Basement Floor 4" Thickx1200 Sq. Ft. _____			6 Pcs., 2x6x4'4" _____		
Patio Floor 4"Thick x 225 Sq. Ft. _____			4 Pcs., 2x8x6'4" _____		
Concrete Platforms on Ground (@ garbage cans), 4" Thick x 15 Sq. Ft. _____			Roof Sheathing 1/2" Plywood, 3850 Bd. Ft. _____		
Concrete Sidewalks (under flagstone walk), 4" Thick x 70 Sq. Ft. _____			Ridge Boards, 2x10, 110 Ft. _____		
Garage Floor, 4" Thick x 600 Sq. Ft. _____			Rafters		
Concrete Steps (under flagstone), 7 Sq. Ft. _____			60 Pcs., 2x8x22'0" _____		
Concrete Hearth setting bed for flagstone for fireplace, 3" Thick x 6 Sq.Ft _____			97 Pcs., 2x8x16'0" _____		
Flue Lining			14 Pcs., 2x8x12'0" _____		
12"x16" T.C., 21 Ft. _____			4 Pcs., 2x8x10'0" _____		
8"x8" T.C., 19 Ft. _____			Fascia Cornice 1x10, 340 Ft. _____		
220 Firebrick _____			Porch Steps		
2400 Common Brick and Chimney _____			2 Pcs., 2x12x10'0" _____		
Mortar, 8.2 Cu. Yds. _____			Waterproof Roofing Paper, 38-1/2 Sqs. _____		
Drain Tile (depends on site), as required _____			Building Paper under Wood Floor, 21-1/2 Sqs. _____		
Chimney Cap, 15 Sq. Ft. _____			Posts		
Supported Concrete Slabs, 1" setting bed x 185 Sq. Ft. _____			1 Pc., 4x4x8'0" _____		
Supported Concrete Slabs, 4" Thick x 175 Sq. Ft. _____			Girders Laminated Beams		
Stone Veneer, 8" Thick x 34'0"x10'0" _____			1 Pc., 5-1/4x14-1/2x24'0" _____		
Pea Gravel Patio and Walk, 3 Cu. Yds. _____			1 Pc., 5-1/4"x14-1/2"x24'0" _____		
19,000 Exterior Face Brick _____			Porch Posts		
Flagstones, 250 Sq. Ft. _____			8 Pcs., 4x4x8'0" _____		
6 Vents in Foundation Walls _____			Porch Railing 2x4, 128 Lin. Ft. _____		
Cement Block Quoins			Porch Cap 2x6, 64 Lin. Ft. _____		
160, 8" Blocks _____			Exterior Sheathing 1/2" Insulating Board, 2400 Sq. Ft. _____		
15, 10" Blocks _____			Siding, 1250 Sq. Ft. _____		
45, 12" Blocks _____			Basement Stair Posts		
Water Proofing Foundation Walls, 850 Sq. Ft. _____			1 Pc., 4x4x8'0" _____		
			Basement Stair Railings		
Material Sub Total _____			1 Pc., 2x4x6'0" _____		
Labor Sub Total _____			Soffits or Roof Overhang		
			1/2" Plywood, 3'4"x205' _____		
Carpenter's Lumber List			1/2" Plywood, 2'0"x145' _____		
			Scaffolding and Extra Joists (approx.), as required _____		
Joists			Plastic Ceiling at Kitchen and Master Bath		
42 Pcs., 2x12x20'0" _____			3 Pcs., 1x12x14'0" _____		
38 Pcs., 2x12x18'0" _____			Valance		
23 Pcs., 2x12x16'0" _____			1x6, 126 Ft. _____		
3 Pcs., 2x12x8'0" _____			1x10, 132 Ft. _____		
Bridging 1x4, 340 Sq. Ft. _____			Furring Strips, as required _____		
Sub Flooring, 2010 Sq. Ft. _____			Wind Stops at Eaves, 300 Ft. _____		
Ceiling Joists			Battens 1x2, 1100 Ft. _____		
13 Pcs., 2x8x20'0" _____			Shelving		
27 Pcs., 2x6x18'0" _____			10 Pcs., 1x10x10'0" _____		
8 Pcs., 2x6x16'0" _____			8 Pcs., 1x10x8'0" _____		
50 Pcs., 2x6x12'0" _____			Rafter Ties		
23 Pcs., 2x6x8'0" _____			2x4, 70 Ft. _____		
8 Pcs., 2x6x14'0" _____			24 Pcs., 2x4x10'0" _____		
Deck Beams					
2 Pcs., 2x10x14'0" _____			Material Sub Total _____		
2 Pcs., 2x10x12'0" _____			Labor Sub Total _____		
4 Pcs., 2x10x8'0" _____					
2 Pcs., 2x8x18'0" _____			**MILLWORK**		
12 Pcs., 2x8x14'0" _____					
10 Pcs., 2x8x10'0" _____			Windows And Screens (as selected)		
4 Pcs., 2x8x6'0" _____					
Deck Flooring			Window Frames		
21 Pcs., 2x6 (redwood) x14'0" _____			4 4'0"x6'0" Vertical Sliding Steel Windows _____		
18 Pcs., 2x6 (redwood) x12'0" _____			(Continued on next page)		
18 Pcs., 2x6 (redwood) x10'0" _____					
18 Pcs., 2x6 (redwood)x 8'0" _____					

Typical list for materials, fixtures and finishes.

Article And Description	Price	Amount

Windows and Screens (Cont'd.)

3   Double 4'0"x6'0" Vertical Sliding Steel Windows _____
4   4'0"x5'0" Vertical Sliding Steel Windows _____
1   3'0"x3'0" Horizontal Sliding Steel Windows _____
Fixed Plastic Screens (weather resistant)

Note: Provide frames for above plastic screens.
Storm Sash and Window screens or Rolling Metal Screens, as required _____
Doors And Trim

Exterior Door Frames
4   Frames for 2'8"x6'8"x1-3/4" Solid Core Wood Doors _____
1   Frame for 2-2'8"x6'8"x1-3/4" Solid Core Wood Doors _____
1   Frame for 2'8"x6'8"x1-3/8" Hollow Core Wood Doors _____
1   Frame for 16'0"x8'0" Sliding Glass Door _____
3   Frames for 8'0"x6'8" Sliding Glass Door _____
Interior Door Frames
8   Frames for 2'8"x6'8"x1-3/8" Hollow Core Wood Doors _____
7   Frames for 2'4"x6'8"x1-3/8" Hollow Core Wood Doors _____
3   Frames for 4'0"x6'8"x1-3/8" Hollow Core Wood Doors (folding)
2   Frames for 6'0"x6'8"x1-3/8" Hollow Core Wood Doors (folding)
Special Door Frames
1   Frame for 2'0"x6'8" Shower Door (master bath) _____
Exterior Doors
6   2'8"x6'8"x1-3/4" Solid Core Doors _____
1   2'8"x6'8"x1-3/8" Hollow Core Door _____
1   16'0"x8'0" Sliding Glass Door _____
3   8'0"x6'8" Sliding Glass Doors _____
Interior Doors
8   2'8"x6'8"x1-3/8" Hollow Core Doors _____
7   2'4"x6'8"x1-3/8" Hollow Core Doors _____
6   2'0"x6'8"x1-3/8" Hollow Core Folding Doors (louvered) _____
4   3'0"x6'8"x1-3/8" Hollow Core Folding Doors (louvered) _____
Interior Door Trim, 330 Lin. Ft. _____
Screen Doors, as required _____

Cabinets and Miscellaneous Millwork

Room Base, 375 Ft. _____
Clothes Closet Hook Strips, 75 Ft. _____
(Including Storage Closet but not Kitchen)
At other shelving, 125 Ft. _____
Closet Shelving, 1'6"x115 Ft. _____
Closet Shelving, 1'8"x12'6" _____
Closet Poles, 50 Ft. _____
Outside Door Thresholds, Entry – Bronze Thresholds,x5'4" _____
Ceiling Mold around Chimney, 30'0" _____
Kitchen Broom Closet and Pantry _____
5 Shelves 1'8"x3/4"x2'6" _____
2 Sides 1'8"x3/4"x8'0" _____
10 Cleats, 1'2"x1'8" _____
Kitchen Cupboards
Doors and Exposed Faces, 180 Sq. Ft. _____
Sides and Partitions, 100 Sq. Ft. _____
Shelves, 115 Sq. Ft. _____
Backs, Sides and Bottom, 90 Sq. Ft. _____
Tops (Plastic Laminated), 65 Sq. Ft. _____
1x2 Framing, 220 Ft. _____
Wood Legs at Island, 7 _____
Drawer Track, 20 Ft. _____
Basement Stairs
16 Pine Risers 7-1/2"x3/4"x3'4" _____
15 Oak Treads 10-1/2"x1-1/4"x3'4" _____
Decorative Screen–In Foyer, 7'0"x11'0" _____
Clothes Chute Door 3/4" Plywood, 1'0"x2'6" _____
Bathroom Cabinets (1st floor)
1x2 Frame, 53' _____
1x4 Kickboard, 12'4" _____
Doors, etc., 31 Sq. Ft. _____
Shelves, etc., 67 Sq. Ft. _____
Special Beams (false)
2 Pcs., 2x4x18'0" _____
5 Pcs., 4x4x18'0" _____
Window Valances
1x10, 130 Ft. _____
1x6, 130 Ft. _____
China Closets
3   16"x28"x1/4" Plate Glass Shelves _____
2   54" Adjustable Shelf Standards _____
6   16" Adjustable Shelf Brackets _____
3"x1-1/8"x2'4" Plate Glass Shelves _____
2-1/4"x1-1/8"x4'8" Plate Glass Shelves _____
3/4"x3/4"x9'0" Plate Glass Shelves _____
15"x24"x1/4" Frosted Plastic Top _____
3/4" Plywood, 40 Sq. Ft. _____
2x6 – 4'8" _____
1x3 – 5'0" _____
2x3 – 2'4" _____
Breakfast Room Cabinets
Kickboard 1x4, 8 Ft. _____
Doors and Sides, 56 Sq. Ft. _____

Cabinets and Miscellaneous Millwork (Cont'd.)

Shelves, 53 Sq. Ft. _____
Frame 1x2, 53 Sq. Ft. _____
Full Length Mirror
Baths
1   80x50 _____
1   68x50 _____
Basement
1   68x50 _____

Material Sub Total _____
Labor Sub Total _____

Insulation

Batt Type Ceilings, 2230 Sq. Ft. _____
Batt Type Walls, 1650 Sq. Ft. _____

Material Sub Total _____
Labor Sub Total _____

Weatherstripping and Calking

Windows, 275 Ft. _____
Exterior Doors, 205 Ft. _____

Material Sub Total _____
Labor Sub Total _____

Plastering or Dry Wall

Living Room Walls, 340 Sq. Ft. _____
Living Room Ceiling, 530 Sq. Ft. _____
Dining Room Walls, 290 Sq. Ft. _____
Dining Room Ceiling, 215 Sq. Ft. _____
Foyer Walls, 31 Sq. Ft. _____
Foyer Ceiling, 102 Sq. Ft. _____
Hall Walls, 250 Sq. Ft. _____
Hall Ceiling, 80 Sq. Ft. _____
Basement Stairway Walls, 300 Sq. Ft. _____
Basement Stairway Ceiling, 35 Sq. Ft. _____
Kitchen Walls, 490 Sq. Ft. _____
Kitchen Ceiling, 290 Sq. Ft. _____
Bathroom Walls
Basement, 65 Sq. Ft. _____
1st Floor, 230 Sq. Ft. _____
Bathroom Ceiling
Basement, 50 Sq. Ft. _____
1st Floor, 85 Sq. Ft. _____
Bedroom Walls
Basement, 410 Sq. Ft. _____
1st Floor, 780 Sq. Ft. _____
Bedroom Ceilings
Basement, 245 Sq. Ft. _____
1st Floor, 480 Sq. Ft. _____
Closet Walls
Basement, 120 Sq. Ft. _____
1st Floor, 610 Sq. Ft. _____
Closet Ceilings
Basement, 16 Sq. Ft. _____
1st Floor, 105 Sq. Ft. _____
Garage Walls, 600 Sq. Ft. _____
Garage Ceiling, 515 Sq. Ft. _____
Laundry Walls Basement, 195 Sq. Ft. _____
Laundry Ceiling Basement, 65 Sq. Ft. _____
Storage Room Walls, 120 Sq. Ft. _____
Storage Room Ceiling, 21 Sq. Ft. _____
Study Walls, 350 Sq. Ft. _____
Study Ceiling, 170 Sq. Ft. _____

Material Sub Total _____
Labor Sub Total _____

Finish Flooring

Living Room, 408 Sq. Ft. _____
Dining Room, 201 Sq. Ft. _____
Foyer, 102 Sq. Ft. _____
Halls, 80 Sq. Ft. _____
Basement Stairway, 50 Sq. Ft. _____
Kitchen, 290 Sq. Ft. _____
Bathrooms, 115 Sq. Ft. _____
Bedrooms, 450 Sq. Ft. _____
Closets, 100 Sq. Ft. _____
Storage Room, 22 Sq. Ft. _____
Study, 155 Sq. Ft. _____

Material Sub Total _____
Labor Sub Total _____

(Continued on next page)

Typical list for materials, fixtures and finishes. (Continued)

Material List

Article And Description	Price	Amount	Article And Description	Price	Amount

Painting And Finishing

Exterior Siding, 1250 Sq. Ft. _____
Exterior Cornice, 360 Ft. _____
Exterior Doors (both sides), 230 Sq. Ft. _____
Basement Doors (both sides), 270 Sq. Ft. _____
Basement Stairs (top sides), 94 Sq. Ft. _____
Interior Doors (both sides), 720 Sq. Ft. _____
Interior Door Trims, 330 Ft. _____
Sheet Metal Items
  Chimney Flashing, 16 Ft. _____
  Wall Flashing @ Decks, 41 Ft. _____
  Ridge Vent, 116 Ft. _____
Kitchen Cupboards (including Shelves and Interior), 650 Sq. Ft. _____
Linen Closets (including Shelves), 145 Sq. Ft. _____
Broom Closet and Pantry (including Shelves), 200 Sq . Ft. _____
Closet Shelving (both sides), 150 Sq. Ft. _____
Closet Poles, 50 Ft. _____
Closet Hook Strip (clothes closets), 75 Ft. _____
Wood Base, 375 Ft. _____
Porch Posts (pipe columns), 35 Ft. _____
Garage Doors (both sides), 225 Sq. Ft. _____
Exposed Bricks
  Interior, 200 Sq. Ft. _____
  Exterior, 1250 Sq. Ft. _____
Interior Beams
  4x4 False Beams, 112 Ft. _____
  5-1/4x14-1/2 Laminated Beams, 48 Ft. _____
Exterior Cinder Block Walls, 60 Sq. Ft. _____
Living Room Walls, 340 Sq. Ft.
Living Room Ceiling (including top side of Valance), 615 Sq. Ft. _____
Living Room Floor
  Flagstone, 38 Sq. Ft. _____
  Carpeted, 408 Sq. Ft. _____
Dining Room Walls, 290 Sq. Ft.
Dining Room Ceiling, 215 Sq. Ft. _____
Dining Room Floor
  Flagstone Passage, 14 Sq. Ft. _____
  Carpeted, 201 Sq. Ft. _____
Foyer Walls, 31 Sq. Ft. _____
Foyer Ceiling, 102 Sq. Ft. _____
Foyer Floor Flagstone, 102 Sq. Ft. _____
Hall Walls, 250 Sq. Ft. _____
Hall Ceiling, 80 Sq. Ft. _____
Hall Floor, 80 Sq. Ft. _____
Basement Stairway Walls, 300 Sq. Ft. _____
Basement Stairway Ceiling, 35 Sq. Ft. _____
Kitchen Walls, 325 Sq. Ft. _____
Kitchen Plastic Ceiling, 48 Sq. Ft. _____
Kitchen Ceiling, 240 Sq. Ft. _____
Kitchen Floor, 290 Sq. Ft. _____
Bathroom Walls
  Basement, 60 Sq. Ft. _____
  1st Floor, 230 Sq. Ft. _____
Bathroom Ceilings
  Plastic Ceiling, 51 Sq. Ft. _____
  Basement, 50 Sq. Ft. _____
  1st Floor, 105 Sq. Ft. _____
Bathroom Floors
  Basement, 20 Sq. Ft. _____
  1st Floor, 115 Sq. Ft. _____
Bedroom Walls
  Basement, 410 Sq. Ft. _____
  1st Floor, 780 Sq. Ft. _____
Bedroom Ceilings (including valances)
  Basement, 245 Sq. Ft. _____
  1st Floor, 480 Sq. Ft. _____
Bedroom Floors
  Basement, 245 Sq. Ft. _____
  1st Floor, 450 Sq. Ft. _____
Closet Walls
  Basement, 120 Sq. Ft. _____
  1st Floor, 520 Sq. Ft. _____
Closet Ceilings
  Basement, 16 Sq. Ft. _____
  1st Floor, 90 Sq. Ft. _____
Closet Floors
  Basement, 18 Sq. Ft. _____
  1st Floor, 90 Sq. Ft. _____
Garage Walls, 600 Sq. Ft. _____
Garage Ceiling, 515 Sq. Ft. _____
Laundry Walls
  Concrete Block, 80 Sq. Ft. _____
  Other, 195 Sq. Ft. _____
Laundry Ceiling, 65 Sq. Ft. _____
Laundry Floor, 65 Sq. Ft. _____
Breakfast Room Walls, see Kitchen _____
Breakfast Room Ceiling, see Kitchen _____
Breakfast Room Floor, see Kitchen _____
Storage Room Walls, 120 Sq. Ft. _____
Storage Room Ceiling, 21 Sq. Ft. _____
Storage Room Floor, 21 Sq. Ft. _____

Painting And Finishing (Cont'd.)

Study Walls, 350 Sq. Ft. _____
Study Ceiling (including Valance), 170 Sq. Ft. _____
Study Floor, 155 Sq. Ft. _____
Special Mold Quarter Round, 500 Ft. _____
Bathroom Cabinets (including shelves and interior)
  Basement, 105 Sq. Ft. _____
  1st Floor, 210 Sq. Ft. _____
China Cabinet (including shelves and interior), 35 Sq. Ft. _____
Deck Steps (one side), 20 Sq. Ft. _____
Full Length Mirrors
Baths
  1   80x50 _____
  1   68x50 _____
Basement
  1   68x50 _____
Square Edge Trim 3/4x3/4, 10 Ft. _____
Battens 1x2, 1100 Ft. _____
Wood Decks
  2x6 Flat 3/16" Spacers, 365 Sq. Ft. _____
  2 2x10 Beams, 42 Sq. Ft. _____
  2 2x8 Beams, 132 Ft. _____
  1 2x8 Beams, 14 Ft. _____
Guard Rail, 190 Ft. _____

          Material Sub Total _____
          Labor Sub Total _____

Miscellaneous Hardware

40 Foundation Anchor Bolts 1/2" Diam.   A.B.'s to Sill _____
1 Clean out Door Frame Unit _____
1 Ash Dump Unit _____
1 Fireplace Damper Unit _____
2 Angle Iron Fireplace Lintels 3-1/2"x3-1/2"x1/2"x5'4" _____
1 Angle Iron Fireplace Lintel 3-1/2"x3-1/2"x1/2"x6'0" _____
Nails approximately 400 Lbs. _____
1 Dowel for Wood Post Anchors and Footings _____
Lally Columns 3" Diam. Pipe Columns
  1   2'0" _____
  1   7'0" _____
  3   8'6" _____
Miscellaneous Builders Hardware, as required _____
250 Wall Ties _____
Roof Beams Flitch Plates
  4   11"x3/8"x18'0" _____
  1   11"x3/8"x15'0" _____
  1   Angle 3-1/2"x3-1/2"x3/8"x3'0" _____
  1   Angle 3-1/2"x3-1/2"x1/2"x4'4" _____
5 Column Caps for 3" Diam. Pipe Column Units _____
5 Column Bases for 3" Diam. Pipe Column Units _____
Wire Mesh Reinforcement, (see Masonry Section) _____
Steps down to Living Room Floor
  4 Angles 1-1/2"x1-1/2"x3'0" _____
  2 Junior Channels 12"x1-1/2"x5'0" _____
Miscellaneous Bolts at Deck Rail 32 Machine Bolts 3/4" Diam. x 6"___
Extra Heavy Corrugated Sheets Metal Forming, 180 Sq. Ft._____
Reinforcement Bars, see Masonry Section _____

          Material Sub Total _____
          Labor Sub Total _____

Finish Hardware

2 Basement Doors
  2 Pr. 3-1/2x3-1/2 Butts _____
  2 Latch Sets _____
1 Pr. Front Entrance Doors
  3 Pr. 4x4 Butts _____
  1 Lockset _____
1 Rear Entrance Doors
  1-1/2 Pr. 4x4 Butts _____
  1 Lockset _____
4 Side Doors (including Doors from Garage)
  6 Pr. 4x4 Butts _____
  4 Locksets _____
Screen Doors (as required) _____
4 Bathroom Doors
  4 Pr. 3-1/2x3-1/2 Butts _____
  4 Locksets (Bath) _____
  3 - 8'0"x6'8" Glass Sliding Door Unit _____
  1 - 16'0"x8'0" Glass Sliding Door Unit _____
Double Acting Doors
  1   2'8"x6'8" _____
  1   Pr. 3-1/2x3-1/2 Double Acting _____
  1   Push Plate each Side _____
9 Interior Doors
  9 Pr. 3-1/2x3-1/2 Butts _____
  9 Latch Sets _____
Storm Sashes, as required _____

(Continued on next page)

Typical list for materials, fixtures and finishes. (Continued)

Material List

Article And Description	Price	Amount	Article And Description	Price	Amount

Finish Hardware (Cont'd.)

Kitchen Cabinets (Storage and Bathroom included)
  41 Pr. Cabinet Hinges _____
  95 Knobs or Pulls _____
  42 Friction Catches _____
Closets Folding Wood (4 panel)
  3 4'0"x6'8" _____
  2 6'0"x6'8" _____
  20 Pr. 3-1/2x3-1/2 Butts _____
  10 Pulls _____
  10 Catches _____
Miscellaneous Cabinets - Dining Room
  2 Pr. Cabinet Hinges _____
  2 Pulls _____
  2 Catches _____
1 Mail Box Unit _____
5 Floor Door Stops _____
16 Regular Door Stops _____
1 Doz. Coat and Hat Hooks _____
Miscellaneous Small Hardware, as required _____
1 Overhead Garage Door Unit 16'0"x7'0" _____
Shower Door (Master Bath)
  1 Pr. Metal Hinges _____
  1 Knob Set Unit _____
  1 Friction Catch _____

                    Material Sub Total _____
                    Labor Sub Total _____

Sheet Metal Work

Flashing around Chimney, 16 Lin. Ft. _____
Flashing at Vertical Walls at Exterior Decks, 41 Ft. _____
Exhaust Fan Grills
  3 Bathroom required _____
  1 Kitchen required _____
4 - 8" Diam. Ducts to Roof Vents _____
Valleys, 40 Ft. _____
Ridge Vent, 116 Ft. _____
1 Metal Clothes Chute Unit 12"x16" _____
Metal Lined Bread Drawer, 12 Sq. Ft. _____

                    Material Sub Total _____
                    Labor Sub Total _____

Floor Finishing Material

Resilient _____
Tile _____
Wood _____
Carpet _____
Tile Fireplace Hearth _____
Cove Base _____
Miscellaneous _____

                    Material Sub Total _____
                    Labor Sub Total _____

Wall Finishing Material

Work Table Tops and Backs Plastic Laminated, 90 Sq. Ft. _____
Tile Base in Bathroom, 80 Ft. _____
Tile or Chrome inserts in Bathroom
  3 Toilet Paper Holders _____
  3 Soap Dishes and Grab Bars _____
  10 Towel Bars _____
  3 Robe Hooks _____
Bathroom Tile Wainscot, 270 Sq. Ft. _____

                    Material Sub Total _____
                    Labor Sub Total _____

Roofing

38-1/2 Sqs. Owner' Choice _____

                    Material Sub Total _____
                    Labor Sub Total _____

Plumbing

Note: This survey does not list the quantities of each item required
       for the mechanical equipment, as there is a variation in any
       system chosen. However, the form given will be of assistance
       to your dealer in arriving at an accurate estimate.

1 Double Kitchen Sink _____
3 Water Closet Units _____
2 Bath Tubs _____
3 Shower Head Units _____
3 Floor Drain Units _____
4 Top Mounted Lavatories _____
Automatic Washer Outlet _____
4 Hose Bib Units _____
Hot Water Heater 40 Gallons Gas Fired Unit (50 Gallons Electric) ____
1 Garbage Disposer Unit _____
Miscellaneous
  Gas Range, Grill with Cover and Rotisserie, Hood with 2 Dual
  Blowers (1200 CFM), Built-In Refr.-Freezer _____

                    Material Sub Total _____
                    Labor Sub Total _____

Electric Wiring

21 Ceiling Outlets (6 Spots) _____
4 Bracket Outlets, Outside Fixtures _____
57 Duplex Receptacles _____
10 Water-proof Receptacles _____
32 Wall Switches _____
1 Dimmer Switch Dining Room Spots _____
10 Three-way Switches _____
1 Set Entrance Chime _____
1 Ceiling Outlet (vapor-proof) over Master Bath Shower _____
2 Push Buttons _____
7 Porch Lights Twin Floods @ each Unit _____
7 Hall and Entrance Lights 150 W Ceiling Flush Mounted Units ____
1 Kitchen Fan - Hood-Fan Combination Unit _____
1 Bathroom Exhaust Fan _____
1 Bathroom Combination Heater and Ventilator _____
1 Bathroom Combination Heater, Ventilator and Light _____
2 - 220V Receptacles (Dryer and Range) _____
Special Tubular Light Installations
  2 2'0" Single Tube Units (20W) _____
  11 4'0" Single Tube Units (40W) _____
  2 23'0" Single Tube Units (Living Room) _____
  1 14'0" Single Tube Unit (Bedroom) _____
  1 13'0" Single Tube Unit (Bedroom) _____
  1 12'6" Single Tube Unit (Bedroom) _____

                    Material Sub Total _____
                    Labor Sub Total _____

Telephone Wiring

Note: Call the nearest telephone company business office for
       assistance in planning adequate built-in telephone facilities.
       These will include the following items:

1. Entrance pipe or underground entrance conduit _____
2. Galvanized iron protector cabinet _____
3. Interior thin-wall conduit to all outlets _____
4. Standard outlet boxes with telephone cover _____
5. Telephone or jack locations _____
6. Miscellaneous or special items _____

                    Material Sub Total _____
                    Labor Sub Total _____

Heating

A heating unit will be required of sufficient size for a house with
3490 Sq. Ft. and/or 30250 Cu. Ft. _____

                    Material Sub Total _____
                    Labor Sub Total _____

Typical list for materials, fixtures and finishes. (Continued)

Now that the cost of materials has been determined, the labor cost must be calculated. As recent as a few years ago the labor cost was less than half the total cost of building a house, but today in most sections of the county it ranges from 60 to 80 percent of the total cost. The labor cost involved in building a house has steadily increased year after year and it would be wise to research this area carefully before trying to estimate that cost. Publications such as the Building Construction Cost Data Book are available which give detailed information on labor costs for various areas of the county. General contractors and sub-contractors also can provide help in arriving at the projected cost. Their experience will enable them to make an accurate estimate of labor costs for a given job.

Another cost which must be included is the fee for permits. Most areas require a building permit, a plumbing permit, an electrical permit and a health permit. The cost of these permits may be as small as a few dollars or as much as several hundred dollars. Also, there may be a fee for electrical, gas, sewer, telephone and water hook up. Again, this may be a small amount or total several hundred dollars. Investigate these areas to determine their exact costs.

Many builders add the cost of insurance to protect materials and workers in the event of an accident or damage. This cost should also be added to the cost of construction. Once all these elements have been evaluated, the total cost of building the house may be calculated.

This estimate will most likely be more accurate than the approximate methods presented earlier, but it may still be a few hundred dollars off. It is impossible to calculate exactly the cost of building a house. Even builders who have been in the business for years sometimes fail to accurately estimate the cost of a job. Therefore, it is extremely important that you learn to prepare drawings and specifications accurately. Be sure all specifications are complete and easy to understand.

REVIEW QUESTIONS – CHPATER 29

1. Two methods commonly used for preliminary cost estimates are:
   a. _____.
   b. _____.
2. If the estimated cost of a house with 1524 sq. ft. is $32,000 what would be the cost per square foot? _____.
3. Explain how a more accurate estimate than the square or cubic foot method may be computed. _____
   _____.
4. Permits usually required for building a new home are:
   a. _____.
   b. _____.
   c. _____.
   d. _____.
5. The cost of labor to construct a house may be determined accurately by _____.
6. The cost of materials required to build a house may be secured from _____.

SUGGESTED ACTIVITIES

1. Using a plan that you have designed or one supplied by your instructor, calculate the cost using the square foot method. Your instructor will help you determine the price per square foot in your area.
2. Using the same plan in No. 1 above, calculate a more accurate estimate for materials only by listing the materials to be used and pricing them in detail. Use prices from a local lumber company and other material suppliers.
3. Establish the current rate for carpenters, plumbers, electricians, masons, and all other skilled tradesmen who work together to build a house. Record the rates and sources used and prepare a report to be presented to your class.

Checking the final details of a residential plan to determine cost specifications.

Chapter 30

FINANCING THE HOME

Very few families are financially able to build a new home and pay cash. The home is usually one of the largest investments that a family ever makes. Therefore, a source of financing other than personal savings is generally required. The purpose of this chapter is to bring about an increasing awareness of home financing.

One of the first questions to be dealt with when a family decides to build a new home is, "how much can we spend"? This will vary from family to family depending on income, number of children and other obligations. However, a "rule of thumb" has been proposed to determine the amount that one should spend for a house. The rule states that an amount between 1 1/2 and 2 1/2 times the yearly gross income of the head of the household may be spent for housing. The chart below shows the amount which may be spent for a home for several earning levels when this rule is applied.

GROSS INCOME AND HOUSE COST RELATIONSHIP

GROSS INCOME YEARLY BEFORE DEDUCTIONS	TOTAL COST OF HOUSE 1 1/2 TIMES TO 2 1/2 TIMES	
8,000	12,000	20,000
9,000	13,500	22,500
10,000	15,000	25,000
11,000	16,500	27,500
12,000	18,000	30,000
15,000	22,500	37,500
20,000	30,000	50,000
30,000	45,000	65,000
40,000	60,000	100,000

Other home financial experts say that a family may spend between 1/4 and 1/5 of monthly income on housing. If this rule is used, then a family whose income is $12,000 a year or $1,000 a month would have between $200 and $250 a month to spend on housing. If this same family wished to borrow $20,000 at 10 percent interest to build a home, their monthly payments would be approximately $193 a month if financed over 20 years. This figure does not include insurance and property taxes which would add several hundred dollars to the housing cost. This would increase the monthly allowance above the prescribed level. They could, however, finance the loan over a 30 year period. This would reduce the monthly payments to about $175 per month. (It would cost them $16,865 more to borrow the money for 30 years as compared to 20 years.)

Each family should examine their own situation to de-termine how much money they have to spend for housing. The most accurate way is to add up all expenses including money for clothes, medical, dental, life insurance, food, utilities, education, transportation, etc. and subtract this from take-home income. The amount left will be the maximum that should be spent on housing.

INCOME:
Husband's take-home pay _____
Wife's take-home pay _____
Bonuses _____
Other income from dividends, interest,
    rental property, etc. _____
                    TOTAL INCOME - - - _____ *
*This is the amount you have to operate the total budget.

MONTHLY EXPENSES:
Food (including meals out) _____
Transportation (include gas, average
    repair costs, etc.) _____
Clothing (add cleaning and laundry) _____
Medical and Dental (do not include those
    items covered by insurance) _____
Household Operations (include utilities,
    maintenance, etc.) _____
Insurance _____
Personal Loans _____
Installment Loans _____
Credit Cards and Charge Accounts _____
Regular Savings _____
Entertainment _____
Contributions and Dues _____
Allowances _____
Baby-sitters and/or household help _____
Miscellaneous job expenses _____
Personal Care _____
Other _____ _____
            TOTAL MONTHLY EXPENSES - - - _____

Subtract the Total Monthly Expenses from your Total Income to determine the amount remaining for housing.

TOTAL Take-home Income _____
TOTAL Monthly Expenses _____

Available for Housing - - - - - - - - - - - - - - - _____

HOME LOANS

Most people who plan to build a home make a down payment and borrow the remainder from a lending agency, obtaining a mortgage on the property as security. Before proceeding any further, several terms should be identified to clarify the discussion.

AMORTIZED MORTGAGE. Has fixed monthly payments which include both interest due and a portion of the principle. As the payments proceed, the amount going to the principal gradually increases and the amount allocated to interest decreases.

CLOSING COSTS. Closing costs are paid by the borrower to the lender for making the loan. The amount is variable, but may be several hundred dollars.

ESCROW. Escrow is money held by a third party until conditions of the contract are met. Frequently, payments into an escrow fund are required to pay the property taxes.

FORECLOSURE. If the terms of a mortgage contract are not met, the mortgagee has a right to sell the property in public auction to recover his investment.

INTEREST. Interest is cost of borrowing money. It is the same as rent.

LIEN. A lien is a legal right to hold property or to have it sold or applied for payment of a claim. Anyone may file a claim (lien) for labor or materials which have not been paid.

MORTGAGE: A mortgage is a pledge of property as a security for a loan.

MORTGAGEE. The mortgagee is the one who loans the money.

MORTGAGOR. The mortgagor is the one who is borrowing the money.

NOTE. A note is a written promise to back the money borrowed.

SECOND MORTGAGE. A second mortgage is one made on a piece of property which already has a mortgage. The first mortgage is always paid first and usually has a lower interest rate due to the position of increased security.

STRAIGHT MORTGAGE. A straight mortgage or fixed mortgage is a loan at a given interest rate for a definite period of time with a promise to pay the full amount on a specified date. This is in contrast to the amortized mortgage which calls for fixed monthly payments, which include both the interest due and a portion of the principal.

Most families should probably seek an amortized mortgage for financing their new home since the terms are definitely fixed in advance to fit the family's financial position and ability to pay. Some people prefer a package loan which is a variation of the amortized mortgage. A package loan allows for the cost of equipment that is an integral part of the house to be included in the mortgage. This is an advantage because it spreads the cost of these items over a long period of time and makes them immediately available.

Another type of mortgage that a prospective home builder might be interested in is the open-end mortgage. An open-end mortgage contains a clause which allows the mortgagor to borrow more money and add it to the present mortgage under the original conditions. This would make possible early expansion or repairs if needs arose. This type of mortgage holds a definite advantage over others if interest rates were to rise significantly during the life of the mortgage.

Any family who plans to build a home may apply for an FHA (Federal Housing Administration) insured loan. The FHA does not lend the money itself, but it insures various lending institutions which have been approved by the FHA. Terms of an FHA insured mortgage are fixed by law and are usually quite liberal.

Veterans may want to apply for a VA (Veterans Administration) loan. The VA also insures mortgage loans against loss. Both the VA and FHA prescribe the terms and arrangements of the loans they insure. VA loans are usually less expensive than other type loans.

In some states, savings banks are a source for home loans. Some lend up to 90 percent of the appraised value of the house and extend the mortgage over a 30 year period. The usual amount is 75 percent for 25 years. In most instances, the larger the down payment on a loan from many sources, the lower the interest rate.

Insurance companies also loan money for new homes. Ordinarily they do business through established mortgage companies which they feel are best suited for each individual case. They make loans up to 75 or 80 percent of the approved value for 25 or 30 years. Their rates are comparable to other sources.

Mortgage contracts are not all identical. Some have penalties if the debt is paid off before a prescribed time. Others have no-penalty clauses. Some mortgage contracts allow for paying off the construction (construction loan) as the work progresses. This is an important feature if one is building a new house rather than buying an existing house. The cost of executing the loan varies broadly from institution to institution.

Some people are only interested in how much the monthly payments will be. However, it may be very surprising to see how much money you will pay in interest during the life of the loan. In the following chart, the interest paid on a $19,000 loan is shown for various periods of time at different interest rates.

HOME LOAN INTEREST COSTS FOR A $19,000 LOAN

LENGTH OF LOAN	INTEREST RATE	INTEREST PAID	TOTAL REPAYMENT
20 Years	6%	13,671	32,671
20 Years	8%	19,143	38,143
20 Years	10%	25,006	44,006
25 Years	6%	17,726	36,726
25 Years	8%	24,995	43,995
25 Years	10%	32,798	51,798
30 Years	6%	22,111	41,111
30 Years	8%	31,191	50,191
30 Years	10%	41,026	60,026

This chart shows the increasing cost of a loan if the payments are stretched out over a long period of time. Few people stop to think that they would pay back over 3 dollars for each dollar borrowed if the interest rate were 10% over a 30 year period. The lowest interest rate and best terms are definitely worth discussion with a number of lending institutions.

REVIEW QUESTIONS — CHAPTER 30

1. How much (by generally accepted standards) should an average family spend for the construction of a house?

   _____.

2. The standard lengths of time that most mortgage contracts are made for are:
   a. _____.
   b. _____.
   c. _____.

3. What is interest?_____.

4. The advantage of an amortized mortgage is _____
   _____.

5. The role the FHA plays in mortgages for new homes is
   _____.

6. VA loans may be obtained by_____
   _____.

7. Identify two other sources of loans for homes.
   a. _____.
   b. _____.

8. One should shop around before making application for a loan to _____.

SUGGESTED ACTIVITIES

1. Make an appointment to take a plan that you have drawn to a local lending institution which makes loans for home construction. Ask them to explain the procedure they would use to determine how much money to loan for the construction of this house. Record the procedure and discuss with the class.

2. Determine the sources for home loans and their requirements in your immediate area. Compare the requirements and prepare a written report from your research.

This home is typical of the many construction-design opportunities for the career architect. He brings together a combination of materials, shapes and colors to present ideas for comfortable residential living.

Chapter 31
CAREER OPPORTUNITIES

The fascinating world of architecture and residential construction has been illustrated throughout this text by many related career and job opportunities. Home construction requires the knowledge and skills of a variety of tradesmen and professionals. To some people, certain occupations will be more interesting and exciting than others. It is this concept that a person should carefully analyze as he contemplates a career in any phase of architecture and the variety of related occupational fields.

Take a close look at the duties, functions, responsibilities and educational requirements of a number of possible employment opportunities in residential architecture. If your interests and abilities lie in any of the architecture and residential construction areas, a close examination of the qualifications for particular job opportunities should be made. The following brief descriptions of a number of career opportunities should prove of value in gaining an over-all picture of man's role in residential architecture, designing and construction.

ARCHITECT

The architect's job includes a great deal of creativity and sensitivity to form and materials, Fig. 31-1. He generally works closely with the client in making preliminary drawings, sketches and suggestions for materials to be used. When the architect and client mutually agree upon a final design for the structure, working drawings are prepared as described throughout the previous chapters.

An architect may also have the responsibility of assisting the client in selecting a building contractor and represent the owner in dealing with the contractor during construction. It is usually his duty to periodically check construction as it proceeds to see that the plan is being followed and the materials specified are being used.

Educational requirements for an architect may vary according to the background of the individual. However, the general practice requires a bachelor's degree from an accredited college

Fig. 31-1. An architect's work is very rewarding.

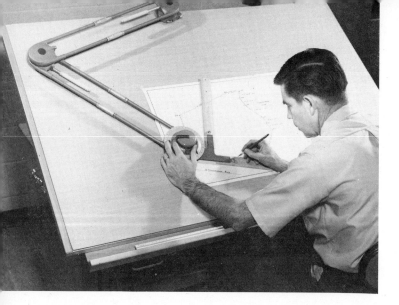

Fig. 31-2. An architectural draftsman completing the details of a plot plan to become part of a set of drawings prepared by the architect.

or university. In many cases a master's degree for advanced study is obtained. In some instances a two year program along with a number of years of practical experience will meet the necessary requirements. All states require an examination to obtain a license. The license indicates that the person is a registered architect. This means that he is qualified to design structures that meet the standards for safety, health and property. Job opportunities for an architect appear to be very favorable. However, relatively few architects are employed full time in residential home design. Most architects work for large firms which design commercial buildings.

ARCHITECTURAL DRAFTSMAN

An architectural draftsman generally draws the details of working drawings and makes tracings from original drawings

Fig. 31-3. Architectural illustrators use many techniques to communicate the plan to others.   (Smith, Hinchman, and Grylls, Assoc.)

that the architect or designer has prepared, Fig. 31-2. He often begins as a junior draftsman and as he gains experience is given more difficult assignments in the architectural firm.

Many architectural draftsmen who are satisfied with their position retain this job as a career. Others may take the licensing examination with the goal of becoming an architect or beginning a new firm on their own.

Educational requirements for the architectural draftsman usually require graduation from high school with some courses in architectural drawing. Extensive study at a technical institute, vocational school or community college is desirable for further experience and better job placement.

Fig. 31-4. A specification writer checking the exacting details of all requirements to go into the contract of an architectural project.

ARCHITECTURAL ILLUSTRATOR

Architectural illustration requires a high degree of skill and study to become readily employable. The architectural illustrator usually begins his study in architectural drawing or art and branches off into this specialized field, Fig. 31-3. The chapter on presentation drawings provides a good opportunity to recognize the various techniques used by architects and illustrators in preparing presentations and renderings. Drawings, sketches, renderings and illustrations are generally prepared to present ideas to potential clients and as advertisements for commercial catalogs and publications.

In more recent years, the use of photographs and models has replaced some of the work the architectural illustrator has done. However, there is still great need for people who are highly skilled in this area. As a person studies architectural designing and finds he has a flair for preparing illustrations, it may well be occupationally profitable to pursue this goal. Educational requirements are similar to those of the architectural draftsman or commercial artist and resulting job opportunities are normally found in larger architectural firms.

Fig. 31-5. An estimator reviewing a set of plans to prepare the cost of materials. (Smith, Hinchman, and Grylls, Assoc.)

SPECIFICATION WRITER

The job of the specification writer is to prepare all the necessary written information needed to describe materials, methods and fixtures to be used in the structure, Fig. 31-4. A review of the chapter on residential specifications provides a broad coverage of the specification writer's responsibilities.

Just as the architect, the specification writer must be knowledgeable in all phases of construction, building materials, hardware, workmanship and fixtures. He will normally need a college degree with emphasis on drawing, industrial materials and building construction. In some cases a specification writer may advance to this position from experience in the construction industry and related study. There are many job opportunities for people with skill in specification writing.

ESTIMATOR

A person who calculates the costs of materials and labor for a building structure is called an estimator, Fig. 31-5. His responsibilities are extremely important, since any error in judgment or material estimates could prove very costly to the company. He must prepare all the paperwork necessary to inform the architect or builder of what the total cost of the structure will be. Selling prices and profits are then determined from this information.

Fig. 31-6. Surveying a parcel of property for a new residence. A surveying team usually includes a rod man, chain man, instrument man and party chief. (David Knox)

An architectural estimator for a large company will normally have a college degree with emphasis on mathematics. A good background in economics and structural materials is also of extreme value. In smaller concerns, an estimator is often selected from drafting work or the building trades and given additional training to master the necessary skills required of the job.

SURVEYOR

In architectural work, the land surveyor is primarily concerned with establishing areas and boundaries of real estate property. He is involved with the planning and subdivision of land, Fig. 31-6, and the preparation of descriptions of property. It is also has responsibility to prepare maps and plats which show defined areas as well as natural or man-made features above and below the ground level. These include both drawings and written specifications, Fig. 31-7. The American Society of Civil Engineers identify four major categories in the field of surveying: land surveying, engineering surveying, geodetic surveying, and cartographic surveying.

Fig. 31-7. A surveyor checks the accuracy of previous field work using a computer.

The surveyor should be skilled in the use of surveying equipment, be exacting in collecting data, knowledgeable about mapping, and know the principles of real estate property law. Many features of a residential structure will be dependent upon the skills of the surveyor as to grade level, property lines, and building code requirements.

Educational requirements to become a surveyor normally require a bachelor's degree in surveying or civil engineering. Many technical institutes and community colleges offer two year programs which, along with practical experience, one may become a surveying technician.

TEACHING ARCHITECTURAL DRAWING

A teaching career in architectural drawing is a very interesting and rewarding experience for many people. There are considerable opportunities to teach architecture in high schools, trade or vocational schools, community colleges and universities, Fig. 31-8.

The educational requirements will vary according to the type of school and program. However, one should possess a bachelor's degree in architecture or industrial education. Teaching in architectural engineering or graduate programs in architectural drawing will normally require an advanced degree, either a master's or doctorate and practical experience.

REVIEW QUESTIONS — CHAPTER 31

1. An architect usually checks the progress of the construction of a residence to see that_____ _____ and _____ _____.
2. Give the reasons why state laws require an architect to be registered (licensed)._____.
3. Some of the career opportunities for teaching architecture are in:
   a. _____.
   b. _____.
   c. _____.
4. A person who calculates the costs of materials and labor for a residential structure is known as an _____ _____.
5. Four areas of work in which the surveyor must be highly skilled are:
   a. _____.
   b. _____.
   c. _____.
   d. _____.
6. The architectural draftsman usually has the following duties.
   a. _____.
   b. _____.
7. Many architects have the responsibility of assisting the client in selecting _____.
8. A person who prepares all the written information needed to describe the materials, methods and fixtures to be used for a house is known as_____.

SUGGESTED ACTIVITIES

1. Using library references, such as the Occupational Outlook Handbook, select a career related to architecture and write a report including such topics as job opportunities, educational requirements, job responsibilities and predicted factors for success.
2. Prepare a bulletin board display that depicts the many jobs involved in architecture. Make use of pictures, magazine clippings, industrial literature and actual drawings to illustrate the ways in which the architect influences the construction of a residential structure.

Fig. 31-8. Teaching architectural drawing is a very interesting and rewarding career.

3. Make a visit to a local architect's office or an architectural firm to ask questions and observe their operation. Prepare a list of the various responsibilities and skills required by those involved with residential architecture and construction. Make note of the use of any new techniques or equipment in architectural designing.

4. To become better acquainted with educational offerings in architecture, obtain catalogs from community colleges, technical schools and universities and write down the names of courses available. Discuss with your class the many directions a person may take in making architecture a career.

REFERENCE SECTION

BUILDING MATERIAL SYMBOLS

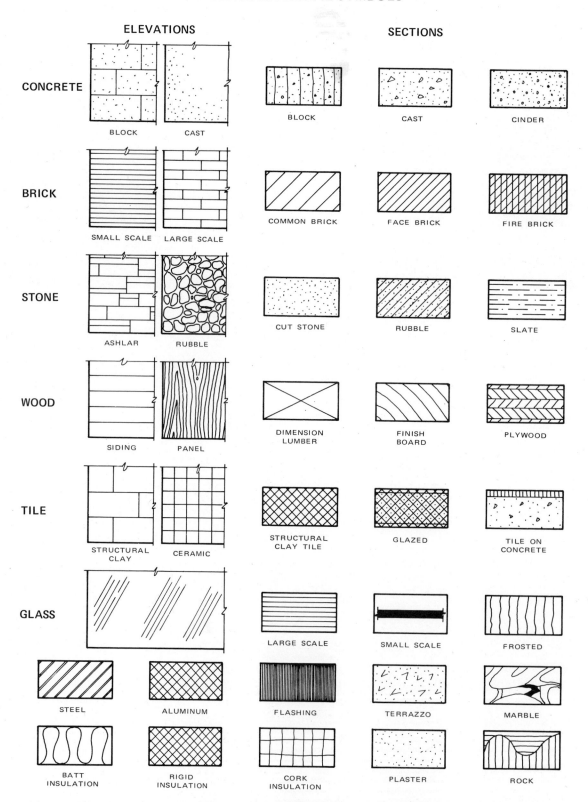

ELEVATIONS

SECTIONS

CONCRETE — BLOCK, CAST | BLOCK, CAST, CINDER

BRICK — SMALL SCALE, LARGE SCALE | COMMON BRICK, FACE BRICK, FIRE BRICK

STONE — ASHLAR, RUBBLE | CUT STONE, RUBBLE, SLATE

WOOD — SIDING, PANEL | DIMENSION LUMBER, FINISH BOARD, PLYWOOD

TILE — STRUCTURAL CLAY, CERAMIC | STRUCTURAL CLAY TILE, GLAZED, TILE ON CONCRETE

GLASS | LARGE SCALE, SMALL SCALE, FROSTED

STEEL, ALUMINUM | FLASHING, TERRAZZO, MARBLE

BATT INSULATION, RIGID INSULATION | CORK INSULATION, PLASTER, ROCK

TOPOGRAPHICAL SYMBOLS

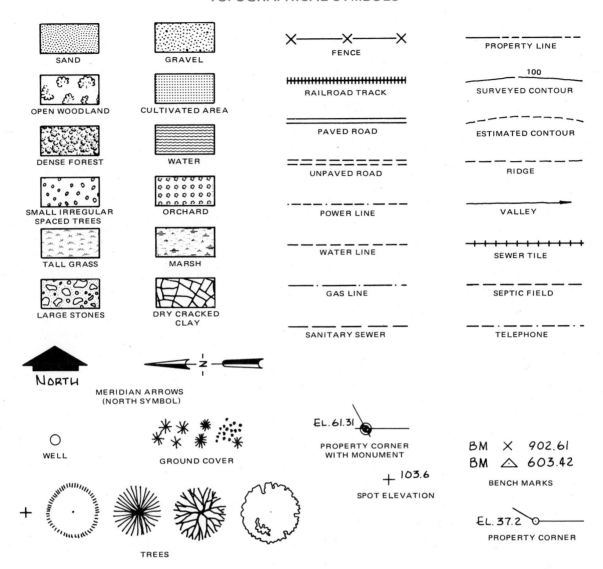

SAND   GRAVEL

OPEN WOODLAND   CULTIVATED AREA

DENSE FOREST   WATER

SMALL IRREGULAR SPACED TREES   ORCHARD

TALL GRASS   MARSH

LARGE STONES   DRY CRACKED CLAY

FENCE   PROPERTY LINE

RAILROAD TRACK   100   SURVEYED CONTOUR

PAVED ROAD   ESTIMATED CONTOUR

UNPAVED ROAD   RIDGE

POWER LINE   VALLEY

WATER LINE   SEWER TILE

GAS LINE   SEPTIC FIELD

SANITARY SEWER   TELEPHONE

NORTH   MERIDIAN ARROWS (NORTH SYMBOL)

WELL   GROUND COVER

EL.61.31   PROPERTY CORNER WITH MONUMENT

+ 103.6   SPOT ELEVATION

BM X 902.61
BM △ 603.42
BENCH MARKS

EL. 37.2   PROPERTY CORNER

TREES

PLUMBING SYMBOLS

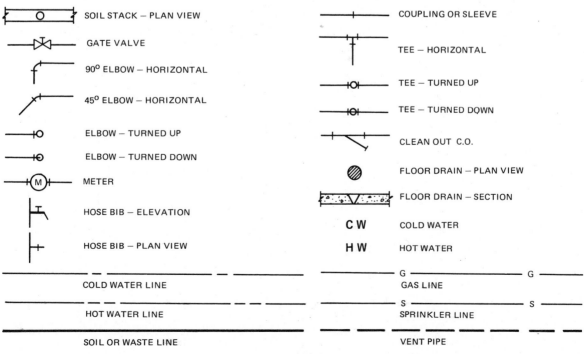

SOIL STACK – PLAN VIEW

GATE VALVE

90° ELBOW – HORIZONTAL

45° ELBOW – HORIZONTAL

ELBOW – TURNED UP

ELBOW – TURNED DOWN

METER

HOSE BIB – ELEVATION

HOSE BIB – PLAN VIEW

COLD WATER LINE

HOT WATER LINE

SOIL OR WASTE LINE

COUPLING OR SLEEVE

TEE – HORIZONTAL

TEE – TURNED UP

TEE – TURNED DOWN

CLEAN OUT C.O.

FLOOR DRAIN – PLAN VIEW

FLOOR DRAIN – SECTION

C W   COLD WATER

H W   HOT WATER

G   GAS LINE   G

S   SPRINKLER LINE   S

VENT PIPE

CLIMATE CONTROL SYMBOLS

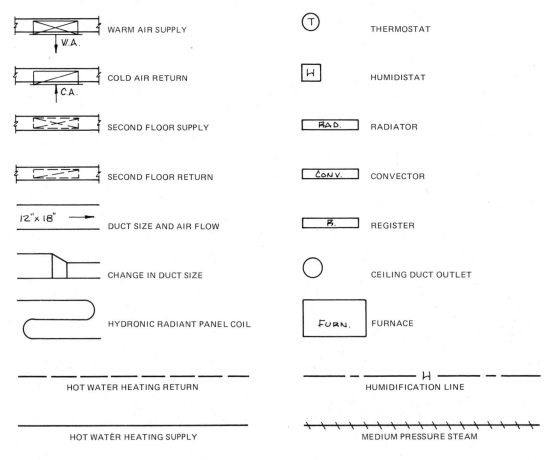

WARM AIR SUPPLY

W.A.

COLD AIR RETURN

C.A.

SECOND FLOOR SUPPLY

SECOND FLOOR RETURN

12"x 18" DUCT SIZE AND AIR FLOW

CHANGE IN DUCT SIZE

HYDRONIC RADIANT PANEL COIL

HOT WATER HEATING RETURN

HOT WATER HEATING SUPPLY

T THERMOSTAT

H HUMIDISTAT

RAD. RADIATOR

CONV. CONVECTOR

R. REGISTER

CEILING DUCT OUTLET

FURN. FURNACE

H HUMIDIFICATION LINE

MEDIUM PRESSURE STEAM

ELECTRICAL SYMBOLS

CEILING OUTLET FIXTURE

RECESSED OUTLET FIXTURE

DROP CORD FIXTURE

FAN HANGER OUTLET

JUNCTION BOX

FLUORESCENT FIXTURE

TELEPHONE

INTERCOM

CEILING FIXTURE WITH PULL SWITCH

THERMOSTAT

SPECIAL FIXTURE OUTLET
A.B.C ETC.

SINGLE RECEPTACLE OUTLET

DUPLEX RECEPTACLE OUTLET

TRIPLEX RECEPTACLE OUTLET

QUADRUPLEX RECEPTACLE OUTLET

SPLIT-WIRED DUPLEX RECEPTACLE OUTLET

SPECIAL PURPOSE SINGLE RECEPTACLE OUTLET

230 VOLT OUTLET

WEATHERPROOF DUPLEX OUTLET
WP

DUPLEX RECEPTACLE WITH SWITCH

FLUSH MOUNTED PANEL BOX

SPECIAL DUPLEX OUTLET
A.B.C ETC.

SINGLE-POLE SWITCH

DOUBLE-POLE SWITCH

THREE-WAY SWITCH

FOUR-WAY SWITCH

WEATHERPROOF SWITCH

LOW VOLTAGE SWITCH

PUSH BUTTON

CHIMES
CH.

TELEVISION ANTENNA OUTLET

DIMMER SWITCH

SPECIAL SWITCH
A.B.C ETC.

STANDARD VANITY SIZES AND DESIGNS

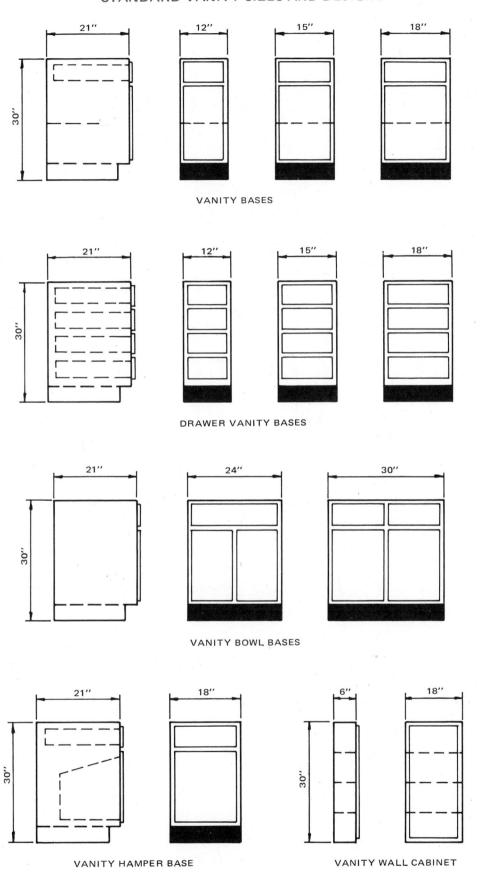

VANITY BASES

DRAWER VANITY BASES

VANITY BOWL BASES

VANITY HAMPER BASE   VANITY WALL CABINET

WALL CABINETS

STANDARD WALL CABINET SIZES AND DESIGNS

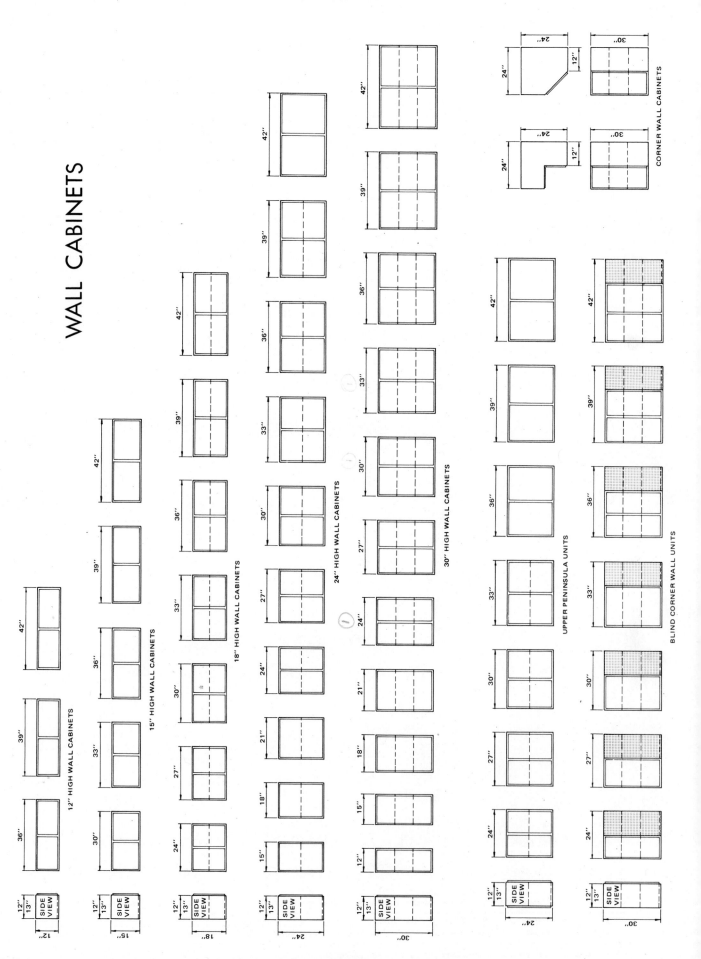

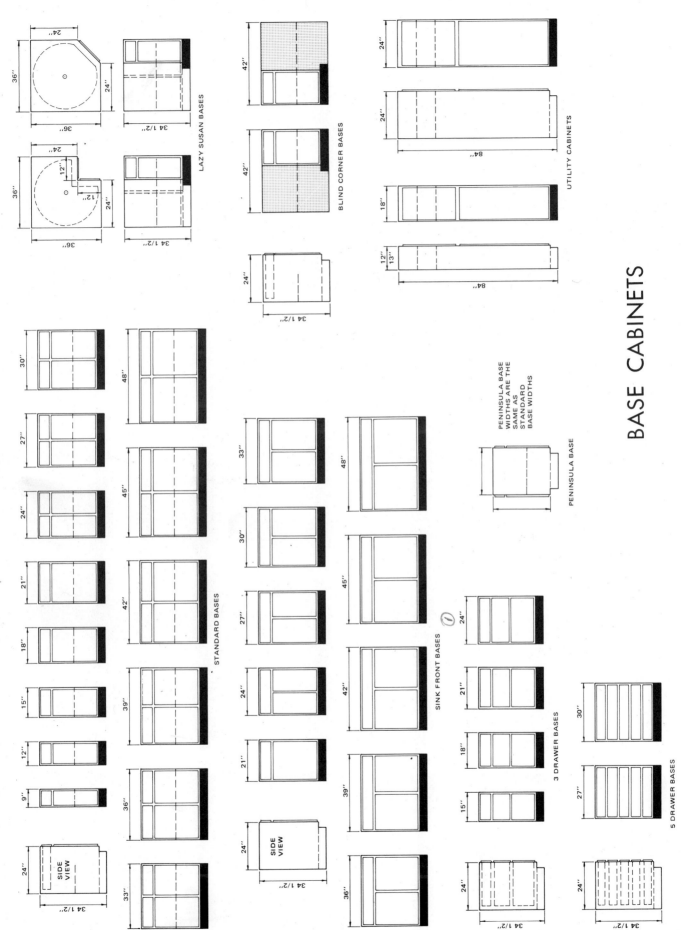

STANDARD BASE CABINET SIZES AND DESIGNS

LAZY SUSAN BASES

BLIND CORNER BASES

UTILITY CABINETS

STANDARD BASES

SINK FRONT BASES

PENINSULA BASE WIDTHS ARE THE SAME AS STANDARD BASE WIDTHS

PENINSULA BASE

3 DRAWER BASES

5 DRAWER BASES

BASE CABINETS

DOUBLE HUNG WINDOWS — STANDARD SIZES

*Unobstructed glass sizes shown

HORIZONTAL SLIDING WINDOWS — STANDARD SIZES

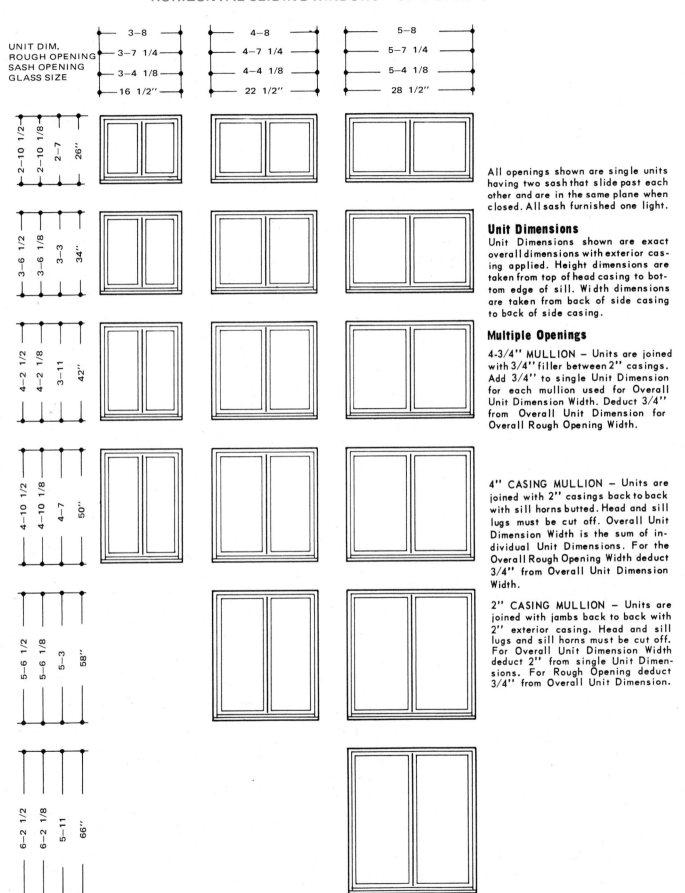

UNIT DIM.
ROUGH OPENING
SASH OPENING
GLASS SIZE

3—8
3—7 1/4
3—4 1/8
16 1/2"

4—8
4—7 1/4
4—4 1/8
22 1/2"

5—8
5—7 1/4
5—4 1/8
28 1/2"

2—10 1/2
2—10 1/8
2—7
26"

3—6 1/2
3—6 1/8
3—3
34"

4—2 1/2
4—2 1/8
3—11
42"

4—10 1/2
4—10 1/8
4—7
50"

5—6 1/2
5—6 1/8
5—3
58"

6—2 1/2
6—2 1/8
5—11
66"

All openings shown are single units having two sash that slide past each other and are in the same plane when closed. All sash furnished one light.

Unit Dimensions

Unit Dimensions shown are exact overall dimensions with exterior casing applied. Height dimensions are taken from top of head casing to bottom edge of sill. Width dimensions are taken from back of side casing to back of side casing.

Multiple Openings

4-3/4" MULLION — Units are joined with 3/4" filler between 2" casings. Add 3/4" to single Unit Dimension for each mullion used for Overall Unit Dimension Width. Deduct 3/4" from Overall Unit Dimension for Overall Rough Opening Width.

4" CASING MULLION — Units are joined with 2" casings back to back with sill horns butted. Head and sill lugs must be cut off. Overall Unit Dimension Width is the sum of individual Unit Dimensions. For the Overall Rough Opening Width deduct 3/4" from Overall Unit Dimension Width.

2" CASING MULLION — Units are joined with jambs back to back with 2" exterior casing. Head and sill lugs and sill horns must be cut off. For Overall Unit Dimension Width deduct 2" from single Unit Dimensions. For Rough Opening deduct 3/4" from Overall Unit Dimension.

CASEMENT WINDOWS — STANDARD SIZES

GRILLE PATTERNS

UNIT DIM.
ROUGH OPENING
SASH OPENING
GLASS *

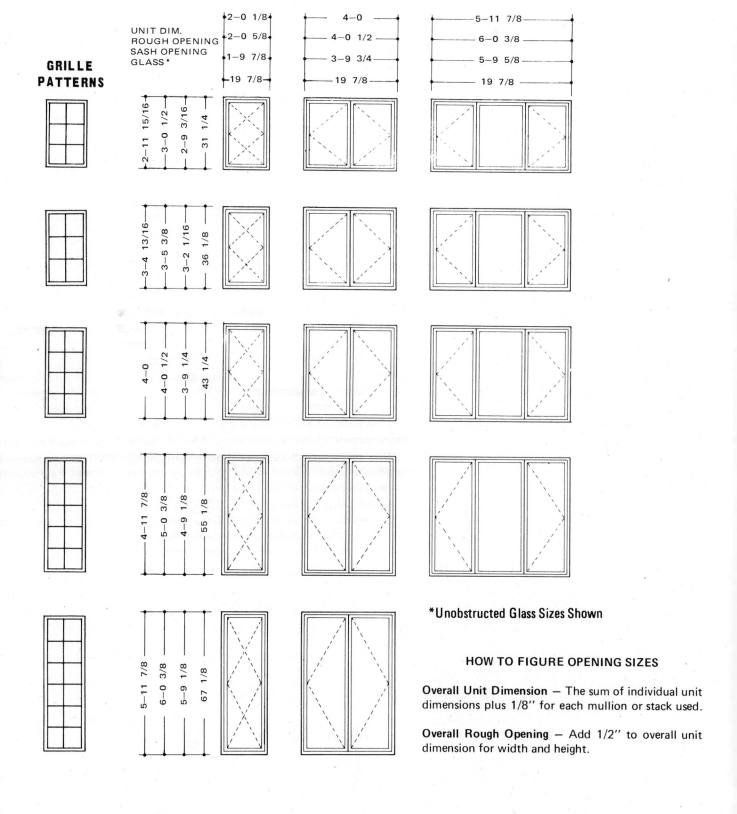

*Unobstructed Glass Sizes Shown

HOW TO FIGURE OPENING SIZES

Overall Unit Dimension — The sum of individual unit dimensions plus 1/8″ for each mullion or stack used.

Overall Rough Opening — Add 1/2″ to overall unit dimension for width and height.

AWNING WINDOWS — STANDARD SIZES

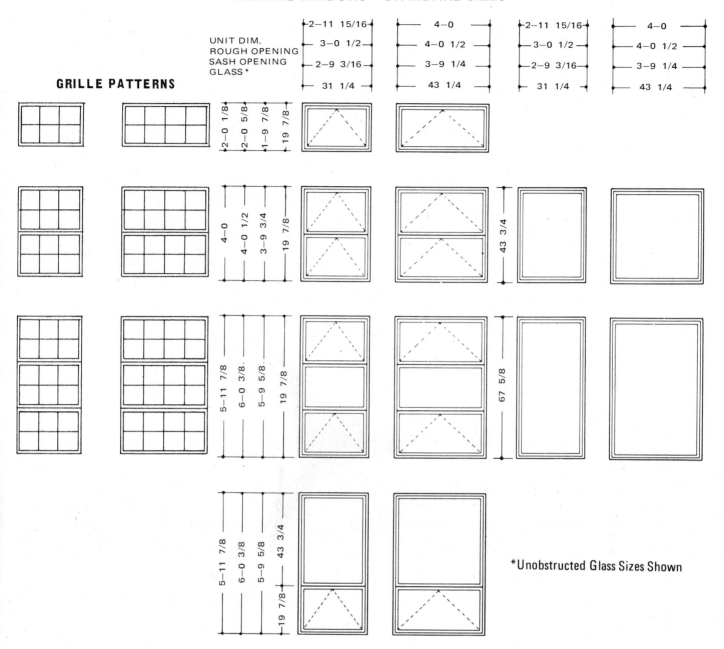

UNIT DIM.
ROUGH OPENING
SASH OPENING
GLASS *

GRILLE PATTERNS

*Unobstructed Glass Sizes Shown

HOPPER WINDOW SIZES

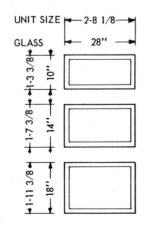

UNIT SIZE 2-8 1/8
GLASS 28"

PICTURE WINDOWS — STANDARD SIZES

GLASS RABBET	EXACT GLASS SIZE FOR	
	1" INSULATING	1/4" PLATE
44 15/16 x 36 9/16	44 1/2 x 36	44 3/4 x 36 1/4
69 3/16 x 36 9/16	68 3/4 x 36	69 x 36 1/4
93 7/16 x 36 9/16	93 x 36	93 1/4 x 36 1/4
44 15/16 x 48 3/4	44 1/2 x 48 1/8	44 3/4 x 48 1/2
69 3/16 x 48 3/4	68 3/4 x 48 1/8	69 x 48 1/2
93 7/16 x 48 3/4	93 x 48 1/8	93 1/4 x 48 1/2
44 15/16 x 60 15/16	44 1/2 x 60 3/8	44 3/4 x 60 5/8
69 3/16 x 60 15/16	68 3/4 x 60 3/8	69 x 60 5/8
93 7/16 x 60 15/16	93 x 60 3/8	93 1/4 x 60 5/8
44 15/16 x 73 3/8	44 1/2 x 72 3/4	44 3/4 x 73
69 3/16 x 73 3/8	68 3/4 x 72 3/4	69 x 73
93 7/16 x 73 3/8	93 x 72 3/4	93 1/4 x 73

GLASS SLIDING DOORS — STANDARD SIZES

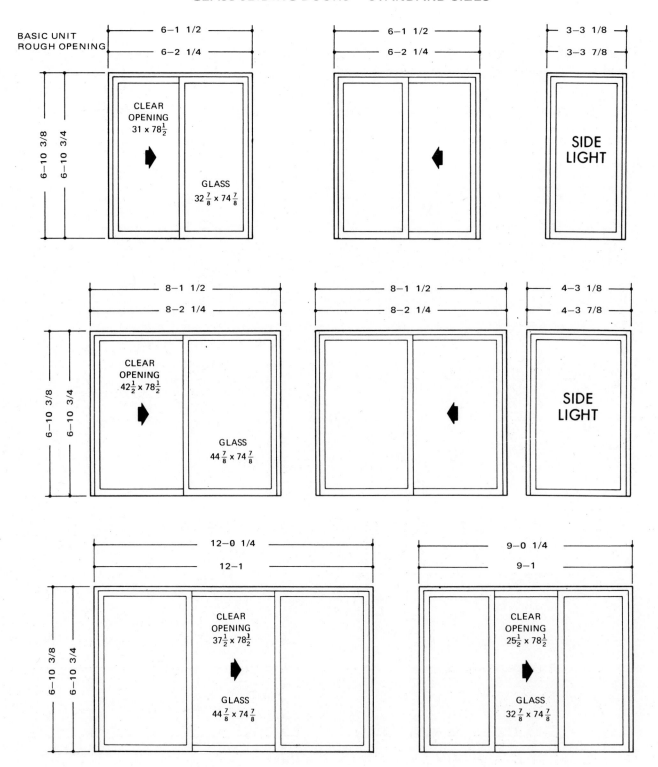

DESIGN DATA FOR W-TYPE, KING-POST, AND SCISSORS TRUSSES

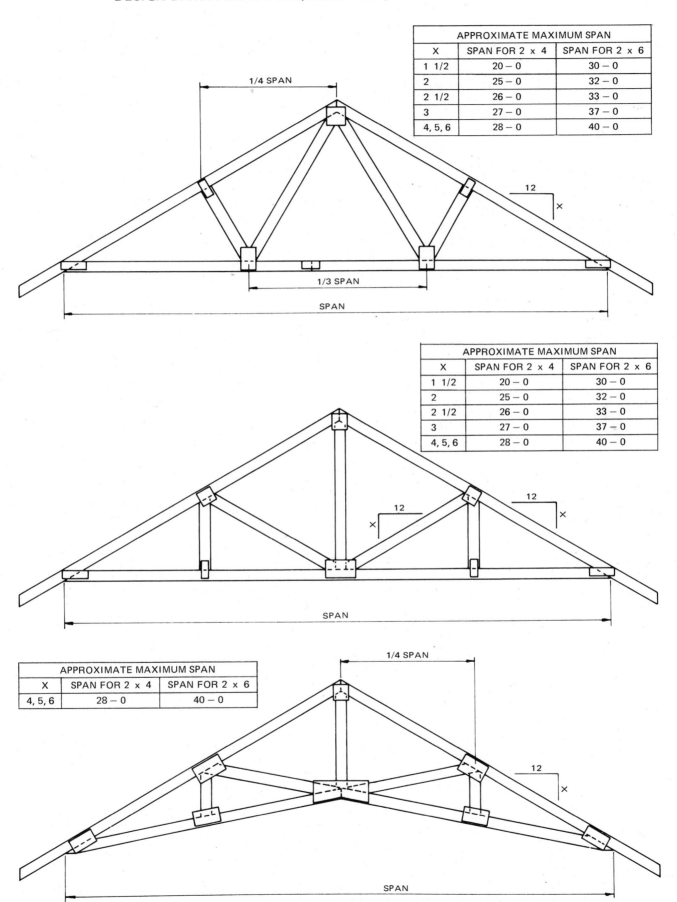

APPROXIMATE MAXIMUM SPAN		
X	SPAN FOR 2 x 4	SPAN FOR 2 x 6
1 1/2	20 — 0	30 — 0
2	25 — 0	32 — 0
2 1/2	26 — 0	33 — 0
3	27 — 0	37 — 0
4, 5, 6	28 — 0	40 — 0

1/4 SPAN

1/3 SPAN

SPAN

12

APPROXIMATE MAXIMUM SPAN		
X	SPAN FOR 2 x 4	SPAN FOR 2 x 6
1 1/2	20 — 0	30 — 0
2	25 — 0	32 — 0
2 1/2	26 — 0	33 — 0
3	27 — 0	37 — 0
4, 5, 6	28 — 0	40 — 0

12

12

SPAN

APPROXIMATE MAXIMUM SPAN		
X	SPAN FOR 2 x 4	SPAN FOR 2 x 6
4, 5, 6	28 — 0	40 — 0

1/4 SPAN

12

SPAN

FLOOR JOIST SPAN DATA

SOUTHERN YELLOW PINE — 30 LB. LIVE LOAD					
JOIST SIZE (NOMINAL)	SPACING OF JOISTS O. C. IN INCHES	LUMBER GRADES			
		NO. 1 DENSE KILN-DRIED 2″ DIM.	NO. 2 DENSE KILN-DRIED 2″ DIM.	NO. 1 DENSE 2″ DIM.	NO. 2 DENSE 2″ DIM.
2 x 6	12	12'- 5″	12'- 5″	12'- 5″	12'- 5″
	16	11'- 4″	11'- 4″	11'- 4″	11'- 4″
	24	10'- 2″	10'- 2″	10'- 0″	9'- 2″
2 x 8	12	16'- 1″	16'- 1″	16'- 1″	16'- 1″
	16	14'- 9″	14'- 9″	14'- 9″	14'- 9″
	24	13'- 1″	13'- 1″	13'- 1″	12'- 4″
2 x 10	12	19'- 11″	19'- 11″	19'- 11″	19'- 11″
	16	18'- 3″	18'- 3″	18'- 3″	18'- 3″
	24	16'- 2″	16'- 2″	16'- 2″	15'- 7″
2 x 12	12	23'- 9″	23'- 9″	23'- 9″	23'- 9″
	16	21'- 9″	21'- 9″	21'- 9″	21'- 9″
	24	19'- 2″	19'- 2″	19'- 2″	18'- 11″

SOUTHERN YELLOW PINE — 40 LB. LIVE LOAD					
JOIST SIZE (NOMINAL)	SPACING OF JOISTS O. C. IN INCHES	LUMBER GRADES			
		NO. 1 DENSE KILN-DRIED 2″ DIM.	NO. 2 DENSE KILN-DRIED 2″ DIM.	NO. 1 DENSE 2″ DIM.	NO. 2 DENSE 2″ DIM.
2 x 6	12	11'- 5″	11'- 5″	11'- 5″	11'- 5″
	16	10'- 5″	10'- 5″	10'- 5″	10'- 1″
	24	9'- 2″	9'- 2″	8'- 11″	8'- 3″
2 x 8	12	14'- 9″	14'- 9″	14'- 9″	14'- 9″
	16	13'- 6″	13'- 6″	13'- 6″	13'-6″
	24	12'- 0″	12'- 0″	11'- 11″	11'- 0″
2 x 10	12	18'- 3″	18'- 3″	18'- 3″	18'- 3″
	16	16'- 9″	16'- 9″	16'- 9″	16'- 9″
	24	14'- 10″	14'- 10″	14'- 10″	14'- 10″
2 x 12	12	21'- 9″	21'- 9″	21'- 9″	21'- 9″
	16	19'- 11″	19'- 11″	19'- 11″	19'- 11″
	24	17'- 7″	17'- 7″	17'- 7″	16'- 11″

LARCH AND DOUGLAS FIR — 30 LB. LIVE LOAD					
JOIST SIZE (NOMINAL)	SPACING OF JOISTS O. C. IN INCHES	LUMBER GRADES			
		SELECT STRUCTURAL	DENSE CONSTRUCTION	CONSTRUCTION	STANDARD	UTILITY
2 x 6	12	11'- 4″	11'- 4″	11'- 4″	11'- 4″	8'- 4″
	16	10'- 4″	10'- 4″	10'- 4″	10'- 4″	7'- 2″
	24	9'- 0″	9'- 0″	9'- 0″	9'- 0″	5'- 10″
2 x 8	12	15'- 4″	15'- 4″	15'- 4″	15'- 4″	12'- 4″
	16	14'- 0″	14'- 0″	14'- 0″	14'- 0″	10'- 8″
	24	12'- 4″	12'- 4″	12'- 4″	12'- 4″	8'- 8″
2 x 10	12	18'- 4″	18'- 4″	18'- 4″	18'- 4″	16'- 10″
	16	17'- 0″	17'- 0″	17'- 0″	17'- 0″	14'- 8″
	24	15'- 6″	15'- 6″	15'- 6″	15'- 6″	12'- 0″
2 x 12	12	21'- 2″	21'- 2″	21'- 2″	21'- 2″	19'- 8″
	16	19'- 8″	19'- 8″	19'- 8″	19'- 8″	17'- 0″
	24	17'- 10″	17'- 10″	17'- 10″	17'- 10″	14'- 0″

LARCH AND DOUGLAS FIR — 40 LB. LIVE LOAD					
JOIST SIZE (NOMINAL)	SPACING OF JOISTS O. C. IN INCHES	LUMBER GRADES			
		SELECT STRUCTURAL	DENSE CONSTRUCTION	CONSTRUCTION	STANDARD	UTILITY
2 x 6	12	10'- 6″	10'- 6″	10'- 6″	10'- 6″	7'- 4″
	16	9'- 8″	9'- 8″	9'- 8″	9'- 8″	6'- 4″
	24	8'- 4″	8'- 4″	8'- 4″	8'- 2″	5'- 2″
2 x 8	12	14'- 4″	14'- 4″	14'- 4″	14'- 4″	10'- 0″
	16	13'- 0″	13'- 0″	13'- 0″	13'- 0″	9'- 6″
	24	11'- 6″	11'- 6″	11'- 6″	11'- 0″	7'- 10″
2 x 10	12	17'- 4″	17'- 4″	17'- 4″	17'- 4″	15'- 2″
	16	16'- 2″	16'- 2″	16'- 2″	16'- 2″	13'- 0″
	24	14'- 6″	14'- 6″	14'- 6″	14'- 0″	10'- 8″
2 x 12	12	20'- 0″	20'- 0″	20'- 0″	20'- 0″	17'- 8″
	16	18'- 8″	18'- 8″	18'- 8″	18'- 8″	15'- 4″
	24	16'- 10″	16'- 10″	16'- 10″	16'- 10″	12'- 6″

CEILING JOIST SPAN DATA

SOUTHERN YELLOW PINE					
JOIST SIZE (NOMINAL)	SPACING OF JOISTS O. C. IN INCHES	LUMBER GRADES			
		NO. 1 KILN-DRIED 2" DIM.	NO. 2 KILN-DRIED 2" DIM.	NO. 1 2" DIM.	NO. 2 2" DIM.
LIMITED ATTIC STORAGE					
2 x 6	12	14'- 4"	14'- 4"	14'- 4"	14'- 4"
	16	13'- 0"	13'- 0"	13'- 0"	12'- 10"
	24	11'- 4"	11'- 4"	11'- 4"	10'- 6"
2 x 8	12	18'- 4"	18'- 4"	18'- 4"	18'- 4"
	16	17'- 0"	17'- 0"	17'- 0"	17'- 0"
	24	15'- 4"	15'- 4"	15'- 4"	14'- 4"
2 x 10	12	21'- 10"	21'- 10"	21'- 10"	21'- 10"
	16	20'- 4"	20'- 4"	20'- 4"	20'- 4"
	24	18'- 4"	18'- 4"	18'- 4"	18'- 4"
NO ATTIC STORAGE					
2 x 6	12	17'- 2"	17'- 2"	17'- 2"	17'- 2"
	16	16'- 0"	16'- 0"	16'- 0"	16'- 0"
	24	14'- 4"	14'- 4"	14'- 4"	14'- 4"
2 x 8	12	21'- 8"	21'- 8"	21'- 8"	21'- 8"
	16	20'- 2"	20'- 2"	20'- 2"	20'- 2"
	24	18'- 4"	18'- 4"	18'- 4"	18'- 4"
2 x 10	12	24'- 0"	24'- 0"	24'- 0"	24'- 0"
	16	24'- 0"	24'- 0"	24'- 0"	24'- 0"
	24	21'- 10"	21'- 10"	21'- 10"	21'- 10"

DOUGLAS FIR AND LARCH					
JOIST SIZE (NOMINAL)	SPACING OF JOISTS O. C. IN INCHES	LUMBER GRADES			
		SELECT STRUCTURAL	DENSE CONSTRUCTION	CONSTRUCTION	STANDARD	UTILITY
LIMITED ATTIC STORAGE					
2 x 6	12	14'- 4"	14'- 4"	14'- 4"	14'- 4"	9'- 6"
	16	13'- 0"	13'- 0"	13'- 0"	12'- 10"	8'- 4"
	24	11'- 4"	11'- 4"	11'- 4"	10'- 6"	6'- 8"
2 x 8	12	18'- 4"	18'- 4"	18'- 4"	18'- 4"	14'- 4"
	16	17'- 0"	17'- 0"	17'- 0"	17'- 0"	12'- 4"
	24	15'- 4"	15'- 4"	15'- 4"	14'- 4"	10'- 0"
2 x 10	12	21'- 10"	21'- 10"	21'- 10"	21'- 10"	19'- 6"
	16	20'- 4"	20'- 4"	20'- 4"	20'- 4"	16'- 10"
	24	18'- 4"	18'- 4"	18'- 4"	18'- 4"	13'- 10"
NO ATTIC STORAGE					
2 x 6	12	17'- 2"	17'- 2"	17'- 2"	17'- 2"	13'- 6"
	16	16'- 0"	16'- 0"	16'- 0"	16'- 0"	11'- 8"
	24	14'- 4"	14'- 4"	14'- 4"	14'- 4"	9'- 6"
2 x 8	12	21'- 8"	21'- 8"	21'- 8"	21'- 8"	20'- 2"
	16	20'- 2"	20'- 2"	20'- 2"	20'- 2"	17'- 6"
	24	18'- 4"	18'- 4"	18'- 4"	18'- 4"	14'- 4"
2 x 10	12	24'- 0"	24'- 0"	24'- 0"	24'- 0"	24'- 0"
	16	24'- 0"	24'- 0"	24'- 0"	24'- 0"	22'- 6"
	24	21'- 10"	21'- 10"	21'- 10"	21'- 10"	19'- 6"

GLUED LAMINATED FLOOR AND ROOF BEAMS — SPAN DATA

SPAN DATA FOR GLUED LAMINATED ROOF BEAMS*
MAXIMUM DEFLECTION 1/240TH OF THE SPAN

BEAM SIZE (ACTUAL)	WGT. OF BEAM PER LIN. FT. IN POUNDS	SPAN IN FEET											
		10	12	14	16	18	20	22	24	26	28	30	32
		POUNDS PER LIN. FT. LOAD BEARING CAPACITY											
3 x 5 1/4	3.7	151	85										
3 x 7 1/4	4.9	362	206	128	84								
3 x 9 1/4	6.7	566	448	300	199	137	99						
3 x 11 1/4	8.0	680	566	483	363	252	182	135	102				
4 1/2 x 9 1/4	9.8	850	673	451	299	207	148	109					
4 1/2 x 11 1/4	12.0	1,036	860	731	544	378	273	202	153				
3 1/4 x 13 1/2	10.4	1,100	916	784	685	479	347	258	197	152	120		
3 1/4 x 15	11.5	1,145	1,015	870	759	650	473	352	267	206	163	128	104
5 1/4 x 13 1/2	16.7	1,778	1,478	1,266	1,105	773	559	415	316	245	193	154	124
5 1/4 x 15	18.6	1,976	1,647	1,406	1,229	1,064	771	574	438	342	269	215	174
5 1/4 x 16 1/2	20.5	2,180	1,810	1,550	1,352	1,155	933	768	586	457	362	290	236
5 1/4 x 18	22.3	2,378	1,978	1,688	1,478	1,308	1,113	918	766	598	478	382	311

```
EXAMPLE:  CLEAR SPAN    = 20'- 0''
          BEAM SPACING  = 10'- 0''
          DEAD LOAD     = 8 LBS./SQ. FT. (ROOFING AND DECKING)
          LIVE LOAD     = 20 LBS./SQ. FT. (SNOW)
          TOTAL LOAD    = LIVE LOAD + DEAD LOAD  x  BEAM SPACING
                        = (20 + 8)  x  10 = 280 LBS./LIN. FT.
THE BEAM SIZE REQUIRED IS 3 1/4'' x 13 1/2'' WHICH SUPPORT 347 LBS./LIN. FT. OVER A SPAN OF 20'- 0''
```

*BEAMS MAY BE DOUGLAS FIR, LARCH OR SOUTHERN YELLOW PINE.

SPAN DATA FOR GLUED LAMINATED FLOOR BEAMS*
MAXIMUM DEFLECTION 1/360TH OF THE SPAN

BEAM SIZE (ACTUAL)	WGT. OF BEAM PER LIN. FT. IN POUNDS	SPAN IN FEET											
		10	12	14	16	18	20	22	24	26	28	30	32
		POUNDS PER LIN. FT. LOAD BEARING CAPACITY											
3 x 5 1/4	3.7	114	64										
3 x 7 1/4	4.9	275	156	84	55								
3 x 9 1/4	6.7	492	319	198	130	89							
3 x 11 1/4	8.0	590	491	361	239	165	119						
4 1/2 x 9 1/4	9.8	738	479	298	196	134	96						
4 1/2 x 11 1/4	12.0	900	748	541	359	248	178	131	92				
3 1/4 x 13 1/2	10.4	956	795	683	454	316	228	169	128	98			
3 1/4 x 15	11.5	997	884	756	626	436	315	234	178	137	108		
5 1/4 x 13 1/2	16.7	1,541	1,283	1,095	732	509	367	271	205	158	123	96	
5 1/4 x 15	18.6	1,713	1,423	1,219	1,009	703	508	376	286	221	173	137	109
5 1/4 x 16 1/2	20.5	1,885	1,568	1,340	1,170	939	678	505	384	298	235	187	151
5 1/4 x 18	22.3	2,058	1,710	1,464	1,278	1,133	886	660	503	391	309	247	200

```
EXAMPLE:  CLEAR SPAN    = 20'- 0''
          BEAM SPACING  = 10'- 0''
          DEAD LOAD     = 7 LBS./SQ. FT. (DECKING AND CARPET)
          LIVE LOAD     = 40 LBS./SQ. FT. (FURNITURE AND OCCUPANTS)
          TOTAL LOAD    = LIVE LOAD + DEAD LOAD x BEAM SPACING
                        = (40 + 7) x 10 = 470 LBS./LIN. FT.
THE BEAM SIZE REQUIRED IS 5 1/4'' x 15'' WHICH WILL SUPPORT 508 LBS./LIN. FT. OVER A SPAN OF 20'- 0''
```

*BEAMS MAY BE DOUGLAS FIR, LARCH OR SOUTHERN YELLOW PINE.

ALLOWABLE RAFTER SPAN

RAFTER SPAN DATA

ROOF SLOPE OF 3:12 OR LESS*

NOMINAL SIZE IN INCHES	SPACING IN INCHES O.C.	NONSUPPORTING FINISHED CEILING					SUPPORTING FINISHED CEILING				
		DOUGLAS FIR AND LARCH									
		SELECT STRUCT.	DENSE CONSTR.	CONSTR.	STANDARD	UTILITY	SELECT STRUCT.	DENSE CONSTR.	CONSTR.	STANDARD	UTILITY
		SOUTHERN YELLOW PINE									
		NO. 1 K. D.	NO. 2 K. D.	NO. 1	NO. 2		NO. 1 K.D.	NO.2 K.D.	NO. 1	NO. 2	
2 x 6	12	14 4	14 4	14 4	14 4	9 6	13 8	13 8	13 8	13 8	8 10
	16	13 0	13 0	13 0	12 10	8 4	12 4	12 4	12 4	11 10	7 8
	24	11 4	11 4	11 4	10 6	6 8	10 10	10 10	10 8	9 8	6 2
2 x 8	12	18 4	18 4	18 4	18 4	14 4	17 8	17 8	17 8	17 8	13 2
	16	17 0	17 0	17 0	17 0	12 4	16 4	16 4	16 4	16 2	11 6
	24	15 4	15 4	15 4	15 4	10 0	14 8	14 8	14 6	13 2	9 4
2 x 10	12	21 10	21 10	21 10	21 0	19 6	21 0	21 0	21 0	21 0	18 0
	16	20 4	20 4	20 4	20 4	16 10	19 6	19 6	19 6	19 6	15 8
	24	18 4	18 4	18 4	18 4	13 10	17 8	17 8	17 8	16 8	12 10
2 x 12	12	24 0	24 0	24 0	24 0	22 8	24 0	24 0	24 0	24 0	21 0
	16	23 6	23 6	23 6	23 6	19 8	22 6	22 6	22 6	22 6	18 2
	24	21 2	21 2	21 2	21 2	16 2	20 4	20 4	20 4	20 2	14 10

SPANS ARE IN FT. AND INCHES.

(National Forest Products Assoc.)

*CALCULATIONS ARE BASED ON:

LIGHT ROOFING – LESS THAN 4 POUNDS PER SQ. FT.

A DEAD LOAD OF 15 POUNDS PER SQ. FT. AND A LIVE LOAD OF 20 POUNDS PER SQ. FT. FOR A FINISHED CEILING.

DEFLECTION NOT TO EXCEED 1/240TH OF THE CLEAR SPAN

ROOF SLOPE OVER 3:12*

NOMINAL SIZE IN INCHES	SPACING IN INCHES O.C.	LIGHT ROOFING					HEAVY ROOFING				
		DOUGLAS FIR AND LARCH									
		SELECT STRUCT.	DENSE CONSTR.	CONSTR.	STANDARD	UTILITY	SELECT STRUCT.	DENSE CONSTR.	CONSTR.	STANDARD	UTILITY
		SOUTHERN YELLOW PINE									
		NO. 1 K. D.	NO. 2 K. D.	NO. 1	NO. 2		NO. 1 K.D.	NO.2 K.D.	NO. 1	NO. 2	
2 x 6	12	16 10	16 10	16 10	16 10	11 2	15 6	15 6	15 6	14 10	9 6
	16	15 8	15 8	15 8	15 0	9 8	14 4	14 4	14 0	12 10	8 4
	24	13 10	13 10	13 6	12 2	7 10	12 6	12 6	11 6	10 6	6 8
2 x 8	12	21 2	21 2	21 2	21 2	16 8	19 8	19 8	19 8	19 8	14 4
	16	19 10	19 10	19 10	19 10	14 4	18 4	18 4	18 4	17 6	12 4
	24	17 10	17 10	17 10	16 8	11 0	16 6	16 6	15 8	14 4	10 0
2 x 10	12	24 0	24 0	24 0	24 0	22 10	23 6	23 6	23 6	23 6	19 6
	16	23 8	23 8	23 8	23 8	19 8	21 10	21 10	21 10	21 10	16 10
	24	21 4	21 4	21 4	21 0	16 2	19 8	19 8	19 8	18 8	13 10

SPANS ARE IN FEET AND INCHES

(National Forest Products Assoc.)

*CALCULATIONS ARE BASED ON:

LIGHT ROOFING WHICH IS LESS THAN 4 POUNDS PER SQ. FT. OR HEAVY ROOFING – OVER 4 POUNDS PER SQ. FT.

A DEAD LOAD OF 15 POUNDS PER SQ. FT. AND A LIVE LOAD OF 15 POUNDS PER SQ. FT. FOR HEAVY ROOFING

DEFLECTION NOT TO EXCEED 1/240TH OF THE CLEAR SPAN

I-BEAM DATA

MAXIMUM ALLOWABLE UNIFORM LOADS FOR AMERICAN STANDARD I-BEAMS WITH LATERAL SUPPORT

SIZE OF BEAM	WEIGHT OF BEAM PER FT.	4	6	8	10	12	14	16	18	20	22	24	26	28	30	32	34	36	38	40
4 x 2 3/4	7.7	10	7	5																
	9.5	11	7	6																
5 x 3	10.0	16	11	8	6															
	11.3	20	13	10	8															
6 x 3 1/8	12.5	24	16	12	10	8														
	17.3	29	19	15	12	10														
7 x 3 3/4	15.3	35	23	17	14	12	10													
	20.0	40	27	20	16	15	13													
8 x 4	18.4	47	32	24	19	16	14	12												
	23.0	53	36	27	21	18	15	13												
10 x 4 3/4	25.4	80	54	41	33	27	23	20	18	16										
	35.0	97	65	49	39	32	28	24	22	20										
12 x 5	31.8	110	80	60	48	40	34	30	27	24	22	20								
	35.0	126	84	63	50	42	36	32	28	25	23	21								
12 x 5 1/4	40.8	144	100	75	60	50	43	37	33	30	27	25								
	50.0	168	112	84	67	56	48	42	37	34	31	28								
15 x 5 1/2	42.9	160	131	98	79	65	56	49	44	39	36	33	30	28	26	25				
	50.0	214	143	107	86	71	61	54	48	43	39	36	33	31	29	27				
18 x 6	54.7		196	147	118	98	84	74	66	59	54	49	45	42	39	37	35	33	31	
	70.0		226	170	136	113	97	85	76	68	62	57	52	49	45	43	40	38	36	
20 x 6 1/4	65.4		260	195	156	130	111	97	87	78	71	65	60	56	52	49	46	43	41	39
	75.0		281	211	169	140	120	105	94	84	77	70	65	60	56	53	50	47	44	42

LOADS ARE IN KIPS. 1 KIP = 1,000 POUNDS   (American Institute of Steel Construction)

MAXIMUM ALLOWABLE UNIFORM LOADS FOR WIDE FLANGE I-BEAMS WITH LATERAL SUPPORT

SIZE OF BEAM	WEIGHT OF BEAM PER FT.	4	6	8	9	10	12	14	18	20	22	24	26	28	30	32	34	36	38	40
8 x 5 1/4	17	47	31	24	19	16	13	12												
8 x 6 1/2	24		46	35	28	23	20	17												
8 x 8	31		60	46	37	30	26	23	20	18	16									
10 x 5 1/4	21	62	48	36	29	24	21	18	16	14										
10 x 8	33		74	58	47	39	33	29	26	23										
10 x 10	49			88	73	61	52	46	40	36	33	30	28	26						
12 x 6 1/2	27		74	57	45	38	32	28	25	23	21	19								
12 x 8	40		87	69	58	49	43	38	35	32	29									
12 x 10	53			108	94	79	67	59	52	47	43	39								
12 x 12	65				117	98	84	73	65	59	53	49	45	42	39					
14 x 6 3/4	30		93	70	56	46	40	35	31	28	25	23	21	20	19					
14 x 8	43			105	84	70	60	52	46	42	38	35	32	30	28					
14 x 10	61				123	102	88	77	68	62	56	51	47	44	41					
14 x 12	78				156	135	115	101	90	81	73	67	62	58	54					
14 x 14 1/2	87				152	132	115	102	92	84	77	71	66	61	57	54	51			
16 x 7	36		124	94	75	63	54	47	42	38	34	31	29	27	25	24	22			
16 x 8 1/2	58			157	126	105	90	78	70	63	57	52	48	45	42	39	37			
16 x 11 1/2	88				202	168	144	126	112	101	92	84	78	72	67	63	59			
18 x 7 1/2	50			148	119	99	85	74	66	59	54	49	46	42	40	37	35	33	31	
18 x 8 3/4	64				188	156	130	111	98	87	78	71	65	60	56	52	49	46	43	41
18 x 11 3/4	96				224	189	176	154	137	123	112	103	95	88	82	77	72	68	65	
21 x 8 1/4	62			211	169	141	120	105	94	84	77	70	65	60	56	53	50	47	44	42

LOADS ARE IN KIPS. 1 KIP = 1,000 POUNDS   (American Institute of Steel Construction)

PLANKING SPAN DATA

SPAN DATA FOR ROOF DECKING
WITH A MAXIMUM DEFLECTION OF 1/240TH OF THE SPAN
LIVE LOAD = 20 LBS./SQ. FT.

THICKNESS IN INCHES (NOMINAL)	LUMBER GRADE	SIMPLE SPANS	
		DOUGLAS FIR, LARCH, SOUTHERN YELLOW PINE	WESTERN RED CEDAR
		SPAN	SPAN
2	CONSTRUCTION	9'-5''	8'-1''
2	STANDARD	9'-5''	6'-9''
3	SELECT DEX.	15'-3''	13'-0''
3	COMPL. DEX.	15'-3''	13'-0''
4	SELECT DEX.	20'-3''	17'-3''
4	COMPL. DEX.	20'-3''	17'-3''

THICKNESS IN INCHES (NOMINAL)	LUMBER GRADE	RANDOM LENGTHS	
		DOUGLAS FIR, LARCH, SOUTHERN YELLOW PINE	WESTERN RED CEDAR
		SPAN	SPAN
2	CONSTRUCTION	10'-3''	8'-10''
2	STANDARD	10'-3''	6'-9''
3	SELECT DEX.	16'-9''	14'-3''
3	COMPL. DEX.	16'-9''	13'-6''
4	SELECT DEX.	22'-0''	19'-0''
4	COMPL. DEX.	22'-0''	18'-0''

THICKNESS IN INCHES (NOMINAL)	LUMBER GRADE	COMB. SIMPLE AND TWO-SPAN CONTINUOUS	
		DOUGLAS FIR, LARCH, SOUTHERN YELLOW PINE	WESTERN RED CEDAR
		SPAN	SPAN
2	CONSTRUCTION	10'-7''	8'-9''
2	STANDARD	10'-7''	6'-9''
3	SELECT DEX.	17'-3''	14'-9''
3	COMPL. DEX.	17'-3''	13'-6''
4	SELECT DEX.	22'-9''	19'-6''
4	COMPL. DEX.	22'-9''	18'-0''

RESISTIVITY TO HEAT LOSS OF COMMON BUILDING MATERIALS

	MATERIAL	RESISTIVITY		MATERIAL	RESISTIVITY
4''	CONCRETE OR STONE	.32	1/2''	PLYWOOD	.65
6''	CONCRETE OR STONE	.48	5/8''	PLYWOOD	.80
8''	CONCRETE OR STONE	.64	3/4''	PLYWOOD	.95
12''	CONCRETE OR STONE	.96	3/4''	SOFTWOOD SHEATING OR SIDING	.85
4''	CONCRETE BLOCK	.70		COMPOSITION FLOOR COVERING	.08
8''	CONCRETE BLOCK	1.10	1''	MINERAL BATT INSULATION	3.50
12''	CONCRETE BLOCK	1.25	2''	MINERAL BATT INSULATION	7.00
4''	COMMON BRICK	.82	4''	MINERAL BATT INSULATION	14.00
4''	FACE BRICK	.45	2''	GLASS FIBER INSULATION	7.00
4''	STRUCTURAL CLAY TILE	1.10	4''	GLASS FIBER INSULATION	14.00
8''	STRUCTURAL CLAY TILE	1.90	1''	LOOSE FILL INSULATION	3.00
12''	STRUCTURAL CLAY TILE	3.00		SINGLE THICKNESS GLASS	.88
1''	STUCCO	.20		GLASSWELD INSULATING GLASS	1.89
15 LB.	BUILDING PAPER	.06		SINGLE GLASS WITH STORM WINDOW	1.66
3/8''	SHEET ROCK OR PLASTERBOARD	.33		METAL EDGE INSULATING GLASS	1.85
1/2''	SAND PLASTER	.15	4''	GLASS BLOCK	2.13
1/2''	INSULATION PLASTER	.75	1 3/8''	WOOD DOOR	1.92
1/2''	FIBERBOARD CEILING TILE	1.20		SAME WITH STORM DOOR	3.12
1/2''	FIBERBOARD SHEATHING	1.45	1 3/4''	WOOD DOOR	1.82
3/4''	FIBERBOARD SHEATHING	2.18		SAME WITH STORM DOOR	2.94
	ROLL ROOFING	.15			
	ASPHALT SHINGLES	.16			
	WOOD SHINGLES	.86			
	TILE OR SLATE	.08			

THE METRIC SYSTEM

LINEAR MEASURE

10 millimeters	=	1 centimeter
10 centimeters	=	1 decimeter
10 decimeters	=	1 meter
10 meters	=	1 decameter
10 decameters	=	1 hectometer
10 hectometers	=	1 kilometer

LIQUID MEASURE

10 milliliters	=	1 centiliter
10 centiliters	=	1 deciliter
10 deciliters	=	1 liter
10 liters	=	1 decaliter
10 decaliters	=	1 hectoliter
10 hectoliters	=	1 kiloliter

SQUARE MEASURE

100 sq. millimeters	=	1 sq. centimeter
100 sq. centimeters	=	1 sq. decimeter
100 sq. decimeters	=	1 sq. meter
100 sq. meters	=	1 sq. decameter
100 sq. decameters	=	1 sq. hectometer
100 sq. hectometers	=	1 sq. kilometer

WEIGHTS

10 milligrams	=	1 centigram
10 centigrams	=	1 decigram
10 decigrams	=	1 gram
10 grams	=	1 decagram
10 decagrams	=	1 hectogram
10 hectograms	=	1 kilogram
100 kilograms	=	1 quintal
10 quintals	=	1 ton

CUBIC MEASURE

1000 cu. millimeters	=	1 cu. centimeter
1000 cu. centimeters	=	1 cu. decimeter
1000 cu. decimeters	=	1 cu. meter

WEIGHTS AND MEASURES CONVERSION TABLE

LINEAR MEASURE

1 inch	=		= 2.54 centimeters
1 foot	= 12 inches		= 0.3048 meter
1 yard	= 3 feet		= 0.9144 meter
1 rod	= 5 1/2 yds. or 16 1/2 ft.		= 5.029 meters
1 furlong	= 40 rods		= 201.17 meters
1 mile (statute)	= 5280 ft. or 1760 yds.		= 1609.3 meters
1 league (land)	= 3 miles		= 4.83 kilometers

CHAIN LINEAR MEASURE (FOR SURVEYOR'S CHAIN)

1 link	= 7.92 inches	=	20.12 centimeters
1 chain	= 66 feet or 100 links	=	20.12 meters
1 furlong	= 10 chains	=	201.17 meters
1 mile	= 80 chains	=	1609.3 meters

SQUARE MEASURE

1 sq. inch	=		= 6.452 sq. centimeters
1 sq. foot	= 144 sq. inches		= 929 sq. centimeters
1 sq. yard	= 9 sq. feet		= 0.8361 sq. meter
1 sq. rod	= 30 1/4 sq. yards		= 25.29 sq. meters
1 acre	= 43,560 sq. feet or 160 sq. yds.		= 0.4047 hectare
1 sq. mile	= 640 acres		= 259 hectares or 2.59 sq. kilometers

CHAIN SQUARE MEASURE

1 sq. pole	=	625 sq. links	= 25.29 sq. meters
1 sq. chain	=	16 sq. poles	= 404.7 sq. meters
1 acre	=	10 sq. chains	= 0.4047 hectare
1 sq. mile or section	=	640 acres	= 259 hectares
1 township	=	36 sq. miles	= 9324.0 hectares

CUBIC MEASURE

1 cu. inch	=		= 16.387 cu. centimeters
1 cu. foot	= 1728 cu. inches		= 0.0283 cu. meter
1 cu. yard	= 27 cu. feet		= 0.7646 cu. meter

ANGULAR AND CIRCULAR MEASURE

1 minute	=	60 seconds
1 degree	=	60 minutes
1 right angle	=	90 degrees
1 straight angle	=	180 degrees
1 circle	=	360 degrees

WEIGHTS OF BUILDING MATERIALS

MATERIAL	WEIGHT		MATERIAL	WEIGHT	
CONCRETE			WOOD CONSTRUCTION (CONTINUED)		
With stone reinforced	150	pcf	Ceiling, joist and plaster	10	psf
With stone plain	144	pcf	Ceiling, joist and 1/2'' gypsum board	7	psf
With cinders, reinforced	110	pcf	Ceiling, joist and acoustic tile	5	psf
Light concrete (Aerocrete)	65	pcf	Wood shingles	3	psf
(Perlite)	45	pcf	Spanish tile	15	psf
(Vermiculite)	40	pcf	Copper sheet	2	psf
			Tar and gravel	6	psf
METAL AND PLASTER			STONE		
Masonry mortar	116	pcf	Sandstone	147	pcf
Gypsum and sand plaster	112	pcf	Slate	175	pcf
			Limestone	165	pcf
BRICK AND BLOCK MASONRY (INCLUDING MORTAR)			Granite	175	pcf
4'' brick wall	35	psf	Marble	165	pcf
8'' brick wall	74	psf			
8'' concrete block wall	100	psf	GLASS		
12'' concrete block wall	150	psf	1/4'' plate glass	3.28	psf
4'' brick veneer over 4'' concrete block	65	psf	1/8'' double strength	1.63	psf
			1/8'' insulating glass with air space	3.25	psf
WOOD CONSTRUCTION			4'' block glass	20.00	psf
Frame wall, lath and plaster	20	psf			
Frame wall, 1/2'' gypsum board	12	psf	INSULATION		
Floor, 1/2'' subfloor + 3/4'' finished	6	psf	Cork board 1'' thick	.58	psf
Floor, 1/2'' subfloor and ceramic tile	16	psf	Rigid foam insulation 2'' thick	.3	psf
Roof, joist and 1/2'' sheathing	3	psf	Blanket or bat 1'' thick	.1	psf
Roof, 2'' plank and beam	5	psf			
Roof, built-up	7	psf			

BRICK AND BLOCK COURSES

BLOCK NO. OF COURSES	BRICK NO. OF COURSES	HEIGHT OF COURSE	BLOCK NO. OF COURSES	BRICK NO. OF COURSES	HEIGHT OF COURSE
	1	0' − 2 5/8''		37	8' − 2 5/8''
	2	0' − 5 3/8''		38	8' − 5 3/8''
1	3	0' − 8''	13	39	8' − 8''
	4	0' − 10 5/8''		40	8' − 10 5/8''
	5	1' − 1 3/8''		41	9' − 1 3/8''
2	6	1' − 4''	14	42	9' − 4''
	7	1' − 6 5/8''		43	9' − 6 5/8''
	8	1' − 9 3/8''		44	9' − 9 3/8''
3	9	2' − 0''	15	45	10' − 0''
	10	2' − 2 5/8''		46	10' − 2 5/8''
	11	2' − 5 3/8''		47	10' − 5 3/8''
4	12	2' − 8''	16	48	10' − 8''
	13	2' − 10 5/8''		49	10' − 10 3/8''
	14	3' − 1 3/8''		50	11' − 1 3/8''
5	15	3' − 4''	17	51	11' − 4''
	16	3' − 6 5/8''		52	11' − 6 5/8''
	17	3' − 9 3/8''		53	11' − 9 3/8''
6	18	4' − 0''	18	54	12' − 0''
	19	4' − 2 5/8''		55	12' − 2 5/8''
	20	4' − 5 3/8''		56	12' − 5 3/8''
7	21	4' − 8''	19	57	12' − 8''
	22	4' − 10 5/8''		58	12' − 10 5/8''
	23	5' − 1 3/8''		59	13' − 1 3/8''
8	24	5' − 4''	20	60	13' − 4''
	25	5' − 6 5/8''		61	13' − 6 5/8''
	26	5' − 9 3/8''		62	13' − 9 3/8''
9	27	6' − 0''	21	63	14' − 0''
	28	6' − 2 5/8''		64	14' − 2 5/8''
	29	6' − 5 3/8''		65	14' − 5 3/8''
10	30	6' − 8''	22	66	14' − 8''
	31	6' − 10 5/8''		67	14' − 10 5/8''
	32	7' − 1 3/8''		68	15' − 1 3/8''
11	33	7' − 4''	23	69	15' − 4''
	34	7' − 6 5/8''		70	15' − 6 5/8''
	35	7' − 9 3/8''		71	15' − 9 3/8''
12	36	8' − 0''	24	72	16' − 0''

MORTAR JOINT IS 3/8''

CONVERSION DIAGRAM FOR RAFTERS

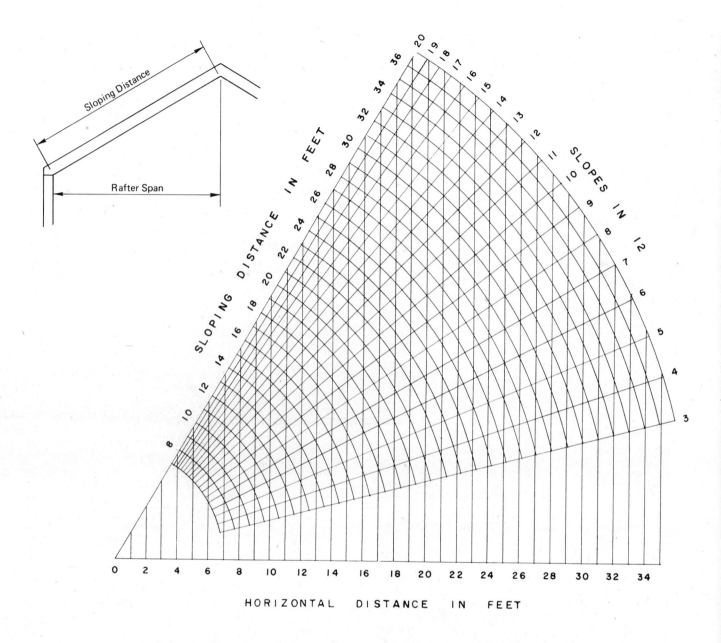

HORIZONTAL DISTANCE IN FEET

To use the diagram select the known horizontal distance and follow the vertical line to its intersection with the radial line of the specified slope, then proceed along the arc to read the sloping distance. In some cases it may be desirable to interpolate between the one foot separations. The diagram also may be used to find the horizontal distance corresponding to a given sloping distance or to find the slope when the horizontal and sloping distances are known.

Example: With a roof slope of 8 in 12 and a horizontal distance of 20 feet the sloping distance may be read as 24 feet.

How to read the four basic grade-trademarks of the American Plywood Association

Product Standard PS 1-74 is a performance standard for clear understanding between buyer and seller. To identify plywood manufactured by association member mills under the requirements of Product Standard PS 1-74, four types of grade-trademarks and one typical edge mark are used to illustrate the plywood's type, grade, group, class, and identification index. Here's how they look together with notations on what each element means.

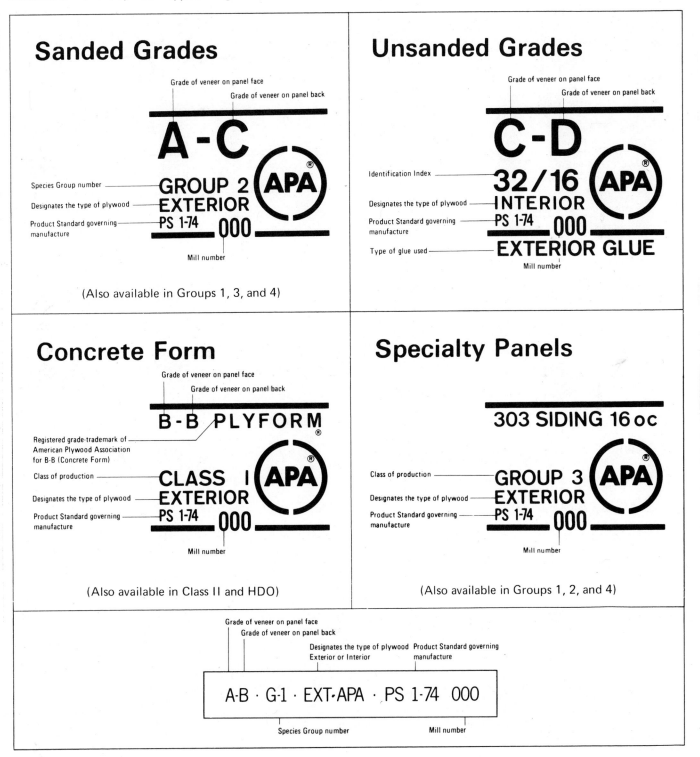

Sanded Grades

Grade of veneer on panel face
Grade of veneer on panel back

A - C

Species Group number — **GROUP 2**
Designates the type of plywood — **EXTERIOR**
Product Standard governing manufacture — **PS 1-74 000**

Mill number

(Also available in Groups 1, 3, and 4)

Unsanded Grades

Grade of veneer on panel face
Grade of veneer on panel back

C - D

Identification Index — **32/16**
Designates the type of plywood — **INTERIOR**
Product Standard governing manufacture — **PS 1-74 000**
Type of glue used — **EXTERIOR GLUE**

Mill number

Concrete Form

Grade of veneer on panel face
Grade of veneer on panel back

B - B PLYFORM

Registered grade-trademark of American Plywood Association for B-B (Concrete Form)
Class of production — **CLASS I**
Designates the type of plywood — **EXTERIOR**
Product Standard governing manufacture — **PS 1-74 000**

Mill number

(Also available in Class II and HDO)

Specialty Panels

303 SIDING 16 oc

Class of production — **GROUP 3**
Designates the type of plywood — **EXTERIOR**
Product Standard governing manufacture — **PS 1-74 000**

Mill number

(Also available in Groups 1, 2, and 4)

Grade of veneer on panel face
Grade of veneer on panel back
Designates the type of plywood Exterior or Interior
Product Standard governing manufacture

A-B · G-1 · EXT·APA · PS 1-74 000

Species Group number
Mill number

GRADE-USE GUIDE FOR APPEARANCE GRADES OF PLYWOOD [1]

Use these terms when you specify plywood (2)	Description and Most Common Uses	Typical Grade-trademarks	Face	Back	Inner Plies	1/4	5/16	3/8	1/2	5/8	3/4
Interior Type											
N-N, N-A, N-B INT-APA	Cabinet quality. For natural finish furniture, cabinet doors, built-ins, etc. Special order items.	N N G1 INT APA PS1 74 / N A G2 INT APA PS1 74	N	N,A, or B	C						3/4
N-D-INT-APA	For natural finish paneling. Special order item.	N D G3 INT APA PS1 74	N	D	D	1/4					
A-A INT-APA	For applications with both sides on view. Built-ins, cabinets, furniture and partitions. Smooth face; suitable for painting.	A A G4 INT APA PS1 74	A	A	D	1/4		3/8	1/2	5/8	3/4
A-B INT-APA	Use where appearance of one side is less important but two smooth solid surfaces are necessary.	A B G4 INT APA PS1 74	A	B	D	1/4		3/8	1/2	5/8	3/4
A-D INT-APA	Use where appearance of only one side is important. Paneling, built-ins, shelving, partitions, and flow racks.	A-D GROUP 1 INTERIOR PS1 74 000 (APA)	A	D	D	1/4		3/8	1/2	5/8	3/4
B-B INT-APA	Utility panel with two smooth sides. Permits circular plugs.	B B G3 INT APA PS1 74	B	B	D	1/4		3/8	1/2	5/8	3/4
B-D INT-APA	Utility panel with one smooth side. Good for backing, sides of built-ins. Industry: shelving, slip sheets, separator boards and bins.	B-D GROUP 3 INTERIOR PS1 74 000 (APA)	B	D	D	1/4		3/8	1/2	5/8	3/4
DECORATIVE PANELS—APA	Rough-sawn, brushed, grooved, or striated faces. For paneling, interior accent walls, built-ins, counter facing, displays, and exhibits.	DECORATIVE B D G1 INT APA PS1 74	C or btr.	D	D		5/16	3/8	1/2	5/8	
PLYRON INT-APA	Hardboard face on both sides. For counter tops, shelving, cabinet doors, flooring. Faces tempered, untempered, smooth, or screened.	PLYRON INT APA PS1 74			C & D				1/2	5/8	3/4
Exterior Type (7)											
A-A EXT-APA (4)	Use where appearance of both sides is important. Fences, built-ins, signs, boats, cabinets, commercial refrigerators, shipping containers, tote boxes, tanks, and ducts.	A A G3 EXT APA PS1 74	A	A	C	1/4		3/8	1/2	5/8	3/4
A-B EXT-APA (4)	Use where the appearance of one side is less important.	A B G1 EXT APA PS1 74	A	B	C	1/4		3/8	1/2	5/8	3/4
A-C EXT-APA (4)	Use where the appearance of only one side is important. Sidings, soffits, fences, structural uses, boxcar and truck lining, farm buildings. Tanks, trays, commercial refrigerators.	A-C GROUP 1 EXTERIOR PS1 74 000 (APA)	A	C	C	1/4		3/8	1/2	5/8	3/4
B-B EXT-APA (4)	Utility panel with solid faces.	B B G1 EXT APA PS1 74	B	B	C	1/4		3/8	1/2	5/8	3/4
B-C EXT-APA (4)	Utility panel for farm service and work buildings, boxcar and truck lining, containers, tanks, agricultural equipment. Also as base for exterior coatings for walls, roofs.	B-C GROUP 2 EXTERIOR PS1 74 000 (APA)	B	C	C	1/4		3/8	1/2	5/8	3/4
HDO EXT-APA (4)	High Density Overlay plywood. Has a hard, semi-opaque resin-fiber overlay both faces. Abrasion resistant. For concrete forms, cabinets, counter tops, signs and tanks.	HDO AA G1 EXT APA PS1 74	A or B	A or B	C or C plgd		5/16	3/8	1/2	5/8	3/4
MDO EXT-APA (4)	Medium Density Overlay with smooth, opaque, resin-fiber overlay one or both panel faces. Highly recommended for siding and other outdoor applications, built-ins, signs, and displays. Ideal base for paint.	MDO BB G4 EXT APA PS1 74	B	B or C	C		5/16	3/8	1/2	5/8	3/4
303 SIDING EXT-APA (6)	Proprietary plywood products for exterior siding, fencing, etc. Special surface treatment such as V-groove, channel groove, striated, brushed, rough-sawn.	303 SIDING 16oc GROUP 1 EXTERIOR PS1 74 000 (APA)	(5)	C	C			3/8	1/2	5/8	
T 1-11 EXT-APA (6)	Special 303 panel having grooves 1/4" deep, 3/8" wide, spaced 4" or 8" o.c. Other spacing optional. Edges shiplapped. Available unsanded, textured, and MDO.	303 SIDING 16oc T1-11 GROUP 1 EXTERIOR PS1 74 000 (APA)	C or btr.	C	C					5/8	
PLYRON EXT-APA	Hardboard faces both sides, tempered, smooth or screened.	PLYRON EXT APA PS1 74			C				1/2	5/8	3/4
MARINE EXT-APA	Ideal for boat hulls. Made only with Douglas fir or western larch. Special solid jointed core construction. Subject to special limitations on core gaps and number of face repairs. Also available with HDO or MDO faces.	MARINE AA EXT APA PS1 74	A or B	A or B	B	1/4		3/8	1/2	5/8	3/4

(1) Sanded both sides except where decorative or other surfaces specified.
(2) Available in Group 1, 2, 3, 4, or 5 unless otherwise noted.
(3) Standard 4x8 panel sizes, other sizes available.
(4) Also available in Structural I (all plies limited to Group 1 species) and Structural II (all plies limited to Group 1, 2, or 3 species).
(5) C or better for 5 plies; C Plugged or better for 3-ply panels.
(6) Stud spacing is shown on grade stamp.
(7) For finishing recommendations, see form V307.

SPECIFIC GRADES AND THICKNESSES MAY BE IN LOCALLY LIMITED SUPPLY.
SEE YOUR DEALER FOR AVAILABILITY BEFORE SPECIFYING.

	Use these terms when you specify plywood	Description and Most Common Uses	Typical Grade-trademarks	Veneer Grade Face	Veneer Grade Back	Veneer Grade Inner Plies	Most Common Thicknesses (inch) (1)				
Interior Type	C-D INT-APA (2) (3)	For wall and roof sheathing, subflooring, industrial uses such as pallets. Also available with intermediate glue or exterior glue. Specify intermediate glue for moderate construction delays; exterior glue for better durability in somewhat longer construction delays, and for treated wood foundations.	C-D 32/16 APA INTERIOR PS 1-74 000	C	D	D	5/16	3/8	1/2	5/8	3/4
	STRUCTURAL I C-D INT-APA and STRUCTURAL II C-D INT-APA	Unsanded structural grades where plywood strength properties are of maximum importance: structural diaphragms, box beams, gusset plates, stressed-skin panels, containers, pallet bins. Made only with exterior glue.	STRUCTURAL I C-D 24/0 APA INTERIOR 000 EXTERIOR GLUE	C (6)	D (7)	D (7)	5/16	3/8	1/2	5/8	3/4
	UNDERLAYMENT INT-APA (3) (2) (9)	For underlayment or combination subfloor-underlayment under resilient floor coverings, carpeting in homes, apartments, mobile homes. Specify exterior glue where moisture may be present, such as bathrooms, utility rooms. Touch-sanded. Also available in tongue and groove.	UNDERLAYMENT GROUP 1 APA INTERIOR PS 1-74 000	C Plugged	D	(8) C & D	1/4		3/8	1/2	5/8	3/4
	C-D PLUGGED INT-APA (3) (2) (9)	For built-ins, wall and ceiling tile backing, cable reels, walkways, separator boards. Not a substitute for UNDERLAYMENT as it lacks UNDERLAYMENT's punch-through resistance. Touch-sanded.	C-D PLUGGED GROUP 2 APA INTERIOR PS 1-74 000	C Plugged	D	D	5/16	3/8	1/2	5/8	3/4
	2·4·1 INT-APA (2) (5)	Combination subfloor-underlayment. Quality base for resilient floor coverings, carpeting, wood strip flooring. Use 2·4·1 with exterior glue in areas subject to moisture. Unsanded or touch-sanded as specified.	2·4·1 GROUP 1 APA INTERIOR PS 1-74 000	C Plugged	D	C & D	(available 1-1/8" or 1-1/4")				
Exterior Type	C-C EXT-APA (3)	Unsanded grade with waterproof bond for subflooring and roof decking, siding on service and farm buildings, crating, pallets, pallet bins, cable reels.	C-C 42/20 APA EXTERIOR PS 1-74 000	C	C	C	5/16	3/8	1/2	5/8	3/4
	STRUCTURAL I C-C EXT-APA and STRUCTURAL II C-C EXT-APA	For engineered applications in construction and industry where full Exterior type panels are required. Unsanded. See (9) for species group requirements.	STRUCTURAL C-C 32/16 APA EXTERIOR PS 1-74 000	C	C	C	5/16	3/8	1/2	5/8	3/4
	UNDERLAYMENT C-C Plugged EXT-APA (3) (9) / C-C PLUGGED EXT-APA (3) (9)	For underlayment or combination subfloor-underlayment under resilient floor coverings where severe moisture conditions may be present, as in balcony decks. Use for tile backing where severe moisture conditions exist. For refrigerated or controlled atmosphere rooms, pallets, fruit pallet bins, reusable cargo containers, tanks and boxcar and truck floors and linings. Touch-sanded. Also available in tongue and groove.	UNDERLAYMENT C-C PLUGGED GROUP 2 APA EXTERIOR PS 1-74 000 / C-C PLUGGED GROUP 3 APA EXTERIOR PS 1-74 000	C Plugged	C	C (8)	1/4		3/8	1/2	5/8	3/4
	B-B PLYFORM CLASS I & CLASS II (4) EXT-APA	Concrete form grades with high re-use factor. Sanded both sides. Mill-oiled unless otherwise specified. Special restrictions on species. Also available in HDO.	B-B PLYFORM CLASS I APA EXTERIOR PS 1-74 000	B	B	C				5/8	3/4

(1) Panels are standard 4x8-foot size. Other sizes available.
(2) Also available with exterior or intermediate glue.
(3) Available in Group 1, 2, 3, 4, or 5.
(4) Also available in STRUCTURAL I.
(5) Available in Group 1, 2, or 3 only.
(6) Special improved C grade for structural panels.
(7) Special improved D grade for structural panels.
(8) Ply beneath face a special C grade which limits knotholes to 1 inch or D under Group 1 or 2 faces 1/6 inch thick.
(9) Also available in STRUCTURAL I (all plies limited to Group 1 species) and STRUCTURAL II (all plies limited to Group 1, 2, 3 species).

Veneer Grades

N — Smooth surface "natural finish" veneer. Select, all heartwood or all sapwood. Free of open defects. Allows not more than 6 repairs, wood only, per 4x8 panel, made parallel to grain and well matched for grain and color.

A — Smooth, paintable. Not more than 18 neatly made repairs, boat, sled, or router type, and parallel to grain, permitted. May be used for natural finish in less demanding applications.

B — Solid surface. Shims, circular repair plugs and tight knots to 1 inch across grain permitted. Some minor splits permitted.

C — Tight knots to 1-1/2 inch. Knotholes to 1 inch across grain and some to 1-1/2 inch if total width of knots and knotholes is within specified limits. Synthetic or wood repairs. Discoloration and sanding defects that do not impair strength permitted. Limited splits allowed.

C Plugged — Improved C veneer with splits limited to 1/8 inch width and knotholes and borer holes limited to 1/4 x 1/2 inch. Admits some broken grain. Synthetic repairs permitted.

D — Knots and knotholes to 2-1/2 inch width across grain and 1/2 inch larger within specified limits. Limited splits are permitted.

©1974 American Plywood Association

VENEER GRADES USED IN PLYWOOD

Veneer Grade	Defect Limitations
N — Intended for Natural Finish	Presents smooth surface. Veneer shall be all heartwood or all sapwood free from knots, knotholes, splits, pitch pockets, other open defects, and stain, but may contain pitch streaks averaging not more than 3/8″ wide blending with color of wood. If joined, not more than two pieces in 48″ width; not more than three pieces in wider panels. Joints parallel to panel edges and well-matched for color and grain. Repairs shall be neatly made, well-matched for color and grain, and limited to a total of six in number in any 4′ x 8′ sheet. • Maximum of three "router" patches not exceeding 3/4″ x 3-1/2″ admitted. No overlapping. • Shims admitted not exceeding 12″ in length but may occur only at ends of panel. (Examples of permissible combinations: 3 router patches and 3 shims, 2 router patches and 4 shims, 1 router patch and 5 shims, or 6 shims). Suitable synthetic fillers may be used to fill 1/32″ wide checks, splits up to 1/16″ x 2″, and chipped areas or other openings not exceeding 1/8″ x 1/4″.
A	Presents smooth surface. Admits—Pitch streaks blending with color of wood and averaging not more than ⅜″ in width. —Sapwood. —Discolorations. Veneer shall be free from knots, knotholes, splits, pitch pockets and other open defects. If of more than one piece, veneer shall be well joined. Repairs shall be neatly made, parallel to grain, and limited to 18 in number in any 4′ x 8′ sheet, excluding shims; proportionate limits on other sizes. Patches of "boat," "router," and "sled" type only, not exceeding 2-1/4″ in width, and may be die-cut if edges are cut clean and sharp. Radius of ends of boat patches shall not exceed 1/8″. • Multiple patching limited to 2 patches, neither of which may exceed 7″ in length if either is wider than 1″. • Shims admitted except over or around patches or as multiple repairs. Suitable synthetic fillers may be used to fill 1/32″ wide checks, splits up to 1/16″ x 2″, and chipped areas or other openings not exceeding 1/8″ x 1/4″.
B	Presents solid surface. Admits—Knots up to 1″ across the grain if both sound and tight. —Pitch streaks averaging not more than 1″ in width. —Discolorations. —Slightly rough but not torn grain, minor sanding and patching defects, including sander skips not exceeding 5% of panel area. Veneer shall be free from open defects except for splits not wider than 1/32″, vertical holes up to 1/16″ in diameter if not exceeding an average of one per square foot in number, and horizontal or surface tunnels up to 1/16″ in width and 1″ in length not exceeding 12 in number in a 4′ x 8′ sheet (proportionately on other sizes). Repairs shall be neatly made and may consist of patches, plugs, synthetic plugs and shims. • Patches may be "boat," "router," and "sled" type not exceeding 3″ in width individually when used in multiple repairs or 4″ in width when used as single repairs. • Plugs may be "circular," "dog-bone," and "leaf-shaped," not exceeding 3″ in width when used in multiple repairs or 4″ in width when used as single repairs. • Synthetic plugs shall present a solid, level, hard surface not exceeding above dimensions. Suitable synthetic fillers may be used to fill small splits or openings up to 1/16″ x 2″, and chipped areas or other openings not exceeding 1/8″ x 1/4″.
C	Admits—Tight knots up to 1½″ across the grain. —Knotholes not larger than 1″ across the grain. Also an occasional knothole not more than 1½″ measured across the grain, occurring in any section 12″ along the grain in which the aggregate width of all knots and knotholes occurring wholly within the section does not exceed 6″ in a 48″ width, and proportionately for other widths. —Splits ½″ by one-half panel length; ⅜″ by any panel length if tapering to a point; ¼″ maximum where located within 1″ of parallel panel edge. —Worm or borer holes up to ⅝″ x 1½″. Repairs shall be neatly made and may consist of patches, plugs, and synthetic plugs. Patches ("boat," including die-cut) not exceeding 3″ in width individually when used in multiple repairs or 4″ in width when used as single repairs. Plugs may be circular, "dog-bone" and leaf-shaped. Synthetic plugs shall present a solid, level, hard surface not exceeding above dimensions.
C (plugged)	Admits—Knotholes, worm or borer holes, and other open defects up to ¼″ x ½″. —Sound tight knots up to 1½″ across the grain. —Splits up to ⅛″ wide. —Ruptured and torn grain. —Pitch pockets if solid and tight. —Plugs, patches and shims.
D	D veneer used only in Interior type plywood and may contain plugs, patches, shims, worm or borer holes. Backs: Admits tight knots not larger than 2½″ measured across the grain and knotholes up to 2½″ in maximum dimension. An occasional tight knot larger than 2½″ but not larger than 3″ measured across the grain or knothole larger than 2½″ but not larger than 3″ maximum dimension, occurring in any section 12″ along the grain in which the aggregate width of all knots and knotholes occurring wholly within the section does not exceed 10″ in a 48″ width and proportionately for other widths. Inner Plys: Knotholes limited as for backs. All Plys: Pitch pockets not exceeding 2-1/2″ measured across the grain. Splits up to 1″ except in backs only not more than one exceeding 1/2″; not exceeding 1/4″ maximum width where located within 1″ of parallel panel edge; splits must taper to a point. White pocket in inner plys and backs, not exceeding three of the following characteristics in any combination in any area 24″ wide by 12″ long. (a) 6″ width heavy white pocket. (b) 12″ width light white pocket. (c) One knot or knothole or repair 1-1/2″ to 2-1/2″, or two knots or knotholes or repairs 1″ to 1-1/2″.

Thickness (inch)	C-D INT - APA C-C EXT - APA			NOTES:
	Group 1 & Structural 1	Group 2 or 3 & Structural II*	Group 4**	
5/16	20/0	16/0	12/0	* Panels with Group 2 outer plies and special thickness and construction requirements, or STRUCTURAL II panels with Group 1 faces, may carry the Identification Index numbers shown for Group 1 panels.
3/8	24/0	20/0	16/0	
1/2	32/16	24/0	24/0	** Panels made with Group 4 outer plies may carry the Identification Index numbers shown for Group 3 panels when they conform to special thickness and construction requirements detailed in PS 1.
5/8	42/20	32/16	30/12†	
3/4	48/24	42/20	36/16†	
7/8	--------	48/24	42/20	† Check local availability.

Key Definitions:

Plywood is manufactured in two types: Exterior type with 100% waterproof glueline and Interior type with highly moisture-resistant glueline. Interior type plywood may be bonded with exterior, intermediate, or interior glue. Specify Exterior type plywood for all permanent outdoor applications and those subject to continuing moist conditions or extreme high humidity. For other applications, Interior type may be used.

Group:

Wood from more than 70 species of varying strength may be used in plywood manufacture. The species are grouped on the basis of stiffness and strength, and divided into five classifications—Groups 1 through 5. Stiffest and strongest woods are in Group 1. The group number in the American Plywood Association grade-trademark refers to the weakest species used in face and back, except in decorative and sanded panels 3/8 inch thick or less. These are identified by the face species group. PS 1 lists species in all groups.

Appearance Grades:

Within each type of plywood are grade designations based on an appearance grading system for the veneer. Grades are N, A, B, C, and D, with N and A veneers the best looking. Panel grades are generally designated by veneer grade of panel face and back and by glue line (i.e., interior or exterior). PS 1 details allowable characteristics and repairs.

Engineered Grades:

Engineered grades are designed for demanding construction applications where properties such as nail bearing, shear, compression, tension, etc., are of maximum importance and appearance is secondary to strength.

C-D INTERIOR and C-D INTERIOR WITH EXTERIOR GLUE (CDX) are Interior type panels for uses such as sheathing. They will withstand considerable exposure to outdoor moisture conditions during construction, but must not be mistaken for Exterior plywood. STRUCTURAL I C-D is limited to Group 1 species throughout. STRUCTURAL II C-D permits Group 1, 2, or 3 species. Both are bonded with exterior glue.

Identification Index:

The basic unsanded grades of plywood—C-D sheathing, C-C Exterior, and STRUCTURAL I and II C-C and C-D carry an Identification Index of two numbers in the American Plywood Association grade-trademark, for example 24/0 or 32/16. The left-hand number refers to maximum recommended spacing of roof framing in inches when the panel is used as roof sheathing. The right-hand number refers to maximum spacing of floor framing when the panel is used for subflooring. In each case, face grain is across supports and panel is continuous across two or more spans.

IMPORTANT NOTE: The spans referred to in the Index numbers are accepted by most major building codes. Local interpretations may vary, however. So make sure your specifications comply with the local code under which you are building.

Class I, Class II:

Applies only to Plyform grade for concrete form plywood. Indicates species mix permitted. Plyform Class I is limited to Group 1 faces, Group 1 or 2 crossbands, and Group 1, 2, 3, or 4 center ply. Plyform Class II is limited to Group 1 or 2 faces (Group 3 under certain conditions) and Group 1, 2, 3, or 4 inner plies.

Method of Ordering:

Appearance grades: Designate the species group, number of pieces, width, length, number of plies, type, grade, finished thickness and agency certification of quality:
"Group 2 plywood: 100 pcs., 48" x 96", 3-ply Interior type, A-D grade, sanded 2 sides to 1/4" thickness, APA grade-trademarked"

Engineered grades: Designate grade, Identification Index, number of pieces, width, length, number of plies, thickness, and agency certification of quality:
"C-D, 24/0, 100 pcs., 48" x 96", 3-ply, 3/8" thick. APA grade-trademarked. (If exterior glue or intermediate glue are desired, note 'exterior glue' or 'intermediate glue'.)"

Concrete form: Designate the Class, number of pieces, width, length, thickness, grade, and agency certification of quality. Concrete form panels are mill-oiled, unless otherwise specified:
"Plyform, Class I, 100 pcs., 48" x 96", 5/8" thick, B-B Exterior type, APA grade-trademarked.

PLYWOOD

Classification of species

Group 1	Group 2	Group 3	Group 4	Group 5
Apitong[a][b]	Cedar, Port Orford	Maple, Black	Alder, Red	Aspen	Basswood
Beech, American	Cypress	Mengkulang[a]	Birch, Paper	Bigtooth	Fir, Balsam
Birch	Douglas Fir 2[c]	Meranti, Red[a][d]	Cedar, Alaska	Quaking	Poplar, Balsam
Sweet	Fir	Mersawa[a]	Fir, Subalpine	Cativo	
Yellow	California Red	Pine	Hemlock, Eastern	Cedar	
Douglas Fir 1[c]	Grand	Pond	Maple, Bigleaf	Incense	
Kapur[a]	Noble	Red	Pine	Western Red	
Keruing[a][b]	Pacific Silver	Virginia	Jack	Cottonwood	
Larch, Western	White	Western White	Lodgepole	Eastern	
Maple, Sugar	Hemlock, Western	Spruce	Ponderosa	Black (Western Poplar)	
Pine	Lauan	Red	Spruce	Pine	
Caribbean	Almon	Sitka	Redwood	Eastern White	
Ocote	Bagtikan	Sweetgum	Spruce	Sugar	
Pine, Southern	Mayapis	Tamarack	Black		
Loblolly	Red Lauan	Yellow Poplar	Engelmann		
Longleaf	Tangile		White		
Shortleaf	White Lauan				
Slash					
Tanoak					

(a) Each of these names represents a trade group of woods consisting of a number of closely related species.

(b) Species from the genus Dipterocarpus are marketed collectively: Apitong if originating in the Philippines; Keruing if originating in Malaysia or Indonesia.

(c) Douglas fir from trees grown in the states of Washington, Oregon, California, Idaho, Montana, Wyoming, and the Canadian Provinces of Alberta and British Columbia shall be classed as Douglas fir No. 1. Douglas fir from trees grown in the states of Nevada, Utah, Colorado, Arizona and New Mexico shall be classed as Douglas fir No. 2.

(d) Red Meranti shall be limited to species having a specific gravity of 0.41 or more based on green volume and oven dry weight.

Identification Index of Plywood Sheathing

Thickness (inch)	C-C EXTERIOR C-D INTERIOR			STRUCTURAL I C-C and C-D STRUCTURAL II** C-C and C-D	STRUCTURAL II C-C and C-D
	Group 1 Group 2*	Group 2 or 3 Group 4*	Group 4	Group 1	Group 2 or 3
5/16	20/0	16/0	12/0	20/0	16/0
3/8	24/0	20/0	16/0	24/0	20/0
1/2	32/16	24/0	24/0	32/16	24/0
5/8	42/20	32/16	30/12	42/20	32/16
3/4	48/24	42/20	36/16	48/24	42/20
7/8†	----	48/24	42/20	----	48/24

*Panels conforming to special thickness provisions and panel constructions of Paragraph 3.8.6 of PS 1.
**Panels manufactured with Group 1 faces but classified as STRUCTURAL II by reason of Group 2 or Group 3 inner plies.
†Panels thicker than 7/8 inch shall be identified by group number.

The Identification Index numbers placed on the panel by the manufacturer in the grades shown in this table are based on panel thickness and the stiffness of species used on the face and back. Since stiffness varies with different species, the same index number may appear on panels of different thickness. For example, 24/0 appears on both 3/8 inch and 1/2 inch C-D INT sheathing. In the latter, species of lesser stiffness have been used on the face and back.

Conversely, panels of the same thickness may be marked with as many as three different index numbers. For example 3/8 inch C-D INT may be marked with 16/0, 20/0 or 24/0 depending on the species used on the face and back. In general, the higher the index number, the greater the stiffness.

PRODUCT	Approx. Shipping Weight Per Square	Packages Per Square	Length	Width	Shingles Per Square	Side or End Lap	Top Lap	Head Lap	Exposure
3 Tab Self Sealing Strip Shingle	235 lb. 300 lb.	3 or 4	36" 36"	12" 12"	80 80		7" 7"	2" 2"	5" 5"
2 and 3 Tab Hex Strip	195 lb.	3	36"	11-1/3"	86		2"	2"	5"
Individual Lock Down	145 lb.	2	16"	16"	80	2½"			
Individual Staple Down	145 lb.	2	16"	16"	80	2½"			
Giant Individual American	330 lb.	4	16"	12"	226		11"	6"	5"
Giant Individual Dutch Lap	165 lb.	2	16"	12"	113	3"	2"	2"	10"

PRODUCT	Approx. Shipping Weight Per Square	Packages Per Square	Length	Width	Units Per Square	Side or End Lap	Top Lap	Head Lap	Exposure
Saturated Felt	15 lb. 30 lb.	1/4 1/2	144' 72'	36" 36"		4" to 6" 4" to 6"	2" 2"		34" 34"
Smooth Roll	65 lb. 50 lb.	1 1	36' 36'	36" 36"		6" 6"	2" 2"		34" 34"
Mineral Surfaced Roll	90 lb. 90 lb. 90 lb.	1.0	36'	36"	1.0 1.075 1.15	6" 6" 6"	2" 3" 4"		34" 33" 32"
Pattern Edge Roll	105 lb. 105 lb.	1 1	42' 48'	36" 32"			2" 2"		16" 14"
19" Selvage Double Coverage	110 lb. to 120 lb.	2	36'	36"			19"	2"	17"

RECOMMONDED STYLES OF WELDED WIRE FABRIC REINFORCEMENT FOR CONCRETE

TYPE OF CONSTRUCTION	RECOMMENDED STYLE	REMARKS
Barbecue Foundation Slab	6x6-8/8 to 4x4-6/6	Use heavier style fabric for heavy, massive fireplaces or barbecue pits.
Basement Floors	6x6-10/10, 6x6-8/8 or 6x6-6/6	For small areas (15-foot maximum side dimension) use 6x6-10/10. As a rule of thumb, the larger the area or the poorer the sub-soil, the heavier the gauge.
Driveways	6x6-6/6	Continuous reinforcement between 25- to 30-foot contraction joints.
Foundation Slabs (Residential only)	6x6-10/10	Use heavier gauge over poorly drained sub-soil, or when maximum dimension is greater than 15 feet.
Garage Floors	6x6-6/6	Position at midpoint of 5- or 6-inch thick slab.
Patios and Terraces	6x6-10/10	Use 6x6-8/8 if sub-soil is poorly drained.

Porch Floor
  a. 6-inch thick slab up to 6-foot span
  b. 6-inch thick slab up to 8-foot span
	6x6-6/6
	4x4-4/4
		Position 1 inch from bottom form to resist tensile stresses.

Sidewalks	6x6-10/10 6x6-8/8	Use heavier gauge over poorly drained sub-soil. Construct 25- to 30-foot slabs as for driveways.
Steps (Free span)	6x6-6/6	Use heavier style if more than five risers. Position fabric 1 inch from bottom form.
Steps (On ground)	6x6-8/8	Use 6x6-6/6 for unstable sub-soil.

GYPSUM WALLBOARD APPLICATION DATA

THICKNESS	APPROX. WEIGHT LBS./SQ. FT.	SIZE	LOCATION	APPLICATION METHOD	MAX. SPACING OF FRAMING MEMBERS
¼″	1.1	4′ x 8′ to 12′	Over Existing Walls & Ceilings	Horizontal or Vertical	
⅜″	1.5	4′ x 8′ to 14′	Ceilings	Horizontal	16″
⅜″	1.5	4′ x 8′ to 14′	Sidewalls	Horizontal or Vertical	16″
½″	2.0	4′ x 8′ to 14′	Ceilings	Vertical Horizontal	16″ 24″
½″	2.0	4′ x 8′ to 14′	Sidewalls	Horizontal or Vertical	24″
⅝″	2.5	4′ x 8′ to 14′	Ceilings	Vertical Horizontal	16″ 24″
⅝″	2.5	4′ x 8′ to 14′	Sidewalls	Horizontal or Vertical	24″
1″	4.0	2′ x 8′ to 12′		For Laminated Partitions	

SIZES AND DIMENSIONS FOR REINFORCING BARS

WEIGHT LB PER FT	NOMINAL DIAMETER INCHES	SIZE	NUMBER	NOMINAL CROSS SECT AREA SQ IN.	NOMINAL PERIMETER
.376	.375	⅜	3	.11	1.178
.668	.500	½	4	.20	1.571
1.043	.625	⅝	5	.31	1.963
1.502	.750	¾	6	.44	2.356
2.044	.875	⅞	7	.60	2.749
2.670	1.000	1	8	.79	3.142
3.400	1.128	1*	9	1.00	3.544
4.303	1.270	1⅛*	10	1.27	3.990
5.313	1.410	1¼*	11	1.56	4.430
7.650	1.693	1½*	14	2.25	5.320
13.600	2.257	2*	18	4.00	7.090

These sizes rolled in rounds equivalent to square cross section area.

RECOMMENDED FOOT CANDLE LEVELS

AREA	LEVEL
TV Viewing	5 FC
Storage	10 FC
Stairway	20 FC
Dining	20 FC
Bedroom	20 FC
Bath	30 FC
Living	30 FC
Den	30 FC
Reading	50 FC
Sewing	50 FC
Kitchen	50 FC
Shop	70 FC
Drawing	100 FC

ABBREVIATIONS

Acoustic	ACST	Drawing	DWG	Perpendicular	PERP
Acrylonitrile butadiene styrene	ABS	Drywall	DW	Plaster	PLAS
Actual	ACT	Elbow	ELL	Plate glass	PL GL
Addition	ADD	Electric	ELEC	Plates	PLTS
Adhesive	ADH	Elevation	EL or ELEV	Platform	PLATF
Aggregate	AGGR	Entrance	ENT	Plumbing	PLMB
Air conditioning	AIR COND	Estimate	EST	Plywood	PLY
Alternate	ALT	Excavate	EXC	Polyvinyl chloride	PVC
Aluminum	AL	Exterior	EXT	Prefabricated	PREFAB
American Association of Registered Architects	ARA	Fabricate	FAB	Property	PROP
American Institute of Architects	AIA	Family room	FAM R	Push button	PB
American Society for Testing Materials	ASTM	Federal Housing Authority	FHA	Radiator	RAD
American wire gage	AWG	Finish	FIN	Random length and width	RL & W
Amount	AMT	Fire brick	FBRK	Range	R
Ampere	AMP	Fireproof	FP	Receptacle	RECP
Anchor bolt	AB	Fitting	FTG	Recessed	REC
Approximate	APPROX	Fixture	FIX	Reference	REF
Architectural	ARCH	Flange	FLG	Refrigerator	REF
Area	A	Flashing	FLSHG	Register	REG
Asbestos	ASB	Floor	FL	Reinforce	REINF
Asphalt	ASPH	Floor drain	FD	Return	RET
Assembly	ASSY	Flooring	FLG	Riser	R
Automatic	AUTO	Footing	FTG	Roof	RF
Average	AVG	Foundation	FDN	Roofing	RFG
Balcony	BALC	Frame	FR	Rough	RGH
Basement	BSMT	Full size	FS	Round	RD
Bathroom	B	Gallon	GAL	Schedule	SCH
Beam	BM or BMS	Galvanized	GALV	Section	SECT
Bedroom	BR	Glass	GL	Self-closing	SC
Bench mark	BM	Grade	GR	Service	SERV
Between	BET	Gypsum	GYP	Sewer	SEW
Blocking	BLKG	Hall	H	Sheathing	SHT'G
Board feet	BD FT	Hardware	HDW	Sheet metal	SM
Bottom	BOT	Header	HDR	Shelves	SHLV'S
Bracket	BRKT	Heater	HTR	Shower	SH
British thermal unit	BTU	Horizontal	HORIZ	Siding	SDG
Broom closet	BC	Hose bib	HB	Sill cock	SC
Building	BLDG	Inside diameter	ID	Sink	SK
Buzzer	BUZ	Insulation	INS	Socket	SOC
Cabinet	CAB	Interior	INT	Soil pipe	SP
Casing	CSG	Joint	JT	Specification	SPEC
Cast iron	CI	Joist	JST	Square	SQ
Caulking	CLKG	Kiln dried	KD	Stairs	ST
Ceiling	CL	Kitchen	K	Standpipe	ST P
Cement	CEM	Kitchen cabinets	KC	Station point	SP
Center line	CL or ℄	Kitchen sink	KS	Steel	STL
Center to center	C to C	Laminated	LAM	Structural	STR
Ceramic	CER	Landing	LDG	Surface	SUR
Circuit	CKT	Laundry	LAU	Surface four sides	S4S
Circuit breaker	CIR BKR	Lavatory	LAV	Surface two sides	S2S
Cleanout	CL or CO	Leader	LDR	Suspended ceiling	SUSP CLG
Closet	CLOS or CL	Level	LEV	Switch	S or SW
Clothes dryer	CL D	Light	LT	Symbol	SYM
Column	COL	Linen closet	L CL	Tee	T
Composition	COMP	Linoleum	LINO	Telephone	TEL
Concrete	CONC	Living room	LR	Television	TV
Concrete block	CONC B	Lumber	LBR	Temperature	TEMP
Construction	CONST	Manufacture	MFR	Terra-cotta	TC
Copper	COP or CU	Material	MATL	Thermostat	THERMO
Counter	CTR	Maximum	MAX	Thickness	THK
Courses	C	Medicine cabinet	MC	Tongue and groove	T & G
Cross section	X–SECT	Metal	MET	Tread	TR
Cubic feet	CU FT	Minimum	MIN	Unfinished	UNFIN
Cubic yard	CU YD	Modular	MOD	Vanishing point	VP
Damper	DMPR	Molding	MLDG	Vanity	VAN
Decorative	DEC	National Electric Code	NEC	Ventilation	VENT
Detail	DET	National Lumber Manufacturer's Association	NLMA	Ventilator	V
Diagram	DIAG	Nominal	NOM	Vertical	VERT
Diameter	DIA	North	N	Wall cabinet	W CAB
Dimension	DIM	Number	NO	Wall vent	WV
Dining room	DR	Office	OFF	Water	W
Dishwasher	DW	On center	OC	Water closet	WC
Door	DR	Opening	OPG	Water heater	WH
Double hung	DH	Outside diameter	OD	Waterproof	WP
Down	DN	Painted	PTD	Weep hole	WH
Downspout	DS	Panel	PNL	Wide flange	WF
Drain	D or DR	Parallel	PAR	Window	WDW
		Partition	PTN	With	W/
				Wood	WD
				Wrought iron	WI
				Zinc	Z or ZN

GLOSSARY

ACRE: A plot of land comprising 43,560 sq. ft.

ADHESIVE: A natural or synthetic material, generally in paste or liquid form, used to fasten or glue boards together, lay floor tile, fabricate plastic laminates, etc.

AIR-DRIED LUMBER: Lumber that has been piled in yards or sheds for length of time. The minimum moisture content of thoroughly air-dried lumber is usually 12 to 15 percent.

ALCOVE: A recess opening off of a wall of a larger room. Often used as a sitting area, coat room or storage area.

ANCHOR: Any fastener (usually metal) used to attach parts, such as joists, trusses, posts, etc., to masonry or masonry materials.

ANCHOR BOLT: A threaded rod inserted in masonry construction to anchor the sill plate to the foundation.

APRON: Trim used under the stool on interior windows.

ARCADE: A series of arches supported by columns or piers to provide an open passageway.

ARCH: A curved structure that will support itself and the weight above its curved opening by mutual pressure.

AREAWAY: Recessed area below grade around the foundation to allow light and ventilation into basement window.

AROMATIC RED CEDAR: Similar characteristics to (Western) red cedar. Primarily used in construction for chests and closet linings for its mothproof value.

ARRIS: A sharp edge formed when two planes or surfaces meet. Found on edges of moldings, doors, shelves and in cabinet construction.

ASH PIT: The area below the hearth of a fireplace, which collects the ashes.

ASPHALT SHINGLES: Composition roof shingles made from asphalt impregnated felt covered with mineral granules.

ASSESSMENT: The levy of a tax or charge on property, usually according to established rates.

ASSESSOR: A public official responsible for the evaluation of property for the purposes of taxation.

ASSIGNEE: A person to whom a transfer of interest is made in connection with a mortgage or contract for a home or piece of property.

ASSIGNOR: A person who makes an assignment for a mortgage or contract for a home or piece of property.

ASTM: American Society for Testing Materials.

ATRIUM: A central hall or open court within a structure.

ATTACHMENT: The legal seizure of property to require payment of a debt.

ATTIC: The space between the roof and the ceiling.

ATTIC VENTILATORS: In houses, screened openings provided to ventilate an attic space. They are located in the soffit area as inlet ventilators and in the gable end or along the ridge as outlet ventilators. They can also consist of power-driven fans used as an exhaust system. See LOUVER.

AWNING WINDOW: An outswinging window hinged at the top.

BACKFILL: The replacement of excavated earth into a trench around and against a basement foundation.

BALCONY: A deck projecting from the wall of a building above ground level.

BALUSTERS: Usually small vertical members in a railing used between a top rail and the stair treads or a bottom rail.

BALUSTRADE: A series of balusters connected by a rail; generally used for porches and balconies.

BANISTER: A handrail with supporting posts used alongside a stairway.

BASEBOARD: The finish board covering the interior wall where the wall and floor meet.

BASE SHOE: A molding used next to the floor in interior baseboards.

BATT: A roll or sheet of insulation designed to be installed between members of frame construction.

BATTEN: Narrow strips of wood used to cover joints or as decorative vertical members over plywood or wide boards.

BATTER BOARD: One of a pair of horizontal boards nailed to posts set at the corners of an excavation, used to indicate the desired level, also as a fastening for stretched strings to indicate outlines of foundation walls.

BAY WINDOW: Any window space projecting outward from the walls of a building, either square or polygonal in plan.

BEAM: A structural member transversely supporting a load.

BEAM CEILING: A ceiling in which the ceiling beams are exposed to view.

BEARING PARTITION: A partition that supports any vertical load in addition to its own weight.

BEARING WALL: A wall that supports any vertical load in addition to its own weight.

BEECH: A whitish to reddish brown hardwood used especially in construction for interior and exterior cabinet parts. Blends well with birch for stained kitchen cabinets and vanities.

BENCH MARK: A mark on some permanent object fixed to the ground from which land measurements and elevations are taken.

BIRCH: Hard and heavy light reddish brown hardwood. The most widely used hardwood veneer for flush doors, cabinetwork and paneling. Mill products include interior trim, flooring, sash and trim.

BLIND NAILING: A method of nailing so that the nail is not visible.

BOARD FOOT: A method of lumber measurement using nominal dimensions of 1 in. thick, 12 in. wide, and 12 in. long, or the equivalent.

BRICK: A solid masonry unit composed of clay or shale. Formed into a rectangular prism while soft and burned or fired in a kiln.

BRICK VENEER: A facing of brick laid against and fastened to sheathing of a frame wall or tile wall construction.

BRIDGING: Small wood or metal members that are inserted in a diagonal position between the floor joists at midspan to act both as tension and compression members for the purpose of bracing the joists and spreading the action of loads.

BUILT-UP ROOF: A roofing composed of three to five layers of asphalt felt laminated with coal tar, pitch or asphalt. The top is finished with crushed slag or gravel. Generally used on flat or low-pitched roofs.

BUREAU OF LAND MANAGEMENT: The branch of government in charge of surveying public lands.

CARPORT: A garage not fully enclosed.

CASEMENT WINDOW: A hinged window, usually metal, that opens out.

CASING: Molding of various widths and thicknesses used to trim door and window openings at the jambs.

CAULKING: A waterproof material used to seal cracks.

CENTRAL HEATING: A system by which the heat from a single source is distributed with ducts.

CHAIN: A unit of land measurement 66 ft. in length.

CHAMFER: A beveled edge on a board formed by removing the sharp corner. Generally used on moldings, edges of drawer fronts, and cabinet doors.

CHASE: A slot or continuous groove built in a masonry wall to accommodate ducts, pipes or conduits.

CHIMNEY: A vertical flue for passing smoke from a heating unit, fireplace or incinerator.

CHIPPED GRAIN: Wood surface that has been roughened by the action of cutting tools. Considered a defect when surfaces are to be smoothly finished.

CHORD: The horizontal member of a truss connecting the lower corners.

CLEAR TITLE: A title to property that is free of any defects.

CLEAT: A piece of wood, normally used in frame construction, fastened to another member to serve as a brace or support.

COLLAR BEAM: Nominal 1 or 2 in. thick members connecting opposite roof rafters. They serve to stiffen the roof structure.

CONCRETE: A mixture of cement, sand and gravel with water.

CONDITIONS AND RESTRICTIONS: The term used to designate any conditions to which the use of land may not be put and the penalties for failure to comply.

CONDUIT, ELECTRICAL: A pipe, usually metal, in which wire is installed.

CONTRACT: An agreement between a seller and purchaser. The title is withheld from the purchaser until all required payments to the seller have been completed.

COPING: A cap or top course of a masonry wall to protect lower areas from water penetration.

CORBEL: A ledge or shelf constructed by laying successive courses of masonry out from the face of the wall.

CORE: The inner layer or layers of plywood. The core may consist of veneer, solid lumber or composition board.

CORNER BRACES: Diagonal braces at the corners of frame structure to stiffen and strengthen the wall.

CORNICE: The part of a roof that projects out from the wall.

CORNICE RETURN: That portion of the cornice that returns on the gable end of a house.

COUNTERFLASHING: A flashing used under the regular flashing.

COVE: Molded trim of a concave shape used around cabinet construction and other built-ins.

CRAWL SPACE: The shallow space below the floor of a house built above the ground. Generally it is surrounded with the foundation wall.

CRICKET: A device used at roof intersections to divert water.

CRIPPLE: A structural member that is cut less than full length, such as a studding piece above a window or door.

CROSS BRACING: Boards nailed diagonally across studs or other boards to make framework rigid.

CROWN MOLDING: A decorative molding used at the top of cabinets, at ceiling corners and under a roof overhang.

CUL-DE-SAC: A street or court with no outlet which provides a circular turn around for vehicles.

CULL: Building material (especially boards) that is rejected because of defects or below usable grade.

CUPOLA: A small, decorative structure built on the roof of a house. It is often placed over an attached garage and may also be used for ventilating purposes.

CURTAIN WALL: An exterior wall which provides no structural support.

DADO JOINT: A groove cut across the face of a board to receive the end of another board. Often used in quality shelf and cabinet construction.

DAMPER: A movable plate which regulates the draft of a stove, fireplace, or furnace.

DEAD LOAD: All the unmovable weight in a structure and the weight of the structure itself.

DEED: A document indicating that the ownership of land has been transferred from one person to another.

DIMENSION LUMBER: Framing lumber which is 2 in. thick and from 4 to 12 in. wide.

DOME: A roof used over an entryway or a complete structure in the form of a hemisphere.

DOORJAMB: Two vertical pieces held together by a head jamb forming the inside lining of a door opening.

DOORSTOP: The strips on the doorjambs against which the door closes.

DORMER: An opening in a sloping roof, the framing of which projects out to form a vertical wall suitable for windows or other openings.

DOUBLE GLAZING: Making a pane of two pieces of glass with air space between and sealed to provide insulation.

DOUBLE HEADER: Two or more timbers joined for strength.

DOUBLE HUNG: Refers to a window having top and bottom sashes, each capable of movement up and down.

DOUGLAS FIR: A yellow to pale reddish soft wood. The leading veneer wood primarily converted into plywood and widely used in building and construction. Lumber used in general construction. Mill products used for sash, flooring and doors.

DOWNSPOUT: A pipe, usually of metal, for carrying rainwater from roof gutters.

DRESSED SIZE: The actual size of lumber after jointing and surfacing.

DRIP CAP: A molding placed on the exterior top side of a door or window frame to cause water to drip beyond the outside of the frame.

DRY WALL: Interior covering material, such as gypsum board or plywood, which is applied in large sheets or panels.

DRY WELL: A pit located on porous ground, walled up with rock, which allows water to seep through; used for the disposal of rain water or as the effluent from a septic tank.

DUCTS: In a house, usually round or rectangular metal pipes for distributing warm air from the heating plant to rooms, or air from a conditioning device or as cold air returns. Ducts are also made of asbestos and composition materials.

DUPLEX OUTLET: Electrical wall outlet having two plug receptacles.

DWARF WALL: A low wall built to retain an excavation or embankment.

EARNEST MONEY: A partial payment made as part of the purchase price to bind a contract for property.

EASEMENT: An area of a piece of property given rights to another for the purpose of placing power lines, drains and other specified uses.

EASTERN FIR: A softwood similar to spruce in its general characteristics. Used for siding, moldings and general construction.

EAVES: The lower portion of the roof that overhangs the wall.

ELL: An extension or wing of a building at right angles to the main section.

ESCUTCHEON: Door hardware which accommodates the knob and keyhole.

EXCAVATION: A cavity or pit produced by digging the earth in preparation for construction.

EXPANSION JOINT: A bituminous fiber strip used to separate blocks or units of concrete to prevent cracking due to expansion as a result of temperature changes.

FACADE: The front elevation or face of a structure.

FACE BRICK: Brick of better quality used on the face of a wall.

FACE SIZE: The exposed width of a molded piece of lumber after installation.

FACE VENEER: Veneer selected for exposed surfaces in plywood. Especially selected for fancy paneling.

FACING: Any material attached to the outer portion of a wall used as a finished surface.

FASCIA: A vertical board nailed onto the ends of the rafters.

FIBERBOARD: A building board made with fibrous material and used as an insulating board.

FILL: Sand, gravel or loose earth used to bring a subgrade up to a desired level around a house.

FILLED INSULATION: A loose insulating material poured from bags or blown by machine into walls.

FIREBRICK: A brick that is especially hard and heat-resistant; used in fireplaces.

FIRECLAY: A refractory mortar used to lay firebrick in the bed and walls of a fireplace.

FIRE CUT: The angular cut at the end of a joist designed to rest on a brick wall.

FIRE STOP: A solid, tight closure of a concealed space, placed to prevent the spread of fire and smoke through such a space. In a frame wall, this will usually consist of 2 by 4 cross blocking between studs.

FIRE WALL: Any wall designed to resist the spread of fire between sections of a house. Fire walls are commonly used between the main structure and an attached garage. Fire resistant materials are designed specifically for this purpose.

FLAGSTONE: Flat stone used for floors, steps, walks or walls.

FLASHING: Sheet metal or other material used in roof and wall construction to protect a building from water seepage.

FLUE: The space or passage in a chimney through which smoke, gas or fumes ascend. Each passage is called a flue, which together with any others and the surrounding masonry make up the chimney.

FLUE LINING: Fireclay or terra-cotta pipe, round or square, usually made in all ordinary flue sizes and in 2 ft. lengths, used for the inner lining of chimneys with the brick or masonry work around the outside. Flue lining in chimneys runs from about a foot below the flue connection to the top of the chimney.

FLY RAFTERS: End rafters of the gable overhang supported by roof sheathing and lookouts.

FOOTING: A masonry section, usually concrete, in a rectangular form wider than the bottom of the foundation wall or pier it supports.

FORM, CONCRETE: A temporary structure built to contain concrete during pouring and initial hardening.

FOUNDATION: The supporting portion of a structure below the first-floor construction, or below grade, including the footings.

FRAMING, BALLOON: A system of framing a building in which all vertical structural elements of the bearing walls and partitions consist of single pieces extending from the top of the foundation sill plate to the roof plate and to which all floor joists are fastened.

FRAMING, PLATFORM: A system of framing a building in which floor joists of each story rest on the top plates of the story below or on the foundation sill for the first story, and the bearing walls and partitions rest on the subfloor of each story.

FRIEZE: In house construction, a horizontal member connecting the top of the siding with the soffit of the cornice.

FROSTLINE: The depth of frost penetration in soil. This

depth varies in different parts of the country. Footings should be placed below this depth to prevent movement.

FURRING: The use of wood strips (or other materials) as a method of finishing the interior face of a masonry wall. Furring provides a space for insulation, helps prevent moisture transmission, and provides a level surface for paneling or other surface finishing treatment.

GABLE: The portion of the roof above the eave line of a double-sloped roof.

GAIN: A recess or notch into which a door hinge fits flush with the surface.

GARRETT: An attic or unfinished part of a house just under the roof.

GIRDER: A large or principal beam of wood or steel used to support concentrated loads at isolated points along its length.

GLAZING: Placing of glass in windows or doors.

GRADE: The surface of the ground around a building.

GRADE, WOOD: A designation given to the quality of manufactured lumber.

GRAVEL STOP: A strip of metal with a vertical lip used to retain the gravel around the edge of a built-up roof.

GROUT: A plaster-like material used to seal between ceramic and other tile in kitchens, showers and baths.

GUSSET: A plywood or metal plate used to strengthen the joints of a truss.

GUTTER: A trough for carrying off water.

HANGER: A metal strap used to support piping or the ends of joists.

HARDWOOD: Wood produced from broad-leaved trees or trees that lose their leaves. Examples include oak, maple, walnut and birch.

HEADER: (a) A beam placed perpendicular to joists and to which joists are nailed in framing for chimney, stairway or other opening. (b) A wood lintel.

HEARTH: The inner or outer floor of a fireplace, usually made of brick, tile or stone.

HICKORY: A hard and heavy brown to reddish brown hardwood. Used as face veneer for decorative interior plywood paneling and as solid lumber in special flooring applications. Pecan, a variety of the hickory family, has similar properties and construction applications.

HIP RAFTER: The diagonal rafter that extends from the plate to the ridge to form the hip.

HIP ROOF: A roof that rises by inclined planes from all four sides of a building.

HOSE BIB: A water faucet made for the threaded attachment of a hose.

HOUSE DRAIN: A horizontal sewer piping within a building, which receives waste from the soil stacks.

HOUSE SEWER: The watertight soil pipe extending from the exterior of the foundation wall to the public sewer.

HUMIDIFIER: A device, generally attached to a furnace, to supply or maintain humidity in a home.

HUMIDSTAT: A controlling device to regulate or maintain the desired degree of humidity in a house.

I-BEAM: A steel beam with a cross section resembling the letter I. It is used for long spans as basement beams or over wide wall openings, such as a double garage door, when wall and roof loads are imposed on the opening.

IMPROVEMENTS: Any additions to property which tends to increase its value, such as buildings, streets, sewers, etc.

INCANDESCENT LAMP: A lamp in which a filament gives off light when sufficiently heated by an electric current.

INSULATING BOARD: Any board suitable for insulating purposes, usually manufactured board made from vegetable fibers, such as fiberboard.

INSULATION: Materials for obstructing the passage of sound, heat, or cold from one surface to another.

INTERIOR TRIM: General term for all the finish molding, casing, baseboard and cornice applied within the building by finish carpenters.

JACK RAFTER: A rafter that spans the distance from the wall plate to a hip, or from a valley to a ridge.

JALOUSIE: A type of window consisting of a number of long, thin, hinged panels.

JAMB: The side and head lining of a doorway, window or other opening.

JOIST: A horizontal structural member which supports the floor or ceiling system.

KILN-DRIED LUMBER: Lumber that has been kiln-dried, generally to a moisture content of 6 to 12 percent.

KING POST: The central upright piece in a roof truss.

KNEE WALL: A low wall resulting from one-and-one-half-story construction.

LALLY COLUMN: A steel column used as a support for girders and beams.

LAMINATED BEAM: A beam made of superimposed layers of similar materials by uniting them with glue and pressure.

LANDING: A platform between flights of stairs or at the termination of a flight of stairs.

LATH: A building material of wood, metal, gypsum or insulating board that is fastened to the frame of a building to act as a plaster base.

LATTICE: A framework of crossed wood or metal strips.

LEADER: A vertical pipe or downspout that carries rainwater from the gutter to the ground or storm sewer.

LEASE: A contract for the use of land for a period of years with a designated payment of a monthly or annual rental.

LEDGER STRIP: A strip of lumber nailed along the bottom of the side of a girder on which joists rest.

LEGAL DESCRIPTION: A written indication of the location and boundaries of a parcel of land. Reference is generally made to a recorded plat of survey.

LINTEL: A horizontal structural member that supports the load over an opening such as a door or window.

LOOKOUT: A short wooden framing member used to support an overhanging portion of a roof. It extends from the wall to the underside surfacing of the overhang.

LOT: A measured amount of property (land) having fixed boundaries.

LOT LINE: The line forming the legal boundary of a piece of property.

LOUVER: An opening with a series of horizontal slats so arranged as to permit ventilation but to exclude rain, sunlight, or vision. See ATTIC VENTILATORS.

MANTEL: The shelf above a fireplace. Also used in referring to the decorative trim around a fireplace opening.

MAPLE: Both hard and soft maple are generally light tan and used in construction where hardness is a major factor. Used for expensive cabinetwork, flooring, doors and trim. Often used for interior railings, posts and furniture.

MASONRY: Stone, brick, concrete, hollow-tile, concrete-block, gypsum-block or other similar building units or materials or a combination of the same, bonded together with mortar to form a wall, pier, buttress or similar mass.

MASTIC: A flexible adhesive for adhering building materials.

METAL WALL TIES: Strips of corrugated metal used to tie a brick veneer wall to a framework.

MILLWORK: Lumber that is shaped to a given pattern or molded form. It includes dressing, matching and machining. Examples include casing, base, panel door parts and stair rails.

MITER JOINT: A joint made with the ends or edges of two pieces of lumber cut at a 45 deg. angle and fitted together.

MODULAR CONSTRUCTION: Construction in which the size of all the building materials is based on a common unit of measure.

MOISTURE BARRIER: A material such as specially treated paper that retards the passage of vapor or moisture into walls, and prevents condensation within the walls.

MORTAR: A mixture of cement, sand and water, used by the mason as a bonding agent for bricks and stone.

MORTGAGE: A document used to hold property as security for a debt.

MORTISE: A slot cut into a board, plank or timber, usually edgewise, to receive the tenon of another board, plank or timber to form a joint.

MULLION: A vertical bar or divider in the frame between windows, doors or other openings.

MUNTIN: A small member which divides the glass or openings of sash or doors.

NEWEL: A post supporting the handrail at the top or bottom of a stairway.

NOMINAL SIZE: The size of lumber before dressing, rather than its actual size.

NONBEARING WALL: A wall supporting no load other than its own weight.

NOSING: The rounded edge of a stair tread.

OAK, RED: Hard and tough hardwood used for flooring, interior trim, stair treads and railings. Popular as a face veneer plywood for paneling and cabinetwork. A rich light to medium brown in color. White oak has similar characteristics and applications.

OAK, WHITE: See OAK, RED.

O.C., ON CENTER: The measurement of spacing for studs, rafters, joists and other framing members from the center of one member to the center of the next.

OUTLET: Any type of electrical box allowing current to be drawn from the electrical system for lighting or appliances.

OVERHANG: The projecting area of a roof or upper story beyond the wall of the lower part.

PALLET: An inexpensive wood skid used to stack and ship construction materials such as brick or concrete block.

PANEL: In house construction, a thin flat piece of wood, plywood, or similar material, framed by stiles and rails as in a door or fitted into grooves of thicker material with molded edges for decorative wall treatment.

PAPER, BUILDING: A general term for papers, felts, and similar sheet materials used in buildings without reference to their properties or uses.

PARAPET: A low wall or railing around the edge of a roof.

PARGE COAT: A thin coat of cement plaster applied to a masonry wall for refinement of the surface or for damp-proofing.

PARTICLE BOARD: A composition board made of wood chips or particles bonded together with an adhesive under high pressure.

PARTITION: A wall that subdivides spaces within any story of a building.

PECAN: See HICKORY.

PERIPHERY: A boundary or complete outside edge of a parcel of land or an object on a drawing.

PIER: A masonry pillar usually below a building to support the floor framing.

PILASTER: A portion of a square column, usually set within or against a wall for the purpose of strengthening the wall; also, a decorative column attached to a wall.

PINE, PONDEROSA: Light reddish colored softwood used especially for sash, doors and screens in the softer grades. Harder grades are used for joists, rafters, studdings, sills, sheathing, porch columns, posts, balusters and stair rails.

PINE, WHITE: Softwood of light tan color used for door, sash, interior and exterior trim, siding and panels. Lower grades are used for sheathing, subflooring and roofing.

PINE, YELLOW: Softwood of medium texture, moderately hard, and a yellow to reddish brown color. Used for joists, rafters, studding and general construction where extra strength and stiffness are required.

PITCH: The slope of a roof usually expressed as a ratio.

PLASTER: A mortar-like composition used for covering walls and ceilings, usually made of portland cement mixed with sand and water.

PLAT: A drawing of surveyed land indicating the location, boundaries and dimensions of the parcel. The recorded plat, usually sent to an appropriate governmental office or the county recorders office, also contains information as to easements, restrictions and lot number.

PLATE: Sill plate is a horizontal member anchored to a masonry wall. Sole plate is bottom horizontal member of a frame wall. Top plate is top horizontal member of a frame wall supporting ceiling joists, rafters or other members.

PLENUM SYSTEM: A system of heating or air conditioning in which the air is forced through a chamber connected to distributing ducts.

PLUMB: Exactly perpendicular; vertical.

PLYWOOD: A piece of wood made of three or more layers of veneer joined with glue, and usually laid with the grain of adjoining plies at right angles. Almost always an odd number of plies are used to provide balanced construction.

PORTICO: A covered entryway attached to house, usually open on three sides and supported by posts or columns.

POST AND BEAM CONSTRUCTION: Wall construction consisting of posts rather than studs.

PRECAST: Concrete shapes which are made before being placed into a structure.

PREFABRICATED HOUSES: Houses that are built in sections or component parts in a plant, and then assembled at the site.

PREFRAMED PANELS: Fabricated panels consisting of pre-cut lumber and plywood manufactured to standard dimensions ready for structural use.

PRESERVATIVE: Any substance that, for a reasonable length of time, will prevent the action of wood-destroying fungi, borers of various kinds and similar destructive agents when the wood has been properly coated or impregnated with it.

PURLINS: Horizontal roof members laid over trusses to support rafters.

QUARTER ROUND: A small molding that has the cross section of a quarter circle.

QUARTER-SAWED: Lumber which has been sawed so that the medullary rays showing on the end grain are nearly perpendicular to the face of the lumber.

QUOINS: Stone or other building materials set in the corners of masonry sections of a house for appearance.

RABBET: A groove cut along the edge of a board producing an L shaped strip. Used as trim and in joint work in cabinet construction.

RADIANT HEATING: A method of heating, usually consisting of a forced hot water system with pipes placed in the floor, wall or ceiling; or with electrically heated panels.

RAFTER: One of a series of structural members of a roof designed to support roof loads. The rafters of a flat roof are sometimes called roof joists.

RANDOM RUBBLE: Stonework having irregular shaped units and no indication of systematic course work.

RED CEDAR: A reddish to dull brown softwood. The premier wood for shingles used in the United States because of its durability, ease of working and light weight. Also used for interior and exterior trim, sash, doors and siding.

REDWOOD: Light to deep reddish brown softwood. Mill products include sash, doors, blinds, siding and trim. Extensively used for garden furniture and exterior decking.

REGISTER: The open end of a duct for warm or cool air; usually covered with screening.

REINFORCED CONCRETE: Concrete with steel bars or webbing embedded for strength.

RETAINING WALL: A wall which holds back an earth embankment.

REVEAL: The side of an opening for a window or door, between the frame and the outer surface of the wall.

RHEOSTAT: An instrument used for regulating electric current.

RIDGE: The top edge of the roof where two slopes meet.

RIDGE BOARD: The board placed on edge at the ridge of the roof into which the upper ends of the rafters are fastened.

RIPRAP: A sustaining wall or foundation of random stone to prevent erosion on an embankment.

RISE: In stairs, the vertical height of a step or flight of stairs.

RISER: Each of the vertical boards closing the spaces between the treads of stairways.

ROOF SHEATHING: The boards or sheet material fastened to the roof rafters on which the shingles or other roof covering is laid.

ROUGH OPENING: A framed opening in a structure into which doors, windows and other finished trim are set.

RUN: In stairs, the net width of a step or the horizontal distance covered by a flight of stairs.

SADDLE: Two sloping surfaces meeting in a horizontal ridge, used between the back side of a chimney or other vertical surface and a sloping roof. Also called a cricket.

SASH: A single light frame containing one or more lights of glass.

SCUTTLE: A small opening in a ceiling which provides access to an attic or roof.

SECTION: A rectangular area of land used in the survey system which is approximately one mile square bounded by section lines. The section system may then be divided into halves, quarters or smaller units. One square mile comprises 640 acres.

SEPTIC TANK: A concrete or steel tank where sewage is partially reduced by bacterial action.

SETBACK: A zoning restriction which applies to the location of the home on a lot.

SETBACK LINES: Lines which indicate the required distances for the location of a structure in relation to the boundaries of the property.

SHEATHING: The structural covering, usually wood boards or plywood, used over studs or rafters of a structure. Structural building board is normally used only as wall sheathing.

SHED ROOF: A flat roof, slanting in one direction.

SHIPLAP: Wood sheathing which is rabbeted so that the edges of the boards make a flush joint.

SHOE MOLD: The small mold against the baseboard at the floor.

SIDING: The finish covering of the outside wall of a frame building, whether made of horizontal weatherboards, vertical boards with battens, shingles or other material.

SILL: The lowest member of the frame of a structure, resting on the foundation and supporting the floor joists or the uprights of the wall. The member forming the lower side of an opening, as a door sill.

SKYLIGHT: An opening in a roof covered by glass or plastic material to admit natural light.

SLEEPER: Usually, a wood member embedded in concrete, as in a floor, that serves to support and to fasten subfloor or flooring.

SMOKE CHAMBER: The portion of a chimney flue located directly over the fireplace.

SOFFIT: Usually the underside of an overhanging cornice.

SOFTWOOD: Wood produced from coniferous trees or trees that bear cones. Most commonly used are the pines, but also includes such trees as fir, spruce, redwood and cedar. The term has no reference to the actual hardness or softness of the wood.

SOIL STACK: The main vertical pipe which receives waste water from fixtures in a building.

SOLID BRIDGING: A solid member placed between adjacent

floor joists near the center of the span to prevent joists from twisting.

SPAN: The horizontal distance between supports for joists, beams or trusses.

SPRUCE: Pale yellowish softwood used for general building purposes as planks, dimension stock and joists. Millwork products include doors, sash, casing and trim.

SQUARE: A unit of measure — 100 sq. ft. — usually applied to roofing material. Sidewall coverings are sometimes packed to cover 100 sq. ft. and are sold on that basis.

STOOL: The horizontal ledge or strip as part of the frame below an interior window.

STRETCHER COURSE: A row of masonry in a wall with the long side of the units exposed to the exterior.

STUCCO: Most commonly refers to an outside plaster made with portland cement as its base.

STUDS: The vertical framing members of a wall.

SUBFLOORING: Any material, usually 1/2 in. plywood, nailed directly to floor joists. The finish floor is attached over the subflooring.

SUBGRADE: A fill or earth surface upon which concrete is placed.

SUGAR PINE: Similar in physical properties and uses in construction as white pine. See WHITE PINE.

SUMP: A pit in a basement floor which collects water and into which a sump pump is placed to remove the water.

SURVEY: A description of the measure and marking of land, including maps and field notes which describe the property.

SUSPENDED CEILING: A ceiling system supported by hanging it from the overhead structural framing.

TAIL BEAM: A relatively short beam or joist supported in a wall on one end and by a header at the other.

TERMITE SHIELD: A shield, usually of noncorrodible metal, placed in or on a foundation wall or other mass of masonry or around pipes to prevent passage of termites.

TERRAZZO FLOORING: Wear-resistant flooring made of marble chips or small stones embedded in cement and polished smooth.

THERMOSTAT: Automatic device for controlling temperature.

THRESHOLD: A strip of wood or metal with beveled edges used over the finish floor and the sill of exterior doors.

TITLE: Evidence indicating the rights a person has to the ownership and possession of land.

TRACT: A specified area of land.

TRANSOM: A window placed above a door or permanent window which is hinged for ventilation.

TRAP: A U-shaped pipe below plumbing fixtures designed to create a water seal and prevent sewer odors and gases from being released into the habitable areas.

TREAD: The horizontal board in a stairway on which the foot is placed.

TRIM: The finish materials in a building, such as moldings, applied around openings (window trim, door trim) or at the floor and ceiling of rooms (baseboard, cornice).

TRIMMER: The longer floor framing member around a rectangular opening into which a header is joined.

TROWELING: The finishing operation which produces a smooth, hard surface on concrete slab.

TRUSS: Structural members arranged and fastened in triangular units to form a ridge framework for support of loads over a long span.

UNDERLAYMENT: A material placed under finish coverings, such as flooring or shingles, to provide a smooth, even surface for applying the finish.

VALLEY: The internal angle formed by the junction of two sloping sides of a roof.

VALLEY RAFTER: The diagonal rafter at the intersection of two intersecting sloping roofs.

VENEER: Extremely thin sheets of wood produced by slicing or rotary-cutting a log.

VENEERED CONSTRUCTION: Type of wall construction in which frame or masonry walls are faced with other exterior surfacing materials.

VENT STACK: A vertical soil pipe connected to the drainage system to allow ventilation and pressure equalization.

WAINSCOT: Surfacing on the lower part of an interior wall when finished differently from the remainder of the wall.

WALL TIE: A small metal strip or steel wire used to bind tiers of masonry in cavity-wall construction, or to bind brick veneer to the wood-frame wall in veneer construction.

WARPAGE: Twisting or distortion of a board from its true plane, normally as a result of seasoning.

WATER CONDITIONER: A device used to remove dissolved minerals from water to make it soft. Generally used in houses supplied by well water, which contains calcium, magnesium and other minerals, to remove hardness that causes scale buildup in plumbing.

WEATHERSTRIP: Strip of metal or fabric fastened along the edges of windows and doors to reduce drafts and heat loss.

WEEP HOLE: An opening at the bottom of a wall which allows the drainage of water.

WYTHE: Pertaining to a single-width masonry wall.

ZONING: Building restrictions which regulate size, location and type of structures to be built in specific areas.

ACKNOWLEDGMENTS

The author wishes to thank the many individuals, organizations and companies who contributed time, materials and information toward the preparation of this book. Their contributions proved to be invaluable.

Many thanks are given the following individuals for their assistance: Mr. Larry Bauman, Mr. John Berry, Miss Arlene Brown, Mr. Loren W. Campbell II, and Mr. Harry Smith.

Appreciation is acknowledged to Professor Raymond LaBounty, Assistant Vice President for Instruction, Eastern Michigan University, for his encouragement in the preparation of the manuscript.

Sincere gratitude is extended to my wife, Joan, for her untiring support and assistance throughout the writing.

Tremendous credit is due Dr. Ronald J. Baird, my friend and consulting editor. His expert judgment, guidance and assistance played a very large part in the writing of this text. I am truly grateful for his contribution and will be forever indebted to him.

INDEX